SSADM Version 4:
A Practical Approach

Mike Goodland
*Senior Lecturer, School of Information Systems,
Kingston University*

with

Caroline Slater
Managing Consultant, CraySystems AIMS

McGRAW-HILL BOOK COMPANY

London · New York · St Louis · San Francisco · Auckland · Bogotá
Caracas · Lisbon · Madrid · Mexico · Milan · Montreal · New Delhi
Panama · Paris · San Juan · São Paulo · Singapore · Sydney · Tokyo
Toronto

Published by

McGRAW-HILL Book Company Europe

Shoppenhangers Road
Maidenhead, Berkshire, England SL6 2QL
Telephone 01628 23432
Fax 01628 770224

British Library Cataloguing in Publication Data

The CIP data of this title is available from the British Library.

Library of Congress Cataloguing-in-Publication Data

The LOC data of this title is available from the Library of Congress, Washington DC, USA.

12345 CUP 998765

Typesetting and artwork created by Mike Goodland
and printed and bound in Great Britain at the University Press, Cambridge.

Contents

Preface

The Structured Systems Analysis and Design Method (SSADM) was developed by the United Kingdom government in 1982 for development of information systems by government departments. Since then its use has spread to the commercial market and to other countries. The only 'open' method available for information systems development, SSADM is supported by many training organizations, consultancies, independent contractors, and CASE tools. SSADM is the most widely used method in the UK (surveys suggest that around 70% of organizations using structured methods use SSADM or one of its variants). Throughout its life SSADM has been refined and improved through changing technology and the experiences of its users. Version 4 of the method was released in early 1991 to an enthusiastic reaction from its users.

SSADM is a very comprehensive method and, although the techniques are not particularly difficult to learn, it is often difficult to apply them correctly without guidance from an experienced user. In this book we have tried to distil some of that experience into a form which will both teach the basic principles of the method and also demonstrate how it can be applied.

This book is the successor to 'SSADM: A Practical Approach' by the same authors (although Caroline Slater was then Caroline Ashworth) which described Version 3 of SSADM. This book follows the structure and examples of the earlier book—updating them to Version 4. We have developed the practical nature of the book; using more examples and discussing further how the method can be applied in practice. This book describes SSADM as defined by the SSADM Reference Manuals and has been assessed by the Technical Committee of the International SSADM User Group as conforming with SSADM Version 4. Throughout the book we have used footnotes to discuss areas for improvement or extension of SSADM—some of these are under consideration for upgrades to Version 4. Another improvement over the earlier book is a new chapter that discusses the management aspects of an SSADM project.

Many undergraduate and postgraduate courses in Information Systems, Business, and Computing teach SSADM in some detail. SSADM is a good example of structured method as the techniques employed are used in all major structured methods for analysis and design. The materials in this book can be used in various ways. Most obviously following the structure of the book to give a 'pure' SSADM course but also by teaching topics that are simpler such as Data Flow Models in the early part of an undergraduate course and dealing with more 'difficult' techniques such as Entity Life Histories and Physical Design in later years when the students have greater experience of databases and software engineering. In this way SSADM can be taught in small chunks over a three-year course, enabling students to graduate with an integrated and critical view of a systems development method.

This book covers the syllabus set by the Information Systems Examination Board of the British Computer Society for the Certificate in SSADM Version 4. It has been used as the basis for commercial training courses delivered in both distance learning and conventional modes. We hope that this book will be of use to professionals taking the SSADM Certificate examination and to other professionals interested in using SSADM.

Structure of the book

Part 1, SSADM Concepts, consists of two chapters. An introductory chapter describes the need for SSADM, shows how it fits into the systems development life cycle, and describes briefly the structure, techniques and documentation used by SSADM. Chapter 2, Three views of the system, describes the basic views that SSADM takes of an information system and explains their inter-relationships.

Part 2, Working through SSADM, follows the structure of SSADM with a separate chapter on each of the modules of SSADM. Each chapter begins with an introductory section describing the module. The remainder of each chapter is divided into several sections each describing a step. The overall objective of Part 2 is to show how SSADM might be used on a typical project. The reader is taken through the development of the major SSADM end-products and shown how they should be developed. To illustrate the development of an SSADM project we have used a case study. This concerns the activities of a fictional vehicle rental company, Yorkies.

The book ends with Chapter 7, Management Aspects. This discusses the project management issues affecting an SSADM project, how SSADM might be customized to particular project circumstances, and the use of CASE (Computer Assisted Software Engineering) tools on an SSADM project. Please note that the ideas expressed in Chapter 7 are those of Mike Goodland alone—they have not been reviewed by the Technical Committee of the International SSADM User Group.

A glossary of SSADM terms is given in Appendix A (we thank NCC Blackwell for allowing us to use the Glossary from the SSADM Reference Manual). A bibliography in Appendix B lists some books referred to in the text and others of interest to an SSADM practitioner. A description of the Yorkies case study is given in Appendix C. Exercises are given at the end of many of the sections. These test the techniques used in the step described in the section. Suggested answers are given in Appendix D. The optional Feasibility module of SSADM is briefly described in Appendix E. Details of the International SSADM User Group, the SSADM Certificate, and of further teaching materials available to universities, colleges, and training organizations are given in Appendix F.

Acknowledgements

Acknowledgements and thanks are due to a large number of individuals and organizations who have helped with this book. The help of Louise Pearce with word processing and diagram drawing was invaluable. Our respective employers (Kingston University and AIMS Systems) during the time of writing provided support, encouragement, and facilities. Students from the commercial SSADM courses run by

University of Westminster, Kingston University, and Metadata have provided a useful testing ground for many of the ideas and examples used in the book. Karel Riha from Kingston University contributed words, SQL, and advice. Several people have usefully reviewed parts of the manuscript at various stages including John Wurr, David Robinson, Anthony Lucas Smith, Jim Laflin, and Karel Riha (again). Jennifer Stapleton and John Hall reviewed the book on behalf of the Technical Committee of the International SSADM User Group and made several useful suggestions. Lastly, on a more personal note, I thank my partner, Liz Hart, for her often tested patience, love, and support during the over-long period of gestation.

Mike Goodland

Part 1 SSADM Concepts

1 Introduction

1.1 Why use SSADM?

SSADM is one of the most mature and widely used methods in the UK. However, it requires a significant investment in training and learning, so why should an organization consider taking it on? Some may not acknowledge the need for systems analysis, some may see the need, but not know why a structured method is better than traditional methods, and others may need to be convinced that SSADM has advantages over the other methods available. This section addresses all three standpoints and explains the underlying principles of the method.

Why have systems analysis at all?

It is often difficult to explain what is achieved by systems analysis and design—especially when talking to a user who wants a system tomorrow! After all, their 14-year-old son can knock together a quick program on his PC in a couple of hours. Surely, a larger system is just the same but a bit bigger? Why should it take so long to design a system? And then there are the traditionalists to whom systems analysis consists of refining a design that is laid down from the start. To examine the reasons for using a method, perhaps the subject is best tackled from the point of view of something that is a comparable investment: building a house.

Imagine that you have bought a plot of land in order to build yourself a house. This is a big investment and you want to be sure that you end up with the house that you want. How do you proceed?

Start constructing it straightaway?
You could go to your local do-it-yourself superstore and buy some materials and start laying the foundations straightaway. After all, houses are pretty standard and you have recently built a shed (with some help from your 14-year-old son), so you are quite an expert. Unfortunately, you get carried away and find out when it is finished that the walls are not strong enough to support the roof and you forgot to put the electricity cables in the walls, so there is no light! The whole thing fails because a lack of planning meant that even simple standard parts of the design of a house were missed (Fig. 1.1).

Fig. 1.1 What you (and your son) built!

Go directly to a builder?

You look in the Yellow Pages and find a builder who seems to have the right qualifications. Surely, if you go to someone who has had a lot of experience in building houses, he won't make the same mistakes you made? You show the builder your plot of land and he agrees to go ahead and start building. You tell him you want some bedrooms, a living room, a kitchen and a bathroom, and then you go away and leave him to it. Six months later he tells you he has finished and you go to look at the house (Fig. 1.2).

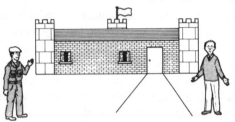

Fig. 1.2 What the builder did!

Oh dear! The builder's tastes in house design are not very conventional and he has built you a bungalow with turrets! He has built a house that meets your instructions but there are all sorts of things about it that you hate—the rooms are small and dark whereas you have always liked large light rooms. The place is habitable but you certainly don't want to live there. You have a house that doesn't meet your requirements because you didn't tell the builder exactly what you wanted and he never came and checked with you that what he was doing was what you wanted. You assumed that because he is an expert in building a house, he didn't need to be told what to build.

Employ an architect to design it first?

You have managed to sell your monstrosity and bought another plot of land. This time you have learnt your lesson! You employ an architect. You have a series of meetings together. There are several things you tell him about your requirements. Then he goes away, draws a few plans and shows them to you to clarify a few points. To help you envisage it, he produces a few artist's impressions and non-technical drawings that you can all understand. He asks you some searching questions about how you want the rooms laid out, and makes absolutely sure he understands your requirements. Also, he points out to you that there are certain building regulations that must be adhered to so you have a good understanding of the constraints. He finally draws plans from several viewpoints and if there is anything you don't understand, he is there to explain it to you. Finally, you are happy that the plans he has drawn will meet your requirements. He asks you to authorize him to go ahead and develop the system. You sign the necessary papers and he gives the plans to a builder who proceeds to build your dream house (Fig. 1.3). You are happy at last!

Fig 1.3 Your dream house—with the help of an architect

This rather simplistic example illustrates the need to specify requirements before construction of a house (or system) is started. Although it may seem that the requirements are fairly straightforward, constraints may be missed or interdependencies overlooked during development. A problem is far cheaper to put right early in the process than leaving it until the final day of the implementation!

How do we find out exactly what the requirements are? The future users are no more expert in expressing their needs to a programmer than the hapless landowner was in expressing what he wanted to the builder! Left to their own devices, computer people will implement the system that is most convenient to build, which will not necessarily be what the user wanted. The systems analyst takes a similar role to that of the architect—as communicator between client and builder. Some of the underlying principles of systems analysis, which are also principles of SSADM, help make sure that the user requirements are fully specified.

User involvement During the design process, the architect constantly made sure he understood the requirements by producing non-technical plans for the customer to look at and discuss. It is a basic principle of SSADM that the users have involvement in, and commitment to, the development of their system from a very early stage. By ensuring that the specification and design match the user's requirements at each stage of analysis and design, the risks of producing the 'wrong' system are very much reduced and possible problems can be sorted out before they become unmanageable.

Quality assurance The architect needed authorization from the customer to go ahead once the plans were agreed. In SSADM, formal quality assurance reviews are held at the end of each stage where the user is asked to 'sign off' the design so far. The end products for the stage are scrutinized for quality, completeness, consistency, and applicability by users, developers, and by experienced systems staff external to the project.

Separation between logical and physical specifications The requirements were expressed in logical terms first before the final architecture was known. This helped the architect to determine the best way to satisfy the requirements before going into the physical details. SSADM separates logical design from physical design. A hardware/software-independent logical design is produced which can easily be translated into an initial physical design. This helps the developers to address one problem at a time and prevents needless constraints being added at too early a stage in development. This also helps communication with users who may not be computer literate but are perfectly able to validate a logical specification or design of their system.

It is important to investigate what is required It is rare for any users to be able to describe in detail everything that is required without a lot of prompting. The architect in the example above played a vital role, using his experience of other designs and his knowledge of the techniques of planning, in asking about many of the details. Similarly, the systems analyst will need to ask the users many questions about what is required.

Why use a structured method?

Structured methods share these characteristics:

- they structure a project into small, well-defined activities and specify the sequence and interaction of these activities;
- they use diagrammatic and other modelling techniques to give a more precise (structured) definition that is understandable by both users and developers.

Why can a systems analyst not use his or her experience and just ask all the right questions? Some of the advantages of structured methods are given here.

Structured analysis provides a clear requirements statement that everyone can understand and is a firm foundation for subsequent design and implementation Part of the problem with a systems analyst just asking 'the right questions' is that it is often difficult for a technical person to describe the system concepts back to the user in terms the user can understand. Structured methods generally include the use of easily understood, non-technical diagrammatic techniques. It is important that these diagrams do not contain computer jargon and technical detail that the user won't understand—and does not need to understand.

More effective use of experienced and inexperienced staff Another part of the problem with this approach is the availability of staff with enough experience to ask all the right questions. A structured method does not remove the need for experienced staff, but it does provide the option of spreading the experience more thinly. The use of structured techniques means that certain tasks can be delegated to inexperienced staff who can then be guided by the more experienced.

Improved project planning and control The use of a structured approach allows the more effective management of projects. Splitting a project down into stages and steps allows better estimation of the time taken to complete the project. Also, by following a detailed plan, it will be possible to detect slippage as it occurs and not just before the system is due to be implemented.

Better quality systems By making the specification very comprehensive, it is possible to ensure that the system built will be of a high quality. The use of structured techniques has been found to lead to a system that is very flexible and amenable to change. Within SSADM, users participate in formal quality assurance reviews and informal walk-throughs and 'sign off' each stage before the developers progress to the next. This means that the analysts can be confident that the new system will meet the user's requirements before it is built.

Why choose SSADM?

As stated above, SSADM is one of the most mature methods in the UK. The experience gained in the first few years after it was introduced as a government standard has been fed back into the method to ensure its usability and practicality. Because of this, and because of the way SSADM has taken on the best ideas from other methods, it has several significant advantages over its nearest rivals.

One of the main advantages is that SSADM builds up several different views of the system which are used to cross-check one another. In the building example above, to help the customer visualize the final building, the architect drew several different representations—a cross-sectional view, artist's impressions, etc. This probably helped the architect to validate the plans as he made sure that each view was consistent with the others. In SSADM, three different views of the system are developed in analysis. These views are closely related to one another and are cross-checked extensively for consistency and completeness. The equal weight given to these three techniques and the prescriptive procedures for checking them against one another is a great strength of the SSADM approach. The three views are:

- the underlying structure of the system's data (the Logical Data Structure);
- how data flows into and out of the system and is transformed within the system (Data Flow Diagrams);
- how the system data are changed by events over time (Entity Life Histories).

Another advantage of SSADM over a number of methods is that it combines techniques into a well-established framework, and so, as well as providing the techniques for the analyst, it gives guidance on how and when to use them. Even though SSADM adopts this rather prescriptive approach, there is still a large amount of flexibility within the method and it should be tailored to specific project circumstances.

1.2   Overview of SSADM

This section describes how SSADM fits into an overall systems development life cycle. It gives a brief overview of the structure of SSADM, and explains what each of the stages are. The major techniques of SSADM are also briefly described and the documentation standards explained.

SSADM and the system development life cycle

SSADM is used in the development of systems, but it does not cover the entire system life cycle. Figure 1.4 shows a typical system life cycle, indicating where SSADM fits into the entire procedure. We describe below what is meant by each of these phases and explain how SSADM fits into them.

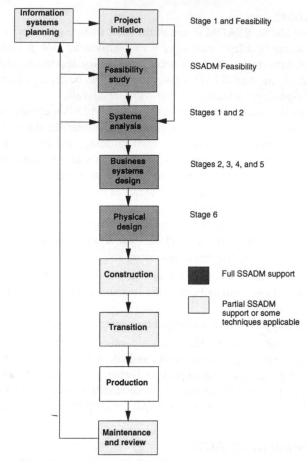

Fig. 1.4 SSADM and the system development life cycle

Information systems planning

Many organizations, recognizing the contribution of information systems to their success, have invested in strategic planning for the development of future and existing information systems. Recently many methods for information systems planning have been put forward. These take a variety of approaches but generally the result from the planning exercise will be an analysis of the organization's present position, recommendations as to which systems should be developed or enhanced, a plan showing the order in which these projects should be done, and outline project plans and terms of reference for each project.

Three of the techniques used by SSADM—Requirements Definition, Data Flow Diagrams and Logical Data Structures—are used, in some form, by many of these methods. Many projects which have used SSADM have been initiated by an information systems planning study. To this extent SSADM offers partial support to this activity. There is no information systems planning component within SSADM, though it is desirable that some planning has been done before an SSADM project starts.

Project initiation

This is the phase where the project is set up, terms of reference agreed, team members assigned, and plans drawn up. SSADM provides some guidelines for this activity. In this book we develop a case study through the steps and stages of SSADM—this initiation activity is discussed in Sec. 3.2.

Feasibility study

This is the phase where it is decided whether the project is technically possible, whether it can be financially and socially justified, and whether the new system will be accepted by the organization. Feasibility studies have become less popular recently with the activity either being part of an information systems planning study or the project being a 'must have'. SSADM provides detailed guidelines on the conduct of feasibility studies detailing the steps and stages required. In this book we concentrate on 'one-pass' analysis and design, without a feasibility study (Appendix F briefly describes the Feasibility stage in SSADM). However, the techniques and approach used by SSADM for feasibility is very similar to that described in this book for the systems analysis and early business systems design phases of the project.

Systems analysis

Here the current system is analysed in great detail to determine the requirements for a new system. SSADM does not give guidelines on such basic systems analysis skills as interviewing and other data collection methods but provides the means of recording and analysing the results of the investigation. Stage 1 of SSADM deals with the analysis of the current system, stage 2 produces outline systems designs, and stage 3 specifies the requirements for the new system. These stages are fully described in Chapters 3 and 4.

Business systems design

The requirements for the new system will have been broadly specified in the previous phase. In this phase various technical solutions that meet the requirements are evaluated and one selected. A detailed logical design of the new system is developed which shows clearly, in a non-technical way, how the new system will operate within the business. This phase is dealt with by SSADM stages 2, 3, 4, and 5. They are fully described in Chapters 3, 4, and 5.

Physical design

The logical design is converted to a design that fits the computer hardware and software selected. This is known as the physical design and is dealt with by stage 6 of SSADM. Physical design involves the specification of files (or database definitions), the specification of programs, and the detailed operating and manual procedures that support them. This phase is described in detail in Chapter 6.

Construction

This concerns the programming, the assembly of programs into a system, and the testing of the system. SSADM does not address this phase. However, the plans for system building and testing are laid in SSADM stages 4 and 6. Many projects are now using fourth-generation environments for systems development and have integrated their use into stages 5 and 6 of SSADM; some of these ideas are discussed in Chapters 5 and 6. Prototyping has also become an important component of SSADM and this is discussed in Chapter 4.

Transition

This phase involves the transition from operating the old system to operating the new. It involves the installation of equipment, the conversion of old system data to the formats required by the new system, and the training of users. Some systems' life cycles join the construction and transition phases together to form an implementation phase. SSADM does not fully address the transition phase although the plans for it are developed in stage 4.

Production

This phase begins when the system has been completely handed over to the users. The term production conveys that the system is operating and producing the information that was required of it. This activity is not supported by SSADM.

Maintenance and review

Throughout the production phase the system will require maintenance in various ways: correction of errors, adaptation to new software and hardware releases, and minor enhancements. The system will need to be reviewed to show how well it has met the requirements and objectives set for it and whether it continues to meet the users' requirements. These enhancements and reviews may lead into further system studies as shown in Fig. 1.4. Guidelines are available as to how SSADM can be employed in a maintenance environment, although these are beyond the scope of this book.

Basic principles of SSADM

SSADM is a data-driven method. This means that there is an basic assumption that systems have an underlying, generic, data structure which changes very little over time, although processing requirements may change. Within SSADM, this underlying data structure is modelled from an early stage. The representation of this data structure is checked against the processing and reporting requirements and finally built into the system's architecture.

The structured techniques of SSADM fit into a framework of steps and stages, each with defined inputs and outputs. Also, there are a number of forms and documents that are specified which add information to that held within the diagrams. Thus, SSADM consists of three important features:

- Structures   define the frameworks of steps and stages and their inputs and outputs.
- Techniques   define how the steps and tasks are performed.
- Documentation   defines how the products of the steps are presented.

Each of these features is described below.

Structure of SSADM

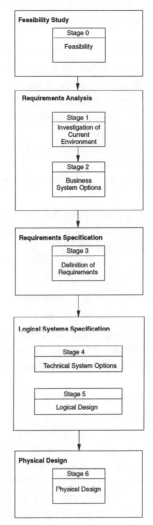

Fig. 1.5 Modules and stages of SSADM

Figure 1.5 shows that the modules of an SSADM project contain stages. Each module is designed to be self-contained, with the idea that projects might choose to use SSADM for one module and not for others. The first module is an optional feasibility stage (earlier we explained that this is often omitted and is not dealt fully with in this book). Each stage is broken down into a number of steps which define inputs, outputs, and tasks to be performed. The products of each step and the interfaces between steps are clearly defined.

SSADM is divided into five modules; Feasibility Study, Requirements Analysis, Requirements Specification, Logical Systems Specification, and Physical Design. Each of these is divided into stages. Each stage is then divided into steps. In this book we take you through the structure of a typical SSADM project following the modules, stages, and steps of the method.

The structure of the method illustrates several features of the SSADM approach:

1. The current system, in its current implementation, is studied first in order to gain an understanding of the environment of the new system.
2. This view of the current system is used to build the specification of the required system. However, the required system is not constrained by the way in which the current system is implemented.
3. The specification of requirements is defined to the extent that detailed technical options can be formulated.
4. The detailed design is completed at the logical level before implementation issues are addressed.
5. The logical design is converted into physical design by the application of simple (first cut) rules. The resulting design is tuned using the technique of physical design control before implementation.

Requirements Analysis

Stage 1: Investigation of Current Environment

The current system is investigated for several reasons, including the following:

- the analysts learn the terminology and function of the users' environment;
- the old system may form the basis of the new system;
- the data required by the system can be investigated;
- it provides the users with a good introduction to the techniques;
- the boundaries of the investigation can be clearly set.

The third reason illustrates one of the principles of SSADM that the underlying structure of the data of a system will not change much over time. Even though the introduction of a new computer system may change the functions—a computer system can significantly increase what can be tackled by the users—the underlying data required to perform the functions will not change very much.

If there is no current system, for example where there is a new law that requires support, this stage consists of just initiating the project and beginning to document the new requirements.

The current system view built up in Stage 1 is redrawn to extract *what* the system does without any indication of *how* this is achieved. The resulting picture is the logical view of the current system. This allows the analyst to concentrate on what functions are performed in the current system and to make decisions about what must be included in the new system.

Stage 2: Business System Options

The current system is left far behind by the Business System Options which are completed next. They reflect the different ways (options) in which the system might be organized to meet the requirements. A decision is made by the users as which option or combination of options best meets their needs. The decision is not an implementation decision (although it may constrain the way the system is implemented). Instead, this is a way of taking a fresh view of what the system is required to do and how it can be organized to meet the underlying business objectives.

Requirements Specification

Stage 3: Definition of Requirements
Based upon the selected Business System Option, a detailed specification of the required system is built up and checked extensively. In order that the new system will not be constrained by the current implementation, there are a number of steps within this stage to lead the analysts gradually away from the current system towards a fresh view of the requirements.

This stage builds up the data design so that all the required data will be included. It applies a relational analysis technique to groups of data items in the system to act as a cross-check on the data definitions.

Logical Systems Specification

The two stages in this module are often performed in parallel.

Stage 4: Selection of technical options
At this stage, if the purchase of new computer equipment is required, the development team have enough information to compile the different implementation options for the system. Each option is costed out and the benefits weighed against the costs to give the user some help in choosing the final solution. This might form the basis for selecting the final system hardware.

Stage 5: Logical design
The specification developed in Stage 3 is expanded to a very high level of detail so that the constructor can be given all the detail necessary to build the system.

Physical Design

Stage 6: Physical design
Here, the complete logical design—both data and processing—is converted into a design that will run on the target environment. The initial physical design is tuned before implementation so that it will meet the performance requirements of the system.

Customizing SSADM

We have described above and concentrate, in this book, on the basic structure of SSADM. However, every project is different and to a certain extent requires its own customized method. Towards this end, customized versions of SSADM have been developed for common project circumstances. These include versions for use with application packages, for designing systems with Graphical User Interfaces (GUIs), and 'fast path' templates for use when a solution is required 'yesterday' and risks have to be taken. These use the SSADM techniques and principles described in this book; their differences with basic SSADM are that some steps are omitted or added and that the order of steps will be different. There may also be some adaptation of the techniques— we give some guidance on customization in Chapter 7, Management Aspects.

Structured techniques

The techniques of SSADM give standards for how each step and task is to be performed. The rules of the syntax and notation of each technique are supplemented with guidelines on how they should be applied in a particular step. The diagrammatic techniques of SSADM are:

- Data Flow Modelling;
- Logical Data Modelling;
- Event- Entity Modelling;
- Dialogue Design;
- Logical Database Process Design

In addition, there are techniques and procedures that are not diagrammatic including:

- requirements definition;
- function definition;
- relational data analysis;
- specification prototyping;
- physical data design;
- physical process specification;

This book gives clear guidelines on each of the techniques and shows how they are inter-related and can cross-check one another. These techniques and procedures are briefly described below and explained in more detail in subsequent chapters.

Requirements Definition

A requirement is a feature or facility that is desired by some of the users of the current or future system. The technique of Requirements Definition involves eliciting those requirements, defining and refining them, and documenting them in the Requirements Catalogue. Throughout this process the analyst tries to develop a consensus amongst users regarding the definition of each requirement and its importance in the new system. When considering different ways forward for the project these requirements provide a checklist against which different options can be measured. This happens in both the Business Systems Options and the Technical Systems Options stages.

Logical Data Modelling

This is a method for describing what information should be held by the system. The approach used in SSADM is very similar to entity modelling in other methods. A diagram is produced showing the entities and their relationships, this is further documented by a set of entity description forms detailing their data contents.

A Logical Data Model is produced for the current system. This is extended to meet the requirements of the new system, resulting in a Required System Logical Data Model. The Required System Logical Data Model is used as the basis for the physical data design.

Another part of the technique defines the navigation required for enquiries using a diagram known as an Enquiry Access Path. These are used later to define the detailed processing in an Enquiry Process Model.

Data Flow Modelling

Data Flow Diagrams are a widely used technique for representing the information flows of a system. The diagrams represent the external agents sending and receiving information; the processes that change information; the information flows themselves; and where information is stored. (They should really be called 'Information Flow Diagrams'.) The diagrams are hierarchical in nature with a single, top-level diagram decomposing to many lower-level diagrams, each representing different parts of the system.

Data Flow Diagrams are used in the early stages in systems analysis to help understand the present system. As the project proceeds they are used to represent the required system. They are used to identify functions, described below, which become part of the final specification

Function Definition

The concept of functions is central to SSADM. Functions are the basic blocks of processing through which we build the whole system. Ultimately all of the processing is defined through functions. They collect together other SSADM specifications: process models, input/output structures, dialogue designs and the interim products used to develop these. Functions are initially defined from the Required System Data Flow Diagrams and then refined as the specification becomes more detailed.

This technique also involves the initial definition of the structure and content of the information input to and output from the system. These Input/Output Structures later become dialogues, reports or input forms.

Specification Prototyping

The SSADM approach to prototyping is characterized by careful management control, by clearly defining the scope of prototyping, and by being 'throw away' but accepting that some aspects of the prototype may be retained in the delivered system. Step 350, *develop specification prototypes*, deals with the selection, construction, demonstration, evaluation, review, and re-specification of the core critical functions subjected to prototyping. The results of prototyping are fed back into the systems design.

Event-Entity Modelling

Entity Life Histories are models of how the system's data is changed over time by events acting on entities. For each entity the sequence, selection, and iteration of events affecting it are shown using a graphical notation.

An event is whatever triggers a process to update system data. As it would be too complicated to model the entire set of events for a whole system at once, the effects of the events on each entity are modelled. For each event we produce an Effect Correspondence Diagram showing the data changed by the event.

Dialogue Design

The SSADM technique of dialogue design includes the identification of the end-users of the computer system, the identification of which functions will be on-line, the identification of critical dialogues which may be prototyped. We define the detailed structure of each dialogue showing how the user navigates within the dialogue and how he or she navigates from the dialogue to other dialogues via menus and commands. 'Help' facilities are also defined for dialogues. An Application Style Guide is produced which contains guidelines for the developer on screen design, 'help' messages, etc.

Relational data analysis

Relational data analysis, based upon relational theory, is used in the Requirements Specification module of SSADM where it complements and checks logical data modelling. The merging of the two techniques results in a Required System Logical Data Model which is the basis for database design.

In contrast to logical data modelling, relational data analysis is a bottom-up technique—using data items, the atomic units of data. We start from groups of data items that are commonly used together: input forms, screens, and reports; analysing the inter-relationships between data items on the inputs to or from the system.

Relational data analysis consists of a progression from the original, unnormalized, data through several refinements (normal forms) until the data items are arranged to eliminate any repeating items or duplication. The results of performing this analysis on several different groups of data items are merged, or rationalized, to give sets of data items that should correspond to the entities on the Logical Data Model.

The process of relational data analysis ensures that all data items required by the system are included in the system's data structure. Also, it is a good way to ensure that the system data is fully understood.

Logical Database Process Design

This technique is closely related to Jackson structured programming in that input (from Effect Correspondence Diagrams or Enquiry Access Paths) and output data structures are defined and merged to produce Update and Enquiry Process Models. These process models also contain operations and conditions forming a very detailed specification of the processing—but one which is independent of the physical implementation.

Physical Data Design

The conversion of the Logical Data Model into a workable physical design takes place in two phases. First, simple rules are applied which crudely convert the logical design into a corresponding design for the target environment. This design might work, but would probably not be very efficient or exploit the features of the particular hardware or software that will be used. Therefore, the 'first-cut' design is tuned using a process called physical design control. This consists of successively calculating the performance of the system (time taken to execute certain critical transactions, space requirements, and recovery times), then modifying the design slightly and recalculating until the performance objectives are met.

Physical Process Specification

This first identifies how the Physical Design stage of the project is to be done by developing a Physical Design Strategy. The technique concentrates on mapping the logical process design represented by functions, and Update and Enquiry Process Models into the physical environment chosen in Technical System Options.

Documentation

Documentation standards define how the products of this development activity should be presented. Several different kinds of document will be produced during a project: diagrams, forms, matrices, and narrative reports. Working documents are produced as a means of developing some of the diagrams. Other documents are part of the formal documentation standards of SSADM and are carried forward into later steps of the project. Some of these will need to be maintained throughout the system's life cycle.

An important part of the diagrammatic techniques are the standards that govern their layout, symbols, and content. This standardization facilitates understanding of the diagrams within the project team, with users, and with others interested in the project.

In addition to the diagrams there is a considerable amount of highly structured information that needs to be developed. Some of this is necessary to support the diagrams, for instance each data entity shown on a Logical Data Structure diagram needs to be defined, and its constituent attributes specified. Some of this structured information is not directly related to the diagrams, for example a Requirements Catalogue is developed which describes and gives a priority weighting to each requirement identified in analysis. To help record this structured information a number of standard forms are suggested. We have used these forms throughout the book, although these forms should be modified for specific projects.

In addition to forms, matrices are used to help start some of the diagrams. An entity matrix is used to identify relationships between entities as an initial step in the logical data modelling technique and an entity/event matrix is used as a basis for Entity Life Histories. Matrices are also sometimes useful in cross-checking one technique with another.

Often formal reports such as feasibility study reports or full study reports will be required. SSADM provides no detailed recommendations on the content or format of such reports; these will often be set by the organization. However, much of the SSADM documentation, both diagrams and forms, will need to be integrated into these formal reports.

Finally, although the emphasis of this book is in describing a paper-based method, we should stress that very few projects will use only manual methods of documentation. There are now many computer-aided systems engineering (CASE) tools on the market. Many of these support SSADM and some support some of the SSADM techniques. These tools are invaluable in producing high-quality documentation, in checking consistency and completeness, in enabling rapid amendment of diagrams and other structured information, and in many other ways. We have chosen to present the method as a manual one for two main reasons. First, because we wished to concentrate on the method itself rather than its software implementations. Second, the market is changing very rapidly and our use of any particular product or range of products could soon be out of date. In Chapter 7, Management Aspects, we describe some of the features of CASE and discuss how CASE tools might be used in an SSADM project.

2 Three views of the system

SSADM takes three basic views of information:

- Logical Data Models   show what information is stored and how it is inter-related;
- Data Flow Models   show how information is passed around;
- Entity Life Histories   show how information is changed during its lifetime.

Each of these views is developed in the Requirements Analysis and Requirements Specification Modules before development of a detailed logical process design and conversion to an executable physical design. Throughout the analysis and design phases of SSADM all three of these views are used and inter-related. It is therefore important to gain a good understanding of each view and how they fit together as a whole. In this chapter we discuss each view separately; concentrating on the notation and the conceptual information represented. In the final section of the chapter we describe how the views inter-relate and can be cross-checked against each other. Some readers may find it easier to skim this section and return to it after seeing how the different views are used in practice in Chapters 3 and 4.

Note that we do not attempt to describe how the different views are developed in this chapter. This is explained in detail in the rest of the book where we take a case study through all the stages of SSADM.

2.1 Logical Data Models

Introduction

Computer systems are much better than human beings at storing and retrieving large amounts of data. This characteristic has led to the development of large, computer-based information systems. All organizations of any size possess vast quantities of information which may be stored in a number of ways: in people's heads, in filing cabinets, on card indexes, on microfiche, and on computer-readable media. To design computer-based information systems for these organizations it is necessary to know exactly what information should be held by the computer and to specify how that information should be organized.

SSADM makes a fundamental split between a logical and a physical view of data. The physical view represents how the system's data is held in particular technological environments. For example, if the system was currently implemented using many card indexes and paper-based files, then the way its data would be organized to maximize efficiency would be very different from the same system implemented using serial and index sequential files or using a relational database. The logical view of the system's data is completely independent of how it is physically implemented; it could use any computer file or database organization, or even a manually based file organization.

The result of the first four modules of SSADM is a complete specification of the logical data design and the logical processing design. To achieve this logical data design SSADM uses two techniques: logical data modelling and relational data analysis. Thus two separate views of the system's data are derived. The view from relational data analysis is used to validate the Logical Data Model.

Relational data analysis is a 'bottom-up' technique where the smallest meaningful components of information—the attributes or data items—are rigorously analysed to produce a complete and flexible organization of data. Logical data modelling is a 'top-down' technique where things about which we might want to hold information are modelled.

Logical data modelling is a very widely used technique. Originally devised for database design, it is now also used in many systems development methods. The terms entity modelling, data modelling, and entity relationship modelling are all used by different methods to describe a similar approach to SSADM's logical data modelling.

In this section we describe the components of a Logical Data Model: entities, relationships, and attributes. We then describe how the diagram (known as the Logical Data Structure) is presented as a whole.

Entities and attributes

A Logical Data Model of a system models the entities and their inter-relationships.

Definition of an entity
An entity is something of significance to the system about which information is to be held.

Some examples of information systems and their entities are:

* Hospital information   patients, wards, diseases.
* Library systems   books, borrowers, loans, reservations, fines.
* Personnel systems   employees, jobs, grades, skills.
* Banking systems   customers, bank accounts, loans.

Type and occurrence
In each of the above examples we described the entity type representing a number of entity occurrences. For example, in the bank the entity type Customer represents all the occurrences of the Customer entity—Maurice Moneybags, Percy Penniless, etc. It is important to distinguish between type and occurrence as it often causes confusion.

Entity Type	*Entity occurrence*
Customer	M. Moneybags and associated information
	P. Penniless and associated information

In this book we always use 'entity' to refer to the entity type and always use 'entity occurrence' to refer to a specific entity occurrence. When we are referring to the entity type the name is begun with a capital, as in Customer.

Representation of entities
An entity is represented as a box on a Logical Data Structure diagram with the name of the entity inside it as shown in Fig. 2.1. The singular form is used to emphasize that it is the entity type rather than the number of occurrences that is being represented.

Fig. 2.1 Notation for entity types

Real world entities and system entities
The definition of an entity began: 'An entity is something of significance to the system...' A real world 'something'—a book, a person, a job—may be important to a number of different systems. The real world Maurice Moneybags may be a system entity occurrence in a number of systems: patient in the hospital example, borrower occurrence in the library, employee occurrence in the personnel, and customer occurrence in the bank. In logical data modelling we ignore the real world aspects of entities and concentrate on things about them that are important to the system. It is therefore system entities rather than real world entities that are described in Logical Data Models, although the distinction is rarely made. The real world existence of these entities is a convenient handle which enables us to get to grips with their importance to the system being considered. Thus customers, bank accounts, loans arc all real world things of significance to the banking system.

Real world attributes and system attributes
'An entity... about which information is to be held': when designing information systems we need to say precisely what that information is. The real world Maurice Moneybags has a name, a wife called Joyce, a house (at Acacia Avenue), a Rolls-Royce car, blue eyes, three cats, and a credit card. These could all be thought of as real world attribute occurrences of the attribute types: name, wife's name, home-owner or not, home address, make of car, colour of eyes, number of cats, credit card holder or not. However, for the banking system we are not interested in the colour of our customers' eyes or the number of cats they own but in their names and home addresses. So for each system entity we can define a set of system attribute types. In SSADM these system attribute types are known simply as attributes.

Definition of an attribute
A attribute is the smallest discrete component of the system information that is meaningful.
Other approaches to data modelling sometimes use the terms 'data item', 'logical data item', and 'data element' to mean much the same thing.

When an attribute is implemented in a file-based computer system it is usually referred to as a field. Different database management systems use a variety of terms to refer to their implementation of attributes.

Attributes are important not only in logical data modelling in SSADM; the contents of the system inputs and outputs are also described in terms of their constituent attributes. In this context the attributes are sometimes referred to as data items.

In the early steps and stages of SSADM only the major attributes for each entity may be loosely described; however, before physical design can commence all attributes should be fully described by a text description, a format specification, sizes (average and maximum), and by validation information.

Keys

It must be possible to identify uniquely each entity occurrence. For each entity this means that there must be one attribute or group of attributes whose value determines the value of all the other items in the entity. In other words if the value of this key attribute is known it is possible to find the values of all the other attributes in that entity. For example, let us take an occurrence of the entity Bank Account in Cash & Grabbs Bank:

Account No.	1234
Date Opened	12 June 1978
Branch	The Strand, London
Current Balance	£20 000

The Current Balance clearly cannot uniquely determine the values of the other attributes as there obviously may be several accounts with balances of £20 000. In a similar way neither Date Opened nor Branch could determine the other values. The only attribute that could uniquely determine the values of the other attributes is Account No. This is then referred to as the *primary key*. Through the primary key we can find all of the data associated with a particular entity occurrence.

Sometimes a combination of attributes is required as the primary key. For example, if each branch of the Bank set their own Account Nos., it would then be possible for the same account number to occur at several branches. A combination of Account No. and Branch would be needed to identify uniquely each Bank Account occurrence.

This definition of keys is dealt with in much more detail in the section on relational data analysis. The important thing to remember here is that each entity occurrence must be capable of being uniquely identified, and it is through the identifying attributes that we have immediate access to all the data for the particular entity occurrence.

Relationships

Real world entities have relationships with other real world entities. Maurice Moneybags has *borrowed* the books 'How to be a Millionaire' and 'Tax Saving Guide' from the library, *is treated* in Ward 10 of the hospital, *has* a grade of Senior Accountant at work, and *has* a current bank account and a deposit bank account. These are all examples of real world relationship occurrences that are also system relationship occurrences in the library, hospital, personnel, and banking systems. Relationships are normally described as verbs (borrowed, treated, has) and entities as nouns (borrower, book, patient, ward, etc.). As with entities and attributes, relationship type is always referred to in this book as relationship and relationship occurrence is always referred to as relationship occurrence.

Definition of a relationship
A relationship is an association between two entities that is important to the system.

Relationships are important when designing information systems because they define access from one entity occurrence to another. Thus a relationship between say Patient and Ward implies that from an occurrence of Patient, say Mr Moneybags, we can find the occurrence of the Ward in which they are treated, Ward 10. Similarly we can find which patients are in a particular ward by going from the Ward occurrence to the Patient occurrences. We must remember that when we draw a relationship on a Logical Data Structure then we are saying that when we develop an information system, we will always be able to access occurrences by navigating from either end of the relationship.

Just as entities are accessed by keys so the link between entities can be managed by attributes acting as keys. This makes perfect sense in that we would naturally associate, with the Patient entity, the attribute of the Ward No. that he or she was treated in. Ward No. would thus appear as a *foreign key* attribute in the list of attributes associated with the Patient entity, which would have a primary key attribute of Patient No. It is called a foreign key because it also appears as the primary key of another entity, in this case the Ward entity.

Note that it is very poor data modelling to include all the Patient Nos. (in other words, a repeating group) associated with the Ward in the list of its attributes. The list of patients in a given ward can be obtained by looking at all the Patients and finding those with the right Ward No. In Chapter 4 we discuss relational data analysis and explain that an entity which can have multiple occurrences of some of its attributes is not in First Normal Form.

Representation of relationships
The relationship described above is a one-to-many relationship in that *one* occurrence of ward may have *many* occurrences of patient associated with it. Figure 2.2 shows diagrammatically the relationships between a ward and its patients.

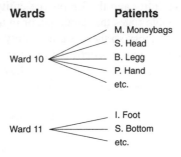

Fig. 2.2 Occurrence diagram showing relationships between wards and patients

These occurrence diagrams are useful for explaining ideas but a more concise notation is required for specifying systems. Figure 2.3 shows entity types and relationship types.

The line with the crow's foot describes the relationship, called a *one-to-many* relationship. The crow's foot is always shown at the many end. The entity at the *one* end is often referred to as the *master entity* and the entity at the *many* end referred to as the *detail entity*. We sometimes say that 'Ward *owns* Patient'; this means that Ward is the master entity related to the detail entity, Patient.[1]

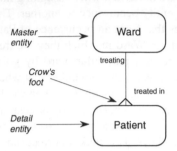

Fig. 2.3 SSADM notation showing relationship between Ward and Patient

We can think of the relationship as two relationships:

> each **ward** must be **treating** one or more **patients**
> each **patient** must be **treated in** one and only one **ward**

Each of these relationships is separately named. In the first case we are going from the master entity to the detail entity, in the second case we are going from the detail entity to the master entity.

Optional and mandatory relationships

A relationship is said to be optional between two entities if an occurrence of one may exist without associated occurrences of the other. A mandatory relationship is where if one occurrence of an entity must be associated with an occurrence of the other entity. Mandatory relationships are shown by solid lines, optional relationships are shown by broken lines (dashed or dotted).

A concrete example of optional and mandatory relationships could be the relationship between the Office entity and the Employee entity for a personnel system. Figure 2.4 shows the four possible states that could occur in the system. In state 1 both ends of the relationship are mandatory so there are no empty offices or no 'homeless' employees. In state 2 there may be empty offices but there are no 'homeless' employees. In state 3 all offices are occupied, but some employees have no office. In state 4 offices may be empty and some employees may have no office.

---

[1] It is worth getting used to this jargon; analysts always use it when they are discussing Logical Data Structures.

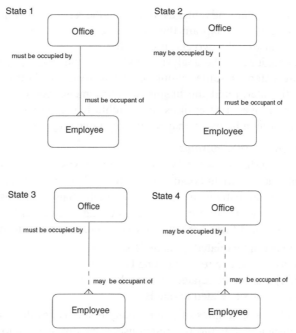

Fig. 2.4 Possible optional and mandatory relationships between Office and Employee

Relationship names

You will have noticed that we name each relationship at each end. The names are constructed so that a sentence may be formed linking both entities together, hence:

each **ward** must be **treating** one or more **patients**

each **patient** must be **treated in** one and only one **ward**

The syntax for each sentence is always exactly the same:

each <subject entity name> *must be/may be* <link phrase closest to subject entity> *one and only one/one or more* <object entity name> (plural if the many end)

must be is used if the relationship is mandatory

may be is used if the relationship is optional

one and only one is used if the object entity is at the *one* end

one or more is used if the object entity is at the *many* end

At first it is quite difficult to find useful names for the relationship that conform to this syntax. Using 'must be/may be' (necessary to show the optionality of relationships) means that relationship names often take particular verb forms: 'treating', 'treated in', 'author of', 'holder', 'employer of', 'employing', 'employed in', 'credit or debit to', are all examples. With practice, it becomes much easier to find meaningful names that conform to this syntax. In your first attempts at naming relationships it is better to put something which is meaningful and definite rather than something vague and unspecific just to conform to the syntax rules. Phrases such as 'owned by', 'related to', 'associating', 'part of' should generally be avoided.

There are many advantages to naming the relationships in these ways. First, it makes it much easier to explain the models to users. Each relationship may be read as a sentence linking the two entities together.

Second, it helps the analyst to understand the business environment. The process of naming enforces some rigour on the analyst and helps ensure that he or she has correctly interpreted the business environment. Some projects have data structures containing over 100 entities and double that number of relationships; it improves communication between analysts in such large projects when relationships are named.

The degree of relationships

The relationship between Ward and Patient was a one-to-many relationship in that at any one time a patient could only be treated in one ward, and that in any one ward there could be many patients treated. These one-to-many relationships between two different entities are the most common type occurring on Logical Data Structures. Between two entities A and B there are four possible degrees of relationship:

1. One A can be related to many B's.
2. Many A's can be related to one B.
3. Many A's can be related to many B's.
4. One A can be related to one B.

1 and 2 are examples of one-to-many relationships discussed before. Many-to-many relationships and one-to-one relationships are discussed below.

Many-to-many relationships

Example 3 above is a many-to-many relationship, although these often emerge in the early stages of data modelling, they can nearly always be resolved into one-to-many relationships. An example will make clear why this is so.

Consider the relationship between a patient and drugs in the hospital.

A patient may be prescribed many drugs and a drug may be prescribed to many patients (Fig. 2.5).

Fig. 2.5 Many-to-many relationship between Patient and Drug

So we have a many-to-many relationship. However, when we investigate this relationship more deeply it becomes apparent that there is information associated with the relationship 'prescribed'. In fact, the more we think about it the more obvious it becomes that 'Prescription' is itself an entity, containing information such as the date of prescription, the dosage, and strength. Further analysis shows that a prescription can only be for one patient, although each patient may have many prescriptions. Hospital rules state that a prescription can be for one and only one drug and, obviously, the same drug may appear on many prescriptions This gives Fig. 2.6 as a better representation of the relationships.

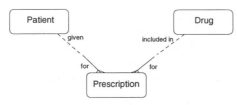

Fig. 2.6 Many-to-many relationship resolved using the entity Prescription

Thus the many-to-many relationship can be broken into two one-to-many relationships. It is normally the case that what appear to be many-to-many relationships can, on further analysis, be broken into new entities and relationships. Any many-to-many relationships should be very carefully examined. SSADM allows them to be shown as many-to-many in the early stages of a project but insists that they are resolved before Stage 5, Logical Design.[1]

There are rare cases where true many-to-many relationships exist. When this occurs a link entity and two one-to-many relationships are created. An example of this comes from the banking system where a customer can have many bank accounts and a particular bank account may be owned by several customers. The link entity could be called 'Ownership', 'Participation', or 'Signatory' but none of these accurately describe the link entity—this is a true many-to-many relationship as there is no information associated with the link. If no suitable name can be found then the link entity could be called 'Customer/Bank Account Link' as in Fig. 2.7.

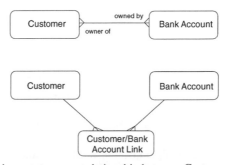

Fig. 2.7 Resolving a 'true' many-to-many relationship between Customer and Bank Account

It is important to note that the 'many' means 'one or more' Most people will only have one bank account and most bank accounts will only be owned by one person. So there will, in most cases, be only one occurrence of Customer/Bank Account Link for each customer. What is being represented in the Logical Data Structure is the general case.

---

[1] Very few database management systems can directly implement many-to-many relationships. If they were retained until the logical design is converted to a physical implementation, major changes to the process design would be needed to handle the processing of the new entity types required to resolve the many-to-many relationships.

One-to-one relationships

This is where one A is related of only one B. Consider the entities Borrower and Book in the library example; further thought might lead us to another entity, Loan. Examining the relationships between these three entities it becomes clear that the relationship between Book and Borrower is maintained though the Loan entity (Fig. 2.8).

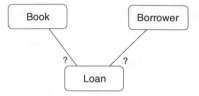

Fig. 2.8 Relationships between Book, Borrower, and Loan

This library is a very poor one and has only one copy of each book—this makes the example more straightforward. A borrower occurrence may at one time have several loan occurrences. Each of these loan occurrences can be associated with only one borrower occurrence. So there is a one-to-many relationship between Borrower and Loan.

A loan occurrence can only be for only one book occurrence and a book occurrence can only have, at any one time, one loan occurrence associated with it (in this case we only need to record the current loan). So we have a one-to-one relationship between Book and Loan (Fig. 2.9).

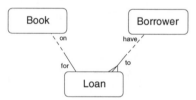

Fig. 2.9 One-to-one relationship between Book and Loan

We can, however, amalgamate the entities Book and Loan, adding to the attributes associated with Book (e.g. title, ISBN, author, date of publication) the attributes associated with Loan (e.g. date borrowed, date due back). This could be represented as shown in Fig. 2.10.

Fig. 2.10 Book/Loan entity resolving a one-to-one relationship

SSADM recommends that one-to-one relationships are resolved before logical design. In this example Book and Loan can be merged to form one entity Book/Loan with a single key of ISBN. In other cases it may be more appropriate to show the one-to-one relationship as a one-to-many relationship.[1]

The merging of entities makes it almost impossible to find sensible names for the relationships.

Exclusive relationships
This is when the existence of one relationship precludes the existence of another. In Fig. 2.11 an occurrence of *B* can be owned by *either* an occurrence of *A or* by an occurrence of *C* but *never* by *both*. This is represented by drawing an arc linking the two relationships that exclude each other.

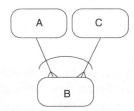

Fig. 2.11 Exclusive relationships shown by exclusion arc

Individual arcs, linked by identifiers ('a's in Fig. 2.12), are sometimes used when the drawing of a continuous arc would cause crossing lines or otherwise confuse the diagram.

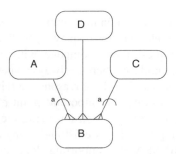

Fig. 2.12 Individually identified arcs showing an exclusive relationship

Figure 2.13 shows that a patient occurrence can be treated either in a ward or in an outpatient department but not in both. The relationship statement associated with exclusive relationships will include the either/or phrase so:

---

[1] We feel that this removal of one-to-one relationships is undesirable since it prejudges the physical design. There are many different ways of physically implementing the one-to-one relationship and we feel the best approach is to treat each case on its particular merits considering the opportunities provided by the physical environment chosen. Combining entities also makes Entity Life Histories much more difficult.

each **patient** must be **either** treated in one and only one **ward or** treated in one and only one **outpatient department**

Sometimes exclusivity can occur across several relationships (e.g. the patient could be treated in a ward, an outpatient department, or by a community nurse)—this is shown using the same notation.

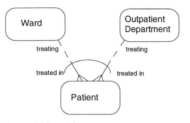

Fig. 2.13 Example of an exclusive relationship

Recursive relationships

Previously we have discussed the relationship of entity occurrences of one type with entity occurrences of a different type. Often entity occurrences have direct relationships with other entity occurrences of the same type.

Consider the Personnel system in which Maurice Moneybags is an entity occurrence of the type Employee. Maurice has a manager, J. Pounds, who is also an occurrence of Employee, Maurice also manages I. Shilling and A. Penny. An employee can manage many employees but is managed by one and only one employee. Thus the Employee entity has a one-to-many relationship with itself (Fig. 2.14). This recursive relationship is shown by the 'crow's leg' looping round—often referred to as a 'pig's ear'. This kind of relationship is very common in administrative systems.

These recursive relationships display a peculiar kind of optionality. At the top of the structure there is presumably someone without a manager (unless we invoke the Ultimate Being!). Similarly, there is always someone at the bottom of the structure who doesn't manage anyone. For these reasons the relationship is shown as optional in both directions. This illustrates an important point about Logical Data Models—it is not possible to represent every constraint using the modelling notation. More advanced semantic modelling techniques exist and many are described in academic papers. In cases like this the SSADM supporting documentation can be used to annotate any particular conditions or constraints that may apply which are beyond those represented by the diagrammatic notations.

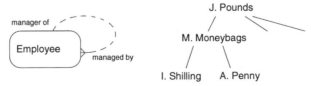

Fig. 2.14 Employee recursive relationship and corresponding occurrence diagram

Entities also may appear to have many-to-many relationships with themselves. When this happens a double-lobed pig's ear (sow's purse) is not drawn. Instead, as in other many-to-many relationships, a link entity is created (Fig. 2.15).

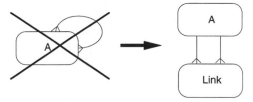

Fig. 2.15 Resolving a recursive many-to-many relationship

Consider a delivery system to supermarkets; if one product is out of stock then alternative products can act as substitutes. So each product can be substituted by many other products and can, in turn, act as a substitute for many other products (Fig. 2.16).

Fig. 2.16 Occurrence diagram for product substitution

Thus it appears that the Product entity has a many-to-many relationship with itself. A link entity is therefore created (Fig. 2.17). On closer inspection it is clear that there are attributes associated with the link entity such as the price adjustment required and the equivalent quantity.

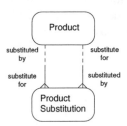

Fig. 2.17 Resolved many-to-many relationship of Product with itself

Multiple relationships
These are when there are more than one relationship between the same pair of entities. Each relationship is different and this is reflected in their names. Multiple relationships are quite common and are often a convenient way of avoiding creation of unnecessary link entities.

Suppose we are trying to model the relationship between teams and fixtures in a sport such as football. Each team may have many fixtures and each fixture involves two teams. So it appears that we have a many-to-many relationship for which we can create an artificial link entity: Participation (see Fig. 2.18).

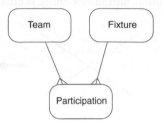

Fig. 2.18 Unsatisfactory modelling of relationship between Team and Fixture

However, a better way of modelling this is to say that as only two teams can be involved in a fixture then Fixture has two relationships with Team (Fig. 2.19).

Fig. 2.19 Multiple relationships between Team and Fixture

A very frequent occasion when a multiple relationship occurs is when the movement of something is being modelled (see Fig. 2.20). An example like this occurs in the Yorkies case study later in this book.

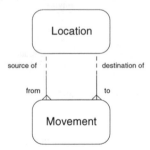

Fig. 2.20 Multiple relationships modelling movement

Entity sub-types and super-types
This technique is not formally part of SSADM but is discussed in the SSADM Reference Manual. It is a very useful construct which is used in several other systems

development methods and is closely related to the object-oriented approach.[1] The idea is that an entity sub-type may inherit attributes from an entity super-type.

In the example shown below in Fig. 2.21 the super-type is Patient and the sub-types are In Patient and Out Patient. Certain attributes belong to Patient such as Patient No., Patient Surname, Patient Address, Date of Birth, etc. Other attributes will be specific for each sub-type. For example, for In Patient: Dietary Requirements, Visiting Regulations, Bed No.; and for Out Patient: Transport Requirements, Home Circumstances. There are no separate occurrences of In Patient and Patient, it is simply that the In Patient will always inherit the attributes of Patient.

Super-types and sub-types can both participate in relationships. For example, all patients must be given treatment (shown by the link to the super-type box). However, only out-patients must be given out-patient treatment and only in-patients occupy beds (shown by the sub-types' relationships).

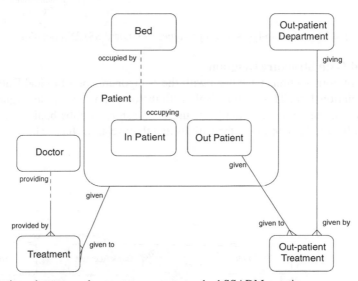

Fig. 2.21 Entity sub-types and super-types—not standard SSADM notation

The notation does not allow sub-types to overlap and so this model does not cater for a patient being both an in-patient and out-patient. The notation used here is not that suggested by SSADM but is similar to the notation used by some other methods, including the Oracle CASE* Method. The SSADM notation, shown below in Fig. 2.22 for exactly the same example, uses exclusive mandatory one-to-one relationships to show sub-types. We prefer the non-SSADM notation since it is less geared to a specific physical implementation and because we feel it is more elegant to use different notations for different semantic information.

---

[1] Object-oriented modellers would refer to a sub-type as *inheriting* the characteristics of the super-type. A sub-type is a *specialization* of a super-type, and a super-type is a *generalization* of a sub-type.

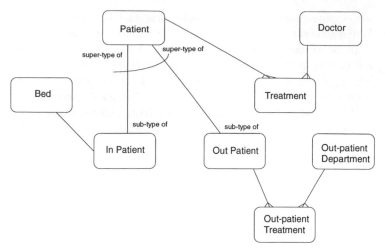

Fig. 2.22 Entity sub-types and super-types—standard SSADM notation

The Logical Data Structure Diagram

Previous sections have dealt with the components of a Logical Data Structure and their relationships. This section deals with the diagram as a whole. Figure 2.23 below shows a complete Logical Data Structure for Cash & Grabbs bank. Certain conventions are followed in positioning the entities and their relationships. These are explained below.

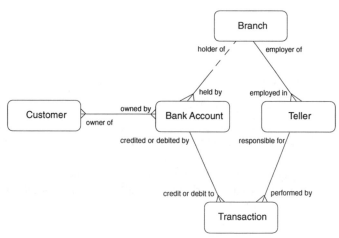

Fig. 2.23 Logical Data Structure for Cash & Grabbs Bank

Layout (or presentation)

For a very large and complex system these diagrams can contain more than 100 entities and more than 200 relationships. Even simple systems have 20 or 30 entities. It is important that these diagrams are presented in a way that makes them easy to read and understand.

Crossing lines If at all possible the diagram should be drawn so that relationship lines do not cross. This can often be easily managed by rearranging the position of entities, as shown, for example, in Fig. 2.24.

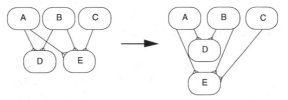

Fig. 2.24 Avoiding crossing relationship lines

Sometimes it is necessary to place a kink or 'dog leg' a line to avoid crossing an entity or another line (Fig. 2.25).

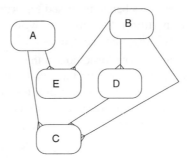

Fig. 2.25 Kinking relationship lines to avoid crossings

Some practitioners and some CASE tools show only orthogonal relationship lines (Fig. 2.26). This makes the diagrams look neat but in the opinion of the authors makes it harder, in complex diagrams, to sort out which entities are related to which others.

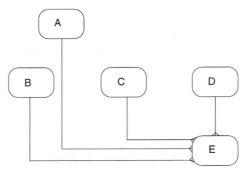

Fig. 2.26 Orthogonal relationship lines

If it is impossible to avoid crossing lines then the neatest way of drawing this to build a 'bridge' over which one of the relationship lines passes. This is shown in Fig. 2.27.

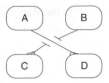

Fig. 2.27 'Bridges' to handle crossing lines

Positioning the entities Some complex Logical Data Structures may cover several areas of the organization. Entities that fall into the same business area should then be drawn physically close to each other. This will often happen anyway because their relationships will tend to be with other entities in the same business area.

There are several advantages of presenting the information in this way:

- it is easier to understand;
- it is easier to present (the diagram can be presented in a top-down fashion with particular business areas being discussed separately);
- it is easier to partition the project, with different people or teams having responsibility for different business areas.

A convention of Logical Data Structures is that they are drawn so that the 'crow's feet' are placed so that the crow stands on the detail entity (see Fig. 2.28). This makes it easy to view the diagram since all master entities are above their detail entities. This convention cannot always be followed—sometimes it will lead to crossing lines or placing entities out of context.

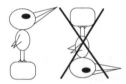

Fig. 2.28 No dead crows!

Validation
The Logical Data Structure must be able to support the processing requirements of the system. Every bit of processing defined on the Data Flow Diagrams and every retrieval documented must be capable of being performed on the Logical Data Structure. This means that the attributes required for the processing must be included in entities and that the relationships exist between those entities to enable the navigation from one entity occurrence to another for that bit of processing to be performed. Validation is discussed further in Sec. 3.5 and again in Sec. 4.8.

Supporting documentation—Entity and Relationship Descriptions
The Logical Data Structure diagram is a summary of the data that the system must hold. It gives the groupings of attributes and their inter-relationships. To document fully the system's data it is necessary to go into further detail on each entity, each relationship,

and each attribute that has been included in an entity. In Sec. 3.5, Investigate current data, we explain this supporting documentation and give examples.

SUMMARY
- The Logical Data Structure is the means of describing the information held by the system and its inter-relationships.
- The components of the Logical Data Structure are entities and relationships.
- The Logical Data Structure deals with entity and relationship types rather than their occurrences.
- Entities are things about which the system holds information.
- Each entity is made up of a number of attributes, which are the smallest meaningful chunks of information in the system.
- Relationships relate one entity to another and indicate access from one entity occurrence to all the related ones.
- One-to-many relationships are drawn on Logical Data Structures.
- One-to-one and many-to-many relationships need to be considered very carefully.
- Exclusive, recursive, and multiple relationships often occur.
- Entity sub-types and super-types show an inheritance hierarchy where sub-types inherit attributes from super-types.
- Diagram layout is important—minimize crossing lines and show masters above details.

2.2   Data Flow Models

Introduction

A Data Flow Model consists of a set of Data Flow Diagrams and of supporting information that further describe the information shown on the diagrams.[1] A Data Flow Diagram is a diagrammatic representation of the information flows within a system, showing:

- how information enters and leaves the system;
- what changes the information;
- where information is stored.

Data Flow Models are an important technique of systems analysis (they are an important part of most systems development methods) as a means of:

- *Boundary definition.* The diagrams clearly show the boundaries and scope of the system being represented.
- *Checking the completeness of analysis.* The construction of the diagrams, and their cross-comparison with the other major SSADM techniques, helps to ensure that all information flows, stores of information, and activities within the system have been considered.

---

[1] Generally in SSADM the term *model* is used to refer to a set of documentation that reflects a particular view of the system world. The 'model' will normally contain diagrams and supporting textual information.

- *Basis for systems design.* Data Flow Diagrams show the major functional areas of the system, and therefore different designs with differing functionality can be discussed. Following agreement on the high-level design further Data Flow Diagrams can then be used to specify the detailed design.

Stages of data flow modelling in SSADM
Data Flow Models may be used to represent a physical system or a logical abstraction of a system. In SSADM, three sets of Data Flow Models are developed, in turn:

- *Current Physical.* The current system is modelled in its present implementation.
- *Logical.* The essential activities of the current system are extracted from the Current Physical Data Flow Diagrams.
- *Required System.* From the Logical Data Flow Diagrams and a list of prioritized requirements, a high-level design is produced—called the Selected Business System Option. This is then developed into a full set of Data Flow Diagrams representing the new system.

The relationship between the different stages of the Data Flow Model is represented in Fig. 2.29.

Fig. 2.29 Development of different types of Data Flow Diagrams

Data Flow Diagrams are developed during the analysis and early design stages of a project. In design, during the Requirements Specification module, they are used to identify *functions* around which the detailed processing design is built.

Benefits of Data Flow Diagrams
Data Flow Diagrams are a pictorial but non-technical representation of a system, so can be used by both technical and non-technical staff. They are used in discussions between analysts and users, and are easy to draw or amend in addition to being easily understood and verified.

One of the great strengths of Data Flow Diagrams is that it is possible to describe a system at several levels. A top-level Data Flow Diagram may show a complete system in very little detail. Each process can be separately decomposed to show the detail within. These processes can be subsequently decomposed and so on until the desired level of detail has been reached. Each level is useful to the analyst:

- the top-level diagram shows clearly the overall system boundaries, and the interfaces to other systems and users of the system;
- the detail of each individual area may be investigated in relative isolation from the rest of the system.

The management of staff within a project is helped by the segmentation of the system as individuals or teams may be assigned a single top-level Data Flow Diagram process to investigate knowing that work is not being duplicated. It is a relatively simple matter to recombine work undertaken in this way.

Components of Data Flow Diagrams

External entities
An external entity is whatever or whoever donates information to the system or receives information from it. All information represented within a system must have been obtained initially from an external entity. An external entity is represented on a Data Flow Diagram as an oval containing the name and an identifier. The convention is that the identifier is a lower-case letter, as shown in Fig. 2.30. An external entity may be a user of the system, an external organization, a computer system, or any other source or recipient of information.

Fig. 2.30 Notation for external entities

Process
A process transforms or manipulates data within the system. Processes are represented by rectangles on a Data Flow Diagram. Each process box contains the name of the process, an identifier, and possibly a location:

- The process name is an imperative statement: 'do this' or 'do that'. It describes the processing performed on the data received by the process. For example, a process may be named 'Register new customer', but may not be named 'Manager' or 'Registration Section'.
- Process identifiers are numerical.
- In the Current Physical Data Flow Diagrams, the location of the process is placed at the top of the box. This might be a physical location, but is more often used to denote the staff responsible for performing the process. The Logical and Required System Data Flow Diagrams do not show the locations of the different processes.

Figure 2.31 shows where each of these elements are placed in a process box.

Fig. 2.31 Notation for processes in Data Flow Diagrams

Data store
A data store is where information is held for a time within the system. A data store is represented on a Data Flow Diagram by an open-ended box as shown in Fig. 2.32.

Fig. 2.32 Notation for data stores

In the Current Physical Data Flow Diagrams, the data stores represent real-world stores of information such as computer files, card indexes, ledgers, etc. Manual data stores are shown on these physical diagrams by using the identifier, 'M'; computer-based data stores are shown by using the identifier, 'D'. In contrast to these main stores where data is held permanently, transient data stores hold data for a short time before it is used. Transient stores are identified by a 'T', if they are also manual then 'T(M)' is used.

In the Logical and Required System Data Flow Diagrams, each main data store is regarded as computerized and identified by a 'D'. Some transient stores may remain and retain their 'T' identifier.

Data flow

A data flow represents a package of information flowing between objects on the Data Flow Diagram. A data flow is represented by a line and an arrow to denote the direction of the flow of information. It is labelled with the name or details of the information represented by the data flow. Figure 2.33 illustrates data flows on a Current Physical Data Flow Diagram.

Fig. 2.33 Data flows on a Current Physical Data Flow Diagram

Points to note about data flows are:

- Information always flows to or from a process. The other end of the flow may be an external entity, a data store, or another process.
- Occasionally there are relevant data flows between external entities. Though, strictly speaking, these are outside the system; it can make the diagram more understandable if they are shown. The convention is to use a dashed line for these external data flows.
- In the Current Physical Data Flow Diagrams, the data flows represent real-world flows of information. For example, these could be forms sent from one part of the system to another or telephone conversations between someone within the system and a customer.
- In the Logical and Required Data Flow Diagrams, these flows represent the attributes required by a process or an output from a process.

Construction of Data Flow Diagrams

The top-level Required System Data Flow Diagram of a simple banking system is shown in Fig. 2.34. Here, the main activities are the registration of new customers, the recording of deposits or withdrawals, and the closing of accounts. New customers are registered and accounts are closed by the bank manager, represented here as an external entity. When an account is closed, the customer is notified by the system. Cash deposits into the account are made by the customer, and salary cheques are paid in by the employer. The bank clerk performs a balance check before allowing a withdrawal by the customer at the bank counter. Notice the external flows (shown by dashed lines) between Customer and Clerk indicating the information passing before entry into the computer system.

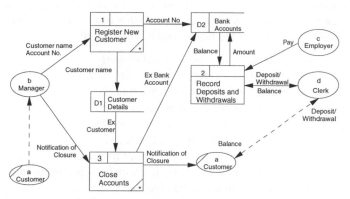

Fig. 2.34 Example Data Flow Diagram for Cash & Grabbs Bank

Some general principles about Data Flow Diagrams arise from Fig. 2.34

External entities

It is sometimes difficult to decide exactly where the system boundary lies. In the early stages of analysis the boundary should be wide to ensure that all possibilities are explored. So when investigating the current physical system the current operators are normally shown inside the boundary as part of the processes (usually named in the 'location'). Figure 2.33 shows the current physical version of Process 1 in Fig. 2.34 (which is the required system). In the current system, the manager is performing the Process 'Register New Customer', so is shown in the location area of the process box. The external entity is the customer.

The logical view of this is also that the customer is the external entity for the process 'Register New Customer'; since he or she is the 'owner' of the information and could conceivably be directly responsible for input into the computer. Our feeling is that it is best to keep the boundary wide when developing the Logical Data Flow Diagrams and so avoid constraining possible designs later.

The Required System Data Flow Diagrams show the design of the automated system. Thus Fig. 2.34 above shows the manager as the external entity as he or she is responsible for entering the information into the computer system. The customer is shown, via a dashed external data flow, supplying the manager with the information. We could have designed the system differently and allowed the customer to enter their details directly; there would then be a direct flow into the process from the customer. We have also used a dashed data flow to describe the interaction the clerk has with the customer for a deposit or withdrawal.

Further details of the Current Physical, Logical, and Required System Data Flow Diagrams are given in Secs 3.4, 3.6, and 4.2 respectively.

Process numbering

Although the processes are numbered sequentially, this does not imply that they are executed in any particular sequence. Data Flow Diagrams do not imply sequence. Processes 1, 2, and 3 could be renumbered in another sequence and remain meaningful. Even where a process-to-process data flow exists, this need not imply that the second process must wait for the first to end before it begins.

Duplication of data stores and external entities

It has been necessary to duplicate certain external entities and data stores to avoid overcomplicating the diagram with crossing lines. To denote that a particular data store has been duplicated in the diagram, an extra vertical line is placed at the left side of the box. Duplicated external entities are denoted by an oblique bar to one side of the oval, as in the Customer external entity in Fig. 2.34.

Where objects are duplicated, it is easy to make mistakes in rewriting the names of the objects wherever they occur. If identifiers are present we can easily reconcile different appearances of the same objects.

Layout of the diagram

To make the diagram more readable, the external entities have been arranged around the edges of the diagram, and the data stores placed towards the centre of the diagram. This is good practice rather than a particular rule. For clarity, no more than 12 processes should be shown on a single Data Flow Diagram. It is important to remember that one of the main purposes of a diagram is to act as a means of communication, so legibility and clarity are as important as the technical content of a diagram.

Levels of Data Flow Diagrams

Each process on a Data Flow Diagram may be broken down into several processes which are shown on another Data Flow Diagram. This is described as decomposing the Data Flow Diagrams. The Data Flow Diagram which is a result of this decomposition is one level below the Data Flow Diagram containing the original process.

The Data Flow Diagram that describes the entire system within a single diagram is the 'top-level' or 'level 1' Data Flow Diagram. The Data Flow Diagrams that are expansions of processes at the top level are 'level 2' Data Flow Diagrams (see Fig. 2.35). Levels below this are called 'level 3', 'level 4', etc. Processes that are not further decomposed are 'bottom-level' processes. Processes from the top-level Data Flow Diagram may be broken down to a number of levels if they are complex or may not be broken down at all if they are relatively simple. Thus, it is possible to have bottom-level processes appearing at all levels of the Data Flow Diagrams. Bottom-level processes are shown on the diagrams by marking them with a '*' as Processes 1 and 3 in Fig 2.34 and all the processes in Fig. 2.36.

If a process is decomposed, the identifiers of the lower-level processes are prefixed by the identifier of the higher-level process. For example, if Process 5 is decomposed, the lower-level processes will be identified as 5.1, 5.2, etc. Similarly, if Process 5.1 is subsequently decomposed, the lower-level processes will be 5.1.1, 5.1.2, and so on.

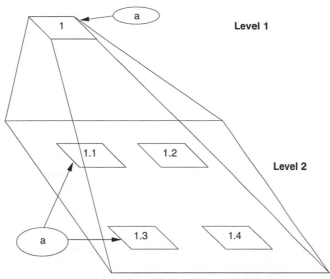

Fig. 2.35 Decomposition of processes and data flows in Data Flow Diagrams

Notice that data flows also decompose as we go down the levels of Data Flow Diagrams; the level 1 flow 'a—1' in Fig. 2.35 splits into two flows, 'a—1.1' and 'a—1.3', at level 2.

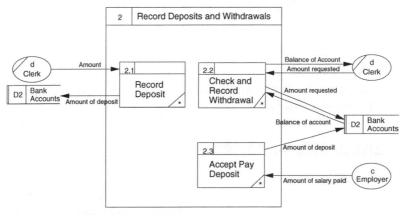

Fig. 2.36 Level 2 Data Flow Diagram for Process 2

The second-level Data Flow Diagram of Process 2 is shown in Fig. 2.36. The frame surrounding the lower-level Data Flow Diagram denotes the boundary of the higher-level process. The identifier of the higher-level process and the name of the process are put at the top of the frame.

Note that all of the flows to and from the higher-level box have been either duplicated or broken down into several flows at the lower level. If new data flows are identified at the lower level which cross the frame, these should be reflected at the higher level so that consistency between the levels is maintained. To simplify level 1 diagrams 'to' and 'from' data flows between objects are often combined into one double-headed arrow (see '2—d' on Fig. 2.34). These should always be split into the constituent data flows at the lowest level as with '2.2—d' and 'd—2.2' in Fig. 2.36.

So that it is clearly understood what is represented by each bottom-level process, it is useful to write a brief description of the process with an indication of when the process is triggered into action. This description is called an Elementary Process Description.

External entities are normally described further in External Entity Descriptions. Data flows are further described by Input/Output Descriptions (usually shortened to I/O Descriptions) which gives the data content (i.e. which attributes it uses) of the flow. Examples of this supporting information that, together with the Data Flow Diagrams, comprise the Data Flow Model are given in Sec. 4.2.

SUMMARY

Data Flow Models are an important systems analysis technique for representing the flows of information within a system.

The Data Flow Models produced in SSADM are:

- Current Physical;
- Logical;
- Required System.

The components of a Data Flow Diagram are:

- external entities;
- processes;
- data flows;
- data stores.

Each process may be further described by:

- decomposition to another level of Data Flow Diagrams;
- Elementary Process Descriptions.

2.3   Entity Life Histories

What is an Entity Life History?

A major reason for building computer-based information systems is to provide up-to-date and accurate information. Information is constantly changing, for example the number of beds available in a hospital, the price of petrol, and people's names and addresses. An information system must be able to keep track of these changes. The previous sections have described how the system is modelled from the viewpoint of information flows (Data Flow Diagrams) and from the viewpoint of the information that is held (Logical Data Structures). Entity Life Histories model the system from the viewpoint of how information is changed. What the Entity Life Histories show is the full set of all information changes that can possibly occur within the system, together with the context of each change.

Initially, each entity within a system is examined in isolation as this is a manageable unit of information to model. It is the stimuli of the changes that are modelled rather than the processes that operate to cause those changes. By specifying the set of changes to each entity, a composite picture is formed, eventually specifying the full set of changes that will occur within the system.

An Entity Life History is a diagrammatic representation of the life of a single entity, from its creation to its deletion. The life is expressed as the permitted sequence of events that can cause the entity to change. An event may be thought of as whatever brings a process into action to change entities, so although it is a process that changes the entity, it is the event that is the cause of the change.

An example will explain Entity Life Histories more clearly. Imagine that Maurice Moneybags has decided he wants to open a bank account at Cash & Grabbs Bank. When Maurice has persuaded Mr Cash, the manager, that he would be suitable as a customer, Mr Cash turns to his computer terminal and records Maurice's new bank account code in the system. The Logical Data Structure of the bank computer system contains an entity called Bank Account. The event occurrence that creates the Maurice Moneybags occurrence of the entity Bank Account is the opening of the account by Mr Cash. This event occurrence and the ones that follow it are:

- Account opened for M. Moneybags
- Cash Deposit £2000
- Cheque Cashed for £20
- Direct Deposit £1000
- Cheque Cashed for £20
- Direct Deposit £2000
  etc.

Percy Penniless is another customer at the bank, and the event occurrences that affect his bank account are:

- Account Opened for P. Penniless
- Pay Deposit by Credit Transfer £500
- Cheque Cashed for £200
- Cheque Cashed for £300
- Cheque Cashed for £300

Other accounts may behave in similar ways, none of which are precisely the same. However, it is possible to build up a general picture that will fit all occurrences of Bank Accounts at the Cash & Grabbs Bank. Basically, all accounts are opened, and several deposits and several withdrawals may be made. The way that these events affect the entity Bank Account can be summarized using a diagrammatic notation, as shown in Fig. 2.37.

Figure 2.37 is read from left to right, and wherever there is a structure going down the page, this is followed through before continuing along the left-to-right progression. This Entity Life History shows that the first event to affect the entity Bank Account will be Account Opened for all occurrences. (The first effect in the life will always be the creation of the occurrence.) Next, the Account has a life which is a series of Balance

Changes. Each Balance Change is either a Credit of a Debit. After an undefined number of Balance Changes have taken place, the Account will be closed and finally deleted.

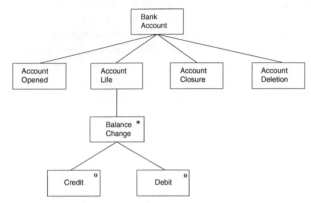

Fig. 2.37 Entity Life History for Bank Account

The elements of the notation used in this example are:

- *Sequence:* the boxes read left to right from Account Opened to Account Deletion. Thus Account Closure must happen before Account Deletion.
- *Selection:* the boxes with small circles in the top right corners are alternatives for one another, so each Balance Change is either a Credit or a Debit.
- *Iteration:* the box with the asterisk in the top right corner represents an iteration, many Balance Changes can occur one after another.

Diagrams that use these three components in the way used above are known as Jackson structures (or Jackson diagrams) after Michael Jackson who pioneered their use as a technique for program design in the early 1970s. In SSADM, Jackson structures are used in Entity Life Histories, I/O Structure Diagrams, and in Update and Enquiry Process Models.

In each of these diagrams the Jackson structure is used to model different things. In Entity Life Histories the notation models the ordering of events affecting data held by the system. The I/O Structure models the position of data in the input to or output from the computer. In Update and Enquiry Process Models the notation is used to show the controlled sequence of procedures carried out by the computer to perform a particular process.

The elements of Jackson structures, with particular emphasis on Entity Life Histories, are described in detail later in the section. These structures warrant careful study as they are used widely in SSADM.

Terms and notation

An entity may be affected by several different events. In the banking example the events Account Opened, Credit, Debit, Account Closure, and Account Deletion all affect the entity Bank Account.

An event may also affect several entities. For example, when the Bank Account of Maurice Moneybags was opened, a 'Maurice Moneybags' occurrence of the entity Customer would also have been created. The event Account Opened affects two entities: Bank Account and Customer. Similarly the event Credit (and Debit) modifies the Bank Account occurrence, by changing the balance, and creates an occurrence of Transaction. Figure 2.38 below is an Event/Entity Matrix which shows the effects of events on entities.

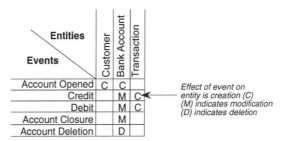

Fig. 2.38 Event/Entity Matrix showing the effects of events on entities

Thus an entity can be affected by a number of events, and an event may affect a number of different entities. To describe the particular interaction between a single event and a single entity, the term 'effect' is used. The box on the Entity Life History of Bank Account represents the effect of the event Account Opened on the entity Bank Account (see Fig. 2.39). Although the box represents the effect of the event the name inside the box is always the name of the event.

Within an Entity Life History diagram, the effect boxes have no other boxes directly beneath them. Intermediate boxes with other boxes directly beneath them are called 'nodes'. Nodes have no significance other than in expressing the valid event sequences within the context of the Entity Life History diagram. Within an Entity Life History, the names in the boxes will reflect the names of events if they are effect boxes and the names will reflect a particular section of the Entity Life History if they are node boxes.

An Entity Life History diagram is constructed for each entity in the Logical Data Structure. The entity is placed in a box at the top of the diagram, and all possible progressions through the life of the entity are overlaid on one another, to form a picture that fits every occurrence. Figure 2.39 shows the components used to build an Entity Life History diagram.

Note that this notation has a similar meaning whenever Jackson structures are used in SSADM. The node at the very top of the structure represent the whole diagram. The nodes only have significance by combining elements (effects or 'leaves') of the same type together. The leaves are what actually happens, do something, or contain some data (depending on whether the Jackson structure is an Entity Life History, a Process Model, or an I/O Structure).

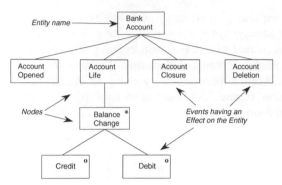

Fig. 2.39 Notation used in Entity Life Histories

Entity Life History diagrams use the following diagramming components:
- Sequence
- Selection
- Iteration.

All Entity Life Histories can be built up using just these three components, which are the basic components of Jackson structures. However, certain complex situations can be simplified by the use of two other conventions:

- Parallel structures
- Quit and resume.

The component types are described here, but their use within SSADM is described in later sections.

Sequence
A sequence is represented by a series of boxes reading from left to right as shown in Fig. 2.40.

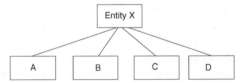

Fig. 2.40 Sequence in Entity Life Histories

The box labelled A will always be the first to occur, followed by B which in turn is followed by C then D. This is the only possible sequence. Although the sequence may be thought of as a progression through time, there is no indication of the time intervals between the boxes within a sequence. These could span minutes, hours, days, or years.

Selection
A selection defines a number of effects or nodes that are alternatives to one another at a particular point in the Entity Life History. A selection is represented by a set of boxes with circles in the top right corners as shown in Fig. 2.41.

Note that the selection node is A, and the selection components (or 'leaves') are E, F, or G. In a similar way the box at the top of the structure, with the entity name inside, is, in this example, a sequence node. Later we discuss further how the components are merged to form an overall structure. The basic rule is that all boxes must be either elements ('leaves' or effects in Entity Life Histories) or nodes of one, and only one, component type.

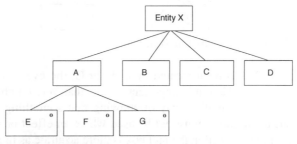

Fig. 2.41 Selection in Entity Life Histories

As node A is at the beginning of the Entity Life History, this diagram shows that an occurrence of entity X must be created by only one of three events: E, F or G. If there is a requirement to show that one of the options need not be selected, a 'null' box may be added as shown in Fig. 2.42. This extension to the banking example shows that a Bank Account could start with a Pay Deposit, a Direct Deposit, or neither of these.

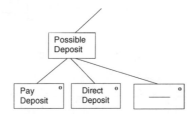

Fig. 2.42 A null box in a selection

The null box does not represent an effect or node, but is a notational device to indicate the situation where something may or may not happen. If the null box is selected, the Entity Life History continues directly to the next node or effect.

Iteration
An iteration is where an effect or node may be repeated any number of times at the same point within an Entity Life History. An iteration is represented by an asterisk in the top right-hand corner of a box as shown in Fig. 2.43.

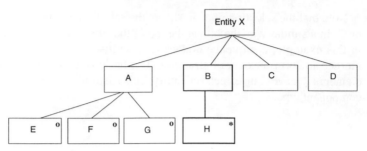

Fig. 2.43 Iteration in Entity Life Histories

After entity X has been created by E, F, or G, the event H may affect the entity any number of times. Here it is important to note that 'any number of times' includes none, so an iteration is another way of showing that something may occur or it may not. However, the iteration must not be used where an effect or node occurs either once or not at all. In this situation the null box is more accurate as in Fig. 2.42.

A restriction upon the iteration is that each occurrence of the iteration must be complete before the next begins. This is most relevant where there are several elements in a node which iterates. (If iteration H consisted of effects 1, 2, and 3 in that sequence then the iteration could not restart with 1 until the previous iteration had completed with 3 occurring.)

Parallel structures

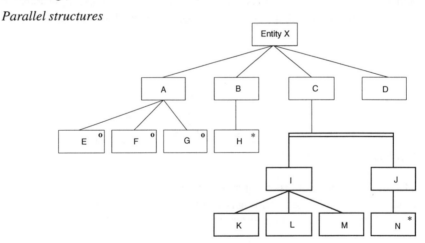

Fig. 2.44 Parallel structures in Entity Life Histories

A parallel structure is used in the situation where effects or nodes occur in no predictable sequence.[1] A parallel structure is shown as a parallel bar on the Entity Life

---

[1] Note that it does not represent concurrence which is when two events, or parts of the structure, affect the occurrence at exactly the same time. This means that the same data is updated at exactly the same time; in conventional computing this is probably impossible but is certainly undesirable from a data integrity

History diagram as in Fig. 2.44. This represents the situation where the sequence of K, L, and M occurs at this point in the Entity Life History, and the event N may affect the entity a number of times during this sequence. The node I, representing the sequence, and the node J, representing the iteration, are shown under the parallel bar.

Figure 2.44 could be drawn without the use of the parallel structure, as shown in Fig. 2.45. In order to show that the event N may occur anywhere in the sequence of K, L, and M, the iteration of N must be repeated several times. The diagram is made clearer by the use of the parallel structure.

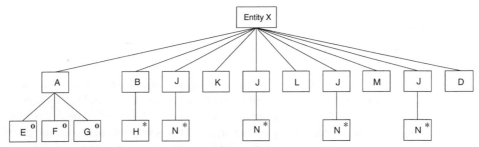

Fig. 2.45 Fig. 2.44 redrawn to avoid using the parallel structure

Quit and resume

The quit and resume convention is used in situations where the diagramming conventions excessively constrain the Entity Life History, or force a very complex artificial structure in an attempt to model a particular situation. The use of this convention allows a quit from one part of an Entity Life History diagram to resume in another part of the diagram. In the simple case, a Q and a number are placed by the right-hand side of a box on the diagram, and a corresponding R and the same number are placed by the left-hand side of a box in another part of the diagram (Fig 2.46). This shows that if the quit event occurs, then instead of processing the event marked with the Q, the life jumps to the quit event which is marked R.

In Fig 2.46 this means that if, after event B occurring, instead of the normally occurring next event, C, event E can occur. Some possible event sequences are (using lower case italics to indicate event occurrences): *abcbcde*, *ade*, *abe*, *abcbe*. This sort of quit is known as a *disciplined conditional quit*.

perspective. Real-time systems development methods and concurrent programming languages cope with this kind of problem.

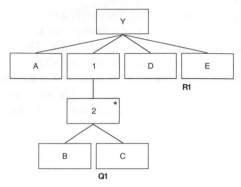

Fig 2.46 Quit and resume

We sometimes discover, while developing an Entity Life History, that the structure we have drawn doesn't cater for all of the possible sequences. In Fig. 2.47, below, we have identified that if event F occurs it will always be followed immediately by event D—showing this schematically by the arrow. This is an example of an *unconditional quit*[1] where the quit event must always be followed by the resume effect. We cannot handle this using the standard quit and resume notation—if we place a quit on F and a resume on D, it would imply that after F occurred then the iteration of H could occur, or D could occur instead of F.

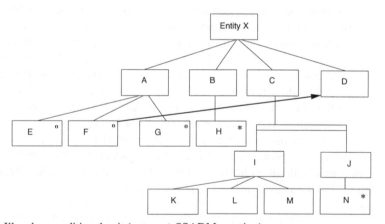

Fig. 2.47 Illegal unconditional quit (note **not** SSADM notation)

Unconditional quits should not be shown in SSADM diagrams—they can always be avoided by redrawing the structure. We have redrawn Fig. 2.47 to give Fig. 2.48 below

---

[1] There has been some debate in the SSADM community about the use of quits and resumes. The dust seems to have settled now. The approach outlined above is now the standard one which will be defined by future versions of the SSADM Reference Manual. A full account of the different kinds of quit and their pros and cons is given by Ashworth, C., Le Marchant, J., and Lomax, P. (1994) Quits and Resumes on Entity Life Histories: A Comparison of Alternative Approaches. *SSADM Journal*.

which avoids the unconditional quit. Two new nodes, P and Q, have been introduced into the diagram to ensure that each parent node has children of only one type.

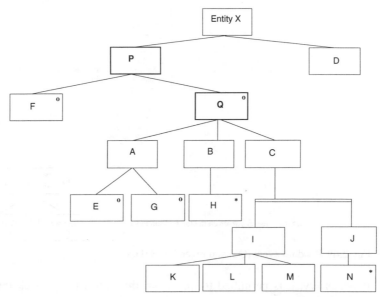

Fig. 2.48 Avoiding the quit and resume

In the banking example, it is possible to reopen a bank account that has been closed, but not yet deleted. In this case, the event Account Reopened causes a quit back to the part of the Entity Life History before Account Closure. This backwards quit is shown by Q1 and R1 in Fig. 2.49. The backwards quit is known in SSADM as a *reversion* as on the quit the occurrence reverts to an earlier part of its life (they can also be modelled using an iteration).

Another use of the quit and resume convention allows a quit from the main structure of an Entity Life History, and a resume at a box on a stand-alone structure. This is used where an event might occur at any time, altering the sequence of the Entity Life History. These are known as *random events* in SSADM. As it is impossible to predict where on the diagram the quit might occur, no Q is placed on the structure. Instead, a sentence indicating the area of the Entity Life History the quit might occur from and the circumstances that cause the quit is placed at the bottom of the diagram. The stand-alone box or substructure is annotated with the R that corresponds to the Q detailed in this sentence.

An example of this random quit is shown by Q2 and R2 in Fig. 2.49. Here, the death of a customer may occur at any time after the account has been opened. If a customer dies, the normal sequence is no longer applicable and this account is placed into suspension. The account is deleted when the customer is finally deleted from the system. Note that in this example we are showing the effects of Customer Death and Customer Deletion on the Bank Account entity. Customer Death will close the account and Customer Deletion will delete the account—both events will do other things to the account also. These events will also occur in the Customer Entity Life History.

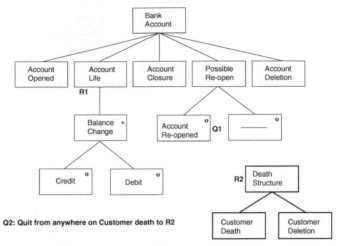

Fig. 2.49 Random event (Q2) and reversion (Q1)

If necessary, it is permitted to quit from this substructure back into the body of the Entity Life History.

In general, it is possible to have more than one quit point with the same identifier on the same diagram, but there must only be one resume point with the same identifier to avoid ambiguity.

Combining the components
When sequences, selections, iterations, and parallelism are combined into a structure then a particular rule always applies. Each node or elementary component (leaf) can only be combined with other nodes or leaves of the same type under one 'parent' node. Figure 2.50 below shows an incorrect Jackson structure.

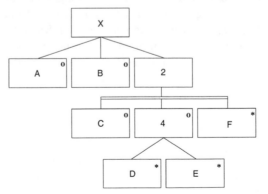

Fig. 2.50 Incorrect Jackson structure

This structure is incorrect for the following reasons:

- Node X, combines ('parents') a selection (A and B) with a sequence (A, B, and 2)
- Node 2 combines a selection (C and 4) and an iteration (F) with a parallel structure
- Node 4 combines two iterations (D and E) with a sequence.

Each of these causes slight ambiguity and doubt when interpreting the structure. The most likely correct structure (though this does require assumptions about what is meant by Fig. 2.50) is shown by Fig. 2.51 below, and the letters correspond to those in Fig. 2.50. Each node now only 'parents' components of the same type:

- Node X parents a sequence;
- Node 2 parents a parallel structure;
- Node 3 parents a selection;
- Node 4 parents a sequence;
- Nodes 5, 6, and 7 parent iterations.

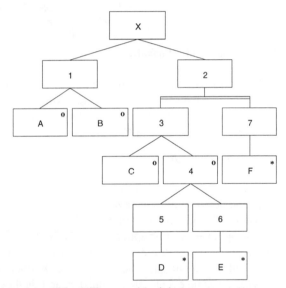

Fig. 2.51 Corrected version of Fig. 2.50, to avoid mixing component types

Effect qualifiers (optional effects)

This is where the same event can affect an entity occurrence in two or more ways. For example, a Debit; this will have a different effect on the overdrawn account to the account in credit. If the account is overdrawn, then the bank will put a stop on the account and write a nasty letter to the customer.

So one event, Debit, can take on two roles depending on the state of the Bank Account occurrence that it affects. The roles are distinguished by placing them, in round brackets, after the event name—shown in Fig. 2.52. The term, *optional effects*, is also used—this is perhaps a better description than *effect qualifiers* since there is a selection of effects that could result from the event.

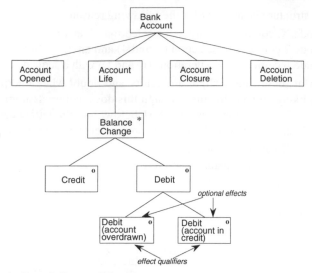

Fig. 2.52 Optional effects (effect qualifiers)

Optional effects are particularly important when we come to define the processing because for one event occurrence the processing can follow different directions depending on the state of the entity. We will look at this particular example again when we develop processing structures in Chapter 4.

Entity roles (simultaneous effects)
This is where one event occurrence affects more than one entity occurrence of the same type in different ways. For example, in the banking system one account may be closed by transfer to another account. One event, Transfer, affects two entity occurrences: the account closed and the new account opened. Because we are looking at one entity type, Bank Account, the event has to appear twice in its life history as shown in Fig. 2.53 below.[1] These are two *simultaneous effects* of one event occurrence: one effect is closing a particular account, and the other effect is opening another account. So we show them with the same event name, Transfer, and then qualify this with the name of the *entity role* affected. Entity role names are shown in square brackets, [New Account] and [Closed Account], to distinguish them from effect qualifiers, which use round brackets.

---

[1] Note that the diagram is not suggesting that all accounts are both closed and opened by Transfer, it is indicating the possibilities. Some accounts will be opened by cheque and closed by transfer, some will be opened by transfer and closed by withdrawal, some will be opened by cheque and closed by withdrawal, and some will be opened by transfer and closed by transfer.

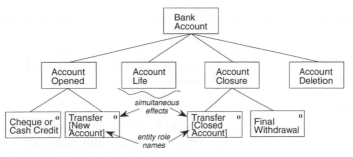

Fig. 2.53 Simultaneous effects (entity roles)

Operations

Operations are included on the Entity Life History to show what actually happens to an entity occurrence as a result of each event. These operations show the processing, in a detailed way, performed on the data. Each operation changes the value of at least one attribute in the entity and/or modifies a relationship occurrence. Figure 2.54 shows the Entity Life History of Bank Account with a separate Operations List; each operation is cross-referred to the diagram by the numbers in small square boxes attached to the larger effect boxes.

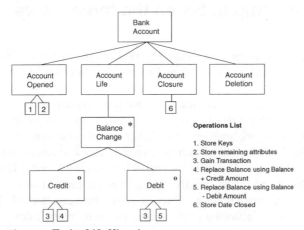

Fig. 2.54 Operations on Entity Life Histories

A specific syntax is recommended for operations—we describe this in detail in Sec. 4.7. Operation 1, shown attached to the event 'Account Opened', is 'Store Keys'—the first operation is always to store the value of the key attributes. Often, the second operation is to store values to all of the remaining attributes. Operation 3 is a 'gain'—it refers to creating a relationship occurrence with a detail entity occurrence. On the bank's Logical Data Structure (Fig. 2.23) the entity Bank Account has many Transactions. So the 'gain' operation is adding a new transaction to that particular bank account. (We also use 'lose', if the transaction is removed from a particular account.) Operations 4 and 5 are changing the value of the Balance attribute, replacing it with a new value after the credit or debit.

Operations, first defined for Entity Life Histories, are carried forward to Update Process Models, which are an important part of the detailed process specification[1] that SSADM produces (see Chapter 5).

SUMMARY

- Entity Life Histories model the changes to the information held in a system.
- Events that cause the system to update entities are reflected within Entity Life Histories.
- The particular set of changes in an entity caused by an event is an effect.
- Sequences, selections, and iterations are shown by Jackson diagrams, which are used in SSADM for Entity Life Histories, I/O Structures, Update Process Models, and Enquiry Process Models.
- An Entity Life History diagram shows the sequences, selections, and iterations of the effects of events on a single entity.
- Two additional conventions—parallel structures, and quit and resume—are used to simplify the diagrams.

2.4   Relationship between the three views

Overview

It is a very important principle of SSADM that the different views of the system should be closely related to one another. Each view is built up, sometimes from another view and sometimes separately, and is then checked for consistency and completeness by comparison with the other views. The Required System Data Flow Model, Logical Data Model, and Entity Life Histories are related to one another in defined ways and can be checked against one another before being signed off as correct.

The degree to which the techniques can be checked against one another depends upon the SSADM stage. The rules for cross-checking the Logical Data Model with the Data Flow Model cannot be strictly applied for the current physical system as they will reflect the current situation which may not be very logical. Thus, the relationships described in the following sections concentrate upon the rules that apply in the required system definition with some indication of how they can be used in earlier stages.

Relationship between the Data Flow Model and the Logical Data Model

Logical Data Models reflect the structure of stored data. A Data Flow Diagram shows data moving about the system and being stored in data stores. All attributes should appear in an Entity Description if they are held within the system and will probably be shown flowing around the system on data flows. The rules that govern the relationship between the two views are described here.

---

[1] We expect that, in the future, CASE tools will be developed which use these operations, and an extended operations syntax, to generate program code. Such products already exist to support the Information Engineering Method—these use action diagrams as the basis for code generation.

Each data store should represent a whole number of entities.

As both entities and data stores represent stored data, there is a very close relationship between them. As an entity is a grouping of related attributes, it would not be logical that it could be split across more than one data store. Also, as the Logical Data Structure is the more detailed view of data, it is unlikely that a data store would represent a smaller grouping than a single entity. These principles have been translated into the following rules:

* A data store is related to one or more entities.
* An entity may not appear in more than one data store.

The only exceptions to these rules are:

* In the current system, data is often duplicated, so it is possible for an entity to appear in more than one data store.
* Transient data stores do not represent stored data and will therefore not be related to any entities on the Logical Data Structure.

The precise relationship between particular entities and data stores is formally documented using a Logical Data Store/Entity Cross-Reference form (see Fig. 3.50 in Sec. 3.6). This form is referred to when checking either technique for consistency.

Attributes on data flows should belong to entities.

Another relationship between the Data Flow Model and the Logical Data Model is in relating the attributes flowing around a system to the attributes attached to entities. This can be used when checking the data flows into and out of data stores to ensure that the attributes shown on the data flows appear in the Entity Descriptions relating to the data store.

The only data flowing that may not appear in the Logical Data Model are:

* Transient items such as partial results.
* Derived items for output from the system.

Also, some data flows may just have a label (such as 'Errors') which will not have a direct relationship to any attributes.

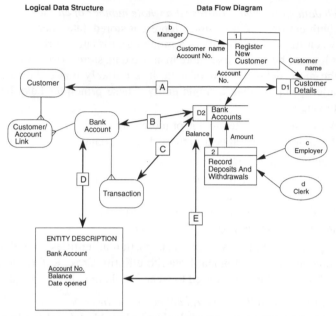

Fig. 2.55 Relationship between Logical Data Model and Data Flow Model

The relationships between the Data Flow Model and the Logical Data Model are shown in Fig. 2.55 which shows how some areas of the banking example are related:

A. The Customer and Customer/Account Link entities relate to the Customer Details data store.

B. The Bank Account entity relates to the Bank Accounts data store.

C. The Transaction entity relates to the Bank Accounts data store.

D. The Bank Account entity is described by an Entity Description showing a set of attributes.

E. The Balance attribute on the Entity Description relates to the Balance attribute on the data flow.

Relationship between the Logical Data Model and Entity Life Histories

An Entity Life History is constructed for each entity in the Required System Logical Data Model.[1] The starting point for Entity Life Histories is the Event/Entity Matrix in which all entities from the Logical Data Structure are listed down one side of the matrix and events added to the other side. The Entity Description and relationships to other entities are examined to ensure the completeness of the Entity Life History:

• Each attribute must be created, possibly amended, and deleted by events and their associated operations on the Entity Life History.

---

[1] This use of Entity Life Histories takes SSADM close to the object-oriented approach which requires that objects *encapsulate* both data and behavioural properties. The SSADM **entity type** maps to the object-oriented *class*, **entity occurrence** maps to *object* or *instance*.

- Changes in relationships, e.g. change of master entity, may be events that should be considered.
- The Entity Life Histories of entities may be affected by the Entity Life Histories of entities related to them as masters or details.

Thus, the construction of Entity Life Histories is done by referring constantly to the Logical Data Structure and the supporting Entity Descriptions.

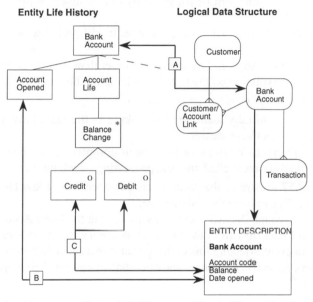

Fig. 2.56 Relationship between Entity Life History and Logical Data Model

Figure 2.56 illustrates the relationships between an Entity Life History and the Logical Data Model:

A. An Entity Life History is drawn for each entity on the Logical Data Structure. Here, the Bank Account Entity Life History is for the Bank Account entity on the Logical Data Structure.

B. In creating the entity, the event Account Opened will set a value for the attribute Date Opened. This attribute will not be updated by any subsequent event.

C. The Credit and Debit events will update the Balance attribute each time they affect the Bank Account entity (they will also create an occurrence of the Transaction entity).

Relationship between the Data Flow Model and Entity Life Histories

The events reflected in the Entity Life Histories are triggers to the Data Flow Diagram processes that update the system data. Therefore, there should be some indication of the events on the Data Flow Diagrams. If the event is the arrival of input data, then events can be directly related to input data flows. If the events are not associated with particular data flows (as for time-based events), the relationship between events and the

Data Flow Diagrams is not so clear cut. However, each process that updates a main data store (i.e. one or more entities on the Logical Data Structure) must have an event (or events) associated with it.

To summarize, the relationships between Entity Life Histories and Data Flow Diagrams are:

• Each bottom-level process on the Required System Data Flow Diagram that updates a main data store will be triggered by one or more events that appear on the Entity Life Histories.
• If an event is from an external source, it will probably be associated with an input data flow.
• If a process is triggered by something other than the arrival of data, the event will not be shown explicitly on the Data Flow Diagram but can be inferred by inspection.

The way that this works in practice is:

• Events are initially identified by looking at the Data Flow Diagrams and deciding what triggers the processes.
• After Entity Life Histories have been completed, any new events that have been identified are reconciled with the processing which might require new functions.

Figure 2.57 illustrates the relationship between Data Flow Diagrams and Entity Life Histories. The relationships shown are:

A. The Account Opened event shown affecting the Bank Account entity is represented by the data flow from the Manager external entity to Process 1. This was identified as an event affecting this entity because there is a data flow from the process to the Bank Accounts data store, showing that an entity is being updated.
B. The Credit and Debit events are related to the inputs to Process 2.

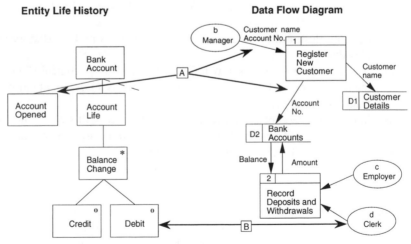

Fig. 2.57 Relationship between Entity Life History and Data Flow Diagram

SUMMARY

The Data Flow Model, the Logical Data Model, and Entity Life Histories are all related to each other in some way. It is important that the diagrams are made consistent at all times so that at any stage in a development project the three views are showing different aspects of the same thing.

This is a very important aspect of SSADM. At each stage, each diagram can be used to check the consistency and completeness of the others. If a CASE tool is to provide adequate support for SSADM, it is important that these relationships are reflected in the underlying structure so that the relationships described here can be checked automatically.

Part 2 Working through SSADM

Part 2 follows the structure of SSADM with a separate chapter on each of the four modules of SSADM. Each chapter begins with an introductory section describing the modules. The remainder of each chapter is divided into several sections each describing a step.

The overall objective of Part 2 is to show how SSADM might be used on a typical project. The reader is taken through the development of the major SSADM end-products and shown how they should be developed.

The remainder of the book works through the whole of SSADM using a fictional, but realistic, case study. This is based upon a vehicle hire company called Yorkies and a brief description is given in Appendix C. You should read through this before starting Sec. 3.1.

Note that we have followed exactly the structure of SSADM as laid down by the Reference Manual. In practice, most projects will vary from this structure which should really be regarded as a default. SSADM is a flexible method and needs to be tailored for every project situation. An important part of project managing a development using SSADM is deciding how to tailor and adapt the method. However, you can only do this when you have a good and detailed understanding of the method as a whole and therefore this course follows rigorously and religiously the default structure of the method. Tailoring the method is advised only for the experienced systems developer.

3 Requirements Analysis

3.1 Introduction

Requirements Analysis involves us (systems analysts, systems designers, IT professionals, consultants, or whatever we like to call ourselves) in analysing (discovering, understanding, clarifying, documenting, and focusing) the requirements (what the new system must be able to do and how well it is able to do it) that they (users, clients, customers, purchasers, managers) have of the future system (bounded set of inter-related parts to achieve a set of inter-related objectives).

This analysis is based on an understanding of what currently happens in the environment. The people who operate and manage the current system often have the best ideas about what could be improved. The focus of Requirements Analysis is strongly on the future system; the current system is only analysed in sufficient depth to provide requirements for the new system. The module ends with a range of possible business solutions being presented to senior users, who decide the future directions that the system (and the project) should take.

Many projects start using SSADM with the Requirements Analysis module. Sometimes this will follow a feasibility study (carried out using SSADM) but often this is unnecessary (e.g. if a strategy study has performed the feasibility role or if the project is a 'must have').

As is shown below in Fig. 3.1 the module falls into two stages: Investigation of Current Environment and Business Systems Options. Sections 3.2 to 3.7 discuss the steps of Stage 1 and Sec. 3.8 discusses the Business Systems Options Stage.

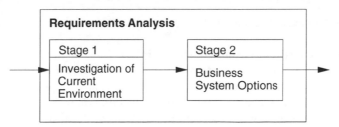

Fig. 3.1 Stages in the Requirements Analysis module

Objectives of Requirements Analysis

The emphasis is on determining the requirements for the future system rather than on understanding the problems and the operations of the current system. By the end of the module the boundary of the future computerized system should have been clearly set and agreed with the users. Both the users and the project team will have a good understanding of how the future system meets business needs. Costs and benefits of the system proposed should be understood and a clear decision to proceed with the project will have been made. Through the use of techniques such as Business Systems Options the users should gain clear ownership of the system and its requirements—the users are responsible for making all of the significant decisions regarding the directions of the project.

Products of Requirements Analysis

Figure 3.2 below shows the Product Breakdown Structure of the Analysis Of Requirements which is the end product of this module. The Current Services Description shows how the data and processes of the current system are logically organized: represented by Logical Data Models and Logical Data Flow Models. The User Catalogue describes the jobs performed by the on-line users of the future system. The Requirements Catalogue itemizes and prioritizes each requirement agreed with the users; it covers both functional and non-functional requirements. The Selected Business System Option shows the optimum solution to the business requirements and is expressed in business terms using cost benefit analysis, impact analysis and textual descriptions of functionality.

This set of products is carried forward to the Requirements Specification where the selected Business System Option is refined in great detail to provide a full specification of the required system. The other end products of Requirements Analysis are used to help build the detail of the specification.

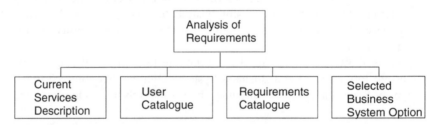

Fig 3.2 Product Breakdown Structure Analysis of Requirements

Investigation of current environment (Stage 1)

Figure 3.3 shows the six steps of Stage 1, and their relationship to one another.

The analysis is initiated in step 110, then three steps are carried out in parallel. A Requirements Catalogue, initiated in step 110, is expanded within step 120. The current system processing is described by the Current Physical Data Flow Model (step 130). The data held in the current system is documented by the Current Environment Logical Data Model (step 140). These two models are then used to derive a logical view of the current system processing which is expressed as the Logical Data Flow Model (step 150). The results of the current system investigation are assembled together, and checked for completeness and consistency (step 160) before proceeding to Stage 2.

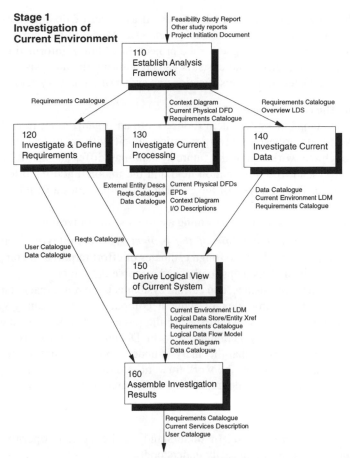

Fig. 3.3 Structure of Stage 1: Investigation of Current Environment

Techniques of Stage 1

Throughout Stage 1 of SSADM, the development team must find out about the system by a number of fact-finding techniques:

- interviewing;
- studying the current system's documentation;
- circulating questionnaires;
- observing the system in practice;
- looking at the results of previous studies;
- conducting surveys.

These are well-known techniques described in many textbooks (e.g. Yeates *et al*., 1994) and will not be described here. Certainly, whatever other techniques are chosen, it will be necessary to interview one or more users in order to understand their perspective and to appreciate the problems associated with the current operations.

The information collected is expressed as: a set of detailed Data Flow Diagrams representing the current system, a Logical Data Model of the current system's data, and the Requirements Catalogue for the project. In addition, information about the project, especially volumetrics and costs, is gathered during the analysis of the current system. This is used later for cost justification and sizing of the new system.

Why investigate the current system?

When a computer system is introduced into an organization, it is often to support the work already done by that organization, albeit with modifications or enhancements. Although the workings of the future system may differ substantially from those of the current system, the information held and the major functions often remain relatively unchanged. Thus analysis of the existing system provides a firm basis for the design of the future system.

Additional reasons for performing a current system investigation are:

- *To understand the scope of the project.* The complexity of the system can be determined, enabling the rough estimates of effort required to complete the project to be determined. This helps to plan and resource the project.
- *To increase confidence.* The current system is known in great detail by the users who may not have any idea of what a computer system can give them. It is the development team's task to specify the job that must be done and how that job can best be supported by a computer system. Documenting the current system is a way of reassuring the users that the analysts understand the nature of the problem fully and are competent to carry the work forward into the design of the required system. The analysts become confident that they understand the business of the system.

To design and justify the new system, several aspects of the current system are investigated:

- *Operations and data.* In understanding the current operations and data, the requirements are more easily understood.
- *Problems inherent in the current system.* Examining the problems found in the current system ensures that they will not be replicated in the new system.
- *Boundaries of the system.* It is important, throughout the project, to attempt to draw accurate boundaries around the area of investigation to avoid needless effort on areas that lie outside the boundaries or, more importantly, to ensure that all the areas inside the boundaries are investigated. The boundary of the current system investigation should be explicitly stated and agreed with all those concerned.
- *Costs and volumes.* These act as a basis for system justification and sizing in the analysis of requirements.

It is important to note that an investigation of the current system does not constrain the project to reimplement the current system. In the second stage of Requirements Analysis, the Business System Options step takes a fresh approach to meeting the objectives of the system. This may lead to a complete restructuring of processes and data; thus designing a new system that is nothing like the old.

Types of current system

The different types of current system may be classified under the following headings.

Fully clerical

Fig. 3.4 Fully clerical system

The new system might be required to either:

- Replace a system currently using manual procedures and paper files. An example of this might be a personnel system that is implemented entirely on card indexes. The new computer system would be required to store the records on computer media.

Or

- Monitor a system that will remain in place. An example of this might be a system that monitors stock in a warehouse. The stock will continue to be bought and distributed in the same way, but the new system would be required to monitor the levels of stock and to control reordering of stock.

Although the requirements of these two types of system will be different, the investigation of their current systems follow the same pattern. All the information currently held or currently monitored and all the procedures are modelled using the SSADM techniques.

Partly computerized

Fig. 3.5 Partly or currently computerized system

The new system may be required to replace an existing computer system because it:

- does not meet the user's requirements;
- has reached the end of its maintained life;
- requires major enhancements.

An example of this might be where a payroll system is already computerized, and the corresponding personnel system is clerical. A new requirement to computerize the personnel records might prompt the requirement for a fully integrated personnel and payroll system, even though the payroll is already implemented as a computer system.

The computer system forms only a part of the current system modelled by SSADM. The clerical procedures surrounding the system will also form a part of the investigation, although the precise boundaries will be set by the user.

No apparent current system

Fig. 3.6 No apparent current system

Sometimes, a completely new requirement will arise, for example when new legislation is introduced or an organization moves into a new business area. It may appear, in these cases, that there is no current system to investigate. However, if a similar system already exists within the organization, it is useful to perform a brief investigation on this system to establish common areas of information and of procedures.

An example of this is where an organization that is currently archiving and retrieving paper records decides it has a need for a similar system to archive and retrieve files stored on computer media. Although the requirement has no real current system, the system for archiving and retrieving paper files might provide a useful basis for the investigation.

In cases where there is no similar system within the organization it may be necessary to look at how other organizations deal with similar problems. If the requirement arises from a new law then it will be necessary to analyse the requirement expressed within the legislation and supporting documentation.

Often it appears that there is no existing system although the activities are currently performed. This may indicate that the current system is a highly informal one.[1] All systems have both a formal and an informal component. The formal component operates through rigid rules and uses highly structured information such as computer files and manual forms. The informal component operates through intuition, value judgements, and unstructured information such as conversations and prose. If the objective is to develop a computer system to support a largely informal system then analysis and formalization of the current informal system is essential. Stage 1 of SSADM in this case would require analysis of the current informal system as well as the formal one.

---

[1] See the article by Land and Kennedy-McGregor in Galliers, R. (ed.) (1987) *Information Analysis: Selected Readings* (Addison-Wesley, Reading, Mass.).

3.2   Establish analysis framework (step 110)

Overview of the step

This first step of Requirements Analysis (which may also be the first step of the project) may be thought of as two separate, but related, parts:

- General project set-up.
- Initiation of analysis.

The objective of this step is to provide a firm foundation for the whole of the development with a detailed framework for the early stages of the project. The scope and size of the project are agreed and plans are drawn up for the first three stages of the project. Much of the activity described in this section belongs under the heading project management and control—this is discussed further in Chapter 7, Management Aspects.

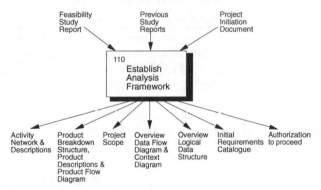

Fig. 3.7 Inputs and outputs from step 110, *establish analysis framework*

Figure 3.7 shows the inputs and outputs of this first step of Requirements Analysis (which may also be the first step of the project). The products produced by this step fall into two categories:

- project management products
- early analysis products

Project management products (those on the left side of Fig. 3.7) are largely pre-defined by SSADM. Product Breakdown Structures, Product Descriptions, and Product Flow Diagrams are provided by the SSADM Reference Manual and can be used directly unless SSADM is being modified in some way for this particular project. The Activity Descriptions and Activity Network are also defined by the SSADM Reference Manual, they can be extended to show timescales and individuals involved. These project management products are discussed further in Chapter 7, Management Aspects.

Project Initiation Document

This is a short document (often known as the terms of reference in conventional systems development) which is drawn up and agreed between the senior users (usually the people who requested the system and who have the financial authority to pay for it) and the development team. If a strategy or feasibility study has been done, then this could be a very detailed document, giving clear boundaries for the project, and precise budgets and timescales. The recommendations of the previous study would form the basis of the terms of reference for the next study. If no previous studies have been performed then the Project Initiation Document might contain rather vague statements about scope, constraints, budgets, and timescales.

Project Initiation Document

1. To design a computer system to support the vehicle rental, driver administration, customer records, and invoicing areas of Yorkies Ltd.

2. To investigate ways of improving the efficiency of the operations of the company in the areas specified in 1.

3. To investigate extending the system to include the administration of one-way hires and the acceptance of non-registered customers.

4. The system will not be required to replace existing staff but the increased efficiency will be expected to increase the income from customers with less wastage of resources in the use of agency drivers.

5. The team of a contract senior systems analyst and a junior analyst are required to use SSADM for the analysis and design of the system. They will report back to the Yorkies finance director. The team should report back with their proposals for a new system (end of Requirements Analysis in SSADM) within two months of starting the study.

Fig. 3.8 Project Initiation Document for the Yorkies project

It is important that some sort of contract should be agreed between the users and the developers. This is often the first formal statement by the users of what they want and thus forms the basis for the subsequent work. This is not to say that the document is 'cast in stone'—often the early steps of analysis will clarify the boundaries of the project which will require modifications (regarded as improvements) to the Project Initiation Document. It is important that the Project Initiation Document is sufficiently detailed and clear for the project team to be confident that they can proceed.

As an example of the type of document that might be agreed, the Project Initiation Document for the Yorkies project is given in Fig. 3.8. In this case no previous studies had been performed.

Previous studies

The tasks to be performed will depend upon the depth of any previous studies. For instance, the users may have independently produced a detailed description of their requirements or the application may have been the subject of a feasibility study or part of a strategic study.

If SSADM Feasibility has been followed then this will have produced a Feasibility Study Report which contains much of the documentation required for this step (such as overview Logical Data Structure and Data Flow Diagrams). This feasibility documentation needs to be checked to ensure that it is still valid.

If other (non-SSADM) approaches have been used to study this system before then the resulting documentation will need to be translated to a SSADM style. Again some investigation will be necessary to re-establish its validity.

Definition of boundaries and scope of investigation

It is important, from the outset of a project, to be as clear as possible about the boundaries and scope of the investigation. This ensures that only the areas of interest are studied and that nothing is left out. It is often the case that a much larger proportion of the system is investigated than is necessary, extending the timescales of the project needlessly and wasting time and resources. Missing areas out can have similar effects as much effort will be wasted later in the project trying to cover the areas missed earlier.

In this step some of the basic SSADM techniques are used to clarify the boundaries of the project:

Overview Logical Data Structure and Data Flow Diagrams

The techniques of Data Flow Diagrams and Logical Data Models help in the definition of boundaries and scope:

- Data Flow Diagrams show data flowing across the boundaries of the system from processes within the system to external sources and recipients, and vice versa. This shows clearly where the boundaries of the investigation will lie.
- Logical Data Models show the objects, or entities, within the system that will be investigated.

In large systems, a single user with detailed knowledge of every part of the system is difficult to find. If this is the case, an overall picture of the current system might be built up from a set of partial views obtained from a range of users. Data Flow Diagrams and a Logical Data Structure of each partial view are easy to combine to give the complete picture. Alternatively, a single Data Flow Diagram and Logical Data structure might be drawn in consultation with a group of users together.

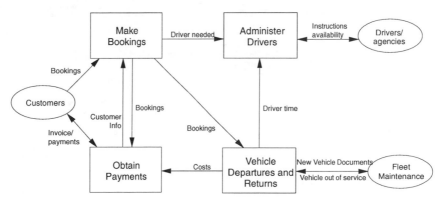

Fig. 3.9 Overview Data Flow Diagram for Yorkies

The overview Data Flow Diagram produced for the Yorkies system from these initial discussions with users from both the local offices and the head office is shown in Fig.

3.9. Only the processes and a few external entities are shown, but it does give a fairly clear picture of the scope and boundary of the system under investigation. The supporting overview Logical Data Structure is shown in Fig. 3.10.

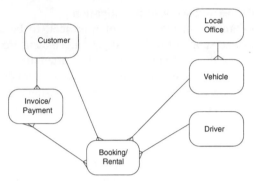

Fig. 3.10 Overview Logical Data Structure for Yorkies

The conventions of Logical Data Structuring have not been adhered to rigidly as the purpose of Figs 3.9 and 3.10 is to give an outline of the task. Sometimes these early models can be used as the basis for estimating the complexity of the project and thereby the effort required for the development—estimating techniques based on this approach are described briefly in Chapter 7, Management Aspects. The full Data Flow Diagrams and Logical Data Model of the current system are constructed in later steps as described in Secs 3.4 and 3.5.

Context Diagram

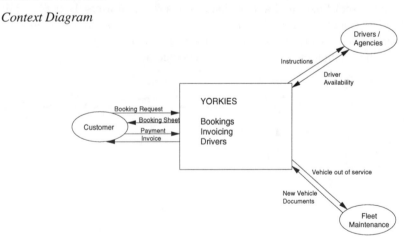

Fig. 3.11 Context Diagram

This is where the system is represented as a single process—it is sometimes known as a 'Level 0 Data Flow Diagram'. All flows into and out of the system are shown around the edge of the process. This helps ensure that the boundaries are correct and well understood.[1] A Context Diagram for the Yorkies system is shown in Fig. 3.11. Although trivial in this instance, this type of diagram can be very useful for large projects.

Initial Requirements Catalogue

Previous studies (if there were any) will have identified requirements. A major SSADM product is the Requirements Catalogue which defines all requirements by: describing them, giving them a priority, suggesting possible solutions, and describing the business benefits of them being met. In this step the formal documentation of requirements in the Requirements Catalogue is begun, initially by examining the previous studies and the Project Initiation Document. (A full description of the development of the Requirements Catalogue is given in Sec. 3.3.)

There will be some initial discussions with users and further problems and new requirements will begin to emerge. Their comments may take the form of 'The way this works is a real nuisance...' or 'If only I could do this...'. These comments should be documented in the Requirements Catalogue—if they are documented only as part of a discussion record for the whole interview, then they are likely to be missed later.

Planning the analysis

Once all of the parameters of a project are set, the development team is able to prepare for the investigation of the current system. The tasks and products required here are:

Decide on areas for and methods of investigation The areas for investigation will largely be determined by the boundaries and scope defined in the Project Initiation Document. However, it may be necessary to consider certain aspects in greater detail than others. Appropriate investigation techniques need to be determined for each area (see Sec. 3.1 for a brief discussion of the analyst's armoury).

Detailed allocation of project team members to tasks Although an overall project plan has been drawn up, it remains to detail the actual tasks to be performed by the analysts, and to allocate individuals or teams to tasks.

Identify users Users will be involved in the analysis in a variety of different ways: as interviewees, as reviewers, as representatives of other users, as questionnaire respondents, and even possibly as part of the analysis team. These people need to be identified and their roles explained to them.

Interview plans It is important to interview a good cross-section of users, at all levels of the organization, to be able to build a complete picture of the system. A plan should be drawn up for agreement with the user management, detailing the interviewers and interviewees for each interview, and giving a timetable for the interviews.

---

[1] As the project develops the boundaries will inevitably change. Tight well-controlled project boundaries help project managers to achieve their goals of 'on-time and on-budget': whether they help users to achieve their goals is a different question. By the end of the Requirements Analysis module the system/project boundary should be clearly defined.

Authorization to proceed

As the products produced in this step are so critical to the success of the project they are normally the subject of a quality assurance review. This should result in a formal agreement that is made with the senior users or the project board[1] to proceed with the project.

SUMMARY

- Step 110, *establish analysis framework*, produces project management products and early analysis products.
- As the step sets up the framework for the whole project it is critical for its success.
- The Project Initiation Document is a major input to the step and describes the terms of reference.
- The step involves planning the analysis in great detail and the whole project in lesser detail.
- Previous studies of the system are checked for consistency, completeness, and to ensure that they are still valid. Early versions of analysis products are developed from these studies.
- Early versions of the Logical Data Structure, the Requirements Catalogue, and the Data Flow Diagrams are developed and used to help clarify the systems boundary.
- The various plans developed are subject to a formal review which should result in authorization for the project.

3.3   Investigate and define requirements (step 120)

Introduction

A requirement is a feature or facility that is desired by some of the users of the current or future system. The technique of *requirements definition* involves eliciting those requirements, defining and refining them, and documenting them in the Requirements Catalogue. Throughout this process the analyst tries to develop a consensus amongst users regarding the definition of each requirement and its importance in the new system. In this step the objective is to define and agree requirements and their relative importance in sufficient detail to produce Business System Options.

The requirements will fall into two main categories: first, those resolving or reducing deficiencies in the current system and, second, those for new facilities not provided in the current system. The Requirements Catalogue can be seen as a list of the factors that must be accounted for in the new system. As the project progresses each requirement becomes defined in more detail. Eventually the requirement will be fully resolved; then documented as part of the Requirements Specification, or discarded. When considering different ways forward for the project these requirements provide a powerful checklist against which different options can be measured. This happens in both the Business Systems Options stage and the Technical Systems Options stage. It is useful to give

---

[1] This is a term used in the PRINCE project management method to describe the steering committee that has overall control over the project. See Chapter 7 for further details.

priorities to the requirements to help in the production and evaluation of different options.

The emphasis is on defining requirements for the future system rather than on describing the problems of the old system. Each requirement should ideally be expressed in a quantifiable or measurable way so that it can be tested when the eventual system is delivered.

Approach to Requirements Definition

The Requirements Catalogue is started in step 110, *establish analysis framework,* or in a feasibility study. Step 120, *investigate and define requirements,* refines the Requirements Catalogue in much more detail.

Step 120, *investigate and define the requirements,* is carried out in parallel with step 130, *investigate current processing,* and step 140, *investigate current data.* Predominantly standard investigation techniques are used such as interviewing, questionnaires, observation and studying previous reports. When trying to give priorities to different requirements it may be necessary to have brainstorming sessions with a group of senior users. Achieving consensus between users on requirements and their relative priorities is often a difficult activity and may require more sophisticated techniques[1] than those of conventional systems analysis or of SSADM.

There is considerable interaction between requirements definition and other techniques. For instance, problems may be identified during the development of the Current Physical Data Flow Models which need to be described in the Requirements Catalogue. Later these may be resolved in the Required System Data Flow Models or in the Function Definition; and then reflected back in the Requirements Catalogue.

Sometimes a formal user requirement is produced by the users independently (this often happens as a prelude to involving specialist staff). They are usually expressed purely in narrative and are a useful input into the development of the Requirements Catalogue. However, such user requirements often prejudge the design with such statements as 'I need a terminal linked to a central mainframe' (suggesting a technical solution without describing the problem or the requirement). The underlying requirement might be that the user needs data to be up-to-date at all times and will need to be able to access the data during working hours. It is the analyst's responsibility to make sure that the real requirements are identified and expressed in an implementation-independent way. It is important to have this 'logical' statement of requirements so that the solution is not needlessly constrained. It must be left to the project team to specify the best solution to fit the users' requirements without allowing the users' preconceptions to be carried through to an ill-judged implementation.

Functional requirements

These are activities that the new system is required to perform. They cover the normal range of functional requirements: storing and retrieving data, updating data, producing reports, answering enquiries, interacting with other systems, etc. As an example we

---

[1] e.g. the Soft Systems Methodology, see Checkland, P. and Scholes, J.E. (1991) *Soft Systems Methodology in Action* (Wiley, Chichester).

have developed the Requirements Catalogue entry for the Vehicle Availability Enquiry requirement in Fig. 3.12. Many of these functional requirements will be documented further in Data Flow Models for the current physical and current logical system. However, enquiries are not normally shown on Data Flow Diagrams (particularly unpredictable or on demand enquiries, known as *ad hoc* enquiries) so special care is needed to ensure that functional requirements for enquiries are fully documented.

Non-functional requirements

As the name suggests, these are not functions or capabilities of the new system. They cover other important requirements such as performance, security, recovery, archive, and audit. They are often associated with particular functional requirements, e.g. the response time for a Vehicle Availability Enquiry must be less than five seconds. Other non-functional requirements may be system-wide, e.g. hardware must be able to operate in Yorkies' depots (particularly dirty and smelly places). Ideally non-functional requirements should be quantifiable so that conformance to requirements can later be tested. For example, after thirty minutes' formal training, a user should be able to perform a Vehicle Availability Enquiry in less than two minutes unaided.

Types of non-functional requirements

Service Level Requirements These are related to the performance of the required system. They cover such factors as the times of the day when a particular function will be available, response times, turnaround times for batch processing, and reliability considerations (e.g. acceptable downtime,[1] number of failures, and maximum amount of downtime per failure). These Service Level Requirements are important inputs to Technical Systems Options work which may involve capacity planning expertise. During Physical Design they can act as targets for the performance of the system and can form the basis of Service Level Agreements with suppliers.

Access Restrictions These are developed in outline during this stage. They describe which users have access rights to which data. Later, in the Requirements Specification module, they are refined to describe access to entity occurrences, attribute values, and relationships; these are further documented in Entity Descriptions, Attribute Descriptions, and Relationship Descriptions. Other security aspects, such as physical protection and data encryption, could also be described. Some particularly sensitive projects may need to use sophisticated risk management techniques such as CRAMM (CCTA Risk Analysis and Management Method).

Recovery This is a complex issue with rapid recovery being very expensive. Pragmatic consideration needs to be given to issues such as, how long we could cope without the system after a 'crash' or how much data can be 'lost' in a system failure. The recovery requirements will have a considerable impact on the kind of hardware and software required and on planning for contingencies such as back-up manual systems or agreements with other computer installations. Again sophisticated risk analysis techniques may be appropriate.

---

[1] Downtime is the period when the function is unavailable.

Audit and control For financial systems, audit requirements are very important. These may have an impact on how particular functions are allocated to users and on access to the system. It may also be necessary to specify audit trails.

Constraints There may be complex conversion requirements particularly if the current system is a manual system. Other important constraints could be associated with interfaces with other computer systems or particular human–computer interaction (HCI) requirements (e.g. use by disabled staff or the environmental conditions under which the hardware has to operate).

Archive Archival requirements are broadly described in this step. They will be considered in greater detail during the development of the Required System Logical Data Model. They are then added to Entity Descriptions and will cover factors such as/when data is to be archived and later destroyed, and what physical media will hold archive data.

Requirements Catalogue documentation

An example of a Requirements Catalogue entry is shown below in Fig. 3.12. The majority of the information shown below is developed early in a project, particularly in step 120, *investigate and define requirements*. As the project progresses and the requirements are resolved much of this detailed information is transferred and extended to formal Requirements Specification documentation (e.g. functional requirements and their associated performance requirements are often transferred to Function Definitions, requirements covering access restrictions and archival are transferred to Entity Descriptions).

Source Where the requirement was originally identified—this could be a user, a document, a previous study or feasibility report. The source may cross-refer to the User Catalogue. This describes the current system users and their particular responsibilities— it is developed in this step and is discussed later in this section (see page 81).

Priority Describes the priority assigned by the user. Various forms of classification are possible such as: high/low, mandatory/desirable/optional, or use of a numerical rankings or weightings scheme. Some projects may use a systematic approach to the determination of priorities similar to the critical success factor approach often used in information systems planning.[1]

Owner The name of the user or the part of the organization responsible for negotiating the requirement described. Again this may cross-refer to the User Catalogue.

Requirement ID An identifier given to the requirement. The official SSADM form does not have a space for requirement name. In our example we have named the requirement Vehicle Availability Enquiry and have shown that as the name of the functional

---

[1] See the article by Rockart in Galliers, R. (ed.) (1987) *Information Analysis: Selected Readings* (Addison-Wesley, Reading, Mass.).

requirement. If stand-alone non-functional requirements are being described then it would be sensible to name these on the form in the appropriate place.[1]

Functional requirements Description of the feature or facility required. This will be extended and further developed during Requirements Analysis. Obviously for some requirements considerable explanation may be required—this will necessitate changing the form or adding continuation sheets.

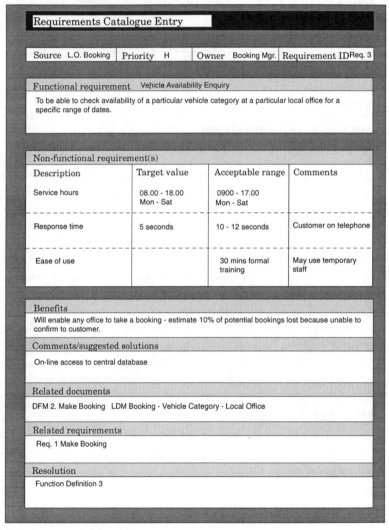

Fig. 3.12 Requirements Catalogue Entry form

---

[1] It should be stressed that the SSADM forms are a guideline only and often need adapting for specific projects.

Non-functional requirements Generally these are only developed in outline form in the early steps of the project. Often they may be related, as in Fig. 3.12, to functional requirements. Alternatively they may be stand-alone non-functional requirements such as system constraints. The detailed Service Level Requirements are later transferred to Function Definitions (see Sec. 4.4). Archival and access requirements are later transferred to Entity Descriptions (see Sec. 4.3). Ideally these non-functional requirements should be measurable.

Benefits A brief description of any business benefits expected from meeting the requirements.

Comments/suggested solutions A brief description of any possible solutions that may be suggested by the users or the project team. This is simply to ensure that valuable ideas are not lost—there is no commitment to meeting the requirement in this way.

Related documents Cross-refers to any other documents, e.g. Project Initiation Documents, Feasibility Report, Data Flow Models, and the Logical Data Model.

Related requirements Cross-refers to any other requirements which may be associated with this particular one. The Vehicle Availability Enquiry requirement is closely related to the Make Booking requirement in that availability enquiries often precede making of bookings. This cross-referring helps avoid duplication of requirements and helps to assess the impacts of any changes to requirements.

Resolution This is completed after the Business Systems Options stage and shows how the requirement is met. It may cross-refer to other specification documents such as Function Definitions, parts of the Logical Data Model or Technical System Options. If the chosen Business System Option does not satisfy this requirement then the reasons for its rejection can be discussed.

User Catalogue

Job title	Job activities description
Depot Clerk	Select vehicle from required category for customer on collection. Record mileage, condition, etc. on departure and return of vehicles.
Driver administrator (Local office)	Find suitable drivers from Driver/Agency Register. Determine availability. Find agency if no Yorkies driver available. Record driver details on Booking Sheet.

Fig. 3.13 User Catalogue

One of the great strengths of SSADM is its treatment of user concerns. During this step the User Catalogue is built—this describes the current system users and their activities.

For each *job title* a *job activities description* is given showing their current responsibilities. As the project progresses user roles for the required system are defined, based upon the current system activities. A partial User Catalogue for Yorkies is shown in Fig. 3.13.

Large systems may have complex user organizations with users organized into departments. It may then be necessary to organize the User Catalogue on a departmental or business area basis and supplement it by diagrams and organization charts. Sometimes development of the User Catalogue identifies problems with the organization's management structure. As the project progresses new jobs may be identified. Both of these problems belong to user management—it is not the responsibility of SSADM or the analyst to try and sort these out, although they must be raised—the success of the future system may depend upon the user organization.

SUMMARY

- The major product of step 120, *investigate and define requirements,* is the Requirements Catalogue.
- Each entry in the Requirements Catalogue describes a requirement, which may be either an improvement to a current facility or a new facility.
- The Requirements Catalogue describes functional and non-functional requirements.
- Non-functional requirements cover service levels, access restrictions, security, system constraints, audit and control and archival. Non-functional requirements may be system-wide (e.g. constraints) or specific to a functional requirement (e.g. service levels).
- Each requirement is given a priority to help identify and evaluate possible Business System Options.
- After Business System Options the requirements are defined in greater detail with much of the information formalized in other SSADM documents.
- The User Catalogue is also developed in this step. This describes current system jobs and their responsibilities.

3.4   Investigate current processing (step 130)

Objective

The objective of this step is to represent the workings of the current physical system using Data Flow Diagrams and to agree these with the users.

Approach

The Data Flow Diagram is a meeting-point of the analysts and users. The use of a diagrammatic model gives a precise and concise representation of the current system that can be used as the basis for further analysis and design. The diagrams use the language of the current system so that, for example, if a 'Pink form 13A' is used it will be shown on the Data Flow Diagrams as a 'Pink Form 13A'.

The development of the Data Flow Diagrams is done jointly by the users of the system and the analysts. Typically, the Data Flow Diagrams would be started by the analysts after being given a description of the current system by its users. Then would follow a number of further discussions in which the users would work closely with the analysts to refine the diagrams until they represent the current system accurately.

As the users are so closely involved with the development of the Data Flow Diagrams, it follows that they must understand the notation and their purpose. This may require some training.

Starting the Data Flow Diagrams

With the amount of detailed information available, it can be difficult to comprehend the whole system at first. To assist in the development of the initial Data Flow Diagram, several approaches have been formulated. We describe three: starting from the physical documents, starting from the actual goods passing around the organization, and starting from the organization's management structure. Each approach splits the task of drawing the diagrams into a series of manageable steps. In practice, a combination of the three may be the most appropriate, with most analysts finding their own approach with experience. Some analysts will produce partial Data Flow Diagrams while they are interviewing, validate them at the same time, and later compile the partial diagrams into one 'big' picture.

Below we demonstrate the three approaches—these are based upon the description of the Yorkies system given in Appendix C.

Physical document flows
This approach is appropriate if the current system consists principally of flows of information in the form of documents or computer input and output. The initial Data Flow Diagrams are arrived at by:

Listing the major documents and their sources and recipients In addition to actual documents in this list, major information flows of other kinds are listed, e.g. information communicated over the telephone or through computer dialogues. The list compiled for the Yorkies system is:

> Booking Sheet
> Invoice
> Customer Payment
> Booking Request
> Customer List
> Driver Request
> Driver Confirmation
> Driver Instructions
> New Vehicle Documents

Obviously, these are not the full set of information flows within the system, but they are the major ones needed to start the Data Flow Diagrams.

Drawing the document flows Each source or recipient is represented as an oval in a diagram with the documents represented as flows between them. A source or recipient might be:

• a section within the relevant area of the organization;

- an office in another part of the organization;
- an outside organization or person;
- a computer system.

The relevant sources and recipients for the Yorkies system are initially identified as:

> Local Office Reception Staff
> Local Office Booking Staff
> Local Depot Staff
> Local Office Driver Administration
> Head Office
> Vehicle Fleet Maintenance
> Customers
> Drivers
> Driver Agencies

These sources and recipients are scattered over a page, and each of the main documents listed before are matched to the relevant sources and recipients. The resulting diagram is shown in Fig. 3.14. The four different copies of the Booking Sheet are separated to show which copies are used in which areas of the organization.

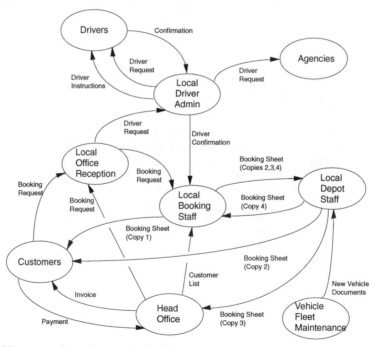

Fig 3.14 Document flow diagram for Yorkies

Agree the system boundary The diagram produced is shown to the users for comments on its accuracy and to check that nothing is left out. The boundaries of the investigation are defined on this diagram, showing which areas should be included in the investigation, and which should be considered as external to the system. In Fig. 3.14, the sources and recipients that are obviously going to be external to the system are the Customers and Agencies, as they belong to external organizations. Also, the users decide that the activities of the Driver Administration Section should be included, but not the activities of the Drivers themselves, making the Drivers external, but Driver Administration internal. Although an important part of the organization, it is also decided that the Vehicle Fleet Maintenance should be excluded from the system, as this is a large but self-contained section of the organization. The resulting system boundary is drawn onto the diagram as shown in Fig. 3.15.

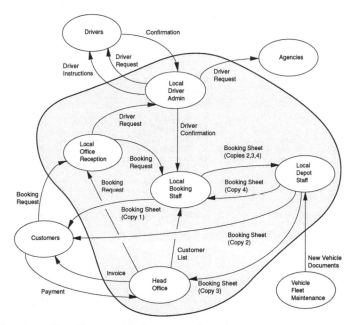

Fig. 3.15 Document flow diagram showing system boundary

In some projects this definition of system boundary will have been completed in an earlier stage, perhaps as part of an information systems strategy or by a feasibility study. At the moment we are only considering the boundary of the investigation—we focus on the eventual computer system boundary when we have agreed an initial design with the users as the Selected Business System Option at the end of the Requirements Analysis module.

Identify processes within the system The activities relating to the sending or receiving of the major documents within the system boundary are represented as processes, forming the basis of the top-level Data Flow Diagram. Where these documents are held within files or other means of storage, data stores are added to the diagram. For example, Fig. 3.16 demonstrates how the Booking Request form sent in by the Customers to Local Office Reception and Local Office Booking Staff is now represented as being received by a process, Receive Booking Request, performed by the

Reception Staff. The process passes the Booking Request to another process, Fill Bookings, performed by the Booking Staff. The Booking Requests are transformed into Booking Sheets by this process, and these Booking Sheets are put into the Booking Sheets File, shown as a data store. Note that the section responsible for performing the process is indicated at the top of each process box. This emphasizes the physical mapping of current system functions within the Data Flow Diagrams.

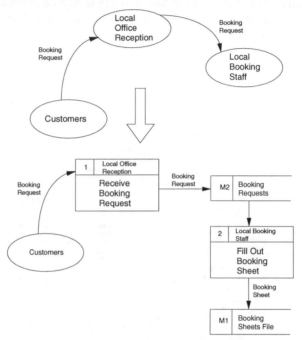

Fig. 3.16 Converting the document flow diagram to a Data Flow Diagram

Resources Flow Diagrams
This technique can be a good way of developing the Data Flow Diagrams if the current system consists principally of flows of goods. The Resources Flow Diagram concentrates on following the movement of the physical objects of interest. This flow of goods is represented by broad arrows. Physical objects at rest are shown by naming them in an elongated box—the resource store, equivalent to the data store. The progress of the goods is shown from when they arrive within the boundaries of the system, through the various points at which something is done to them or recorded about them (represented as processes), to their departure from the system.

A diagram that could be used to model the purchasing, rental, and sales of vehicles for Yorkies is shown in Fig. 3.17 (this area is actually outside the system boundary in the case study—we are using it for illustration only). In this case, the physical resources are vehicles. This shows how the vehicles are tracked from their purchase, through to their eventual sale.

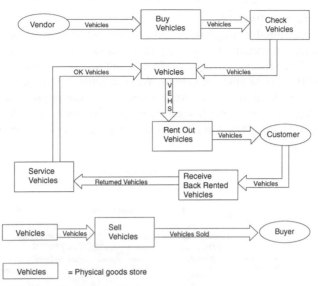

Fig. 3.17 Resources Flow Diagram for Yorkies

The reason for representing the physical flows is that information will normally follow the same paths. For example, the vehicle documents will accompany a vehicle when it is bought and sold, and the Booking Sheets will initiate a rental, and be sent when a rental is terminated, as shown in Fig. 3.18. In this way, the information flows and processes of the current system are determined.

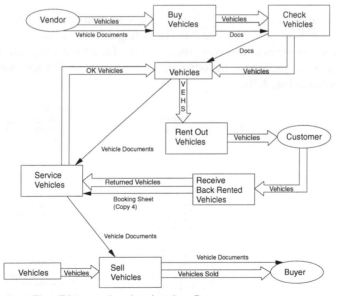

Fig. 3.18 Resources Flow Diagram also showing data flows

Organization structure

Often, the simplest way to develop a top-level Data Flow Diagram is to use the current organization structure for defining the processes. This approach starts from the point of view of the processes that are performed in the organization, rather than the information that is flowing around the system. When dealing with large systems which have many significant documents and information flows, the physical document flow approach may lead to very complicated diagrams. By looking at the relevant functions of different areas of the organization, a simpler initial picture may be produced, with the detail added later.

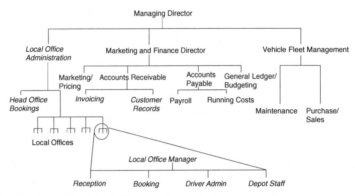

Fig. 3.19 Organization chart for Yorkies

The organization structure of the Yorkies system is shown in Fig. 3.19. Here, the user has decided which of the areas of the organization should be included in the investigation, as shown in italics. The main function of the Local Office Booking staff is to fill the bookings that have been requested by customers. A process Fill Booking Sheet becomes a top-level process on the Data Flow Diagram. By a similar procedure, the main functions of the other areas of the organization are represented as processes, as shown in Fig. 3.20.

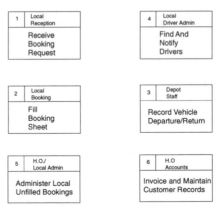

Fig. 3.20 Processes from the organization chart

The information flows between these processes, and between the processes and external entities, together with the stores of information are determined and added to the diagram to give the top-level Data Flow Diagram shown in Fig. 3.21. This top-level diagram could have been derived whichever approach had been taken. Remember that there is no such thing as a 'perfect' Data Flow Diagram—what is important is that analysts and users agree that it is a reasonable and understandable view of the current system. Try to avoid over refining the diagrams; we have seen projects developing 'paralysis by analysis'—Data Flow Diagrams are a means to an end.

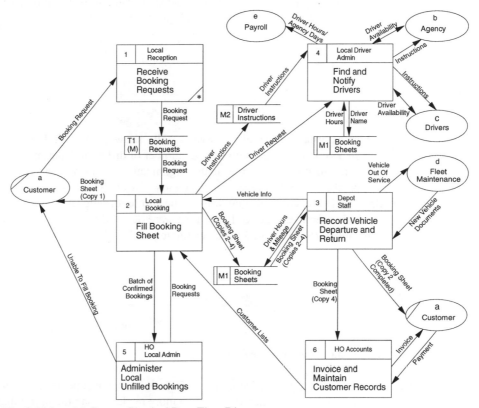

Fig. 3.21 Level 1 Current Physical Data Flow Diagram

Simplifying complex diagrams

The top-level Data Flow Diagram produced by the approaches above might become very complex and confused. (Remember that a Context Diagram was produced in step 110, *establish analysis framework*, to show clearly the system boundary.) It is important that the level 1 (or top-level) Data Flow Diagram is easily understood, as this is a very useful overview of the whole area of investigation, to be used for discussions with users and managers. If the level 1 Data Flow Diagram is unclear, then it should be simplified until the overall diagram is intelligible.

This simplification may be done in one of three ways (or a combination):

1. Combine some of the process boxes, until there are a maximum of 12 boxes on one diagram.[1] The processes that are combined can be split again at a level 2 Data Flow Diagram.
2. Combine data stores at level 1 only, showing them individually at lower levels. This might be done if a number of data stores are holding very similar information: in clerical systems, it is often necessary to hold the same information filed under different headings. The identifiers of the new data stores are 'Dn', where n is a number, and when they are broken down at lower levels, the identifiers of the lower-level data stores are 'Dna', where n is the same number as the top-level data store and a is an alpha character, as shown in Fig. 3.22.

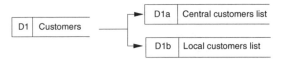

Fig. 3.22 Decomposition of data stores

3. Combine external entities at the level 1 only, showing them individually at lower levels. In a system dealing with a large number of different departments of the same overall organization, the name of the organization could be used at the top level, with a breakdown of the departments at a lower level. The composite external entity is denoted in the conventional way at the top level with an alpha character. The individual external entities at lower levels are denoted by the same alpha character and a number. (See Fig. 3.23 for an example.)

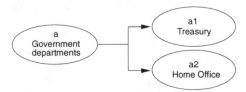

Fig. 3.23 Decomposition of external entities

The tidying up of a top-level Data Flow Diagram is shown schematically in Fig. 3.24. The final diagram is less cluttered and much more readable than the initial diagram.

---

[1]Experienced analysts vary in what they consider to be too complex; we have seen level 1 diagrams with more than 20 processes. In our view the 7±2 rule is generally a good one to follow. The 7±2 rule was devised by the American psychologist Miller, who observed that people could remember and understand a maximum of 7±2 'things' in one 'go'. The 7±2 rule applied to SSADM would state that no diagram should be presented with more than 9 major objects (processes, entities, etc.) in it when the objective is first-time understanding.

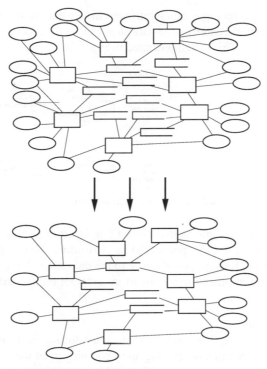

Fig. 3.24 Schematic simplification of complex diagrams

Data flows to and from data stores

Where an update to a data store is required, it is often tempting to show a data flow from the data store to the process in addition to the flow from the process to the data store. It seems to be logical, especially for those from a conventional programming background, that the required information should be retrieved from the data store before it can be updated. However, unless there is some real reason to extract the record first, only the data flow performing the update should be shown. This is demonstrated in Fig. 3.25.

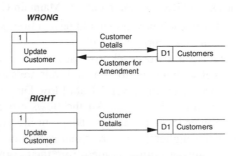

Fig. 3.25 Data flows should indicate the direction of information flow

Similarly, if a record is being retrieved from a data store, it is not necessary to show the selection criteria entering the data store before the record being retrieved is output from the data store. This is demonstrated in Fig. 3.26.

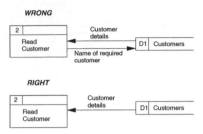

Fig. 3.26 Information flow and not selection criteria

The general principle is that Data Flow Diagrams show the direction of information flow necessary for the process to be performed. Thus a process that is changing data will show the information flowing **to** the data store. A process that is retrieving data, to pass it onto another process or to an external entity, will show information flowing **from** the data store.

Updates and retrievals

Normally only updates to system data are documented on the Data Flow Diagrams. It may appear that this is ignoring an important part of the system in the area of enquiries. All but the most major enquiries are omitted from the Data Flow Diagrams to avoid confusing the diagrams needlessly. The others are documented in the Requirements Catalogue. At a later stage, the retrievals documented are specified for the required system or discarded if no longer required.

Decomposition to lower levels

To describe fully the current system in the form of Data Flow Diagrams, it is necessary to expand most of the top-level Data Flow Diagram process boxes to a second level, or possibly to a third or fourth. As a general guideline, processes are decomposed if:

- there are more than eight data flows into or out of the process;
- the process name is complex or very general, e.g. 'Record Customer Information, Send Invoices, and Receive Payment' or 'Maintain Customer Information'.

At the bottom level, each process should have a brief specific name and have between two and eight data flows surrounding it.

Data flows between lower-level processes and other objects should be reflected back up to the top level so that data flows at all levels are shown in summary at the top level. This is demonstrated by the level 2 Data Flow Diagram of process 4 of the Yorkies Data Flow Diagram in Fig. 3.27. All the flows crossing the boundary (shown as a frame) of the lower-level Data Flow Diagram are shown as flows to and from the process box at the higher level. Error and exception handling data flows shown on lower-level diagrams are often omitted from their corresponding higher levels to help keep these simple.

While data flows at higher levels often use the double-headed arrow, those at the lowest level should be split into separate flows and labelled. This helps ensure that the current physical system processing is fully documented.

If a data store is used by only one top-level process, then it is said to be internal to that process. To avoid confusing the level 1 Data Flow Diagram, internal data stores are not shown. They are shown inside the frame of the level 2 Data Flow Diagram, and their identifiers reflect the identifier of the top-level process.

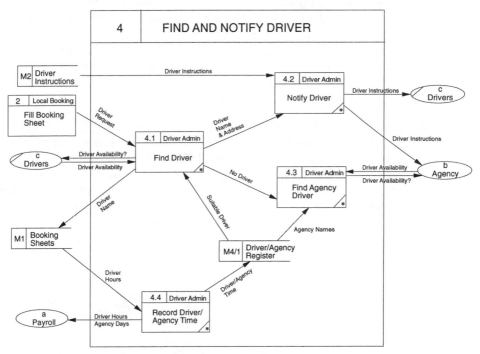

Fig. 3.27 Level 2 Data Flow Diagram

In Fig. 3.27. the data store M4/1 is internal to process 4 so appears only at the second level. If other internal data stores were shown, they would be identified as M4/2, M4/3, and so on. Consider also that no main data store associated with customers appears on the level 1 diagram (Fig. 3.21)—this is because the two data stores, the computerized central Customer File and the Local Customers List are maintained internally to processes 6 and 2 respectively. The Customers List is both a data flow and a data store, it is printed by process 6 and sent to the Local Offices. Because it cannot physically be shared between different offices it would be wrong to show it as a physical data store accessed by processes 2 and 6 which happen in different locations.

Validation of Data Flow Diagrams

It is important to realize that there is no such thing as a perfect Data Flow Diagram— unlike some of the other SSADM techniques they are quite subjective. What looks understandable and pleasing to one eye looks messy or over-simplified to another. Data Flow Diagrams are wrong if they inaccurately represent what happens in the current system. However, this can only be discovered by referring to the users or to the original description of the environment and checking that the diagram reflects what is described. Obviously common-sense checks can be applied; the processes should be 'walked-through' by the analyst to ensure that they make sense in terms of his or her understanding of how the system operates. More mechanical checks can be applied by looking at the data flows; any processes or data stores that do not both send and receive data flows should be queried. These may not necessarily be wrong but they suggest something unusual about the current system.

Current Physical Data Flow Diagrams should be reviewed informally with the users (some projects may decide on a formal quality assurance review). This review should concentrate on ensuring that the current system has been shown accurately and that no important functional areas have been omitted.

Data Flow Model Product Description

Figure 3.28 shows the Data Flow Model Product Breakdown Structure which shows that the Data Flow Model consists of Data Flow Diagrams and their supporting information. External Entity Descriptions show in a narrative way the responsibilities of, the constraints upon, and the functions of all external entities. Input/Output (I/O) Descriptions show the data content of bottom-level data flows across the system boundary (by naming all attributes contained in the flow).

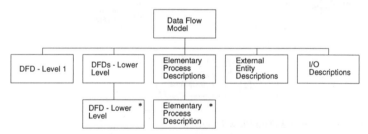

Fig. 3.28 Product Breakdown Structure for the Data Flow Model

Elementary Process Descriptions are used to describe the bottom-level processes. These are usually brief narrative descriptions of the processes and often cross-refer to existing current system documentation. If the processing is complex then a variety of techniques (none of which are specific to or are described by SSADM—see the systems analysis books listed in the Bibliography) could be used to describe the process. What is important is that an appropriate and accurate means of documentation is used (ideally, one that enables an accurate and complete description yet is fully comprehensible to the users). Appropriate techniques include: mathematical formulae, pseudo-code, Structured English, Action Diagrams, decision tables and trees, and formal specification languages. Examples of Elementary Process Descriptions, External Entity Descriptions and Input/Output Descriptions are given in support of the Required System Data Flow Diagrams in Sec. 4.2.

SUMMARY
- Current Physical Data Flow Diagrams are built up by users and analysts jointly.
- Three methods of starting the Data Flow Diagrams are described: Physical Document Flow Diagrams, Physical Resources Flow Diagrams, and using the organization structure.
- A level 1 Data Flow Diagram is built and, if necessary, simplified by combining processes, data stores, and external entities.
- Each level 1 process is expanded to second- and, possibly, third-level diagrams, maintaining consistency between the levels.
- Elementary Process Descriptions may be completed for some or all of the bottom-level processes.
- Reports and enquiries are documented in the Requirements Catalogue.

Exercises

3.4.1   CABA—CAt Breeding Agency

CABA specialize in finding mates for pedigree cats. They advertise in magazines such as *Pedigree Cat* and in response to enquiries owners are sent an application form. On the application the owner sends in details of the cat they wish to breed (name, age, sex, pedigree) and their preferences for a mate. Owners may also send in details of their membership of various cat organizations which may entitle them to discounts.

This information is transferred to two card index files—one detailing the cat and its preferred mates, the other holding the owner's details. The original application form is filed by date received.

CABA guarantees to send the owner details of five possible mates. After the cat and owner have been registered the cat card index is examined for potential mates. When the best five mates have been found, details of their owners are extracted from the owner's card index and the names of the potential mates are recorded on the cat card. The owner of the cat is then sent details of the five cats and their owners. The owner may make later applications for the same cat if they are unsuccessful—in this case CABA ensure that different mates are found.

Use a Data Flow Diagram to represent this system.

3.4.2   Reckitt Repairs

In order to control the Reckitt Repairs projects there will be a system to track the work and movement of parts. The current system includes a small computer system to track the movement of parts but does not interface this with the control of work.

The types of machine repaired by Reckitt consist of a number of different parts that are removed from the machine, cleaned, and inspected for defects. If defects are found, the parts need to be re-manufactured. Finally, all the different parts need to be replaced in the correct machine in the right place. This entire process needs to be monitored and controlled carefully to ensure that parts are not lost and that projects are completed on time and within budget.

The current operation of Reckitt Repairs can be broken up into the following activities:

- Customers send in requests for repairs to the Project Office.
- The Project Office replies to confirm acceptance of the request and plans the work.
- The Project Office also monitors and programs the work (detail planning of work packages and phases). It sends progress reports to Customers, notifies Finance when the work is done and the Management of any changes in the work plans.
- The Project Manager allocates staff to work, controls and monitors (with the help of a computer) the movement of parts in and out of machines and reports to the Management.
- The computer generates reports from the Parts File for the Management.
- The Factory manufactures new parts and informs the Project Office about their progress and records the movement of the parts in the Machine/Parts Book.
- The Cleaning Room cleans parts and informs the Project Office about their progress and records the movement of the parts in the Machine/Parts Book.

The following data is held manually, with the exception of the Parts File:

Job Order Book   List of all projects and customers. The status of the project is monitored here under the headings Planned Start Date, Planned End Date, Actual Start Date, and Actual End Date.

Project Plans   These are set up by the project office to show the different work packages and the phases within the work packages.

Staff Records   A card index of all staff with their qualifications.

Work Plans   Detailed plans of the work with staff allocations and details of parts to be worked on in a work package.

Machine/Parts Book   The machine details and all parts are detailed in this book with any special requirements for any particular part. All movements are recorded here under standard location headings.

Parts File   Computer-based file showing the parts and their current and planned locations.

Use a level 1 and one level 2 Data Flow Diagram to represent this system.

3.5   Investigate current data (step 140)

Introduction

This step produces the Logical Data Model for the current environment. It is carried out in parallel with the development of the Current Physical Data Flow Diagrams (step 130) and with the development of the Requirements Catalogue (step 120). This section describes how the Current Environment Logical Data Model is developed with particular reference to the Yorkies case study. Section 2.1 described the components of the Logical Data Model and showed how they were related together.

During the first step of Requirements Analysis, *establish analysis framework* (Section 3.2, step 110), an overview Logical Data Structure was drawn; this was used to agree the area of investigation and to help estimate the resources required for the project. This overview Logical Data Structure would normally act as input to step 140, although in this section the development of the Logical Data Model from its inception is demonstrated. The end-products of the step are the Current Environment Logical Data Model and the Data Catalogue. The Logical Data Model consists of the Logical Data Structure (the diagram), Entity Descriptions, and Relationship Descriptions.

As the step is carried out at the same time as the other investigation steps, the information for the production of the Logical Data Model should be collected at the same time as that for the Data Flow Diagrams and the Requirements Catalogue. The means of information gathering are the standard systems analysis tasks of interviewing, questionnaires, sampling, document collection, etc. Studying documents used in the current system is particularly useful for identifying attributes and entities.

The development of the Logical Data Model is often best carried out by two or three analysts pooling their ideas together in a 'brainstorming' session. They would then spend some time checking their ideas with users (these users would need to have had some instruction in SSADM) and validating the diagram against the processing requirements detailed on the Data Flow Diagrams. This step should not involve a significant effort, taking about one working day on a small project and about five days on a medium-sized project.

In this section a systematic approach to developing the Logical Data Model is described: selecting the entities, identifying the relationships, drawing the diagram, developing the supporting documentation, and then validation of the Logical Data Model. These are only guidelines to logical data structuring; experienced practitioners will develop an approach that suits them and the particular task best.

Selecting entities

The first step is to identify some of the entities of the current system. Remember that an *entity is something of significance to the system about which information will be held and which is capable of being uniquely identified.*

From the description of the Yorkies current system given in Appendix C we can identify the following as possible entities:

Customer, Booking, Driver, Invoice, Vehicle, Agency

All of these are things that information is held about in the current system. For instance, information about the Customer is held in the Customer List and the Customer File. Note that the Customer File and List are not themselves entities—they are both ways in which the current system implements the Customer entity and both appear as data stores on the Current Physical Data Flow Diagram. Other current system data stores may have no obvious entity counterpart: the Vehicle Booking Diary and the Empty Vehicle Log use data that spans several entities.

There are other potential entities that do not match data stores in the current system: Payment, Vehicle Category, Local Office.

It is difficult to decide whether these are entities or attributes which belong to the entities listed above. Vehicle Category is obviously very important to the system; customers book for a vehicle category, and vehicles belong to a vehicle category. But is it an entity itself or should the Vehicle Category Code just belong as an attribute to Booking and Vehicle? There are two factors that point to it being an entity:

- There are several attributes that could be associated with Vehicle Category: Vehicle Category Code, Vehicle Category Description, Type of Driver's Licence Required, Capacity Range, and others. Vehicle Category Code could uniquely identify each entity occurrence.
- An occurrence of the Vehicle Category entity is related to many occurrences of both the Vehicle and the Booking entities. This is an important point; if there are many occurrences of one potential entity associated with one occurrence of a different potential entity then both are likely to be entities.

A similar argument could be applied to the Local Office entity.

Payment is a slightly different case. There are several items that we would associate with it, such as Amount Paid, Date Paid, Method of Payment—indicating a Payment entity. However, there seems to be no unique identifier for a Payment and there could be only one payment for each Invoice—indicating that the payment details belong in the Invoice entity. Resolving this question with the user indicates that a customer may pay for an invoice in several instalments or pay for several invoices with one cheque—suggesting a separate Payment entity.

It is a common mistake to identify an attribute as an entity— remember that an entity is made up of attributes. Thus Booking No. is not an entity, it is the attribute that uniquely identifies an occurrence of the Booking entity (i.e. the primary key).

Another common mistake is to make the organization itself an entity—in this case Yorkies would appear as an entity on the Logical Data Structure diagram with relationships to every other entity. For something to be an entity there must be multiple occurrences of it, and there must be information that would be held for it. In a system like this there is only one occurrence of Yorkies and the information which would be held about it is all the information shown in the Logical Data Structure. The whole Logical Data Model is Yorkies—it is wrong to show it as a separate entity.

Four tests of an entity

1. It should be of importance to the system being studied.
2. There should be information associated with the entity. This means that you should be able to think of a number of attributes that belong to the entity.
3. There should be several occurrences of the entity.
4. Each occurrence should be uniquely identifiable. In other words it must be possible to define a primary key for each entity.

The attributes defined for each entity should not repeat. In other words, for one value of the key attributes there should not be multiple values of other attributes. If this happens the entity is not in First Normal Form (explained in more detail in relational data analysis described in Chapter 4). A new entity should be created and the repeating group removed to that entity. The original entity will be master to the entity formed by the repeating group.

Having identified the entities, we now go on to investigate the relationships between them. Selecting the entities may seem at first like a black art, but with experience it becomes easier. It is not too critical if mistakes are made at this point: new entities are often identified and old ones removed in the later stages of logical data modelling.

Identifying relationships

Each combination of selected entities needs to be examined to establish whether there is a direct relationship between them. Two approaches are described for doing this: a rigorous approach using an entity grid, and an informal approach building the diagram directly.

The entity grid

A rigorous approach which uses a grid to force analysis of every pair of entities and determine the relationship between them. The entities selected previously were:

Customer, Booking, Driver, Invoice, Vehicle, Agency, Payment, Vehicle Category, and Local Office.

These can be drawn up on an initial grid as shown in Fig. 3.29.

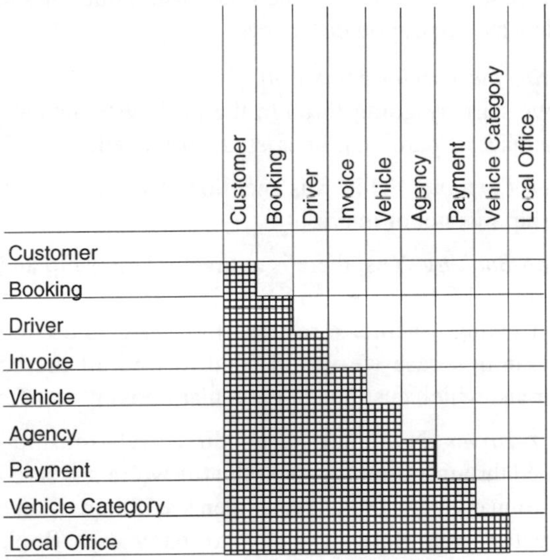

Fig. 3.29 Entity grid for Yorkies

The bottom left corner of the grid has been hatched to avoid considering relationships twice; the Customer/Booking relationship would be considered in the Customer row and so has been hatched out to avoid consideration in the Booking row. (There are several possible ways of laying out these grids but each should force analysis of all possible pairs of entities.)

Each box on the grid represents a possible relationship between a pair of entities. So for the top row we consider all the possible relationships that a Customer could have, for the next row we consider all the possible relationships that Booking could have (apart from the one with Customer considered in the Customer row). By proceeding systematically through the grid every possible relationship is analysed.

For each pair of entities the following questions must be asked.

*Are there occurrences of entity A that are **directly** related to occurrences of entity B?* It is important that only direct relationships are identified. For instance, when analysing Customer and Vehicle, we might think 'Customers rent and drive Vehicles therefore there must be a direct relationship between them'. However, the relationship is an indirect one that is maintained through the Booking entity.

If the answer is *Yes* then a further question is asked.

Is that direct relationship of interest to the system? In some cases there may be a direct relationship but one which is of no interest to the system. For example, some occurrences of the Customer entity may have a relationship with other Customer occurrences perhaps as subsidiary companies or as clients. However, this relationship is not of interest to the system (although really only the user can say this).

If the answer to both these questions is *Yes* then a relationship exists between the pair of entities, and the appropriate box on the grid is marked with a cross. If you're not certain then it is best to leave the relationship out—it's easier to add relationships than to decide which ones you don't need.

Completing the Yorkies entity grid
Below we start by going through the grid systematically although after the first row only examples of particular interest are discussed.

Customer–Customer This was mentioned above and it was decided that the direct relationship was not of interest.

Customer–Booking Yes, there is a direct relationship and it is of interest to the system. Customers make bookings and bookings are made by customers. Sometimes a good way of deciding whether a relationship exists and is of interest is whether access is required; in this case we would want to find all the bookings made by a particular customer and which customer a particular booking was for.

Customer–Driver No, there is no direct relationship—an indirect relationship is maintained through Booking. Note that if we're not sure then asking if the relationship is many-to-many can help—if it is, then see if there is an entity already identified which could be the link. Here the many-to-many uses Booking as the link. Even if the relationship had been incorrectly identified; further examination of the nature of the relationship or validation of the diagram would have identified and corrected the error.

Customer–Invoice Yes, customers are sent invoices and this is of definite interest to the system. Sometimes another good way of identifying relationships is to ask if we would hold any data belonging to the other entity in either of the two entities being considered. Here the Customer No. would be associated with the Invoice, thus indicating the relationship.

Customer–Vehicle No, considered previously—no direct relationship.

Customer–Agency No, similar to the Customer–Driver considered previously.

Customer–Payment Yes, customers make payments which are of interest to the system.

Customer–Vehicle Category No, although customers book for a vehicle category, this relationship is maintained through the Booking entity.

Customer–Local Office Customer lists are held at local offices but they include all customers on them. Customers do not deal with just one particular office, they could book at any office. Thus there is no direct relationship, only an indirect one via Booking.

Only relationships of particular interest are considered below.

Driver–Payment Drivers presumably receive a payment for work done. However, the Payment entity in this case refers to a payment made by a customer for a completed booking. It is therefore important to be clear exactly what is meant by each entity name. In this case study the payment of drivers and agencies is not included in the area under study, otherwise a new entity might have had to be introduced.

Driver–Vehicle Category There seems to be a relationship in that only drivers with certain licences can drive certain vehicle categories. Although this could be an indirect relationship through another entity it does not appear to be via any of the entities identified so far. It is marked in on the grid with a '?' and considered later.

Local Office–Local Office There could be a relationship between different Local Offices, for instance one could manage a group of smaller Local Offices. It is marked on the grid with a '?' and considered later.

The completed grid is shown Fig. 3.30. The next step is to draw each entity as a box on a diagram and draw in the relationships. Each relationship identified on the grid should be examined to determine its precise nature. This is described in the section, 'Drawing the diagram'.

	Customer	Booking	Driver	Invoice	Vehicle	Agency	Payment	Vehicle Category	Local Office
Customer		X		X			X		
Booking			X	X	X	X			X
Driver								?	X
Invoice							X		
Vehicle								X	X
Agency									
Payment									
Vehicle Category									
Local Office									?

Fig. 3.30 Completed entity grid

Building the diagram directly

This is a more informal approach based upon drawing the entities on a diagram and considering the likely relationships. The disadvantage of this approach is that it does not force consideration of every possible relationship. Its advantage, apart from being slightly quicker, is that it is easier to identify indirect relationships. There is a temptation when building the grid to mark in a relationship between almost every pair of entities—this will lead to a 'spaghetti' style diagram that will be very hard to sort out. However, if only few indirect relationships have been identified these should be easily corrected when a closer examination of the relationships is made and when the diagram is validated.

The relationship between Customer and Vehicle discussed previously was not obviously indirect when the grid was being used. When all the entities are shown on a diagram it is easier to see that the relationship is maintained through the Booking entity, especially if the relationships of Booking with Vehicle and with Customer have already been shown.

The questions asked of the possible relationships are the same whether the grid is used or not:

*Are there occurrences of entity A that are **directly** related to occurrences of entity B?*

Is that direct relationship of interest to the system?

There is really very little difference between the two approaches and personal preference should decide which is used.

In the next section the relationships identified are further examined to determine their nature. When the diagram is built up directly without the use of a grid the identification and examination of relationships are normally performed at the same time. The activities have been separated here because it is easier to explain the rather more formal approach.

Drawing the diagram

After identifying the relationships, the next step is to draw each entity as a box on a diagram and draw in the relationships. There are no precise rules for positioning the entities though it is obviously best to try to place entities close to each other if there is a relationship. The entities identified on the grid are drawn in Fig. 3.31.

Each relationship identified on the grid should be examined to determine its precise nature. It is necessary to determine the degree and the existence of each relationship (both discussed in Sec. 2.1).

To determine the degree of the relationship between entities A and B we ask two questions:

> *Can **one** occurrence of A be related to **more than one** occurrence of B ?*
>
> and
>
> *Can **one** occurrence of B be related to **more than one** occurrence of A ?*

The answers to these questions will determine whether the relationship is one-to-many, many-to-one, many-to-many, or one-to-one.

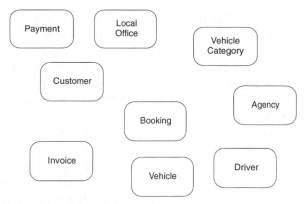

Fig. 3.31 Initial set of entities for Yorkies

Taking the first row of the grid we examine the relationships of Customer with Booking, Invoice and Payment.

Customer–Booking
To determine the degree of the relationship we ask:

*Can **one** occurrence of **Customer** be related to **more than one** occurrence of **Booking** ?*
Yes
and
*Can **one** occurrence of **Booking** be related to **more than one** occurrence of **Customer** ?*
No
This means that there is a one-to-many relationship with the many at the Booking end. This is represented by a line with a 'crow's foot' on the Booking entity (Fig. 3.32).

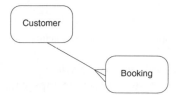

Fig. 3.32 One-to-many relationship between Customer and Booking

We name each relationship at both ends to form two sentences (see Sec. 2.1).

> Each **customer** ~~must~~ /may be **maker of** one or more **bookings**
> Each **booking** must/~~may~~ be **made by** one and only one **customer**

Strong descriptive names should be used which follow the users' terminology if possible. Generally phrases such as 'associated with', 'related to', 'belonging to', 'for', and 'part of' should be avoided. It is often difficult, at first, to come up with reasonable names but with practice naming becomes much easier. Constructing the sentence using the word 'be' can also prove problematic; again with practice you develop a repertoire of verb conjunctions such as 'employer of', 'employing', 'employed by', 'working for' and many others. The following endings of phrases are particularly useful: '...er of', '...ed by', '...ed at', '...ing', '...ing to', and '...ing for'.

The name of the relationship is shown, on the diagram, closest to the entity which forms the subject of the sentence describing that relationship. Thus, **maker of** is shown at the **Customer** end, and **made by** is shown at the **Booking** end.

The optional/mandatory nature is determined by asking:

Can an occurrence of one entity exist without a related occurrence of the other entity?

- Can an occurrence of **Customer** exist **without** a related occurrence of **Booking**? Yes—because customers are accepted before they make any bookings.

- *Can an occurrence of **Booking** exist **without** a related occurrence of **Customer**?* No—because bookings can't be made unless they are for an accredited customer.

This means that the relationship is optional (dashed line at the Customer end) from the Customer (master entity) to the Booking (detail entity) but is mandatory from the Booking to the Customer (solid line at the Booking end).

Another way of deciding whether the relationship is mandatory or optional is to consider the use of must/may in the relationship sentence:

> Each customer ~~must~~ /may be maker of one or more bookings
>
> Each booking must/~~may~~ be made by one and only one customer

Using **may** indicates an **optional** relationship, and using **must** indicates a **mandatory** relationship. Figure 3.33 below shows the Customer–Booking relationship; named and showing optionality.

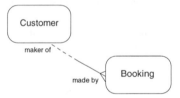

Fig. 3.33 Named relationship showing optionality

Customer–Invoice and Customer–Payment

These are both one-to-many relationships with the Customer being at the one end. Neither an invoice nor a payment can exist without a corresponding customer. However, customers can be accepted before being invoiced or paying Yorkies. So both relationships are marked as optional at the 'one' end and mandatory at the 'many' end.

Booking–Driver and Booking–Agency

A driver may have many bookings but a particular booking will only be for one driver—this is then a one-to-many relationship with Booking at the many end. A similar relationship exists between Agency and Booking. These two relationships exclude each other in that if a booking is for a driver it cannot be for an agency and vice versa. However, this case is more complex than the simple exclusivity described in Sec. 2.1 in that a booking may not require a driver at all if the customer is supplying his own. Thus a Booking occurrence may be owned by a Driver occurrence or by an Agency occurrence or by neither of them. So both are shown as optional relationships linked by an exclusive arc. These exclusive relationships use either/or in their statements:

Each **booking** *either* may be **driven by** one and only one **driver**
or may be **driven by** one and only one **agency**

Booking–Invoice
A booking will only appear on one invoice. In this system Yorkies invoice their customers on individual bookings so each invoice will be for one booking. Thus we have a one-to-one relationship between Booking and Invoice. One-to-one relationships are not usually shown in Logical Data Models since it normally means that the entities can be merged. In this case both Booking and Invoice could be uniquely identified by the Booking No. and the attributes associated with Invoice such as Invoice Date and Invoice Amount could be included in the merged Booking/Invoice entity. The two entities are then merged. (Note that it would also be acceptable not to merge the two entities—later in this project we will split the Booking/Invoice to meet a requirement for the new system.) The relationship Invoice had with Customer has similar optionality to the one that Booking had with Customer and therefore both become a fully optional Customer–Booking/Invoice relationship. One of the problems with merging entities like this is that it becomes difficult to find names for the combined relationship (the names used here are really only appropriate to the Customer–Booking relationship).

Vehicle–Booking/Invoice and Vehicle Category–Booking/Invoice
The booking is initially made for a vehicle category and then when the booking is confirmed it is allocated to a particular vehicle. Booking/Invoice is therefore at the many end of two one-to-many relationships. (Note that there is no redundancy in these relationships—see pages 118–9.) The relationship with Vehicle is optional at the many end until confirmation when it becomes mandatory. This illustrates one of the characteristics of Logical Data Models: it's not possible to show all business rules in the model, this sort of time-based constraint is best described in Entity Life Histories. As the relationship is optional for part of its life it's shown as optional on the diagram. The relationship of Booking with Vehicle Category is mandatory at the Booking end because a booking is made for a specific vehicle category.

Booking/Invoice–Payment
The identification of a Payment entity was discussed earlier under the heading 'Selecting entities'. A customer may pay an invoice in several different instalments. Similarly a payment may cover several invoices. There is then a many-to-many relationship between Booking/Invoice and Payment. This is resolved by the creation of a link entity, called Allocated Payment, which is owned by both Booking/Invoice and Payment.

Local Office–Local Office
This was marked with a '?' on the grid for further consideration. If each office was managed by another office then Local Office would have a one-to-many relationship with itself. This would be shown by the crow's leg from Local Office looping back,

sometimes known as the 'pig's ear'. In the Yorkies system further discussion with the users reveals that the inter-relationships between local offices are not relevant.

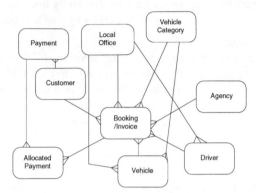

Fig. 3.34 Yorkies Logical Data Structure before tidying up

Some other relationships which are 'one-to-many' have not been discussed but are shown in Fig. 3.34. This is Fig. 3.31 with the one-to-many relationships drawn in, and we've not shown the relationship names or optionalities in this first draft diagram. It also has many crossing lines and some master entities shown below their details. The layout of Logical Data Structure diagrams was discussed in Sec. 2.1. By repositioning some entities it is possible to avoid all crossing lines and show all masters above their details. The improved complete diagram is shown in Fig. 3.35.

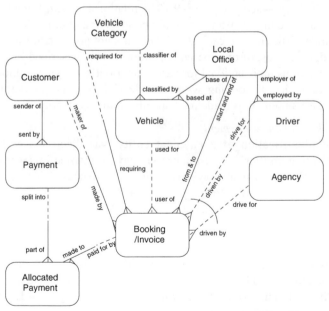

Fig. 3.35 Yorkies Logical Data Structure showing optionality and relationship names

Supporting documentation

The previous section ended with the production of a neat first version of the current environment Logical Data Structure diagram. The production of the documentation necessary to support that diagram is now discussed.

The Logical Data Structure diagram is a summary of the data that the system must hold. It gives the groupings of attributes and their inter-relationships. To document fully the system's data it is necessary to go into further detail on each entity, each relationship, and each attribute that has been included in an entity. This can either be presented using the standard SSADM forms or using a CASE tool—in either case the information held is the same.

Logical Data Model Products

The Logical Data Model Product Breakdown Structure, shown below in Fig 3.36, shows that the Logical Data Model is composed of a Logical Data Structure (the diagram), a number of Entity Descriptions and a number of Relationship Descriptions. Entity Descriptions and Relationship Descriptions are described below and examples from the Yorkies case study given.

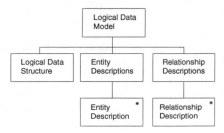

Fig. 3.36 Product Breakdown Structure for Logical Data Model

Entity Description

The Entity Description is developed in two parts: Part 1 shown below is initially developed in Step 140 for the Current Environment Logical Data Model; Part 2 is developed for the Required System Data Model in step 320 (see Sec. 4.3). The complete set of documentation for the data model is further reviewed and extended in later steps throughout SSADM. An Entity Description (Part 1) for the Vehicle entity is given in Fig. 3.37 and shows the following information:

Current/Required/Enhanced This shows which version of the data model is being documented. Usually the same form can be amended as it goes through the project. The information could be held on a CASE tool, word processor, or manually.

Entity Name and *Entity ID* Used to identify the entity and cross-referenced to the name given on the diagram. Some large projects may find it useful to use entity identifiers (IDs) particularly if these are supported by a CASE tool or data dictionary.

Location Useful in distributed applications where some entity occurrences may be stored at differing physical locations. In centralized applications this is not applicable (N/A) as shown here.

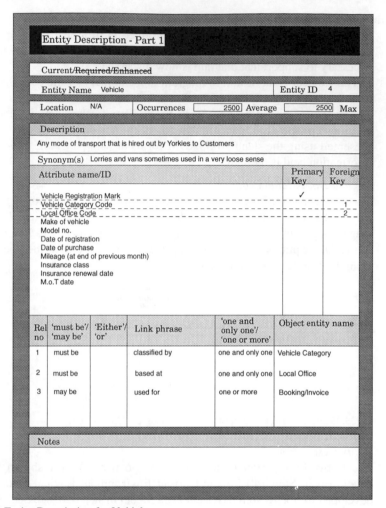

Fig. 3.37 Entity Description for Vehicle

Occurrences Estimate the average and maximum numbers of entity occurrences to be permanently stored at any one time on the system. This information can be used to calculate how much storage is required. Obviously these are often imprecise figures and any assumptions about how they are determined can be given in the notes shown at the end of the form.

Description It is important to clarify exactly what is meant by the name of the entity. Often people in other parts of the organization may have a different understanding of the same word (homonyms), e.g. the marketing department might think of a customer as someone who has expressed an interest in opening an account, whereas the rest of Yorkies would only regard someone as a customer when they had opened an account.

By formally describing or defining every entity there is a better chance that these kind of ambiguities can be identified and resolved. You may also describe why the entity was included in the model and help the reader to visualize occurrences. A description of the entity is most important, very helpful to the user, and should always be given.

Synonyms The names (including abbreviations) and an explanation of any synonyms can be recorded here. For example, different departments of Yorkies might use 'customer' and 'client' to mean exactly the same.

Attributes A list of the attributes that make up the entity must be included. Attribute identifiers may be used instead to save space or time, or may be included to clarify. Every attribute should be described fully in the Data Catalogue. At this stage only the most significant attributes would be included with each entity—if any items discovered in analysis obviously belong to a particular entity they should be included; it is silly to discard any information collected. However, an exhaustive exercise to discover all attributes and assign them to entities is not necessary.

Primary keys A attribute or group of attributes that uniquely define an occurrence of an entity is known as its primary key. Relational data analysis (see Sec. 4.5) is used in Requirements Specification to define formally the keys of every entity. However, it is useful to nominate keys earlier, when developing the Logical Data Model, because it makes it easier to validate the model against the processing requirements. To indicate that an attribute is a notional primary key (or part of one) it is marked with a tick. Here Vehicle Registration Mark has been ticked.

Foreign keys Some attributes shown here clearly do not belong to the Vehicle entity. Vehicle Category Code and Local Office Code are the primary keys of the Vehicle and Local Office entities. As they are the primary keys of other entities they are acting in the Vehicle entity as foreign keys. Relationships between entities are maintained through foreign keys appearing in the detail entities—so as Vehicle Category (Rel. No. 1) and Local Office (Rel. No. 2) are masters of Vehicle the foreign key column is marked with the appropriate relationship numbers (the '1' shown for Vehicle Category Code cross refers). In some circumstances the primary key and/or foreign keys may be composed of several attributes (explained in more detail in Sec. 4.5).

Relationship information This describes how key attributes link entities. It is also on the Logical Data Structure diagram but it is also useful to have a complete, separate view of each entity. The components of a relationship are:

> *Relationship No.* Cross-refers the relationships on the diagram with those on the form and cross-refers to the attributes identified as foreign keys.

> *'must be'/'may be'* Used to indicate whether the relationship is mandatory or optional.

> *'either'/'or'* Used for exclusive relationships.

> *Link phrase* Name given to the relationship from the perspective of the entity being described. This will always be the phrase closest to the entity on the

diagram, thus 'classified by' is closest to the Vehicle end of the relationship with Vehicle Category.

'one and only one'/'one or more' Indicates whether the subject entity, in this case Vehicle, is at the one or many end.

Object entity name The name of the other entity participating in the relationship.

Notes Any additional remarks about the entity, e.g. assumptions about volumetrics and explanations of its derivation. Do not include any access, security, or archive information—these are added when Part 2 is completed.

Relationship Descriptions

Every relationship shown on the Logical Data Structure diagram should be further documented by Relationship Descriptions. They would be started in this step using information gathered while analysing the present system. Several advantages of describing relationships are

- relationships are often identified to fit a particular requirement, drawn on the diagram and then some time later that requirement and discussion will be forgotten and revisited;
- it helps users and analysts to understand and agree the diagram;
- there is often more information about the relationship than could be recorded on the diagram, for instance with optional or exclusive relationships there will be conditions under which the optionality or exclusivity occurs (some database management systems can support these rules);
- volumetric information can be collected and held.

An example Relationship Description is given in Fig. 3.38 for Vehicle–Booking/Invoice. Notice that two descriptions are needed, one for each link phrase used on the diagram. Figure 3.38 shows the relationship from the Vehicle end, another description would be produced for the Booking/Invoice end.[1]

Current/Required/Enhanced The particular version of the Logical Data Model referred to.

Entity name The name given to the entity closest to the relationship being described, in other words the subject entity. In this case each Vehicle may be used for one or more Bookings/Invoices.

Mandatory, Optional, % Optional Indicates whether the relationship is mandatory or optional. The % figure shows, for an optional relationship, the number of occurrences of the subject entity not participating in the relationship. In this case this means that 1% of the vehicles have no associated bookings/invoices.

Link phrase The phrase used on the diagram to describe the relationship from the perspective of the subject entity, in other words the phrase closest to the subject entity.

---

[1] In practice, this seems to be a case of over-documentation—one Relationship Description per relationship, with further description of each end, would probably be sufficient for most projects.

Relationship Description

Current/Required/Enhanced

Entity name Vehicle

Mandatory ☐   Optional ☑   % Optional 1%

Link phrase used for

Description A vehicle is only assigned to a booking when the booking is confirmed. The booking was made for the vehicle category.

Synonym(s)

Object entity name   Booking/Invoice

One(1:) ☐ Many (m:) ☑	Minimum 0	Average 18	Maximum 40

Cardinality description   Most relationships will be close to the average

Growth per period   Probably very slow ca .2% per year

Additional properties   Transferable

User role	Access rights

Owner

Notes

Fig. 3.38 Relationship description for Vehicle to Booking/Invoice

Description Used if further detail to the link phrase is needed to explain the relationship.

Synonym(s) Other phrases that are used instead of the link phrase.

Object entity name The name of the entity at the far end of the relationship described.

One (1:)/Many (m:) Whether the relationship is the one end or the many end.

Minimum/Average/Maximum The number of occurrences at the object end of the relationship for one occurrence of the subject entity. In Fig. 3.38 this is showing the minimum, average, and maximum number of bookings for a vehicle.

Cardinality description May be used to further explain the volumetric information given above.

Growth per period A description of the growth rate referring to the volumetrics given above for a particular period.

Additional properties This is an opportunity to describe further properties of the relationship, such as transferability, which cannot be shown on the diagram. In Fig. 3.38 'Transferable' means that once a vehicle has been used for a booking, then the vehicle can be transferred to another booking by severing the link and connecting to another booking occurrence. [1]

User role Which users will have access to occurrences of the relationship end being described.

Access rights The access rights which a particular user role is to be granted. Can be Insert, Read, Modify, Delete, Archive or All.

Owner The user who is responsible for deciding which types of access will be allowed.

The access information described above will normally be described for a whole portion or total model. Very rarely is it necessary to specify this detailed access information for particular relationships. This information on access would be added as the required system is defined.

Notes Any further discussion of the relationship.

Data Catalogue
Each attribute is separately described in a Data Catalogue. Attributes are the fundamental unit of data in a system; entities are made up from them, Data Flow Diagram processes transform them, inputs to and outputs from the system contain them. The Data Catalogue could be held manually as a card index, as a PC database file, on a data dictionary package, or best of all, on a CASE tool. There is some considerable advantage in automating the maintenance of the Data Catalogue in that there will be many different attributes in a system. Typically a medium-sized project (4–5 man-years for analysis and design) may have over 400 different items and a large project may have 1000 plus. The Data Catalogue is invaluable in ensuring that a consistent set of definitions are used across the project, that ambiguities are resolved, and that synonyms and homonyms are discovered.

The Data Catalogue is refined throughout the project but is mainly developed in the steps involving logical data modelling. Documents used in the current system such as completed forms, reports, or files are the main source from which attributes are identified.

Figure 3.39 shows the Product Breakdown Description for the Data Catalogue; containing Attribute Descriptions and Grouped Domain Descriptions. The Grouped Domain Descriptions group together attributes that share certain characteristics. They

---

[1] This could happen if the vehicle to be used on a booking broke down beforehand and the booking had to be transferred to another vehicle.

avoid repeating definitions of formats, validation checks, ranges and access privileges which are common to several distinct attributes.

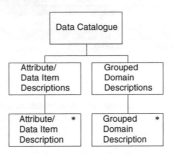

Fig. 3.39 Product Breakdown Structure for the Data Catalogue

Attribute/Data Item Description
The terms 'attribute' and 'data item' are synonyms in SSADM. Some purists use the term attribute for data properties that further describe entities and would argue that these become data items as the system becomes more precisely defined. It is more common to use the term 'attributes' when discussing data models and to use 'data items' when discussing process models. Usually 'attributes' belong to entities, and 'data items' belong to data flows. However, there is no formal standard on this terminology and either term can be used by SSADM in an interchangeable way. We have attempted to be consistent and use the term 'attribute' throughout the book but some specific SSADM forms use the 'data item' and we have followed this convention on those forms.

An example of an Attribute Description for the Vehicle Registration Mark from the Yorkies system is shown below in Fig. 3.40. The following information is held:

Attribute/data item name This is the name given to the attribute. It is best to be as specific as possible; for large projects naming standards will be needed.

Attribute/data item ID This is a code, usually numeric, used to identify uniquely the attribute. These short identifiers can be useful when computer tools are used since they will save typing long names, and make it easier to change the name of the attribute if required.

Cross-reference name/ID and *Cross-reference type* Used to show where the attribute is used in the system. In this example the Veh Reg Mark appears in the Entity Description for Vehicle and Booking/Invoice Entity Descriptions. Later on in the project this cross-reference will show I/O Descriptions, Dialogue Structure Elements, Update and Enquiry Process Models. Even in small projects the number of cross-references for particular data items can be enormous, this cross-referencing alone may justify the use of a CASE tool or data dictionary product.

Synonyms Any synonyms or abbreviations that are used by differing groups of users for the attribute.

Description A definition agreed with the users of what is meant by the attribute name.

Attribute/Data Item Description

Attribute/data item name	Veh Reg Mark	Attribute/data item ID	39

Cross-reference name/ID	Cross-reference type
Vehicle	Entity Description
Booking/Invoice	Entity Description

Synonym(s)   Vehicle Registration Mark, VRM, Registration No

Description

Unique identifier given by the Government to all motor vehicles—used in Yorkies to uniquely identify Vehicles.

Validation/derivation

First character will be in the range A to P excluding I and O

Mandatory ☑	Default value	Optional ☐	Value for null
Logical format	A999AAA	Unit of measure	Char
Logical length	7	Length Description	Fixed

User role	Access rights

Owner

Standard messages

Notes

Mandatory for all Vehicle entity occurrences. Optional for Booking/Invoice until vehicle collected

Fig. 3.40 Attribute Description for Vehicle Registration Mark

Validation/derivation Validation shows ways in which the values of the data can be checked for errors. This could include: range checks, consistency checks with other attributes, sequence checks, format checks, or use of check digits.

Derivation is described if the attribute value is generated by the system (e.g. system generated order numbers) or derived from the values of other attributes (e.g. invoice totals). It is important to distinguish attributes whose value is generated or derived once and then permanently stored from those attributes which are always recalculated. Sometimes validation and derivation rules are common to a number of attributes—these should then be described in the common Grouped Domain Description. Often detailed description of validation is left until Physical Design.

Mandatory and *Default value* Mandatory indicates that the attribute must always have a value for every entity occurrence. This is particularly significant for attributes which act as the primary key which must always have a value to provide uniqueness for the entity occurrence (note that foreign key attributes may have no value if the relationship is optional). Non-key attributes may also be mandatory for clear business reasons. It may be useful to define a default value for cases where no value has been supplied for the attribute.

Optional and *Value for null* This indicates that an attribute value need not be supplied for every entity occurrence. Some database management systems do not support 'null' values and it may be then necessary to specify a value to represent null.

Logical format The type of data that is to be held as the attribute. Some examples are: numeric, alpha, alpha-numeric, date, pounds sterling. In the case of codes the specific format might be given, e.g. AAA99 representing three alphabetical characters followed by two digits.

Logical length, Unit of measure, and *Length description* These describe the space to be taken by the attribute. 'Logical length' in Fig. 3.40 shows that Veh Reg Mark is always seven characters in length. 'Unit of measure' refers to units in which the length is given, this could be characters, bytes, bits or other forms. Where the length is variable it may be useful to include a maximum and an average size since many database management systems can compact these to the space actually occupied.

User role, Access rights, and *Owner* As in the Relationship Descriptions these define access privileges to attribute values. Each user role may have insert, modify, delete, archive, read, or all privileges. The owner is the user responsible for deciding access privileges. It is rare for individual access privileges to be defined at the attribute level, usually they are defined at the entity level. In these cases they will be documented on the Entity Description form (part two—which is completed in step 320, *develop required data model*).

   Broad access requirements are detailed in the Requirements Catalogue and transferred to the Data Catalogue and Logical Data Model in step 320, *develop required data model*.

Standard messages This can be used to specify the name used on particular screens for the attribute. It can also be used to document help and help error and other messages.

Grouped Domain Descriptions
In any system there are often several attributes that share formats, ranges and validation/derivation rules. For example, in Yorkies; Date Collected, Date Returned, and Date of Registration could all belong to the grouped domain Date or, in a hospital system; Patient Name, Doctor Name and Nurse Name could all belong to the domain Person Name. The idea of grouped domains is to avoid unnecessary duplication of derivation and validation processing—each attribute belonging to the domain is cross-referred to the Grouped Domain Description. As can be seen by the example (Fig. 3.41) this description contains similar information to that shown on the Attribute Description.

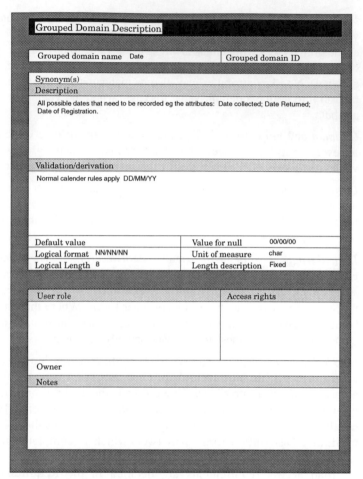

Fig. 3.41 Grouped Domain Description for Date

Validating the Logical Data Model

When the Logical Data Structure diagram has been produced it should be checked to ensure that no redundant relationships have been shown, that the structure can support the processing required by the current system, and that it is acceptable to the user.

Access paths and navigation of the Logical Data Model

Relationships indicate access from one entity occurrence to another—it is therefore possible to access an entity occurrence from other entity occurrences even when many other entities and relationships separate them. This is often referred to as *navigation* of the Logical Data Model and the path taken is often referred to as the *access path*. Consideration of the access paths is an important part of validation of the Logical Data Model. It leads to removal of redundant relationships and ensures that the Logical Data Model supports the processing.

An example of an access path is shown below. Suppose that there is a Yorkies requirement (perhaps identified by the marketing department and known as the Customer Requirements Enquiry) to list the vehicle categories and their prices used by a particular customer in the last year. The part of the Logical Data Structure involved in validating this processing is shown in Fig. 3.42. This shows an informal approach to validation; a diagram of this kind is not an end-product in SSADM—but merely demonstrates the thought processes of an analyst checking that the data structure can satisfy the enquiry. In Sec. 4.7 we use this example to demonstrate Enquiry Access Paths, which is the formal technique for validating enquiries.

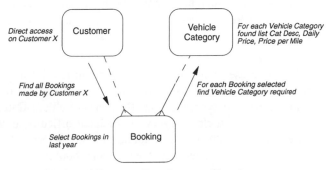

Fig. 3.42 Informal validation of Customer Requirements Enquiry

Access path rationalization
The Logical Data Model should be checked to ensure that no redundant relationships have been created. This is sometimes referred to as access path rationalization since it removes unnecessary or duplicated access paths between entities. Consider Fig. 3.43— there are two paths between entities A and C; one direct and the other through entity B. There are then two ways of satisfying the requirement to find all occurrences of C associated with a particular occurrence of A:

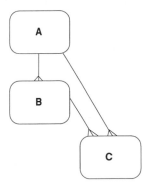

Fig. 3.43 Possible redundant relationships

1. Find the particular occurrence of A.
    Find all the occurrences of C using the relationship A–C.
2. Find the particular occurrence of A.
    Find all the occurrences of B using the relationship A–B.
    From the occurrences of B find all of the associated occurrences of C using the relationship B–C.

Obviously route 1 is simpler and quicker but the Logical Data Model is not concerned with simplicity or speed of access—it is concerned with ensuring that all the necessary inter-relationships are shown. Since route 2 can satisfy the requirement, the relationship A–C is redundant and can be removed.[1] Inexperienced modellers may introduce many redundant relationships, particularly when a grid is used. Careful analysis of the access paths should remove these.

Redundant relationships—warning
Caution should be used when removing redundant relationships. Consider the part of the Yorkies current environment Logical Data Structure shown in Fig. 3.44. Two relationships appear to be redundant: Booking—Vehicle Category, and Booking—Local Office. If the vehicle category or the local office associated with a particular booking were required this could be found through the Vehicle occurrence (or Driver for the Local Office) associated with the particular booking.

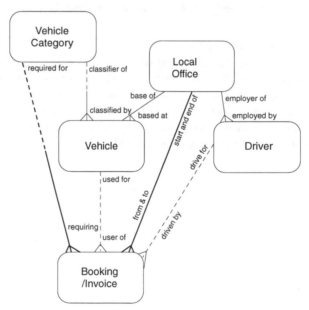

Fig. 3.44 Booking-Vehicle Category and Booking-Local Office relationships are **not** redundant

---

[1]Note that the relationships involving entity B could not be removed since entity B and its relationships would be required by other processing.

This does not consider the changing relationships of the Booking entity over time: a booking is initially made for a category of vehicle—it is only when the booking is confirmed that a particular vehicle is allocated to the booking. Thus the relationship occurrence between a Booking occurrence and a Vehicle occurrence is not created until the confirmation is made. (Changes to relationships over time are best represented in Entity Life Histories which give a dynamic view of the data.) So if the vehicle category associated with a particular booking was required before confirmation then this enquiry could only be satisfied by using the direct relationship between Vehicle and Booking.

Neither does it consider the meaning of the relationships; the link phrases are very helpful in understanding these. Thus the Booking must be **requiring** one Vehicle Category but may be **user of** one Vehicle. So the category required may be different from the category of the vehicle actually used. Similar non-redundancy occurs in the Booking—Local Office relationship: the reader should justify this to himself or herself.

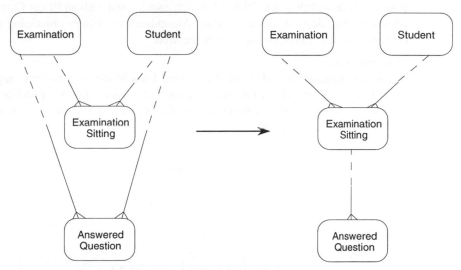

Fig. 3.45 Removing the double 'V' redundant relationships

Another kind of redundancy is frequently met in logical data modelling. This is sometimes known as the 'double V'. Figure 3.45 deals with a system recording examination marks. Two many-to-many relationships between Student and Examination have been resolved with the link entities: Examination Sitting and Answered Question. Further investigation should lead us to the conclusion that a better structure is to link the Answered Question entity to the Examination Sitting and remove the relationships between Answered Question and Student and between Answered Question and Examination. These 'double Vs' are quite common in Logical Data Models and should always be carefully examined to see whether redundant relationships exist. Redundant relationships can also arise when performing relational data analysis (see Sec. 4.5).

Validation against the current system processing
The current system processing will be described by the Current System Data Flow Diagrams, and their supporting Elementary Process Descriptions. Processing that is only enquiry is sometimes only documented in the Requirements Catalogue. The Current Environment Logical Data Model should be checked against the processing to ensure that the access paths can provide the data required for each process.

The validation of the Logical Data Model is performed each time it is developed or modified. In Requirements Analysis and the early steps of Requirements Specification, the validation is informal and consists of walking through each update or enquiry against the Logical Data Model. The informal thought processes that the analyst might have in checking a requirement against the Logical Data Model were shown earlier in this section in Fig. 3.42.

In step 360, *develop processing specification,* formal validation takes place with an Enquiry Access Path being defined for each enquiry and with an Effect Correspondence Diagram being defined for each update. All update and enquiry processing is then fully documented in terms of the navigation required.

Connection traps
A common mistake is to think of the Logical Data Model as a railway map—because every station on the railway network is connected to each other it is possible to get from any one station to another without leaving the network. The route may be tortuous but you will get there in the end.

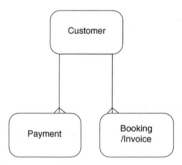

Fig. 3.46 Potential connection trap

Unfortunately it is not true of Logical Data Models that navigation is always possible from one entity occurrence to another related entity occurrence. Suppose there is a requirement to match each particular invoice to a payment made by the customer. The Logical Data Structure fragment shown in Fig. 3.46 appears to satisfy the requirement since Payment is connected to Booking/Invoice through the Customer entity. However, the occurrence diagram (Fig. 3.47) shows that it is impossible given a specific invoice to find the related payment or payments. Given a specific invoice, say Invoice No. 2345, we can find the related customer, Robinsons Ltd. But having found Robinsons Ltd there is no way of determining which of their four payments relates to Invoice 2345. This type of navigation problem is commonly referred to as a *connection trap.*

Fig. 3.47 An occurrence diagram demonstrating a connection trap

In this case the way of resolving the connection trap is to create a direct relationship between Booking/Invoice and Payment. As discussed earlier in the chapter this relationship is many-to-many and an Allocated Payment link entity is created.

Validation with the user
The Logical Data Model should be explained to the users. The users should be able to check that all data held in the current system is reflected in the Current Environment Logical Data Model and supporting Entity Descriptions. They should also be convinced that the Logical Data Model can support the current system processing.

Presenting the Logical Data Model
The users should be involved in the development of the Logical Data Model. Validation will then take place as the Logical Data Model develops. However, on most projects a formal presentation of the Logical Data Model will be necessary at some time. Often, on large projects, the complete Logical Data Structure diagram is built up from several smaller Logical Data Structures, each describing part of the system; a formal presentation will then be required to tie the various parts together.

The Logical Data Model should be presented in such a way as to promote understanding and discussion. Too often users are intimidated by the presentation of a complex diagram showing more than 100 entities with perhaps 200 relationships. The presentation of such a diagram should be carefully planned and the diagram partitioned into smaller chunks for separate discussion.[1] Sometimes the presentation of a summary Logical Data Structure is worth while with each high-level 'entity' expanding into a detailed Logical Data Structure.

When presenting partial Logical Data Structures to users some entities will not show their full set of relationships. The convention is to show these incomplete entities on the diagram as a dashed soft box. There may also be incomplete exclusive relationships— shown by dashed exclusion arcs. The example shown in Fig. 3.48 could be the partial diagram shown to Driver Administration when validating the Yorkies Logical Data Structure.

---

[1]Remember the 7±2 rule discussed in the footnote on page 90.

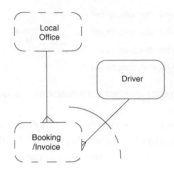

Fig. 3.48 Notation for partial Logical Data Structures

Validating contents
All data held in the current system should be represented in the Current Environment Logical Data Model by either an entity or a attribute detailed on an Entity Description form. Users should ensure that all data used in the current system is described.

Some projects prefer not to define the contents of each entity until relational data analysis has been performed in Requirements Specification. The Entity Description forms may then only detail the major items for each entity. This makes validation of the data content more difficult, since users will need to infer the contents from the entity name. An additional problem is that users often find the concept of an entity harder to grasp than that of a attribute. Without engaging in detailed theoretical argument, the authors prefer the earlier assignment of attributes to entities—this seems to be general practice in most projects using SSADM.

Users should check that the volumetric information given on supporting documentation is correct.

Validating access paths and relationships
Relationships described on the Logical Data Model and possibly further defined on Relationship Descriptions should be checked by the users. The degree and existence of each relationship should be examined to ensure that they represent the user's view of the system data.

The user should be convinced that the Logical Data Model supports the current system processing. Normally the analyst will 'walk through' some of the more complex or critical navigations as part of the presentation of the Logical Data Model.

SUMMARY
Step 140, *investigate system data structure,* is carried out in parallel with the development of the Current Physical Data Flow Diagrams (step 130) and with the development of the Requirements Catalogue (step 120).

The major products of step 140 are the Logical Data Model and the Data Catalogue.
Development of the Logical Data Model involves:

- identification of entities;
- identification of direct relationships between entities;
- creation of a diagram representing the entities and their relationships;

- production of supporting documentation to the diagram;
- validation against the processing requirements;
- validation with the user.

For something to be an entity it should meet the following four criteria:

- It should be of importance to the system being studied.
- There should be information (in the form of attributes) associated with the entity.
- There should be more than one occurrence of the entity.
- Each occurrence should be uniquely identifiable.

Relationships are characterized as follows:

- Relationships should be direct.
- Relationships should be of importance to the system.
- Relationships can be marked on an entity grid or drawn directly onto a diagram.
- The degree of the relationship is determined, if it is many-to-many then a link entity is created or found.
- Relationships are named at both ends.
- Optional relationships are investigated and are shown by broken lines.

The diagram is redrawn with masters above details and avoiding crossing lines.

Supporting documentation to the Logical Data Structure diagram includes:

- Entity Descriptions giving a definition of the entity, volumetric information, and the attributes contained.
- Relationship Descriptions.
- A Data Catalogue which begins to describe each attribute in more detail and any domains that cover several attributes.

The Logical Data Model is validated to:

- remove redundant access paths;
- ensure that the structure supports the processing of the current system.

The Logical Data Model is validated with the user.

Exercises

3.5.1   Scapegoat Systems—project management system

1. An employee can work on several projects at the same time. Each employee belongs to one department and has one manager within the department.
2. Each project has a start date and a finish date and a number of employees assigned to it. One employee is assigned as project manager. Projects are identified by a Project Code but there is a requirement to list all projects due to finish in a certain week.
3. Most projects are carried out for a single customer although there are some internal projects for which there is no client. At any one time a client may have several projects under way.
4. Scapegoat have about 100 customers each identified by a Customer No.

Develop a Logical Data Structure for this system.

3.5.2   Reckitt Repairs

Use the description given for the Current Physical Data Flow Diagram exercise at the end of Sec. 3.4

1. Develop a Logical Data Structure to represent this system.
2. Describe each entity in terms of a definition and some likely attributes
3. Validate the Logical Data Structure against the following requirements:
    (a) Find all parts repaired in a particular project.
    (b) Find out which parts are currently at a particular location and which ones will be received in the next day.

3.5.3   CAt Breeding Agency (CABA)

Use the description given for the Current Physical Data Flow Diagram exercise at the end of Sec. 3.4. Develop a Logical Data Structure to represent this system. (Warning: some parts of this are quite tricky.)

3.6   Derive logical view of current services (step 150)

Introduction

In this step, the Current Physical Data Flow Diagrams are re-expressed as a 'logical' view of what the current system does. The Current Physical Data Flow Diagrams are a powerful tool to help analyse the processing and information flows of the current system, but it is difficult to gain a true view of the functionality of the system, as it is embedded in the description of how it is implemented. In order to design a new system, it is important to take a fresh view, looking at what the current system does, independently of how it is achieved.

To be able to look at what the system does, it is necessary to deal with the inessential duplication of function between different sections of the organization. Logically, all of the information is held only once, and all of the processes in the system are able to access all of that stored information. In the logical view, the data flows contain only the information necessary for use within the relevant process. Many current systems will have 'evolved', so it is common to find a large amount of duplication and illogical groupings of both functions and data. So, the task of logicalization may require a complete restructuring of the Data Flow Diagrams. Although the guidelines for logicalization are relatively straightforward, this is one of the most difficult steps of SSADM as it requires a complete change of emphasis.

The main purposes of logicalizing the Current Physical Data Flow Diagrams are as follows.

To identify problems within the current system The type of problem identified during logicalization is to do with unnecessary duplication of function and/or information in the current system. Duplication of function means that it is possible that resources are being wasted in doing the same job more than once. Duplication of information, particularly common within clerical systems, means that there is a risk of different versions of the same data becoming inconsistent. Where this information is being used to support decision making, the impact of this inconsistency may be very great.

To understand the basic functionality of the current system After the development of the Current Physical Data Flow Diagrams, there will be a very detailed understanding of how the system is currently implemented. This is not always commensurate with understanding the underlying objectives and essential functionality of the system. By producing Logical Data Flow Diagrams, the project team are better equipped to explore ways of supporting the existing environment with a new computer system.

To establish the boundaries of the investigation more closely In Stage 1, the areas of the business to be investigated are identified and modelled using Data Flow Diagrams and Logical Data Models. The logical view of the system allows the identification of the precise functions within each area to be investigated. In Stage 2, Business System Options, differing system boundaries may be presented and the users will decide on a more precise definition of the manual/computer system boundary.

To force a switch in concentration Until now, the investigation has concentrated entirely on the workings of the current system. It is difficult to switch from that viewpoint to a more logical, abstract view. By following the steps in logicalization, the mind is forced away from the 'real-world' view. It is essential to make this mental switch before attempting to specify the required system or it will be difficult to explore the different options available to meet the objectives of the required system: the organization of the old system will persist.

To act as a basis for the specification of the required system Many of the functions of the current system will be required in the new system. The Logical Data Flow Model defines the part of the requirement that is to be carried forward to the new system. Later, in step 310, *define required system processing,* the Logical Data Flow Model is extended to accommodate new requirements—it then becomes the Required System Data Flow Model.

Steps in logicalization

Logicalization involves the 'unravelling' of the Current System Data Flow Diagrams to give an ungrouped set of bottom-level processes. Physical aspects are removed from the bottom-level processes and they are rationalized according to specified guidelines. The easiest starting point is to make the data stores logical, relating them to the Logical Data Model as a way of ensuring consistency between the two diagram types. The processes and data flows are then made logical and grouped to form the top-level processes of the Logical Data Flow Diagram.

Step 1: logicalize data stores

Each data store on the Current Physical Data Flow Diagrams represents either data stored in the permanent base of data (main data stores) or transient data (transient data stores) that is held for a short time before being used by a process and deleted. Each of the main data stores relates to entities on the Current Environment Logical Data Model, as this is where the structure of the permanent data is shown.

In logicalizing the Data Flow Diagrams, it is desirable to establish a precise relationship between the data stores and the entities on the Logical Data Model to facilitate cross-validation of the two diagrams. Thus, the rule is that each main data store on the Logical Data Flow Diagram represents a whole number of entities on the Logical Data Model (one or more) and that each entity on the Logical Data Model belongs to only one main data store. This rule cannot be applied to the current physical diagrams as information is often duplicated in real life.

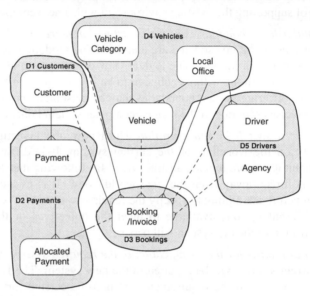

Fig. 3.49 Logical Data Stores in Yorkies

The main data stores are derived from the Logical Data Model. Logically related groups of entities are identified and cross-referenced to a new data store. One way of documenting this is on a Logical Data Store/Entity Cross-Reference form. If there is a problem grouping data logically, it is best to look for entities that are functionally related, i.e. entities that are generally operated on together or that form part of the same major inputs or outputs to the system. Theoretically, a data store could map each entity on the Logical Data Model, but it is preferable to keep the groupings of data at a more summary level on the Data Flow Diagrams, leaving the close definition of data to the Logical Data Model. In the Yorkies system the Current Environment Logical Data Model is subdivided as shown in Fig. 3.49 to form the main data stores. Notice that none of the logical data stores use the prefix 'M'; the 'D' prefix is used for all main logical data stores—there should be no indication of the physical implementation. The resulting Entity/Data Store Cross-Reference form is shown in Fig. 3.50.

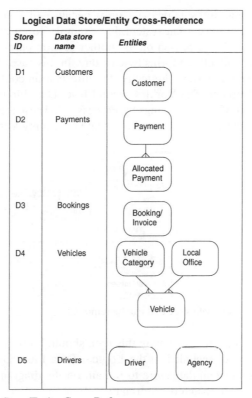

Fig. 3.50 Logical Data Store/Entity Cross Reference

The relationship between the data stores on the Current Physical Data Flow Diagrams and the new 'logical' data stores is shown in Fig. 3.51, which indicates the significant duplication of information on bookings in the current system.

Current physical data store	Logical data store
M1 Booking Sheets M2 Driver Instructions T1 (M) Booking Requests M2/1 Vehicle Bookings Diary T2/1(M) Confirmed Bookings M5/1 Empty Vehicles Log	D3 Bookings
M6/2 Invoices File	D2 Payments
M2/2 Local Customer List M6/1 Customer File	D1 Customers
M4/1 Driver/Agency Register	D5 Drivers
M3/1 Vehicle History Cards	D4 Vehicles

Fig. 3.51 Relationship between Current Physical and Logical Data Stores

Transient data stores may exist only because of constraints that exist within the environment of the current system. For example, forms may be batched together by one section before being passed on to another section purely because the internal mailing system only collects the forms twice a day. In this case, there is no logical requirement for a transient data store: logically, the information could be passed directly from one process to another. The Yorkies second-level Data Flow Diagrams (Fig. 3.52) show a batching of confirmed bookings by Process 2.3. These are then sent every second day to Head Office where they are used to update the Empty Vehicle Log.

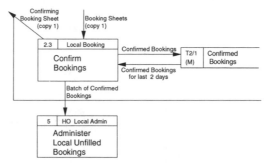

Fig. 3.52 Transient data store that can be removed

There is no logical reason why this data should be stored before transmission, so this data store is not included in the Logical Data Flow Diagrams. The only reason for allowing a transient data store to remain on the diagram is if the subsequent process needs a complete batch of information all at once. For example, if a process needs to compare a number of records, then it will be necessary to hold them in a transient data store for the whole batch to be read at the same time.

Step 2: logicalize bottom-level processes and data flows
1. A logical process is one that transforms or uses data because the business requires it to do so, independently of how it is implemented. For example, 'Print Report' in the Current Physical Data Flow Diagram would become 'Output Report' and 'Record details in Ledger' would be abbreviated to 'Record details'.
2. Those processes in the current system that are not subject to computerization should be separated from those that will be supported or replaced by a computer. (Sometimes, this distinction is very hard to make and there may be several ways of handling a process—Business System Options enables the users to make the decision regarding which design is best.) An example of this is where a decision may be made or Authorization given only by a responsible person. A process in the Current Physical Data Flow Diagrams named 'Authorize Request' can be treated in one of two ways:
    • If the clerical system surrounding the computer system is within the terms of reference, the clerical process 'Authorize Request' should be separated out from the potentially automatable process 'Record Authorization'.

- If the boundary of the system under investigation is synonymous with the boundary of the computer system, the person doing the authorizing should be put outside the system boundary as an external entity, with a data flow being shown entering the process 'Record Authorization'.

3. In the Current Physical Data Flow Diagrams, the location where a process is performed is indicated at the top of the process box. All references to locations are removed in the Logical Data Flow Diagrams. The processes represent what is done independently of where it is being done or who is doing it. The location in a current physical process box may become an external entity. Generally, the external entities shown on the Data Flow Diagrams are the last to have changed information entering the system or the first to use information extracted from the system.

4. If the data entering a process is unaltered on its exit from the process, the process is replaced by a data flow carrying that information. The process is not transforming the data, merely passing it on or reorganizing it in some way. Also, minor retrievals are removed from the Data Flow Diagrams and listed in the Requirements Catalogue.

5. Where several processes are performing exactly the same function, they should be combined. The exception to this is where ambiguity is introduced by doing this or where a large number of additional process-to-process data flows are introduced giving a confused picture. For example, Processes 1 and 2 in the Yorkies Current Physical Data Flow Diagrams both deal with bookings, and may therefore be combined.

6. If two processes are always performed together or serially, they should be combined. For example, one location may perform some initial validation on a piece of information before passing it over to another location for further validation before recording the information on a file. This will have been represented by two processes on the Current Physical Data Flow Diagrams. The Logical Data Flow Diagrams should contain only one process where the two stages of validation form part of the process of recording the information.

7. Where data flows are annotated with document names in the current system Data Flow Diagrams, the actual attributes or groups of attributes on the documents used by the relevant process should be used to annotate the data flows in the Logical Data Flow Diagrams. For example, in the Yorkies system, only a few items are added to the Booking Sheet initially, so instead of showing the data flow 'Booking Sheet (Copy 1)' as shown in Fig. 3.52, the attributes or a group of attributes would be shown in the Logical Data Flow Diagrams, e.g. 'Customer Name, Dates Required, Vehicle Type, etc.'. However, if certain documents or information flows within the current system cannot be changed in the new system (e.g. a legal requirement to produce a particular document), then references to these documents are retained.

8. Any processes that must remain clerical should be excluded from the Data Flow Diagrams unless the clerical system is within the terms of reference for the project. In this case, the clerical processes should be clearly distinguished from potentially automatable processes.

9. Often, processes are organized as they are in the current system because copies of the data are held in different places or because uncontrolled updating means that checks must be made at regular intervals. Given that all information is held only once in the logical system, and all access to it is restricted to the processes shown on the Data Flow Diagrams, many of the current system processes may now be unnecessary. For example, in a system where deliveries are made, a copy of a list sent with the driver may be accepted at the destination and recorded in the files there, but later have to be reconciled with a central register of that information held from the originating depot. This reconciliation should not be necessary logically, as the information is assumed to be available to all processes within the system.

In Step 1 logical data stores replaced physical data stores, in Step 2 there may be considerable redundancy of processing associated with the previously duplicated physical data stores. In practice this means going through the bottom-level current physical data flow diagrams and having replaced the physical stores with their logical equivalents now removing any redundant or duplicated processing that handles these stores.

Step 3: group bottom-level processes to form higher-level Data Flow Diagrams

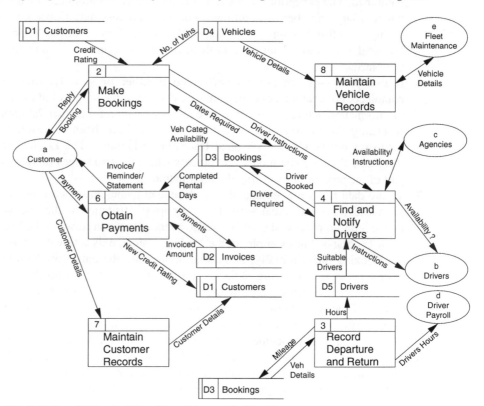

Fig. 3.53 Level 1 Logical Data Flow Diagram for Yorkies

The Yorkies top-level Logical Data Flow Diagram is shown in Fig. 3.53. The top-level Data Flow Diagram shows the logical functional areas of the system. Again, it is difficult to define what is meant here by 'logical'. A useful guideline is that the number of data flows between top-level processes should be minimized, and processes that use the same data should generally be grouped together.

If there is a large number of bottom-level processes to the extent that the logical groupings are not obvious, it may be helpful to draw up a process/data store matrix, showing which processes use which data. In doing this it is possible to identify all of the processes that create, modify, delete, and read the same information. If a group of more than 5–10 processes is identified, then these should be subdivided to give several second-level processes in addition to the single top-level process.

Often in a system, the processes supporting the actual business of the system (such as booking, invoicing, etc.) may be distinguished from those maintaining reference information to support that business (such as maintaining customer information, tables of rules, etc.). These should be clearly distinguished on the Logical Data Flow Diagrams.

Step 4: check for consistency and completeness
Once logicalization has been completed and a set of diagrams developed then it is important to check that a consistent and complete set of documentation has been produced. First, the diagrams should be compared with the Current Physical Data Flow Diagrams and to ensure that all the data flows, processes and data stores have been accounted for in the logical model—in other words everything that was essential in the current physical system is shown in the logical system. Second, common-sense checks should be applied—the analyst should satisfy himself that all inputs are used, stored, and ultimately produce outputs; that the diagrams reflect the analyst's feel for how the system works. Third, check for obvious oddities on the diagrams: data stores having no inputs or no outputs, processes only receiving or only transmitting data, and consistency between different levels of the diagrams. Finally the diagrams should be informally reviewed with users to ensure that no essential functionality of the current system has been omitted. The Logical Data Flow Model is part of the Current Services Description, which is an end product of Stage 1, and is carried forward through Stage 2 to the Requirements Specification Module. Like all end-stage products it is subject to formal quality assurance review (see Sec. 3.7).

Step 5: amend and extend supporting documentation
The Logical Data Flow Diagrams are supported by Elementary Process Descriptions, Input/Output Descriptions and External Entity Descriptions. These were created to support the Current Physical Data Flow Diagrams and any changes resulting from logicalization must be reflected here. The Elementary Process Descriptions should be validated against the Logical Data Model to ensure that all necessary navigation paths are present. More formal validation of the data model occurs in the Requirements Specification module when Enquiry Access Paths are developed (see Sec. 4.6). This may lead to changes in the Logical Data Model. The Requirements Catalogue is annotated to show any physical constraints which are still valid.

SUMMARY

The steps in creating Logical Data Flow Diagrams that represent the current system functions are:

- Logicalize data stores: determine main data stores from the Logical Data Model, some transient stores may be removed.
- Logicalize bottom-level processes and data flows. All references to how or who removed.
- Group into logical top-level processes. Minimize number of inter-process data flows and group together processes that use the same information.
- Check the Logical Data Flow Model for completeness and consistency. Informally review with users.

Exercise

3.6.1   Reckitt Repairs

This exercise is based on the Current Physical Data Flow Diagrams and Logical Data Structure provided as answers to the exercises in Secs 3.4 and 3.5.

1. Identify logical data stores from the Logical Data Structure, and name them. Produce a Logical Data Store/Entity Cross-Reference and Logical Data Stores/ Physical Data Stores Cross-Reference.

2. Rationalize bottom-level process (this may take several iterations).
   a) Replace processes which only retrieve data by entries in the Requirements Catalogue.
   b) Split processes containing subjective decision-making into an external entity (representing the subjective decision-making part of the process) interacting with a process.
   c) Ensure that no duplicate processing occurs in the logical system.

3. Draw a Logical Data Flow Diagram based upon parts 1 and 2,

3.7   Assemble investigation results (step 160)

Introduction

Each of the SSADM stages, from Stage 0, Feasibility, through to Stage 6, Physical Design, is completed by a formal process involving the users (and other experts) in making decisions and in accepting end-products. The Business Systems Options and Technical System Options stages are completed by the users making a decision regarding the future directions of the system (and project). All the other stages end with a step called 'Assemble...'. This 'Assemble...' step involves checking the accuracy, completeness, and consistency of the end-products of the stage. The products are checked both individually and as a whole. This checking is normally performed by a formal quality assurance review. Techniques for quality control are outside the remit of SSADM and are the responsibility of the project management method (e.g. PRINCE) used. Further discussion of an approach to quality control is given in Chapter 7,

Management Aspects. As a result of quality control, some end-products may need amendment and further review.

All SSADM end-products are defined by Product Descriptions in the SSADM Reference Manual. This contains quality criteria for each product: at the lowest level of each Product Breakdown Structure, quality criteria are defined for individual parts of the product; at higher levels of the breakdown structure, quality criteria define consistency and completeness of logically related groups of products. In each of the sections dealing with the 'Assemble...' steps we discuss the objectives of the review and identify some of the most important points to which users and technical experts should pay particular attention. For a full description of quality criteria see Part 4 of the SSADM Reference Manual.

Stage 1 products to be reviewed

There are two major products of Stage 1, the Requirements Catalogue and the Current Services Description (Fig. 3.54 shows its Product Breakdown Structure).

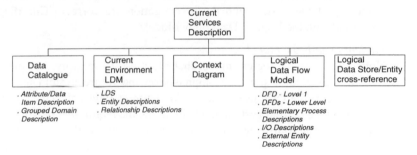

Fig. 3.54 Product Breakdown Structure for Current Services Description

Requirements Catalogue

The entries in the Requirements Catalogue should be reviewed with the appropriate users—those that raised the requirements in the first place and those, perhaps at a more senior level, responsible for a wider area embracing the whole system. It is important to ensure that requirements are consolidated so that duplication and repetition is avoided. The Requirements Catalogue is the most important, determining factor for the following Business Systems Options stage. It must reflect a clear consensus of the differing priorities given to requirements.

The Requirements Catalogue should integrate with and cross-refer to the Current Services Description. For example, functional requirements to be carried forward from the old system to the new should be reflected in and cross-referred to the Logical Data Flow Model.

Data Catalogue

This eventually contains all the information about the attributes used in the system. At this point in the development it is unlikely that a full description will be given to each and every attribute. However, the users need to be satisfied with the names and descriptions given to each attribute.

Current Environment Logical Data Model
Checks that should be applied to the Logical Data Structure might include: that all entities have been identified, that all entities **really are** entities, that no redundant relationships are shown, that all relationships are named at both ends, that entities do not contain repeating information. The model needs to be checked for completeness: ensuring all entities on the diagram have Entity Descriptions, ensuring all relationships shown have Relationship Descriptions.

The Entity Descriptions at this stage may only contain a brief list of attributes (each attribute is also defined in the Data Catalogue). Some of the checks that should be applied at this stage are: is each entity name and textual description meaningful and accurate to the users, are primary and foreign keys correctly defined, is the volumetric information accurate?

Context Diagram
This shows the context in which the system operates; showing all external entities, and the information they receive and transmit. The users must ensure that the scope and the boundary of the system and the investigation are correct. This diagram should be consistent with the Logical Data Flow Model.

Logical Data Flow Model
Notice that it is the logical model that is subject to scrutiny, not the current physical model. This clearly puts the emphasis on the future system and on the essential processing of the current system.[1] (The Current Physical Data Flow Diagrams help understand the current system and help define the requirements—but are only a 'means to an end'.) The following points are worth checking: is the system boundary clear, are all important functional areas shown, are all physical aspects of the current system removed, are all data flows described at the lowest level, are Elementary Process Descriptions complete and accurate, are I/O Descriptions complete and accurate, do external entity names and supporting descriptions reflect the environment outside the system, are the different levels of the diagram consistent, has the notation been used correctly?

The most important criterion is that the users are satisfied that the functionality to be carried forward from the current system to the future system is completely and accurately described by the Logical Data Flow Model.

Logical Data Store/Entity Cross-Reference
This shows which entities are contained in which Logical Data Stores and cross-checks the data model against the data flow model. The following quality criteria should be applied: does every entity belong to one and only one data store, and do all main data stores contain entities?

---

[1] This differs from earlier versions of SSADM which required that the current physical system be formally reviewed. Unfortunately many projects 'overdid' the Current Physical Data Flow Diagrams—a clear case of 'paralysis by analysis'.

3.8   Business System Options (Stage 2)

Introduction

In Stage 1 the current system was analysed in great detail. In Stage 2, Business System Options, tentative designs for the new system are put to the users. In consultation with the project team, a basic design, which may be an amalgam of the designs suggested, is agreed and carried forward for detailed specification in the Requirements Specification module. These tentative designs are known as Business System Options and the design agreed for specification is known as the Selected Business System Option.

A Business System Option describes a system: the boundary, the inputs and outputs, and what it does. It is concerned with *what* the system does rather than *how* it does it. This stage explores several ways of meeting the system requirements—defining different areas and levels of functionality to support the business. It enables the users to decide exactly what they require the new system to do.

The Business System Options break away from the current system completely, and begin to explore the shape of the new system. Several possible ways of meeting the requirements of the new system are considered before Requirements Specification is started. Very rarely is there only one possible design that will meet the requirements of the users. In Business System Options, the creativity of the systems analysts is used to explore the different ways in which a system can be organized, each having its strengths and weaknesses. Obviously, each possible solution will have an impact on the future users of the system, so although the options are devised by the analysts, it must be the users that decide which one to go for.

The Business System Options are not based around physical considerations such as operating system, database management system, etc.—these decisions are made in Stage 3 Technical System Options. Instead, the organization and scope of the system are examined and effects on the working of the business or of the system are considered. The possible solutions take the form of a description of functionality and scope, a cost benefit analysis, and an impact analysis. The users select the design that best meets their business objectives, considering financial and other constraints.

Overview of Business System Options

The Business System Options are formulated after the Requirements Catalogue has been finalized in step 160. Each of the entries in the catalogue is considered during Business System Options, and if any are excluded, the reasons are documented. Any constraints or other factors to be considered have been described in the Project Initiation Document.

Assuming that the majority of functions present in the current system will be required in the new system, the Logical Data Flow Model will provide an idea of the processing required by the new system.

If the scope of the Logical Data Model is likely to change as a result of the Business System Options, the Current Environment Logical Data Model will also be an input to this stage. The structure of the stage is shown in Fig. 3.55.

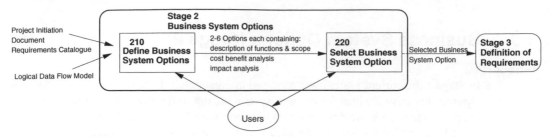

Fig. 3.55 Structure of Stage 2, Business System Options

Step 210, *define business system options,* produces between two and six options. Using the Requirements Catalogue, the project team develop a list of minimum functional and non-functional requirements which all options must satisfy. From this, up to six skeleton Business Systems Options, showing the range of possible functional solutions, are developed. These skeleton options are then discussed with senior users and refined into a shortlist of two or three options for further development. Each option is expressed as a description of the system (possibly supported by Data Flow Diagrams and Logical Data Structures), a Cost/Benefit Analysis, and an Impact Analysis.

In step 220, *select business system options*, the options are presented to senior users and the project board, a decision is made, and the Selected Business System Option is refined to account for any changes made in the selection process. The selected option fixes the system boundary and forms the high-level design on which the detailed specification will be based. The Selected Business System Option is carried forward to Stage 3, Definition of Requirements.

Development of the Business System Options

The suggested approach to developing the Business System Options is to start from the Requirements Catalogue and any other defined constraints that the new system must conform to. From these a list is compiled of minimum functional and non-functional requirements that all options must satisfy. There is a definite intention to escape from thinking about the system in the way that it is currently implemented—the analysts think creatively of ways in which a new system could meet the organization's objectives.[1]

The approach to this creative thinking may take the form of a group discussion in which the project team try to invent as many ideas as possible for the new system, including silly ones (some projects employ a 'brainstorming' technique). This could be followed by a session in which they try to rationalize these ideas into outline Business System Options, expressed as a description and a list of advantages/disadvantages. These options would then be informally discussed with senior users, and then refined into those for formal presentation.

---

[1] Forward-thinking users should also be involved in formulating options. Some research shows that many of the 'strategic' systems, that have enabled companies to improve their competitive position, were first conceived by users.

The range of the Business System Options

The options presented must obviously differ from one another, but by how much? In some circumstances, very radical changes to the practices and structure of the organization can be suggested, e.g. sack the salesmen and install terminals in the customers' offices. In other circumstances the difference between one option and another can be as small as the extension of the human–computer boundary to allow a small group of users to input their own data.

There is always an implicit option of 'do nothing'. The Business System Options stage is, like Feasibility and Technical Systems Options, a point at which decisions are made about the direction of the project. One of those decisions, which should always be considered, is to discontinue the project. The political and economic factors which justified the project at its beginning may no longer apply. At each of these option points, the termination of the project, perhaps with small enhancements to the current system, should be considered.

The number of options produced for formal selection depends on the size and complexity of the project. The bare minimum is to present two options and the suggested maximum is six. Small projects or those highly constrained by the Project Initiation Document may produce two options: a minimal option and an advanced option. Although only two options are presented, by going to the two extremes of the spectrum, the users are presented with a range of alternatives and may pick minimal support for some functions and advanced support for others—leading to selection of a hybrid between the two options. The minimum option put forward should offer a basic solution for only the requirements of the highest priority in the Requirements Catalogue. The priorities given to each Requirements Catalogue entry are the major factors in determining the components of each option. At the other extreme the advanced option should provide a comprehensive solution for every Requirements Catalogue entry. Some of the factors that determine the breadth of the options offered are:

The Project Initiation Document Certain constraints upon the new system were defined from the beginning of the project and documented in the Project Initiation Document. If these constraints are very explicit and limit the project team to, for example, re-implementing the current system without any changes to working practices, the options will be limited. In this case, the user has already specified the outline of the Business System Options before the project was started. Again, the options could be limited if a previous feasibility study has defined the new system in outline. Alternatively, if few constraints are defined, then the options could consider radical changes to meet the objectives specified for the system in the Requirements Catalogue.

Relationships between users and the project team If the users are keen and involved in the project, they will already have influenced the direction of the required system specification by this time and the project team will have a good idea of what is required. The options will be limited in this case because the decisions are made continuously and gradually.

The nature of the system If the project is providing computer assistance to manual processes that are not going to change, the options will be very much more limited than if the computer is actually taking over some of the processes of the system. In this case, there may be several levels of automation possible (some of which are discussed later: 'Levels of automation').

Business System Options for Yorkies

In the Yorkies system, there are two major requirements that the new system must meet:

*   to improve the operations of the parts of the organization studied in Stage 1;
*   to be able to deal with one-way hires of vehicles and to trace the whereabouts of each vehicle.

There is also a more minor requirement:

*   to be able to accept bookings from *ad hoc* (or non-regular) customers.

The Business System Options for Yorkies must be able to meet these requirements. Three such options are described below.

Business System Option 1—centralized system

This involves completely centralizing all the major activities of the company except for the depots for the collection and return of vehicles. All customers would then deal with a Head Office for both bookings and invoicing. Allocation of drivers would also be administered centrally although each driver would only serve a group of nearby depots. Local Offices would be closed down with some staff being transferred to Head Office, some being transferred to the depots, and some being made redundant.

This would involve the purchase of a minicomputer and approximately 35 terminals. Each depot would be informed of their bookings by telephone, and a computer-generated form would be posted to confirm the booking. The mileage covered by the customer would be written on the form, which would then be returned to Head Office. The depots would inform Head Office of any vehicles out of service by telephone.

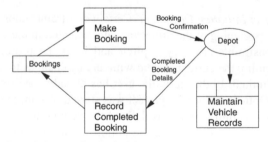

Fig. 3.56 Partial Data Flow Diagram for Option 1

In Fig. 3.56, the Depot becomes an external entity, receiving the printed booking form from the system, completing it, and returning the Booking Details to be entered into the Bookings data store by the system. All the processes shown here would be performed on the central computer at Head Office.

Option 2—local autonomy for the offices

This is almost the complete opposite of Option 1. Each Local Office is responsible for its own bookings, drivers, and invoicing. Information is held centrally and shared by all offices. Almost all data is entered at the Local Offices. Thus customers would deal with their local office for both bookings and invoices. Each office can make a booking at another nearby office if it cannot be satisfied at the originating office.

This option might require the purchase of a computer capable of supporting up to 60 terminals, communications hardware and software, about 55 terminals or PCs (one for each office and some for Head office), and about 52 printers.

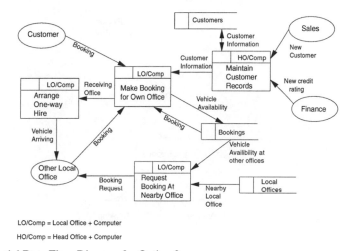

Fig. 3.57 Partial Data Flow Diagram for Option 2

Figure 3.57 shows the parts of the system where Option 2 differs from the Logical Data Flow Diagram (Fig. 3.53). Figure 3.57 shows the distributed nature of the system, with Head Office responsible for the Customer Records and the Local Offices responsible for the bookings. Another way of showing the distribution would have been to draw separate Data Flow Diagrams for Head Office and Local Offices.

Option 3—a distributed system

This is intermediate between Options 1 and 2. In this case Yorkies would be split into five regions each controlled by a Regional Office. Head Office would also become a Regional Office and the largest Local Office in each region would become the Regional Office. In each region five of the Local Offices would be closed down, leaving four Local Offices and ten Depots for each Regional Office to administer.

The Regional Offices would hold all the information for the region and be responsible for invoicing. The Local Offices would enter the bookings and add the mileage and driver time when completed. As in Option 2, each office can make a booking at another nearby office if it cannot be satisfied at the originating office. Communications facilities with other Regional Offices would allow one-way hires to be handled.

Each Regional Office would have a minicomputer and two or three terminals or a network of PCs. Each Local Office would have one terminal or PC linked to the Regional Office machine and a printer.

As before, a Data Flow Diagram would demonstrate how Option 3 would work. This would be very similar to the Logical Data Flow Diagrams. Modifications to the Logical Data Model result from this option. These are shown in Fig. 3.58, where it can be seen that a Regional Office is responsible for several Local Offices and that each Local Office is responsible for several Depots. Vehicles and Bookings are associated with a Depot.

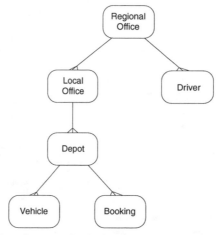

Fig. 3.58 Partial Logical Data Structure for Option 3

A large number of options could have been developed for this system, each varying slightly in its central, regional, and local flavour. The options presented here demonstrate the two extremes and a middle ground—the user need not choose any of these options. Instead a combination of mainly one option and aspects of the other options could be selected.

Differences between the Business System Options

The range of Business System Options was discussed earlier. This section describes the ways in which different options can differ from both the original system and the other options. These differences can be categorized as:

- distribution of the system;
- system boundaries;
- levels of automation.

Distribution of the system

In the Yorkies system, the options have been mainly concerned with the distribution of the system. If chosen, both Options 1 and 3 would have meant a significant restructuring of the company. Distributing or centralizing systems will almost always have a major impact on an organization, the effect of which will need to be carefully considered by senior management.

System boundaries and human–computer boundaries
The boundaries of the investigation are originally set in Stage 1, now in this step in Stage 2 we set the boundaries for design. Each option should have both system and the human-computer boundary clearly defined (this does not mean that they may not be changed later).

If the Yorkies PC system which produces the invoices and customer lists in the current system was considered to be satisfactory, then one possible option would be to leave the invoicing and customer records outside the boundary of the investigation. In this case, an interface with the new system would have to be specified. As this could be a possibility with both Options 1 and 2 it could be regarded as a sub-option of both.

Within the system boundary, the human-computer boundary may be defined. Two examples of possible human-computer boundaries are described here:

- The outgoing and incoming mileages are recorded within the Yorkies system when a vehicle is rented out and returned. The mileage could be entered directly into the system by the depot staff or they could fill in a form for input at the Local or Head Office.
- In a stock control system, it might be suggested that hand-held devices are carried by the person performing a stock count when determining actual stock levels. This would necessitate the use of computer equipment by relatively unskilled workers. Factors to be considered here would be impacts on wages, trades unions, retraining and other related matters.

All of these implications must be made clear so that the user can decide upon the exact boundaries of the computer system.

Levels of automation
In developing computer support for any process, several levels of automation can be defined. For example, a stock control system would require some way of ensuring that stock levels remain above a certain level. A computer system could deal with this in three basic ways each offering a different level of automation.

- The most basic option would be for a report to be produced every week showing all the current stock levels. The warehouse clerk would then raise an order for the low-stock items.
- A prompting option would determine daily whether any stock levels had fallen below the prescribed level and would generate a report to the warehouse clerk telling him to reorder.
- A fully automatic option would determine when stocks had fallen below the prescribed level and automatically reorder from the suppliers offering the best terms.

Contents of a Business System Option

Initially skeleton Business System Options are developed—these are probably best presented in the form of points emphasizing the functionality of each skeleton option and the differences between them. As these skeleton options are refined into full Business System Options for presentation to the users they become a more detailed document. Each option should contain the following:

Description

This is a textual description of the system covering the boundary proposed by the option. It describes the functionality within that boundary and for each function shows the level of IT support provided to it by the option. These descriptions of functionality can be supported by a level 1 Data Flow Diagram and by a Logical Data Structure (if these help explain how the option differs from other options). Technical aspects should be described in terms of the impact that these have on the business. They could include security, operating environment, data communications, and any other technical considerations influencing the design. The description should include details of proposed timescales for development, split into: design, construction, implementation, and procurement.

Cost/Benefit Analysis

This details the development costs and operating costs of the proposed option. It balances these against the expected benefits, both tangible and intangible. Cost/Benefit Analysis is always a difficult activity to perform and has been much criticized within the information systems community. However, there has been no consensus on choosing a satisfactory alternative technique. A full description of the techniques of Cost/Benefit Analysis is outside the scope of this book and the reader is referred to one of the system analysis texts suggested in the Bibliography.

Impact Analysis

This explains the effects of the proposed option on the user environment. It covers: conversion from the old system to the new system, training requirements, any changes required to the organization structure, and any changes in user-operating procedures.

Impact Analysis and Cost/Benefit Analysis are also produced at the other decision point stages in SSADM: Feasibility and Technical System Options. We discuss both techniques further in Chapter 5 which deals with Technical System Options.

Presentation of the Business System Options

The form that the presentation of the two or three favoured options should take will depend on the project. In small projects where the users are closely involved, informal discussions could be sufficient. If the project is large, with several groups of users, then it may be necessary to produce a report and have a formal presentation to the project board. The project board is the senior committee responsible for the project and is composed of an impartial senior executive, a senior user, and a senior IT professional. In many projects the board will authorize a review panel, which may contain people from the project board, to make the decision at each of the SSADM decision points. This panel could involve other senior users and senior staff from other parts of the organization affected by the system. It is also worth while to have an experienced, independent analyst as part of the review panel to ensure that all options are fully explored and that the users have a clear understanding of the impact of each option.

For a presentation of this importance, careful preparation is necessary to ensure that the audience fully understands the consequences of each option. A table could be presented summarizing the relative advantages and disadvantages, referring to entries in the Requirements Catalogue, of each option. The presentation will normally be given by senior analysts who should be able to give further amplification and answer any queries. The intention should be to provoke discussion and exploration of any new ideas rather than a 'rubber stamping' of the analysts' preferred option.

It is important that minutes are taken of the meeting and that decisions made during the selection process are fully documented. It may be necessary later to backtrack and see why a particular decision was made.

Selection of a Business System Option

The users are invited to select one option or a combination of features from all the options presented. If a combination option is selected then this needs to be reworked into a full Selected Business System Option. This selection then becomes the basis for the full specification of the system in the subsequent steps.

As a result of the discussions at Yorkies the users decided to pick Option 2 although elements of the other two options were selected for combination into the required system specification. The chosen combination is described below.

- The organization of the company remains the same as the current system with no offices being closed.
- Information is to be stored centrally on a minicomputer.
- Each Local Office will have a terminal or PC (to be decided at Technical System Options) and printing facilities.
- Head Office will remain responsible for customer records and invoicing.
- No terminals will be installed in the Depots. As the Depots adjoin the Local Offices, printed booking forms will be used to transmit information to and from the Depots.
- Each Local Office will accept bookings for any office.
- Local Offices will be able to modify any non-financial information about the customer and will validate bookings against the customer records.
- Drivers will be organized into regional pools so that each driver might be used by any one of the offices in the region.

SUMMARY

Business System Options:

- take a fresh creative view of the required system;
- are based on the Requirements Catalogue;
- may include 'brainstorming' to generate many possibilities;
- narrow the possibilities down to two or three options for presentation to the user.

Each option includes:

- A description showing the proposed functionality and boundary;

- possibly a level 1 Data Flow Diagram and a Logical Data Model;
- a Cost/Benefit Analysis;
- an Impact Analysis.

Options can vary in:

- distributed nature of new system;
- levels of autonomy;
- position of system boundary.

The options are presented to a review panel authorized by the project board.

The review panel picks one or, more commonly, a combination of features.

The Selected Business System Option is carried forward to the Requirements Specification module.

4 Requirements Specification

4.1 Introduction

Specification follows analysis. When problems are well understood, solutions can be formulated and design can begin in earnest. Requirements Analysis produced a outline design of the future system—this is now specified in great detail. The Requirements Specification module requires both analysis, to understand the detail of the requirements, and design, to specify how those requirements can be met.

The Selected Business System Option was chosen by the project board and senior users as the last step in the Requirements Analysis module. Requirements Specification builds the selected initial design into a very detailed logical specification. This module contains only Stage 3, Definition of Requirements, which is probably the most complex stage of SSADM—both in structure and in the range of techniques employed. The Requirements Specification module results in the production of the Requirements Specification document. This specification is essentially a logical view of the required system, although it will rarely be entirely free of implementation considerations.

The processing of the new system is defined in considerable detail in terms of its inputs and outputs, and deciding whether these are to be produced on- or off-line. A full definition of the system's data is produced and organized into an effective and flexible structure capable of meeting all of the functional requirements. Through the use of Entity Life Histories and associated techniques, a detailed specification of the processing logic is obtained. Any ambiguous or ill-defined requirements are clarified by using specification prototyping and then fed back into the specification. Further work is done on the Requirements Catalogue to ensure that acceptance criteria (e.g. for performance) are fully determined. The module ends with the publication and review of the Requirements Specification which should ensure that it is fully agreed, understood, and accepted by the user community.

Objectives of Requirements Specification

The main objectives of the stage are to produce a specification document that describes fully the requirements in terms of the functions and data, and which can be carried forward for further systems development work. During this stage a very clear idea of the overall shape and structure of the logical system is obtained.

There are significant advantages in specifying the required system in logical terms before deciding how to go about implementing it:

1. It is always best fully to understand a problem before trying to solve it. Consider the design process for a large and complex piece of machinery; before the nuts and bolts

are chosen there is a lengthy period where the purpose of the machinery is agreed, plans are drawn up by draughtsmen, and the overall structure of the machine designed. This is so that the final design is not needlessly constrained by the tools used to implement it—by choosing the nuts and bolts before the specification has been properly stated, the best solution may be ruled out in advance.

2. The users can understand a logical specification and are able to verify that their requirements are being met by the new system at an early stage of development—before it is presented to them as a *fait accompli*!

3. If a system is to be developed by external contractors, a logical specification provides all the required information about the system without constraining the developers to particular technical solutions.

4. The earlier errors can be identified, the less costly it is to correct them. The further through the development life cycle a project is, the greater will be the impact of any change in the terms of reference or underlying specification.

5. The maintenance of the system is helped by the presence of the logical specification. The specification can be used as a basis for adding enhancements to the system. If the system is replaced altogether, the logical design can be used as a basis for the design of the replacement system.

Products of Requirements Specification

Figure 4.1 below shows the Product Breakdown Structure of the Requirements Specification which is the end-product of this module. The Data Catalogue shows all of the attributes used in the required system and defines them in terms of their format, derivation and validation. The Requirements Catalogue is extended in Stage 3 to show more detailed non-functional requirements particularly those that have an impact on the whole system—these are considered in the Technical System Options stage.

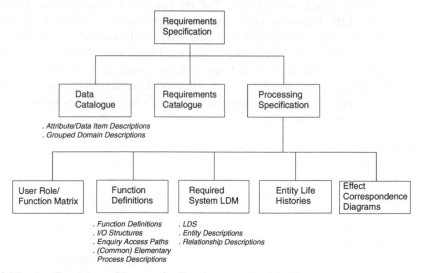

Fig. 4.1 Product Breakdown Structure for Requirements Specification

The User Role/Function Matrix shows which users have on-line access to which functions and is later used to help define menu and command structures. Function Definitions describe the processes of the required system, on-line and off-line. Included with the Function Definitions are: descriptions of the structure and content of any information passing into or out of the system (I/O Structures), Enquiry Access Paths which show the navigation through the Logical Data Model necessary to support enquiries, and any Elementary or Common Process Descriptions which describe the detail of processing (these have been carried forward from the Data Flow Model). The Required System Logical Data Model will be developed into a physical database design which includes complete descriptions of each entity—their keys and their relationships.

Entity Life Histories show for each entity all of the possible events that can affect it; for each event, operations show in detail what is done to the data. Effect Correspondence Diagrams show for each event the correspondence between its effects on various entities; these are used to develop Update Process Models in Stage 5, Logical Design.

Overview of the module

Figure 4.2 shows the steps of Requirements Specification, and their inputs and outputs.

Step 310, *define required system processing,* develops the Required System Data Flow Model from the Selected Business System Option. This model includes External Entity Descriptions, Elementary Process Descriptions, and Input/Output Descriptions which show the data content of system inputs and outputs. The external entities are matched with the users defined for the required system.

Step 320, *develop required data model,* adds any new requirements, defined in the Requirements Catalogue, to the data model developed in Requirements Analysis. The Entity Descriptions are expanded to ensure that a complete set of attributes have been identified and to include non-functional requirements (access, security, archive, etc.).

Step 330, *derive system functions,* groups together the lowest-level Data Flow Diagram processes to form update functions. Enquiry functions are developed from Requirements Catalogue entries. Functions are the main groupings of processing that are carried forward to Physical Design in SSADM. For each function considerable additional documentation is built up through the stages of the project to produce a complete processing specification. In this step this process is begun by developing Input/Output Structures to show the detailed structure of system inputs and outputs.

Step 340, *enhance required data model,* uses relational data analysis, applied to the inputs and outputs of the required system, to check and extend the Required System Logical Data Model. Relational data analysis is a bottom-up technique that looks at the inter-relationships between attributes and from that derives a model similar to that of a Logical Data Structure.

Step 350, *develop specification prototypes,* identifies critical dialogues and reports, and for these quickly produces working software which is demonstrated to users. The results of their evaluation are fed back into Requirements Specification.

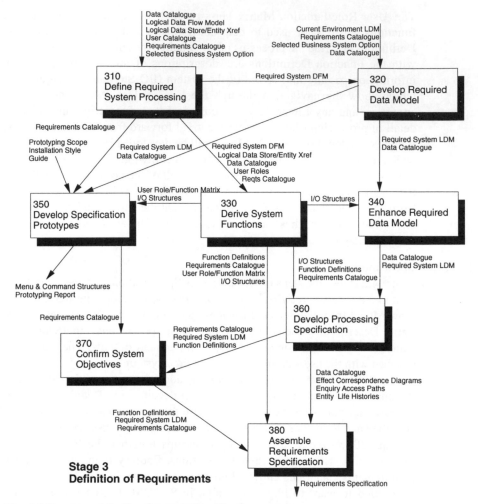

Fig. 4.2 Structure of the Requirements Specification module

Step 360, *develop processing specification,* uses the technique of entity-event modelling. This involves: identifying events from Function Definitions, developing Entity Life Histories for each entity, developing Effect Correspondence Diagrams for each event, and developing Enquiry Access Paths for complex enquiry functions.

Step 370, *confirm system objectives,* re-examines the Requirements Catalogue, particularly looking at non-functional requirements (performance, security, operational constraints, etc.), to ensure that all have been resolved.

Step 380, *assemble requirements specification,* brings together all of the products included in the Requirements Specification and checks their internal consistency and completeness, and cross-checks them against each other. A formal quality assurance review of the Requirements Specification is held.

4.2   Define required system processing (step 310)

Objective

The objective is to define the processing using a Data Flow Model for the Selected Business System Option. The processing of the required system is specified by:

- a set of Data Flow Diagrams;
- descriptions of the content of the data flows across the system boundary;
- descriptions of the external entities and users of the new system;
- detailed descriptions of the bottom-level processes (Elementary Process Descriptions).

The external entities on the Data Flow Model are used to define the different roles that users may take in interacting with the future system. The Requirements Catalogue is brought into line with the Selected Business System Option by ensuring that each requirement is either incorporated into the new system or, if rejected in the chosen option, then the reasons for rejection are given in the Requirements Catalogue. This helps ensure that a fully agreed specification is carried forward with no later recriminations regarding 'missing parts of the system'.

Approach

Although preceding development of the Required System Logical Data Model (step 320), the two steps interact quite closely and may be done in parallel. The two steps are linked in that the Logical Data Model must be able to support the required system processing, and the main data stores on the Required System Data Flow Diagrams must correspond to entities in the data model. The main activity of the step involves the development of the Required System Data Flow Model. This includes the Data Flow Diagrams (levels 1-2, and possibly beyond), the External Entity Descriptions, the Input/Output Descriptions and the Elementary Process Descriptions. Each of these is described with examples later in this section.

The basic approach is to build upon the selected Business System Option. This may have been represented as a level 1 Data Flow Diagram but in many cases a hybrid option may have been picked—needing considerable rework of the level 1 diagram. If the options are not represented by Data Flow Diagrams then the required system diagrams are developed from the narrative describing the Selected Business System Option and the Logical Data Flow Diagrams. Often the diagrams need not be developed from scratch—the Logical Data Flow Diagrams are modified. They need to exclude any processing outside the Selected Business System Option boundary and to include any processing defined or changed by the selected option.

Required System Data Flow Diagrams

In the previous step Business System Options were developed and represented as level 1 Data Flow Diagrams. One, or a combination, of these was chosen by the users for development into the new system. The first part of this development involves the production of a full set of Data Flow Diagrams.

In the Yorkies case study a combination of mainly Option 2 (local autonomy) with some elements of Option 1 (centralized system) was selected. The relevant elements are taken from the appropriate Business System Option diagrams to form the level 1 Required System Data Flow Diagram. This is shown in Fig. 4.3. Process 3 interacts with the Depot as an external entity as in the Option 1 Data Flow Diagram (Fig. 3.5). The chosen solution has a PC in each Local Office (from Option 2) which is used to make the bookings.

Notice that the system boundary now clearly defines the human-computer interface of the new system. Comparison with the Logical Data Flow Diagram (Fig. 3.53) shows that for process 1, Make Booking, it is now 'Booking Clerk' that interacts directly with the system instead of 'Customer' in the logical diagram. It is important that the system boundary is not set until after the options have been explored—in this case, an option might consider the customer interacting directly with the computer system. The level 1 Required Data Flow Diagram shows the booking clerk interacting, outside the computer system, with customers, drivers and agencies (dashed or broken data flow lines show them to be outside the boundary). These external data flows help show the user how the *manual* system would work.

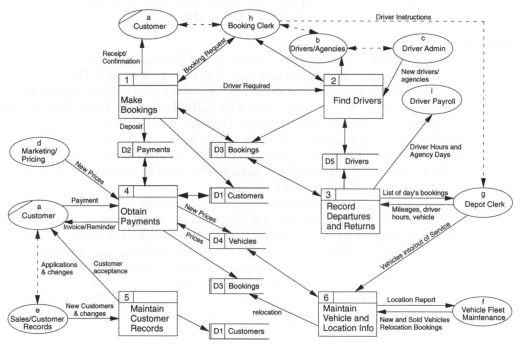

Fig. 4.3 Yorkies Required System Data Flow Diagram (level 1)

The Data Flow Diagrams should include appropriate solutions for entries on the Requirements Catalogue. This may mean that some additions have to be made to the diagrams. For example, the requirement for accepting unknown customers involves obtaining a deposit from them, issuing a receipt, and recording the payment. This is shown on both the level 1 diagram (Fig. 4.3—Process 1) and on the level 2 diagram (Fig. 4.4—Process 1.1).

Decomposition of the Required Data Flow Diagrams follows the same principles as in the current and logical diagrams; i.e. processes that are complex, cover a multiplicity of functions, and deal with a large number of data flows should be decomposed.

The development of the lower-level Data Flow Diagrams should follow the spirit of the Selected Business System Option. However, in some areas the chosen option may not differ very significantly from the logical view. In this case, processes from the logical diagrams can be incorporated directly.[1] The logical processes Obtain Money, Maintain Customer Records, and Maintain Vehicle Records are substantially unchanged by the Business System Options step and are shown in a very similar way in the level 1 and level 2 Required Data Flow Diagrams. It is worth going through the Logical Data Flow Diagrams systematically to ensure that all processing required from the old system is included in the new.

Note on the level 2 diagram that no double-headed arrows are shown inside the system—these could obscure the detail on this lowest-level diagram. Again the interactions of 'Booking Clerk' with 'Customers' and 'Depot Clerks' outside the system are shown. Although SSADM does not include specific techniques for defining the manual processing of the system, these diagrams are helpful to the designers of manual procedures.

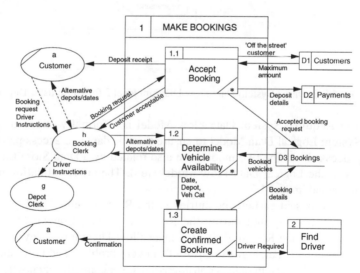

Fig. 4.4 Required System Data Flow Diagram level 2 for Make Booking

---

[1]Often it is unnecessary to redraw the Logical Data Flow Diagrams, a few amendments can convert them to the required structure. Of course, this depends on how radical the Selected Business System Option is.

Process 3, Administer Departures and Returns, shows the system automatically producing a list of departures and returns for each depot and sending that to the depot clerk. At the end of the day the depot clerk records the day's journeys on the PC situated in the depot. This updates the temporary file, T3/1, which is then used in off-line mode for all depots to update the booking and driver information. This is shown in Fig. 4.5.

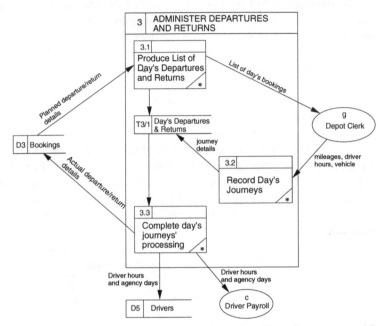

Fig. 4.5 Required System Data Flow Diagram level 2 for Administer Departures and Returns

The Required System Data Flow Model is informally checked against the Required System Logical Data Model to ensure that the data and access paths necessary for each process exist. The two models are also related by a Data Store/Entity Cross-Reference (as in the Logical Data Flow Model step). The cross-validation of the two models is described in Sec. 4.3.

As was said earlier, the entries in the Requirements Catalogue should be resolved during this step and during the Required System Logical Data Model step. While developing the Required System Data Flow Diagrams an eye should be kept on the Requirements Catalogue to ensure that every problem and requirement that is related to updating the system data is considered, resolved, and the catalogue amended.

System boundaries at different times in the project
It is worth digressing briefly to discuss the question of how the system boundary changes during the different phases of the project. Figure 4.6 below shows schematically how this could happen.

The investigation of the current physical environment normally has a broad scope, possibly incorporating areas with only a slight chance of being computerized into the Current Physical Data Flow Diagrams. The Logical Data Flow Diagrams should follow more or less the same boundary with possibly some slight narrowing of scope brought about by a better understanding. The boundaries of the current system study should be wide enough to allow a broad and creative range of options to be put forward. For instance, customers would normally be outside the boundary of the computerized required system but it would be unimaginative to exclude the possibility of allowing the customers direct access to the computer system.

The two Business System Options put forward, shown in Fig. 4.6, have narrowed the scope from the current system study. The Selected Business System Option is intermediate between the minimal and advanced options: the boundary defined by this becomes the boundary of the required system. The human–computer interface is shown explicitly on the Required System Data Flow Diagrams with users interacting with the future computer system shown as external entities.

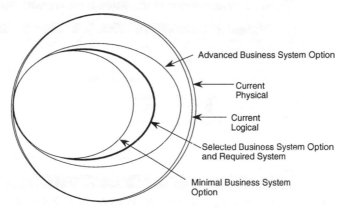

Fig 4.6 System boundaries at different steps of the project

Elementary Process Descriptions

These are used to describe bottom-level processes and any common processes. Common processes are those that are used in different parts of the system. There are no restrictions on the format of this description—use whatever is most appropriate. For complicated decision-making processes use decision tables or decision trees. For complicated mathematical manipulations then use formulae, other algorithmic representations, or formal logic. Otherwise program-like code could be used, such as Structured English or Pseudocode. In most cases a simple narrative description, occasionally supplemented by one of the above, is used. Note that SSADM does not use decomposition of the Data Flow Diagram processes to define the detailed processing structure—this is done from the events identified when developing Entity Life Histories. However, the Elementary Process Descriptions are carried forward and associated with Function Definitions later in Requirements Specification.

Figure 4.7 shows the Elementary Process Description for Process 1.1, Accept Booking. *Common processing cross-reference* enables any descriptions of processing to be identified in one part of the system and cross-referred to other areas where they occur. This is particularly important with Function Definitions. As these common processes are carried forward to Physical Design it is important that they are identified early to avoid any possible duplication of effort (worse still if the same process is implemented twice, inconsistent results may occur and increased maintenance work will be necessary).

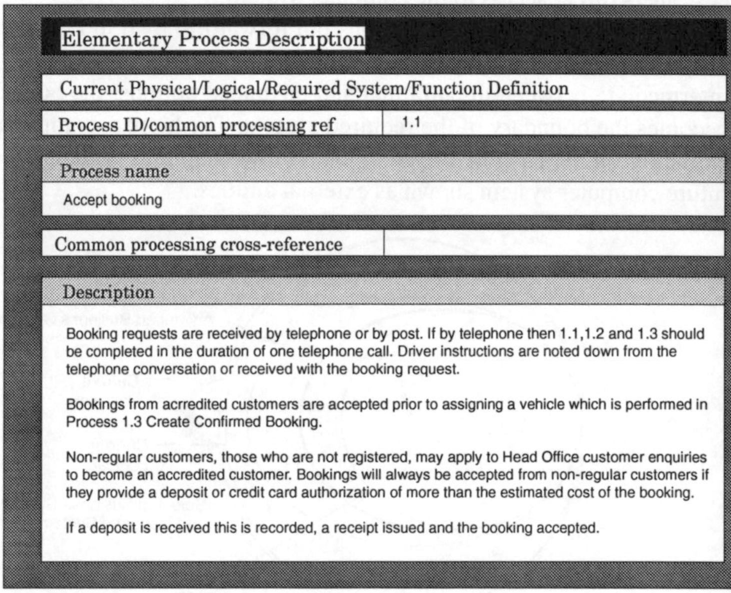

Elementary Process Description

Current Physical/Logical/Required System/Function Definition

| Process ID/common processing ref | 1.1 |

Process name

Accept booking

Common processing cross-reference

Description

Booking requests are received by telephone or by post. If by telephone then 1.1,1.2 and 1.3 should be completed in the duration of one telephone call. Driver instructions are noted down from the telephone conversation or received with the booking request.

Bookings from acrredited customers are accepted prior to assigning a vehicle which is performed in Process 1.3 Create Confirmed Booking.

Non-regular customers, those who are not registered, may apply to Head Office customer enquiries to become an accredited customer. Bookings will always be accepted from non-regular customers if they provide a deposit or credit card authorization of more than the estimated cost of the booking.

If a deposit is received this is recorded, a receipt issued and the booking accepted.

Fig. 4.7 Elementary Process Description for Process 1.1, Accept Booking

Input/Output Descriptions

A description of the data content of every input to and output from the system is developed. This is called an Input/Output Description and is usually shortened to I/O Description, which is the term used in this book. The inputs and outputs concerned with updates map to the data flows to and from external entities on the bottom-level Data Flow Diagrams. Figure 4.8 shows the I/O Description for the output 'Booking Confirmation'. *Data content* lists the attributes contained on the input—these should cross-refer to Attribute Descriptions in the Data Catalogue. *Comments* are given to explain the structure of the data and any other contextual information.

The users of the new system must be deeply involved in the development of I/O Descriptions. They must ensure that the data content is correct and consistent with how they see the new system operating. I/O Descriptions may have been developed earlier in the project, as part of the Current Physical and Logical Data Flow Models. Some projects, particularly those using CASE tools, will record the attributes associated with each bottom-level data flow. These data flow contents will then form the basis for the I/O Descriptions. Otherwise it may be necessary to develop the I/O data content from the information on the data flow lines and from discussions with the users.

The I/O Descriptions will be developed into I/O Structures in the next step—forming the basis for the detailed design of screens, reports, and forms. In SSADM these inputs and outputs are also used for relational data analysis in step 340, *enhance required data model*. A full set of detailed physical formats for input forms, screens, reports, and machine-readable inputs and outputs are developed when the nature of the hardware and software is known in Stage 6 (physical design). The use of prototyping for developing screens and human–machine dialogues is discussed in Sec. 4.6.

I/O Descriptions

From	To	Data flow name	Data content	Comments
1.3 Create Confirmed Booking	a Customer	Booking Confirmation		Customers are sent a Booking Confirmation
			Customer No. Customer Name	The next group of data items may be repeated if there are several bookings being confirmed at the same time
			Booking No. Vehicle Category Code Required Booking Start Date Required Booking Finish Date Driver Requirement (Y/N) Office No. (Start) Office Name (Start) Office No. (Finish) Office Name (Finish)	only inserted if one-way hire

Fig. 4.8 I/O Description for the output Booking Confirmation

External entities

Further descriptions of these are given in External Entity Descriptions, and an example is shown in Fig. 4.9. The Selected Business System Option defined a clear system boundary: all external entities that interact with the computer system must be described. They may be directly linked to the computer system (either on-line or off-line) or can be receiving information (e.g. a document or report) via some minor manual intervention (e.g. putting a letter in an envelope). The external entities should show the on-line users, in Fig. 4.9: 'd', 'h', and 'g' are all Yorkies internal staff who interact with the computer system. These 'internal' external entities should match the job descriptions of the future users of the system—known in SSADM as *user roles.*

ID	Name	Description
a	Customer	A customer of Yorkies who hires out or intends to hire out vehicles.
b	Drivers/Agencies	Yorkies employs drivers on a freelance basis for customers' bookings. If a freelance driver cannot be found a more expensive agency is contacted who will supply a driver.
d	Marketing/Pricing	A department at Yorkies H.Q. who can modify prices for vehicles and will receive some reports from the system.
h	Booking Clerk	Located in the Local Offices they create bookings for customers and liaise with the customers. They also liaise with drivers and agencies, to find those available for customer bookings.
g	Depot Clerk	Located in the depots they enter in mileage and other journey details on completion of bookings.

External Entity Descriptions

~~Current~~/~~Logical~~/Required

Fig. 4.9 External Entity Descriptions

User Catalogue and User Roles

The User Catalogue was developed in step 120, *investigate and define requirements,* to show the job titles and activities of the users of the current system. The example given in Sec. 3.3 is repeated below in Fig. 4.10.

User Catalogue

Job title	Job activities description
Depot Clerk	Select vehicle from required category for customer on collection. Record mileage, condition, etc. on departure and return of vehicles.
Driver administrator (Local office)	Find suitable drivers from Driver/Agency Register. Determine availability. Find agency if no Yorkies driver available. Record driver details on Booking Sheet.

Fig. 4.10 Part of Yorkies User Catalogue

The User Catalogue provides a brief description of the jobs and their activities to be performed by the on-line users of the required system. The User Catalogue acts as an input to the definition of the user roles. In step 310, *define required system processing,* the User Catalogue is expanded to describe the user roles for the required system. A *user role* is defined as a collection of job titles who share a large proportion of common tasks—one way of thinking about user roles is that a set of menus and access privileges will be shared by a given user role. A description of user roles is shown on the User Roles form (Fig. 4.11).

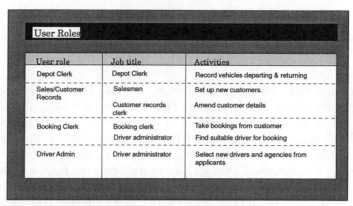

| User Roles | | |

User role	Job title	Activities
Depot Clerk	Depot Clerk	Record vehicles departing & returning
Sales/Customer Records	Salesman	Set up new customers.
	Customer records clerk	Amend customer details
Booking Clerk	Booking clerk	Take bookings from customer
	Driver administrator	Find suitable driver for booking
Driver Admin	Driver administrator	Select new drivers and agencies from applicants

Fig. 4.11 Some user roles documented on the User Roles form

In most cases for one user role there will be one job title as for the Depot Clerk above. In some cases one user role can be taken by several job titles. For example, the Booking Clerk (user role) includes both the Booking Clerk (job title) and Driver Administrator (job title) so that individuals with either job title can take bookings and find drivers. Driver Admin is a separate user role from Booking Clerk because only Driver Admin will have the necessary access privileges to enter new drivers onto the computer system. The user roles should be compared with the external entities to ensure that all 'internal' external entities match a user role—the same names should be used for both.

The development of the User Catalogue and the definition of user roles are the initial stage of dialogue identification—part of *dialogue design*, an important technique in SSADM.

SUMMARY

- The required system is specified in terms of its inputs, outputs, and processing.
- This step is carried out in parallel with and cross-checked against the development of the Required System Data Structure.
- The Selected Business System Option is expanded into a full set of Required System Data Flow Diagrams and supporting documentation.
- The Requirements Catalogue is made consistent with the Selected Business System Option and the Required System Data Flow Model.
- For every input and output from the required system an I/O Description is developed defining its data content.
- Elementary Process Descriptions provide detailed descriptions of the bottom-level processes.
- External Entity Descriptions are used to further explain their role in the system.
- The User Catalogue and User Roles describe their interaction with the system.

4.3   Develop required data model (step 320)

Introduction

In this step the Required System Logical Data Structure and its supporting documentation are developed. This involves extending the Current Environment Logical Data Structure, previously developed in step 140, to support the high-level design described by the Selected Business System Option. Non-functional requirements associated with the system data (access, security, and archive) are further defined in the Entity Descriptions. Figure 4.12 shows the inputs and outputs of the step.

This step follows step 310, *define required system processing,* and closely interacts with it. The Logical Data Store/Entity Cross-Reference (from step 150, *derive logical view*) is extended—each required system data store will contain one or more required system entities. All processing defined is checked against the Logical Data Structure to ensure that the necessary navigation is supported.

The outputs of the step are used extensively in the forthcoming steps of SSADM. The Required System Logical Data Structure is validated and extended by using relational data analysis in step 340, *enhance required data model.* This model is then carried forward to physical data design in Stage 6. An Entity Life History is developed for each required system entity in step 360, *develop processing specification.*

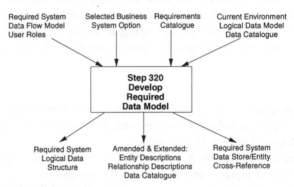

Fig. 4.12 Inputs and outputs from step 320

Modelling the new requirements

The Current Environment Logical Data Structure developed in Stage 1 supports the processing performed in the current system. To satisfy new requirements, changes to the current system data structure may be necessary. These new requirements will come from two sources: the Selected Business System Option and the Requirements Catalogue. Both should be examined to identify any necessary changes to the data structure. These changes may involve addition of new entities and relationships to the Current Environment Logical Data Structure diagram or only minor changes to the supporting documentation. The development of the Yorkies Current Environment Logical Data Structure into the required view is described below.

New structures

The Requirements Catalogue detailed that the new system should be capable of administering one-way hires (when the vehicle does not return to its base) and the tracing of vehicles (so that we know where all vehicles are). This leads to some additional relationships on the Logical Data Structure.

A one-way hire indicates that the starting local office will be different from the finishing local office. There are then two relationships between Booking and Local Office: one indicating the *from* office and the other indicating the *to* office. Another change is in the nature of the relationship of Vehicle with Local Office; in the current system this indicated the base location of a vehicle and in the required system it indicates the office at which the documents for a vehicle are kept. Compare the Required System Logical Data Structure shown in Fig. 4.13 with the Current Environment Logical Data Structure shown previously in Fig. 3.35.

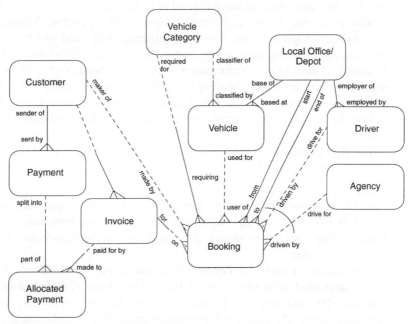

Fig. 4.13 Required System Logical Data Structure

The new system's acceptance of one-way hires causes another problem; some destinations would prove more popular than others so vehicles could get stuck in undesirable locations. To solve this problem a new Process 6 'Maintain Vehicle and Location Information' was shown on the Required System Data Flow Diagram (Fig. 4.5). One of the activities within this process is the relocation of vehicles which have become 'stuck' in undesirable locations. This relocation is managed within the new system by means of an internal one-way booking. The internal booking will be very similar to the ordinary booking except that there will be no corresponding customer and no invoice. The internal and external bookings both belong to the same entity type

Booking.[1] The internal booking makes the relationship of Booking with Customer optional from the Booking end.

In the current system one invoice is created for each booking and so the Invoice and Booking entities are merged. A requirement for the new system is that each customer is invoiced (provided they have had bookings) every two weeks. This means that an invoice can be for many bookings and therefore leads to the separation of Invoice and Booking as shown. The relationship is optional at the Booking end because a booking will be created before the invoice and must then be able to exist without the master invoice (also internal bookings won't be invoiced).

Changes to supporting documentation
Any changes to the Logical Data Structure diagram will also result in changes to the supporting documentation. For instance, the new Invoice entity will require an Entity Description, modifications will have to be made to the Booking Entity Description, and new Relationship Descriptions will need to be created.

New requirements may also force changes to the supporting documentation without any changes to the diagram. Thus new attributes will need to be added to the Entity Description of Customer to enable the processing of 'off-the-street' Customers. One Business System Option requirement is that the freelance drivers be organized into regional groups thereby increasing flexibility in driver allocation and reducing the use of expensive agency drivers. This results in a new attribute: Driver Region. This is defined in the Data Catalogue and added to the Entity Descriptions of Driver and Local Office.

The Requirements Catalogue is one of the driving documents behind this step—as problems are solved and requirements met it should be amended to include solutions.

Extending the Entity Descriptions
Figure 4.14 below shows the second part of the Entity Description for the Vehicle entity (part 1 is Fig. 3.37). In this step the non-functional requirements associated with the system's data (previously identified in the Requirements Catalogue) are defined in the Entity Descriptions.
User roles, access rights, and owner This information is included on all of the SSADM forms associated with system data: Entity Descriptions, Relationship Descriptions, Attribute Descriptions, and Grouped Domain Descriptions. Very rarely will it be necessary to specify access information in great detail—only complex systems with many users and requiring high levels of security will need to define access privileges at all levels. In most cases access privileges will be common to many entities, attributes and relationships—they can be described in one description and cross-referenced in the others. It is in this step that these access requirements are fully defined from those previously outlined in the Requirements Catalogue.
Growth per period This describes the expected growth (or decline) in the number of occurrences of the entity described for over a period. The type of period (day, week, month, year, etc.) must be specified.

---

[1] They could be modelled using entity sub-types.

Additional relationships Sometimes the entity may partake in relationships with other entities which the logical data modelling notation cannot document. An example of this could be where an entity of one type becomes an entity of another type when certain things happen—both entities would be shown separately on the Logical Data Structure (for example, an Order could become a Delivery).

Archive and destruction Describes the time frame and conditions under which occurrences of the entity are to be archived, and then those under which the archive occurrences are to be destroyed. The archive media should also be described.

Security measures This shows any measures necessary to protect the data against unauthorized access, e.g. use of encryption.

State Indicator Values These are added in Stage 5, Logical Design. They are developed from Entity Life Histories to show the various states that an entity occurrence can be in after it has been changed by an event occurring. A full description of State Indicator Values is given in Sec. 5.7.

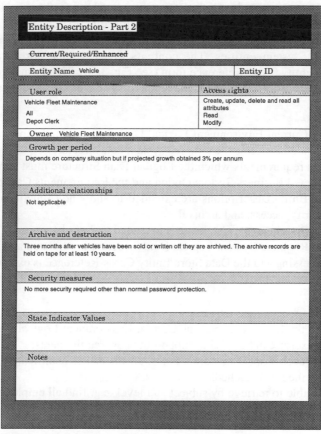

Fig. 4.14 Part 2 of Entity Description for Vehicle (part 1 shown in Fig. 3.37)

Validation against required system processing

In Sec. 3.5 the validation of the current system processing against the Current Environment Logical Data Model is described. The way in which the Required System Logical Data Model is validated in this step is exactly the same—it is not described here. Later in step 360, *develop processing specification*, formal validation is provided by the use of Effect Correspondence Diagrams and Enquiry Access Paths.

The Logical Data Structure should be validated against the update and enquiry processing. The update processing is detailed by the Required System Data Flow Diagrams and their supporting Elementary Process Descriptions. The enquiry processing is detailed by the Requirements Catalogue. Although some of the processing will be similar to that previously validated during the development of the current Logical Data Structure, an informal check should be made to ensure that all processing carried through into the new system can be supported by the new data structure. The new processing requirements should be thoroughly checked.

Data Store/Entity Cross-Reference

The Data Store/Entity Cross-Reference provides a further check that the data structure supports the processing. This cross-reference is first developed in the definition of the logical system (step 150 described in Sec. 3.6). Each logical main data store contains current system entities. The contents of each data store are recorded on a Data Store/Entity Cross-Reference form (see Fig. 3.50). This form should be extended during steps 310 and 320 to include the required system entities and data stores.

SUMMARY

- The Current Environment Logical Data Structure and supporting documentation are extended to define the required system data structure.
- New requirements which the Logical Data Structure must support are defined by the Selected Business System Option and the Requirements Catalogue.
- The Entity Descriptions are extended to show non-functional requirements such as security, access, and archival.
- The Requirements Catalogue is amended to describe any solutions adopted.
- The Required System Logical Data Structure is validated against the required system processing and the Data Store/Entity Cross-Reference is extended.

Exercise

4.3.1   Scapegoat Systems

Extend the Scapegoat Systems Current Environment Logical Data Structure developed in the exercise in Sec. 3.5 to support the new requirements:

a) For each employee store a list of all his or her qualifications including the subject and the level reached.
b) Be able to retrieve by subject and level, e.g. find all employees with an 'A' level or degree in French.

4.4   Derive system functions (step 330)

Introduction

What is a function?
The concept of functions is central to SSADM. Functions are the basic blocks of processing through which we build the whole system. Ultimately all of the processing is defined through functions. They collect together other SSADM specifications: process models, input/output structures, dialogue designs and the interim products used to develop these. Each function can be thought of as a distinct set of system processing which will normally be performed continuously from start to finish. One way of imagining a function is as a menu option in the final system. (This is, of course, a naive view—some functions will be implemented off-line or by command-driven interfaces.) SSADM defines a function as:

> *A set of system processing which the users wish to
> schedule together, to support their business
> activity.*

This is rather a vague definition and the SSADM approach to deciding how processing should be grouped is also rather nebulous—ultimately these decisions are made by the user. Functions are carried through to Physical Design where they become the 'packages' of processing specification that are passed to the programmer for construction.

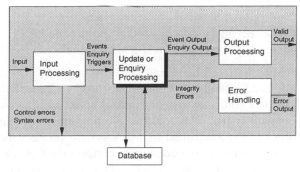

Fig. 4.15 The Universal Function Model

Figure 4.15 shows the Universal Function Model, which is a conceptual way of understanding functions, showing their various components. Every input is verified, results in updates and/or enquiries, and then produces outputs and possibly errors. The update or enquiry processing shown in Fig. 4.15 is initially documented by events or enquiries, then by Effect Correspondence Diagrams or Enquiry Access Paths, and finally by Update Process Models or by Enquiry Process Models. Input and output processing is documented by I/O Structures and their supporting descriptions. Ultimately these will become screen or report formats.

The various components of a function are tied together by the Function Definition form, described fully later in this section, which cross-references a brief description of the function with its associated SSADM documentation.

Basic approach in the step

First using the lowest-level Data Flow Diagrams, functions are identified—each bottom-level process is allocated to at least one function. Enquiry functions are defined from the Requirements Catalogue (some may be described on the Data Flow Diagrams or may be obtained directly from users). The Data Flow Diagrams also help identify events (the 'real-world' causes of changes to system data). Each event is also allocated to a function.

Each function is given a brief description and a decision made (based on the Selected Business System Option) whether it is to be performed on-line or off-line. Next, the user interface for each function is specified in more detail by expanding upon the I/O Descriptions to show the detailed structure. On-line functions will require dialogue design—a User Role/Function Matrix shows which users have access to which functions. Those dialogues critical to the success of the new system are identified (and may be used for specification prototyping in step 350). The Requirements Catalogue outlined performance requirements for the new system, and these are expanded to become Service Level Requirements. As the project progresses each component of the function is defined in more detail to build up a full logical specification of the system processing—this is complete by the end of Stage 5.

Types of functions

Functions can be classified in three ways:

1. By their mode of initiation—user or system
2. By their effect on the system's data—update or enquiry
3. By their mode of operation—off-line or on-line

User or system initiated functions

A user initiated function is one that is activated by a system user or other external entity (including other computer systems) making some decision and indicating that decision to the computer system. This could be selecting a menu option, clicking a mouse or any other form of user controlled input. A system initiated function is one where the computer system makes the decision to perform the function. This may result from a date or particular time being reached or may result from a process that the system has performed. For example, it may check to see which invoices have been paid and produce reminders for those outstanding.

User initiated functions can be often identified from the Required System Data Flow Diagrams where there will be a data flow from an external entity into the system (user initiated enquiries will normally be described in the Requirements Catalogue). System initiated functions may have no associated input data flows but will result in an update to a data store shown by an input flow. System generated enquiries, if shown in the Data Flow Diagrams, will have an output data flow. Most system initiated enquiries will be described in the Requirements Catalogue.

Update or enquiry functions

Update functions change system data. They will always result in changes to occurrences of entities described in the Logical Data Model. All update processing has been described using the Required System Data Flow Diagrams where it is shown by data flow arrows pointing at data stores.

Enquiries retrieve system data, supplying it to users or to other systems. Normally enquiries are not documented in Data Flow Diagrams, but are described in the Requirements Catalogue. Sometimes regular enquiries which are associated with update processing are shown on the Data Flow Diagrams. This classification into update and enquiry should not be followed too rigidly; often update processing involves some minor enquiries—do not artificially create separate functions for these.

On-line or off-line functions

On-line—interactive mode with user involved in dialogue with the computer.

Off-line—initiated and then left to run its course without intervention or interaction with the end-user.

Most systems being developed today have a large proportion of on-line processing. This means that the user can interact directly with the computer system via a terminal, PC, or other workstation. Unlike off-line processing (often referred to as batch processing), where predefined information is entered in large batches to be processed in a predefined way, on-line processing offers much more flexibility, allowing the user to control their interaction with the computer. To underline the difference between the two types of processing, imagine that you want to communicate some information to a friend. This information is sent:

- *Off-line*, if you enclose all of the information in a letter. You perhaps plan the letter, decide what you want to say, then write it and mail it. Once the letter has been sent, there is no possibility of changing the information in it. If you do want to amend the information in the letter, you will have to send a second letter contradicting the first. If your spelling is wrong, or the address is incomplete, the postal service and your friend will have to cope, based upon their knowledge of geography and spelling.
- *On-line*, if you phone your friend. No planning is required—you dial the number, and blurt out all your news as you think about it. If there is anything that you friend does not understand, you will be asked to repeat or rephrase your news. During the conversation, your friend may give you information that causes you to modify some of the news you were about to impart.

In a similar way, off-line processing is relatively straightforward when designing the input stream of data, but processing must be built in to cope with error data. This can be a very complex part of the design of off-line processing. An on-line process is more complex when designing the facilities to input data. The user might want a combination of ease of use and sophisticated control over the course of dialogues with the system. Error handling is much easier in on-line systems. As the user is sitting at the terminal when the data is first input, if the computer detects errors, it can ask the user to re-key the information until it is correct.

Early computerized information systems worked only in an off-line mode. In the past batch systems were cheaper to build and use, but current hardware and software costs mean that there is now little cost difference between batch and on-line processing. Direct interaction with the computer via a terminal was expensive and complex input systems were devised and used. Nowadays terminals and PCs are cheap and on-line processing is the norm rather than the exception. As on-line processing offers more accurate and timely information it is now generally favoured.

However, some processes are best handled in off-line mode. It is the most efficient means of processing very large numbers of similar transactions (e.g. producing large numbers of payments or invoices). Many modern information systems combine on-line and off-line processing to maximize the efficiency of both the human and computer operations. In SSADM decisions about whether processes are to be performed on- or off-line are made at the Business Systems Options stage (or possibly in the Feasibility stage).

As a general rule, the normal mode of processing should be on-line. The exceptions, where off-line processing should be considered, are:

- if very high volumes of the same sort of data are required to be input or output;
- if there is a very regular demand for a particular form of output, e.g. payments or invoices;
- if input data can be provided in a machine readable format, e.g. through electronic data interchange or through optical character recognition;
- if system performance is a problem then on-line processing for validation and creation of transaction files during the day followed by off-line update of the main database at night can be very effective.

These guidelines can help determine which processes should be handled off-line at any of the options stages of SSADM. Sometimes it is necessary to have a process operate in both off-line and on-line modes. In this case separate functions are defined for on- and off-line.

Identification of functions

Functions are first identified from the Required System Data Flow Diagrams and the Requirements Catalogue. By looking at the lowest-level Data Flow Diagrams we can identify an initial set of update functions. Most of the enquiries will be described in the Requirements Catalogue but some may also be shown on the Data Flow Diagrams.

It is hard to be specific about the relation of Data Flow Diagram processes to functions. In many cases each lowest-level process can become a single function. However, this depends greatly on how the Data Flow Diagrams have been constructed; if the lowest-level is very detailed then one function may cover several processes. Conversely, if the lowest-level is rather general then one process may require several functions. Below we repeat the lowest-level Data Flow Diagram for the process Make Booking. There are several possibilities regarding the allocation of functions to this diagram: one function could cover Processes 1.1, 1.2 and 1.3; a separate function could be defined for each of the three processes; or other combinations could form a function.

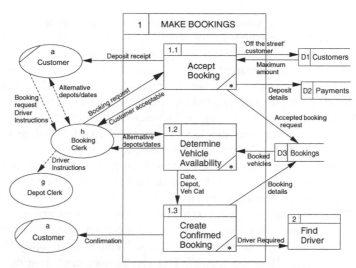

Fig. 4.16 Level 2 Required System Data Flow Diagram for Make Booking

We cannot be too specific about the method for grouping processes into functions but some general guidelines are:

Users decide The users must feel that the activities should be scheduled together; that they belong in the same menu option or batch process.

Separate on-line and off-line processing Many operating systems are unable to combine on-line processing with off-line processing. In any case the great difference in operation would make a combination of the two undesirable. If the same function needs to be performed both on-line and off-line then separate functions are defined for each mode, although there will be common processing used by both functions.

Group together processes performed together If a process is always performed in conjunction with another process then these should be combined into a single function. Conversely, processes which are carried out independently should form separate functions. Figure 4.16 repeated above shows the lowest-level Data Flow Diagram for the process Make Booking. We will use this as an example for showing how we can group processes into functions. All of these processes will be performed on-line and obviously fit together in that they will be performed by the same user and are in the same functional areas (this should always be the case because they are following the process hierarchy described by the Data Flow Diagrams). Process 1.2, Determine Vehicle Availability, is an enquiry which is frequently invoked separately. However, Processes 1.1, Accept Booking, and 1.3, Create Confirmed Booking, are always carried out together. Because the enquiry is frequently invoked separately, a separate function is created for this named 'Vehicle Availability Enquiry'. A second function is created to cover the other two functions and named 'Make Booking'.

Groupings of processes to functions is obviously rather subjective and it should be pointed out that the consequences of minor 'mistakes' are small. Obviously it would be radically wrong to group together processes that are completely different and this could have serious consequences for the system's design. However, the consequences of grouping the three processes above into a single function would be minor. (If not rectified before construction, we would develop a system in which the Vehicle Availability Enquiry could not be invoked separately. This problem could then be 'solved' by duplicating processing in the combined function and the separate enquiry function—this could cause inconsistencies if the code was written twice.) Grouping of processes into functions should be relatively straightforward, providing: the structures of the Data Flow Diagrams are followed, the users are consulted, and the above guidelines roughly followed. There will be many opportunities later to revisit these function groupings and modify them in the light of further design.

Enquiries are normally described only in the Requirements Catalogue. Each enquiry will normally be the subject of a separate entry in the Catalogue and normal practice will be to create a separate function for each enquiry. Some enquiries will be associated with particular update functions (e.g. the Vehicle Availability Enquiry is associated with the Make Booking update). This can be documented on the Function Definition form.

An initial list of functions, their associated Data Flow Diagram processes and their types is shown in Fig. 4.17 below. Note that this is not an official SSADM form but is a useful way of summarizing all of the functions in the system. Notice that user initiated functions are usually performed on-line and system initiated functions are usually performed off-line. This is not always the case since off-line functions could be requested by a user and the computer system could require the user to perform an on-line function. Notice also that some of these enquiries were defined in the Data Flow Diagrams and others were defined only in the Requirements Catalogue. Those enquiry functions shown on the Data Flow Diagrams are regular reports which are associated with important update processing (remember that these diagrams are subjective and a main objective is to describe the system to the user).

Function Name	DFD Processes	Function Type		
		Initiation	Mode	Update or Enquiry
Produce invoices	4.2	System	Off-line	Update
Produce reminders	4.4	System	Off-line	Update
Make Booking	1.1,1.3	User	On-line	Update
Find Driver	2	User	On-line	Update
Record Journey Details	3.3	User	On-line	Update
Departure/Return list	3.1	System	Off-line	Enquiry
Depot VehicleUsage report		System	Off-line	Enquiry
Vehicle Location Report		System	Off-line	Enquiry
Booking Enquiry		User	On-line	Enquiry
Vehicle Availability Enquiry	1.2	User	On-line	Enquiry

Fig. 4.17 Functions in Yorkies

Events and functions

Events cause the computer system to update the data it holds. The concept of an event is very important in SSADM as the update processing is based around the events. Entity Life Histories show all of the events affecting a particular entity. In step 330, *derive system functions*, we identify the events from the Data Flow Diagrams and allocate them to functions. Often the allocation of events helps check the function groupings. Later, when we develop Entity Life Histories, we may identify further events and thus revisit our functions.

Types of event
There are generally three types of event that can be identified in this way:

Externally sourced The Data Flow Diagram will show a data flow from an external entity to the process updating a data store (Fig. 4.18). This represents someone (or something) external to the system starting up a process because of something that has happened outside the system. An example of this would be the receipt of a booking request by an office of Yorkies. The office staff would wish to record this receipt on the system so would start up a process called 'Accept Booking'. The event identified here could be called 'Booking Request'.

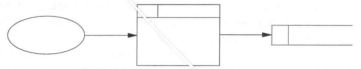

Fig. 4.18 External event on a Data Flow Diagram

Time based This type of event will normally be identified by an update to a data store from a process that has no apparent triggering data flows (Fig. 4.19). (Alternatively, it can be indicated by an input to a process from a 'Diary' or 'Actions' data store.) This represents a process being triggered at a particular time or on a particular date.

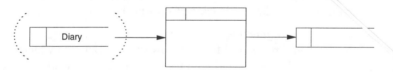

Fig. 4.19 Time-based (System) event

Internally recognized This type of event will be identified by an update to a data store from a process that has no apparent triggers in the same way as for the time-based event except that it will not be time or the calendar that is the trigger but some circumstance recognized by the system as a prerequisite to a process being triggered. This could be thought of as the computer system monitoring something internal such as a stock level or a payment received marker. The distinction between a 'time-based' and an 'internally recognized' event is rather arbitrary as both will probably be physically implemented by triggering a process to look at the system clock and perform the enquiry/update at a prescribed frequency.

Identification of events

In this step we identify events from the bottom-level Required System Data Flow Diagrams. As each process has been allocated to a function the allocation of events to processes and thus to functions follows easily. (In simple systems, the mapping of processes, events and functions will often be one-to-one-to-one. It is only in more complex systems that complicated relationships evolve between processes, events and functions.)

A Data Flow Diagram process that is updating system data will be shown by a data flow going from the process box to a main data store (i.e. a data store which corresponds to one or more entities from the Logical Data Model). By examining the process, it is possible to identify the events by deciding what will cause the process to be performed.

Figure 4.16 showed the level 2 Data Flow Diagram of Process 1 from the Required System Data Flow Diagrams. The events are identified first by looking for updates (input data flows) to data stores. In this diagram, there are updates to the following data stores: D1, Customers; D2, Payments; D3, Bookings.

What caused these updates to be made? By tracing the flows back, first to the processes and then beyond, to the inputs to those processes, it is possible to find the events that must have caused these updates.

D1 (Customers) and D2 (Payments) are updated by Process 1.1 (Accept Bookings). The input to this process comes (indirectly) from the customer. From the labels on the data flows, we can deduce that the event that causes these data stores to be updated is the receipt of a booking request. The Customer and Payment data store will only be updated if the booking request is received from an 'off-the-street' customer, in which case a new customer record will be created as the system will not have any previous record of this customer. (Booking requests received from customers already known to us will not cause an update to this data store.)

D3 (Bookings) is updated by Process 1.3 (Create Confirmed Booking). The event that triggers this update is 'Booking Confirmed'.

Grouping events to functions

As the functions are derived from the lowest-level Data Flow Diagram processes and as the events are also associated with these processes, it is a simple matter to allocate the events to functions. The process Accept Booking handles the event Booking Request. This process belongs to the function Make Booking so the event Booking Request belongs also to the function Make Booking. In Fig. 4.20 below we show the functions, their Data Flow Diagram processes and their events; this is not a formal SSADM document but is a useful way of seeing the groupings of events across the whole system. The relationship between events and functions is formally documented on the Function Definition form (see Fig. 4.23).

Function Name	DFD Processes	Events
Produce invoices	4.2	Invoice Issued
Produce Reminders	4.3	Reminder Sent
Make Booking	1.1,1.3	Booking Request, Booking Confirmed, Vehicle Relocation
Find Driver	2	Driver Allocated, Agency Allocated
Record Journey Details	3.3	Vehicle Depart, Vehicle Return, Vehicle Written-off

Fig. 4.20 Functions and events

In this step events are allocated to functions following their identification from the Data Flow Diagrams. Later, when a complete set of events are identified in step 360, *develop processing specification,* the event/function groupings are checked. Obviously new events will be identified by event/entity modelling for which functions will not have been defined—they will need to be added to existing functions or to newly created functions. For a set of events to belong the same function they should:

- communicate with similar external entities or be performed by the same users;
- occur together or closely following each other;
- affect the same entities and attributes;
- in an off-line function the events must be performed in the same time frame (it would be impossible to operate a function that combined weekly batch processing with daily batch processing).

These guidelines for grouping events into functions are, of course, similar to those used to group processes into functions.

Identification of dialogues

Decisions about whether functions are to be handled on-line or off-line are normally made in conjunction with the user in the Business Systems Options stage. (General principles for deciding whether functions should be performed on- or off-line were discussed previously.) Any functions to be performed on-line will require dialogue design. In earlier steps of SSADM user roles were defined (see Sec. 4.2) to show the activities that individual users could perform.

The User Roles/Function Matrix, shown in Fig. 4.21, links the user roles with the functions that they can perform. Each 'X' on the matrix represents a dialogue for a function being performed by a particular user role, thus Booking Clerk performs Make Booking, and Find Driver, etc. It may be necessary in large systems, with many different users, to define different dialogues for the same function for each user role. However, in simpler systems this is rarely necessary and one dialogue will be appropriate for all users of the function. This matrix should be discussed with the users to ensure that it meets their requirements.

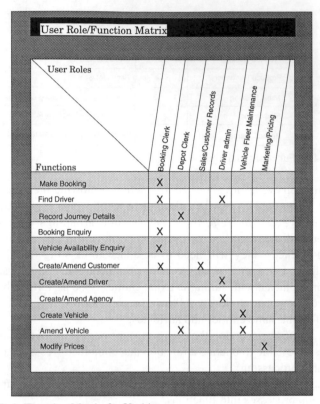

Fig. 4.21 User Role/Function Matrix for Yorkies

Critical dialogues
Some parts of the system will be more significant to its success than others. Typically we may find that a small number of dialogues are performed very frequently and will have a great impact on the system.[1] SSADM attempts to identify these critical dialogues with a view to ensuring that they are well designed. In step 350, *develop specification prototypes*, a working version of these dialogues is produced and evaluated with the users. In step 330, *derive system functions*, we identify those critical dialogues, and a

---

[1] Most systems development methodologies are very weak on the 80/20 rule. The 80/20 rule states that with 20% of the effort you get 80% of the results. The remaining 20% of the results cost you 80% of the effort. Some effort is worth while to identify the 20% of effort that you need to get 80% of the results. In SSADM, maybe at the Business Systems Option stage, there could be a specifically focused activity to say 'Look for the essential parts of this system where you've really got to put the work in, where you've got to put your best analysts, your best programmers, where you've got to put most time in, because those are the things that are going to make or break your system'. SSADM treats the transaction that is performed 10 000 times a day in the same way as it treats the transaction that is going to be performed five times a day. Some good suggestions on how these ideas can be applied are given by Tom Gilb in his book *Principles of Software Engineering Management* (Addison-Wesley, Reading, Mass.).

decision is then made by project management as to the extent of prototyping in step 350.

The following criteria can be applied to decide which dialogues are critical:

Seen by users as critical The users will have a view on which dialogues are most critical to the system. This should be the primary consideration given to deciding on which functions are candidates for prototyping. Usually the users will identify dialogues which meet other criteria, given below, such as being high volume or central to the business, but it may be that some dialogues are regarded as critical which meet none of the other criteria. For instance, if a particular dialogue is used by a very senior manager to supply him or her with information critical to the running of the organization, then the dialogue producing this information would be regarded as critical.

Frequently used Dialogues which are performed most often will dominate the performance of both the machine and of the users. It is essential to design these dialogues well so that efficient and effective use is made of the staff operating the dialogue and of the computer resources supporting it. Often careful design of a dialogue can minimize dissatisfaction with relatively poor response times.

Requiring complex processing Some dialogues will require complicated retrievals and display many different data items on the screen. When asked what information is required users may glibly say 'All of it'. If they are shown prototypes then this information can often be pared down to simpler screens. The retrieval processing for these complex dialogues may result in poor response times. Some dialogues may require complicated navigation through several screens or have complex error handling or complex help facilities. Again these features may make them good candidates for prototyping.

Shared by many users In large systems some dialogues may be performed by a range of users of differing abilities and skill levels which are indicated by their differing user roles. Again prototyping these can help to decide whether different dialogues need to be designed for each user role.

Some dialogues may be identified as critical, although they would not be considered for prototyping. However, they may affect the technical environment chosen for the system. For example, if sophisticated help facilities are required or if use in unusual environments (e.g. on workshop floors or on ships) then these environments can influence decisions made about the hardware and software made in Technical Systems Options.

Documenting critical dialogues
The User Role/Function matrix is annotated to show the critical dialogues. In Fig. 4.22 the critical dialogues have been identified by 'ringing'. (An alphabetic code could be used to indicate them, e.g. 'C' for critical dialogues replacing the 'Xs'—obviously more sophisticated ranking systems of criticality could also be devised.) In the example above the critical dialogues fulfil many of the criteria previously defined; all of them are high volume and are central to the main objective of the system, which is to take and record information about bookings.

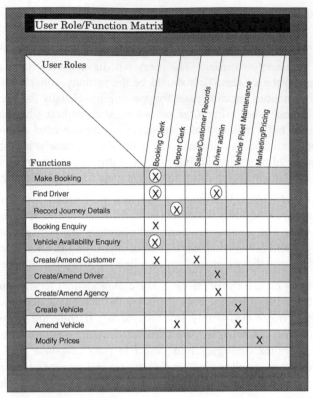

Fig. 4.22 User Role/Function Matrix annotated to show critical dialogues

Common processing

Identification of common processing starts with the development of the Current Physical Data Flow Diagrams. As these are being produced the analyst should look for any processes or routines which are common to different areas of the system. These are documented as Common Elementary Process Descriptions, being described once and cross-referenced thereafter. As we progress through Current Logical Data Flow Diagrams and Required System Data Flow Diagrams these Common Elementary Process Descriptions are maintained. In this step we rationalize the common processing.

High-level common processing defined in the Data Flow Diagrams will probably map to events or functions defined later. As the events and functions form the basic units for defining processing they need no longer be regarded as common processing—each event and each function is defined once and once only. Much of the common processing previously defined will be low-level, and this now needs to be included in the appropriate functions. The Common Elementary Process Descriptions are annotated with the function, event, or enquiry names that use them and cross-referenced on the Function Definition form.

Function volumetrics

It is extremely important to collect information about how often a function occurs. This information is documented on the Function Definition form. This volumetric information is used in various ways: for sizing and costing the system, for determining high volume and therefore critical functions, and for measuring the detailed performance of the system during Physical Design. Figures should be collected to show how often the function will be performed within a given period (e.g. 10,000 per day). Any predictable fluctuations should also be recorded, e.g. seasonal peaks and troughs or daily variations.

Volumetric information must also be collected about each function's components. A function may be composed of several different events and enquiries. We must record how often each event or enquiry occurs each time the function is performed. In simple, mainly on-line, systems this is rarely a problem since events and functions usually map one-to-one. However, if complex off-line processing occurs then one function may handle several different events. In on-line processing, enquiries may precede events as part of the same function—again we need to record how often the enquiries and the events occur each time the function is performed. All this volumetric information is extremely important when sizing the system. Detailed sizing will take place in the Technical System Options stage. Later, during the Physical Design stage, we attempt to predict the performance of critical functions and measure these against the Service Level Requirements agreed with the users. Again this detailed volumetric information is necessary to produce good estimates of performance.

Often this volumetric information is collected during the Investigation of the Current Environment stage: users are interviewed, current documentation is studied, and records are searched and sampled. However, further investigation and discussion with users will be necessary during Requirements Specification to clarify volumetric information.

Documentation

The Function Definition form, shown in Fig. 4.23, serves two main purposes. First, it briefly describes the function and its performance requirements. Second, it provides a way of linking together all of the associated documentation that eventually provides a full processing specification for the function. For example, we could use the reference to the Data Flow Diagram process, 1.1 Accept Booking, to find the Elementary Process Description which gives the detail.

As functions are composed of many components, built during the various steps of the project, this form will likewise develop. Some parts of the form are completed in step 330, *derive system functions*; other parts are completed later, and other parts may only be required for certain functions. In Fig. 4.23 we show a complete form at the end of Stage 5—the descriptions of the various parts of the form, given below, explain when (or if) the section is completed (no explanation is given if the section must be completed in step 330).

Function name Short name given to the function. This may be the same as the Data Flow Diagram process names; in Fig. 4.23 we have used the level 1 process name 'Make Booking'.

Function Definition	
Function name Make booking	**Function ID** 4

Type   Update/On-line/User
User roles   Bookings clerk

Function Description

This is carried out daily on demand as customers send in or make telephone bookings. Each period for which a vehicle is required is assigned a vehicle of the required category, a depot from which it may be collected and the dates for the booking.

Error handling

The function will be terminated if the customer is marked as a bad debtor.

DFD processes: 1.1 Accept Booking 1.3 Create Booking

Events: 1.1 Booking Received 1.3 Booking Confirmed	**Event frequency** 1 1

I/O descriptions: a-1.1,1.1-a,1.3-a

I/O structures: 1.1/1, 1.1/2,1.3/1

Requirements Catalogue ref. Requirement 1 Make Booking

Volumes: Average 1400 per day, maximum 2000 per day (peaks with post at 10am & 2pm)

Related functions: Function 2 Find Driver

Enquiries Vehicle Availability Enquiry (Function 1.2)	**Enquiry frequency:** 1.2 One in six enquiries do not result in a booking

Common processing: None

Dialogue names: Booking

Service level requirements

Description	Target value	Range	Comments
On-line response time	5 seconds	5-10 seconds	response time is critical as customer on telephone

Fig. 4.23 Sample Function Definition form

Function ID A unique identifier given to the function. This might be related to process, event, or enquiry identifiers. In large projects, naming standards will need to be set for all identifiers. Some CASE tools may follow a specific convention.

Type There are three ways of classifying functions. Process type—update (U) or enquiry (E). Implementation type—on-line (On) or off-line (Off). Initiation type—user (U) or system (S). All functions must be classified in all three ways.

User roles On-line functions may be carried out by several end users. Each end user may belong to one or more user roles. These user roles will have security levels defined for them. The user roles must be completed for all on-line functions.

Function description Brief description of what the function does, how it is invoked, what the system does and what output is produced.

Error handling An overview of the error handling associated with the function. This may cross-refer to other documents for fuller description of error handling, e.g. Required System Data Flow Diagram Elementary Process Descriptions, validation checks in the Data Catalogue, further documentation in the Update or Enquiry Process Models (developed in Stage 5). The error handling section is optional on the form and usually not completed until the later stages of the project.

DFD processes The lowest-level Required System Data Flow Diagram process(es) where the processing required for the function is shown. A function may cover several lowest-level processes or two or more functions may be necessary for one lowest-level process. The correspondence between processes and functions depends on the level of detail in the Data Flow Diagrams. Often, correspondence will be one-to-one between functions and processes. This section must be completed for all update functions.

Events Events were briefly described in Chapter 2 and their allocation to functions was discussed earlier. They are initially identified from the Required System Data Flow Diagrams in this step. Further events are usually identified in step 360, *develop processing specification*, so it often necessary to revisit this allocation of events. This section must be completed for all update functions.

Event frequency The frequency of the event relative to the function—how many times does the event happen each time the function is invoked? In most cases one function occurrence will handle one event occurrence. Sometimes, there are several events being handled by one function. There may be one event type handled first followed by an iteration of another event type. Alternatively there may be one primary event followed by another event which may or may not happen. So the event frequency can vary between less than one and greater than one. This section must be completed before Technical System Options in order for sizing to be performed.

I/O Descriptions Input and output data flows are initially documented by I/O Descriptions (during step 310, *define required system processing*) and later by I/O Structures. Note that the identifiers given here map to required system data flows (e.g. from external entity 'a' to process '1.1').

I/O Structures and I/O Structure Descriptions Refer to the diagrams that show the structure of the inputs to and outputs from the function. The I/O Structure Descriptions show the data content of the groupings on the inputs or outputs. (Examples are given later in this section.)

Requirements Catalogue reference Cross-refers to the Requirements Catalogue entry associated with the function.

Volumes How frequently the function is performed in a given time period. Any peaks or troughs should be shown. This information is needed for sizing in Technical System Options and to check Service Level Requirements. It also helps to identify critical functions for prototyping.

Related functions References any related functions. In the example above, the function Find Drivers is often performed immediately after the Make Booking function. There may be no related functions so this section is optional.

Enquiry Names of any enquiries required by the function. This will cross-reference the access paths required for the enquiry. This section must be completed for any functions containing an enquiry.

Enquiry Frequency As in the events frequency section above, this is the number of times an enquiry is performed for each time the function is performed. Mostly this will be one-to-one.

Common processing Cross-refers to any common processing at a low level that may be used by the function. This common processing will be described in the Elementary Process Descriptions. Again, this section is optional.

Dialogue Names Once the on-line functions have been identified the dialogues required to perform that function are named. Usually there is only one dialogue per on-line function but if several user roles can perform the function then different dialogues may be designed for different skill levels. This section must be completed by the end of step 330, *derive system functions*, for all on-line dialogues.

Service Level Requirements
These were originally identified in the Requirements Catalogue and are considered and added to this form before step 370, *confirm system objectives*, because they are required for Technical System Options. If several dialogues support the function then each dialogue may have different Service Level Requirements. They describe response times and batch turnaround times expected by the user for the function.

Description A description of what the Service Level Requirement is about.

Target Value A quantitative expression of performance, size, cost, satisfaction levels etc.

Range This details the maximum and minimum target values in the range.

Comments Explanation or qualification of the target value and acceptable ranges.

Sequencing input data

In large systems the handling of input data can be particularly complex, especially when off-line processing is used. The order in which data arrives and is input can be critical to the integrity of the systems data. Common problems that arise if data arrives in the wrong sequence are amendments to entity occurrences that haven't yet been created, and addition of new detail occurrences to a master entity occurrence which doesn't yet exist. Careful consideration of the order in which data is input can minimize such problems and reduce the need for complex error processing. At this stage in the project we do not consider the overall performance of the software—this is left until detailed Physical Design in Stage 6.

Complex batch processing can be designed with low-level Required System Data Flow Diagrams. These will often show several transient data stores being created and used. The way in which we order updates to the main system data (the main data stores containing entities) is critically important. If the input data is coming from one source, normally a transient data store, then we might consider re-ordering the input data so that it follows the precise order in which the data came in (i.e. time stamp the data, sort on the time stamp, then apply changes in the order in which the data arrived). This gives the same sequence as on-line processing and avoids errors caused by data arriving at the wrong time. In all cases we must be very careful to anticipate errors and investigate their consequences.

Functions after step 330

Step 350, *develop specification prototypes,* and step 360, *develop processing specification,* can each identify functions that were missed in the first pass through step 330. Step 350, by demonstrating prototype software to the users, may revise some of the functions designed in step 330. Step 360, by examining the processing from the perspective of the system's data, may also lead to changes in the functions. Thus there is an iterative aspect to steps 330, 350, and 360 which will lead the project to revisit step 330 in the light of prototyping and event-entity modelling. In large projects these steps will often overlap, with different analysts working on different steps at the same time.

As the project progresses, different components are defined for each function and the Function Definition form becomes complete. In step 360, *develop processing specification,* we develop further specification of the update processing (using Effect Correspondence Diagrams) and of the enquiry processing (using Enquiry Access Paths). In step 370, *define system objectives,* we examine in detail the Service Level Requirements for each function. In Stage 5, Logical Design; update and enquiry process design (using Update Process Models and Enquiry Process Models) and dialogue design (based on I/O Structures) complete the logical specification of the functions. In Stage 6, Physical Design, the Function Component Implementation Map defines how each component of the function is physically implemented.

Input/Output Structures

These define the data content and structure of all system inputs and outputs. In step 310, *define required system processing*, Input/Output Descriptions were developed to show the content of data flows crossing the system boundary. In step 330, *derive system functions*, the content and structure of all inputs and outputs from functions are defined.

Below we repeat the I/O Description for a booking request that was given in Sec. 4.2. These I/O Descriptions should cross-reference their data content with the Data Catalogue and informally describe the data input and output from each Data Flow Diagram process. It is important to realize that this data content may not be complete and it is not possible to define its full structure, particularly when the data flow is representing an on-line dialogue. Now we develop a more formal definition of each input, output, or dialogue with a diagrammatic representation known as an I/O Structure and a supporting description of the attributes included in the input/output.

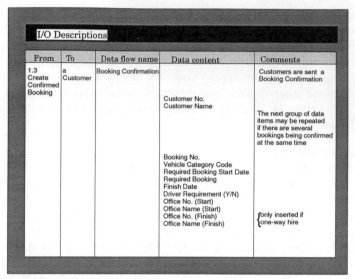

Fig. 4.24 I/O Description for Booking Confirmation

Notation for I/O Structure diagrams

These are represented using Jackson structures. Jackson structures were first used by Michael Jackson as a technique for program design in the early 1970s.[1] They are one of many ways of representing sequence, selection, and iteration that are popular in different program design methods (Nassi–Shneiderman charts and action diagrams are other examples).

In SSADM, Jackson structures are used in I/O Structure Diagrams, Entity Life Histories, and in Update and Enquiry Process Models. In each of these diagrams the Jackson notation is being used to model different things. The I/O Structure models the position of data in the input to or output from the computer. In Entity Life Histories the notation models the ordering of events affecting data held by the system. In Update and Enquiry Process Models the notation is used to show the procedures carried out by the computer to perform a particular process.

Through all the different uses of the notation the same basic rules apply—these were described in Chapter 2 for Entity Life Histories. With I/O Structures the parallel construct (which allowed events to occur in an unpredictable sequence) is not used.

The example given below shows the structure diagram for Booking Confirmation. The name of the input/output is shown at the top of the structure. Each of the leaves (the boxes that have no children) represents data input to or, in this example, output from the system. This data is documented in more detail with a supporting description. The null selection (the box with the '—' in it) shows that there will be no details of a return office if a one-way hire is requested. The iteration of booking details shows that one customer may have many separate bookings on one confirmation.

---

[1]The way they are used in SSADM is very much a development of Jackson's original technique.

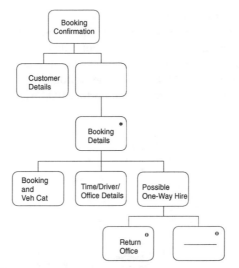

Fig. 4.25 I/O Structure diagram

In Fig. 4.26 below we show the I/O Structure Description which supports the I/O Structure Diagram. Each of the leaves on the diagram is represented by an I/O structure element which contains attributes (often called data items). Thus the Customer Details leaf consists of the data items: Customer No. and Customer Name. The Comments column can be used to further describe the conditions associated with the element. Notice that we have separated the elements by a horizontal dashed line—to avoid any ambiguities. Obviously the I/O Structure form (Fig. 4.26) has a great deal in common with the I/O Descriptions form (Fig. 4.24)—in practice, the I/O Description is annotated to contain the I/O Structure Description information.[1]

I/O Structure Description		
Data flows represented Create Confirmed Booking (1.3)–Customer (a) Booking Confirmation		
I/O structure element	**Data item**	**Comments**
Customer details	Customer No. Customer Name	
Booking and Veh Cat	Booking No. Vehicle Category Code	Usually only one but possibly several
Time/Driver/Office details	Required booking start date Required booking finish date Driver Requirement (Y/N) Office No. (Start) Office Name (Start)	bookings in same confirmation
Return office	Office No. (Finish) Office Name (Finish)	Only if one-way hire

Fig. 4.26 I/O Structure Description

---

[1] Most systems developments would be supported by a CASE tool which would ease the transformation of the documentation between the different steps of SSADM.

I/O Structures for dialogues

To represent a dialogue we need to show both inputs and outputs together. The I/O Structure interleaves inputs and outputs: distinguishing them by writing 'input' and 'output' inside the boxes (after the I/O Structure element name). An example is shown in Fig. 4.27 below which shows the dialogue for the Vehicle Availability Enquiry function. Figure 4.28 shows the supporting I/O Structure Description.

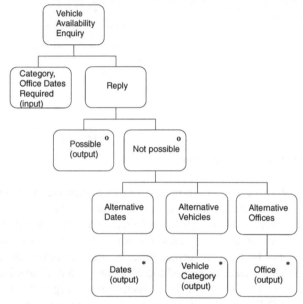

Fig. 4.27 I/O Structure for dialogue

Notice that the I/O Structure Element has no associated data items but describes the message, 'Possible'. SSADM is rather vague on the handling of messages in dialogues. In practice, projects use the Comments column or enter into the Data Item column the message given in quotes. The input of conditional data (for example, 'Do you want to enter another screen?' expecting the answer 'Yes' or 'No') can be handled by showing conditions on the I/O Structure Diagram or by adding comments to the I/O Structure Description.

This representation of dialogues follows from the separation of functions into on-line and off-line. Further dialogue design continues with critical dialogues being considered in step 350, *develop specification prototypes*. Specification prototyping may lead to changes to the I/O Structures which will be carried forward to detailed dialogue design in Stage 5 of SSADM.

I/O Structure Description		
Data flows represented Booking Clerk(h)—Determine Vehicle Availability(1.2) Availability Information		

I/O structure element	Data item	Comments
Category Office Dates Required	Vehicle Category Code Office Number Start Date Finish Date	
Possible		Message saying vehicle available on those dates
Dates	Required Booking Start Date Required Booking Finish Date	Other dates within 3 days of required start date
Vehicle Category	Vehicle Category Code Vehicle Category Description	Other categories similar to one requested available from same office on same dates
Office	Office number Office Name Office Address	Nearby offices where category requested is available on required dates

Fig. 4.28 I/O Structure Description

SUMMARY

- A function is a set of system processing which the users wish to schedule together, to support their business activity.
- Functions are first identified from Data Flow Diagrams.
- Group processes/events into functions by timeframe, mode of operation, and by similarity of activity, or data, or users.
- Functions 'collect' other SSADM products to become the processing specification
- Function Definition forms document functions, cross-refer to other SSADM products, and show Service Level Requirements.
- I/O Structures are defined for each function.
- I/O Structures use a Jackson diagram supported by data content definitions.

Exercises

4.4.1 I/O Descriptions —Scapegoat
Create I/O Descriptions for the staff allocation sheet and invoice from Scapegoat Systems. (This would normally be performed as part of step 310, *define required system processing*—you might prefer to go straight to the I/O Structure in the next part of the exercise.)

Staff allocation sheet This indicates which staff are allocated to a project. A staff allocation sheet is drawn up for each project as the contract is awarded. This maps to dataflow: Allocate Staff (3.2)—Project Manager (d) and is an output from the system. The No. of Days column relates to the planned number of days that an employee will spend on the project. A project is assigned a unique code and each project will be carried out for a single customer. If a project is carried out internally (i.e. not for a customer) then Customer Number and Customer Name are replaced by the words 'Internal Project'.

Proj Code	3411	Proj Desc	New Accounts
Cust No.	3475	Cust Name	British Bakers
Staff No.	Name	Grade	No. of Days
34	Bloggs	S.Prog	12
12	Jones	Analyst	3
23	Brown	Manager	9

Proj Code	2356	Proj Desc	Betting System
Cust No.	5134	Cust Name	Bobs Bookies
Staff No.	Name	Grade	No. of Days
34	Bloggs	S.Prog	3
12	Jones	Analyst	32
45	Williams	Teaboy	12

Fig. 4.29 Two sample staff allocation sheets

Invoice Each active customer is invoiced once a month for the work performed by Scapegoat in a previous month. The start and finish dates refer to the overall project but the Man Days column refers only to those worked in that particular month. This dataflow is from Produce Invoices (5.1) to Customer (a).

Invoice No:	3412	**Date of Invoice**	23/12/88
From:		SCAPEGOAT Systems	
		Acacia St	
		London	
		W14 3RT	
Cust No.		3475	
Cust Name		British Bakers	
Address		Bread House	
		Albert Square	
		London	
		E12 6TY	

Proj Desc	Start Date	Finish Date	Man Days	Cost
New Accounts	12/8/88	11/11/88	13	£13,000
Delivery System	13/3/88	30/11/88	58	£42,000
		Total Cost		£55,000

Fig. 4.30 Sample invoice from Scapegoat

4.4.2   Scapegoat Systems—I/O Structures and I/O Structure Descriptions

a) Create an I/O Structure and an I/O Structure Description for the staff allocation sheet.

b) Create an I/O Structure and an I/O Structure Description for the invoice.

c) Develop an I/O Structure for the New Employee dialogue for the user role Personnel Manager. The Elementary Process Description associated with the function Record New Staff is given below:

'The basic employee details are entered such as Name, Grade and Department No and the system generates a Staff No. Further personal details are then added such as Full Name, Address and Date of Birth.'

'The employee needs to be assigned to a manager in the same department. The system should be able to display a list of possible managers. This could be staff one or two grades above the grade of the new employee. When a suitable manager has been identified, either previously or by selecting from this list, then their staff number is entered.'

'The new employee may also be allocated some staff for him- or herself to manage. The system should be able to display a list of potential staff to be managed by the new employee. These could be all staff one and two grades below the employee in the same part of the department. The Personnel Manager then inputs Staff Nos. of those employees to be managed by the new employee (most new employees will have no staff so the input of possible staff only occurs in approximately 20% of cases).'

'The Personnel Manager then enters a variable number of qualifications that the employee has. A qualification number is entered and then validated by displaying the qualification name and the subject area. Providing this is satisfactory then the date qualification passed and the level attained are entered.'

4.4.3   *Given the I/O Description shown below from the Yorkies system develop an I/O Structure Diagram and I/O Structure Description.*

I/O Descriptions

From	To	Data flow name	Data content	Comments
		Local Office Vehicle Report	Local Office ID Local Office Name Local Office Address Depot Address	This printed report details all of the vehicles registered at a particular local office broken down by their vehicle categories It is produced on demand for the local office managers and for vehicle maintenance staff.
			Veh Cat Code Veh Cat Description No. of Vehicles	For each Vehicle Category these items may occur several times
			Veh Reg Mark Make of Veh Model No. Date of Reg Date of Purchase End Month Mileage Insurance Class Insurance Renewal Date MOT Date Condition	Then a list of vehicles for each category registered at that office. The following items for each vehicle.

Fig. 4.31 I/O Description for Local Office Vehicle Report

4.5   Enhance required data model (step 340)

In step 320, *develop required data model*, we were concerned with defining the major objects about which data was to be held (entities) and their inter-relationships. These were documented by a Logical Data Structure diagram supported by Entity Descriptions and Relationship Descriptions. The Logical Data Model was produced by a top-down approach of identifying the entities and relationships, and their major attributes were assigned to each entity. This model was informally validated to ensure that the processing for the required system could be performed.

Logical data structuring is a top-down technique that determines the real-world things (entities) about which we want to hold information in a computer system. In this step we enhance this top-down model by using a bottom-up technique, relational data analysis, which examines the most detailed information about the system (the data items or attributes).

Objectives

There are two major objectives of the step.

1. To produce a detailed data design that will fully meet the user's requirements and is flexible enough to incorporate future requirements.
2. To produce a design that is sufficiently detailed to be converted to a physical database design or file design.

Comparison of logical data modelling with relational data analysis

The Logical Data Model produced in step 320 has some major limitations which mean that, by itself, it may be unsatisfactory as the final data design. These are:

*   Only the major attributes were identified for each entity.
*   A sub-optimal, inflexible assignment of attributes to entities may have occurred since formal techniques were not used.
*   There may be undiscovered inherent relationships between attributes which could be invaluable for some retrievals.

The degree to which the Required System Logical Data Model, produced in step 320, will be subject to these limitations is quite dependent on the effort expended then.

To overcome these limitations an additional approach to defining the system's data is used, relational data analysis. This is a bottom-up technique in that the relationships between attributes are rigorously analysed in a way that is independent of the processing. This analysis results in groups of attributes organized in a flexible, non-redundant way. These are known as normalized relations. The differences between relational data analysis and logical data modelling are summarized in Fig. 4.32.

Logical data modelling	*Relational data analysis*
Top-down	Bottom-up
Based on analysis of entities and their inter-relationships	Based on analysis of attributes and their inter-relationships
Intuitive subjective technique	Formal, rigorous, mathematically based technique[1]
Based on and validated against the processing requirement	Based on the data contents of system input and outputs
May produce simple, inflexible structures	Produces highly flexible, complex structures
Model is represented as a diagram showing entities and relationships	Model is represented by groups of attributes, with key attributes identified known as normalized relations

Fig. 4.32 Comparison of logical data modelling and relational data analysis

To produce the detailed logical data design the results of relational data analysis are combined with the required Logical Data Model. Thus the strengths of both techniques are used to ensure that the Required System Logical Data Model is as complete and accurate as possible.

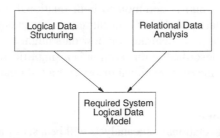

Fig. 4.33 Using both techniques to produce the Required System Logical Data Model

Approach
In step 330, *derive system functions*, we defined the structure of inputs and outputs to the required system. Now we apply relational data analysis to the data content of these inputs and outputs. This produces, for each function, groups of attributes with primary and foreign key attributes identified, known as normalized relations.

The Required System Logical Data Model also describes groupings of attributes. In order to merge the two representations of the system's data, both representations must be put into a comparable form. Thus the normalized relations are, by the application of simple rules, represented by a Logical Data Structure type diagram.

Differences between the two diagrams are then resolved by discussion with the users and by considering the processing requirements. A new version of the Required System Logical Data Structure is produced. Differences between the Entity Descriptions and

---

[1] However, there is some subjectivity in deciding upon the inter-dependence of attributes.

the data content of the normalized relations are resolved in a similar way and a set of revised Entity Descriptions produced.

This Required System Logical Data Model is used in step 360, *develop processing specification*. Entity Life Histories are developed for all entities and we validate, in a formal way, that the Required System Logical Data Model can support the processing required.

Relational data analysis

Section 4.5 is separated into two parts. The first part deals with relational data analysis in a general sense, explaining the background, underlying theory, terminology, and demonstrating the technique. The second part deals with the approach taken to relational data analysis in SSADM, illustrating this with examples from the Yorkies case study.

Background to relational data analysis

Relational data analysis is a very widely used technique, and several modern systems development methodologies use it in some form. The ideas behind it stem from theoretical work published by Codd in the early 1970s. This work led to the development of relational database theory and to the development of the relational data analysis technique for database design. The basic ideas of viewing all data in simple tables (or relations) is common to both relational database theory and to relational analysis. The database theory concentrates on the manipulation of these tables, whereas relational analysis concentrates on how data might best be organized into these tables. The approach described in this section is a simplification of some of the more abstract and theoretical ideas of relational theory (for a full treatment the reader is referred to the database books listed in the Bibliography and the references they contain).

Tables, columns, and rows

The product of relational data analysis will be a set of tables in which all of the systems data can be represented. These tables, often called relations, are equivalent to entities. (The terminology is confusing; relations are nothing to do with relationships in Logical Data Models.) The mathematical origins of relational theory give rise to a number of specific mathematical terms whose meaning is not obvious to the less mathematically minded. We use the more informal equivalents but give the formal relational terms.

Table or relation

This comprises both the actual data occurrences and the heading information at the top of the table. Figure 4.34 shows two tables from the hospital example used in Chapter 2.

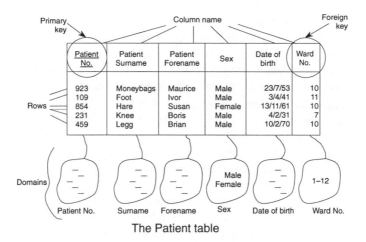

The Patient table

Ward No.	Ward Name	Type	Number of beds
3	Nightingale	Medical	8
11	Fleming	Medical	12
10	Barnard	Surgical	21

The Ward table

Fig. 4.34 Two well-normalized tables for a hospital

Rows (equivalent to occurrences)
The rows[1] of the table show the various occurrences of the patient. For instance, the first row shows the various values associated with Maurice Moneybags' stay in hospital.

Two important properties of relations are concerned with rows.

1. In any table there can be no duplicate rows. It follows from this that each row must be uniquely identifiable. In the most complex case it may require a combination of all the values in the row to identify it. However, in most cases it requires only one value or a combination of two or three values to identify each row. In the Patient table, only the value of Patient No. is required to identify the row. The column (attribute name or names) whose value identifies each row are referred to as the *primary key*. Thus Patient No. is the primary key of the Patient relation and Ward No. the primary key of the Ward relation. As there can be no duplicate rows the primary key must always exist.

2. The order in which the rows appear in the table must *not* be significant. This follows from the principle that in relations all data is represented explicitly, i.e. in terms of values rather than position. Thus if the Patient table was in order of when the patients were to be operated on, then this should be shown explicitly by adding a new column, Operation Sequence No.

---

[1]Tuple is the mathematical term, equivalent to row, used in some of the literature.

Columns (equivalent to attributes)

Each column has a heading or column name and a set of values that are taken by the attribute in different rows. The column name is equivalent to the attribute type and each value is equivalent to a attribute occurrence in the Logical Data Model.

Two important properties of columns in relations are:

1. The order of columns must not be significant. We have shown, as is the convention, the primary key columns as the first column in the table, but the relation has to be represented on paper in some order. This property is less important in relational analysis than in relational database theory where the unordered nature of the relations enhances data independence.

2. The second important property is that only one value should be associated with each column/row intersection in the table. So if we were to add a column to the patient table in Fig. 4.34 of Drug Prescribed, then because a patient may be prescribed several drugs during their stay there could be several values for, say, Maurice Moneybags' Drug Prescribed, e.g. penicillin, aspirin. This breaks the rule of one value per column/row intersection. Another way of expressing this rule is that there can be no repeating groups of attribute occurrences for one occurrence of the primary key. This rule is important as it means that a relation must at least be in what is called *First Normal Form*. The normal forms of data are discussed later.

Domain

This represents a pool of possible values from which the actual values appearing in the columns of the table are drawn. Thus the domain of Patient Nos. includes all of the possible Patient Nos., not just the ones currently in the hospital. The domain of Sex has just two possible values—male and female. The importance of domains is shown when we compare values from different tables. Thus if we wanted to find the name of the ward a particular patient was in we would have to compare the values of Ward No. in the Patient table with the values of Ward No. in the Ward table. This could only sensibly be done if the two Ward Nos. came from the same pool of values.

Another example of this could be if we had another table called 'Doctor' which had column names Doctor No., Doctor Surname, Doctor Forename, Doctor Date of Birth, etc. To find out if we had any doctors who might also be patients we could compare the attribute values: Patient Surname with Doctor Surname, Doctor Forename with Patient Forename, Patient Date of Birth with Doctor Date of Birth. This can be done because the columns being compared share the domains: surname, forename, date of birth.

In SSADM we develop Grouped Domain Descriptions (see Fig. 3.41 for an example) for attributes with common domains. These are included, with the Attribute Descriptions, in the Data Catalogue.

Normalized relations

The object of relational data analysis is to organize all of the system's attributes into a set of well-normalized relations. Well-normalized relations avoid certain undesirable properties:

- unnecessary duplication of attributes in different relations (i.e. no redundant data);

- problems with modifying, inserting, and deleting data (sometimes referred to as the update anomalies).

To illustrate the problem we will extend the hospital example described earlier. Suppose that each patient has, at the end of their bed, a Drug Card showing all drugs prescribed during their stay and the dosage required. Two sample cards, with information typed onto them, are shown in Fig. 4.35.

Drug Card

Patient No.: 923   **Surname:** Moneybags   **Forename:** Maurice

Ward No.: 10   **Ward Name:** Barnard

Drugs prescribed:

Date	Drug Code	Drug Name	Dosage	Length of Treatment
20/5/88	CO2355P	Cortisone	2 pills 3 x day after meals	14 days
20/5/88	MO3416T	Morphine	Injection every 4 hours	5
25/5/88	MO3416T	Morphine	Injection every 8 hours	3
26/5/88	PE8694N	Penicillin	1 pill 3x day	7

For additional drugs continue on another card

Drug Card

Patient No.: 109   **Surname:** Foot   **Forename:** Ivor

Ward No.: 11   **Ward Name:** Fleming

Drugs prescribed:

Date	Drug Code	Drug Name	Dosage	Length of Treatment
15/5/88	AS473A	Aspirin	2 pills 3 x day after meals	7 days
20/5/88	VA231M	Valium	2 per day	5

For additional drugs continue on another card

Fig. 4.35 Sample Drug Cards in the hospital system

This data could be organized into several ways depending on which requirements we are trying to satisfy. If we want to simply recreate the information on the Drug Card then the organization of attributes into one table as shown in Fig. 4.36 is ideal—with one retrieval the drug card can be recreated for each patient.

Pat No.	Surname	Fore-name	Wd No.	Ward Name	Prescr Date	Drug Code	Drug Name	Dosage	Lgth Treat
923	Moneybags	Maurice	10	Barnard	20/5/88	CO2355P	Cortisone	2 pills 3 x day after meals	14
923	Moneybags	Maurice	10	Barnard	20/5/88	MO3416T	Morphine	Injection every 4 hours	5
923	Moneybags	Maurice	10	Barnard	25/5/88	MO3416T	Morphine	Injection every 8 hours	3
923	Moneybags	Maurice	10	Barnard	26/5/88	PE8694N	Penicillin	1 pill 3 x day	7
109	Foot	Ivor	11	Fleming	15/5/88	AS473A	Aspirin	2 pills 3 x day after meals	7
109	Foot	Ivor	11	Fleming	20/5/88	VA231M	Valium	2 per day	5

Fig. 4.36 Possible (unnormalized) table design for the Drug Card

However, when we look at the data in the table there seems to be considerable unnecessary duplication: Moneybags appears four times, Ward Name and Drug Name have the same value appearing several times. This duplication means that some, apparently very simple, queries will be rather inefficient and difficult to perform. For example:

• How many patients are there in the hospital?

This would mean that our program would need to maintain a list of Patient Numbers it had already met and check each number against this list in order to avoid counting the same patient several times.

• How many patients in Ward 10 have been given morphine?

This could be programmed in several different ways but would always be more complex than it need be if the file(s) were better designed. A skilful programmer could make the program more efficient by exploiting the way the data was ordered in the file. This could cause serious problems in maintaining the program if the file structure was changed.

There are also some problems when we come to update the data in Fig. 4.36. For example:

• If Foot dies and is deleted we lose important information (that Ward 11 is called Fleming and that Valium is VA231M).

• If Moneybags is moved from Ward 10 to 11 we need to find each row connecting Moneybags to Ward 10 and change it *otherwise* we will get an inconsistent result when we query the data.

These problems can be avoided by organizing the data into 'well-normalized' tables, like those shown at the beginning of this section in Fig. 4.34. These provide a structure which is inherently flexible and should enable all enquiries and updates to be performed in a simple and natural way. Because the data structure is 'right' then even unexpected queries can be easily programmed.

To build these well-normalized relations the analyst take the raw system's data going through several stages of normalization known as normal forms:

There are further normal forms (Boyce–Codd, Fourth, and Fifth Normal Forms) but, in practice, relations which are in what SSADM calls Third Normal Form are almost always also in the further normal forms. Very rarely, relations are identified which are in Third Normal Form but not in Fourth Normal Form—this problem will invariably be identified and resolved by comparing the relation with the Logical Data Structure. Relations which have been defined in their 'ideal' state, referred to as *well-normalized relations*, will be in First, Second, Third, Boyce–Codd, Fourth, and Fifth Normal Forms. Normal forms beyond third are not discussed here nor in the SSADM reference manual.[1] As the SSADM approach formally analyses data to Third Normal Form the technique is often referred to as Third Normal Form (TNF) data analysis.

The Patient and Ward tables shown in Fig. 4.34 are well-normalized relations. Each well-normalized relation must have a *primary key* attribute (or combination of attributes) whose value can identify the values of the other attributes in the relation. Thus the primary key value (923) of Patient No. identifies or determines the associated Patient Surname (Moneybags) and the Ward No. (10). In SSADM we show primary key attributes by underlining. Ward No. appears in both the Ward and Patient tables: in Ward as the primary key and in Patient as a *foreign key*. Non-primary key attributes in a relation which are the primary key(s) of another relation(s) are known as foreign keys.

Earlier in this book we discussed Logical Data Models—these contained relationships between entities. We showed a one-to-many relationship between the Ward and Patient entity—in relational tables this relationship would be managed through equating common values of the attribute Ward No. We could *join* Patient and Ward together on Ward No. to discover that patient Moneybags was in a Surgical ward. A set of well-normalized relations can easily be converted into a Logical Data Structure by showing relationships between entities (which are equivalent to well-normalized relations) where they can be joined on key attributes. The precise rules for this conversion are given later in this section.

---

[1] The interested reader should consult one of the many comprehensive database textbooks—these tend to use slightly different approaches and terminology to normalization (and entity modelling) to SSADM. Date (1995) is the classic textbook; clear, succinct, accurate, but too mathematical for some. Howe (1990) has a very detailed tutorial on normalization. Bradley has a long and clear explanation of Fourth and Fifth Normal Forms showing how they arise in both normalization and logical data models. See Date, C. J., (1995) *An Introduction to Database Systems: Volume 1* 6th edn (Addison-Wesley, Reading, Mass); Howe, D.R., *Data Analysis for Data Base Design* 2nd edn (Edward Arnold, London); Bradley, J.,(1987) *Introduction to Data Base Management in Business* 2nd edn (Holt, Rinehart & Winston, New York).

How to perform relational data analysis

Relational data analysis can be applied to any set of attributes. One could, theoretically, take all of the attributes of the system, analyse them, and produce a data design for the system all in one step. In practice this is almost impossible to do (unless the system is very small) since it involves comparing every attribute with every other. The practical approach taken in SSADM is to analyse separately small 'chunks' of the system data and then synthesize the results of each separate analysis. The 'chunks' of data selected for analysis are often referred to as *data sources*. Normally the inputs and outputs from the system are used; these could be forms, screen formats, or reports.

To illustrate the technique we will use the hospital example described earlier. The Drug Card is our data source and we use as samples, representing all of the drug card data for all patients, the two cards shown in Fig. 4.35. It is important to realize we are analysing all existing data and all possible data associated with the data source chosen (in other words; the sample data may not cover all possibilities so we must look further in our analysis).

1. Represent the data in unnormalized form and pick a key   The first step is to represent all of the data in a table. Some of the column headings (attribute names) have been abbreviated to save space. As the dates given on the Drug Card are the dates on which the particular drug was prescribed we have renamed Date to the more meaningful Prescription Date. Note that the table is not strictly speaking a relation since there are several possible values for, say, patient 923's Drug Code.

We can select any attribute or combination of attributes to act as primary key. However, it makes the analysis rather more straightforward if a 'reasonable' key is selected. Criteria for selecting a reasonable key are:

- ideally the key should be unique (only one possible value) for the particular data source;
- use the smallest combination of attributes possible;
- avoid textual keys.

The Patient No. is a good choice of key since each Drug Card is for one and only one patient, and the other criteria are satisfied. The convention is that primary keys are underlined. Figure 4.37 shows the Drug Card data in unnormalized form.

Pat No.	Surname	Fore-name	Wd No.	Ward Name	Prescr Date	Drug Code	Drug Name	Dosage	Lgth Treat
923	Moneybags	Maurice	10	Barnard	20/5/88	CO2355P	Cortisone	2 pills 3 x day after meals	14
					20/5/88	MO3416T	Morphine	Injection every 4 hours	5
					25/5/88	MO3416T	Morphine	Injection every 8 hours	3
					26/5/88	PE8694N	Penicillin	1 pill 3 x day	7
109	Foot	Ivor	11	Fleming	15/5/88	AS473A	Aspirin	2 pills 3 x day after meals	7
					20/5/88	VA231M	Valium	2 per day	5

Fig. 4.37 Drug Card data in unnormalized form

2. Represent the data in First Normal Form by removing any repeating groups of attributes to separate relations. Pick keys for any relations identified A repeating group is defined as any *attribute or group of attributes* that may occur with *multiple values* for a *single value of the primary key attribute.*

Thus in the table shown in Fig. 4.37 there are several values of Drug Code, Drug Name, Prescription Date, Dosage, and Treatment Length for one value of the Patient No. These attributes form a repeating group and are removed to a separate relation.

The new relation has the column headings Patient No., Drug Code, Drug Name, Prescription Date, Dosage, and Treatment Length. The Patient No. is required to make each row unique across the whole of the system data; it is quite likely that two patients could be given exactly the same prescription on the same day.

We now have to decide on the primary key of the new relation. This will always be a combination of the key selected in step 1 and one or more additional attributes necessary to identify a particular row. Patient No. is therefore part of the key and further analysis shows that it is necessary to have both Drug Code and Prescription Date included in the key. (A patient may be prescribed several drugs on the same day or may be prescribed same drug on separate occasions.) When several attributes are required for the key of a relation this is known as a *compound key.* The new relation shown in Fig. 4.38 has a compound key of Patient No., Drug Code, and Prescription Date. (This assumes a hospital rule that a patient cannot be given different dosages of the same drug several times in the same day. What could the key be if there was no such rule?)

Pat No.	Presc Date	Drug Code	Drug Name	Dosage	Lgth Treat
923	20/5/88	CO2355P	Cortisone	2 pills 3 x day after meals	14
923	20/5/88	MO3416T	Morphine	Injection every 4 hours	5
923	25/5/88	MO3416T	Morphine	Injection every 8 hours	3
923	26/5/88	PE8694N	Penicillin	1 pill 3 x day	7
109	15/5/88	AS473A	Aspirin	2 pills 3 x day after meals	7
109	20/5/88	VA231M	Valium	2 per day	5

Fig. 4.38 Separated repeating group now in First Normal Form

With the repeating group removed to a separate relation, we now consider the attributes left behind. These are the attributes that do not repeat for a single value of the key selected in step 1. Each row is therefore uniquely identified by the value of the key previously selected.

Thus Patient No., Surname, Forename, Ward No., and Ward Name remain as a relation with a key of Patient No. This is shown in Fig. 4.39. The data is now represented by two tables in First Normal Form (Figs 4.38 and 4.39).

Pat No.	Surname	Fore- name	Wd No.	Ward Name
923	Moneybags	Maurice	10	Barnard
109	Foot	Ivor	11	Fleming

Fig. 4.39 Non-repeating information in First (and Second) Normal Form

3. Represent the data in Second Normal Form by removing any attributes that only depend upon part of the key to separate relations This only affects relations that have compound keys. We have to decide whether any attributes in a compound key relation are dependent on only part of that compound key.

This concept of dependency, often referred to as *functional dependency*, is very important in relational data analysis.

For any two attributes A and B, A is dependent on B if and only if:

> For a given value of B there is associated with it precisely one value of A at any one time.

Thus the attribute Patient Surname is dependent on the attribute Patient No. since for a given value of Patient No., say 923, there is associated with it precisely one value of Patient Surname, in this case Moneybags.

Another way of describing this is to say that:

> Attribute B *determines* attribute A

> Patient No. *determines* Patient Surname

Notice that the opposite is false:

> Patient Surname *does not determine* Patient No.

For a given value of Patient Surname, say Moneybags, there may be several associated values of Patient No., as there may be several patients called Moneybags in the hospital at the same time.

Functional dependency diagrams (Figs 4.40 and 4.41) are a useful way of understanding dependency and of sorting out complex dependencies. An arrow is drawn from the determining attribute(s) to the dependent attribute. Figure 4.40 emphasizes the common-sense view of dependency: if you know the Patient No, then you can find the Patient Surname.

Fig. 4.40 Functional dependency diagram: Patient No. *determines* Patient Surname

Dependency can also occur with groups of attributes. In the table shown in Fig. 4.42 the combination of attributes—Patient No., Prescription Date, and Drug Code—determines each of the attributes—Dosage and Treatment Length. This compound key relation can also be shown by a dependency diagram as in Fig. 4.41 below.

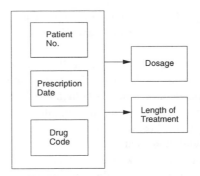

Fig. 4.41 Functional dependency diagram showing a compound key relation

To put a relation into Second Normal Form we check that each attribute in the relation depends on the whole key of the relation that it is in. Any attributes not depending on the whole key are removed to separate relations using their determining attributes as primary key.

The First Normal Form relation, shown in Fig. 4.38 above, includes the attribute Drug Name. This is only determined by the Drug Code. Thus the relation is not in Second Normal Form and the attribute, Drug Name, which is only dependent on part of the key, is removed from the relation. Drug Code and Drug Name form a new relation with Drug Code as the key. The modified relation and the new relation are shown in Fig. 4.42.

Pat No.	Presc Date	Drug Code	Dosage	Lgth Treat
923	20/5/88	CO2355P	2 pills 3 x day after meals	14
923	20/5/88	MO3416T	Injection every 4 hours	5
923	25/5/88	MO3416T	Injection every 8 hours	3
923	26/5/88	PE8694N	1 pill 3 x day	7
109	15/5/88	AS473A	2 pills 3 x day after meals	7
109	20/5/88	VA231M	2 per day	5

Drug Code	Drug Name
CO2355P	Cortisone
MO3416T	Morphine
PE8694N	Penicillin
AS473A	Aspirin
VA231M	Valium

Fig. 4.42 Second Normal Form relations from the Drug Card

The systematic way of deciding whether there are any part-key dependencies is to go through each compound key relation and ask of each attribute:

*Does it depend on the **whole** key?*

If the answer is *No* then which attribute(s) it depends upon must be decided. An additional relation is created with the determining attribute(s) as the key and the dependent attribute(s) as the data. The dependent attributes are removed from the original relation.

In the example Drug Name is only dependent on Drug Code, so an additional relation is created with Drug Code as key and Drug Name as data. Drug Name is removed from the original relation.

Note that we should also examine the key attributes and ask for a compound key whether any parts of the key directly depend on other parts of the key? If any parts of the key are dependent on other parts then the dependent attributes should be relegated to non-key attributes with the determining attributes remaining as keys. In the case of our compound key in the hospital example there is no dependency within the key. However, dependencies within keys are quite common, particularly in key-only relations, and we shall meet some in the Yorkies case study.

Any relations that have single keys are not affected by step 3. They are already in Second Normal Form.

4. Represent the data in Third Normal Form by removing any attributes not directly dependent on the key to separate relations This step is similar to the previous one in that we are looking at dependency between attributes. The difference is that here we are looking for attributes that might be dependent on other attributes instead of looking for non-key attributes that might be dependent on only part of the key.

Therefore for each attribute we should ask the questions:

> *Is the attribute directly dependent on the key*
> *attribute(s) of the relation it is in?*

and

> *Is it directly dependent on any other*
> *attribute(s) in the system?*

If the answer to the first question is *No* then the answer to the second must be *Yes*. These two questions act as a cross-check on each other in trying to find any undetected inter-data dependencies. These are always difficult to find since to ask the second question systematically we would have to compare each attribute in the system with every other attribute or combination of attributes. This systematic approach is obviously impossible in practice so a more intuitive approach has to be taken. The intuitive approach relies on the analyst's skill and knowledge of the system in being able to spot possible inter-data dependencies and then to investigate them formally. In most cases the inter-data dependencies will be obvious and will occur within the relations being analysed together—it is those rare cases where a dependency occurs between attributes analysed on separate data sources that are hard to find.[1]

If an inter-data dependency is detected, say between attributes A and B, then we must decide whether attribute A determines attribute B or vice versa. The following questions should be asked:

---

[1] The technically minded reader should note that these questions ensure that the relations are in Boyce–Codd Normal Form, sometimes referred to as Strong Third Normal Form. We are following the conventions described by the SSADM Reference Manual; which makes no distinction between Third Normal Form and Boyce–Codd Normal Form, and describes the latter as Third Normal Form.

Given a value for attribute A is there just one
possible value for attribute B?

and

Given a value for attribute B is there just one
possible value for attribute A?

If the first question is answered *Yes* and the second *No* then attribute A determines attribute B. Attribute A is then key to attribute B. Item B is removed from the relation it was previously in to a new separate relation whose key is attribute A. Item A is left in the previous relation.

If the first question is answered *No* and the second *Yes* then attribute B determines attribute A.

If both questions are answered *No* then there is no inter-data dependency.

If both questions are answered *Yes* then the two attributes determine each other. These are sometimes known as *candidate keys* as either could act as primary key to the other. Normally the more appropriate attribute would be selected as the key and it would be treated in a similar way to the first case above. Occasionally it happens that the two attributes are also candidates for the primary key of the relation they are already in. Then no significant redundancy is involved and they can both be left in the Third Normal Form relation. Care should be taken that the same candidate is always chosen as the primary key whenever the relation occurs. (A good example of this could occur in a personnel system. We might have a relation Employee with a primary key of Employee No. This could have non-key attributes of Pay Reference No. and National Insurance No. All three attributes are candidate keys with Employee No. being chosen as primary key.)

In the Drug Card example, examining our three Second Normal Form relations indicates a possible inter-data dependency in the relation with the key Patient No. This relation is repeated in Fig. 4.43.

Pat No.	Surname	Fore-name	Wd No.	Ward Name
923	Moneybags	Maurice	10	Barnard
109	Foot	Ivor	11	Fleming

Fig. 4.43 Second Normal Form relation not in Third Normal Form

Each non-key attribute is dependent on the primary key of Patient No. in that there is precisely one value of each attribute associated with a given Patient No. However, there appears to be an inter-data dependency between Ward No. and Ward Name. In other words Ward Name does not seem to depend directly on Patient No. Asking the questions:

Given a value for Ward No. is there just one
possible value for Ward Name?

Yes, each ward can only have one name.

Given a value for Ward Name is there just one possible value for Ward No.?

No, in this hospital it is possible for several wards to share a name.

This means that Ward No. determines Ward Name and therefore forms a new relation with Ward No. as the primary key. Ward No. is left in the Patient relation as its value is determined by the Patient No. Ward No. is acting as a *foreign key* in the Patient relation.

Pat No.	Surname	Fore-name	Wd No.
923	Moneybags	Maurice	10
109	Foot	Ivor	11

Wd No.	Ward Name
10	Barnard
11	Fleming

Pat No.	Presc Date	Drug Code	Dosage	Lgth Treat
923	20/5/88	CO2355P	2 pills 3 x day after meals	14
923	20/5/88	MO3416T	Injection every 4 hours	5
923	25/5/88	MO3416T	Injection every 8 hours	3
923	26/5/88	PE8694N	1 pill 3 x day	7
109	15/5/88	AS473A	2 pills 3 x day after meals	7
109	20/5/88	VA231M	2 per day	5

Drug Code	Drug Name
CO2355P	Cortisone
MO3416T	Morphine
PE8694N	Penicillin
AS473A	Aspirin
VA231M	Valium

Fig. 4.44 Third Normal Form relations from the Drug Card

The new relations, Patient and Ward, arising from further normalization of the Second Normal Form relations are shown in Fig. 4.44 with the other relations. The Prescription and Drug relations, developed at Second Normal Form, were already in Third Normal Form.

If we had answered to the second question: *'Yes, for a given value of Ward Name there is only one possible value of Ward No.',* then we could select either Ward No. or Name as the key of the new relation, and both would be candidate keys. Ward No. is a better primary key because it is non-textual.

The process of normalization is now complete and to ensure that the data is well-normalized two tests are applied.

5. Apply the TNF tests to check that the relations are well-normalized

TNF Test 1:   *Given a value for the key(s) of a TNF relation, is there just one possible value for each attribute in that relation?*

Applying this test to each of the relations defined above we ask:

For a given value of Patient No. is there just one possible value of: Patient Surname? Patient Forename? Ward No.?

> *For a given combination of values for Patient*
> *No., Date of Prescription, and Drug Code is*
> *there just one possible value of: Dosage?*
> *Length of Treatment?*

Similar questions are asked for the relations identified by Ward No. and Drug Code.

To all these questions the answer is *Yes,* indicating that the relations are in First Normal Form and that each attribute is dependent on the key of the relation (but not necessarily wholly and directly dependent on the key).

TNF Test 2:   *Is each attribute in a TNF relation directly and wholly dependent on the key(s) of that relation?*

Applying this test to each of the relations defined above we ask:

> *Is Patient Surname/Patient Forename/Ward*
> *No. directly and wholly dependent on Patient*
> *No.?*

> *Is Dosage (Length of Treatment) directly and*
> *wholly dependent on Patient No., Date of*
> *Prescription, and Drug Code?*

Similar questions are asked for the relations identified by Ward No. and Drug Code.

To all these questions the answer is *Yes,* indicating that the relations are in Second and Third Normal Form.

To illustrate further the use of these tests we will modify the hospital example slightly. Suppose each patient belongs to a Patient Weight Type which can take values: 'Very Underweight', 'Underweight', 'Normal', 'Overweight', and 'Obese'. The amount of each drug given to a patient will depend on which Weight Type they are.

Applying the two tests to the Dosage attribute:

> *For a given combination of values for Patient*
> *No., Date of Prescription, and Drug Code is*
> *there just one possible value of Dosage?*

Yes, the relation is in First Normal Form and Dosage is dependent on the key attributes.

> *Is Dosage directly and wholly dependent on*
> *Patient No., Date of Prescription, and Drug*
> *Code?*

No, Dosage is directly dependent on a combination of Drug Code and Patient Weight Type. Thus the relation is not in Third Normal Form and the Dosage attribute should be removed from the relation to a new relation with a compound key of Drug Code and Patient Weight Type.

This kind of redundancy is quite common and is known as *transitive dependency* since the dependency has been transferred from one attribute to another. In this case the Patient Weight Type is dependent on the Patient No. Test 2 detects the transient dependencies.

Test 2 can be rephrased to the relational oath for each attribute in a relation:

*'I swear to be dependent on the key, the whole
key, and nothing but the key so help me Codd'*

A further test that should be applied is that attributes should not appear in several different relations *unless* they are primary keys (or parts of primary keys) in a relation. In other words, if an attribute appears more than once in a normalized set of relations it must be acting (somewhere) as a primary key. In the other relations it will be either a part of a primary key or a foreign key.

SSADM notation

We have illustrated the process of normalization using sample tables of data. Although this technique makes the process easy to visualize it is rather cumbersome when analysing large tables and many data sources. A simpler notation is to use only the column headings (attribute names) from the tables. These are listed down the page with the primary keys, underlined and shown at the top of each relation. Note that the foreign key of Ward No. is marked in the 3NF relation by an asterisk.

UNF	1NF	2NF	3NF
<u>Patient No.</u> Patient Surname Patient Forename Ward No. Ward Name Prescription Date Drug Code Drug Name Dosage Length of Treatment	<u>Patient No.</u> Patient Surname Patient Forename Ward No. Ward Name <u>Patient No.</u> <u>Prescription Date</u> <u>Drug Code</u> Drug Name Dosage Length of Treatment	<u>Patient No.</u> Patient Surname Patient Forename Ward No. Ward Name <u>Patient No.</u> <u>Prescription Date</u> <u>Drug Code</u> Dosage Length of Treatment <u>Drug Code</u> Drug Name	<u>Patient No.</u> Patient Surname Patient Forename *Ward No. <u>Ward No.</u> Ward Name <u>Patient No.</u> <u>Prescription Date</u> <u>Drug Code</u> Dosage Length of Treatment <u>Drug Code</u> Drug Name

Fig. 4.45 SSADM notation for showing normalization

6. Rationalize relations obtained from all data sources Relational data analysis is performed on a number of data sources and will yield from each source a number of normalized relations. The process of combining those relations, to form the full set of normalized relations, is known as *rationalization*. All relations that have exactly the same primary key are merged together and the new merged relation given a name. Figure 4.46 shows the four relations obtained by normalization of the Drug Card and the two relations shown previously in Fig. 4.34 being merged.

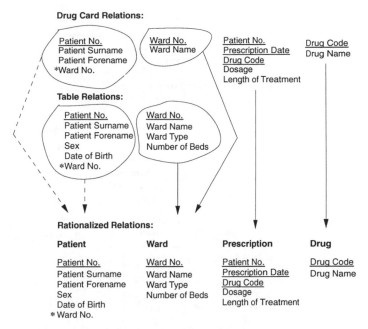

Drug Card Relations:

Patient No.
Patient Surname
Patient Forename
*Ward No.

Ward No.
Ward Name

Patient No.
Prescription Date
Drug Code
Dosage
Length of Treatment

Drug Code
Drug Name

Table Relations:

Patient No.
Patient Surname
Patient Forename
Sex
Date of Birth
*Ward No.

Ward No.
Ward Name
Ward Type
Number of Beds

Rationalized Relations:

Patient

Patient No.
Patient Surname
Patient Forename
Sex
Date of Birth
* Ward No.

Ward

Ward No.
Ward Name
Ward Type
Number of Beds

Prescription

Patient No.
Prescription Date
Drug Code
Dosage
Length of Treatment

Drug

Drug Code
Drug Name

Fig. 4.46 Rationalizing relations with the same primary keys

After rationalization has been performed, the TNF tests described previously should be performed to ensure that the merged relations are still in Third Normal Form.

Creating a data structure diagram from normalized relations

In order to compare the results of relational data analysis with the Logical Data Model the normalized relations must be represented in a form that makes comparison easy. It is very simple to represent a set of normalized relations as a Logical Data Structure style diagram. SSADM prescribes a set of rules for this conversion. However, before applying these rules to the case study we demonstrate how a set of relations can be represented as a data structure.

In Fig. 4.47 the four relations identified from the hospital example are shown. The relationships are shown by crow's feet linking the common keys in each relation. Notice that the 'one' end of the relationship is where the attribute appears as the sole primary key of the relation. Thus the Ward relation, which has Ward No. as its single primary key, 'owns'[1] the Patient relation, which has Ward No. as a foreign key. Also the Patient relation 'owns' the Prescription relation, which has Patient No. as part of its primary key. This clearly fits in with the data—for one row in the Patient relation (923, Moneybags, etc.) there are four rows in the Prescription relation with the same value of Patient No.

---

[1]This terminology was explained in Chapter 2. An entity at the 'one' end (the master) of a one-to-many relationship is said to 'own' the entity at the 'many' end (the detail).

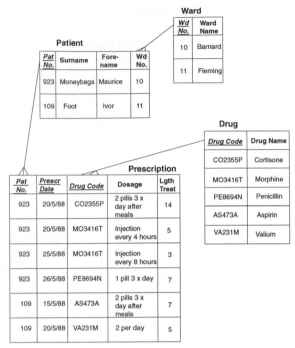

Fig. 4.47 Drug Card relations shown as a data structure type diagram

Below we show the conventional SSADM representations for this data: first, the set of relations and second, the data structure diagram (Fig. 4.48). From these the basic rules for representing a set of relations as a data structure diagram clearly emerge (the Prescription Date entity is a bit of an oddity and will be explained later).

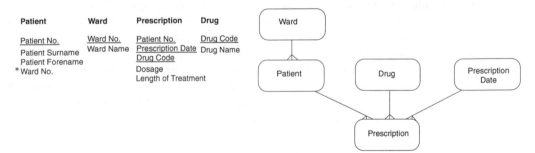

Fig. 4.48 Relations shown as a Logical Data Structure

Rules for producing a relational structure

1. Relations are shown as entities Each relation is shown as an entity on a Logical Data Structure diagram with the name of the relation inside the box. Often the primary and foreign keys of the relation are also written inside the box—this can help identify which relationships need be drawn. The Logical Data Structure diagram can help in placing the boxes. Another good guideline is to show relations that have large compound keys or many foreign keys at the bottom of the diagram.

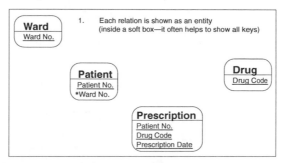

Fig. 4.49 Applying Rule 1 to the Drug Card relations

1a. If a part of a compound key does not exist as a primary key of another relation then this attribute is shown as an entity and is marked as a foreign key in any other relations it occurs in. If the compound key is also a hierarchic key then do not apply Rule 1a, instead apply Rule 1b. Thus Prescription Date is shown as an entity. This seems at first to be a rather odd rule in that we are creating entities which only contain one attribute. Its significance becomes apparent when we realize that this attribute may occur in other entities (as part of primary keys or, after rule 1a, as foreign keys). Creating the new entity and linking other entities to it ensures that all the relationships implied by the normalized relations are shown on the diagram.

A hierarchic key is a special case of a compound key in that one or more of the attributes participating in the key have no unique significance in the system. (In other words they are incapable of acting as primary and foreign keys on their own.) Hierarchic keys and their application in rule 1b are discussed in more detail later in this section using an example from the Yorkies case study (see Fig. 4.64).

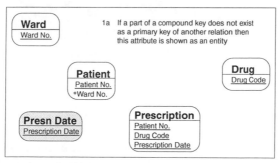

Fig. 4.50 Applying Rule 1a to the Drug Card relations

2. Compound key relations are owned by the relations which have the attributes of the compound key as their primary key attribute (little keys own big keys) Thus Patient, Drug, and Prescription Date own Prescription.

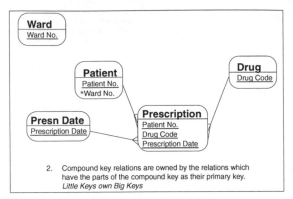

2.   Compound key relations are owned by the relations which have the parts of the compound key as their primary key.
Little Keys own Big Keys

Fig. 4.51 Applying Rule 2 to the Drug Card relations

So if a relation, *ABC*, has a compound key, *abc*, then it could be owned by relations *A* (with a key of *a*), *B* (with a key of *b*), and by *C* (with a key of *c*). Alternatively if there were another compound key relation *AB* (with a key of *ab*), then this should own *ABC* (as in Fig. 4.52) rather than relations *A* and *B*. The number of relationships should always be minimized in this way if possible. Note that it would also be wrong to show *ABC* linked to *A, B,* and *AB*—each key attribute can only be assigned to a relationship **once** and only once.

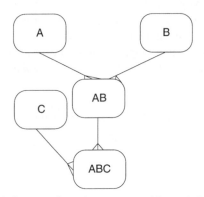

Fig. 4.52 Compound key relations owning other compound key relations

3. Relations that have foreign keys are owned by those relations that have the foreign key as their primary key (crow's feet grab the asterisks) A foreign key in a relation indicates that it should be a detail of the relation which has that attribute as its primary key. Thus the foreign key of Ward No. in the Patient relation indicates that the Ward relation is master of the Patient relation.

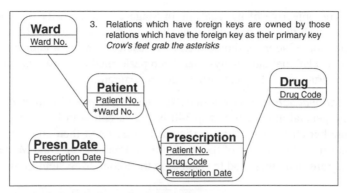

Fig. 4.53 Applying Rule 3 to the Drug Card relations

Some relations that have many foreign key attributes can have these attributes combined into foreign compound keys. For example, a relation *D* which has foreign keys *a, b,* and *c,* should be owned by a relation *AB* (with key *ab*), if it already exists, rather than be separately owned by the *A* and *B* relations. This follows the general principle of minimizing the number of relationships.

Application of rule 3 completes the conversion of a set of relations into a data structure type diagram. The analyst should check that the diagram makes sense in terms of his or her understanding of the system by asking such questions as 'Does a drug have many prescriptions?' and 'Is a prescription for one and only one drug?'

Once a satisfactory diagram has been produced it should be compared with the Required System Logical Data Structure and any differences between the two diagrams resolved. This comparison will be illustrated by examples from the Yorkies case study in the next part of the section.

Relational data analysis in SSADM

Logical data modelling and relational data analysis are very widely used techniques in systems development. However, the way in which information systems methods use these techniques is variable. Relational data analysis could be performed at any time in a project to produce a database design. Some projects may chose to use relational data analysis as the only technique needed to produce the data design. Other approaches use only entity modelling to produce the data design.

Normally in SSADM, relational data analysis is based on the required system and is used as a complementary technique to entity modelling. Because performing relational data analysis can be very time consuming it is often used as a confirming, checking activity that supports the building of the Required System Logical Data Model.

Relational data analysis in Requirements Analysis

It is sometimes difficult to identify entities and produce the Current Environment Logical Data Model. Normalization of the current system data may help. The sources for analysis will then be the documents of the existing system such as the input forms, output forms, and reports. The files of the existing system are also a useful source as they contain much of the data used by the existing system.

The objective of the analysis in Stage 1 is to identify the major entities and their relationships—an exhaustive analysis to discover all attributes is unnecessary. The selection of sources should then be restricted to a few major inputs, outputs, and files. After relational data analysis has been performed on these, the rationalized relations are converted into a Logical Data Structure diagram.

Relational data analysis in step 340, enhance required data model
The general approach in step 340 is shown below in Fig. 4.54. The idea is to analyse together all the data for a particular function and then compare the resulting diagram with the relevant part of the Required System Logical Data Model. Comparing the two diagrams may then lead to changes in the Required System Logical Data Model.

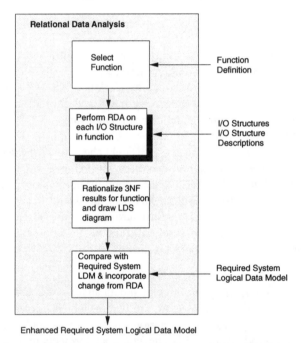

Fig. 4.54 Approach to relational data analysis in Requirements Specification

We first identify the functions whose inputs and outputs we wish to analyse. The success of the data analysis step in SSADM is greatly dependent on the inputs selected for analysis. If insufficient or unrepresentative sources are selected then not all attributes will be discovered and potentially useful data inter-relationships may be missed. If too many sources are selected then the task can be enormous and exhausting.

Each project team needs to decide which functions are subjected to data analysis. Some project managers may feel that their Required System Logical Data Model is detailed and accurate enough to be carried forward without the rigorous checking of relational data analysis. Others may feel less confident in their data model and decide to analyse all the system inputs and outputs. Most projects will decide that some relational data analysis is necessary and select the functions related to the parts of the Required System Logical Data Model in which they have least confidence.

The major data sources for relational data analysis will be the I/O Structures and their supporting I/O Structure Descriptions produced during step 330, *derive system functions*. These detail the data contents and structure of each major input to and output from the system. Sometimes reports or screens produced in step 350, *develop specification prototypes*, are valuable data sources. (Step 340 does not usually precede step 350—they are often performed at the same time by different analysts.) In general, the more structured the definitions of system inputs and outputs are, the easier they will be to analyse. This is because the underlying semantics of the data are often apparent from the way that the data is structured on the inputs and outputs.

It is often suggested that a good source for analysis are the required system Entity Descriptions, which detail the data content of each entity. However, in most projects these will already have been informally normalized. The benefit of a fresh view of the system data provided by analysing inputs and outputs would also be lost. However, project teams *not* performing a thorough analysis on all functions should ensure that all Entity Descriptions are fully normalized.

The comparison between the two diagrams, necessary for their merger, will show many differences in structure which need to be resolved with the future users of the system and against the processing requirements. These differences may result from errors in one of the structures; this error detection demonstrates one of the strengths of employing two distinct techniques for data design. Differences will also result from the ways in which the structures are developed; the relational structures will usually be more complex and flexible to future requirements, whereas the Logical Data Model will usually be simpler and tailored to the specific business requirements identified in systems analysis.

Relational data analysis in the Yorkies case study

The previous sections illustrated the use of relational data analysis with a simplified example. We now demonstrate its use in a more typical SSADM environment using the case study.

The I/O Structures selected for relational data analysis from the Yorkies case study are listed below:

> Booking Confirmation
> Daily Departure and Return List
> Local Office Vehicle Report
> Invoice
> Reminder
> Driver Application/Acceptance

Obviously this is not a complete list—although they cover most areas of the system, analysis of additional I/O Structures would result in a more thorough data design. These examples have been picked to illustrate some of the more common problems with relational data analysis.

Normalization of Booking Confirmation

We will systematically apply the rules of normalization to the system output, Booking Confirmation, whose I/O Structure and I/O Structure Description are repeated in Fig. 4.55. The result of this analysis is shown in Fig. 4.56, which shows each of the stages of normalization.

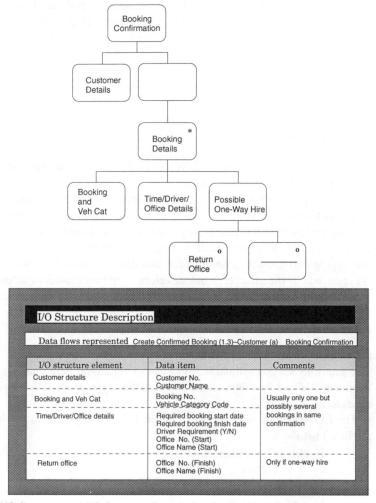

Fig. 4.55 I/O Structure and I/O Structure Description for Booking Confirmation

1. Represent the data in unnormalized form and pick a key Following the SSADM notation described previously, we list the attributes in an unnormalized form (UNF). Naming of attributes can cause quite a problem. Ideally attributes should be named once, the name and the associated data definitions being held in the Data Catalogue. The same name should then be used whenever the same attribute appears on an Entity Description or an I/O Description. This consistency is easy to manage on small projects if CASE tools are used, but with large teams communication can be a problem, particularly if no multi-user CASE facilities are available. If actual screen, report, or form designs are used as data sources then the names of fields on the designs may not correspond to the names used on other SSADM documentation—care must be taken to ensure that consistent names are used for analysis. Whatever support tools are employed some sort of naming convention should be used, giving guidelines on standard abbreviations and on the position of frequently used words (e.g. date, name, description) within attribute names. Some abbreviations have been used below in Fig. 4.56, e.g. *Vehicle* becomes *Veh, Required* becomes *Req,* and *Category* becomes *Cat.*

Note that had we analysed the input Booking Request the attribute, Booking No., would be missing—making normalization difficult. This could then be added to the list of UNF attributes. This kind of addition is very common when analysing system inputs. We only hold confirmed bookings on the system so there is little point in analysing an enquiry prior to update when by adding the Booking No. we can analyse the update.

As each customer will presumably have only one Booking Confirmation with Yorkies at any time, we have selected and underlined Customer No. as the key.

2. Represent the data in First Normal Form by removing any repeating groups of attributes to separate relations. Pick keys for any relations identified The I/O Structure (Fig. 4.55) shows an iteration which indicates the repeating group—it can be useful to show the level of iteration alongside the unnormalized column. In this case the level of the non-repeating information is '1' and the level of the repeating information is '2'. The repeating relation for each booking the customer has made is removed to a new relation. Part of the key must be the key defined in step 1, Customer No., and the other part(s) must identify each occurrence of the repeating group. The only attribute that can do this is Booking No, so the compound key of the new relation is Customer No. with Booking No. The only attribute that does not repeat is Customer Name so this is left in the relation identified by Customer No.

3. Represent the data in Second Normal Form by removing any attributes that only depend upon part of the key to separate relations Second Normal Form is only applicable to compound key relations, so we ask:

> *Do any of the attributes in the relation*
> *identified by Customer No. with Booking No.*
> *depend on either Customer No. alone or on*
> *Booking No. alone?*

Yes, all attributes in that relation are dependent upon Booking No. alone, these are therefore removed to new relation with Booking No. as the key. Note that Customer No. also depends upon Booking No. so that it goes into this relation. (Always look inside compound keys at Second Normal Form to see if any of the key attributes depend on each other.)

4. Represent the data in Third Normal Form by removing any attributes not directly dependent on the key to separate relations Looking at the relation identified by Booking No. we see that there is an inter-data dependency between Office No. and Office Name, these therefore form a separate relation with Office No. as the key. It is not necessary to show two separate relations for the start and finish offices, they can be combined (rationalized) together as all offices act as both starts and finishes. However, both Office No. (Start) and Office No. (Finish) must be left in the relation identified by Booking No. else information would be lost. These are marked with asterisks in Fig. 4.56 to indicate that they are acting as foreign keys.

UNF	1NF	2NF	3NF
<u>Customer No.</u> Customer Name Booking No. Veh Cat Code Req Bookg Start Date Req Bookg Finish Date Driver Req (Y/N) Office No. (Start) Office Name (Start) Office No. (Finish) Office Name (Finish) Date Booking Reciv	<u>Customer No.</u> Customer Name <u>Customer No.</u> <u>Booking No.</u> Veh Cat Code Req Bookg Start Date Req Bookg Finish Date Driver Req (Y/N) Office No. (Start) Office Name (Start) Office No. (Finish) Office Name (Finish) Date Booking Reciv	<u>Customer No.</u> Customer Name <u>Booking No.</u> Customer No. Veh Cat Code Req Bookg Start Date Req Bookg Finish Date Driver Req (Y/N) Office No. (Start) Office Name (Start) Office No. (Finish) Office Name (Finish) Date Booking Reciv	<u>Customer No.</u> Customer Name <u>Booking No.</u> *Customer No. Veh Cat Code Req Bookg Start Date Req Bookg Finish Date Driver Req (Y/N) *Office No. (Start) *Office No. (Finish) Date Booking Reciv <u>Office No.</u> Office Name

Fig. 4.56 Normalization of Booking Confirmation

Customer No. is also a foreign key and is marked with an asterisk to give the Third Normal Form relations shown in Fig. 4.56. Applying the TNF tests to these relations confirms that they are in Third Normal Form.

The next step is to represent the set of relations as a partial Logical Data Structure. We have named the three relations: Customer, Booking, and Local Office. Applying rule 3 ('crow's feet grab the asterisks') shows Booking to have two relationships with Local Office, one indicating the 'from' office and the other indicating the 'to' office. Figure 4.57 is then compared with the complete Required System Logical Data Structure (Fig. 4.58). The partial Logical Data Structure built from the normalization of Booking Confirmation is consistent with the data structure built in step 320, *develop required data model*, so no change is required

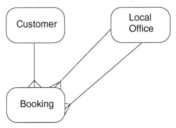

Fig. 4.57 Partial Logical Data Structure from Booking Confirmation

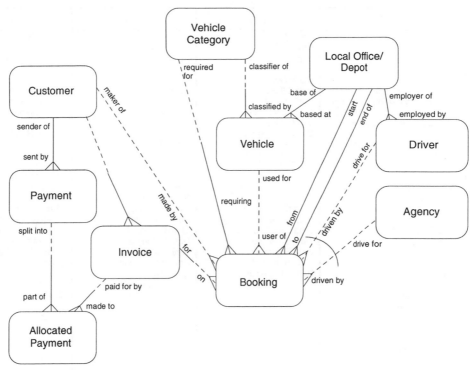

Fig. 4.58 Required System Logical Data Structure before 'enhancement'

Daily Departure and Return List
This is a list of the vehicle departures and returns expected at a particular depot on a particular day. This list is printed at the end of the previous day's business in the office and collected by the depot staff before starting work in the morning. To save space we have included the I/O Structure and Description information in the UNF column of Fig. 4.59.

Date of Report has been removed prior to normalization as it is assumed that this will correspond to either Date Booking Starts or Date Booking Ends. No distinction has been made between the departing bookings and the returning bookings as this distinction is implied by the various dates.

There are several optional fields in this report: Driver No., Driver Name, and Agency Name. They are optional because a booked vehicle may be driven by a customer, by a Yorkies driver, or by an agency driver. Some analysts mark optional attributes with a preceding 'O'. This can give rise to optional foreign keys e.g. O* Driver No. These would then result in optional or exclusive relationships on the Logical Data Structure.

The partial Logical Data Structure (not shown—you may wish to develop it as an exercise) developed from the relations is consistent with the Required System Logical Data Structure.

UNF	1NF	2NF	3NF
Office No.	Office No.	Office No.	Office No.
Office Name	Office Name	Office Name	Office Name
Depot Address	Depot Address	Depot Address	Depot Address
Date of Report			
	Office No.	Booking No.	Booking No.
Then a list of Bookings	Booking No.	Customer No.	*Customer No.
separated into departures and	Customer No.	Customer Name	Veh Cat Req
returns. The following items are	Customer Name	Veh Cat Req	Date Booking Starts
included for each Booking.	Veh Cat Req	Date Booking Starts	Date Booking Ends
Some will be blank on the	Date Booking Starts	Date Booking Ends	Driver Req (Y/N)
report and be completed on	Date Booking Ends	Driver Req (Y/N)	Veh Reg Mark
return or departure.	Driver Req (Y/N)	Veh Reg Mark	Agency Name
	Veh Reg Mark	Agency Name	*Driver No.
Booking No.	Agency Name	Driver No.	Start Mileage
Customer No.	Driver No.	Driver Name	Finish Mileage
Customer Name	Driver Name	Start Mileage	Date Collected
Veh Cat Req	Start Mileage	Finish Mileage	Time Collected
Date Booking Starts	Finish Mileage	Date Collected	Date Returned
Date Booking Ends	Date Collected	Time Collected	Time Returned
Driver Req (Y/N)	Time Collected	Date Returned	Return Condition
Veh Reg Mark	Date Returned	Time Returned	*Office No. (Start)
Agency Name	Time Returned	Return Condition	*Office No. (Finish)
Driver No.	Return Condition	Office No. (Start)	
Driver Name	Office No. (Start)	Office No. (Finish)	Customer No.
Start Mileage	Office No. (Finish)		Customer Name
Finish Mileage			
Date Collected			Driver No.
Time Collected			Driver Name
Date Returned			
Time Returned			
Return Condition			
Office No. (Start)			
Office No. (Finish)			

Fig. 4.59 Normalization of Daily Departure and Return List

Normalization of Local Office Vehicle Report
This printed report details all of the vehicles registered at a particular Local Office broken down by their Vehicle Categories.

In this example we have a nested repeating group, shown by the iteration within an iteration on the I/O Structure. We have indicated the levels of nesting: on the I/O Structure in Fig. 4.60, by slightly indenting and separating each nested group in the unnormalized form column, and by using a separate 'Level' column in the normalization (Fig. 4.61).

These 'Levels' can help us sort out First Normal Form:

• Level 1 is the non-repeating group and has the initial key identified in UNF;
• Level 2 is a repeating group and will have the key of the Level 1 group plus at least one additional key attribute;
• Level 3 is a repeating group within the Level 2 group and will have the key of the Level 2 group plus at least one additional key attribute;
• further levels are treated in the same way.

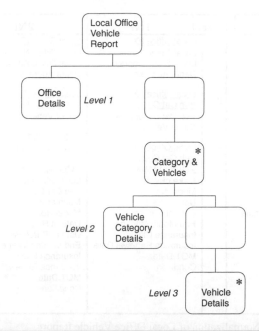

Fig. 4.60 I/O Structure and I/O Structure Description for Local Office Vehicle Report

Thus First Normal Form produces the two-attribute and three-attribute compound keys shown in Fig. 4.61. Part key dependencies are removed from both of these compound key relations. The three-attribute key relation has inter-key dependencies in that Local Office ID and Veh Cat Code both depend on Veh Reg Mark. These give the Second Normal Form relations which are also in Third Normal Form.

UNF	Level	1NF	2NF	3NF
Local Office ID	1	Local Office ID	Local Office ID	Local Office ID
Local Office Name		Local Office Name	Local Office Name	Local Office Name
Local Office Address		Local Office Address	Local Office Address	Local Office Address
Depot Address		Depot Address	Depot Address	Depot Address
Veh Cat Code	2	Local Office ID	Local Office ID	Local Office ID
Veh Cat Description		Veh Cat Code	Veh Cat Code	Veh Cat Code
No. of Vehicles		Veh Cat Description	No. of Vehicles	No. of Vehicles
		No. of Vehicles		
			Veh Cat Code	Veh Cat Code
Veh Reg Mark	3	Local Office ID	Veh Cat Description	Veh Cat Description
Make of Veh		Veh Cat Code		
Model No.		Veh Reg Mark	Veh Reg Mark	Veh Reg Mark
Date of Reg		Make of Veh	Local Office ID	*Local Office ID
Date of Purchase		Model No.	Veh Cat Code	*Veh Cat Code
End Month Mileage		Date of Reg	Make of Veh	Make of Veh
Insurance Class		Date of Purchase	Model No.	Model No.
Insurance Renewal Date		End Month Mileage	Date of Reg	Date of Reg
MOT Date		Insurance Class	Date of Purchase	Date of Purchase
Condition		Insurance Renewal Date	End Month Mileage	End Month Mileage
		MOT Date	Insurance Class	Insurance Class
		Condition	Insurance Renewal Date	Insurance Renewal Date
			MOT Date	MOT Date
			Condition	Condition

Fig. 4.61 Normalization of Local Office Vehicle Report

The No. of Vehicles attribute can be calculated by counting the occurrences in the Vehicle relation with the particular Local Office ID and the particular Veh Cat Code. Attributes whose value can be found by examining the values of other attributes are known as *derived attributes*. These attributes can often be removed from the normalized relations without loss of information (the No. of Vehicles attribute could be removed). Sometimes, the value is derived on a particular date and then the data it is derived from is deleted or amended—then removing the derived attribute will lose important information.[1]

In many physical database designs, derived attributes are retained to avoid repeated recalculations, though this sacrifices space and risks inconsistent data to improve performance. It is recommended that derived attributes are kept until the completion of the Required System Logical Data Model at the end of step 340 and then reconsidered with respect to the whole system's data. All derived attributes should be described in the Data Catalogue with the method of derivation described on the Attribute Description or on the Grouped Domain Description.

We now need to build the partial Logical Data Structure from the normalized relations. First, we need to name the relations. The single key relations are straightforward and follow from the names of the keys. The compound key relation (Local Office ID, Veh Cat Code, No. of Vehicles) is more difficult to name; if we

---

[1] A good example is the Balance attribute in an Account entity—clearly the Balance could be derived but none of the individual debits or credits on which it is based could be archived. Take particular care with financial information to ensure audit trails are preserved.

couldn't think of anything suitable we would resort to 'Office/Category Link' or something similar. We have named the relation, 'Number at Depot', because it shows the number of vehicles of a particular category at a particular depot at any time.

The Number at Depot relation is detail to the two relations that have Local Office ID and Veh Cat Code as their primary keys (Rule 2). The Local Office ID and Veh Cat Code foreign key attributes in the Vehicle relation indicate the masters of Local Office/Depot and Vehicle Category (Rule 3). (We could link Vehicle directly to Number at Depot but we know that the other relationships already occur in the required data model so there is no chance of removing them.) The partial Logical Data Structure from Local Office Vehicle Report is shown in Fig. 4.62.

The Number at Depot entity does not appear on the Required System Logical Data Structure (Fig. 4.58) produced in step 320, *develop required data model*. We need to investigate whether the new entity is required. The attribute No. of Vehicles, contained in the Number at Depot entity, can be derived (as discussed above). The information about whether vehicles of a particular category are at a particular depot can be determined from other entities and relationships. The Number at Depot entity is therefore redundant and is omitted from the Required System Logical Data Model.

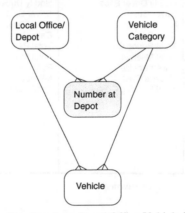

Fig. 4.62 Partial Logical Data Structure from Local Office Vehicle Report

Normalization of invoice
Invoices are produced every two weeks and for active customers several bookings may be included on the same invoice. To save space we have included the I/O Structure and Description information in the UNF column of Fig. 4.63. Normalization of the invoice is straightforward to Second Normal Form but some interesting points arise at Third Normal Form. Veh Cat Code is dependent on Veh Reg Mark and so is removed to a separate relation. There are several attributes associated with the prices for a category which are removed to the relation identified by Veh Cat Code. The Office Name attributes are not directly dependent on the Booking No., they depend on Office No. (shown in the normalization of Booking Confirmation). These are therefore replaced by the directly dependent foreign key attributes of Office No.

UNF	1NF	2NF	3NF
Invoice No.	Invoice No.	Invoice No.	Invoice No.
Invoice Date	Invoice Date	Invoice Date	Invoice Date
Customer No.	Customer No.	Customer No.	*Customer No.
Customer Name	Customer Name	Customer Name	Invoice Amount
Customer Address	Customer Address	Customer Address	
Invoice Amount	Invoice Amount	Invoice Amount	Customer No.
			Customer Name
An invoice may be for several	Invoice No.	Booking No.	Customer Address
bookings. These items are	Booking No.	Invoice No.	
included for each Booking:	Veh Cat Code	Veh Cat Code	Booking No.
	Veh Cat Description	Veh Cat Description	*Invoice No.
Booking No.	Veh Reg Mark	Veh Reg Mark	*Veh Reg Mark
Veh Cat Code	Office Name (Start)	Office Name (Start)	*Office No. (Start)
Veh Cat Description	Date Collected	Date Collected	Date Collected
Veh Reg Mark	Time Collected	Time Collected	Time Collected
Office Name (Start)	Start Mileage	Start Mileage	Start Mileage
Date Collected	Office Name (Finish)	Office Name (Finish)	*Office No. (Finish)
Time Collected	Date Returned	Date Returned	Date Returned
Start Mileage	Time Returned	Time Returned	Time Returned
Office Name (Finish)	Finish Mileage	Finish Mileage	Finish Mileage
Date Returned	Return Condition	Return Condition	Return Condition
Time Returned	Damage Charges	Damage Charges	Damage Charges
Finish Mileage	Driver Hours	Driver Hours	Driver Hours
Return Condition	Hourly Driver Price	Hourly Driver Price	Driver Cost
Damage Charges	Driver Cost	Driver Cost	No. of Days
Driver Hours	No. of Days	No. of Days	Total Period Cost
Hourly Driver Price	Daily Price	Daily Price	Total Mileage
Driver Cost	Total Period Cost	Total Period Cost	Mileage Cost
No. of Days	Total Mileage	Total Mileage	Total Booking Cost
Daily Price	Price per Mile	Price per Mile	
Total Period Cost	Mileage Cost	Mileage Cost	Veh Reg Mark
Total Mileage	Total Booking Cost	Total Booking Cost	*Veh Cat Code
Price per Mile			
Mileage Cost			Veh Cat Code
Total Booking Cost			Veh Cat Description
			Hourly Driver Price
			Daily Price
			Price per Mile

Fig. 4.63 Normalization of Invoice

The data structure resulting from the normalization of Invoice matches the relevant part of the Required System Logical Data Structure (Fig. 4.58). The partial structure is not shown here but may be developed by the reader as a simple exercise.

Normalization of Reminder

To identify uniquely each reminder we need a combination of the Invoice No. and the Reminder No. attributes because the Reminder No. is just a sequence number for that invoice (e.g. Invoice No. 34567; Reminder No. 2). The Reminder No. cannot therefore identify a reminder on its own, it needs the qualifying attribute of Invoice No. This special case of a compound key, where one or more of the key attributes has no unique significance throughout the system, is known as a *hierarchic key*. The attribute that is required to make the combination unique is known as the *qualifying element*, thus Invoice No. is the qualifying element of Reminder No. The SSADM convention is to

show hierarchic keys by surrounding each attribute with brackets and to show the
qualifying elements first, as shown in Fig. 4.64.

Fig. 4.64 Notation for a hierarchic key

When we go from First to Second Normal Forms we cannot have part key dependency
on the non-unique part of the key. So in this example the only part key dependency is
on the qualifying attribute, Invoice No. (see Fig. 4.65).

UNF	1NF	2NF	3NF
(Invoice No.) (Reminder No.) Customer No. Customer Name Customer Address Invoice Date Invoice Amount Reminder Date	(Invoice No.) (Reminder No.) Customer No. Customer Name Customer Address Invoice Date Invoice Amount Reminder Date	(Invoice No.) (Reminder No.) Reminder Date Invoice No. Customer No. Customer Name Customer Address Invoice Date Invoice Amount	(Invoice No.) (Reminder No.) Reminder Date Invoice No. *Customer No. Invoice Date Invoice Amount Customer No. Customer Name Customer Address

Fig. 4.65 Normalization of Reminder

To draw the partial Logical Data Structure we need to use Rule 1b:

> *If a compound key is also a hierarchic key then*
> *the qualifying unique attribute(s) is marked as*
> *a foreign key in that relation and in any others*
> *where it occurs. Do not create an entity for the*
> *non-unique attribute(s) of the hierarchic key.*

The key of Reminder is a hierarchic key of Invoice No. (the qualifying attribute) and
Reminder No. (the non-unique part). So we mark the Invoice No. component of the
hierarchic key as a foreign key. When we apply Rule 3 ('crow's feet grab the asterisks')
the Reminder entity becomes the detail entity of the Invoice entity as shown in Fig.
4.66.

Fig. 4.66 Partial Logical Data Structure from normalization of Reminder

Reminder does not appear on the Required System Logical Data Structure (Fig. 4.58). After discussion with the users it is decided that, as only three reminders are issued before legal action is started, the Reminder Dates could be held in the Invoice entity. The Reminder entity is not included in the Required System Logical Data Model but the Entity Description of Invoice is amended to include the three extra attributes.

Normalization of Driver Application/Acceptance
This represents the information entered into the system when a new driver is employed by Yorkies. Notice that the First Normal Form relations are also in Second and Third Normal Forms—rather than repeat the relations in those columns we have used arrows as a shorthand.

UNF	1NF	2NF	3NF
Driver No Driver Name Driver Address Driver Tel No Date Appointed Local Office No Region Code *Then information about the various licences the driver holds.* Driving Licence Type Date Passed	Driver No Driver Name Driver Address Driver Tel No. Date Appointed Local Office No. Region Code Driver No. Driver Licence Type Date Passed	' '	' '

Fig. 4.67 Normalization of Driver Application/Acceptance

To produce the partial Logical Data Structure from the normalized relations we need to use Rule 1a:

> *If a part of a compound key does not exist as a primary key of another relation then this attribute is shown as an entity and is marked as a foreign key in any other relations it occurs in.*

Driving Licence Type does not appear as the primary key of any other entities or relations so it becomes a separate entity which becomes the master of Driver under Rule 2 as shown in Fig. 4.68 below. Driving Licence Type is also an attribute in the Vehicle Category entity and so is marked as a foreign key there. This results in the Driving Licence Type entity becoming master to the Vehicle Category entity (shown in the finalized Required System Logical Data Structure, Fig. 4.69).

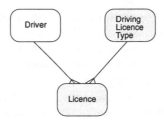

Fig. 4.68 Partial Logical Data Structure from Driver Application/Acceptance

Licence Type and Licence do not appear in the Required System Logical Data Structure. The users decide they prefer the extra flexibility offered by their inclusion. They will help Driver Administration staff to assign drivers to bookings. Thus the Required System Logical Data Structure is amended to include the new entities and relationships.

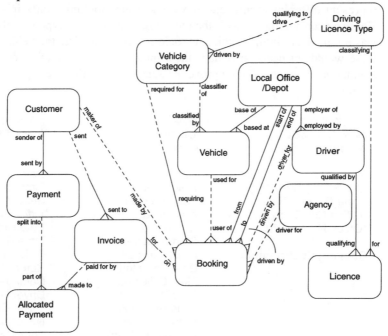

Fig. 4.69 Required System Logical Data Structure after 'enhancement'

Rationalization of Yorkies relations
We have demonstrated the normalization of the following Yorkies I/O Structures: Booking Confirmation; Daily Departure and Return List; Local Office Vehicle Report; Invoice; Reminder and Driver Application/Acceptance. In each case the resulting relations were turned into a partial data structure, compared with the Required System Logical Data Structure, and differences resolved. Normally several I/O Structures from a particular function are normalized, the resulting relations are rationalized and the data

structure built. As none of the functions examined included more than one I/O Structure no rationalization was necessary. We concentrated on merging the diagrams but it was also necessary to examine the content of the relations and compare this with the Entity Descriptions. As a demonstration we will rationalize the three relations that have Booking No. as their primary key.

These three relations (Fig. 4.70) can be rationalized together to form one relation which we shall call the Booking relation. The easiest way of doing this is to take the relation with most attributes (i.e. the one from Invoice) and merge the other relations into it.

Merging the relation from Daily Departure and Return List, we see that there are several attributes that do not correspond exactly (shown in *italics*). These should be examined carefully to ensure that they are not synonyms (the same attribute but with a different name). When merging attributes of the same name from different relations care should be taken to recognize homonyms (attributes that have the same name but represent different things; e.g. if we had Date Booking Starts in both the Booking Confirmation and the Invoice, then in the request it would represent the date the vehicle was required and in the Invoice it would represent the date the vehicle was collected— these would not necessarily have the same value). The use of a good Data Catalogue, manual or automated, should prove invaluable in avoiding these problems with attribute definition.

Booking No.	Booking No.	Booking No.
Veh Cat Code	*Customer No.*	*Invoice No.
Customer No.	*Veh Cat Req*	*Veh Reg Mark
Req Booking Start Date	*Date Booking Starts*	*Office No. (Start)
Req Booking Finish Date	*Date Booking Ends*	Date Collected
Driver Req (Y/N)	*Driver Req (Y/N)*	Time Collected
Date Booking Reciv	Veh Reg Mark	Start Mileage
*Office No. (Start)	*Agency Name*	*Office No. (Finish)
*Office No. (Finish)	* *Driver No.*	Date Returned
	Start Mileage	Time Returned
Booking Confirmation	Finish Mileage	Finish Mileage
	Date Collected	Return Condition
	Time Collected	Damage Charges
	Date Returned	Driver Hours
	Time Returned	Driver Cost
	Return Condition	No. of Days
	*Office No. (Start)	Total Period Cost
	*Office No. (Finish)	Total Mileage
		Mileage Cost
	Daily Departure and	Total Booking Cost
	Return List	
		Invoice

Fig. 4.70 Relations to be rationalized into one Booking relation

When we merge in the attributes from the Booking Confirmation we see that we have several synonyms that can be combined (these are only synonyms if we are dealing with the confirmation rather than the request since it may not be possible to provide what is requested). These are then merged and the most appropriate attribute name used. This gives the Booking relation shown in Fig. 4.71.

When we have produced our rationalized relations we must apply the two TNF tests to them to ensure that redundancy has not been introduced during rationalization. Applying the first test:

> *Given a value for the key(s) of a TNF relation,*
> *is there just one possible value for each*
> *attribute in that relation?*

Yes, this relation passes the first test.

Applying the second test:

> *Is each attribute in a TNF relation directly and*
> *wholly dependent on the key(s) of that*
> *relation?*

BOOKING

Booking No.
*Invoice No.
*Veh Reg Mark
*Veh Cat Code Req
*Office No. (Start)
*Office No. (Finish)
*Customer No.
*Driver No.
 Agency Name
 Date Collected
 Time Collected
 Start Mileage
 Date Returned
 Time Returned
 Finish Mileage
 Return Condition
 Damage Charges
 Driver Hours
 Driver Cost
 No. of Days
 Total Period Cost
 Total Mileage
 Mileage Cost
 Total Booking Cost
 Veh Cat Code Req
 Date Booking Starts
 Date Booking Ends
 Driver Req (Y/N)
 Date Booking Reciv

Fig. 4.71 Rationalized Booking relation

This relation appears to fail the second test in that we seem to have returned the relation to Second Normal Form by including the Veh Cat Code and Customer No. foreign key attributes. These were directly dependent upon Veh Reg Mark and Invoice No. when the invoice was analysed. However, Customer No. is directly dependent on Booking No. in the early life of a booking as an Invoice No. will not be assigned until later. The Veh Cat Code Req will also be directly dependent in the early life of Booking since the particular vehicle is not assigned until later. It is also possible that the Veh Cat Code Req might be different from the vehicle category actually used, so the removal of this attribute could mean the loss of valuable information. Therefore this relation does pass the second TNF test.

When the results of this rationalization are combined with the relation that results from the analysis of the Vehicle Relocation Booking (normalization of this was not demonstrated previously) another typical problem arises. We are merging two relations that have the same key but represent different things. One represents a booking by a customer and the other an internal booking; by merging them we risk losing the information that distinguishes them. Relational theory does allow us to have several different relations that have the same primary key but only if each relation has a different name. However, this is generally not recommended. (They might have been modelled using entity sub-types in the early versions of the Logical Data Structure.) The usual solution is to merge the two relations but to include a new attribute which is simply an indicator to which population the particular occurrence belongs. Thus in this case we create a new attribute called Internal Booking Ind to indicate the internal vehicle relocation bookings.

Support documentation

When the Required System Logical Data Structure has been produced its support documentation can be finalized. This will require production of Entity Descriptions from a merger of the Entity Descriptions from step 320 and of the normalized relations.

The Entity Descriptions will be used to define the detailed data content of the new system and will be used for physical data definition of records, files, tables, and so on in Stage 6, Physical Design, and in the construction phases of the development. The production of these Entity Descriptions requires several activities:

- Extending the Entity Descriptions developed in steps 140 and 320 to include the data content identified by relational data analysis.
- Developing Entity Descriptions for any new entities identified by relational data analysis.
- Ensuring that the entities identified by logical data modelling alone have their primary and foreign keys correctly defined.
- Ensuring that the Data Catalogue (described in Sec. 3.5) is complete, new entries may be required for attributes identified in step 340.

This documentation of entities, attributes, and relationships is best held in a computerized data dictionary package. This could be the repository of a CASE tool or could be the data dictionary employed by the database management system to be used for the development.

SUMMARY

Relational data analysis is a bottom-up technique based on analysing the inter-relationships between attributes.

The product of relational data analysis is a set of normalized relations (or tables) which minimize redundancy of data and avoid consistency problems.

Each relation is composed of rows and columns:

- Columns map to attributes identified in the early stages of SSADM.
- Each occurrence of a row can be uniquely identified by a combination of attributes known as the primary key.

Relational data analysis is applied to set of attributes, known as data sources, which are usually required system inputs or outputs.

A normalized set of relations is produced from each data source by following these steps:

- Represent the attributes in unnormalized form and pick attribute(s) to act as key.
- Put the data in First Normal Form by removing repeating groups to separate relations.
- Put the data in Second Normal Form by removing part-key dependent attributes to separate relations.
- Put the data in Third Normal Form by removing attributes not directly dependent on the key to separate relations.

The above process is often called normalization.

The results of normalization of each data source are combined together by merging all relations with the same key. This process is known as rationalization.

After rationalization two tests are applied to ensure that the data is in Third Normal Form.

- Given a value for the key(s) of a TNF relation, is there just one possible value for each attribute in that relation?
- Is each attribute in a TNF relation directly and wholly dependent on the key(s) of that relation?

The relations are represented as a data structure diagram to aid comparison with the Logical Data Structure.

- The two diagrams are merged and differences resolved with reference to the processing requirements and to the users.
- The Entity Descriptions are extended to show the full data content defined by the relations.
- Any remaining documentation of the system's data, such as Entity Descriptions, Attribute Descriptions, and Relationship Descriptions, is completed.

Exercise

4.5.1   Scapegoat Systems

Apply relational data analysis to the Staff Allocation Sheet and the Invoice from Scapegoat Systems. I/O Structures were produced for these in the exercises at the end of Sec. 4.4. You may also find it useful to look at the sample documents supplied in this previous exercise.

The following end-products are required:

a) A normalized set of relations from the analysis of the Staff Allocation Sheet.
b) A normalized set of relations from the analysis of the Invoice.
c) The rationalized set of relations.
d) A data structure diagram representing the rationalized relations.
e) Compare this with the Required System Logical Data Structure, developed in Sec. 4.3. Identify any differences and combine to produce a new (enhanced) Required System Logical Data Structure.

4.6   Develop specification prototypes (step 350)

Introduction

Prototyping has been described as an approach 'lacking tightly written systems design specifications' which is capable of 'providing the user with a tentative system for experimental purposes at the earliest possible time' and which can evolve into the production system. Prototyping in information systems design has been subject to much discussion recently, with many articles and books being published. There are two major reasons for this recent interest:

Users find it impossible to specify their requirements The future users of a system find it very difficult to imagine what it will look like until it is in front of them. It is very common for a project team to feel sure that a thorough analysis has been performed, but after implementation many enhancements are requested by the users. Only by seeing what the system looks like and experimenting with some of the facilities can users decide what is really required.

Modern tools enable rapid systems development Many projects now use fourth-generation software for systems development. This software provides a number of facilities that make rapid construction of business information systems possible. They provide some or all of the following facilities: relational database management systems, data dictionaries, very high-level languages, end-user query languages, report writers, tools for building interactive systems such as screen painters, and CASE tools for analysis and design and sometimes generation of code.

Although prototypes are built early in the systems development life cycle, most authors agree that some basic data and function modelling are necessary first. It is also widely accepted that prototyping should be controlled as part of a systems development method.

There are basically two kinds of prototype: ones which will be thrown away and ones which will eventually be developed into a full production system. The 'throw away' variety are used as a learning medium between the developer and the user to help them converge on an adequate set of requirements. Typically 'throw away' prototypes are built very rapidly, very early in requirements analysis but will sacrifice certain aspects of the system such as error handling, security, and performance. The 'developable' prototype will evolve into a working system; sometimes 'throw away' prototypes turn into 'developable' ones.

The SSADM approach to prototyping is characterized by careful management control, by clearly defining the scope of prototyping, and by being 'throw away' but accepting that some aspects of the prototype may be retained in the delivered system. Step 350, *develop specification prototypes*, deals with the selection, construction, demonstration, evaluation, review, and re-specification of the core critical functions subjected to prototyping.

SSADM has learnt much from recent experience with prototyping in including it within the core of SSADM. It is important to distinguish the SSADM approach from other variations on the prototyping theme such as: 'rapid prototyping', 'evolutionary prototyping', and 'incremental prototyping'.[1] Rapid prototyping is performed very early, perhaps after only two or three days investigation, and is usually 'throw away' with the results being incorporated into the specification. Evolutionary prototyping occurs when there is more initial investigation leading to the building of a prototype which evolves and grows into the delivered system. Incremental prototyping occurs when the project is partitioned into smaller sub-projects which are delivered one-at-a-time to the user until the whole system is assembled. Each of these approaches has an important place in systems development.[2]

---

[1] There is little consensus and much ambiguity about these terms—many authors, including ourselves, feel that the word 'prototyping' has been misused and can often be replaced by the word 'development'.

[2] See CCTA (1993) *Prototyping within an SSADM Environment* (HMSO, London).

Why build prototypes?

To test technical or operational feasibility   There may be doubt about whether certain functions, specified in the required system, are technically feasible. This is unlikely with the typical information system but there may be some advanced features (e.g. knowledge-based aspects of the system) that stretch the available technology. Other functions may be unworkable for operational reasons, such as functions requiring the user to enter a lot of data very quickly. These 'doubtful' functions should be prototyped and different approaches to them explored.

To ensure that the requirements are correctly specified   A lot of effort has been spent trying to identify the requirements; building the Requirements Catalogue, developing Business Systems Options, and specifying them using Function Definitions. Providing the user with an animated specification is a good way of checking these requirements; demonstrating menus, screens, and the navigation between them. Errors identified will be corrected and fed back into the specification.

Prototyping helps break down the traditional barriers between IT staff and users. The mutual learning process can generate confidence in each other, improve co-operation, increase the feeling of being part of the same team, and give feelings of ownership and commitment to both users and developers.

When is prototyping most effective?

If users are uncertain of their requirements   This is particularly likely if there is little previous experience with computerized information systems or if there is no current system. The users may find it difficult to visualize the new systems functions from the SSADM documentation such as Data Flow Diagrams, Function Definitions, and I/O Structures.

The project might have a huge list of requirements and when the prototype is demonstrated the users may say that certain ones aren't really necessary. The formal process that SSADM uses in Business System Options should have filtered the unnecessary requirements out. If a prototype is built that covers 'frill' requirements then some effort has been wasted but it's preferable that these are identified early. (More effort would be wasted if the 'frills' are delivered.)

If certain dialogues have a great impact   Often system performance is dominated by a few transactions. These critical dialogues will be those that occur most frequently, and/or those that where failure, errors, or user dissatisfaction can lead to disastrous consequences.

If a dialogue occurs very frequently then prototyping can help design an efficient dialogue by considering both the user and the computer sides of the interaction. The dialogue may be designed so that, while a transaction is being performed by the computer, the user can do other tasks. Often the users and the designers only become aware of these possibilities when the prototype is demonstrated. Getting the design right provides great savings and greater efficiency, and getting it wrong loses these. Worse still the wrong design may alienate the users so much that they reject the system.

Prototyping might identify that the computer's response time is critical in a particular dialogue. Finding the problem at this point ensures that later: in Technical System Options, hardware and software is specified that is able to provide the performance; in Physical Design, the program design is tuned to obtain that performance; and finally, that the problem does *not* surface when the system 'goes live'.[1]

Risks of prototyping

Raised user expectations are, of course, a big problem. Here are some typical reactions from users at the prototype demonstration:

'Lovely, I'll have one tomorrow' Or the user might ask: 'If you can do this in two weeks, why are you planning two years to build the system?' Often the user has a point—we do take too long to build systems.[2] Users must be educated to understand the process of developing systems and software. They need to know that writing bug-free, consistent software that meets requirements, that preserves the integrity of data when the plug is pulled, and that supports 1000 users simultaneously is a difficult, expensive, highly skilled, and time-consuming process. There is more to the system than a few menus and screens.

'Nice (inter)face' The interface demonstrated to the user may be more (or less) flexible, intuitive, and user friendly than the eventual interface.[3] Some tools, like Visual Basic, can be used to rapidly produce prototype graphical user interfaces (GUIs). These can raise user expectations only to have them dashed when they are delivered a character based interface. On the other hand, some prototyping tools, particularly those included in CASE products, may offer limited facilities for demonstrating the interface (typically screen and menu painting with some navigation). Then the prototype may be unable to demonstrate many features of the eventual system—demoralizing the user, and making it harder for them to visualize the dialogue and suggest improvements. Ideally the prototype should mirror as closely as possible the eventual interface style.

'It's very fast' The prototype may appear to work dazzlingly quickly to the user, due to dedicated facilities, absence of large amounts of data, etc. This can also raise expectations of the performance of the future system—again user education is the answer. (However, programmers have been known to build in delays to avoid this problem.)

There are other potential problems frequently encountered when prototyping which are more concerned with the process than with the user. Most of these risks are minimized by the SSADM approach, which carefully controls specification prototyping.

---

[1] A tragic example of this problem was the recent implementation of a computer system for the London Ambulance Service that left casualties waiting for up to five hours.

[2] Our feeling is that projects should be designed to be able to deliver something usable, not necessarily the whole system, within one elapsed year.

[3] The kind of technical environment used to build the system is not finally decided until the Technical System Options stage but in practice, many projects decide on the type of product, if not the actual product, to be used for developing dialogues during project initiation, during Feasibility, or during Business System Options.

Constant redefinition of project boundaries The users might say 'Oh yes, well that's nice, but could you do this, and could you do that?' and thus extend the project boundary. An SSADM project is less likely than most to have this problem as careful requirements definition and options work has been performed. However, if it does occur it's better that the new requirements are identified now rather than when the system is delivered. User and project management must agree that the change in boundary is fully justified.

Excessive iteration of prototypes Often the analyst (who now has the opportunity to revisit his or her earlier life as a programmer) is tempted, egged on by a sympathetic user, to produce a 'perfect' prototype. This leads to many iterations around the define/redefine, implement, demonstrate, review loop shown later in Fig. 4.73. This problem often occurs when incremental or evolutionary prototyping (i.e. a developable prototype) rather than when specification prototyping is used.

Lack of documentation This can be a serious problem with 'developable' prototypes. When the system is delivered there may be little documentation of the design, and the program code may be unstructured and poorly commented. This makes maintenance of the system very difficult. Documentation after construction is unlikely to be completed. Because specification prototypes are thrown away and the results of prototyping documented in the Requirements Specification, the problem is less likely to occur in SSADM.

Lack of standardization between dialogues If several analysts each develop prototypes for a particular functional areas then inconsistencies in the interfaces can develop (e.g. in use of function keys, menus, or colour). SSADM recommends the use of a *style guide* to define interface standards and help ensure that a consistent interface is built. When the detail of the technical environment is decided in the Technical System Options stage then an Application Style Guide is built. Before then the organization may have defined general standards in an Installation Style Guide, which can be used to give a consistent look to the prototype. (Or the project might use standards defined by the manufacturer or software supplier, e.g. IBM's Common User Access standards.) Style guides are described in more detail in Sec. 5.4.

Place in SSADM

The major decision that has to be made by senior users and project management is whether prototyping should be performed at all. Step 350, *develop specification prototypes*, is an optional step in SSADM—prototyping is inappropriate for some projects. Typically inappropriate projects are those where all of the user requirements are very clear, where the users have a very good understanding of the future system and can visualize it well, where great changes to working practices are not envisaged, and where great costs and risks to the development are not expected. Thus a rewrite of a currently computerized system onto new hardware and software would usually not prototype. Other projects showing some of the counter-indications might only use specification prototyping for a very small number of functions providing that the exercise could be cost justified.

Specification prototyping follows on from step 330, *derive system functions*, where critical functions were selected as good candidates for prototyping. The prototyping step is usually carried out in parallel with relational data analysis (step 340) and with entity-event modelling (step 360). It is usually performed by different staff. The results of prototyping may feed back into Function Definitions or may lead to the definition of new events. In this way it may be necessary to revisit steps 330 and 360 after prototyping to ensure a full set of functions and events are defined. Figure 4.72 below shows the inputs and outputs to step 350.

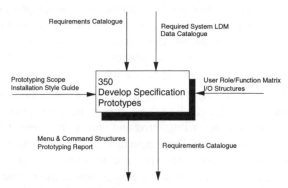

Fig. 4.72 Inputs and outputs to step 350, *develop specification prototypes*

Inputs to and outputs from prototyping
A major input to the step is the Prototyping Scope decided by project management and senior users. This describes the objectives of the prototyping, the functions to be prototyped, and the resources available (development staff, users, and equipment). Ideally, measurable ways of evaluating the prototype should be defined. The scope of prototyping could vary from none at all, to the majority of system functions. Management need to judge the relative advantages, risks, and costs of developing prototypes for each of the functional areas.

General interface standards covering aspects such as screen positions, use of function keys, and use of colour are important to provide a consistent design for the prototype. These may be described by a style guide. The Required System Logical Data Model and the Data Catalogue provide the definitions of the system's data attributes needed to build screens and reports.

In step 330, *derive system functions*, the User Role/Function Matrix was used to identify critical dialogues (see Fig. 4.22). Most of these are good candidates for prototyping; some may not be, usually those that are only critical for performance reasons. The users may identify additional dialogues that they regard as critical. For all dialogues, I/O Structures and supporting descriptions were developed during function definition; these form the basic designs for the prototype. Menus and navigation between dialogues are often prototyped and will give rise to formal Menu Structures and Command Structures to be passed to step 510, *define user dialogues*.

The Requirements Catalogue helps to identify critical dialogues for prototyping but may also identify critical reports. It is often useful to prototype the layout of important reports such as: those conforming to legal regulations, those outputs passing to other computerized information systems, and those used in a formal way by other organizations. These report prototypes are shown to the relevant external entities (or user roles) for comment and approval.

Many of the changes identified by specification prototyping will require amendment to the Requirements Catalogue. Particular attention should be given to some of the non-functional requirements associated with dialogues such as ease of use or response time—these will be examined in greater detail in step 370, *confirm systems objectives*.

The Prototyping Report is to management. This details the changes identified by prototyping, discusses and evaluates the approach taken, and assesses the general impact on the project.

Management and control of prototyping

Prototyping is an iterative activity and needs tight management control to define objectives, to ensure that these are followed, and to evaluate results. It is also important to select the right staff to develop and demonstrate the prototype, and the right users to evaluate it.

The prototyping cycle

Figure 4.73 shows the iterative prototyping cycle. The prototype is defined, then it is implemented or constructed, then demonstrated to the user, and finally reviewed to see what improvements or changes are necessary. This review may lead into another cycle. SSADM gives clear guidelines on each of these phases within the cycle—these are discussed later in this section. Obviously it is important to control this cycle otherwise the iteration never ends.

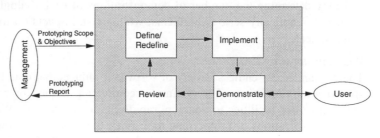

Fig. 4.73 The iterative nature of prototyping

Prototyping team

The suggested minimum team is two analysts and a team leader, who may be part time. Obviously this presupposes a medium sized project as other members of the project team will probably be simultaneously working on relational data analysis and entity-event modelling—small projects would have to manage with a smaller prototype team (however, demonstrations and reviews seem to work better with two development staff involved).

Normally analysts develop prototypes but obviously some experience in the tool is desirable and programmers may be used for construction. Two project staff should always be involved in each demonstration; this helps to ensure objectivity. The prototype might be demonstrated by the person who constructed the software; while another analyst takes notes, observes the user reaction, and probes the user more deeply. The developer of the software is naturally over-protective of his or her own work.

It is also important to select carefully which users to demonstrate to. They should be the people who will perform the dialogue in the future system, and possibly their immediate managers. It is best to select users who are supportive of the new system and can think creatively about how it may be designed.

The prototyping team are responsible for selecting the dialogues and reports for implementation, demonstration, and review. They also will feed back any changes required to the Function Definitions, the Requirements Catalogue, and any other SSADM documentation. The team leader will usually be responsible for producing prototyping reports and for reporting any serious problems, either associated with the prototyping process or identified by prototyping, to overall project management and ultimately to the project board.

Management control
Project management defines the scope and objectives of the prototyping exercise. It is important to be clear about the objectives and to communicate these to the users involved in the demonstrations. Typical objectives will be to ensure that the right data is displayed on the screens, that the navigation between screens is appropriate, that the right processes are automated and that the right processes are left under the users' manual control. The objectives are unlikely to include determining the exact screen layouts or contents of messages.

The Prototyping Scope defines the functional areas which prototyping should address and may determine the number of demonstrations of each dialogue. The prototyping team will report any serious problems, which have impacts on the whole project, to management.

Which prototyping tool?
There is an almost endless variety of software products that could be used to develop specification prototypes. The minimum requirement is that the potential prototyping tool must offer facilities to develop, rapidly, a demonstration. We will look at three broad classifications of prototyping tool. First, the CASE tool with some prototyping facilities; second, a PC based package designed specifically for prototyping or for small systems development; and third, Fourth Generation Environments which may be used for the eventual construction. Each has advantages and disadvantages which are discussed below.

CASE tools These often have basic prototyping facilities in addition to the normal CASE facilities of diagram drawing and dictionary support. Using Attribute Definitions held on the CASE tool and I/O Structures or I/O Descriptions (often associated with data flows) the analyst can paint screens, add labels for the fields, and add messages and titles. Simulation of data entry and validation can thus be achieved. Most products also have menu builders and methods of navigating from one screen to another through menus or commands. These limited facilities are useful to develop quickly simple simulations for demonstration to the user. These simulations lack the facilities to store and retrieve information or to perform any complicated logic or arithmetic functions. Thus the prototype could not be tried out by the user in a working environment.

PC packages A variety of PC packages may be used to develop specification prototypes such as spreadsheets, databases, and visual programming languages. Typically the most frequently used, package type for information systems prototyping in SSADM projects will be a database package, e.g. Paradox, Foxbase, Access etc. These packages offer the following advantages: they are widely used so expertise is easy to come by, working solutions can be delivered to the user for them to evaluate in their own time with live data, and they are built using popular hardware and software meaning that additional purchases are rarely necessary. The main disadvantages of such products are that: the eventual system may use a rather different interface style to the package, the users may become too attached to the prototype and be unwilling to throw it away, the data definitions cannot be preserved into the final system. If a large system is being built these tools offer the best approach to building pilot[1] systems which the users can evaluate over a longish period. Visual Basic offers good facilities for prototyping more sophisticated Graphical User Interfaces (GUIs). Spreadsheet packages are a useful prototyping media for decision support or executive information systems— spreadsheets are also useful to build prototypes of reports.

Fourth Generation Environments These are often used as the eventual construction tool in SSADM projects. If the construction tool is known in advance then using that for the prototype offers significant advantages. The eventual interface and the prototype interface should be very similar, if not exactly the same. Various elements of the prototype such as data definitions, screen definitions, menu structures and report layouts can usually be preserved into the final system. The disadvantages of this approach are minor, but may include: the need to enter data definitions (this may be unnecessary if a 'bridge' exists between the CASE tool and the development environment or if an integrated CASE tool (ICASE) is used), the temptation to start construction before specification is properly completed, the fourth generation environment may not be so conducive to rapid development, and skills in the construction environment may not be available.

---

[1] This is sometimes referred to as 'piloting'. The prototype is used instead of, or in parallel with, the current system usually by small subset of the user population. It can be evaluated by the users over a long period with live data to give very detailed understanding of the requirements for both the computer system and the manual system. It is particularly useful when changes to working practices are required and the requirements are very fuzzy. This 'piloting' approach to prototyping is beyond the scope of core SSADM and not discussed further in this book.

What to prototype?

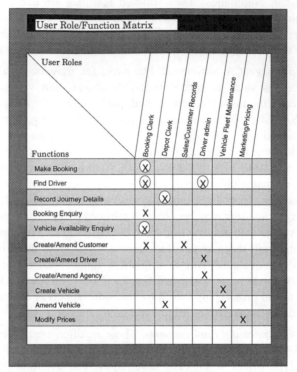

User Role/Function Matrix

Functions	Booking Clerk	Depot Clerk	Sales/Customer Records	Driver admin	Vehicle Fleet Maintenance	Marketing/Pricing
Make Booking	(X)					
Find Driver	(X)			(X)		
Record Journey Details		(X)				
Booking Enquiry	X					
Vehicle Availability Enquiry	(X)					
Create/Amend Customer	X		X			
Create/Amend Driver				X		
Create/Amend Agency				X		
Create Vehicle					X	
Amend Vehicle		X			X	
Modify Prices						X

Fig. 4.74 User Role/Function Matrix showing critical functions

Broad guidelines on the functional areas to be addressed will be provided by the Prototyping Scope. In step 330, *derive system functions*, the User Role/Function Matrix (see Fig. 4.74 above) was annotated to show the critical functions. These critical functions are good candidates for prototyping, although not all critical functions will be appropriate (some will be critical for machine performance or for security reasons). Generally, most critical functions are appropriate for prototyping providing that the resources allow. In this section, we take the Vehicle Availability Enquiry function and discuss how a prototype of that could be built, demonstrated, and reviewed by the user. This is a good example of a critical requirement since it is very high volume, occurring more often than any other transaction in the Yorkies system; it is critical in user performance terms as customers will be enquiring over the telephone; and it is critical to the business of the system.

Designing the prototype

Much work has already been done in defining the functionality of the new system. I/O Structures and their supporting descriptions have been built (step 330) to support Function Definitions—these are our first attempts at dialogue design for the new system. In step 510, *define user dialogues*, the detailed design of dialogues is completed. Normally the techniques used in step 510 are used in specification prototyping for dialogue design. Figure 4.75 (repeated from Sec. 4.4) shows the I/O Structure for the Vehicle Availability Enquiry.

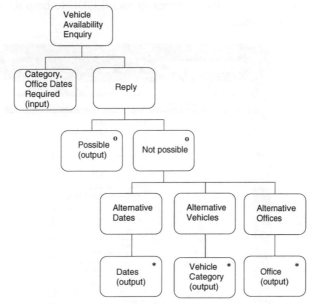

Fig. 4.75 I/O Structure for Vehicle Availability Enquiry.

We might talk through this enquiry with the user as follows:

'A customer telephones, requesting a three ton truck on the 3rd of August from the Yorkies depot in Luton. These details are entered into the system which then replies with either "OK", allowing the user to progress to the booking screen, or a "not possible" message. The system then displays alternative dates, e.g. a three ton truck available from Luton on 4th August followed by alternative vehicle categories, e.g. five ton truck available on 3rd August from Luton and finally, alternative offices, e.g. three ton truck available on 3rd August from Bedford.'

As this is a critical enquiry it is most important to design it 'right'. The user may not be sure of exactly how it will work from the I/O Structure or from the analysts walk-through. Therefore demonstration of a prototype is preferred.

The approach to building the prototype is to determine first the Prototype Pathway. Figure 4.76 is the Prototype Pathway for the demonstration of Vehicle Availability Enquiry to the user role Booking Clerk—it shows the sequence of screens in the order they will be shown. The Prototype Pathway is the script for the demonstration.

The user will first see the main menu, then the vehicle availability option, then the entry screen where the dates, offices and vehicle categories are entered, then the system responses, then the alternative dates information, then the alternative vehicles, and finally the alternative offices. The term 'LGDE' refers to a Logical Grouping of Dialogue Elements. These will be discussed in more detail in Chapter 5 but can be thought of as parts of the I/O Structure which fit together to form a logical screen. The LGDE serves as a screen identifier for the prototype. The components of the pathway are used during demonstration and review to describe where changes are required to the prototype. Screen names are given to each LGDE to help the user understand what is being demonstrated.

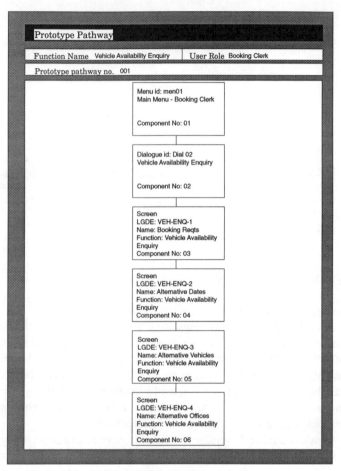

Fig. 4.76 Prototype Pathway for Vehicle Availability Enquiry.

The normal approach is to use the I/O Structure to develop a Prototype Pathway. The prototype is then designed specifically to demonstrate the pathway. Screens should be designed to follow any style guides used by the installation. They should follow general screen design guidelines such as: inputting data from top to bottom and left to right, and being clear and well structured. Earlier specification work performed using SSADM techniques should not be forgotten: use the Attribute Definitions from the Data Catalogue, and follow the Function Definition and its supporting Elementary Process Descriptions.

Preparing to give the demonstration.

On a particular date we may wish to demonstrate to the user a number of Prototype Pathways. We prepare a Prototype Demonstration Objective Document for each demonstration (see Fig. 4.77 below). This acts as an agenda for our demonstration showing any assumptions made and queries to make with the user. This enables the user to know what to expect in the demonstration and raise beforehand any queries or suggestions they may have. The Component Nos cross-refer to the Prototype Pathway and point out specific questions that the development team have about that particular screen. Using the Prototype Demonstration Objective Document helps ensure that the demonstration is well managed and organized with both demonstrators and users being well prepared for the session.

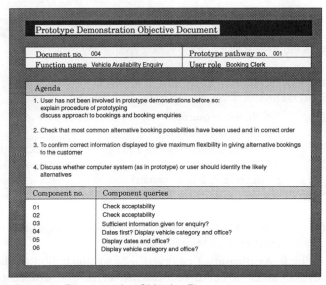

Fig. 4.77 Sample Prototype Demonstration Objective Document

As was discussed previously the prototype will usually be demonstrated by its developer with another analyst taking notes and questioning the user. Ideally live data should be used to give the demonstration a more realistic feel.

Giving the demonstration

The results and comments made during the demonstration can be recorded in a Prototype Result Log[1] (see Fig. 4.78 below). This could be completed after the demonstration and circulated to the users attending the demonstration for agreement. It shows the changes necessary to components in the dialogue, cross-referring these by component number to the Prototype Pathway.

---

[1] Note that all of the standard SSADM forms are guidelines only. Many projects will develop their own standards for prototyping documentation. The examples given throughout this book are based on those in the SSADM Reference Manual but should be treated as guidelines.

Prototype Result Log				
Prototype result log no. 001			Prototype pathway no. 001	
Function name Vehicle Availability Enquiry			User role Booking Clerk	

Component no.	Result no.	Result description	Change grade
01	01	Acceptable	N
02	01	Acceptable	N
03	01	Space out data items more	C
04	01	Prefer choice of alternatives including showing none	P
04	02	Display vehicle category and office address on same screen	D
05	01	Display office and dates	D
06	01	Display vehicle category and dates	D

Fig. 4.78 Prototype Result Log for Vehicle Availability Enquiry

Change grades indicate where and what changes are required to the dialogue and/or to the SSADM products. Suggested codes for change grades are:

N   No change required
C   Cosmetic changes only
D   only affects the particular Dialogue or report being demonstrated
P   affects the Prototype Pathway (may need to revise other SSADM products, e.g. I/O Structure)
S   changes to existing Standards (e.g. Installation Style Guide)
A   Analysis may be incorrect
G   serious Global problems (may require changes to working practice of organization)

The Vehicle Availability Enquiry is a good illustration of the use of specification prototyping since it could be designed in several different ways. The approach suggested in the original Function Definition is an automatic one, where the computer system 'knows' about alternative vehicle categories and local offices.[1] At the prototype demonstration it was clear that the users had sufficient knowledge of nearby offices and of similar categories to make the decisions about which ones to try themselves. They also preferred this approach.

Users suggest that computer generated alternative offices, alternative vehicles and alternative dates may be useful as an option for inexperienced users and that this may be achieved in a simple way by using parts of the Local Office code (the first two digits indicating the region) and part of the Vehicle Category code (the first two characters giving a broad classification). In this way, complex processing can be avoided but the user can be given an option to display system generated alternatives.

---

[1] This obviously requires rather complex processing and needs modifications to the Logical Data Model to incorporate links between a given category and other similar categories, and links between a given local office and other nearby offices. New entities of Vehicle Category Substitution and Local Office Substitution could be required.

The changes suggested by the user require modifications to be made to the I/O Structure diagram. This is reflected in the change grade '4' given to Component No. 4 in Fig. 4.78 above. The modified I/O Structure diagram is used in step 510, *define user dialogues* (see Fig. 5.9 in Sec. 5.6).

Reviewing the prototype

After the demonstration the development team need to decide whether further demonstrations of the prototype are useful. These obviously require more resources—if the time and cost defined in the Prototyping Scope will be exceeded, then authorization is required from the project board. Changes may be required to other SSADM products such as the Requirements Catalogue, the Data Catalogue, the Function Definitions, and the I/O Structures and their supporting descriptions. In the Vehicle Availability Enquiry example, used in this section, the I/O Structure needs to be redrawn to describe the structure preferred by the users at the demonstration.

Sometimes serious problems are identified, indicating that important functional areas of the system have been misunderstood or completely missed. If this kind of problem arises, with significant consequences for the overall project, then project management and ultimately the project board should be told immediately to avoid wasting any further resources. A decision must be taken quickly by those in authority.

The Prototyping Report

A formal Prototyping Report is submitted to the project board at the end of the step. This report summarizes the results of prototyping paying particular attention to the original objectives set in the Prototyping Scope. It summarizes the changes to the SSADM products that result from the step and discusses how the approach to prototyping may be improved in future projects. Much of the information in the Prototyping Report can be derived from the Prototype Result Logs.

SUMMARY
- Prototyping is used in SSADM to help define requirements;
- the Prototyping Scope is clearly defined and may vary from no prototyping to prototyping all of the major functions;
- critical dialogues and reports are prototyped after step 330, *define system functions*;
- tight management control is exercised to overcome some of the typical problems of prototyping;
- the prototype is designed using SSADM dialogue design techniques;
- Prototype Pathways and Prototype Demonstration Objective Documents set scripts and agendas for demonstrations to users;
- the Prototype Result Log records results and changes to specifications required;
- the Prototyping Report goes to user and project management.

4.7   Develop processing specification (step 360)

Introduction

This step produces a detailed specification of the required system processing. Until now this has been defined in terms of Required System Data Flow Diagrams and Function Definitions. In this step, each entity is assigned events to build up an Entity Life History diagram. Effect Correspondence Diagrams show how each event affects different data entities in different ways. Thus the update processing for the required system is specified in more detail during this step.

Enquiry processing is defined in the Requirements Catalogue and in the Function Definitions. In this step, a detailed specification for enquiries is developed using Enquiry Access Paths.

This is a complex step in SSADM involving: the full definition of events and their incorporation into functions, and the development of Entity Life Histories and Effect Correspondence Diagrams. The technique of logical data modelling is used to produce Enquiry Access Paths and to complete the volumetric information about the system's data. This section covers several new techniques and diagrammatic notations and requires careful study. We have divided the section into several parts: first, dealing with entity-event modelling; second, with development of life histories; third, with development of Effect Correspondence Diagrams; fourth, with Enquiry Access Paths; and finally, with the addition of volumetric information to the Logical Data Model.

Entity-event modelling

This is concerned with modelling how entity occurrences are affected by event occurrences (Entity Life Histories) and modelling how event occurrences affect entity occurrences (Effect Correspondence Diagrams). Thus the entity-event modelling technique covers both production of Entity Life Histories and Effect Correspondence Diagrams. The relationship between the two types of entity-event models is shown by the Event/Entity Matrix in Fig. 4.79.

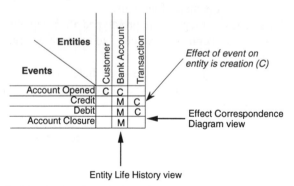

Fig. 4.79 Event/Entity Matrix showing relationships between entity-event models

Section 2.3 described the notation and terminology used in Entity Life Histories. An Entity Life History charts all of the events that may affect an entity during its life within the system. An event is something that happens to trigger a process to update system data. Entity Life Histories are both an analysis and a design tool. We analyse all of the events that can affect the systems data, and their permitted sequences. We design by deciding how the system should process these events and by deciding how it should validate the order in which these events occur.

The technique is often considered to be the most challenging technique of SSADM as the drawing of a single Entity Life History may span several days. This aspect of the technique is not due to any particular difficulty inherent in the technique but is due to the abundance of questions raised that must be answered and the often heated, detailed discussions between members of the development team.

Section 2.4 described the relationship between Entity Life Histories and two other main techniques of SSADM—Logical Data Modelling and Data Flow Modelling. The use of entity-event modelling to validate the other models is summarized here:

- All Data Flow Diagram processes that update the main data stores are triggered by events. We first identify events from the Data Flow Diagrams and then assign these events to functions. Entity-event modelling is used to ensure that a complete set of events has been included in the Function Definitions. When the system is viewed from a purely functional perspective, as with Data Flow Models, it is easy to miss necessary detail. An example of this would be data stores being used by processes without a process to create the data store in the first place. In examining the processing from the point of view of the data, the omission becomes obvious.
- Entity Life Histories are used to validate the Logical Data Model. Difficulties in drawing an Entity Life History may be due to the poor identification of entities. If an entity contains groups of unrelated attributes, its Entity Life History may be very difficult to draw. This prompts a re-examination of the Logical Data Model and new entities may need to be created.

Approach to entity-event modelling

Our recommended approach to entity-event modelling is shown below in Fig. 4.80. Events, previously allocated to functions, are listed on the Event/Entity Matrix and entities are listed from the Logical Data Model—the effect of the event on the entity is shown at the intersection. An initial set of Entity Life Histories is produced, drawing first those of entities at the bottom of the Logical Data Structure (i.e. dealing with the detail entities first). Full lives of each entity are then produced by reviewing first the life histories of entities at the top of the Logical Data Structure (i.e. considering the master entities first). Throughout this process new events will be identified which may result in new requirements and new functions. New entities and attributes may also be identified.

As life histories are completed, operations are added to the effects showing the detailed changes made by the effect on the entity. For each event identified an Effect Correspondence Diagram is produced showing the correspondences between the entities affected by the event. This uses a Jackson style notation to show iterated and selected effects. These Effect Correspondence Diagrams are used in Stage 5 to define the detailed processing using Update Process Models. All of this activity should be completed in step 360, *develop processing specification*. In Stage 5, Logical Design, the Entity Life Histories are further validated by adding state indicators, showing the states that an entity occurrence can have before an event happens. These state indicators can be used in update processing to ensure that the data is in a valid state to accept the update. (Some projects prefer to add state indicators in step 360, finding them a useful way of checking their Entity Life Histories.)

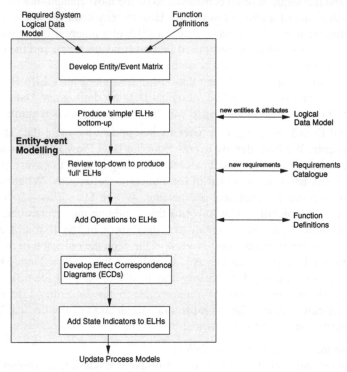

Fig. 4.80 Approach to entity-event modelling

The production of Entity Life Histories

The following sections describe the tasks involved in creating and documenting Entity Life Histories. In summary, these steps are:

- Initial identification of events (performed in step 330).
- Constructing the Event/Entity Matrix.
- Drawing initial Entity Life Histories for all entities.
- Completion of the Entity Life Histories.
- Addition of operations.
- Addition of state indicators (performed in step 520).

Initial identification of events

In step 330, *derive system functions*, we developed an initial list of events and allocated these to functions. The events were identified from the Required System Data Flow Diagrams by looking for all of the updates to data stores. Each update, shown by an arrow pointing into the data store, would signify a change to the system's data. An event is defined as whatever causes the system to change its data so each update to a data store must result from an event. Thus by tracing back through the data flows we can identify the event causing the update.

In step 360, we start from the initial set of events identified during step 330 and build a complete set using the entity-event modelling technique. The initial set of events were identified from the processing of the required system. In this step we look also at the data and consider how that can be changed.

There are several possible approaches to identifying events and using these to build Entity Life Histories. The technique that we prefer is to build a matrix showing all events and all entities identified in the system. However, this Entity/Event Matrix is an optional technique in SSADM and is not used by some practitioners, who feel that it is redundant with Entity Life Histories and Effect Correspondence Diagrams containing all of the required information. They also feel that Entity Life Histories are best developed from scratch.

Constructing the Event/Entity Matrix

As the events are identified, they are listed along one axis of the Event/Entity Matrix. All entities from the Logical Data Model are placed along the other axis of the matrix. There is no standard as to which should be on the horizontal or vertical axis.[1] The intersections of the matrix show the effect of the event on the entity. Thus: create is shown by a 'C', modify by a 'M' and delete by a 'D'.[2] Sometimes one event can have optional effects on the entity requiring two different letters to be shown in the same intersection.

Figure 4.81 shows an incomplete matrix for the Yorkies system—its incompleteness should be immediately apparent since nothing appears to update several entities and no entities are deleted. The matrix is thus a very useful way of initially identifying missing events. By looking down the vertical axis of the matrix we can see the Entity Life History perspective. Thus the Booking column shows the various effects which will form the basis of its life history. Some projects find it worth while to maintain the Event/Entity Matrix throughout the project; finding it a useful summary of the update processing of the system.[3]

---

[1] We usually prefer to show entities along the top of the matrix and events along the side because we are normally using portrait A4 paper and there are usually more events than there are entities. On projects of any size these matrixes get so large that A0 paper can be required, with walls needed to display them.

[2] These matrixes are popular in other methods, notably Information Engineering which often refers to it as a CRUD matrix (Create, Read, Update, and Delete). The main difference is that 'Reads' are shown causing the matrixes to become very complicated.

[3] Other projects find the matrix cumbersome to maintain and only use it to start life histories—all of the matrix information is available from Entity Life Histories and Effect Correspondence Diagrams. The Event/Entity Matrix is also poorly supported by some CASE tools.

Event \ Entity	Customer	Payment	Invoice	Vehicle	Allocated Payment	Vehicle Category	Local Office/Depot	Driver	Agency	Booking	Driving Licence Type	Licence
Invoice Issued			C									
Reminder Sent			M									
Booking Request	C	C								C		
Booking Confirmed										M		
Vehicle Relocation										C		
Driver Allocated										M		
Agency Allocated										M		
Vehicle Depart										M		
Vehicle Return										M		

Fig. 4.81 Partial Event/Entity Matrix for Yorkies

After drawing the Event/Entity Matrix, it is useful to review it before continuing to the Entity Life Histories. By reviewing the matrix from the point of view of the entities, check that each entity has at least one 'C' against it because any data that is in the system must have been created by something. Similarly, by examining the matrix in the knowledge of the requirements, it is often possible to identify events that are missing. Events identified in this way are added to the matrix and effects on other entities explored. If it becomes obvious that there are events for which no functions have been defined then new Function Definitions must be created.

Drawing initial Entity Life Histories
The Entity Life Histories are created in two passes:

- initial (or 'simple') Entity Life Histories are created first;
- final (or 'full') Entity Life Histories are produced afterwards.

This does not mean that two distinct sets of Entity Life Histories are produced in this step. The 'simple' Entity Life Histories are often quite complicated and the changes made to render them 'full' may be fairly trivial.

The first entities for which Entity Life Histories are drawn should be entities that have one or more masters but no details. Second, the masters of these entities are selected and so on until the entities at the 'top' of the Logical Data Structure are chosen. This is so that events that affect the relationships between entities are followed up through from detail to master. The effect of an event on each detail entity is considered first and then the effect from the other end of the relationship is viewed.

On the Yorkies Required System Logical Data Structure (see Fig. 4.69), the only entities without details are:

- Allocated Payment
- Licence
- Booking

Entity Life Histories are drawn for these entities first. From the Event/Entity Matrix, we can see that the events that affect the Booking entity are:

- Vehicle Relocation (C)—one-way hires may leave vehicles in undesirable locations, a relocation is an internal one-way booking to return vehicles to their original offices. As the vehicle is assigned when the relocation is made there is no need for a Booking Confirmation. As with normal bookings, drivers are allocated later.
- Booking Request (C)—this is where an initial booking request is received that is recorded on the system with a provisional status until it has been confirmed.
- Booking Confirmed (M)—this confirms a provisional booking after the vehicle has been allocated and all appropriate authorization received. At this point, it has not been determined whether a Yorkies driver is available or whether an agency driver will be required.
- Driver Allocated (M)—this is where a Yorkies driver is allocated to this booking. Some customers will provide their own driver for a booking—neither the Driver Allocated or Agency Allocated events will affect this occurrence of booking.
- Agency Allocated (M)—this is where a Yorkies driver is not available so an agency is allocated to supply a driver.
- Vehicle Departure (M)—the vehicle rental actually starts at this point; no further amendments can be made to it.
- Vehicle Return (M)—this is when a hired vehicle returns to the depot and the details of the hiring are entered into the system.

The following paragraphs describe how the initial Booking Entity Life History is built up.

1. Identify the creation events There are two: Booking Request and Vehicle Relocation. This means that an occurrence of Booking is created either by the receipt of a Booking Request or by the request to relocate a vehicle. The first thing we draw is a diagram as shown in Fig. 4.82. The entity name is in the box at the top to show which entity this life history belongs to. The box below that (Booking Creation) is called a 'node' as it has no significance within the Entity Life History except that it indicates a particular phase of the life history. The event names are placed in the boxes at the bottom of the structure. These boxes are called 'effects' because they represent the particular effects of the events upon this particular entity. The small circles in these boxes indicate a selection. So, this first portion of the diagram shows that the Booking entity is created either by the Booking Request being received or by the relocation of a vehicle.

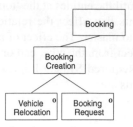

Fig. 4.82 Partial Entity Life History showing creation events

We might then realize that there are two possible optional effects of the event Booking Request: requests from accredited customers are treated differently from requests from new customers. New customers must pay a deposit before their booking is accepted. We show, in Fig. 4.83, the optional effects as alternatives distinguished by their effect qualifiers of 'New Customer' and 'Existing Customer'.

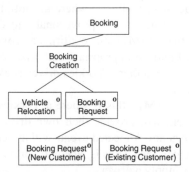

Fig. 4.83 Partial Entity Life History showing optional effects

2. Identify the modification events Next, the events that will modify this entity are considered so that their appropriate position on the diagram can be determined. Are any of the events only going to happen after one of the creation events, or are they going to happen after both of them? Are the modifications going to happen in any particular sequence, will some of them be alternatives for one another?

In the life of Booking, a Booking Confirmation will occur only after a Booking Request, not after Vehicle Relocation. The Driver or Agency Allocation will occur after either of them but will be alternatives—either the customer will drive, or Yorkies will supply a driver, or, if Yorkies cannot, an agency will supply a driver. This leads to a three-way selection, with a 'null' box representing the customer driving as this changes no attribute value in the Booking entity. The structure above needs to have these modifications added in the right place (see Fig. 4.84). There are several things to note:

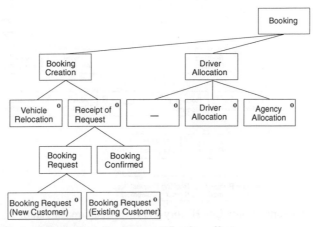

Fig. 4.84 Partial Entity Life History showing modification effects

a) As Booking Confirmed can only happen after the Booking Request and not after Vehicle Relocation, the structure under the Booking Creation node has been amended to show a selection of: *either* the receipt of a request (shown as a node here) which consists of a sequence of the receipt of the request followed by its confirmation; *or* the Vehicle Relocation.

b) Effects must always be at the bottom of the structure which is why the Booking Confirmed box has been put below the new node Receipt of Request. It is not strictly necessary to label node boxes, but it is a useful indication of what is going on in that part of the life.

c) The next thing that happens to the booking is that a driver is allocated; from the Yorkies pool of drivers, or from an agency, or the customer[1] drives following a 'No driver required' request (represented by the 'null' effect). No other changes can be made to the booking before this allocation has been done.

Referring back to the Event/Entity Matrix, there are just two more events that affect this entity: Vehicle Departure and Vehicle Return. It is obvious that the driver must be allocated before the vehicle departs and that the vehicle must depart before it returns! Here is a simple sequence as shown on the Entity Life History in Fig. 4.85.

If you are finding the diagrams difficult to understand, refer back to the explanation of Entity Life Histories in Sec. 2.3.

---

[1] If this follows a Vehicle Relocation then there is still the possibility of a 'null'—often Yorkies internal staff can be persuaded to drive the vehicles back for free. Consider how the structure could be redrawn if a relocation must be followed by a driver allocation.

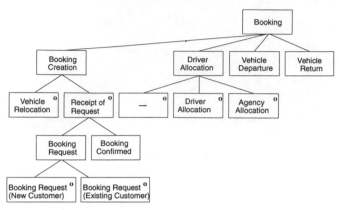

Fig. 4.85 Partial Entity Life History showing departure and return

3. Use the Entity Description to identify further events Now, we have exhausted the events shown on the Event/Entity Matrix affecting the Booking entity. We need to decide whether or not there are events that affect this entity that have been missed.

BOOKING
Booking No.
*Invoice No.
*Veh Reg Mark
*Veh Cat Code Req
*Office No. (Start)
*Office No. (Finish)
*Customer No.
*Driver No.
Agency Name
Date Collected
Time Collected
Start Mileage
Date Returned
Time Returned
Finish Mileage
Return Condition
Damage Charges
Driver Hours
Driver Cost
No. of Days
Total Period Cost
Total Mileage
Mileage Cost
Total Booking Cost
Veh Cat Code Req
Date Booking Starts
Date Booking Ends
Driver Req (Y/N)
Date Booking Reciv
Internal Booking Ind

Fig. 4.86 Attributes in
the Booking entity

The Entity Description of the Booking entity contains a full set of the attributes assigned to it in third normal form. We now ensure that a value for each attribute is created, possibly modified, and deleted. The attributes from the Entity Description of Booking are listed in Fig. 4.86 underlining the primary key and indicating foreign keys by *. Looking through this list, the following attributes would have values when the booking is created:

- Booking No.;
- Customer No.;
- Vehicle Category Requested;
- Date Booking Received;
- Date Booking Starts;
- Office No.(start);
- Office No.(finish);
- Date Booking Ends;
- Driver Required/Not Required.

The Booking No. is the key of this entity, and therefore must have a value for a unique occurrence of the entity to be created. The other attribute values are entered on the receipt of the Booking Request.

The attribute value for Vehicle Registration Mark is added when the booking is confirmed. On Vehicle Relocation a vehicle is assigned immediately and the Internal Booking Ind attribute set to 'Y'.

Driver No./Agency No. is updated when a driver has been allocated or, if a Yorkies driver is unavailable, an agency has agreed to provide a driver.

The Vehicle Departure event would update the Start Mileage and Date and Time Collected attributes, and the Vehicle Return event would update the Date Returned, Time Returned, Finish Mileage, Return Condition, Damage Charges, and Driver Hours attributes.

This quick check has shown us that most of the attribute values are set by one or more of the previously identified events and reflected in the Entity Life History. One attribute that is not yet affected by any events is Invoice No. This is a foreign key, i.e. it is the key of the Invoice entity which is the master of Booking. The reason for the presence of this attribute in the Booking entity is to represent the relationship between the two entities. This means that when the invoice is issued, a relationship between invoice and booking is created, so an update to the Booking entity should be shown. The invoice will only be issued after the vehicle has been returned, so the Entity Life History is amended as shown in Fig. 4.87. (The Total Period Cost, Total Mileage, Mileage Cost, Total Booking Cost, Damage Charges, Driver Hours and Driver Cost attributes are also updated by the Invoice Issued event.)

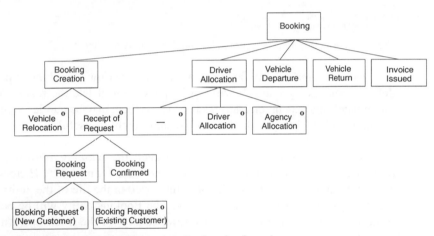

Fig. 4.87 Partial Entity Life History showing Invoice Issued

Next, the attributes should be examined again: are any of these items likely to change after it has been created? (At this point, only the normal things that will cause the items to change should be identified: the more unusual or random events are identified in the next pass of the Entity Life Histories.) As people are often known to change their minds, it seems likely that the customer may wish to alter details of the booking once it has been made. For example, the start and end dates may change, or the driver requirements may change. If the load to be carried increases in size, a different vehicle category may be required. All these changes could take place a number of times before the vehicle actually leaves on hire. This means that the Entity Life History must be changed again to show that amendments can be made to the booking details before the vehicle departure. However, it will be necessary to confirm the amendment after any change has been made. This results in the Entity Life History shown in Fig. 4.88. Here, an iteration of amendments has been added (shown by an asterisk in the top right corner of the box). The repeated element is a sequence of a booking amendment followed by a confirmation of the amendment.[1].

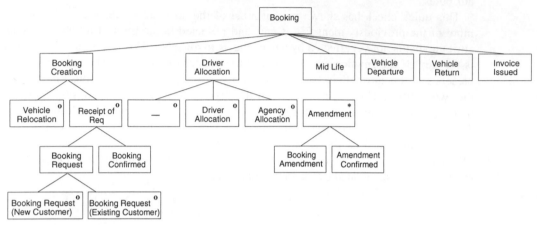

Fig. 4.88 Partial Entity Life History showing Booking Amendment

4. Consider deletions The next question to ask is 'How would the entity normally be deleted from the system?' It will not be possible to delete the record of the booking immediately after an invoice has been issued as there may be queries to resolve with the customer before they pay the invoice. Also, it might be useful to refer to old bookings when a customer makes a new booking. Even after the record is removed from the live system, there may be a requirement to keep the booking information for future reference. This means that the event that finishes this Entity Life History is 'Archive'. This is because this life history is only interested in the life of the entity while it is on the live system's database. After archive, the Booking entity will be held on tape for some time. The final 'simple' Entity Life History for the Booking entity is shown in Fig. 4.89.

5. Ask the users Events are easily understood by users (though they may find the life histories difficult). We can discuss what events affect the entity and change the values of its attributes with the users—they will often identify further events and other possible sequences. Many of the events they identify may be the 'unusual' events that we consider when building the complex or full lives.

---

[1] If this confirmation of the amendment was handled by the system in the same way as the Booking Confirmed event we would show the event appearing twice in the life history. The event would then have two effects upon the Booking entity: the first immediately after the booking is created by a booking request and the second immediately after a booking amendment. It is quite normal for an event to affect an entity at several different points in its life—often effect qualifiers are needed to distinguish them.

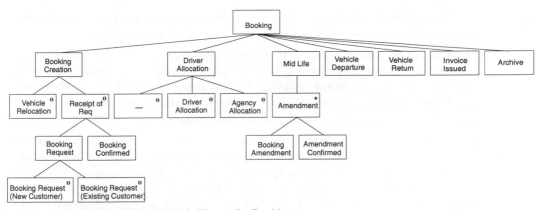

Fig. 4.89 Initial Entity Life History for Booking

Further hints on developing Entity Life Histories

The example developed here for the Yorkies Booking entity illustrates some important points about developing the initial Entity Life Histories. The points, together with some additional hints are summarized here.

Entity Life Histories should be unambiguous The diagram should not be open to several different interpretations. We could have drawn the first part of Fig. 4.89 in the form shown in Fig. 4.90. (The 'null box' under the selection shows that either nothing further will affect the entity after the Booking Creation phase until Driver Allocation or that the Booking Confirmed event will affect the entity. This is a clumsy way of showing that Vehicle Relocation is not followed by a Booking Confirmation.)

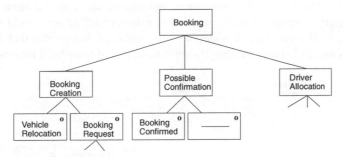

Fig. 4.90 Partial Entity Life History allowing invalid sequences

Figure 4.90 will still allow the same valid sequences to occur:

- Booking Request, Booking Confirmed, Driver Allocation;
- Vehicle Relocation, Driver Allocation.

However, ambiguity has now been introduced as other sequences, which are not valid, are now possible:

- Booking Request, Driver Allocation;
- Vehicle Relocation, Booking Confirmed, Driver Allocation.

So, although the diagram does reflect the required sequences, the diagram is incorrect because ambiguity about valid and invalid sequences has been introduced.

Check selections under iterations If an Entity Life History contains a selection under an iteration, i.e. a selection that may be made any number of times, each box under the selection should be examined to ensure that this really reflects the requirement. It is possible that some may occur only once, or that some may happen in sequence—if so make sure that these are *not* hidden in an iterated selection.

Entity Life Histories as a design tool When we construct a life history in a particular way we are specifying that the computer system will ensure that the defined sequence must be followed. The software will ensure that only valid sequences of events can affect an entity occurrence; events occurring out of sequence will be rejected and error processing invoked. Building an Entity Life History therefore requires important design decisions—to constrain the processing of events in a clearly defined sequence or to allow the events to occur in any sequence. Deciding to constrain involves: the analyst in building a complex Entity Life History, the designer in building complex error processing, and the programmer in constructing and maintaining that software. Alternatively the analyst may prefer to build a simpler system which does not constrain the lives of its entities and in which the user of the system's data is responsible for maintaining its integrity—this may require more work and expertise from the user, and a more complex manual system.

It is important to realize that we are considering system events and not real-world events. System events are those having an impact on system data. Remember that the computer system is a model of the external business world that it is supporting. It is up to the designer to make that model as simple or as complex as is appropriate by considering such factors as resources, time-scales and user requirements. It is often unnecessary to model all of the real-world events and their real-world sequences in our Entity Life Histories and ultimately into our software. Remember that the life history is a design tool and shows the constraints that we intend to be built into the software.

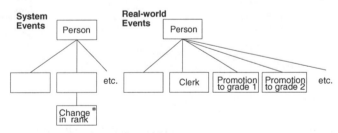

Fig. 4.91 System events rather than real-world events

For example, a real-world payroll system will be interested if a member of staff is promoted as he or she will need to be paid more. However, the exact progression of promotions, and all associated factors, could be of no interest to the payroll computer system. The processing of promotions and the rules concerning pay increases could be handled manually outside the computer system (see Fig. 4.91). If this was agreed with the user; it would be wrong to show a complex structure of promotions in the 'Person' Entity Life History, and correct to show an iteration of 'Change in rank' as that is the only progression event of interest in this payroll system as in Fig. 4.91.

For each entity in the system, many possible life histories could be developed. Some will be exceedingly complex and some will be exceedingly simple. An alternative life history for the Booking entity is shown below in Fig. 4.92. This life history is as 'correct' as the complex one shown in Fig. 4.89. All of the same events are included, it is simply that we have not constrained the order in which the various modification events can occur. This is not an unreasonable design decision. It means that the software will not be able to validate that a vehicle departs before it returns—that responsibility will be left to the user. However, software developed from this life history will be quicker to develop and cheaper to maintain than that following from the complex life history. Ultimately the user has to decide whether to go for complex structures with sophisticated validation or simpler structures with less validation. The important thing to remember is that there are design decisions to be made when developing life histories. Too often projects tie themselves in knots building complex life histories which cannot be justified in terms of their eventual cost in construction and maintenance.

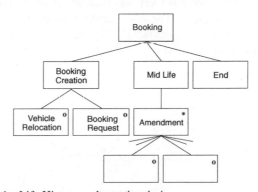

Fig. 4.92 Booking Entity Life History—alternative design

Check that all events have been identified The following list can be used to check that all of the events have been identified in the simple Entity Life Histories:

• Are all of the attributes in the entity given values when the entity is created? If not, what events will give values to them?
• Is it a requirement that individual attributes are updated, and what events will cause them to be updated?
• What will cause the entity to change its relationships with occurrences of the master entities?
• What causes an optional relationship to a master entity to be created or deleted?
• Is it important to know that an event has happened in the life of an entity even if there is not an obvious change in the value of any of the attributes? It may be that certain events set the context for other events, updating only a flag or indicator in the entity.

It is necessary to try to account for all of the events that will normally affect the entity during its life in the system. However, the more unusual events that may occur should be left to the second pass of the Entity Life Histories. Whatever is expected to happen should be reflected in the simple Entity Life Histories.

Complete the Entity Life Histories

We review and extend each life history by considering any unusual events and how events affecting one entity type can also affect entities of other types. In the first pass we started by looking at the entities at the bottom of the Logical Data Structure, in this second pass we review the entities at the top of the structure first (the master entities) and then work down through the data structure. This approach helps to examine the interdependencies between lives of different entity types—e.g. what happens to the occurrences of Booking when their master occurrence, Customer, is deleted.

Interactions Often an event affecting the life of one entity occurrence will also constrain the life of other occurrences. Previously we have considered those 'normal' effects of an event on different entity occurrences—now we look for the abnormal events. Consider the event 'Vehicle Out of Service': this will, apart from affecting the Vehicle occurrence, affect the Booking occurrences associated with the particular vehicle. Those that have not yet departed will need to have another vehicle reassigned before they can depart. (There are several such events we need to consider in the Booking life: 'Driver Unavailable', 'Agency Unavailable', and some deletion events which we will look at later.)

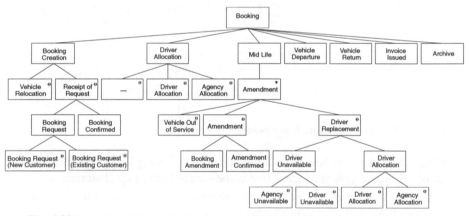

Fig. 4.93 Entity Life History for Booking showing events from the lives of master entities

Deletion of master occurrences The effects of the deletion of an occurrence of master entity on its detail entity occurrences are investigated. (Effects of the deletion of an occurrence of a detail entity on the master entity occurrence are often minor—but they should be considered particularly if the relationship is mandatory at the master end.) For each pair of master and detail entities, only one of the following situations will apply. The deletion of the master occurrence:

- has no effect on the detail occurrence apart from 'cutting' the relationship;
- causes the detail occurrence to be transferred to another master occurrence;
- causes the deletion of the detail occurrences;
- cannot occur until all the detail occurrences have been deleted.

If the deletion of the master does not affect the detail apart from 'cutting' the relationship and the deletion does not constrain the life of the detail, then the deletion (of master) event need not be shown. This can only happen where the relationship is totally optional at the detail end. Often the rules governing the existence of relationships of an entity change over time—a booking is assigned a vehicle on confirmation and thereafter must have a relationship with a vehicle occurrence.

If the relationship is mandatory at the detail end then a deletion of master event may cause the detail occurrence to be transferred to another master occurrence. An example of this would be if a driver left Yorkies, the Driver entity were deleted, then all bookings for that driver would need to be transferred to other drivers or to agencies. (As in the cases of the Driver Unavailable and Agency Unavailable events.)

If the deletion of the master causes the detail to be deleted, then events shown at the end of the Entity Life History of the master should occur at the end of the life of the detail. An example of this in the Yorkies system would be if a customer is deleted, the Booking occurrences belonging to that customer would also be deleted. A Booking occurrence will be deleted either by the normal Booking Archive for a current customer or it will be deleted when a Customer occurrence is archived (see Fig. 4.94).

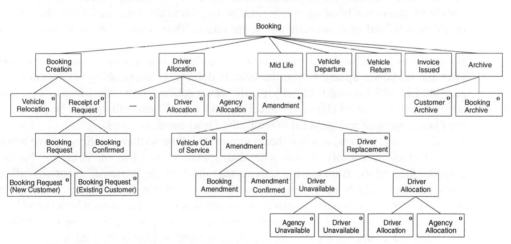

Fig. 4.94 Entity Life History for Booking showing new deletion events

If the master cannot be deleted until the detail has been deleted, then the events that cause the deletion of the detail should be put before the end of the master's Entity Life History. This is known as a *controlled death* since the death of the master is controlled by the death of its details.

In Yorkies, a Vehicle occurrence may not be deleted from the system until all bookings belonging to that vehicle have been deleted. The end of the Vehicle Entity

Life History is shown in Fig. 4.95. This shows that the last booking for this vehicle must have been deleted before the vehicle can be deleted from the system. We have used the effect qualifier notation, '()', to indicate that the effect only occurs when the booking being deleted, either by normal Booking Archive or by Customer Archive, is the last booking still belonging to that vehicle.

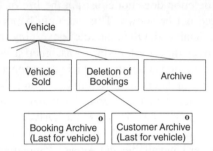

Fig. 4.95 Entity Life History for Vehicle showing last booking deletion before archive

Unusual events Events that occur unusually that alter the sequence of an Entity Life History are added now. We have assumed that the normal course of events is for a customer to make a booking and for that booking to go ahead as planned (the vehicle leaves at the beginning of the hire period and returns at the end of that period). There are quite a few things that might upset this, however. For example, the customer might decide to cancel the booking at any time before the vehicle departs. Also, the vehicle might be involved in an accident and never return. These events, and any other similar events, should be added to the Entity Life History at this stage. The Booking Entity Life History is expanded in Fig. 4.96. This structure shows that a booking can be cancelled after the initial set-up and before the vehicle departs. If the booking is cancelled, the customer is still invoiced. Identifying the cancellation event also leads to two new attributes: Cancellation Date and Cancellation Charge. These will need to be defined in the Data Catalogue and included in the Entity Description for Booking.[1]

If the vehicle departs, it will either return or it will be written off. So we have a new event Vehicle Write-off, which will also appear in the life of Vehicle.[2] Further consideration of the Booking life tells us that the Vehicle Write-off event will affect other bookings which are planned to use the same vehicle. So we have *simultaneous effects* of Vehicle Write-off, an effect on the Booking occurrence on which the vehicle was written off (indicated by [happened on]), and effects on the Booking occurrences which are due to use the written-off vehicle (indicated by [due to be used]).

[1] Very often entity-event modelling changes the Required System Logical Data Model. Because the technique takes a different perspective, events are identified that were missed by the functional perspective taken earlier in the project. These 'new' events can lead to 'new' attributes, relationships, and entities.

[2] We must be careful to use the same name for the event wherever it occurs. This becomes important when we take the next step in entity-event modelling, the building of Effect Correspondence Diagrams. Maintaining consistent names for events can be helped by maintaining the Event/Entity Matrix or by using some form of Event Catalogue or Event Specification.

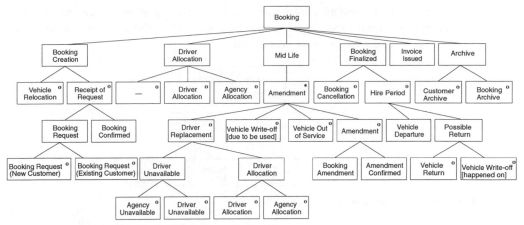

Fig. 4.96 'Full' Entity Life History for Booking

Obviously, there are many more complexities that could be added (e.g. what happens if the customer dies or wishes to extend the period of the booking after the vehicle departs?) but we shall assume that this completes the Booking Entity Life History.

It is worth noting that this life history is likely to be the most complex in Yorkies as the Booking entity is the most 'active' within the system. In our experience most systems have one entity (or a very small group of entities) that is central to the system. Other examples might include personnel systems where the Person entity is central, banking systems where the Account entity is central, order processing systems where the Order entity is central, etc. Thus the Booking entity has been chosen to demonstrate several points about Entity Life Histories. The majority of the other Entity Life Histories will be very simple indeed. Examples are given in Figs 4.97 and 4.98.

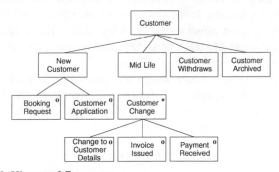

Fig. 4.97 Entity Life History of Customer

In Fig. 4.97 the customer is first notified to our system either by applying to become a regular customer, or by a booking request from an 'off-the-street' customer (this event also creates a booking occurrence and appears in that life history). The only amendments that will be made during the customer's life within the system will be either a change to the customer's details (e.g. the address for invoicing, credit limit, etc.) or will be to do with the total amount owed, i.e. issuing of an invoice and receipt of a payment. At some time the customer may wish to withdraw from custom with Yorkies, after which the customer is archived.

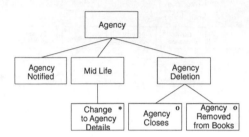

Fig. 4.98 Entity Life History of Agency

In Fig. 4.98 an agency is notified to us, there may be a number of changes in details, such as address, during its life in our system, and then it might close. Alternatively, we may decide that we do not wish to do business with the agency anymore and we delete it from the system.

Operations in Entity Life Histories
Operations are included on the Entity Life History to show what actually happens to an entity as a result of an event. These operations show the processing, in a detailed way, performed on the data. Each operation either changes the value of attribute(s) in the entity or changes the entity's relationship occurrences. Each effect on an entity is performed by a set of operations.

They are shown by an Operations List, describing each operation using a pre-defined syntax, which cross-refers to the life history diagram. Small boxes, containing operation numbers, hang off each effect box in the diagram. The number in the box refers to the corresponding number in the Operations List. Figure 4.99 shows the operations for the Vehicle Relocation effect on the Booking entity. These operations are carried forward to Update Process Models where they can become a type of logical Pseudocode for the program necessary to perform the event.

All the operations occur within a sequence within the effect, thus operation 1 is performed before operation 2. Of course, operations can be re-used both within the same life history or throughout the system. Every attribute included in the entity should be updated by at least one operation.

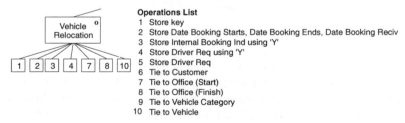

Fig. 4.99 Part of Booking Entity Life History showing operations

Syntax for operations

SSADM recommends a particular syntax for defining operations. Using a standard syntax helps to promote consistency within the project and between projects, there is also the intention that CASE tool suppliers will adopt it. If such a syntax were built into CASE tools it could form the basis of the generation of working program code from operations added to Entity Life Histories.[1] We give the syntax suggested by the SSADM Reference Manual. This syntax seems to us to be incomplete and individual projects using it will need to extend it. Variables are defined in the syntax using < > brackets, so, for example, <attribute> means that the name of the attribute should be inserted inside the bracket.

Store keys This operation sets the primary key values for the entity occurrence. To ensure the uniqueness of the entity occurrence it should always be the first operation in the life of the entity.

Store <attribute> This sets the value of the attribute to that entered by the user. This could happen at any time during the life of the entity.

Store remaining attributes This operation sets the values of any attributes that are not set by other operations (such as the one prescribed above). It is a useful shorthand way of avoiding writing out a long list of all the attributes in the entity and is particularly useful for creation effects. Sometimes it will be helpful to use the phrase 'Store remaining attributes *except* <attributes>'.

Store <attribute> using <expression> This sets a value of the attribute using the expression supplied. There is no notation or syntax given for mathematical expressions or algorithms. Often the expression or formula may be given a name and defined in Common Process Descriptions or defined in the derivation section of the Attribute Description in the Data Catalogue. This is particularly useful for derived attributes which are permanently stored.

Replace <attribute>/Replace <attribute> using <expression> These change the value of the named attribute to that input by the user or that calculated by the expression given.

Tie to <entity> This creates a relationship occurrence between the entity whose life history is being described and the named entity. It is creating the occurrence from the detail entity (many end) to the master entity (one end). Thus Operation 6 links the booking occurrence to its master of local office—there are two relationships between Booking and Office and this deals with the start office. This is equivalent to storing the value of a foreign key in a relational database or to the CONNECT statement used in CODASYL database management systems.[2]

---

[1] However, in our view the SSADM syntax is very much based on using CODASYL or other pointer-based DBMS products. Projects using other products such as relational DBMSs could develop their own standard syntax for operations that may be closer to their implementation language, e.g. SQL. The syntax presented here is that suggested by the SSADM Reference Manual.

[2] It is actually more complex than presented here with the CODASYL designer/programmer having considerable control over the management of relationships (or SETs).

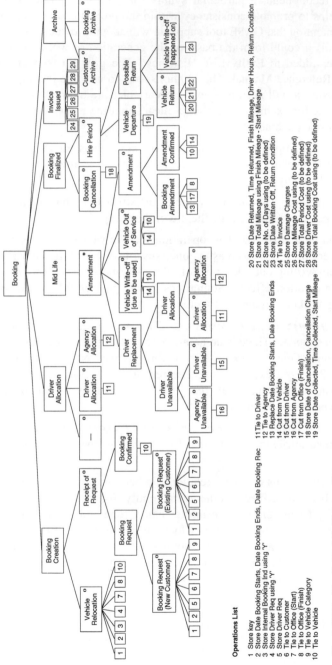

Operations List

1 Store key
2 Store Date Booking Starts, Date Booking Ends, Date Booking Rec
3 Store Internal Booking Ind using 'Y'
4 Store Driver Req using 'Y'
5 Store Driver Req
6 Tie to Customer
7 Tie to Office (Start)
8 Tie to Office (Finish)
9 Tie to Vehicle Category
10 Tie to Vehicle

11 Tie to Driver
12 Tie to Agency
13 Replace Date Booking Starts, Date Booking Ends
14 Cut from Vehicle
15 Cut from Driver
16 Cut from Agency
17 Cut from Office (Finish)
18 Store Date of Cancellation, Cancellation Charge
19 Store Date Collected, Time Collected, Start Mileage

20 Store Date Returned, Time Returned, Finish Mileage, Driver Hours, Return Condition
21 Store Total Mileage using Finish Mileage - Start Mileage
22 Store No. of Days using (to be defined)
23 Store Date Written Off, Return Condition
24 Tie to Invoice
25 Store Damage Charges
26 Store Mileage Cost using (to be defined)
27 Store Total Period Cost (to be defined)
28 Store Driver Cost using (to be defined)
29 Store Total Booking Cost using (to be defined)

Fig. 4.100 Booking Entity Life History with operations

Cut from *<entity>* This deletes the relationship occurrence for the entity whose life is represented and the named master entity occurrence. 'Cut' is often required when transferring an entity occurrence from one master to another; it will then be followed by a 'Tie'. 'Cut' is equivalent to deleting the value of a foreign key attribute in a relational database or to a DISCONNECT statement in CODASYL.

Gain *<entity>* This creates a relationship occurrence between the entity in the life history and the named detail entity (the many end). Each 'Tie' in the detail entity's life should correspond to a 'Gain' in the master entity's life; so the 'Tie to Office' in the Booking history should correspond to 'Gain Booking' in the Office Entity Life History. Relational databases have no equivalent syntax to a 'Gain' and this statement (and the corresponding 'Lose') are rarely used in practice. The CODASYL equivalent is CONNECT.

Lose *<entity>* This deletes the relationship occurrence between the entity whose life is being described and the named detail entity occurrence. This is the opposite of the 'Gain' statement.[1]

Figure 4.100 shows the completed Booking Entity Life History with all operations included.

Effect Correspondence Diagrams

Earlier in this step we developed Entity Life Histories for all entities in the system. These identified all of the events that could affect an entity occurrence and showed the system processing from the perspective of the entity. We now use those Entity Life Histories to develop a view of the processing that is based around the event. Just as an entity may be affected by many different events, an event can affect many entity types and occurrences. So Effect Correspondence Diagrams show diagrammatically the interactions (or correspondences) between the effects of the event on differing entities. These diagrams use a Jackson-like notation; showing iterations by '*' and selections by 'o'. They are used in Stage 5, Logical Design, to develop Update Process Models which show in a procedural way the processing required to perform the update resulting from the event.

Notation used in Effect Correspondence Diagrams
The examples given below to demonstrate the notation are based on the banking example developed in Chapter 2 and cross-refer to some of the life histories explained in Sec. 2.3. Figure 4.101 below shows the Effect Correspondence Diagram for the event 'Credit'.

This diagram is saying that the event 'Credit', triggered by the receipt of several attributes (Account No., Amount Credited, Date of Transaction), has two effects, on one occurrence of 'Bank Account' and on one corresponding occurrence of 'Transaction'.

---

[1] 'Tie', 'Cut', 'Gain', and 'Lose' are all to do with the management of relationships between entities. This is the complex area of referential integrity which is so important in database management systems. (Date, listed in the Bibliography, gives a full description of the referential integrity problem.) DBMS vendors each deal with the problem in different ways and the ramifications of their solutions are significant when it comes to physically implementing these operations in program code.

The one-to-one correspondence of effects is shown by the double-headed arrow connecting the effect boxes. The single-headed arrow into the first effect to be performed, annotated by the attributes whose values are supplied to the event, is known as the *event trigger*.

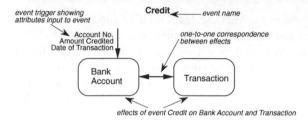

Fig. 4.101 Effect Correspondence Diagram for the event Credit showing notation

Notation for selection in Effect Correspondence Diagrams
Selection occurs when one event occurrence can affect an entity occurrence in two or more exclusive ways. This is shown on Entity Life Histories by the use of *optional effects*. The example given in Sec. 2.3 (repeated in Fig. 4.102) shows that the event Debit can have two optional effects on Bank Account depending upon the state of the occurrence of Bank Account being affected. If the account is overdrawn (shown by the *effect qualifier* '(account overdrawn)') then a 'stop' marker will be placed on the account. If the occurrence to be affected is in credit (shown by the effect qualifier '(account in credit)') then the value of the attribute Balance is simply changed. So the one event Debit can have optional effects on the entity Bank Account.

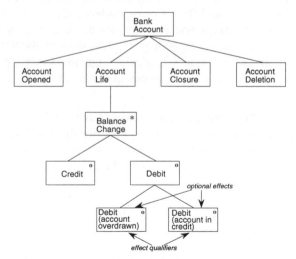

Fig. 4.102 Entity Life History showing effect qualifiers

The optional effects are shown in the Effect Correspondence Diagram for Debit (Fig. 4.103). The same names are given to the optional effects as those used in the Entity Life

History. There are two sorts of line in Fig. 4.103: the one-to-one correspondence line and the Jackson notation plain line. The plain lines show that the effect of Debit on Bank Account depends upon the state of the account occurrence being updated. One-to-one correspondence is shown between Bank Account and Transaction because both possible states of a Bank Account occurrence are effected by the event Debit.

If a Loan Account occurrence was created if the account was overdrawn, then the Effect Correspondence Diagram would also show a one-to-one correspondence between the effect on Loan Account and Debit (account overdrawn). Thus it is possible for correspondence to exist either at the optional effect level or at the level above.

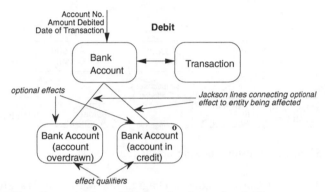

Fig. 4.103 Effect Correspondence Diagram showing optional effects

Iterations in Effect Correspondence Diagrams
Often one event occurrence will have the same effect on many entity occurrences of the same type. In Fig. 4.104 below we show the effects of the event Account Deletion: one account is being deleted along with all of the transactions belonging to that account. One-to-one correspondence of one Bank Account to a number of individual Transactions is obviously a nonsense so we need a Set of Transactions to correspond with the Bank Account. The Set of Transactions is an iteration of Transaction, shown by a Jackson connecting plain line and by the '*'. This sort of Effect Correspondence Diagram structure is quite common, occurring when an event is updating entities down the Logical Data Structure (affecting a master occurrence and its detail occurrences).

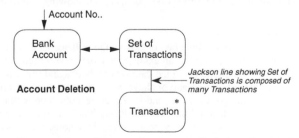

Fig. 4.104 Effect Correspondence Diagram for Account Deletion showing iterated effects

Simultaneous effects in an Effect Correspondence Diagram

Simultaneous effects occur when one event occurrence affects more than one entity occurrence of the same type in different ways. The example given in Sec. 2.3, repeated below in Fig. 4.105, shows that one event, Transfer, has two simultaneous effects on different entity types, one on the occurrence being closed (shown by the entity role name [Closed Account]) and one on the occurrence being opened (shown by the entity role name [New Account]).

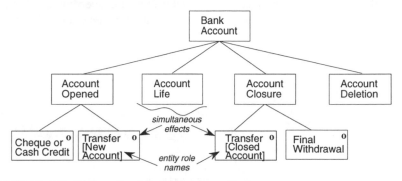

Fig. 4.105 Entity Life History showing simultaneous effects

Part of the Effect Correspondence Diagram for the event Transfer is shown in Fig. 4.106 below. Each simultaneous effect is named on the Effect Correspondence Diagram by the entity name and the entity role name (shown inside square brackets). Each of these effects may show individual correspondences with other effects.[1]

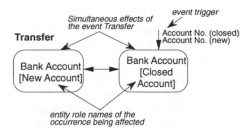

Fig. 4.106 Part of an Effect Correspondence Diagram showing simultaneous effects

---

[1] Many books show simultaneous effects by a box enclosing them. It seems that this is a case of 'Chinese whispers'; the SSADM Reference Manual has an example where two simultaneous effects are surrounded by a larger box to emphasize their simultaneity. Since then several books and training courses have adopted the enclosing box as part of the notation. Some authors have extended it to show grouped correspondences in which several simultaneous effects are shown in one-to-one correspondence with other effects (by pointing the correspondence arrow at the enclosing box). The enclosing box is unnecessary and multiple correspondence can be shown unambiguously by connecting all the correspondences together.

Event triggers on the Effect Correspondence Diagram

The single-headed arrow shown pointing at one of the effects in the diagram represents the data entering the update processing required by the event. This data, known as *event data* or the *event trigger*, is supplied by the function processing the event. Remember that events are allocated to functions during step 330, *derive system functions*. The function defines the input processing and the output processing associated with the event (shown in the I/O Structure), thus passing data to and from the event. The Effect Correspondence Diagram, that represents the event, describes the processing associated with the data held in permanent storage.

So the event trigger constitutes the information being passed to the event by the function. Usually this will consist of a list of attributes and possibly some conditions which must be considered during processing. The attributes supplied often contain the primary key of at least one of the entities to be updated. Sometimes it is necessary to update all of the occurrences of an entity, in this case an unlabelled arrow is shown as the event trigger.

The event data may have been supplied to the function by the outside world, typically if it is a user initiated function, or it may have been supplied by the function itself, typically in system initiated functions. Sometimes some data is supplied externally by the user and some by the function itself. An example of this could be where a booking needs to be created and the event data would be the attribute, Booking No. As the booking is being created no value for this attribute currently exists, therefore the function must generate a valid Booking No. to be supplied to the event for processing—this could be based on other values supplied or be generated by some other algorithmic function.

Developing Effect Correspondence Diagrams

An Effect Correspondence Diagram should be developed for every event identified and shown in the Entity Life Histories. Many Effect Correspondence Diagrams will be incredibly simple with only one entity occurrence being affected by the event. Some will be complex, using many of the notational constructs previously described. The general approach recommended by SSADM is an eight step activity for developing each Effect Correspondence Diagram. In practice, rarely more than four or five of these steps are actually required. Many practitioners find that with experience they develop their own approach to constructing Effect Correspondence Diagrams from the effects shown in life histories. However, even with experience it is useful, particularly with complex examples, to use the systematic approach and ensure that the Effect Correspondence Diagram is complete. We will demonstrate the technique using several events from Yorkies. Each time we will go through the suggested sequence but will find that some of the steps are not required in each example. The eight steps suggested are as follows:

1. Draw a box for each entity affected by the event.
2. Draw separate boxes for simultaneous effects (entity role names).
3. Include optional effects (effect qualifiers).
4. Show iterations where event affects several occurrences.

5. Add one-to-one correspondence between effects.
6. Merge iterative effects.
7. Add any entities required during update only for enquiry.
8. Add input data (event trigger).

Effect Correspondence Diagram for the event New Driver
First we have to identify which entities are affected by this event. This is easy if we are: maintaining our Event/Entity Matrix, using a CASE tool that recognizes events, maintaining an Event Catalogue, or Event Specifications.[1] If we are doing none of these things then we will have to look through all of our Entity Life Histories to ensure that we have found all of the effects of the event.

1. Draw a box for each entity affected by the event Examining the Entity Life Histories for Driver and for Licence shows the event New Driver as a creation effect in both. We show the two effects on the diagram giving it the heading of the event name as shown in Fig. 4.107 below. Note that soft boxes (round cornered) are used—hard boxes are used for pure processing activities. This is a combination of processing and data.

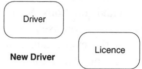

New Driver

Fig. 4.107 Effects of the event New Driver

2. Draw separate boxes for simultaneous effects This is only required if there are simultaneous effects of the event on two or more entity occurrences of the same type. This doesn't happen in the New Driver event, but does in the Vehicle Write-off event discussed later in this section.

3. Include optional effects This is necessary when the event can have optional effects depending upon the state of the entity occurrence—it is not required for New Driver, but is in the Booking Request event discussed later in this section.

4. Show iterations where event affects several occurrences The Required System Logical Data Structure for Yorkies (Fig. 4.69) shows that a driver may have many licences. Thus for one occurrence of the event New Driver, many occurrences of Licence will be created. The iteration of Licences is shown by including a Set of Licences iteration component and indicating the iteration by showing an '∗' in the effect box.

---

[1] The Event Catalogue and Event Specifications are ways of documenting events in more detail and ensuring that consistent names are used throughout the development of Entity Life Histories and Effect Correspondence Diagrams. They are not described in the SSADM Version 4 Reference Manual (though the Event Catalogue was used in Version 3 of SSADM) but many projects find them useful.

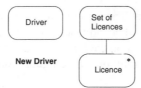

Fig. 4.108 Effects of the event New Driver showing iterated effects

5. Add one-to-one correspondences between effects We identify one-to-one correspondences between the effects on entities. These can occur when entities are connected to each other on the Logical Data Structure. When we are going from a detail occurrence to a master occurrence ('up the crow's leg') the correspondence will normally be one-to-one. However, going from a master occurrence to detail occurrences will involve us in a one-to-many correspondence, so in this case the correspondence has to be with the set of entities. In the New Driver example the correspondence is shown between Driver and Set of Licences.

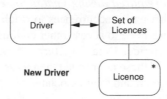

Fig. 4.109 Effects for the event New Driver showing one-to-one correspondence

6. Merge iterative effects This occurs when two or more sets of the same entity occurrences are affected in different ways by the event. This happens very rarely in practice and there are no examples of it in the Yorkies case study. In order to illustrate the problem and its resolution we have extended the New Driver example.

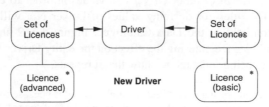

Fig. 4.110 New Driver showing two sets of iterative effects

Suppose that licences come in two types: a basic type and an advanced type. Creating an advanced type requires a different effect on Licence to creating a basic type. As a driver has many licences then there are two sets of iterative effects on Licence as shown in Fig. 4.110.

In this step we consider how these iterative effects can be merged. We have to decide which of the two possible ways shown in Fig. 4.111 best meets the requirements. The structure on the left (as we look at it) describes the situation where many licences can be created of both types. The structure on the right allows creation of many occurrences but of only one type, either 'advanced' or 'basic'. If drivers could hold both types of licences then the solution on the left is correct. If drivers only hold advanced licences or basic licences then the solution on the right is correct.[1]

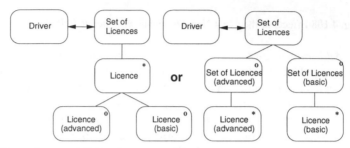

Fig. 4.111 Alternative merged iterative structures

7. Add any entities required during update for enquiry Quite often we will need to navigate through other entity occurrences to reach those entity occurrences we need to update. Sometimes we need to access other entities to retrieve data required for output. By examining the Logical Data Structure we determine whether accesses to other entities are required. If these are needed then these 'read' effects are added to the Effect Correspondence Diagram and their associated one-to-one correspondences shown. They are not required in this example.

8. Add input data This requires us to add the data input to the event by the function to the Effect Correspondence Diagram. It is the last step in development of the diagram. In this case a new driver is being created and the input data is relatively complex. Much of the data will be supplied by the user (and originally by the driver him- or herself). A value for the Driver No. attribute will need to be generated by the function, possibly requiring retrieval of other Driver No. values in order to ensure that a unique value is created. The rules for deriving values of Driver No. will be defined in its Attribute Description held in the Data Catalogue. Figure 4.112 shows the attributes for both Driver and Licence entering the effect on the entity Driver,[2] the information concerning the licences being indented to show that it repeats.

---

[1]One reason that the merging of iterative effects is rarely needed is because they can arise from optional effects which are considered in step 3. In the example in Fig. 4.111 if the solution on the left was appropriate then the structure would have been completed before step 6 was performed.

[2]This implies that the Driver occurrence is updated first but it is meaningless to consider this to be an access path since there can be no navigation with no occurrences of the data present. This is true of many creation events.

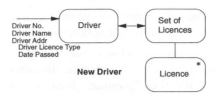

Fig. 4.112 Complete Effect Correspondence Diagram for the event New Driver

The Effect Correspondence Diagram is completed with the adding of the event data. The diagram is now checked to ensure that it is consistent with our understanding of how the update processing would occur for the event—we must ensure that all data processed by the event is input, that all correspondences are shown and that the diagram is consistent with the navigation required by the Logical Data Structure.

Effect Correspondence Diagram for the event Booking Request
As in the New Driver example previously we will work through the eight steps of developing the Effect Correspondence Diagram.

1. Draw a box for each entity affected by the event The Booking, Customer and Payment entities have the event Booking Request as an effect on their Entity Life Histories.

Fig. 4.113 Entities affected by Booking Request

2. Draw separate boxes for simultaneous effects Examining the Entity Life Histories shows no simultaneous effects for this event. Our next example requires us to use simultaneous effects.

3. Include optional effects The Entity Life History of Booking shows two optional effects of Booking Request: one for an Existing Customer and one for a New Customer. Figure 4.114 shows the optional effects or effect qualifiers for the Booking Request.

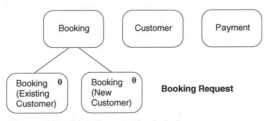

Fig. 4.114 Optional effects of Booking Request included

4. Show iterations where event affects several occurrences Although there are one-to-many relationships between Customer and Booking and between Customer and

Payment, only one occurrence of Customer and only one occurrence of Payment are affected by the event so no iterations need be shown.

5. Add one-to-one correspondences between effects We need to decide whether both options or one option correspond with the other effects. If both optional effects corresponded with the Customer then we would show the double-headed correspondence arrow linking Booking to Customer. In this example, Booking Request (New Customer) creates a Customer occurrence and creates a Payment occurrence by being the deposit for the first booking. The correspondence arrow is therefore shown between Booking Request (New Customer) and the Customer effect. The Payment effect corresponds with the Customer effect as the two entities are directly related on the Logical Data Structure. Figure 4.115 shows the correspondences between effects.

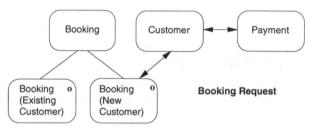

Fig. 4.115 Effects and correspondences of Booking Request

6. Merge iterative effects No iterations are involved here.

7. Add any entities required during update for enquiry only We need to check the customer information for an existing customer although this is only a read, therefore we show a second correspondence with Customer as this is a 'read' effect and as it is a different occurrence it is shown as a separate effect on the diagram.[1] There is also a requirement that the Booking Request is checked for a legitimate vehicle category and it is therefore necessary to read the Vehicle Category occurrence to which the booking occurrence is being linked. So the Vehicle Category read effect is added to the diagram and shows a one-to-one correspondence with Booking (Fig. 4.116).

---

[1]Many projects find it worth while to annotate their Effect Correspondence Diagrams showing the type of effect occurring: Create, Modify, Delete, and Read. These could be indicated by the initial in the top left corner of the effect box. Some projects extend this notation to show a stripe across the box in three parts. The first box shows the type of effect, the second shows the number of occurrences affected (only applicable in iterations and then very useful for estimating the time taken to perform the update), and the third shows whether it is an iterated (∗) or a selected effect (o).

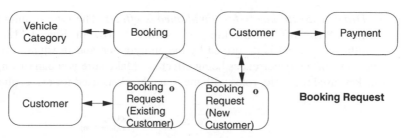

Fig. 4.116 Effect Correspondence Diagram showing 'read' effects

8. Add input data The data input to the event will be the Customer No., the Booking No. and the other booking details such as dates, offices, vehicle category, driver requirements and possibly customer details and payments details (these are shown in an abbreviated form in Fig. 4.117). It will be necessary for the function to generate a Booking No. and possibly a Customer No. and Payment No. A good way of determining the attributes required for the input data is to look at the operations defined on the Entity Life Histories as these will show exactly which attributes are being changed by the effect.

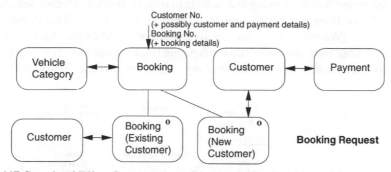

Fig. 4.117 Completed Effect Correspondence Diagram for Booking Request

The diagram is now complete and should be checked to see that it is complete and consistent with both the Function Definition and with the Entity Life Histories.

Effect Correspondence Diagram for the event Vehicle Write-off
Vehicle Write-off was identified during the development of the Entity Life History of Booking (see Fig. 4.100). Simultaneous effects of the event are on the booking occurrence on which the write-off happened and on the booking occurrences which are due to use the written-off vehicle. The event Vehicle Write-off also affects the vehicle entity and would be shown in its life history (not demonstrated in the book, but a good exercise for the interested reader).

1. Draw a box for each entity affected by the event The entities Booking and Vehicle are affected by the event Vehicle Write-off. As we will need to modify the diagram to show the simultaneous effects in step 2 we are not showing the diagram obtained from step 1.

2. Draw separate boxes for simultaneous effects The two simultaneous effects of Vehicle Write-off on Booking are shown below in Fig. 4.118. Note that the simultaneous effect is described by the entity name and in square brackets the entity role name of the occurrences being affected. (Make sure you can distinguish the square brackets used for entity roles with the round brackets used for effect qualifiers.)

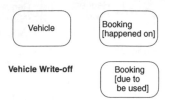

Fig. 4.118 Vehicle Write-off showing simultaneous effects

3. Include optional effects There are no optional effects that update the entity occurrences here. However, some optional 'read' effects are identified in step 6.

4. Show iterations where event affects several occurrences This event first requires the identification of the vehicle that has been written-off. Then we need to identify all of the future bookings using that vehicle to transfer them to another vehicle. So we update a Set of Bookings which contain an iteration of Booking. This is shown in Fig. 4.119 below. (We could show the Set of Bookings linked to the Booking [due to be used] effect but have chosen to show a separate Booking iteration box, realizing that later we will need to select only those bookings which are after the Write-off Date.)

Fig. 4.119 Vehicle Write-off showing iterated effects

5. Add one-to-one correspondences between effects The data structure requires us to go from the detail occurrence of the booking on which the write-off happened to its master occurrence of the vehicle written-off, and then back down the data structure to access all of the occurrences of Booking for that vehicle. Thus the one-to-one correspondences are between Booking [happened on] and Vehicle, and between Vehicle and Set of Bookings (Fig. 4.120).

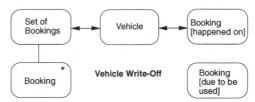

Fig. 4.120 Vehicle Write-off showing all one-to-one correspondences

6. Merge iterative effects There is only one set of iterations here so no merging is required.

7. Add any entities required during update for enquiry only We need to ensure that the bookings being updated are those requiring replacement vehicles. Thus we need to select only those bookings which are due to depart after the write-off date. So we have shown a selection of bookings differentiating between those bookings that have departed and those bookings that are before departure. This is shown using the effect qualifier notation giving the effect qualifiers of '(departed)' and '(before departure)'. The bookings before departure are the same set of occurrences that require updating with the change of vehicle. As these are shown as the entity role '[due to be used]' then the optional 'read' effect and the simultaneous effect are dealing with exactly the same set of occurrences and can be combined into one effect box as in Fig. 4.121. This effect box then shows both an entity role name and an effect qualifier.

Complex enquiry processing is required to determine which vehicles are available to replace the vehicles written-off and may require different replacement vehicles for each booking. These could be documented on the Effect Correspondence Diagram or alternatively a separate Enquiry Access Path could be developed for this part of the function.

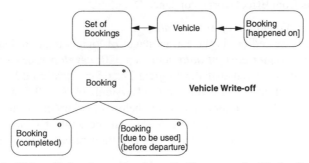

Fig. 4.121 Vehicle Write-off showing optional 'read' effect merged with simultaneous effect

8. Add input data The input data that triggers the event are the values of the attributes Booking No. and Vehicle Write-off Date. The entry point will be the Booking on which the write-off happened. This is shown in Fig. 4.122 which completes the Effect Correspondence Diagram for Vehicle Write-off.

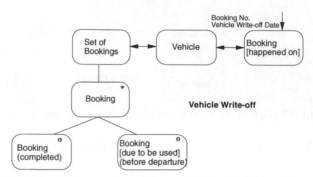

Fig. 4.122 Completed Effect Correspondence Diagram for Vehicle Write-off

Enquiry Access Paths

Introduction

Enquiry Access Paths help us to validate formally that the Logical Data Structure can support the enquiries that are defined for it. Each enquiry is defined initially in the Requirements Catalogue and, if accepted as part of the required system, is further documented in a Function Definition. In this step we develop an Enquiry Access Path for each enquiry. The technique of developing Enquiry Access Paths is considered by the SSADM Reference Manual to be part of the logical data modelling technique.

The notation used for Enquiry Access Paths is quite similar to that used for Effect Correspondence Diagrams: it uses one-to-one correspondence arrows, entry points and Jackson-like iterations and selections. The Enquiry Access Paths are carried forward to step 530, *define enquiry processing,* where they are used to develop Enquiry Process Models (a very similar approach is used to that for development of Update Process Models from Effect Correspondence Diagrams).

Informal Validation of Access Paths

This was carried out in the earlier stages of logical data modelling, particularly in step 140, *investigate current data,* and step 320, *develop required data model.* There we informally checked that the Logical Data Structure could support processing, both enquiry and update, for the required system. In Sec. 3.5 we discussed the informal validation of the enquiry. We repeat below the diagram from Sec. 3.5 which was used to demonstrate the thought processes that the analyst would use when validating an enquiry to list the vehicle categories and their prices used by a particular customer in the last year.

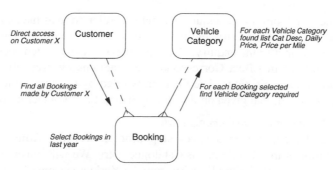

Fig. 4.123 Informal validation of Customer Vehicle Category Enquiry

Enquiry Access Paths—notation

Figure 4.124 below shows the Enquiry Access Path for the Customer Requirements Enquiry for which the informal validation was shown in Fig. 4.123. Each access is represented by a soft box, indicating that it is a data type diagram rather than a process type diagram. The correspondences between accesses are shown by one-to-one correspondence arrows. Unlike the Effect Correspondence Diagram the Enquiry Access Path uses directional single-headed arrows. These directional arrows help to indicate the navigation path taken by the enquiry.[1] These correspondence arrows show one-to-one correspondence so in Fig. 4.124 one Booking occurrence is accessing one Vehicle occurrence and one Customer occurrence is accessing one Set of Bookings.

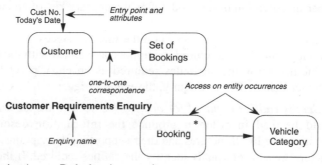

Fig. 4.124 Enquiry Access Path showing notation

---

[1] We feel that it is wrong to indicate the navigation path that the enquiry should take at this stage in design. We have not yet decided on the technology for implementation (done in Technical System Options). With many physical implementations, including relational databases, it is not necessary for the programmer to specify navigation paths. The directional correspondences suggested by SSADM imply a CODASYL or other pointer-based implementation. We prefer the non-directional correspondences suggested by the double-headed bi-directional arrows (or the multi-directional arrows used by some projects) used in Effect Correspondence Diagrams. It is not clear to us why a different notation is used for Effect Correspondence Diagrams and Enquiry Access Paths, possibly the intention is to distinguish the techniques by the arrows used.

The entry point to the enquiry (sometimes referred to as the *enquiry trigger*) is shown by an arrow into the first entity occurrence to be accessed. This is annotated by the attributes input to the enquiry.[1] Iterated accesses and selected accesses are shown in the same way as in Effect Correspondence Diagrams by using the Jackson notation for iterations and selections. The diagram is titled by the enquiry name; which should be consistent with that given on the corresponding Function Definition.

Developing an Enquiry Access Path

SSADM recommends a seven-step process working from initially the Function Definition or the Requirements Catalogue entry. We will illustrate this process with the Customer Vehicle Driver Enquiry from the Yorkies system.

1. Name the enquiry Enquiries were first identified in the Requirements Catalogue and have been further defined, after Business Systems Options, in Function Definitions. During step 330, *derive system functions,* the enquiry was named and described within the Function Definition. The name of the enquiry is used as the name for the Enquiry Access Path.

The Function Definition for the Customer Driver Vehicle Enquiry described it in the following terms: 'Find all vehicles used in departed bookings by a particular customer, and list the registration numbers, makes and models, driver names and addresses or agency names and addresses.'

2. Define the enquiry trigger This comprises the attributes and conditions input to the enquiry. This may be defined in the Function Definition of the enquiry or may require further investigation in step 360. Often the primary key of an entity is used as the entry point. The enquiry trigger is documented as a list of attributes annotating an arrow pointing at the first access shown on the Enquiry Access Path. The I/O Structures and their supporting I/O Structure Descriptions associated with the Function Definition for the enquiry show the attributes required as an entry point for the enquiry. In the Customer Vehicle Driver Enquiry, the enquiry trigger will be Customer No.

3. Identify entities required for access We need to decide which entity occurrences should be read in order to produce the information described by the Function Definition, the I/O Structures and their supporting descriptions. From the Logical Data Structure we can informally identify the entities required. If the structure is very large and complex we may need to examine the Entity Descriptions to find to which entities some attributes belong (a CASE tool holding the Data Catalogue should be able to provide this information rapidly).

---

[1] A similar point to that made in the previous footnote. Defining the entry point in this way seems to determine the navigation path taken by the enquiry. Many database languages do not require the programmer to specify the entry point and several possible entry points are determined by the program code for the enquiry. We would prefer, along with bi-directional correspondences to show multiple access points in the same diagram if these are appropriate. For example, in the example above a possible access point could be on Booking by the attribute Date Booking Starts—this would not normally produce a very efficient enquiry but it should really be left to the physical designer, query optimizer (the software used by relational DBMSs to decide upon the access path) or the programmer to decide upon the most efficient navigation.

This should identify all of the entities required to produce the output, although we may need to navigate through occurrences of other entity types in order to produce the required information. In most simple cases we can use the informal navigation and validation techniques discussed earlier in the section. Below in Fig. 4.125 we show the relevant parts of the Required System Logical Data Structure to satisfy this enquiry.

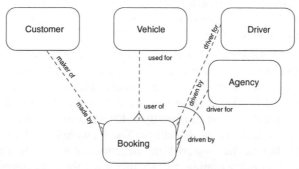

Fig. 4.125 Part of data structure required for Customer Vehicle Driver Enquiry

4. Draw view of Logical Data Structure required for enquiry The recommended technique is to re-draw the Logical Data Structure in a particular way which makes it easier to draw the Enquiry Access Path. Master occurrence to detail occurrence accesses (one-to-many) are shown vertically as in Fig. 4.126 where Customer is directly above Booking. Detail occurrence to master occurrence accesses (many-to-one) are shown horizontally as in Booking to Vehicle.[1]

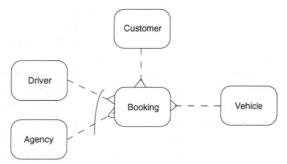

Fig. 4.126 Partial Logical Data Structure required for enquiry showing 'horizontal' and 'vertical' accesses

[1]Our experience is that there is little point in taking this step having identified the entities required for access. It is usually more straightforward to draw the Enquiry Access Path as in step 5. We have described the technique suggested by SSADM. Some CASE tools allow the user to select various entities on the data structure and thereby generate an Enquiry Access Path. It may be that these tools work by first developing a diagram using the rules given in step 4.

5. Redraw as a Jackson-like structure This is where the structure of the Enquiry Access Path is developed. Using the relevant part of the data structure we identify where iterated or selected accesses are required and show the one-to-one correspondences between accesses. Figure 4.127 shows the basic access path for the Customer Vehicle Driver Enquiry. A reasonable approach to developing access paths is:

- identify iterated accesses
- identify selected accesses
- show correspondences

Following this approach with our example, we first deal with iterations. After accessing the Customer occurrence there will be accesses of the many associated occurrences of Booking. This is shown by the iterated access with Set of Bookings containing an iteration of Bookings (note that the notation is exactly the same as that used in all Jackson structures and particularly in Effect Correspondence Diagrams).

Then we identify the selections. These can arise in two ways: by the nature of the relationship on the Logical Data Structure, or from selection criteria imposed by the enquiry.[1] In our example, the enquiry asks for only departed bookings so we have shown a selection that separates the booking occurrences into those before departure and those after departure.

We are also asked to show the drivers and agencies used by the departed bookings. The data structure (see Fig. 4.126) shows Booking participating in an optional exclusive relationship with Driver and Agency. (This reflects the requirement that a booking can be driven by only one of: a Yorkies driver, an agency driver, or the customer themselves. Thus both relationships are optional as well as exclusive.) There are three options each requiring different accesses for the departed bookings: 'Driver Used', 'Agency Used', and '—'. The '—' option indicates that no driver was recorded and implies that the booking was driven by the customer.

Lastly we show the one-to-one correspondences. These can be identified by looking at the data structure. If we are reading from a master occurrence to the detail occurrences (down the crow's leg), we will always find a Set of Detail occurrences. So one Customer access corresponds with one Set of Bookings.

When a selection is used, then where correspondence occurs, it depends completely on the enquiry requirements. As we are only interested in vehicles for bookings that have departed, then each 'After Departure' Booking access corresponds to one Vehicle access. Each 'Driver Used' Booking access corresponds to one Driver access and each Agency Used access corresponds to one Agency access. This produces the diagram shown in Fig. 4.127.

---

[1]Later we formally document these selection criteria and add them to the Enquiry Process Models. However, if specifying these selections in more detail improves the readability of the Enquiry Access Path, there is nothing wrong with documenting at this point and annotating the diagram with these selection criteria.

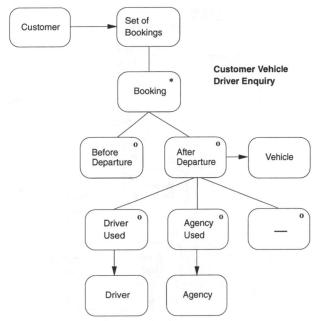

Fig. 4.127 Enquiry Access Path showing correspondences, selections, and iterations

Logical Data Structures sometimes show recursive relationships where an entity occurrence has a relationship with other occurrences of the same type. (The example given in Sec. 2.1 was where an employee could manage many other employees.) In Enquiry Access Paths these recursive accesses can occur in two ways: either from the master to the details or from the details to the master. The master occurrence to the detail occurrences would be shown in the normal way using correspondence to 'Set of..'. The one-to-one correspondence from the detail occurrence to the master occurrence of the same type is shown by an arrow pointing back from the access at itself. (However, it seems more consistent to use the entity role notation showing a one-to-one correspondence between Employee [worker] and Employee [manager].)

6. Show entry point and annotate with attributes input to the enquiry As in the Effect Correspondence Diagrams the entry point is shown by an arrow indicating the attributes whose values are supplied by the function to the enquiry. In this example, the attribute values required are those of the primary key of Customer, Customer No., and Today's Date. The date is needed to apply the selection criteria (or condition) for Before Departure and After Departure bookings. The obvious entry point here is the Customer as we have the primary key of Customer.

Any selection criteria are also added to the entry point so the condition for all departed bookings (Today's Date≥Departure Date) is shown on the arrow pointing into Customer in Fig. 4.128 which shows the completed Enquiry Access Path.

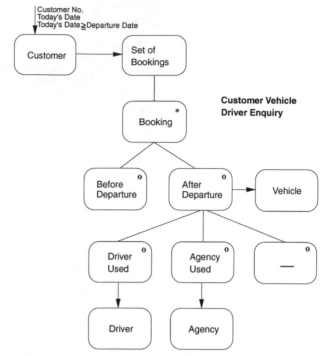

Fig. 4.128 Completed Enquiry Access Path for Customer Vehicle Driver Enquiry

There are various kinds of entry point that can be used. Often access is via the primary key of an entity. This indicates that the value of the primary key of the occurrence is supplied.

Another possibility is for access to be via non-key attributes of the entity. Values of these attributes will be supplied to the enquiry and, as these are not the primary key attributes, it is expected that several occurrences will be identified by the enquiry.

The third type of entry point is to all occurrences of the given entity (implying a serial read). This would be shown by an unlabelled arrow.

Foreign key values should never be used as entry points—the access should always be through the relevant master occurrence. Similarly when the key value of a master entity is required then access to the master occurrence should be shown—to only show access to the detail would suggest that a foreign key value in the detail occurrence must exist. Both of these uses of the foreign key value imply particular physical implementations in which foreign key values are stored in the detail occurrences.[1]

7. Check enquiry We need to ensure that the enquiry can be satisfied using 'normal' database retrieval techniques. The normal database techniques that the access paths

---

[1] Foreign key values would always be required in relational database implementations but they need not be stored in CODASYL and hierarchical databases, since access to the master entity occurrence can be managed through a pointer chain rather than by joining on key values.

should satisfy are that each occurrence required may be read by one of the following access methods:

- read entity occurrence directly via the primary key value;
- read next detail entity occurrence of master entity occurrence within a defined relationship;
- read master entity occurrence of detail entity occurrence within a defined relationship;
- serial reads of entity occurrences.

If the enquiry cannot be satisfied using these access methods then it may be necessary to modify the processing in some way. The Enquiry Access Paths would be annotated to explain the additional processing required (such as sorting). Another alternative, if the normal database accesses cannot satisfy the enquiry, is to modify the Logical Data Model to enable the enquiry to be performed. It may be that important entities and relationships have been missed during development of the data model.

Two problems that occasionally occur when Jackson structures are used to define processing are known as *structure clashes* and *recognition problems*. Structure clashes occur when the output and input data structures do not match each other. Recognition problems occur when the data necessary to satisfy a condition statement cannot be determined until one path following from the condition statement has been performed. These problems are less likely to arise when well-designed databases and fourth generation languages are used as these tools resolve many of these types of problems within their languages. Structure clashes are usually identified when Enquiry Process Models are developed in Stage 5—they are briefly discussed in Sec. 5.5. Detailed discussion of these problems is really beyond the scope of SSADM. The interested reader is referred to the wealth of material on Jackson Structured Programming.

The Function Definition defines the User Roles permitted to make the enquiry. The Entity Descriptions and the Data Catalogue also contain information about the access rights defined for the data—we need to ensure that the functional views and the data views of access rights are consistent.

8. Document all entry points. Before Physical Design all of the entry points on the Logical Data Model need to be identified. One copy of the Logical Data Structure is annotated to show all entry points. Each entry point is shown by arrows pointing at the relevant entity showing the attributes whose values will be supplied by the enquiries or updates. Primary key access is usually shown in a shorthand way by an arrow head without its body or by an arrow with a circular flight. It is important to show both enquiry and update entry points so reference will need to be made to the Effect Correspondence Diagrams as well as to the Enquiry Access Paths.

Enquiry Access Path for Daily Departure and Return List
This is a list of the vehicle departures and returns expected at a particular depot on a particular day. It is printed at the end of a previous day's business at the office and collected by the depot staff before starting work in the morning. The list is separated into departures and returns; detailing the vehicles, drivers, or agencies, or otherwise

used by the booking. This list was used as a example for normalization in Sec. 4.5—the attributes required for the output are listed there.

We will not work through all of the steps required to produce this Enquiry Access Path. However, it is an interesting example in that several possible diagrams could be used to show the retrieval of the same information. Each diagram would produce a different process model and eventually could produce different programs.

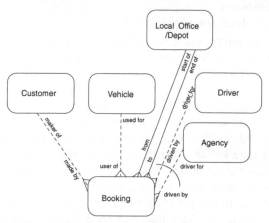

Fig. 4.129 Partial Logical Data Structure showing information required for the Daily Departure and Return List

Figure 4.129 above shows the entities required from the Logical Data Structure to satisfy the enquiry. There are two possible strategies to retrieving the information. First, we can start from the local office and then identify the departing bookings and arriving bookings for the particular day. Second, we could search through all of the booking occurrences to find those that met our criteria of a particular office (as either start or finish) and the date in question as either departure date or arrival date. Each of these strategies gives rise to a different Enquiry Access Path.

The Enquiry Access Path shown below in Fig. 4.130, which is perhaps the 'conventional' SSADM approach, follows from the first strategy. The enquiry data is the required Office No. and the date which the report is for. This identifies one occurrence of Local Office. From this occurrence following the 'start of' relationship to Booking gives the set of all of the departing bookings from that office. Each departing booking either belongs to those 'Departing Today', or to those 'Not Departing Today'. This is shown by the selection under booking. For the booking that is departing today, we find the associated Vehicle and Customer occurrences (these are from the many end to the one end so a one-to-one correspondence occurs). We also have to find the driver. There are three options: either it is driven by the customer, with no driver being recorded; or a Yorkies driver is used, so a Driver occurrence is accessed; or an agency is used, so an Agency occurrence is accessed.

The arriving bookings would be identified by following the 'end of' relationship from Local Office. After identifying these, the remaining accesses are exactly the same as those for the departing bookings. On the Enquiry Access Path shown below in Fig. 4.130 we have extended the effect qualifier notation used on Effect Correspondence Diagrams to indicate the different ('to' and 'from') sets of booking that are identified.

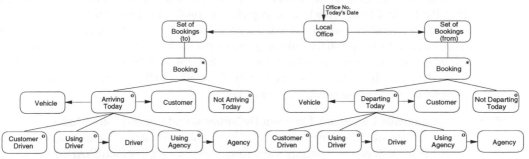

Fig. 4.130 Enquiry Access Path for Daily Departure and Return List (Version 1)

An alternative approach to this enquiry is to retrieve all of the bookings that meet the search criteria that identify those departing from or arriving at the required local office on the required date. This means that the initial access is on a 'Set of Bookings' which is made up of an iteration of Booking, each of which is subjected to the search criteria. In Fig. 4.131 we have shown two options in the selection: 'Not departing or arriving at Local Office' and 'Departing or arriving at the Local Office today'. The latter set could be further separated into the departing set and the arriving set. Notice that our search criteria involves checking the foreign key value of Local Office No. in the Booking occurrence—this is contrary to SSADM's recommendation of not using foreign key values as access points. However, in most physical implementations, particularly relational databases, but also in most CODASYL implementations, this is easily physically achievable. It therefore seems to us to be quite reasonable. Notice also that we have had to show two separate access paths: a simple one to identify the details of the given local office and a more complex one to retrieve the appropriate bookings.

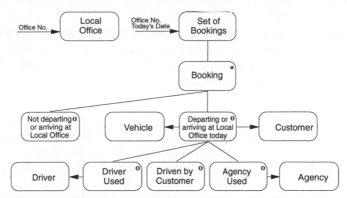

Fig. 4.131 Enquiry Access Path for Daily Departure and Return List (Version 2)

Other access paths could be devised if direct access was possible on the booking by the date. This example demonstrates some of the difficulties in providing an access path as different strategies are appropriate for different physical implementations. Perhaps the major point of the Enquiry Access Path is to show that the information can be retrieved from the Logical Data Model but it is probably unwise to regard these diagrams as a detailed specification. The physical designer or programmer (or in the case of relational databases the query optimizer software) should decide upon the best navigational route for retrieving the required information. If SSADM is followed to the letter then problems can arise from following highly detailed specifications too closely. This example is discussed further in Chapters 5 and 6.

Modify the Requirements Catalogue, Function Definitions, and Logical Data Model

The production of Entity Life Histories, Effect Correspondence Diagrams, and Enquiry Access Paths will almost certainly have identified changes to other SSADM products. We discuss below the sort of modifications that may be required.

Requirements Catalogue

This will need to be modified in two ways. First, we may have identified new requirements by producing the major products of step 360. Second, many of the Requirements Catalogue entries will have been resolved by the techniques employed in the step.

Developing Entity Life Histories can identify new requirements in several ways. In the earlier steps of the project, events were identified using Data Flow Diagrams and Function Definitions. In this step, examining the processing requirements from a data viewpoint might identify additional functional requirements. These new requirements would need to be confirmed with the users and added to the Requirements Catalogue. We also consider the validation requirements of the new system—complex life histories imply that the system must perform complex validations to allow each event to occur. The Entity Life Histories must represent the degree of validation required by the user. This reflects on the use of Entity Life Histories as a design tool and any ways in which the design is being modified should be reflected in a non-technical way in the Requirements Catalogue.

Many of the functional requirements, detailed in the Requirements Catalogue, will be resolved by functions and their associated events. This resolution is noted on the Requirements Catalogue entry (see Fig. 3.12). As each entry becomes resolved, it ceases to be an active requirement.

Function Definitions

Throughout step 360, *develop processing specification*, we extend the specification of the required system processing that we began with the Required System Data Flow Diagrams in step 310 and continued with the identification of functions in step 330. In this step we have built Effect Correspondence Diagrams and Enquiry Access Paths for those events and enquiries identified in step 330 and included on the Function Definitions. The development of Entity Life Histories, by adopting a different perspective, normally leads to the identification of further events. These events will need to be included in existing functions, or alternatively, new functions will need to be defined. Thus throughout step 360 it is necessary to revisit step 330, *derive system functions,* and ensure that the Function Definitions are consistent with the events defined in the Entity Life Histories.

As we develop the processing specification by building Effect Correspondence Diagrams for each event and Enquiry Access Paths for each enquiry, we may identify other changes to the Function Definitions. We may, for instance, recognize that a function needs to create identifiers for new occurrences of entities—the function Make Booking needs to produce a Booking No. to create an occurrence of Booking. Thus there is some degree of overlap and interaction between step 330, *derive system functions,* and step 360, *develop processing specification* (and also with step 350, *develop specification prototypes*).

Logical Data Model

Developing Entity Life Histories will probably lead to changes in the Logical Data Model. Sometimes we will need to create new entities as a result of our analysis. Sometimes a complex, iterated structure in an Entity Life History indicates that, instead of there being one entity type, there are two types. The iterated component occurring in the life history then becomes a separate entity which acts as a detail to the original entity.[1] Sometimes we find ourselves building complex parallel structures each showing independent sequences. This may result from the merger of two independent entities first shown in a one-to-one relationship—often separating back to two entities can simplify processing and enquiries.

Very frequently identification of new events prompts the addition of new attribute types to the Logical Data Model and to the Data Catalogue. For example, the event Cancellation occurring in the life of Booking identified two new attributes: Cancellation Date and Cancellation Charge. These needed to be incorporated on the Entity Description for Booking. Attribute Descriptions for these would be included in the Data Catalogue. Development of Effect Correspondence Diagrams and Enquiry Access Paths can lead to us also identifying new entity types, new relationships and new attributes. These may be necessary to make the processing of the enquiries and the updates possible.

Logical Data Model Volumetrics

Detailed volumetric information is required to determine the amount of disc storage required and to time the transactions performed by the system. This information is needed to develop Technical System Options in the next stage of the project. Earlier in the project, during Feasibility and Business System Options, attempts will have been made to perform rough calculations on data storage and number of transactions and possibly on transaction times.

In this step we can predict more accurately the requirements for data storage space since we are fairly confident that our Logical Data Model will not change significantly throughout the rest of the project. The major changes to it have been incorporated

---

[1] This occurs in one of the exercises at the end of this section.

through relational data analysis and through entity/event modelling. We now assign volumes to all entity types and relationships. These volumes are recorded in the Entity Descriptions and the Relationship Descriptions. These descriptions give detailed volumetric information showing minimum, maximum, and average numbers of occurrences. They also indicate growth rates and any underlying assumptions used to produce the volumetric information.

The Data Catalogue contains Attribute Descriptions and Grouped Domain Descriptions. These also contain volumetric information describing the size and format of the attributes in the required system. This information can be used together with the attributes assigned to each entity (shown on the Entity Description) to calculate the number of characters required to store each entity occurrence. (Note that this will be an approximate figure if there are any variable length attributes.) The actual physical storage space taken up by the entity occurrence will, of course, be considerably larger and depends upon the storage mechanisms used by the database management system software. The total space 'logically' occupied by the average number of occurrences of the entity can be calculated by multiplying the average number of occurrences by the average length. In this step the volumetric information described in the Logical Data Model should be reviewed to ensure that it is complete and consistent.

A good and highly visual way of summarizing the volumetric information is to write it on a copy of the Logical Data Structure diagram (see Fig. 4.132). The average numbers of occurrences and the lengths of each entity can be written inside the boxes. The volumes of relationships can be written on the relationship lines.

The number shown inside the entity box shows the average number of occurrences held on the system at any one time and is taken from the Entity Description. Figure 4.132 shows that there are, on average, 2600 drivers. Of course, archival arrangements need to be taken into consideration in determining these figures. The Entity Life Histories, showing the archival events, and the Entity Descriptions, showing details of the archival requirements for each entity, will help to clarify the figures.

The number on the relationship line shows the average number of dependent occurrences.[1] For example, there are on average 50 vehicles per local office. This information can be taken from the Relationship Descriptions or can be calculated from the ratio of the numbers of detail occurrences and master occurrences.

If the relationships are optional at either end then the number of dependent occurrences may not correspond to the ratio shown on the relationship line. For example, the number of invoices (24000) multiplied by the number of bookings on an invoice (2) does not equal the total number of bookings (52500); this is because the relationship is optional at the booking end (some bookings will not yet have been invoiced).

---

[1] This diagram can be extended to show the average number of characters required for each entity occurrence. These could be put in the top right-hand corner of the entity boxes.

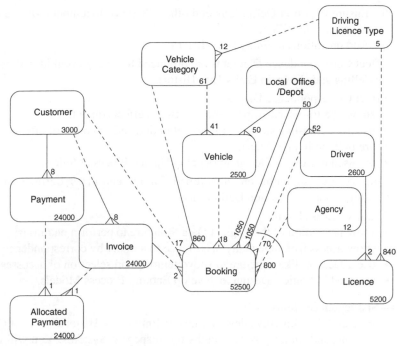

Fig. 4.132 Required System Logical Data Structure showing average volumes

It is often useful to use this kind of diagram in the earlier stages of the project. During the Business System Options and the Feasibility stages, volumetric information can be used to make rough estimates of the performance of certain critical transactions. This will be necessary to size the system and estimate typical hardware and software costs. This kind of information can also be useful in determining critical functions during step 330, *derive system functions*.

SUMMARY
The major end-products of this step are:

- Entity Life Histories;
- Effect Correspondence Diagrams;
- Enquiry Access Paths;
- Logical Data Model volumetrics.

The steps in the production of Entity Life Histories are:

1. Identify events from the Required System Data Flow Model and assign to functions;
2. Develop an Event/Entity Matrix showing all entities from the Required System Logical Data Model and all events identified on Function Definitions;
3. Draw 'normal' Entity Life Histories, working from the bottom of the Logical Data Structure to the top, identifying all events that normally affect the entities;
4. Complete the Entity Life Histories working down the Logical Data Structure to identify events that abnormally affect the entities;

5. Ensure Function Definitions and other SSADM documentation are consistent with the events identified;
6. Add operations to Entity Life Histories.

Effect Correspondence Diagrams are produced for every event identified in entity/event modelling and shown in Entity Life Histories.

Effect Correspondence Diagrams:
- show one-to-one correspondences between effects on entities;
- use a Jackson-like structure to show iteration and selection of effects;
- are built up in eight steps;
- are used in Logical Design to develop Update Process Models.

Enquiry Access Paths are developed for all enquiries defined in Requirements Catalogue and/or Function Definitions.

Enquiry Access Paths:
- show navigation of the Logical Data Structure to perform enquiries;
- show access from one entity occurrence to another by correspondence arrows;
- use a Jackson-like structure to show iteration and selection of accesses;
- are used in Logical Design to develop Enquiry Process Models.

Exercises—Scapegoat Systems

Exercises 4.7.1–3 involve development of Entity Life Histories, Effect Correspondence Diagrams, and Enquiry Access Paths for Scapegoat Systems. You will need to refer to the data structure which is shown below in Fig. 4.133.

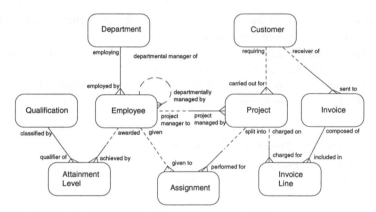

Fig. 4.133 Required System Logical Data Structure for Scapegoat

4.7.1   Entity Life Histories

The Project entity was identified during the Scapegoat data modelling exercises in Secs 3.4., 4.3, and 4.5. The following description was given by a user of the life of a project.

A project is initiated by either a user request (for an internal project) or by negotiation with a customer. When either internal agreement has been reached or a contract has been signed with the customer then the project will be entered onto the system.

A project manager is selected and then staff are allocated to the project. The project manager develops project plans. When these have been agreed, a version number and agreement date are entered onto the system. A project will be made up of several distinct stages: the start date and end date of each stage are entered into the system as they occur. After each stage is completed the work undergoes a quality assurance review, and the QA date and result are then entered.

On completion of the whole project a full review is carried out and the results recorded on the system. One year after the final review the project is archived.

PROJECT
Project Code
* Customer No.
* Staff No. (Project Manager)
Project Description
Proj Start Date
Proj End Date
Plans Agreed Date
Plan Version No.
Stage No.
Stage Name
Stage Start Date
Stage End Date
QA Result
QA Date
Final QA Date
Final QA Result

Fig. 4.134 Attributes in the Project entity

a) Develop an Entity Life History for the Project entity.
b) Add operations to each effect.
c) Consider the handling of stages: what other ways could this be done?
d) Develop an Entity Life History for the Employee entity: you will need to make some assumptions including those necessary to handle redundancy, resignation, dismissal and death.

Note that 'gain' and 'lose' effects have not been shown on our suggested solutions.

4.7.2   Effect Correspondence Diagrams

Use the Entity Life Histories developed previously for Project and Employee to help develop Effect Correspondence Diagrams for the events given below. The effects on other entities are described where necessary.

a) *New Project* The event New Project appears on the Entity Life History of Customer. Apart from linking Project to Customer, the attribute No. of Projects in Customer is incremented.

b) *New Invoice* This event affects the Customer, Invoice and Invoice Line entities. The Customer Balance is amended. Invoice and Invoice Line entity occurrences are created along with their respective relationships

c) *New Employee* An I/O Structure of the dialogue for this event was developed in the exercise at the end of Sec. 3.4. The Elementary Process Description associated with the function Record New Staff is repeated below:

'The basic employee details are entered such as Name, Grade and Department No. and the system generates a Staff No. Further personal details are then added such as Full Name, Address and Date of Birth.'

'The employee needs to be assigned to a manager in the same department. The system should be able to display a list of possible managers: this could be staff one or two grades above the grade of the new employee. When a suitable manager has been identified, either previously or by selecting from this list, then their staff number is entered.'

'The new employee may also be allocated some staff for him or her to manage. The system should be able to display a list of potential staff to be managed by the new employee, and these could be all staff one and two grades below the employee in the same part of the department. The Personnel Manager then inputs Staff Nos. of those employees to be managed by the new employee (most new employees will have no staff so the input of possible staff only occurs in approximately 20% of cases).'

The Personnel Manager then enters a variable number of qualifications that the employee has. A qualification number is entered and then validated by displaying the qualification name and the subject area. Providing this is satisfactory then the date qualification passed and the level attained are entered.'

Consider carefully how you handle the recursive relationship.

4.7.3   Enquiry Access Paths

Develop Enquiry Access Paths for the following enquiries for the Scapegoat system

a) *Customer Project Report.* For a given customer (known customer number) print out the customer name, address and a list of all projects with project code, project name, start date and end date.

b) *Staff Allocation Sheet.* For a given project print out the customer name and number; the project code and description and the staff working on the project; their name, grade and the number of days that they are working on it. (Remember to look for selections using the optional relationships.)

c) *Employee Details Enquiry.* Find out everything about an employee; employee number, employee name, date of birth, home address, home telephone number, qualifications and dates achieved; which projects they are working on and have worked on, with project name, number and the number of days that they are working on that project; which projects they have managed and are currently managing, with code and number, and their departmental manager's number and name.

4.8   Confirm system objectives (step 370)

Overview

This step is concerned with ensuring that the system requirements have been fully identified, considered and, if appropriate, met. Much of the work during Requirements Specification has concentrated on the functional requirements for the new system. In this step, the main emphasis is on the non-functional requirements. The major products which are revised in this step are: the Requirements Catalogue, the Function Definitions, and the Logical Data Model.

Requirements Catalogue

This was created at the beginning of the project and has been maintained throughout. In step 120, *investigate and define requirements*, an attempt was made to capture all of the requirements seen by the users as desirable features of the new system. (Section 3.3 described this step and gave a full description with examples from the Requirements Catalogue.) It was used to develop Business System Options and when an option was selected it was modified to show which requirements were to be incorporated in the new system and which were to be left out.

In step 310 the Requirements Catalogue was modified to indicate which requirements had been left out and the reasoning behind those decisions. The Requirements Catalogue was expanded to include any newly identified requirements and cross-referred to the Required System Data Flow Diagrams and to the Required System Logical Data Model (step 320) showing how particular requirements had been met. Non-functional requirements concerning access restrictions, archival, and security are defined in the Logical Data Model during step 320. Functional requirements for update and enquiry are reflected in functions defined in step 330, *derive system functions*. Performance type objectives, known as Service Level Requirements, were expanded from the Requirements Catalogue and included in the Function Definitions. In step 350, *develop specification prototypes*, the requirements for critical functions were investigated by demonstrating prototypes of those functions to the users and obtaining feedback which could result in further requirements or other changes to the catalogue. In step 360, *develop processing specification*, event-entity modelling might identify further requirements.

In this step 370, *confirm system objectives*, we need to ensure that the Requirements Catalogue is complete. Each entry in the catalogue should be inspected to verify that it has either been discarded (with a reason for the decision being given) or has been resolved (with cross-references to the appropriate specification areas, such as Function Definitions or aspects of the Logical Data Model).

Some entries may be as yet unresolved. These are those that will be resolved by the Technical System Options stage. Generally they will be system-wide non-functional requirements such as: operating conditions, general human–computer interaction considerations, physical security and general software security requirements, conversion requirements, audit requirements, and requirements for interfaces with other systems. Each of these should be fully defined and, if possible, given objective quantifiable measures.

Function Definitions

These were developed from the Required System Data Flow Diagrams in step 330. The Function Definitions should describe how each functional requirement, detailed in the Requirements Catalogue, will be satisfied by the new system. In addition, the Function Definitions document Service Level Requirements (discussed with examples in Sec. 4.4) that quantify the performance expected of the function in ways such as: response times, reliability statistics, and ease of use (measured by learning speeds). In this step it is particularly important to ensure that all Function Definitions include Service Level Requirements, paying particular attention to those functions only identified as a result of entity-event modelling—these will not have been included in the Requirements Catalogue agreed at the end of Stage 2, Business System Options, and investigation of their performance requirements will be needed.

Quantitative Service Level Requirements are an important input to:

• Technical System Options where we estimate how well each option can meet them;

- performance calculations performed during Physical Design;
- acceptance testing by users;
- Service Level Agreements which may contractually bind the provider of the facilities to supply these service levels to the users. These sort of agreements are only practicable if precise levels of service are defined.

Logical Data Model

In step 320, *develop required data model*, we expanded upon access, security, and archival requirements in the Entity Descriptions, Relationship Descriptions, and in the Data Catalogue. In particular, Entity Descriptions were expanded to show access restrictions defining which user roles were allowed which types of access to the data (for an example see Fig. 4.14). In this step, *confirm system objectives*, we review the Logical Data Model and the Data Catalogue to ensure that these access requirements have been fully considered, particularly looking at any entities first identified during relational data analysis or during entity-event modelling. We ensure that the Requirements Catalogue entries are consistent with the access, archival, and security information detailed in the Logical Data Model. Archival requirements are also broadly defined in the Requirements Catalogue, amplified in the Entity Descriptions, and described by the 'deletion' effects in the Entity Life Histories. These should also be reviewed to check they are complete and consistent. Any security measures necessary to protect the data are also considered in the Entity Descriptions—these may have implications for the Technical System Options.

SUMMARY

- This step ensures that the Requirements Catalogue is complete, particularly considering the non-functional requirements.
- All functional requirements, forming part of the new system, should be cross-referenced to other SSADM products, particularly Function Definitions.
- The Logical Data Model is checked to ensure that non-functional data requirements have been defined, particularly access requirements, archival requirements, and security requirements.

4.9 Assemble Requirements Specification (step 380)

Introduction

Each of the SSADM stages, from Stage 0, Feasibility, through to Stage 6, Physical Design, is completed by a formal process involving the users (and other experts) in making decisions and in accepting end-products. The Business Systems Options and Technical System Options stages are completed by the users making a decision regarding the future directions of the system (and project). All the other stages end with a step called 'Assemble...'. This 'Assemble...' step involves checking the accuracy, completeness, and consistency of the end-products of the stage. The products are checked both individually and as a whole. This checking is normally performed by a formal quality assurance review—strictly speaking the actual review is not part of this step which concentrates on the preparation for the review. Techniques for quality control are outside the remit of SSADM and are the responsibility of the project management method (e.g. PRINCE) used. Further discussion of an approach to quality control is given in Chapter 7, Management Aspects. As a result of quality control, some end-products may need amendment and further review.

All SSADM end-products are defined by Product Descriptions in the SSADM Reference Manual. This contains quality criteria for each product: at the lowest level of each Product Breakdown Structure, quality criteria are defined for individual parts of the product; at higher levels of the breakdown structure, quality criteria define consistency and completeness of logically related groups of products. In each of the sections dealing with the 'Assemble...' steps we discuss the objectives of the review and identify some of the most important points to which users and technical experts should pay particular attention. For a full description of quality criteria see Part 4 of the SSADM Reference Manual.

Stage 3 products to be reviewed

In this step all the products that comprise the Requirements Specification are brought together, checked, reviewed formally and published. It is the last step in the Requirements Specification module and ensures that a complete and accurate specification is passed on to the next stages of the project.

A large number of detailed products are produced during this stage and formal review of the complete set is a daunting task. Each of the products should have been subjected to informal review by users and other analysts throughout the module. However, this may be the only point at which the comprehensive set of products can be considered together. Although some products, e.g. the Logical Data Model, will be substantially complete well before the stage ends, later steps, such as the development of Entity Life Histories, may require revisions to these products.

Figure 4.135 shows the Product Breakdown Structure for the Requirement Specification document. The majority of the products developed during the stage are included in this document, but there are some notable omissions. First, the Required System Data Flow Model is missing. The main way in which processing is specified in SSADM Version 4 is using Function Definitions, which carry forward some of the supporting documentation to the Data Flow Diagrams. Thus Elementary Process Descriptions become part of Function Definitions. I/O Structures, which were derived from I/O Descriptions, also become part of Function Definitions.

Another omission is any of the documentation associated with prototyping—any important discoveries in this area are fed into the Requirements Catalogue, Function Definitions, or other SSADM products. Menu and Command Structures agreed during prototyping are passed to Dialogue Design in Stage 5 and are reviewed at the end of that stage. The other product, the Prototyping Report, is considered by management and is not formally reviewed in this step.

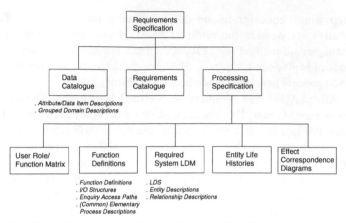

Fig. 4.135 Product Breakdown Structure for Requirements Specification

It is important to consider the set of products as a whole and before discussing the quality criteria that can be applied to each individual product we consider some of the criteria that can be applied to the whole Requirements Specification. The following questions could be asked:

- does the specification conform to the scope and terms of reference set in the Project Initiation Document?
- is the specification consistent with the organization's information systems strategy?
- does it meet the business objectives set in Business Systems Options?
- do the users agree that their requirements have been considered?

Some consistency and completeness checks that could be applied across the whole Requirements Specification are:

- is the Data Catalogue consistent with the Required System Logical Data Model?
- does every entity defined in the Logical Data Model have an Entity Life History?
- are the functional requirements in the Requirements Catalogue supported in the processing specification?
- have Enquiry Access Paths been defined for all enquiry functions?
- have all events shown in Entity Life Histories been allocated to at least one function?
- does every event have an Effect Correspondence Diagram?
- do the attributes described in the operations in an Entity Life History appear as attributes in the appropriate Entity Description?
- is the Requirements Catalogue cross-referenced to the other documentation such as the Function Definitions and the Logical Data Model?
- are the access rights defined in the Logical Data Model consistent with those defined for update and enquiry in the Function Definitions, Effect Correspondence Diagrams, and Enquiry Access Paths?

Having considered some of the general quality criteria looking across the whole of the Requirements Specification; we now consider each of the end-products of the module in turn and discuss the criteria that can be applied to them individually.

Requirements Catalogue

All of the functional requirements and most of the non-functional requirements should have been resolved during the Requirements Specification module. The users should ensure that every functional requirement has been resolved and cross-referenced to specification documents such as Function Definitions and Entity Descriptions. Some non-functional requirements may be unresolved at the end of this stage—these will be those concerned with the technical environment and are addressed in Stage 4, Technical System Options. The users should also ensure that any requirements not carried forward from the Business Systems Options are documented with the reasons for their omission.

Required System Logical Data Model and Data Catalogue

These comprise a complete definition of the required system's data. It is important to ensure that they are consistent with one another and that all attributes described in the Entity Descriptions are fully defined in the Data Catalogue. Some attributes/data items may appear in the Data Catalogue but not in the Entity Descriptions. These will normally be derived information which is supplied on system outputs. Each Attribute Description contains cross-references to where the attribute is used and as such may cross-reference many SSADM products: Entity Descriptions, I/O Structure Descriptions, Elementary Process Descriptions, and operations on Entity Life Histories. Maintaining consistent links with all of these documents is almost impossible without the use of a CASE tool. The technical reviewer needs to be confident that a consistent set of information is provided and may sample these cross-references in order to judge whether consistency has been maintained.

Checks that should be applied to the Logical Data Structure might include: that all entities have been identified, that all entities *really are* entities, that no redundant relationships are shown, that all relationships are named at both ends, that all many-to-many relationships and one-to-one relationships have been resolved, that the entities do not contain repeating information. The model needs to be checked for completeness: ensuring all entities on the diagram have Entity Descriptions and that all relationships shown have Relationship Descriptions.

The Entity Descriptions should contain a complete list of attributes with foreign keys and primary keys fully defined. The keys should be consistent with the relationships shown on the Logical Data Structure. Some other checks that should be applied are:

- is each entity name and textual description meaningful and accurate to the users?
- are access rights correctly assigned to user roles?
- is the volumetric information complete and accurate?
- are archival requirements complete and consistent?

Function Definitions

These comprise the Function Definition forms, the I/O Structures and I/O Structure Descriptions included within each function, any Enquiry Access Paths necessary to perform enquiries within the function, and any Elementary Process Descriptions which further describe how the function is performed. The Function Definitions summarize and incorporate much of the processing specification and cross-refer to other elements within the specification such as events defined in Entity Life Histories and in Effect

Correspondence Diagrams. It is important to ensure that all this information regarding each function is complete and consistent at the end of this stage.

The Function Definition form (see Fig. 4.23) summarizes the function and cross-refers it to associated documentation and products. At the end of this Stage it should cross-refer to events—if it is an update function; or to enquiries—if it is an enquiry function. Service Level Requirements should be defined for each function. These are important when evaluating technical options in the next Stage. Each function must be classified according to all three types: update/enquiry, on-line/off-line and user/system initiated.

The I/O Structure Diagrams and the I/O Structure Descriptions show the data input to and output from the function. If a dialogue is being described for an on-line function then inputs and outputs would be interleaved on the same diagram. The reviewer should check that the diagram is consistent with Jackson conventions and that the descriptions are consistent with the diagrams. User review is particularly important as these structures represent their interface to the system—critical I/Os may have been reviewed by demonstrating prototypes. Users should be convinced that all data needed by the function is input and all necessary data is output. They should also ensure that the control of the dialogue as shown by the I/O Structure is consistent with their working practices.

Enquiry Access Paths defined the navigation of the Logical Data Structure necessary to support any enquiries defined within the function. The following quality criteria should be applied:

- is the diagram consistent with the Enquiry Access Path notation?
- are all input attributes supplied by or to the function?
- is the function named on the access path consistent with the Function Definition?
- are the access rights defined in the Entity and Attribute Descriptions consistent with the accesses defined?

Elementary Process Descriptions were developed as part of the Required System Data Flow Model in step 310. They are carried forward as part of the Function Definitions with particular emphasis on any common processing. There may be organizational standards on their use, e.g. for the representation of mathematical formulae and for algorithms to be performed—these will depend very much on the application and on the organization concerned. In particular, scientific or engineering applications may need detailed standards. Elementary Process Descriptions main use in Function Definitions is to define low-level common processing and each (Common) Elementary Process Description should cross-reference all of the functions that use the common process. The user should be convinced that the process description is accurate and complete for the task that is being described.

User Role/Function Matrix

This shows which users have access to which on-line functions and which of these functions are critical to the success of the system. Some quality criteria that can be applied to the User Role/Function Matrix are:

- have all on-line functions and user roles been included in the matrix?

- are critical functions identified?

Entity Life Histories and Effect Correspondence Diagrams

These are produced in step 360 using the technique of event-entity modelling. They should be consistent in that each effect of an event defined in the life histories should appear on an Effect Correspondence Diagram showing all the effects of the event. Some projects maintain an Event/Entity Matrix and find this a useful document to be reviewed as an end product of this stage. It summarizes the information on the Entity Life Histories and the Effect Correspondence Diagrams but is not formally required by SSADM as an end-product. The following quality criteria can be applied to Entity Life Histories:

- is a complete set of events defined that effect the entity?
- have operations been defined and added to each effect?
- have the Jackson conventions been followed?
- are all creation, modification and deletion events shown?

It can be difficult to review life histories with users as the notation may be difficult to understand in a non-technical way.[1] They may need to be informally presented with the analyst validating the sequences implied by the Entity Life History by describing all of the valid precursors to a particular effect on the entity.

Effect Correspondence Diagrams show the different effects caused by an event and how they inter-relate. Some quality criteria that can be applied to these are:

- does the diagram have an event name?
- are all entities affected by the event shown in the diagram?
- docs the diagram follow the standard notation?

SUMMARY

Step 380, *assemble requirements specification*, checks the completeness and consistency of the following set of end-products:

- Requirements Catalogue;
- Data Catalogue;
- Required System Logical Data Model;
- Function Definitions;
- I/O Structures;
- Elementary Process Descriptions;
- Enquiry Access Paths;
- User Role/Function Matrix;
- Entity Life Histories;
- Effect Correspondence Diagrams.

When a complete and consistent set has passed through quality control then the Requirements Specification is published and the project can move on to Stage 4, Technical System Options.

---

[1] It has been suggested that a good way to see if users understand life histories is to 'seed' the diagrams with mistakes and see if the users correctly identify them.

5 Logical System Specification

5.1 Introduction

The previous chapter finished with the publication of the Requirements Specification which described in great detail what the future system was to do. In this chapter, we look at two aspects of the future system: first, we determine the technical architecture which can be used to build the system (Stage 4, Technical Systems Options); and second, we produce an implementation-independent, detailed specification of the functionality considering dialogues, update and enquiry processing (Stage 5, Logical Design). Figure 5.1 below shows the two stages in the Logical Systems Specification module.

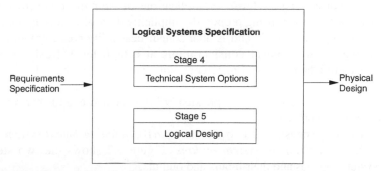

Fig. 5.1 Logical Systems Specification module

These two stages are carried out in parallel with each other, often by separate teams. The team investigating the technical architecture requires specialist technical skills in a variety of areas, but may not require specific knowledge of the requirements. The team performing Logical Design require detailed knowledge of specific SSADM techniques which follow on from those used in Requirements Specification, so ideally this team should include the same analysts who produced the Requirements Specification. There is some interaction between the two stages which may range from the extreme (e.g. if cost/benefit analysis in Technical Systems Options leads the project board to cancel the project) to the minor (e.g. if adoption of particular software in Technical Systems Options influences the design of dialogues in Logical Design). Thus the two teams should keep open communication channels but may, on the whole, work independently of each other.

5.2   Stage 4, Technical Systems Options

Introduction

In every project there comes a time in which we have to move away from a logical implementation-independent specification towards a physical implementation using specific hardware and software. Before we can move to a physical design we need to determine the technical architecture for the future system. In this stage we develop a range of possible technical architectures considering their costs, benefits, and impacts upon the organization and then assist the senior users in determining which architecture is appropriate. This stage can only be completed after a full Requirements Specification has been produced because the costs, benefits, and impacts of the future system will be very dependent upon how we have met requirements and upon volumetric information determined during specification. However, there may be some overlap and work on Technical Systems Options can usually begin before the Requirements Specification is finalized.

There is some similarity to the other options stages within SSADM: Feasibility and Business Systems Options. In all these stages, a range of options are presented to senior users, considering the business implications of the project and reviewing the business case for the system being proposed—implicitly there always is an option that the project is no longer justifiable and is abandoned. Feasibility concentrated on reviewing both business and technical considerations at a high level. Business Systems Options considered the impacts of different solutions and system boundaries on the business in some detail. Now Technical Systems Options considers different ways in which the agreed requirements may be physically implemented and further reviews the business case for the project.

The stage consists of two steps: step 410, *define technical system options,* and step 420, *select technical system options.* Figure 5.2 shows the two steps in Technical System Options and their inputs and outputs.

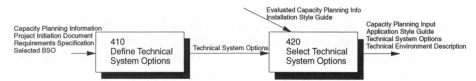

Fig. 5.2 Structure of Stage 4 Technical System Options

Step 410 involves: developing an initial set of constraints which each option should conform to; coming up with a wide range of initial options and discussing these with users to identify those with most potential; fleshing out these preferred options to give detailed technical descriptions, cost/benefit analyses, impact analyses, and development plans. In step 420, the Technical Systems Options are presented to the project board and anybody else who will make the decision, then an option is selected and reworked to reflect the decisions taken. An Applications Style Guide is developed to define user interface standards for the project.

This stage requires a wide variety of skills and knowledge as it brings together both users and technical specialists in the decision-making process. Typically technical expertise is required in: hardware, systems software, DBMS software, programming languages, development platforms, data communications, capacity planning, security, and estimating. The business/user side may involve: risk analysts, financial experts to evaluate cost/benefit analyses, and project board members and senior users to make the final decision on the technical architecture. Occasionally, outside contractors such as hardware and software suppliers are closely involved in developing the options.[1]

5.3   Define Technical System Options (step 410)

Introduction

Several options are prepared for presentation to the users (and others) who are responsible for making the selection. To develop the options the project team need to work through several tasks: first, identifying the basic constraints which all options should meet; second, coming up with a wide variety of loosely defined options; third, with the help of senior users, narrowing this down to two or three viable options; finally, refining each of these options to sufficient detail to be presented to the project board and other decision makers. Refining the option also requires estimating the physical performance of the hardware and software used in the option—experts in this area are known as capacity planners. The decision is made in the next step 420, *select technical system option*. These tasks are shown diagrammatically in Fig. 5.3.

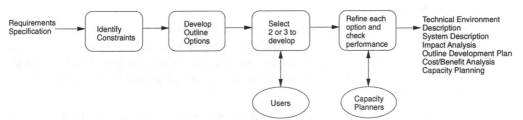

Fig. 5.3 Tasks in step 410, *define Technical System Options*

Identify constraints

The first task is to identify the base constraints that all options must satisfy. These constraints will emerge from a variety of SSADM products such as the Selected Business System Option, the Requirements Catalogue, the Project Initiation Document and the organization's information systems strategy/information technology strategy.

---

[1]This is quite popular in UK government projects where a number of suppliers offer total solutions (hardware, software, user manuals and installation), sometimes known as 'turnkey'. In these cases it is common for potential suppliers to provide 'Technical Design Studies' showing how they would meet the Requirements Specification.

These constraints should be reviewed with the user to ensure that they are still valid and to establish any relevant priorities so that conflicting constraints can be resolved. Below we discuss some typical constraints, dividing them into external and internal constraints.

External constraints

These are imposed from outside the project and will apply to all options. They will often have been set in the Project Initiation Document and strategy documents associated with the project and will have been reflected in the Selected Business System Option. Some examples of external constraints are:

Costs There may be a budget which cannot be exceeded by the project. Sometimes there is a requirement that the business performance of the system will meet certain financial objectives such as achieving an annual saving over current costs of £1 million within 3 years.

Hardware/software The organization may have set certain standards for the use of particular hardware, operating systems software, DBMS software, programming languages, and other development tools. These may have been defined in an information technology strategy. Sometimes the system will have to use existing hardware and currently installed software.

Internal constraints

These are set internally to the project by the user and were originally recorded in the Requirements Catalogue. Some were further detailed in Function Definitions and in the Logical Data Model. Development of the technical options will vary the impacts of these constraints as some may be more important than others. Some examples of internal constraints are:

Mandatory facilities Often the computer system will need to provide other facilities which are not directly associated with the project such as electronic mail, word processing, and spreadsheets. Sometimes these facilities may be linked to the system, for instance the facility to extract data from the system's database into spreadsheets for further manipulation.

Global service levels Minimum levels of service should be set across the system for availability, reliability, and contingency. They should be expressed quantitatively if possible, for example as: mean time between failures, maximum time to restore system, and performance levels of back-up system.

Data storage criteria These are derived from the Required System Logical Data Model to give the maximum file sizes and the utilization of backing storage. Some guidelines to system sizing are given in this section.

Critical timing criteria The Function Definitions will supply information such as the maximum transaction volumes, highest interactive peaks, and the critical on-line responses or off-line processing.

Information objectives The information objectives are implied by the Logical Data Model. However, as a result of the tuning performed in Physical Design, access to certain information might be reduced or sacrificed. For instance, if there is a space constraint one way of meeting it will be to archive data earlier. Thus the data storage criteria may be competing with the information objectives. It is therefore necessary to agree with the users those elements of the system's data to which access should not be reduced.

Other constraints Any other constraints not discussed above need to be specified. These will vary greatly between projects but may include: operating environment conditions (e.g. if the hardware is to be situated in an engineering workshop), data communications line speeds, portability of the software, database management system (DBMS) software characteristics such as hardware independence, reorganization timings, and the performance of interfaces with other systems.

Develop outline options

The approach is similar to the development of outline business options. Often a small group of analysts 'brainstorm' up to six options based around the constraints previously identified. The number of options is then reduced to a more manageable number for further development.

If the current system is manual then one option to be investigated should always be a revised or unchanged manual system. Similarly, if the current system is computerized, then again a no change option or slightly enhanced current system should be considered. In both these cases, we are really considering the possibility that the whole project should be terminated and this can happen at any of the options stages (Feasibility, Business Systems Options and Technical Systems Options).

Some external investigation will be required; collecting technical information from suppliers or independent hardware and software experts. This ensures that the suggested configurations can meet the requirements and constraints—it should not involve collection of detailed information.

The number of outline options will depend upon the size and complexity of the project but should rarely be more than six. This would be too many for a full development of each option and needs to be reduced to a manageable number for formal presentation to the user. Each outline option should be examined critically, with the help of users considering its advantages and disadvantages. The two or three options chosen for refinement will often include features from the other outline options.

Refine each option

Each of the options with most potential is developed into a full Technical System Option for formal presentation to the users. First, we create an initial description of each Technical System Option which includes an overview Technical Environment Description and a System Description. Then we ensure that the technical environment can meet the Service Level Requirements—any variances are noted in the Technical Environment Description. Providing each option can meet the requirements then a complete specification of the Technical System Option is produced by developing an Impact Analysis, an Outline Development Plan, and a Cost/Benefit Analysis. In this step, each of these is developed in sufficient detail only to make the selection in step

420, *select technical system options.* In step 420, we rework the options to reflect the decisions taken and provide one Technical System Option which is the basis for Physical Design (and possibly procurement).

Each of the products comprising a Technical System Option is described below. Note that during the development of technical options these become progressively more detailed—not all of the content will be fully defined at the end of step 410, but all will be defined for the Selected Technical System Option at the end of step 420.

Technical Environment Description

This describes the hardware, software and system sizing for the option being proposed. The emphasis is on describing the general categories of hardware and software rather than on identifying specific products that are to be used. Often the selection of the technical option will precede a procurement of hardware and software services which happens after the completion of the Logical Systems Specification module.

Hardware A diagram showing the overall architecture of the system is very useful. This should show the layout and number of: terminals, personal computers, communication lines, processors, and other devices. Textual descriptions are given covering: communications and networks, environmental and installation requirements (e.g. whether air conditioning required), reliability, serviceability, availability, maintainability, and any upgrade arrangements as well as any standards that the hardware must conform to (e.g. for safety).

Software A description covering: the software facilities required, the number of licences and their provision. The following types of software should be considered: application packages, operating systems software, database management systems software (DBMS), construction software (programming languages, report writers, testing tools), and system utilities (e.g. for recovery and dumping).

System sizing This has two components that the option must satisfy: the space required for storage of the data and the overall processing load. Often the system sizing will be common for all of the technical options but there may be differences in the way the data is distributed or archived.

The size of the data can be estimated by the following procedures.

1. Add together the lengths of each attribute on the Entity Descriptions (make estimates for variable length attributes).
2. Multiply the length of each entity by the average number of occurrences.
3. Add together the total sizes of all entities.
4. Add an extra percentage to this figure to allow for overheads and growth (the usual rule of thumb is to double).

This figure is an estimate of the storage requirements. If there is a requirement to hold historical data on the same database as the current data, then the length of time that data needs to be kept must be considered .

The size of the processing load is most relevant when expressed as a peak and average figure. It is the peak loading that will determine the size of processor required. This is determined in the following way.

1. Ensure that the volumetric information is present on the Function Definitions.

2. If the peak volumes occur only at certain times of the day or on certain days of the month, etc., draw loading graphs, showing where the peaks occur. (An example of this is where orders are received by post: the peak time for entry of orders will occur after the first and second postal delivery.)

3. From the above, estimate the maximum number of events and enquiries to be handled in the worst case.

4. For the most significant events and enquiries, i.e. the most numerous at the peak:
   (a) estimate the number of I/Os (roughly, how many entity occurrences are accessed);
   (b) from this estimate the number of disk accesses per second at the peak time;
   (c) estimate the CPU activity at peak;

These figures comprise the workload base models which are input to capacity planning.

Sometimes it will be necessary to produce a First-cut Physical Design, following the techniques described in Chapter 6. This enables detailed sizing of critical functions but not as detailed as in Stage 6. The emphasis is on identifying the differences between the options.

System Description

This shows how the Requirements Specification is met by the option. Generally there will be little variation between the options as to how they meet the requirements since the major decisions will have been taken at the Business System Options stage. However, sometimes different levels of meeting requirements are proposed, for instance cutting development time by using application packages but thereby reducing the flexibility offered. Maximum use should be made of the SSADM products contained in the Requirements Specification. The following products may be modified to show how each option meets the requirements that they describe: Required System Logical Data Model, Function Definitions, and the Requirements Catalogue. The System Description should make clear what facilities are **not** being provided by the option.

Impact Analysis

An Impact Analysis is produced at each of the options' stages of SSADM: Feasibility, Business Systems Options, and Technical System Options; the analysis becoming progressively more detailed as the project progresses. A thorough Impact Analysis is extremely important to the project; in this way, the effects of the system on the users and on the organization can be fully explored. Although these are not specific SSADM issues, they can have most significant effects on the information system's eventual success. Some of the components in the Impact Analysis become SSADM products in their own right. They are then further defined for the selected option and reconsidered during Physical Design. These are: Training Requirements Description, User Manual Requirements Description, Testing Outline, and Take-on Requirements Description. The Impact Analysis also contains a description of the impact of the option on the organization's structure, the user operating procedures, and a comparison of the option with other options showing advantages and disadvantages. The main components of the Impact Analysis are explained below:

Training Requirements Description In step 410 sufficient information is required to outline the difference between the training requirements for the various options. When an option has been selected then further work on the training requirements can be prepared. From the Training Requirements Description we develop a training strategy for the system. We need to consider who needs to be trained (users, operators, constructors, and management), what they need to be trained in, what costs and resources are required for this training, and when the training should be provided.[1]

User Manual Requirements Description Although design of the manual system that supports the computer system is not formally considered by SSADM, it forms an extremely important part of any information system's project. The user manual will describe the procedures that should be followed by end-users in interacting with the computerized system. In step 410 we are concerned with describing the differences in procedures between the different options. The User Manual Requirements Description provides outline information for inclusion in the final user manual.[2] The user manual can only be completed when Physical Design and possibly testing have been completed. However, some of the components can be started during Logical Systems Specification, after the option has been selected. The sort of factors that should be covered in the user manual are: descriptions of general user facilities; operating timetables; descriptions of each function, including screen displays; guidelines to the user interface; help facilities, security arrangements, error handling, and fall-back facilities.

Testing Outline In step 410, sufficient detail is required to outline the different approaches to testing, if any, required by the various options proposed. After an option has been selected then further work can be started on defining the testing strategy in the Testing Outline.[3] Obviously, testing is a complex area which will absorb a large amount of the overall resources of a project. It is, however, really outside the scope of SSADM, although many of the SSADM products will be used to define the tests.

Take-on Requirements Description Take-on considers how we are going to convert from the existing system to the future system and so is particularly concerned with the conversion of data and the method of conversion. The approach to take-on can have dramatic impacts on a systems' project and should have been considered in the Feasibility and Business Systems Options stages. During Technical Systems Options we first identify any differences in take-on strategy between the options proposed. Following selection of an option we can begin to define the overall strategy for take-on.[4] The Take-on Requirements Description by the end of the Technical System Options stage should cover: resources and costs for take-on; differences in data and file

---

[1] If the project is using PRINCE these will interface with the education products comprising: the Education Strategy, the Education Specification, and the Education Guide.
[2] If the project is using PRINCE this will interface to the User Products which contain a User Guide and User Procedures.
[3] This relates to PRINCE through the Testing Products, particularly the System Test Strategy and the Acceptance Test Strategy.
[4] This interfaces to PRINCE via the Installation and Conversion Products, particularly the Installation and Conversion Strategy.

structures between the existing and the future systems; functions necessary to convert data; strategy for change-over, e.g. parallel running or phased implementation; and resources and plans for conversion. Again, detailed design of take-on procedures is outside SSADM, although in extreme circumstances conversion can be so complex that it may require an SSADM project of its own.

Other considerations which should be considered in the Impact Analysis are discussed below, although these are not specific SSADM products.

Organization and staffing The new system may require a reorganization of personnel. The computer may replace the function of certain staff, or increase their efficiency to the extent that staff numbers might be reduced. A less obvious source of possible discontent is where the same numbers of staff will be needed, but the distribution amongst the grades may change, or new posts specific to the operation of the computer may need to be introduced. All of these factors must be presented to the users at this stage to mitigate possible problems later.

Comparison with other Technical System Options A bullet point summary should be given of the advantages and disadvantages of the option in comparison with other options. Some advantages might include improved efficiency, lower development costs, higher reliability, greater staff savings, better performance, faster implementation. Obviously the option proposed could also be disadvantaged in these areas.

Outline Development Plan

Outline plans will be produced in Feasibility, Business Systems Options, and Technical Systems Options; each in progressively more detail. In step 410, concentration should be on the differences in development plans and schedules between the options. When the option has been selected in step 420, then the plan will become less outline and more detail. The Outline Development Plan should consider: systems design, program design and programming, procurement, testing, and implementation (including conversion and change-over).

Cost/Benefit Analysis

By calculating the cost and benefits of each option we can, in theory, objectively compare one option against another and make a judgement about which is best, based upon sound financial grounds. It should be noted that Cost/Benefit Analysis seems to be a complete minefield[1] with some organizations deciding that, so called, strategic projects must go ahead—whatever the cost. Cost/Benefit Analysis should be carried out in each of the options' stages of SSADM: Feasibility, Business Systems Options, and Technical Systems Options; each time in progressively more detail. The following costs and benefits should be included:

---

[1] A recent survey (*Information Technology Review 1992/93* from Price Waterhouse) showed that 38% of IT directors admitted using 'hidden agendas' and suggested that they were rather optimistic in justifying projects using Cost/Benefit Analyses—optimistic with regard to benefits, particularly intangibles, and pessimistic with regard to costs. The report suggests that IT directors were wary of revealing their 'hidden agendas' fearing misunderstanding of their radical aims and rejection by their fellow directors. This seems to be a fairly alarming indictment of the boards of major UK companies.

Development costs These include the costs of purchasing the hardware and software necessary for the system, thus requiring figures from typical suppliers. They also include the costs of developing the software, including manpower, development software and hardware, training costs for programmers—these costs should have been considered in the Outline Development Plan.

Operating costs These are the running costs of the future system and will include costs of maintenance, costs of stationery and other consumables, and of resources to operate and support the system. This information is related to that given in the Technical Environment Description and in the Impact Analysis for the project.

Benefits This includes tangible and intangible benefits. Tangible benefits are those to which a direct financial cost can be attributed, such as displaced costs—these are costs incurred by the current system (e.g. personnel) which will not be incurred by the new system. Intangible benefits are those for which no accurate figures can be provided. In order to compare options and ultimately to justify the project, we should try to assign some figures to these benefits. However, it may be very hard to be realistic and to quantify benefits of this kind.

Several financial techniques are used to consider and justify projects such as the payback period method (how long does the system take to pay for itself) or the return on investment expressed as a percentage. Sometimes some organizations specify a 'hurdle' rate over which projects must jump in order to be accepted, e.g. a hurdle rate of 10% means that projects would have to show a greater return on investment than 10% to be accepted. All of these approaches require some account to be taken of the varying value of money over time (discounted cash flow is a suitable technique).

Assess performance of each option

Service Level Requirements defined the performance that the user requires of each function; supplied as quantifiable measures such as periods of availability, response times, recovery times, etc. We need to check that each option can meet these requirements. This is a complex and difficult area requiring great knowledge of hardware and software performance as well as detailed information about the volumes of data and transactions in the future system. The technique for estimating the effects of different workloads on hardware/software configurations is known as *capacity planning*—this is not regarded as a specific SSADM technique but one that requires specialist expertise.[1] Capacity planning is used during Technical System Options to help evaluate the different technical environments proposed; during Physical Design, capacity planning is used to assess and tune the system's performance. There are several proprietary software tools available to perform capacity planning calculations, and, hardware and software suppliers have expertise in estimating the performance of their products.

---

[1] CCTA (1992) *SSADM and Capacity Planning* (HMSO, London).

Capacity planning and Technical System Options
For all options there is certain information about the required system that can be fed into capacity planning:

Service Level Requirements These were quantified for each function and are evaluated using capacity planning techniques to give estimated performance levels from the option. Each option should be assessed in outline to ensure that it can broadly meet the Service Level Requirements. On selection of an option, a more detailed investigation should be performed. If it seems that the preferred option cannot meet the Service Level Requirements, then there are three possibilities. First, we could suggest alternative architectures which can meet the Service Level Requirements (usually this means spending more money). Second, we could negotiate a reduction in the Service Level Requirements and maintain the selected architecture. Third, we could change the functionality (usually this means reducing it) so that the Service Level Requirements can be met with the proposed architecture.

Workload base models The workload base model defines the overall requirement for system performance at any one time. We need to consider all transactions that are being performed, the amount of CPU activity they require, and the number of disk accesses. This workload base model is roughly calculated from the volumetric information defined in the Function Definitions. When it becomes clear that the Service Level Requirements are achievable for the selected option then these become the basis for Service Level Agreements. These are negotiated between the users and the IT service providers[1] and may form the basis for a contractual relationship.

SUMMARY
- Before detailed design can begin it is important to agree on the physical architecture of the new system.
- The approach to Technical System Options is very dependent on the project so guidelines are used rather than rules.
- Constraints are identified which all options must satisfy.
- The base constraints will cover such things as costs, timescales, the physical environment, distribution, and basic facilities.
- Up to six outline options are refined to two or three technical options.
- Each option will contain details of: the technical architecture, system sizing, functionality supported, costs and benefits, impacts on the organization, rough plans for construction and implementation.
- The performance of each option is checked by capacity planning experts.

---

[1] IT (Information Technology) service providers are organizations that take responsibility for the operation of the technology associated with the system. With the current fashion for 'outsourcing' this may be a completely separate organization from the users' organization.

5.4   Select Technical System Options (step 420)

Introduction

Once the two or three Technical System Options have been developed so that each includes a Technical Environment Description, an Impact Analysis, a Cost/Benefit Analysis, an Outline Development Plan and a System Description then these options can be presented to a selection panel, usually the project board. The project team will assist the panel to identify the Selected Technical System Option—this is then carried forward for the project. Often the selected option will combine features from the options originally presented; always, further work will be necessary to provide sufficient detail for Physical Design and, possibly, for procurement to go ahead. The full details of the selected option are documented in the Technical Environment Description which is also carried forward (though this needs to be validated by capacity planning experts to check that the option can handle the processing load). Once the technical environment has been decided a style guide can be developed for the application covering user interface guidelines. Figure 5.4 below shows the main tasks involved in step 420.

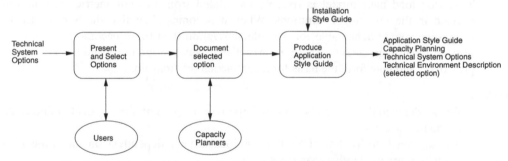

Fig. 5.4 Task in step 420, *select Technical System Options*

Presentation and selection of options

The Technical System Options are presented to a panel responsible for making a selection. Ultimately major decisions about the direction of the project are taken by the project board. They must sanction any decisions made although they may delegate the responsibility to other experts such as senior user managers and technical experts. The selection will be made through a review of written reports, describing the various options, and through formal presentation.

The project board decides who is going to make the decisions—there are several possibilities. They may decide to co-opt senior user representatives to the project board to make up the decision-making panel. They may defer responsibility to user representatives and technical experts from outside the project team but within the organization (e.g. staff from operations or from technical support teams). The project board might defer responsibility to the normal quality assurance review group. In large projects with different user groups, possibly spread over several geographic areas, then there may be different options for groups of users. A wide population of users needs to be involved in the decision-making process, and each user group could report to representatives who will make the eventual selection.

The approach to presenting the options obviously depends upon who is making the selection. In all cases the SSADM end-products comprised within the Technical System Option (Technical Environment Description, Impact Analysis, Cost/Benefit Analysis, Outline Development Plan, and System Description) will be reviewed by the decision makers. Additionally, and perhaps most importantly, formal presentations are made to the decision makers, and informal support provided. This formal presentation will normally be made by the project manager and any technical experts in the team. However, the material should be presented in as non-technical a way as possible, avoiding the use of any jargon that might not be understood. Attempts should always be made to explain the technical issues in a non-technical way so that the panel can understand the business consequences of their decisions. These presentations therefore require careful preparation and skilled communicators. In some cases, several presentations may be necessary if different user groups need to be involved—perhaps repeating the same presentation to several groups or giving different presentations to groups with different interests. The greatest emphasis in the presentations should go on showing the strengths and weaknesses of the various options and ensuring that these are fully understood by the selection panel.

Throughout the selection process various decisions may be made—these should be documented as it is often necessary to revisit these decisions during the Physical Design stage, when detailed sizing is performed, or during testing and other later stages. Throughout the selection process the project team should be available to the panel to provide explanations and amplifications of any technical areas.

Documenting the selection

Often the selected option will not be one of the complete options presented. The panel may choose elements from each of the options, possibly bringing in further ideas of their own or from outline options discarded earlier. Thus it is often necessary for the project team to rework the selected option to provide sufficient detail for the Physical Design stage and sometimes for procurement. The Technical Environment Description is carried forward from this stage for the selected option and now includes the System Description and the Impact Analysis from the selected option. The System Description emphasizes the changes in functionality that have been described in the Requirements Specification. This System Description is mainly textual with cross-references to relevant SSADM documents in the Requirements Specification (such as the Function Definitions and the Logical Data Model). The Impact Analysis is based upon the Impact Analysis within the selected option but may require rework (particularly if a hybrid has been chosen) to ensure that organization impacts, interfaces to other systems, and project objectives related to benefits detailed in the Cost/Benefit Analysis are described. These objectives should be referred to when the system has been delivered to determine whether they have been met.

As the Technical Environment Description is fully fleshed out to describe the selected option then a further check that the Service Level Requirements can be met is made. Capacity planners will estimate the workload required for the proposed option and check whether the technical environment proposed can meet these requirements. Should this further check show that the Service Level Requirements cannot be met by the selected option then the project team needs to go back to the selection panel proposing some changes. They may suggest a different technical architecture with a greater capacity (buying more hardware). They may propose a reduction in the Service Level Requirement's targets (e.g. change the requirement from a 5 second response time to 10 seconds). Or they may propose changes to the Requirements Specification (e.g. removing certain functions from the system or changing them from on-line to off-line). The selection panel will need to decide whether and how much rework is necessary if these recommendations are accepted.

Installation and Application Style Guides

Many organizations use style guides to define how users interact with computer systems. The use of style guides ensures consistency between different applications and within a given application. Generally if software and hardware behave in a consistent way then it is much easier for a user to learn a new application or to switch from one application to another. They also ensure consistent handling of features such as error and help messages. The style guides need not confine themselves solely to screens but also to paper output and input—it is important to provide a consistent design to printed reports, and input forms.

There is little point in developing a style guide until the technical environment has been decided since modern software tools can place great restrictions on the kinds of dialogues that are possible. For example, it would be silly to try to define a set of standards for user interface based upon a GUI (Graphical User Interface) approach when a particular fourth-generation language was adopted which took a form-filling approach.

Some style guides are commercially available and are typically associated with particular hardware and software. Some examples of this are IBM's Common User Access standards, standards for the use of Windows software, and Apple's standards for Macintosh applications. Often an organization, using the same hardware and software across many applications, will have an Installation Style Guide concerning common features such as printing facilities, help facilities, handling of menus, etc. At this point in the project we develop an Application Style Guide which will usually extend the Installation Style Guide to application-specific areas.

Many installations will have no style guide—it is important that the project establishes a style guide, which can then form the basis of an Installation Style Guide to be used by future information systems' projects. Below we describe some of the features that a style guide should contain, many of these could also be covered by an Installation Style Guide.

Keyboard and mouse assignment We might define certain function keys to always perform the same activity, for instance F1 for 'Help', F2 for 'Print Screen', etc. Other key combinations might be defined to do particular functions such as 'Control S' to 'Save to disk'. The use of the mouse button or buttons (if appropriate), speed of tracking, and representation of pointers on the screen should also be defined.

Standard messages These should be defined to cover 'help', 'errors', warnings for delays, standard prompts, 'welcome', and 'goodbye' messages. Standards for showing dates and times are also defined.

Use of colour Colour should be used very carefully to give a pleasing and consistent effect throughout the software. Only a few colours should be displayed at any one time. Each colour should be used in a consistent way; one colour for normal background, another colour for normal text, another colour for warning text, etc.

Menus and Dialogues Standards should be defined for: displaying the titles of menus, the number of options, the method of selecting an option, shortcuts, use of pop-up and pull-down menus, use of buttons in dialogue boxes, cancellation, and escape keys.

Forms Many 4GLs offer a form-based implementation where the user is required to fill in a screen-based form. Standards should be set for: layout, moving the cursor backwards and forwards through the form, field validation, error messages, help information, and for moving between different forms (e.g. a function key may move back to the previously entered form).

Printed reports Standards should be set for: showing dates and times, font styles and sizes, headers and footers, beginnings and ends of reports, and for page widths and lengths.

SUMMARY
- Usually two or three technical options are prepared and presented to the selection panel.
- The selection panel usually involves the project board, senior user representatives, and technical experts.
- The selection of options ensures commitment and approval from user management.
- The Selected Technical System Option often combines features from the options originally presented.
- Documentation from the original options is reworked and extended to become the Selected Technical System Option.
- The Selected Technical System Option contains the following products: Technical Environment Description (including also System Description and Impact Analysis), Outline Development Plan, and Cost/Benefit Analysis.
- Capacity planning experts check that the selected option can meet the Service Level Requirements set by the Requirements Specification.
- An Application Style Guide is developed to define a standard human–computer interface throughout the future system.

5.5   Stage 5, Logical Design

Introduction

Stage 5, Logical Design, complements Stage 4, Technical System Options, to comprise the module Logical Systems Specification. The Logical Design stage develops a more detailed implementation-independent specification of the system. It concentrates on designing the structure of the human–computer interface and on the detail of process design.

Overview of Logical Design

Figure 5.5 shows the structure of this stage.

Step 510, *define user dialogues*, builds upon the earlier identification of dialogues during Stage 3, Definition of Requirements, to provide a full implementation-independent specification of dialogues and the navigation between dialogues. I/O Structures developed in step 330, *derive system functions*, are converted to dialogue structures and navigation paths within a dialogue are defined. The navigations between dialogues are represented by Menu Structures and Command Structures. The requirements for 'help' facilities are also defined. The dialogue designs will be influenced by the findings of specification prototyping performed in step 350 and by the Application Style Guide developed in the Technical System Options stage.

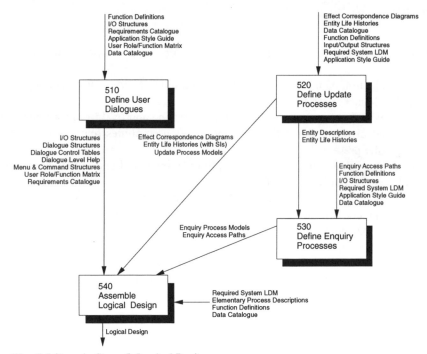

Fig. 5.5 Steps in Stage 5, Logical Design

Step 520, *define update processes*, develops Update Process Models for every event defined in the Requirements Specification. First, Entity Life Histories are extended to show all of the valid states that an entity occurrence can go through during its life and for each of these we indicate what all of the previous states could be. The Effect Correspondence Diagrams developed for each event in step 360, *develop processing specification*, are converted into Update Process Models showing for the event the sequences, selections, iterations, and conditions necessary to process the event. This is represented by a Jackson structure. Operations shown for the events on Entity Life Histories are extended and allocated to the processing shown on Update Process Models.

Step 530, *define enquiry processes*, uses a similar technique to step 520 to develop Enquiry Process Models. The Enquiry Access Paths developed in step 360, *develop processing specification*, are converted to a Jackson structure representing the input processing and merged with the output part of the I/O Structure for the function. This gives one Jackson structure to define the processing for the enquiry; addition of detailed operations and conditions complete the Enquiry Process Model.

Step 540, *assemble logical design*, checks the completeness and consistency of the logical design end-products, ensuring that the products carried through from Requirements Specification are consistent with those products developed during Stage 5. When these products have been checked the Logical Design is published.

5.6   Define user dialogues (step 510)

Introduction

This step continues the process of dialogue design begun in Requirements Analysis and continued through Requirements Specification. In step 510 we define the detailed structure of each dialogue showing how the user navigates within the dialogue and how he or she navigates from the dialogue to other dialogues via menus and commands. 'Help' facilities are also defined for dialogues. Physical aspects of dialogue design are not considered in this step; screen formats are normally not designed until Stage 6, Physical Design.[1]

Dialogues before step 510

The SSADM technique of dialogue design includes the identification of the end-users of the computer system, documented by the User Catalogue and the User Roles; the identification of which parts of the system will be on-line using dialogues; and the identification of critical dialogues which may be prototyped. Each of these activities was described in the relevant steps in earlier chapters of this book. However, we will briefly revisit each of these activities to clarify how the dialogues defined in step 510 have been identified. Figure 5.6 shows the major activities in dialogue identification.

---

[1] Of course, they can be designed earlier but there is always the risk that changes will be required later. Some formats will have been designed for prototypes and these may be retained for the eventual system.

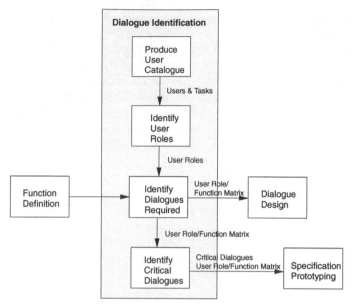

Fig. 5.6 Steps in dialogue identification

The User Catalogue was developed in step 120, *investigate and define requirements*, to define the job titles and their associated activities in the current system which are likely to be carried forward into the future system. An example of the User Catalogue is given in Fig. 3.13 in Sec. 3.3. Once the required system had been identified through selection of a Business System Option, then the user roles for the future system could be identified in step 310, *define required system processing*. A *user role* is a collection of job titles who share a large proportion of common tasks—one way of thinking about user roles is that a set of menus and access privileges will be shared by a given role. The user roles are documented on a form which is repeated below in Fig. 5.7.

User role	Job title	Activities
Depot Clerk	Depot Clerk	Record vehicles departing & returning
Sales/Customer Records	Salesman	Set up new customers.
	Customer records clerk	Amend customer details
Booking Clerk	Booking clerk	Take bookings from customer
	Driver administrator	Find suitable driver for booking
Driver admin	Driver administrator	Select new drivers and agencies from applicants

Fig. 5.7 Some user roles documented on the User Roles form

In step 330, *derive system functions*, we decided which functions were to be performed on-line—each then requires dialogue design. To show which users could perform which functions a User Role/Function Matrix was developed and then used to document which of these on-line functions (dialogues) were critical to the success of the system. Critical dialogues are normally those that occur very frequently and those associated with the most essential functions of the new system. Some of these critical dialogues were passed to step 350, *develop specification prototypes*, for physical implementation, demonstration, and discussion with users. This specification prototyping may have led to changes in the dialogue design to be fed back into Function Definitions and to dialogue design in Stage 5. Figure 5.8 shows the User Role/Function Matrix with the critical dialogues circled.

User Role/Function Matrix

Functions \ User Roles	Booking Clerk	Depot Clerk	Sales/Customer Records	Driver admin	Vehicle Fleet Maintenance	Marketing/Pricing
Make Booking	(X)					
Find Driver	(X)			(X)		
Record Journey Details		(X)				
Booking Enquiry	X					
Vehicle Availability Enquiry	(X)					
Create/Amend Customer	X		X			
Create/Amend Driver				X		
Create/Amend Agency				X		
Create Vehicle					X	
Amend Vehicle		X			X	
Modify Prices						X

Fig 5.8 User Role/Function Matrix showing critical dialogues

In step 330, *derive system functions*, we also defined the structure of inputs to and outputs from the system. These were represented by I/O Structures (using Jackson notation to represent the sequence, selection, and iteration of data input and output) and by I/O Structure Descriptions (showing the detailed data content of the inputs and outputs). For off-line processing these contain either only input or only output data but for dialogues input and output data are interleaved. For critical dialogues the I/O Structure was used to design the prototype which could then lead to a redefinition of the function and its associated I/O Structures.

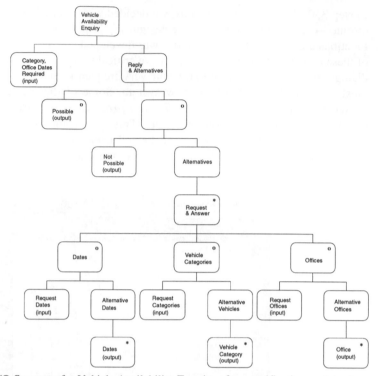

Fig. 5.9 I/O Structure for Vehicle Availability Enquiry after specification prototyping

In Chapter 4 we worked through the development of an I/O Structure for the function Vehicle Availability Enquiry (see end of Sec. 4.4) and then used it as an example for prototyping (see Sec. 4.6). Prototyping identified several problems with the dialogue as first defined in step 330, *define system functions*, which led us to revise the I/O Structure for the dialogue. The original I/O Structure used to design the prototype was shown in Fig. 4.75. In Fig. 5.9 we show the revised I/O Structure after specification prototyping. This structure now reflects the users' requirements extracted through the prototype demonstration.

Technical System Options and dialogue design

Although Stage 4, Technical System Options, and Stage 5, Logical Design, are often carried out simultaneously there is a degree of inter-relation between the two stages. During Stage 4, the performance of critical dialogues will be estimated for each of the options proposed—this may influence the logical design of the dialogue in Stage 5. Performance estimation may show that a dialogue specified in the Requirements Specification is too slow for any of the feasible technology. This could lead to a rethink of how the dialogue can be performed.

Once a technical option has been selected in Stage 4 an Application Style Guide can be developed (see Sec 5.4). This style guide contains guidelines on the amount of information per screen, 'help' messages, etc. Although these guidelines are oriented towards physical dialogue design, (accomplished in Stage 6), some will have a bearing on logical dialogue design.

Dialogue design in step 510, *design user dialogues*

The tasks required to complete logical dialogue design are shown in the shaded area in Fig. 5.10 below. First, we extend the I/O Structure Descriptions to become Dialogue Element Descriptions. This involves copying the data items from the I/O Structure Descriptions. Then we identify Logical Groupings of Dialogue Elements (LGDEs) to form logical screens. From these we identify possible pathways which the end-user can navigate through the dialogue. We also design Menu Structures and Command Structures to show how we can navigate between dialogues. Finally, 'help' facilities are defined for each dialogue. Each of these activities is described in detail with examples below.

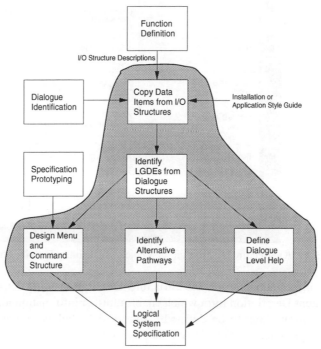

Fig. 5.10 Tasks (in shaded area) in step 510, *design user dialogues*

Copy data items from I/O Structure

The I/O Structures and I/O Structure Descriptions created using the function definition technique in step 330, *derive system functions*, and revised during prototyping, become the dialogue structures. The notation and supporting documentation for these dialogue structures is very similar to that used for I/O Structures. The I/O Structure was shown previously in Fig. 5.9; the I/O Structure Description associated with that I/O Structure is shown below in Fig. 5.11.

I/O Structure Description

Data flows represented	Booking Clerk (h)—Determine Vehicle Availability(1.2) Availability Information	
I/O structure element	**Data item**	**Comments**
Category Office Dates Required	Vehicle Category Code Office Number Start Date Finish Date	
Possible (output)	'A vehicle is available from the office on these dates'	
Not Possible (output)	'No vehicles available, other dates, vehicle categories, or offices?'	
Request Dates (input)	(Alternative) Start Date (Alternative) Finish Date	Default is to enter none
Dates	Required Booking Start Date Required Booking Finish Date	Other dates within 3 days of required start date
Request Categories (input)	(Alternative) Vehicle Category Code	Default is to enter none
Vehicle Category (output)	Vehicle Category Code Vehicle Category Description	Other categories similar to one requested available from same office on same dates
Request Offices (input)	(Alternative) Office No.	Default is to enter none
Office (output)	Office No. Office Name Office Address	Nearby offices where category requested is available on required dates

Fig 5.11 I/O Structure Description for Vehicle Availability Enquiry after prototyping

The information on the I/O Structure Description is now transferred to a Dialogue Element Description form which enables further information about groupings and about navigation paths to be defined.[1] Figure 5.12 below shows the Dialogue Element Description for the Vehicle Availability Enquiry.

---

[1] SSADM suggests copying the information from one form to another—most projects, using manual documentation, would combine the two forms into one. Projects using CASE tools would perform dialogue design in the way prescribed by the tool. It can be useful to keep a catalogue of dialogue elements as they can often be re-used in different parts of the system.

Dialogue Element Descriptions

Dialogue name   Vehicle Availability Enquiry (BC)

User role   Booking Clerk   Function   Vehicle Availbility Enquiry

Dialogue Element	Data item	Logical grouping of dialogue elements ID	Mandatory/ optional LGDE
Category Office Dates Required (input)	Vehicle Category Code Office Number Start Date Finish Date		
Possible (output)	'A vehicle is available from the office on these dates'		
Not Possible (output)	'No vehicles available, other dates, vehicle categories, or offices?'		
Request Dates (input)	(Alternative) Start Date (Alternative) Finish Date		
Dates (output)	Required Booking Start Date Required Booking Finish Date		
Request Categories (input)	(Alternative) Vehicle Category Code		
Vehicle Category (output)	Vehicle Category Code Vehicle Category Description		
Request Offices (input)	(Alternative) Office No.		
Office (output)	Office No. Office Name Office Address		

Fig. 5.12 Dialogue Element Description for the Vehicle Availability Enquiry

Frequently the designer will want to show messages displayed to the user and input information which is not permanently stored (i.e. not an attribute/data item). The convention we have adopted is to show messages in quotes, as in Fig. 5.12 above. Where variable data is entered we have used role names to show how it relates to stored values, thus alternative start dates, finish dates, etc. The convention used here is to show these before the data item name and to enclose the role name in brackets. The name given to the dialogue is normally shown as the function name qualified by an abbreviated user role name—so Vehicle Availability Enquiry (BC) refers to the dialogue related to the function Vehicle Availability Enquiry as performed by the user role Booking Clerk.

Identify Logical Groupings of Dialogue Elements

The dialogue structure is amended to show the Logical Groupings of Dialogue Elements (LGDEs). These comprise the data items that compose a 'logical screen'. They normally form an input/output pair with information being input to the computer system followed by a response. Each logical grouping of dialogue elements is shown on the dialogue structure by a ringing as in Fig. 5.13 below. Note that these 'logical screens' are not the same as physical screens or windows—they can be implemented as part of the screen (e.g. a dialogue box) or as several screens. Dialogue elements cannot overlap and must follow a reasonable sequence.

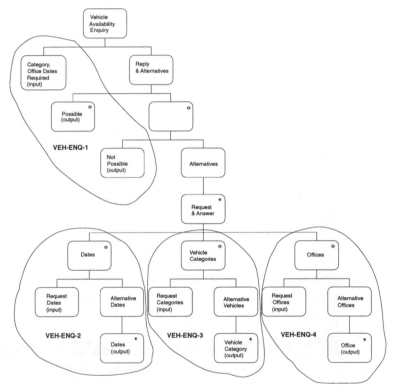

Fig 5.13 Dialogue structure showing Logical Groupings of Dialogue Elements

Each dialogue element is named and the Dialogue Element Description annotated with the identifier of the relevant LGDE. The convention used by SSADM to identify LGDEs is to abbreviate the dialogue name and then use a numeric identifier within the dialogue name: this gives us the VEH-ENQ-1 etc. However, there is no reason why more meaningful names could not be used. The Dialogue Element Description is amended to show the logical groupings as shown in Fig. 5.14 below.

Dialogue Element Descriptions			

Dialogue name   Vehicle Availability Enquiry (BC)

User role Booking Clerk | **Function** Vehicle Availbility Enquiry

Dialogue Element	Data item	Logical grouping of dialogue elements ID	Mandatory/ optional LGDE
Category Office Dates Required (input)	Vehicle Category Code Office Number Start Date Finish Date	VEH-ENQ-1	
Possible (output)	'A vehicle is available from the office on these dates'		
Not Possible (output)	'No vehicles available, other dates, vehicle categories, or offices?'		
Request Dates (input)	(Alternative) Start Date (Alternative) Finish Date	VEH-ENQ-2	
Dates (output)	Required Booking Start Date Required Booking Finish Date		
Request Categories (input)	(Alternative) Vehicle Category Code	VEH-ENQ-3	
Vehicle Category (output)	Vehicle Category Code Vehicle Category Description		
Request Offices (input)	(Alternative) Office No.	VEH-ENQ-4	
Office (output)	Office No. Office Name Office Address		

Fig. 5.14 Dialogue Element Description showing logical groupings

Identify alternative pathways

Within each dialogue we show how the user navigates between each grouping of dialogue elements, under 'normal conditions' using a Dialogue Control Table. This shows the default path and all possible alternatives and provides volumetric information to show how often each path is followed. Figure 5.15 below shows the Dialogue Control Table for Vehicle Availability Enquiry as performed by the Booking Clerk user role. This must fit with the dialogue structure—so VEH-ENQ-1 is always the entry point and must always occur once and once only: the minimum, maximum, and average number of occurrences are all one. The Dialogue Control Table shows this to be the default pathway occurring in 90% of cases—this is because we expect that 90% of enquiries can be met with available vehicles. Alternative pathways are shown in the columns marked alt 1, alt 2, alt 3 (if there are further possibilities then continuation sheets could be used)—we have estimated that 3% of enquiries will look at all possibilities, other dates, other offices and other categories and 7% will look at other combinations.

One of the problems of this form is if you have iterations within a selection, then the number of possibilities becomes very large and it is almost impossible to document in this way—we have chosen to annotate with an explanation rather than show all possibilities on continuation sheets. The maximum number of occurrences allows us to specify that enquiries on alternative dates, categories and offices can each be only performed a maximum of three times. The average figure indicates the average number of times they will occur each time the dialogue is performed. These averages are less than one because they only occur if the booking requested is not possible.

Dialogue Control Table

Dialogue name   Vehicle Availability Enquiry (BC)

Logical grouping of dialogue elements ID	Occurrences			Default pathway	Alternative pathways		
	min	max	ave		alt 1	alt 2	alt 3
VEH-ENQ-1	1	1	1	X	X	X	
VEH-ENQ-2	0	3	0.1		X	any	
VEH-ENQ-3	0	3	0.1		X	combination	
VEH-ENQ-4	0	3	0.1		X	of 2,3,4	
Percentage path usage				90	3	7	

Fig. 5.15 Dialogue Control Table for Vehicle Availability Enquiry (BC)

We also annotate the Dialogue Element Descriptions to show the mandatory and optional Logical Groupings of Dialogue Elements. In Fig. 5.16 below: 'M' indicates that VEH-ENQ-1 is mandatory; the other LGDEs are optional, shown by 'O'. These follow from the dialogue structure and from the Dialogue Control Table.

Dialogue Element Descriptions

Dialogue name	Vehicle Availability Enquiry (BC)		
User role	Booking Clerk	Function	Vehicle Availbility Enquiry

Dialogue Element	Data item	Logical grouping of dialogue elements ID	Mandatory/ optional LGDE
Category Office Dates Required (input)	Vehicle Category Code Office Number Start Date Finish Date	VEH-ENQ-1	M
Possible (output)	'A vehicle is available from the office on these dates'		
Not Possible (output)	'No vehicles available, other dates, vehicle categories, or offices?'		
Request Dates (input)	(Alternative) Start Date (Alternative) Finish Date	VEH-ENQ-2	O
Dates (output)	Required Booking Start Date Required Booking Finish Date		
Request Categories (input)	(Alternative) Vehicle Category Code	VEH-ENQ-3	O
Vehicle Category (output)	Vehicle Category Code Vehicle Category Description		
Request Offices (input)	(Alternative) Office No.	VEH-ENQ-4	O
Office (output)	Office No. Office Name Office Address		

Fig. 5.16 Dialogue Element Description annotated to show mandatory and optional LGDEs

Design Menu and Command Structures

These show how each user role can navigate from one dialogue to another. Menus provide a hierarchical structure through which the user can access dialogues and sometimes off-line functions. The menu will list out the various dialogues available to the user at any one time and may include moving to sub-menus. For the naive or infrequent user menus provide a view of all possibilities available.

Command Structures show, for each dialogue, how a given user role can move to other dialogues—this will include navigation through a Menu Structure and ways in which the user can access other dialogues directly without using menus. The user may issue commands which enable another dialogue to be accessed or the computer system may decide, based upon its own information, that the user should perform a particular dialogue.

Menu and Command Structures complement each other to provide a full design of all the possible paths. There is no requirement that menus be used in a system designed with SSADM although most systems will make some use of menus. However, all on-line systems will require Command Structures.

Menu design

The User Role/Function Matrix (see Fig. 5.17 below) shows for each user role all the dialogues they can perform—giving a first-cut menu design. Thus when an individual logs on to the computer system with a log-on ID that maps to the user role Booking Clerk,[1] they will have available to them the five dialogues listed in Fig. 5.17. These could be presented as a single-level menu—often the case in simple systems. In complex systems, several levels of menus will be needed—the set of dialogues available in each menu being defined by the User Role/Function Matrix.

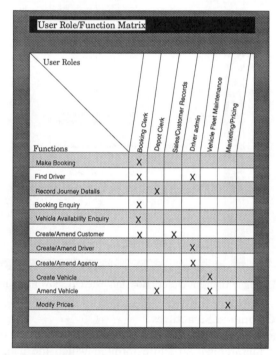

User Role/Function Matrix

Functions	Booking Clerk	Depot Clerk	Sales/Customer Records	Driver admin	Vehicle Fleet Maintenance	Marketing/Pricing
Make Booking	X					
Find Driver	X			X		
Record Journey Details		X				
Booking Enquiry	X					
Vehicle Availability Enquiry	X					
Create/Amend Customer	X		X			
Create/Amend Driver				X		
Create/Amend Agency				X		
Create Vehicle					X	
Amend Vehicle		X			X	
Modify Prices						X

Fig. 5.17 User Role/Function Matrix

Some general guidelines for structuring menus are:
- they should reflect the task requirements of users;
- they should naturally belong together;
- they should reflect the results of specification prototyping;
- the individuals taking on the particular user roles should be consulted about the structure of the menus they will use;
- they should be consistent with the Application and Installation Style Guides.

---

[1] Although we have presented this section as though different Menu Structures or even different dialogues are designed for each user role, in simple systems this will not be the case and most users will see exactly the same menus and dialogues. In very simple systems there will be only one user role.

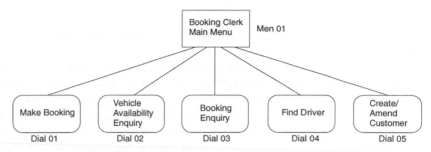

Fig. 5.18 Menu Structure for the user role Booking Clerk

The Menu Structures, which may be uneven, are shown as a hierarchy. Menu options are shown by 'hard' boxes, dialogues are shown by 'soft' boxes (those with round corners). Figure 5.18 shows the Menu Structure for the Booking Clerk.

Command Structures

For each dialogue, designed for a specific user role, there will be several possible paths that can be followed on termination of the dialogue—these are shown using a Command Structure.[1] Although the implementation of Command Structures is left until Stage 6, Physical Design, some mechanisms for passing control may have been defined by the style guides (for instance, a particular function key may always take you back to the higher-level menu). The Command Structure can then be annotated to show these commands. Every dialogue will have an associated Command Structure to show all of the possible paths of control that can follow its completion. Figure 5.19 shows the Command Structure for Vehicle Availability Enquiry (BC).

Command Structure		
Dialogue name	Vehicle Availability Enquiry (BC)	
User role	Booking Clerk	
Option	**Dialogue or menu**	**Dialogue/menu name**
Make another enquiry	Dialogue	Vehicle Availability Enquiry (BC) (Dial 02)
Make booking from enquiry	Dialogue	Make Booking (BC) (Dial 01)
Quit to menu	Menu	Booking Clerk Main Menu (Men 01)

Fig. 5.19 Command Structure for Vehicle Availability Enquiry (BC)

---

[1] If Command Structures are associated with menus then annotation of Menu Structures with arrows to show the paths of control seems to be a better method of communication. These diagrams will then become quite similar to the widely-used technique of state transition diagrams.

Define Dialogue Level Help

We discuss with users any requirements for Dialogue Level Help. This is help for the dialogue as a whole and not screen help which is designed during Stage 6, Physical Design. It will cover: contextual information such as 'Where am I?' and 'What tasks have been performed?'; job related help such as 'How should I perform this?' and 'What should I be doing next?' and navigational help such as 'How do I escape from this dialogue, pause this dialogue, terminate this dialogue?' The 'Help' defined here is not concerned with filling in the individual fields on the screen nor with validation and error handling. Sometimes field-level help is well supported in the development environment. There should be considerable discussion with users to ensure that all Dialogue Level Help requirements are identified and documented. Sometimes the help requirements may have impacts on the dialogue structures, and these should be shown on the Dialogue Element Description form.

The Dialogue Level Help is associated with the other documentation for the particular dialogue. For each dialogue, help messages should be defined which cross-reference the Dialogue Element Description to show when 'Help' may be obtained.

SUMMARY

- Step 510, *define user dialogues*, follows on from earlier dialogue identification work in Requirements Analysis and Requirements Specification.
- I/O Structures for on-line functions become dialogue structures, their supporting I/O Structure Descriptions become Dialogue Element Descriptions.
- Logical Groupings of Dialogue Elements are identified to form 'logical screens'.
- Navigation Paths between Logical Groupings of Dialogue Elements are identified and shown on Dialogue Control Tables.
- Menu Structures are defined for each user role using the User Role/Function Matrix.
- Command Structures are defined for each dialogue.
- Dialogue Level Help is defined with assistance from the users.

Exercises—Scapegoat systems

The I/O Structure Diagram for New Employee was developed in Exercise 4.4.2.

5.6.1   Logical Groupings of Dialogue Elements

Use the answer provided in Appendix D to Exercise 4.4.2 to develop Logical Groupings of Dialogue Elements (LGDEs). Show these by ringing on the I/O Structure.

5.6.2   Dialogue Control Table and Dialogue Element Description

Complete the Dialogue Control Table for the New Employee dialogue. Make reasonable assumptions about alternative pathways and frequencies. Produce a Dialogue Element Description showing the mandatory and optional LGDEs

5.6.3   Menu Structure

Develop a Menu Structure for the user role Personnel Manager. The following functions will be handled on-line by the Personnel Manager (this represents a column of the User Role/Function Matrix). You may choose to group these functions in whatever way seems reasonable.

New Employee
Change Manager
Change Details
Change Department
Allocate to Projects
Employee Details Enquiry
Management Structure Enquiry
Staff Allocation Enquiry
Submit Resignation
Leave on Resignation
Make Redundant
Leave on Redundancy
Employee Death
Employee Dismissal

5.6.4   Command Structure

For the dialogue New Employee complete a Command Structure to show how you may navigate from this dialogue to other dialogues or menus. Make reasonable assumptions about what activities are likely to follow this dialogue.

5.7   Define update processes (step 520)

Introduction

This step defines the detailed update processing at a logical level. Entity Life Histories are extended to show state indicators. These identify each of the possible states that an entity occurrence can be in during its life and show which states can immediately precede each state. Update Process Models are developed for each event identified in step 360. Each Effect Correspondence Diagram is converted into an Update Process Model which shows in great detail how the processing is performed for the update.

Update Process Models and Enquiry Process Models are developed using the SSADM technique of *logical database process design*. After discussing state indicators we describe the general technique of logical database process design giving examples of Update Process Models and Enquiry Process Models. We then give two examples demonstrating how Update Process Models are derived from Effect Correspondence Diagrams. SSADM defines a separate step 530, *define enquiry processes*, for the development of Enquiry Process Models (dealt with in Sec. 5.8). However, the technique for updates and enquiries are very similar and the material given in this section, particularly that discussing logical database process design, is relevant to Sec. 5.8 also.

State indicators

Everything in the real world is dynamic, constantly changing its state as events affect it. Similarly in our model of the world in software, entity occurrences have their state changed by event occurrences. This is depicted in SSADM using Entity Life Histories.

A *state indicator* identifies every state that an entity occurrence could be in—it is an attribute of the entity that is updated every time an event affects it. This means that the value of the state indicator shows where in its life an entity occurrence is at any one time. Using the formal structure defined by the life history, we can also define all of the states that can immediately precede a given state. State indicator values can verify whether an event occurrence can be allowed to affect an entity occurrence.

Figure 5.20 shows part of the Booking Entity Life History; the *set to state* indicates that as a result of the event Booking Confirmed the state indicator of the Booking occurrence becomes '4'. The *valid previous states* show that before a Booking occurrence can reach the state of Booking Confirmed it must have been immediately previously in either state '2' or in state '3'. State '2' indicates that a Booking Request (New Customer) has last been performed. State '3' indicates that a Booking Request (Existing Customer) has last been performed. (This can be seen from the full life history shown in Fig. 5.22.) The values given to the state indicator have no significance provided that each event assigns a unique value to the entity. The convention is to number all the effects of events consecutively, starting with '1'.

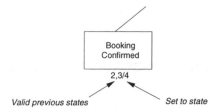

Fig. 5.20 Part of 'Booking' Entity Life History showing state indicators

Assigning state indicators
The first thing to do is to assign a value to each of the effect boxes on the Entity Life History as shown in Fig. 5.21. The basic technique is simply to number all of the effect boxes, starting at the left-hand side of the Entity Life History—some refinements to this are discussed later. The numbers underneath the effect boxes show the value that the state indicator has been set to after the event has affected the entity occurrence. For example, after the occurrence has been created by the Booking Request (Existing Customer) event, the state indicator is set to the value '3'. Therefore, if we find that the state indicator of a Booking occurrence is '3', we know that it has just been created but has not yet been confirmed.

Note that state indicator values are not assigned to the two deletion events, 'Customer Archive' and 'Booking Archive'; this is because the occurrence will then cease to exist and therefore cannot take state indicator values. Later in this section we discuss how operations deal with state indicators and will see that some operations presuppose a special state indicator value of 'deleted'. The non-existence of a state indicator value is shown by '—'.

Null effect boxes indicate that something may not happen; meaning that if the null box is selected then the state of the entity occurrence is unchanged—shown by an asterisk in place of the state indicator value (as in Fig. 5.21) or sometimes by not annotating the null box with any values.

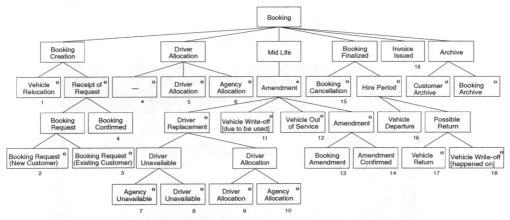

Fig. 5.21 Entity Life History for Booking showing 'set to' state indicators

To allocate the valid previous state indicator values we go through the life history working out for each effect what all the possible values could be from the structure. The Booking Entity Life History including all state indicators is shown in Fig. 5.22.

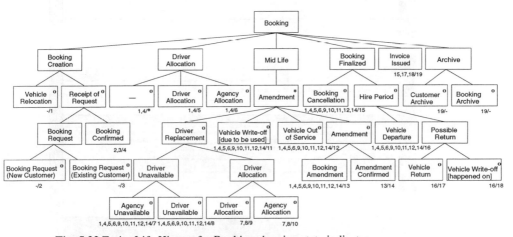

Fig. 5.22 Entity Life History for Booking showing state indicators

The state indicator values depend entirely upon the structure of the Entity Life History:

- Creation effects have a null valid previous value because the state indicator cannot have a value before the occurrence exists.
- When there is a selection, all optional effects that are alternatives to one another have the same set of valid previous state indicator values. (Driver Allocation and Agency Allocation both have the valid previous values of 1 and 4 in Fig. 5.22.)

- When there is an iteration, the value set by the repeating effect will also be included as one of the valid previous values for that effect. (One of the valid previous values for the Vehicle Out of Service effect is '12' which is the value set by the subsequent Vehicle Out of Service effect.)

Documenting state indicators in Entity Descriptions

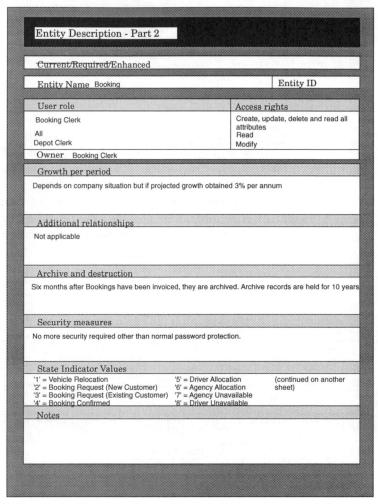

Fig. 5.23 Part 2 of Entity Description for Booking showing meanings of state indicator values

Many projects implement state indicators in the database. The state indicator becomes an attribute of the entity which can take all of the possible state indicator values. The software then checks before the event is processed that the entity occurrence is in the appropriate state for the event to act upon it. It is important that these state indicator values are documented as part of the Entity Descriptions and ultimately as part of the database design so that maintenance of the system is simplified.[1]

The Entity Description Part 2 form developed in step 320, *develop required data model*, is extended to show all of the possible state indicator values and their meanings. Figure 5.23 shows Part 2 of the Booking Entity Description—each of the state indicator values is shown along with the event that causes that state change to the entity occurrence. Thus, state indicator '4' maps to the effect of Booking Confirmed on the Booking occurrence.

State indicators with quits and resumes
Where the Quit and Resume is used, the value set by the effect with the 'Q' is one of the valid previous values for the effect with the 'R'. Figure 5.24 shows that instead of Event B then Event F can occur. Thus the valid predecessors to Event F are '1' and '5'.[2]

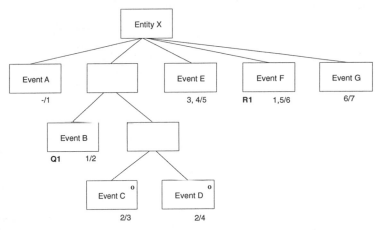

Fig. 5.24 Partial Entity Life History showing state indicators with quits and resumes

State indicators with parallel structures
The rules for parallel structures are more complex. Each leg of a parallel structure is independent of the others, so one state indicator is not sufficient to track the progress of the entity occurrence. There are two ways of dealing with this:

- Only one leg updates the state indicator

---

[1] Imagine what might happen if this is **not** done. Two years after implementation, a program crashes showing an error 'SI <> 12,13, 14'. The maintenance programmer does not understand SSADM, can't find the original Entity Life Histories (which might have been wrong anyway), and the design team who built the system have long departed for greater things. If the meanings of the state indicator values are documented in the database design then at least the programmer can refer to the names of the valid previous events which should relate to the names of other programs or modules and should be meaningful to the users. In other words, documenting the state indicators in the database design reduces the reliance on Entity Life Histories in maintenance.
[2] Note this is a disciplined conditional quit meaning that it depends upon the exception occurring. It does not mean that Event B is always followed by Event F—if this is the case there is an unconditional quit and the structure should be redrawn to avoid using a quit and resume.

or

• A separate subsidiary state indicator is introduced for each leg after the first

Only one leg updates the state indicator In some circumstances, it is necessary only to follow one of the legs using the state indicators: the other legs are unimportant in terms of tracking a particular entity through its Entity Life History. To show that a state indicator remains unchanged after a particular effect, an asterisk is put in the place of the 'set to' value.

Figure 5.25 shows a possible enhancement to the Vehicle life history. A vehicle could have a number of Service Intervals during its life, and parallel with these Insurance Amendments might occur—the Insurance Life is considered to be the subsidiary life having no affect on the other leg. When an Insurance Amendment occurs it does not change the value of the state indicator. This solution is only viable because there is no sequence defined in the Insurance Life leg.

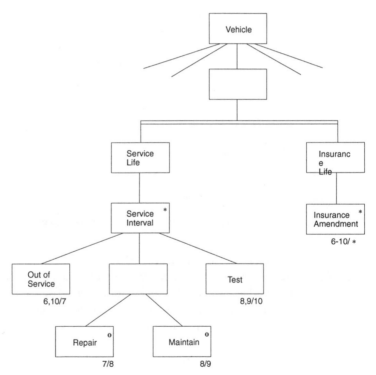

Fig. 5.25 Part of Vehicle life history showing parallel life with one leg's state indicator values unchanged

A separate subsidiary state indicator is introduced for each leg after the first Each subsidiary state indicator may be thought of as an additional attribute in the entity and is updated by one leg of a parallel structure. Possible values of other state indicators may be shown as valid previous values for the leg that uses subsidiary state indicators but only one state indicator value is updated by each leg. The final state indicator values from all legs of a parallel structure are shown as valid previous values for the effect(s) that follow the parallel structure.

Figure 5.26 shows a further enhancement to the Vehicle life history: where we discover that an Insurance Amendment consists of Get Quotation and Assess Quotation. As there is a sequence that must be modelled we introduce subsidiary state indicators. The subsidiary leg then shows two sets of state indicators, one following the main life and being unchanged by the events in the subsidiary leg, the other maintaining the sequence prescribed by the subsidiary leg taking the values of 'null', '1' & '2'. This means that a second state indicator attribute needs to be added to the Entity Description for Vehicle. When events affect a Vehicle occurrence in the subsidiary leg, the primary state indicator value is unchanged—shown by the asterisk.

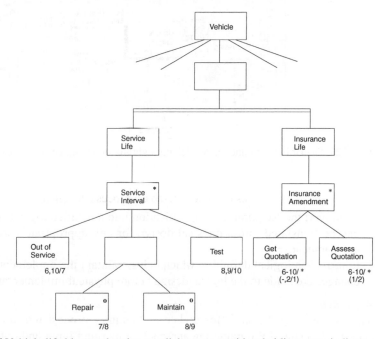

Fig. 5.26 Vehicle life history showing parallel structure with subsidiary state indicators

Logical database process design

Step 520, *define update processes*, and step 530, *define enquiry processes*, both use the technique of *logical process database design* to produce the Update and Enquiry Process Models. The technique is closely related to Jackson structured programming in that input and output data structures are defined and merged to produce a process (or program) structure. These process models also contain operations and conditions forming a very detailed specification of the processing—but one which is independent of the physical implementation.

Figure 5.27 shows the universal function model with the areas covered by logical process database design highlighted. The Update and Enquiry Process Models are cross-referenced on the Function Definitions which detail the events and enquiries involved in the function. Each event will have, at the end of Requirements Specification, an Effect Correspondence Diagram—during Logical Design this is converted to an Update Process Model. Similarly each enquiry has an Enquiry Access Path which becomes in Logical Design an Enquiry Process Model. Logical database process design only covers the processing of permanently stored data, it does not cover input and output of data through the interface (e.g. dialogues and other input and output mechanisms). These would be handled by the techniques of dialogue design or of function definition.

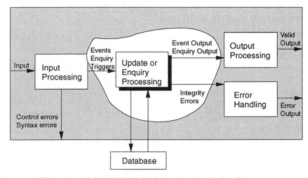

Fig. 5.27 The Universal Function Model highlighting logical database process design activities

Objectives
The two major objectives of logical database process design are:
- to convert the Requirements Specification into a detailed logical specification which can be translated into a physical design for any appropriate hardware or software environment;
- to provide a logical definition which helps maintain the implemented system (ideally changes are made to the logical design before physical implementation).

Approach
This is basically the same for update and enquiry processing, loosely following the Jackson Structured Programming approach of merging input and output data structures to form the processing structure. The following steps are involved:
- convert Effect Correspondence Diagram or Enquiry Access Path to input data structure
- identify output data structures
- merge data structures to form processing structure
- add operations
- add conditions
- specify error conditions and outputs
- check and walk through processing structure

Logical success unit

This is defined as a set of processing which must result in one consistent set of changes to the permanently stored data. This means that the system's data is always in a consistent state as far as the business is concerned whatever has happened to the computer system. So even if the Yorkies' computer crashed in the middle of accepting a booking (i.e. when processing the event Booking Request) then the event would either *succeed* completely or *fail* completely; thus preserving the business integrity of the system's data. So we can think of an *event* as a *logical success unit*.

The term *success unit* is also widely used throughout the database world (although many database authors refer to a *success unit* as a *transaction*[1]). In this sense it means leaving the physical database in a consistent state (which is hopefully consistent for the business also but may not be). In relational (SQL) databases then a completely successful update is achieved through a COMMIT statement[2] and a complete failure is achieved through a ROLLBACK statement. While an individual success unit is being performed the database must prevent other updates to the same entity occurrences involved—consistency is normally preserved by *locking*. The conversion of *logical success units* into *physical success units* during Physical Design has many consequences for the security, recovery, integrity, and performance aspects of the new computer system.

In SSADM we are concerned with the definition of *logical success units* which map to *events,* to *Effect Correspondence Diagrams*, and to *Update Process Models.* Thus when we develop an Update Process Model for an event we are defining a success unit for the future system—this means that though we are operating at a logical level we must be aware of what will happen when the process is physically implemented.

If a *logical success unit* is too large (e.g. consider a Create Order event that updates one Order then 200 Order Lines and 200 Stock Items) then translating this into a physical success unit could cause performance and recovery problems. The logical designer should then consider the best way of splitting the event, and its associated dialogues, rather than leave this problem to be sorted out during physical design (or worse, later).

So far we have discussed success units as update processes. However, consistency is also important with enquiries. If a lengthy enquiry is being performed, accessing many different but inter-related entity occurrences, then the user must be confident that the data it eventually presents provides a consistent picture (e.g. does the Stock Total match the sum of the Stock Item Quantities?). This means that enquiries should also be treated as logical success units. SSADM takes this approach with an *enquiry* becoming an *Enquiry Access Path* then an *Enquiry Process Model.* As with events the logical designer must consider the potential problems of implementing an enquiry as a success unit.

Often a function will combine an enquiry with an update (event). This could be simply establishing that the right customer is about to be updated by displaying their

---

[1] Date, C. J. (1995) *An Introduction to Database Systems* 6th edn (Addison-Wesley, Reading, Mass.).
[2] Some SSADM authors refer to a logical success unit as a *commit unit* but in our view this terminology is best left to the database world.

details in response to user input of the Customer No. A more complex example could involve checking that a vehicle was available before making a booking for it. In both of these cases the data must remain consistent throughout the enquiry and the update. In other words, enquiry-event pairs can become logical success units. During steps 520 and 530 the Function Definitions should be examined to ensure that the events and enquiries defined **do** map to logical success units.

Process Models

Both Update Process Models and Enquiry Process Models use the same Jackson notation. The diagram uses the Jackson constructs of sequence, selection, and iteration. Detailed processing is shown by means of an operations list with each operation attached to a processing box on the diagram. Conditions are attached to selections and to iterations. Figure 5.28 shows a complete Enquiry Process Model.

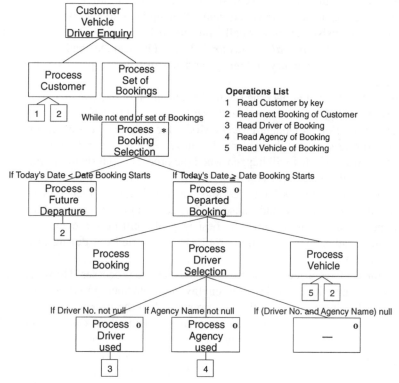

Fig. 5.28 Complete Enquiry Process Model for Customer Vehicle Driver Enquiry

Operations

Entity Life Histories detailed for each entity the *operations* which constitute the effect. These operations are the lowest level of processing specification defined in SSADM, and use a suggested syntax. The operations on the life histories are carried forward to the Update Process Models. Both Enquiry and Update Process Models are supported by an *operations list*; providing a pseudocode which will become part of the program specification.

Operations on Entity Life Histories are specific to the entity being affected. In process models several different entity types and occurrences may be dealt with—each operation must refer specifically to the entity being read or updated. Thus the operation 'store key' on the Booking life history becomes 'store key of Booking' on the Booking Request Update Process Model.

To define the detail processing on process models we need to go beyond the set of operations used on Entity Life Histories. Read operations, validation operations, and operations concerned with the physical storing of data are required. Each of these types of operation has specific syntax which is described below.[1]

Read <Entity> by key This reads the entity occurrence by using the input key value.

Define set of <Entity> matching input data This defines a set of occurrences of the entity matching the criteria given in the input data. Conditions are often supplied in the *event triggers* or *enquiry triggers*.[2] The designer can use this operation to specify a set of entity occurrences matching that condition.

Read next <Entity> in set This must follow a 'define set' operation and reads the next occurrence from the previously defined set. Using these last two operations we can select and read through a set of entity occurrences matching a particular condition.[3]

Read next <Detail Entity> of <Master Entity> [via <Relationship>] This reads the next occurrence of the detail entity related to the master entity occurrence. The process is reading 'down the crow's leg' from the 'one' end to the 'many' end to read the next occurrence associated with the occurrence at the 'one' end. This syntax implies a pointer chain type implementation whereby all occurrences are read in turn starting from the master occurrence then reading the first occurrence, then the second, etc.—all occurrences being related to the same master. The *[via <Relationship>]* syntax is only used where there are several different relationships between the two entity types—it is then necessary to specify which relationship is being used.

Read <Master Entity> of <Detail Entity> [via <Relationship>] This reads the master occurrence of the current detail entity occurrence. In other words, we are going 'up the crow's leg' from the 'many' end to the 'one' end.

Invoke <Common Process> Common processing may be defined at a detailed level in Elementary Process Descriptions, defined initially for Data Flow Diagrams and later transferred to the Function Definitions. Each common process, as it is discovered,

---

[1] *<Entity>* indicates that the name of the entity will be supplied. *[via <Relationship>]* indicates that the syntax in square brackets is optional.
[2] These were shown on the Effect Correspondence Diagrams and Enquiry Access Paths as the entry point arrows, annotated by attributes and conditions.
[3] This is the closest SSADM operations get to accepting that SQL exists. In general, the syntax SSADM suggests is oriented towards CODASYL databases where record-at-a-time processing occurs and records are accessed through pointer chains. Projects using relational databases would be well advised to consider carefully their use of process models and of operations.

should be named, described, and cross-referenced wherever it is used. The description of the common process could be given in free text but more usually would involve mathematical formula, algorithms, or pseudocode.

Create <Entity> This creates the entity occurrence without writing it to permanent storage. Effectively the occurrence is written to working storage, eventually it will be permanently stored through a 'write' operation. 'Create' operations must come before other update operations for an entity occurrence.

Write <Entity> This writes the entity occurrence to permanent storage; it will usually be the final operation in update processing for a particular entity occurrence.

Set state indicator of <Entity> to <Value> This sets the entity occurrence's state indicator value before writing it to storage. State indicators are implemented as attributes within the entity and updates normally change the state indicator value. A special state indicator value of 'deleted' is set. This enables physical records to be logically deleted before they are eventually physically removed from the database. Any read operations will ignore any 'deleted' entity occurrences.

Fail if state indicator of <Entity> outside <value range> Each event affecting the entity occurrence will set the state indicator value. These values can be checked to ensure that the occurrence is in the correct state for the required processing. This operation raises errors if the state indicator value is outside the range specified—this will be the 'valid previous states' defined on the Entity Life History. Any read operations that attempt to read occurrences that have been deleted (but still may physically exist on the database) will ignore those with the state indicator value deleted.

Gain and Lose operations These can be shown on Entity Life Histories of master entities to show the creation of a relationship occurrence with a detail occurrence. These have no equivalent command in many database management systems (e.g. in relational databases, connection is only made by creating a foreign key value at the detail end). However, some products, both primitive ones and the latest object-oriented databases, can implement this kind of sophisticated referential integrity—then gain and lose statements may be useful. In practice most projects using relational databases will not use 'gain' and 'lose' operations.

Conditions
Process models, unlike the other Jackson structures used in SSADM, are annotated by conditions. Conditions are needed in iterations; to decide whether to continue iterating, and in selections; to decide which option to process. The SSADM convention is to show the condition that must be fulfilled in order for the processing to be carried out.

In a selection, each of the options has an associated condition that leads to the particular option happening. The line connecting the option to the node box is annotated with the condition. Thus in Fig. 5.28 the condition, 'If Today's Date < Date Booking Starts', leads to 'Process Future Departure'; and the condition, 'If Today's Date ≥ Date Booking Starts', leads to 'Process Departed Booking'. Every option within a selection must have an associated condition. Selection conditions will often test the values of attributes or of state indicators.

Iteration conditions can also test the value of attributes. They also often test for 'end of set'—typically this is where we are navigating from master entity occurrences to detail occurrences; processing continues until there are no more detail occurrences for the master occurrence.

The conditions governing iterations can be defined in two ways: using *while* or *until* statements. Remember that an iteration can occur zero or more times. A *while* statement ensures that the condition is tested before the processing takes place—thus allowing the iterated processing to be skipped. An *until* condition means that the processing is carried out and then the condition is tested—thus ensuring that one iteration of the processing must occur. So *while* statements are used where the iteration can occur zero times and *until* statements are used where the iteration must occur at least once.

Often, when developing process models, the analyst may discover that a condition is impossible to test because the test data is unavailable at that point in the processing. This is known as a *recognition* problem. The problem is well known and can be resolved by various techniques which are well described elsewhere.[1] There are four basic techniques, briefly described below, which can be used to overcome recognition problems—sometimes a combination of these is necessary.

Store derived data An additional attribute is introduced to anticipate the process which tests its value. An example of this could occur in the Yorkies system if customers were not allowed to go over a pre-set value of bookings when making new bookings. We would then need to calculate the total value of outstanding bookings that each customer had before accepting a new booking; this could be handled by storing an attribute 'Value of Outstanding Bookings' in the Customer entity. The processing would check the value of this attribute first, rather than read through all of the outstanding bookings.

Multiple read ahead This is common in batch processing systems where we need to check that a batch total matches the totals of the individual items that make up the batch. The multiple read ahead would read ahead the individual items to check that their total matched the batch total; if they did not match then an error condition would arise.

Design two processes The input data would be read twice with the first pass setting markers which would be picked up by the second pass through the data—in some ways this is similar to the multiple read ahead technique.

Backtracking This *posits* one option of the selection and starts performing it. At a later point, the program is able to test the condition. If the correct option has been followed then execution can continue until the option is completed. If the wrong option has been followed then the program *admits* its mistake and *quits* to *resume* at another point in the structure—it may be necessary to *backtrack* and undo some of the actions that have been performed in the wrong option.

---

[1] There are many books on Jackson Structured Programming, e.g.: Ingevaldsson, L. (1986) *JSP —A Practical Method of Program Design* (Chartwell-Bratt, Bromley).

Approach to logical database process design

Figure 5.29 shows the general approach to developing Update or Enquiry Process Models. This follows closely the technique of Jackson Structured Programming whereby input and output data structures, both represented using Jackson notation, are merged together to form a processing structure. This processing structure, again represented in Jackson notation, is extended by the addition of operations and conditions.

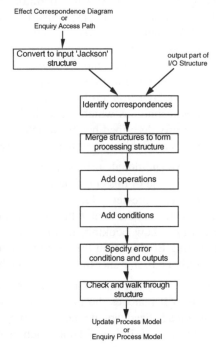

Fig. 5.29 Approach to logical database process design

Earlier in the SSADM project, Effect Correspondence Diagrams were developed for every update to system data (every event, in SSADM terminology). These become the input Jackson structure that is merged with the output Jackson structure represented in SSADM by an I/O Structure. Often the output structure for update processing is exceedingly simple and needs little consideration. In the next part of this section we work through two examples demonstrating the development of Update Process Models using this technique.

Enquiries were specified, earlier in the project, using Enquiry Access Paths. These become the input Jackson structure which is then merged with the output structure. At first, it seems strange that the input is the Enquiry Access Path, representing the navigation of the data structure. The traversal of the Enquiry Access Path is triggered by the enquiry data (or enquiry trigger) supplied by the function—comprising those attributes and conditions required for the processing. The Enquiry Access Path should then supply all of the data required for the enquiry. The result of the enquiry will be a system output, structured as required by the user and represented by an I/O Structure. Thus the processing necessary to produce the input data structure for the function is provided by the Enquiry Access Path—it is this that is merged with the output structures. (Note that exactly the same argument can be applied to explain why Effect Correspondence Diagrams form the input data structure for development of Update Process Models.)

It is important to remember that these steps are only concerned with the update and enquiry processing as related to the Logical Data Model—processing required to organize data before update or to put it into a particular format for output is considered using the function definition technique.[1] Figure 5.27 highlighted the logical database process design activities shown in the universal function model.

Correspondences between the input and output structure are identified. For components of the two structures to correspond they must contain the same, or similar, data and be structurally consistent with each other. If the two structures do not correspond then a *structure clash* arises—various techniques can overcome this. Further discussion of correspondence and structure clashes is given with the examples in Sec. 5.8.

The corresponding components from the two data structures are then merged to form the processing structure. For Update Process Models the operations for the event are transferred from the appropriate Entity Life Histories and extended by further operations of the type detailed above. For Enquiry Process Models read operations are included in the model. Conditions are added to the model for iterations and selections.

Integrity errors may arise when the processing is performed on live data. These may be based upon inconsistencies between entity occurrences at either a software level or at a business level. The processing design must anticipate these potential errors and determine how they should be dealt with. All error messages and codes, whether displayed or printed, should be specified for each error condition.

Finally each Update Process Model and Enquiry Process Model should be reviewed to ensure that it is internally consistent and that it provides the data that the user requires. Some form of review with the user should be performed although it is probably inappropriate to show the user these highly technical diagrams.

Example 1—Booking Request Update Process Model

Before step 520, *define update processes*, various inputs to the Update Process Model were identified. During step 330, *derive system functions*, the event was identified and given a name, in this case 'Booking Request'. This name is used in Function Definitions, Entity Life Histories, Effect Correspondence Diagrams, and Update Process Models. It is most important that the same event name (and identifier, if used) is used throughout the project.

During step 360, *develop processing specification*, the event data (or event trigger) was identified. These are the attributes and conditions that are supplied to the event by

---

[1] Covered at a 'logical' level in Requirements Definition, particularly step 330, *derive system functions*. At a 'physical' level this is done during Physical Design in Stage 6.

the function. The analyst must ensure that the function can generate the necessary data for input. (In this example the function must generate a Booking No. in order for a Booking occurrence to be created—Booking No. is the primary key of Booking.) The event data is shown on the Effect Correspondence Diagram as a single-headed arrow.

Also during step 360 the Effect Correspondence Diagram is built to show the navigation through the data structure necessary to perform the update. The Effect Correspondence Diagram for Booking Request is repeated below.

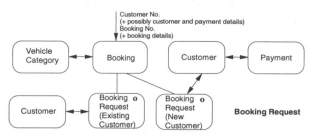

Fig. 5.30 Effect Correspondence Diagram for Booking Request

Specify event output

We need to identify correspondences between the input and output data structures. The Effect Correspondence Diagram will define the input data structure. The event output is usually a simple confirmation message—in this case the Booking Request output is an 'OK' message. If the event output is more complex, perhaps including a report, then its data structure should have been defined by an I/O Structure. If a dialogue is involved then the output half of the I/O Structure will form the dialogue. We do not consider error conditions or error messages at this point, they are considered later in the development of Update Process Models.

Add enquiry only entities to the Effect Correspondence Diagram

If a complex output is required from the event then it may be necessary to extend the Effect Correspondence Diagram to show the additional accesses needed to produce that data. The Effect Correspondence Diagram notation could be used to show the additional enquiry processing. In our Booking Request example during development of the Effect Correspondence Diagram we added enquiry information necessary for the event—no further extensions to the diagram are required now.

Group effects in one-to-one correspondence

We now start to turn the Effect Correspondence Diagram into a formal Jackson structure. This is done by grouping together the effects which are in one-to-one correspondence and naming each one as a process. We can only group together effects which are in one-to-one correspondence—those linked by double-headed arrows.

Thus we cannot group Booking Request (New Customer) with Booking because they are not linked by a one-to-one double-headed correspondence arrow. The names given to the processes should reflect what is being done by the groupings of effects to 'Existing Customer'. Figure 5.31 shows the grouped correspondences on the Booking Request Effect Correspondence Diagram.

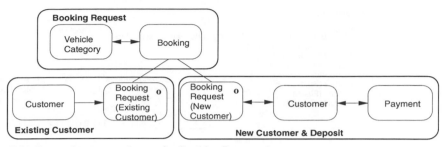

Fig. 5.31 Grouped correspondences for Booking Request

List operations
Each Entity Life History included the operations that could modify an entity occurrence—these operations are carried forward and extended in the process models. The suggestion is to group the operations for each effect shown in the Effect Correspondence Diagram as a prelude to assigning them to the Update Process Model. The suggested order in which the operations are listed, becoming the sequence in which they are performed, is:

1. Any read operations
2. Error operations on invalid state indicator values
3. A create operation
4. Operations shown on the Entity Life History (qualified by the entity name)
5. An operation to set the state indicator value
6. A write operation

Obviously not all these operations will be appropriate for every effect. Read and error operations will only be appropriate if the entity occurrence already exists. Create operations will only be appropriate if the entity occurrence does not exist. Operations setting the state indicator value and write operations will only be appropriate if the entity occurrence is being updated.

The operations shown on the Entity Life History need to be qualified by the entity name—this was not included in the syntax given when the operations were included in the life history. Otherwise it would be unclear as to which entity occurrence is being updated—all references should specify the entity. If different entity occurrences of the same type are being affected in different ways then the different entity roles need to be distinguished (this will occur if simultaneous effects are involved).

Below we show fragments of the Booking and Customer Entity Life Histories (Fig. 5.32) with their relevant operations. Further operations have been extracted from the Payment life history—the Booking Request event would also appear on the Local Office and Vehicle Category life histories if the 'gain' and 'lose' operations had been used.[1]

---

[1] 'Gain' and 'lose' statements are not normally used in process models as they are not supported by the majority of DBMSs. However, SSADM recommends that they are used on Entity Life Histories to cross-validate with their corresponding 'tie' and 'cut' statements, although few projects use them.

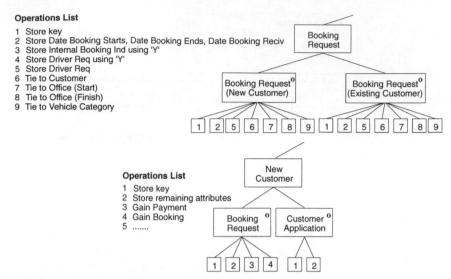

Operations List

1 Store key
2 Store Date Booking Starts, Date Booking Ends, Date Booking Reciv
3 Store Internal Booking Ind using 'Y'
4 Store Driver Req using 'Y'
5 Store Driver Req
6 Tie to Customer
7 Tie to Office (Start)
8 Tie to Office (Finish)
9 Tie to Vehicle Category

Operations List

1 Store key
2 Store remaining attributes
3 Gain Payment
4 Gain Booking
5 ....

Fig. 5.32 Part of Booking and Customer Entity Life Histories

The operations taken from the Entity Life History need to be made more specific about which entity is being updated. Thus 'store key' on the 'Booking' Entity Life History becomes 'store key of Booking' on the Update Process Model. Other examples are illustrated in the operations list given below in Fig. 5.33—the important thing is that each operation should be specific about which entity (and sometimes which occurrence) is being processed. The Operations List has been grouped to each set of effects on an entity. 'Blank' operations have been used to separate the various effects.

Operations List

1 Read Customer by key
2 Fail if SI of Customer <> 1 or 2 or 3 or 4
3
4 Create Customer
5 Store key of Customer
6 Store remaining attributes of Customer
7 Set SI of Customer to 1
8 Write Customer
9
10 Create Payment
11 Store key of Payment
12 Store remaining attributes of Payment
13 Tie Payment to Customer
14 Set SI of Payment to 2
15 Write Payment
16
17 Create Booking
18 Store key of Booking
19 Store Date Booking Starts, Date Booking Ends, Date Booking Reciv of Booking
20 Tie Booking to Customer
21 Tie Booking to Local Office using 'from'
22 Tie Booking to Local Office using 'to'
23 Tie Booking to Vehicle Category
24 Set SI of Booking to 2
25 Set SI of Booking to 3
26 Read Vehicle Category by key
27 Write Booking

Fig. 5.33 Operations list for Booking Request Update Process Model

Convert Effect Correspondence Diagram to Jackson-like notation

The Effect Correspondence Diagram was annotated by grouping effects together in one-to-one correspondence. Each grouping was given a name—this was shown in Fig. 5.30. This diagram is now converted into a Jackson-like structure by making each grouping a node or component on a Jackson diagram. Figure 5.34 shows a 'Booking Request' grouped correspondence with two options 'Existing Customer' and 'New Customer & Deposit' options hanging from it.

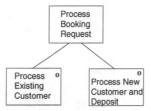

Fig. 5.34 Initial Jackson structure from grouped correspondences

Sometimes the initial Jackson-like structure will break some of the Jackson notation rules. For example, selection nodes may be mixed with iterations or with sequences. To produce a final Jackson structure for the Update Process Model we need to ensure that none of these rules are broken.

In our example, the diagram at first sight appears to be a legal Jackson structure but if we assign operations to it (the next task in building the Update Process Model) we will break one of the Jackson rules—namely that sequence and selection components cannot be mixed. The structure shown below in Fig. 5.35 does not violate the Jackson rules—a sequence follows the selection. This allows us to incorporate the operations that are solely concerned with the Booking to a separate component of the Update Process Model.[1]

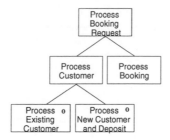

Fig. 5.35 Revised Jackson structure

Note that each of the components has been labelled as a process—this anticipates that this structure will become the processing structure. Normal Jackson Structured

---

[1] This could be overcome by repeating all of the operations for Booking in each of the selection nodes. However, this is bad programming practice since effectively a common routine is being duplicated. It is preferable to adopt the solution given above.

Programming practice is to merge input and output structures. What we have here is the input data structure—the output data structure is often simply a confirmatory message. In these cases, the merging of the two structures is trivial and the output data structure does not really need consideration—the input data structure becomes the processing structure.

Sometimes the output data structure is more complex and correspondence between input and output data structures occurs. This issue will be discussed in the next section dealing with Enquiry Process Models as consideration of both input and output data structures is normally required for enquiries. The technique used for updates and enquiries is similar; it is simply that merging of structures is rarely necessary for updates but is often necessary for enquiries.

Allocate operations to structure
Operations are added to the relevant leaves on the diagram and occasionally to the nodes. The grouping and ordering of operations were discussed previously. The order in which they are added to the leaves is the sequence in which they will be performed. Figure 5.36 shows the Booking Request process structure with operations added.

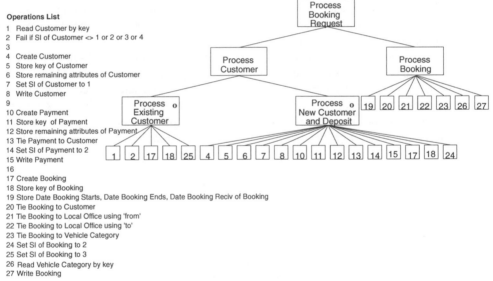

Fig. 5.36 Process structure for Booking Request showing operations

For Process Existing Customer (Fig. 5.36) operations will be performed in the sequence '1', '2', '17', '18', and '25'. Iteration and selection nodes become a condition statement in the eventual program. These therefore cannot include pure processing as specified by operations. It is always wrong to add operations to a node which is a parent of either selection components or an iteration component (in other words no operations on nodes above 'o' or '*'). It is acceptable to add operations to a sequence node (e.g. Process Booking Request at the top of the structure in Fig. 5.36) as operations can be elements in the sequence. However, many experienced programmers would consider this bad practice leading to poorly constructed programs—they would create separate sequence components and hang the operations from these.

Add conditions to structure
Any iterations will require a condition so that the iteration can finish. These will usually take the form of 'while...' or 'until...' statements; examples of these will be illustrated later. If a selection appears each option must be documented with the condition that must be met for the option to be followed. Thus in Fig. 5.37 below the condition 'if Customer No. exists' leads to 'Process Existing Customer' and the condition 'if Customer No. does not exist' leads to 'Process New Customer and Deposit'. Often conditions test the values of attributes; sometimes state indicator values are used to evaluate conditions. Figure 5.37 shows the Update Process Model for Booking Request including conditions.

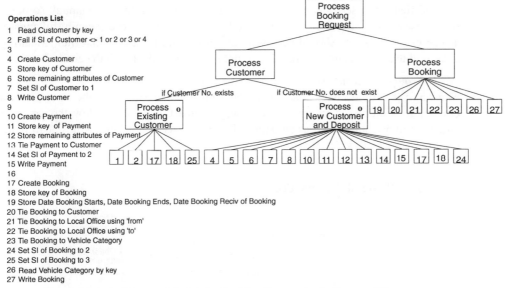

Operations List

1 Read Customer by key
2 Fail if SI of Customer <> 1 or 2 or 3 or 4
3
4 Create Customer
5 Store key of Customer
6 Store remaining attributes of Customer
7 Set SI of Customer to 1
8 Write Customer
9
10 Create Payment
11 Store key of Payment
12 Store remaining attributes of Payment
13 Tie Payment to Customer
14 Set SI of Payment to 2
15 Write Payment
16
17 Create Booking
18 Store key of Booking
19 Store Date Booking Starts, Date Booking Ends, Date Booking Reciv of Booking
20 Tie Booking to Customer
21 Tie Booking to Local Office using 'from'
22 Tie Booking to Local Office using 'to'
23 Tie Booking to Vehicle Category
24 Set SI of Booking to 2
25 Set SI of Booking to 3
26 Read Vehicle Category by key
27 Write Booking

Fig. 5.37 Update Process Model for Booking Request including conditions

Specify integrity error conditions
These are documented in the operations as a number of 'fail conditions'. An integrity error is where the processing will put the data in such a state that it is inconsistent with other data or with the business rules that govern the system.

Usually these business rules that govern the system are embedded in various SSADM models (examples are using state indicators on Entity Life Histories and using mandatory relationships between entities). In Fig. 5.37 above the operation 'fail if SI<> 1 or 2 or 3 or 4' means that the processing can only take place if the entity occurrence is in one of the states which allow this event to affect the entity.

Many integrity errors are associated with 'referential integrity'—this is a term used in database theory to deal with the management of relationships between entity occurrences. Typically, errors can occur when deleting occurrences, e.g. the effects on detail entities if the master occurrence is deleted, the effects on the master occurrence if the detail is deleted (or if the last detail for the master is deleted). Other errors can occur when creating occurrences. For example, if the data structure shows a mandatory relationship at the detail end then a detail occurrence cannot be created without a master occurrence being present. Similarly, a mandatory relationship at the other end ensures that a detail occurrence must be present before the master can be created. Of course, these rules should be reflected in the Entity Life Histories. Sometimes integrity errors can reflect 'pure' business rules such as when the processing could allow the customer to exceed a pre-defined credit limit.

Define error outputs

Each of the integrity errors defined should result in a message to the user. Often these are codified with users having to look up error codes in a reference manual; sometimes the software will trap the error code and replace it by a more meaningful message. These error messages should be discussed with users to ensure that their meaning is clear and that information is provided to help the user to deal with the error situation.

Walk through the structure

The analyst should check that the processing makes sense; that the operations and conditions are defined in a reasonable way. Some CASE tools allow the processing structure to be represented as an action diagram or as pseudocode—these can make it easier for the analyst (and user) to understand the processing that is being performed. An example of an action diagram is given in Fig. 5.49.[1]

Example 2—Vehicle Write-off Update Process Model

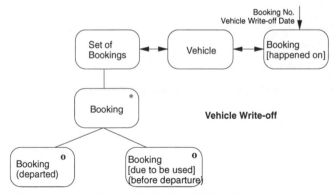

Fig. 5.38 Effect Correspondence Diagram for Vehicle Write-off

---

[1] Note that action diagrams and pseudocode are not part of SSADM but can be very useful in defining processing.

In Sec. 4.7 we identified the event Vehicle Write-off and developed an Effect Correspondence Diagram for it. A Vehicle Write-off occurs when a vehicle does not return from a booking or is so damaged as to be unusable. As a result of this the Booking occurrence is amended, the Vehicle occurrence is amended and all of the Booking occurrences which were due to use that vehicle are also amended. The Effect Correspondence Diagram developed in Sec. 4.7 is repeated in Fig. 5.38.

Specify event output
The output from the event has to be identified. Further consideration of the Effect Correspondence Diagram and particularly of the Booking Entity Life History (the relevant fragment is shown below in Fig. 5.39) suggests that the processing described by these is very difficult to perform.

The Entity Life History shows that when the bookings that are due to use the vehicle are identified, not only is the connection with the associated vehicle 'cut', but also each Booking occurrence is 'tied' to a new Vehicle occurrence. Practically, this seems almost impossible to do automatically. There could be many future bookings for the vehicle (probably an average of 20 but possibly as many as 50). The program would have to identify vehicles that were available to substitute for the written-off one.

The analyst could, of course, have identified this problem at several points during the analysis: while developing the Entity Life History of Booking, while developing the Effect Correspondence Diagram, or as we are illustrating, during development of the Update Process Model. One of the strengths of SSADM is its iterative nature in which a design becomes progressively more detailed; ensuring that each design component is considered several times.

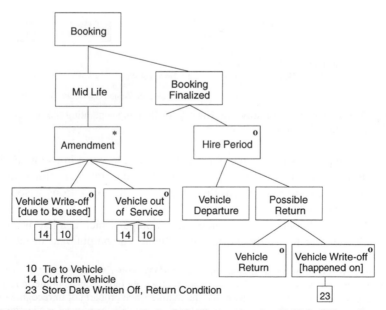

Fig. 5.39 Part of original Booking Entity Life History showing Vehicle Write-off

The most obvious redesign to avoid this problem is to exclude the processing that ties the booking to the new vehicle from the Vehicle Write-off event. This requires a new effect on the Booking Entity Life History which immediately follows the 'Booking [due to be used] (before departure)' effect. This change requires the user to perform a Vehicle Availability Enquiry for each of the bookings now without a vehicle and assign a replacement vehicle to each. The event Replacement Found can then follow Vehicle Write-off.

This approach also seems to be sensible for the event 'Vehicle out of Service'. So the Entity Life History of Booking is now amended to separate the replacement of the vehicle from the vehicle becoming unavailable. The revised part of the Booking Entity Life History, including operations, is shown below in Fig. 5.40.

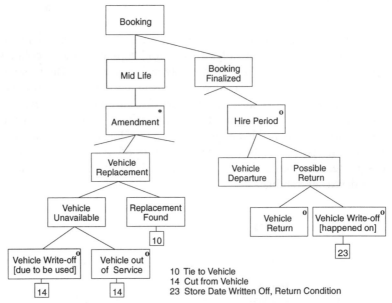

Fig. 5.40 Part of revised Entity Life History for Booking separating the 'replacement' event from the 'unavailable' events

This example illustrates some of the complexities inherent in using SSADM. Amending this Entity Life History causes changes to all of the state indicator values of effects that can follow and therefore requires changes to the operations associated with many Update Process Models.[1]

The event Vehicle Write-off now has an output which is a list of all of the bookings which were due to use the written-off vehicle. The output data structure is very simple

---

[1] In order to manage this kind of modification and use SSADM properly one requires a very sophisticated CASE tool. An alternative, which we prefer, is to not specify state indicators as numeric flags but to name them in a meaningful way. This would ensure that the maintenance problem of unrecognizable flags did not occur. It would also ensure that when modifications to Entity Life Histories were made, their impact on the rest of the design was minimized.

and is shown in Fig. 5.41 below. The other output from the event will simply be a confirmation that the Booking occurrence on which the write-off occurred and the Vehicle occurrence have been updated.

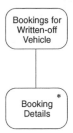

Fig. 5.41 I/O Structure for output from the event Vehicle Write-off

Add enquiry only entities to the Effect Correspondence Diagram
Without the amendments discussed above there would have been some complex enquiry processing associated with the event. This would have involved navigation through several entity occurrences to discover which vehicles were available to replace the one that had been written-off in all its future bookings. With the separation of Vehicle Unavailable and Replacement Found then the enquiry processing no longer becomes part of the update and is dealt with by performing a Vehicle Availability Enquiry.

Group effects in one-to-one correspondence
Where effects are in correspondence with each other they can be grouped into the separate parts of the processing structure. This means that soft boxes linked by double-headed arrows can be grouped together, and soft boxes linked by plain lines must be separated. Each grouped correspondence is given a name appropriate to the data being updated—this gives Fig. 5.42 below.

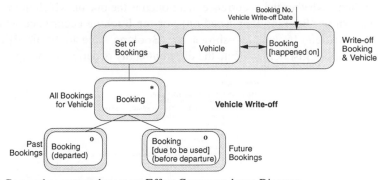

Fig. 5.42 Grouped correspondences on Effect Correspondence Diagram

List operations
The initial set of operations come from the life histories; from the Effect Correspondence Diagram we know that the Vehicle and Booking entities are affected by

the Vehicle Write-off event so we must look for this event on those life histories and identify the operations from them. The relevant parts of the revised Entity Life History for Booking were shown above in Fig. 5.40. The relevant part of the Vehicle life history is shown below with its operations.

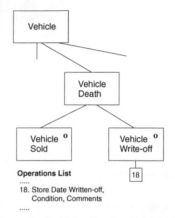

Fig. 5.43 Part of Entity Life History for Vehicle showing Vehicle Write-off

We now list these operations from the Entity Life Histories, plus any additional operations needed to process the Vehicle Write-off event. The order in which operations process the changes to the entity occurrence was discussed previously. Figure 5.44 below shows the operations list for the Vehicle Write-off event. Note that the state indicator values have had to be revised because of the change to the Booking Entity Life History; these are no longer consistent with those on the full Booking Entity Life History shown earlier in this Section (Fig. 5.22).

The Booking entity occurrences have been qualified by the entity role names. These indicate whether the occurrence mentioned is the one on which the write-off occurred—shown by 'Booking [happened on]'; or the Booking occurrence which was due to use the written-off vehicle—shown by 'Booking [due to be used]'. The gaps in the Operations List help indicate the different entity occurrences being affected.

Operations List

```
 1  Read Booking[happened on] by key
 2  Fail if SI of Booking[happened on] <> 18
 3  Replace Return Condition of Booking[happened on]
 4  Set SI of Booking[happened on] to 19
 5  Write Booking[happened on]
 6
 7  Read Vehicle of Booking
 8  Fail if SI of Vehicle <> 4 or 7 or 8
 9  Store Date Written-off, Condition, Comments of Vehicle
10  Set SI of Vehicle to 11
11  Write Vehicle
12
13  Read next Booking of Vehicle
14  Fail if SI of Booking[due to be used] <> 1 or 4 or 5 or 6 or 9 or 10 or 11 or 13 or 15
15  Cut Booking[due to be used] from Vehicle
16  Set SI of Booking [due to be used] to 11
17  Write Booking[due to be used]
```

Fig. 5.44 Operations for Vehicle Write-off

Convert Effect Correspondence Diagram to Jackson-like notation
The grouped Effect Correspondence Diagram (Fig. 5.42) is turned into a Jackson structure by creating a box on the Jackson diagram for each grouped correspondence. Each of these is named as a process followed by the name given to the grouped correspondence. Each grouped correspondence maintains the iteration and selection symbols from the Effect Correspondence Diagram. This gives the Jackson-style diagram shown below in Fig. 5.45.

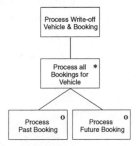

Fig. 5.45 Initial Jackson structure for Vehicle Write-off

This initial Jackson diagram will break some of the formal Jackson rules when we come to add operations to it. As there is processing associated with the box at the very top of the structure then we prefer to split this into two sequence boxes; the first of these becomes a 'leaf' and can have operations assigned to it.[1] This gives the improved Jackson structure shown below in Fig. 5.46.

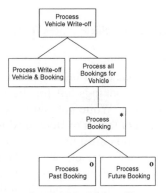

Fig. 5.46 Improved Jackson structure for Vehicle Write-off

Allocate operations to structure
Operations are linked to each of the leaves in the process structure (and occasionally to nodes—we prefer not to do this but would have to if the Jackson structure had not been

---

[1] Some analysts, and other books, assign operations to nodes on the structure but this goes against the spirit of Jackson Structured Programming, and we suggest a more purist approach. However, it can make the diagrams simpler—we've used this approach in some of our answers to the exercises at the end of the section.

'improved' in Fig. 5.46). Remember that the order in which the operations are shown is the order in which they will be performed; so in Fig. 5.47 below, operation 1 will be performed before operation 2.

Note the 'read ahead' with operation 13. This must occur before we enter the iteration so that the condition can be applied to decide whether the iteration can continue. The iteration condition must be tested immediately after the 'read'—if there is no next Booking of Vehicle then the iteration will not be entered. Note also that the next read (operation 13 again) occurs after the processing has been carried out—this is another 'read ahead', before the next cycle of iteration begins.

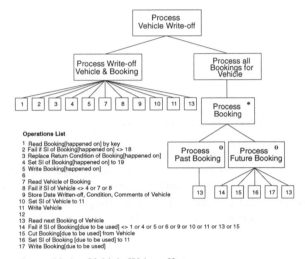

Operations List

1 Read Booking[happened on] by key
2 Fail if SI of Booking[happened on] <> 18
3 Replace Return Condition of Booking[happened on]
4 Set SI of Booking[happened on] to 19
5 Write Booking[happened on]
6
7 Read Vehicle of Booking
8 Fail if SI of Vehicle <> 4 or 7 or 8
9 Store Date Written-off, Condition, Comments of Vehicle
10 Set SI of Vehicle to 11
11 Write Vehicle
12
13 Read next Booking of Vehicle
14 Fail if SI of Booking[due to be used] <> 1 or 4 or 5 or 6 or 9 or 10 or 11 or 13 or 15
15 Cut Booking[due to be used] from Vehicle
16 Set SI of Booking [due to be used] to 11
17 Write Booking[due to be used]

Fig. 5.47 Operations added to Vehicle Write-off structure

Add conditions to the structure

We need to add conditions to all iterations and selections. The iteration will continue until there are no more bookings left for the vehicle that has been written-off—this gives rise to the condition 'While not end of set of Bookings'. Thus the iteration will terminate when the 'end of the set of Bookings' is reached.

Each option in a selection must have an associated condition. Only Bookings which are due to use the written-off vehicle need to be updated so we select them by applying a condition related to the dates on which the Booking is due to start. If the start date is before the current date (i.e. the date on which the write-off occurred) then it is a past Booking and can be ignored. If it is the same as the date on which the vehicle was written off then it will be the 'write-off' booking and can also be ignored. If the date that the booking is due to start is later than the date on which the vehicle was written-off then we need to find a new vehicle for the future booking. The condition that is applied for the option to be followed is written above the option in the diagram; 'If Date Booking Starts ≤ Today' is shown above 'Process Past Booking' and 'If Date Booking Starts > Today' is shown above 'Process Future Booking'. This completes the Update Process Model for Vehicle Write-off which is shown in Fig. 5.48.

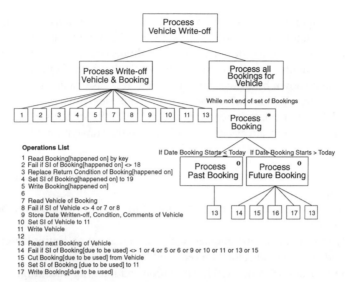

Fig. 5.48 Completed Update Process Model for Vehicle Write-off

Specify integrity error conditions and define error outputs
The major error conditions have been specified by using the state indicator values with the conditions 'fail if state indicator <>...'. The error messages for these should be defined and agreed with the user.

Walk through the structure
The analysts should convince themselves that the process model works. One convenient, alternative view of the processing is given by an action diagram (Fig. 5.49). These are used extensively in the Information Engineering Methodology for all processing structures.

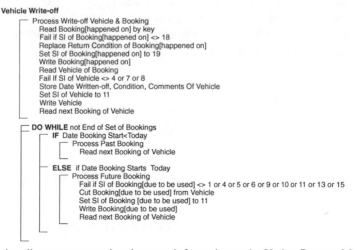

Fig. 5.49 Action diagram representing the same information as the Update Process Model

Action diagrams provide a more compact and program-like documentation of the structure, although it is not so easy to see the conditions and the overall structure. Sequence is shown by the order in which things occur, from top to bottom. Iteration is shown by a double parallel bar at the top of the large bracket and a 'do while' condition. Selection is shown by separate brackets and 'if ... else' statements.

The action diagram shown in Fig. 5.49 represents exactly the same information as that held in the Update Process Model in Fig. 5.48. Some users and some analysts will find the action diagram easier to validate than the conventional Update Process Model.

SUMMARY

- state indicators show the state of an entity occurrence after it has been affected by an event;
- 'valid previous' and 'set to' state indicators are shown below the boxes in Entity Life Histories;
- state indicators are documented with their meaning on Entity Descriptions;
- subsidiary state indicators are required for parallel structures;
- state indicators can be used in validation and integrity checking;
- Logical database process design is the SSADM technique used for producing Update Process Models and Enquiry Process Models;
- Logical database process design follows the techniques of Jackson Structured Programming to develop a detailed logical process design;
- Update and Enquiry Process Models show sequences, selections, iterations, operations, and conditions;
- each event has an Effect Correspondence Diagram which is developed into an Update Process Model;
- each enquiry has an Enquiry Access Path which is developed into an Enquiry Process Model;
- logical success units are integral units of processing which must be fully completed to leave the system's data in a consistent state;
- events and enquiries become logical success units;
- Update Process Models are a major product of step 520, *define update processes*;
- Update Process Models are developed from Effect Correspondence Diagrams in the following way:
  - specify event output—usually a simple confirmation that the update has been processed;
  - add enquiry processing to the Effect Correspondence Diagram;
  - group effects in one-to-one correspondence on the Effect Correspondence Diagram;
  - list operations;
  - convert grouped Effect Correspondence Diagram to Jackson-like structure;
  - allocate operations to structure;
  - add conditions to structure;
  - specify integrity error conditions and error outputs;
  - walk through the structure.

Exercises

5.7.1   State indicators
Add state indicators to the Project Entity Life History developed in Exercise 4.7.1 a)
and b).

5.7.2   Update Process Models
Use the Effect Correspondence Diagrams developed previously in Exercise 4.7.2. You
will need to assume some operations and state indicators from the Entity Life Histories
of Customer, Invoice, and Invoice Line.
a) Develop an Update Process Model for the New Project event (use the operations
    from the Project Entity Life History answer).
b) Develop an Update Process Model for the New Invoice event.

5.8   Define enquiry processes (step 530)

Introduction
In this step we use logical database process design to produce Enquiry Process Models,
a very similar approach is used to that for developing Update Process Models. In this
section we give two examples of the development of an Enquiry Process Model
concentrating on the minor differences between this technique and that for updates.

Example Customer Vehicle Driver Enquiry
This was discussed in Sec. 4.7. During step 360, *develop processing specification*, an
Enquiry Access Path was developed (repeated below in Fig. 5.50). The enquiry trigger
and the full access path are needed to develop the Enquiry Press Model.

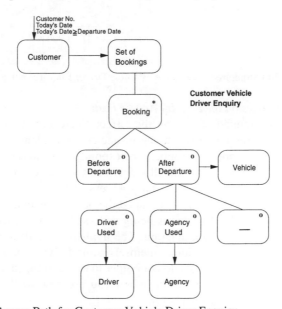

Fig. 5.50 Enquiry Access Path for Customer Vehicle Driver Enquiry

Specify Enquiry Output

In step 330, *derive system functions,* I/O Structures and supporting descriptions were developed for all inputs, outputs, and dialogues in the system. We need to consider the output from the enquiry in order to merge its data structure with that derived from the Enquiry Access Path. This merging is normally a more complex task for enquiries; with updates the output data structure is usually very simple, rarely warranting consideration.

The I/O Structure for the Customer Vehicle Driver Enquiry is shown below in Fig. 5.51. We have shaded the output area and converted the soft boxes to hard— emphasizing that this data structure is about to become a processing structure. We only need consider the output half of this dialogue. The input data should (and does) match the enquiry trigger defined on the Enquiry Access Path. Sometimes a complex I/O Structure may require several Enquiry Access Paths each triggered by separate enquiry triggers—it is probably best to treat these as separate Enquiry Process Models all operating within the same function.

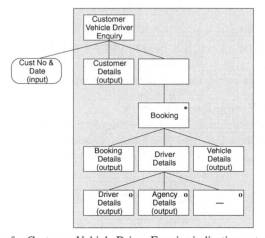

Fig. 5.51 I/O Structure for Customer Vehicle Driver Enquiry indicating output structure

Group accesses on the Enquiry Access Path

Just as we grouped effects on the Effect Correspondence Diagram when designing updates, we group accesses in one-to-one correspondence on the Enquiry Access Path. The same rules apply—grouped correspondences cannot include accesses linked by plain lines; they must include all the associated one-to-one correspondences (shown by single-headed arrows on the Enquiry Access Paths).

In Fig. 5.52 below we have grouped the one-to-one correspondences and named each one to describe the data that is being accessed—this is useful for the next task which turns this into a Jackson diagram. The hyphenated null box indicates that the vehicle may be driven by the customer themselves: no Driver No. or Agency Name would then be recorded. Some analysts do not bother to circle grouped accesses if they only contain one box. However, it is useful when you are new to this technique to indicate all grouped accesses as shown below.

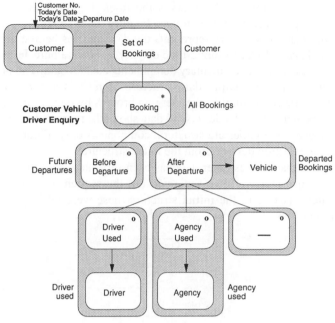

Fig. 5.52 Grouped correspondences on the Enquiry Access Path

Convert to Jackson-like notation

Just as the grouped Effect Correspondence Diagram was converted to a Jackson diagram, so the grouped Enquiry Access Path is converted to a Jackson diagram. Each grouped access becomes a box on the Jackson diagram, maintaining iteration and selection symbols. Thus, 'All Bookings' retains the iteration and 'Future Departures' maintains the selection.

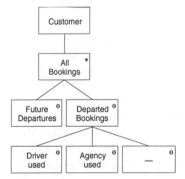

Fig. 5.53 Initial Jackson structure derived from grouped Enquiry Access Path

Sometimes the Jackson diagram that arises does not fully follow the Jackson convention. For instance, several iterations may come from the same parent or iterations and selections may have the same parent. In these cases it is best to develop a further

Jackson structure which observes the rules. Figure 5.53 shows the initial Jackson structure produced from the grouped Enquiry Access Path.

This Jackson structure represents the data that has been extracted by navigating the Logical Data Model to support the enquiry. It is not a pure Jackson structure in that the nodes as well as the elementary components contain data. The next task is to merge this structure with the output data structure—which is a pure Jackson structure. Some analysts prefer to simplify the merging process by developing a pure Jackson structure from the initial one. To do this, all data should be represented in elementary components (the leaves); the nodes are structural components only. Figure 5.54 below shows a pure Jackson structure derived from the initial structure.

Notice that the customer data has been separated from the group handling bookings. Notice also that we have separated out the sequence with 'Booking', 'Driver', and 'Vehicle' boxes; in the initial structure these were all implied within the 'Departed Bookings' box.

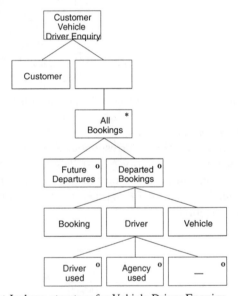

Fig. 5.54 Improved input Jackson structure for Vehicle Driver Enquiry

Identify correspondences between input and output data structures
Parts of the structure are said to be in correspondence if they contain the same data and are structurally consistent with each other. The input data structure from Fig. 5.54 and the output data structure (from Fig. 5.51) are shown below in Fig. 5.55 with correspondences marked by double-headed arrows.[1]

---

[1] This is the normal convention for showing correspondences, although they could equally well be shown by letter codes or by applying different shadings. Do not confuse correspondence between elements in input and output data structures with one-to-one correspondences shown on Effect Correspondence Diagrams and Enquiry Access Paths—the two are quite different.

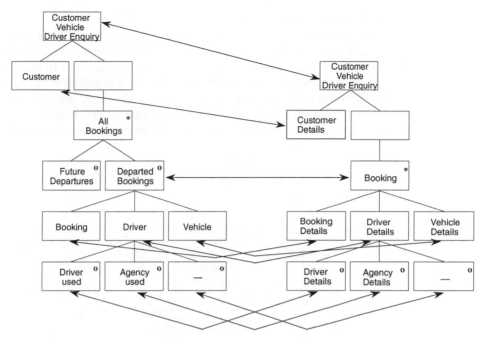

Fig. 5.55 Correspondence between input and output data structures

Figure 5.55 shows only exact correspondences, thus 'Customer' in the input structure corresponds with 'Customer Details' in the output structure. 'Booking' in the input structure corresponds with 'Booking Details' in the output structure. Notice that whole components of a structure can correspond. Thus, 'Departed Bookings' corresponds with the 'Booking' iteration in the output structure—it is only the departed bookings that are required in the output. The input data structure shows 'Future Departures' which are not required in the output data structure. This is where the two structures do not exactly correspond; this is not a problem as there is no clash in structures, the 'Future Departures' can be incorporated into the merged structure without any problems.

We have shown the correspondence between the improved input structure and the output structure. Had we used the original input structure (Fig. 5.53) then correspondences could still have been shown. These would not be the precise correspondences of data achieved above.

Sometimes the two structures do not appear to correspond; this may be due to different sequences being shown in the input and output structures. Usually the input structure can be amended (this only represents the order in which we have chosen to extract the data) to match the output data structure. Sometimes the input and output structures cannot correspond and we have a *structure clash*, and this is discussed further later in the section.

Merge input and output structures

Where correspondence exists the two structures can be merged. The resulting merged boxes are given a name that reflects the processing that occurs. The usual technique is to take one of the two structures and merge the other structure into it, adding any extra boxes that may be required. Figure 5.56 shows the merged structure for Customer Vehicle Driver Enquiry. Note that this has followed the input structure with each box given a name appropriate to the data that it is processing. The structural boxes (nodes) are processing a part of the structure such as a sequence, selection, or iteration.

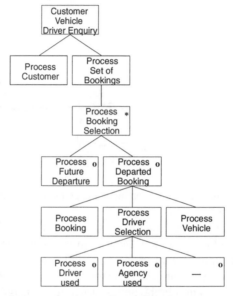

Fig. 5.56 Merged input and output structure to give processing structure

Add operations to structure

We now add the read operations to the structure. No update operations will appear as we are dealing with an enquiry. The following set of operations were previously discussed—these are the ones necessary for all Enquiry Process Models:

- read <entity> by key;
- read next <detail entity> of <master entity> [using <relationship>];
- read <master entity> of <detail entity>;
- define set matching <condition>;
- read next <entity> in set;
- fail if SI<> value;

Figure 5.57 shows the process structure with operations. The first operation to be performed is to read the Customer occurrence using the primary key. This is followed by reading the next Booking occurrence for that Customer. Note that this is a 'read ahead' processed before we enter the iteration. The iteration condition will be applied and if there are no Bookings for the Customer then the iteration will not be entered.

Operation 2 appears again at the end of the iteration as another 'read ahead'. We have only shown read operations here. Printing, writing to temporary files, etc., are considered to be part of the output processing and are handled by the output process of the function. Enquiry and Update Process Models are only concerned with the processing associated with updating and extracting from the main systems' data; input and output processing are handled by other components of the function.

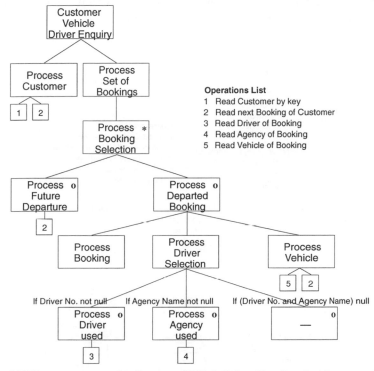

Fig. 5.57 Process structure for Customer Vehicle Driver Enquiry showing operations

Allocate conditions to structure

We now add conditions for all selections and iterations in the structure. The conditions below 'Process Booking Selection' could be defined in several different ways. The enquiry is discriminating between the bookings that have departed and those that have not. One way would be to use the state indicator value of Booking which is changed when the booking departs. Another way would be to test the value of an attribute in the Booking occurrence; we could use Date Booking Starts or Date Collected. We think it is better to use real values rather than state indicators as these will be more meaningful to the maintenance programmer or designer. Either of the two attributes could be used although each has slightly different consequences for potential errors. These should be considered and possibly discussed with the user—we have chosen to use Date Booking Starts as the tested attribute value.

With 'Process Driver Selection' we also have various ways in which the condition could be expressed. Our approach is to test the foreign key values which would be in Booking to decide which option should be followed. An alternative could be the conditions: 'if Driver master' and 'if Agency master'.

When assigning conditions we should be aware of recognition problems which occur when the condition cannot be evaluated without some of the processing within the selection or iteration being performed. Figure 5.58 shows the completed Enquiry Process Model for Customer Vehicle Driver Enquiry.

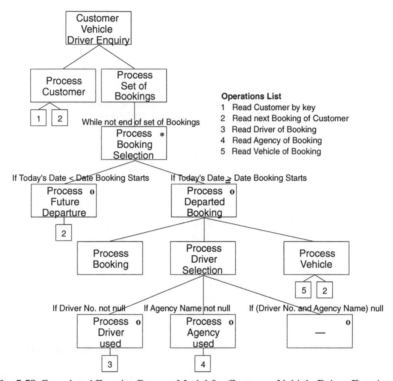

Fig. 5.58 Completed Enquiry Process Model for Customer Vehicle Driver Enquiry

Specify error conditions and output
Error conditions are not so critical with enquiries as with updates but the designer should still ensure that errors are recognized and reported to the user—otherwise the user will be getting erroneous data. One of the most obvious error conditions that could arise is where the input data (often the primary key of an entity) does not match any values in the database. A fail condition should be documented as an operation and a suitable error message defined so that it may be provided to the user. Other error conditions might check the state indicator values for entity occurrences.

In our example, the conditions governing the driver selection are not complete and an error could arise if both Driver No. and Agency No. were supplied for the Booking (this is clearly not correct since the Logical Data Structure shows an exclusive arc on the relationships of Booking with Driver and Agency—either a Driver is used, or an Agency is used, or neither). An error condition could be added to the Enquiry Process Model such as 'if Driver No. and Agency Name not known then error 10'. 'Error Code 10' could be defined as the message 'inconsistent driver information for this Booking'; this message would be picked up by the output process, and displayed or printed.

Walk through the structure
The Enquiry Process Model should be examined to ensure that it makes sense. Ideally this should be done with another designer who is not involved in the development of the particular process model. As with Update Process Models, action diagrams may be a useful alternative way of checking Enquiry Process Models. Some sort of review should be held with the users, probably including both Enquiry Process Models and Update Process Models in the same review. However, it is unlikely that users would welcome the technical detail provided by SSADM's process models and a more user-friendly form of review should be provided.

Example 2 Departure and Return List

This was discussed in Sec. 4.7 where two different Enquiry Access Paths were developed. We take the first solution produced (Fig. 4.130) of these forward to an Enquiry Process Model—we describe the steps in less detail than in the previous example. Figure 5.59 below shows the grouped accesses on the Enquiry Access Path— all those in one-to-one correspondence.

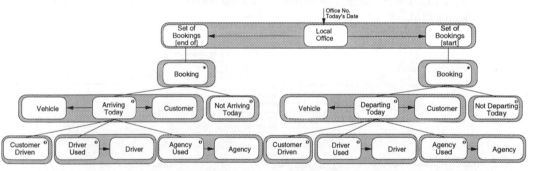

Fig. 5.59 Enquiry Access Path for Departure and Return List showing grouped correspondences

In order to produce an Enquiry Process Model we merge the input and output data structures. Figure 5.60 shows on the left the output structure for the list: local office details are followed by an iteration of the day's departing bookings and an iteration of the day's arriving bookings. The right-hand side of Fig. 5.60 shows the input data structure derived from the grouped Enquiry Access Path. Separate boxes have been shown for the local office, customer and vehicle data to simplify further development of the process model. Exact correspondences between the output and input structure are shown by the double-headed arrows.

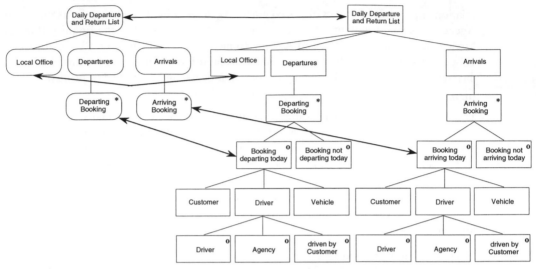

Fig. 5.60 Output and input data structures for the Departure and Return List showing correspondences

The merging of the two structures gives the Enquiry Process Model shown below in Fig. 5.61. To this we have added the operations and conditions. There was not enough room to show all conditions in position on the diagram so a separate conditions list has been added.

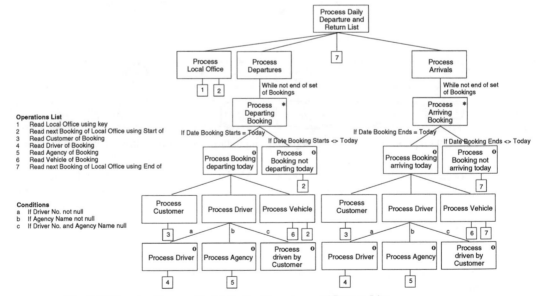

Operations List
1   Read Local Office using key
2   Read next Booking of Local Office using Start of
3   Read Customer of Booking
4   Read Driver of Booking
5   Read Agency of Booking
6   Read Vehicle of Booking
7   Read next Booking of Local Office using End of

Conditions
a   If Driver No. not null
b   If Agency Name not null
c   If Driver No. and Agency Name null

Fig. 5.61 Enquiry Process Model for the Departure and Return List

Notice that the 'read ahead' of the next Booking occurrence of Local Office (operations 2 and 7) is performed before the iteration is entered. This ensures that the 'While not end of set of Bookings' iteration condition can be tested and the iteration not entered if no occurrences of the Booking exist for that Local Office. For a similar reason the read of the next Booking occurrence is performed again at the end of each iteration. This example is discussed further in Chapter 6, Physical Design, where we use it as an example for timing the transactions and show the SQL required to perform this enquiry.

Structure clashes

These arise when there is a mismatch between input and output data structures. In general, they are unlikely to occur in SSADM because the two structures being merged have, to some extent, a common source. We derive Enquiry Access Paths (or Effect Correspondence Diagrams) from the Logical Data Structure, and these are then converted into Jackson structures which are merged with the output structure. The output structures (incorporated in I/O Structures) were normalized to check our Logical Data Structure. Thus the output data structures should be consistent with the Logical Data Structure and with the access paths.

When we appear to have a structure clash we should first determine whether we really do have a clash—sometimes the order in which data is presented is not dependent upon the way that the data is organized but is simply the sequence in which it has been shown. If this is the case then the input data structure derived from the Enquiry Access Path can be changed.

The second action is to consider whether the Logical Data Structure is correct—it is quite possible that we have made an error during its development or during normalization. If we are convinced we have a structure clash then there are several methods that can be used to resolve it.[1] These techniques form a major part of most texts on Jackson structured programming. Detailed treatment of structured clashes is beyond the scope of this book and of SSADM but we will briefly cover the main types of structure clash and their resolution below.

Ordering clash   This is where the sequences of the input and output structures do not match. It may be that the sequence boxes appear in the wrong order or it may be that the information is presented in the wrong order (for instance, displaying bookings in Booking No. order rather than Date Booking Starts order). This can be resolved in two ways. First the Logical Data Model can be modified so that the input structure can match the output structure—i.e. so that the data model can immediately produce the information in the order required for the output. Second, an additional process could be defined to resequence either the input data or the output data—frequently this means sorting the data into the order required for the output.

Boundary clash   This occurs when the groupings of data attributes in the input structure do not match the physical groupings required in the output. For instance, the number of bookings for a particular customer will be unknown and may spread over several pages

---

[1] It may be worth getting specialist help from an experienced programmer to consider how the problem may be resolved.

of print-out or several screens. This kind of structure clash is rarely a problem with modern 4GLs which are good at handling this sort of problem. If more primitive technology is being used then an output process needs to be defined to format the data. An intermediate output data structure is defined which is compatible with the input data structure and a further output process is defined to perform the necessary formatting.

Interleaving clash This occurs when the events for one entity are mixed up with the events for another entity. This causes data structures where the elements belong to different entity occurrences. These frequently occur when we are trying to navigate through recursive relationships (the pig's ear). Some relational databases (e.g. Oracle Version 7) provide mechanisms and commands to help navigate these structures. The normal approach requires designing a process so that it temporarily stores entity occurrences while other entity occurrences are processed. This is the most difficult kind of structure clash to resolve.

SUMMARY
- Enquiry Process Models are a major product of step 530, *define enquiry processes*.
- Enquiry Process Models are developed from:
  - Enquiry Access Paths;
  - output data structures (the output part of the I/O Structure).
- Enquiry Process Models are built up in the following way:
  - group accesses on the Enquiry Access Path;
  - convert to Jackson-like structure—to form input data structure;
  - identify correspondences between input and output data structures;
  - merge input and output structures;
  - add operations to structure;
  - add conditions to structure;
  - specify integrity error conditions and error outputs;
  - walk through the structure.
- Structure clashes occur when input and output structures cannot be merged;
- Structure clashes can be resolved by Jackson techniques not part of core SSADM.

Exercises

5.8.1   Enquiry Process Models
Use the Enquiry Access Path solutions provided for Exercise 4.7.3 in Appendix D.
a) *Customer Project Report.* For a given customer (known customer number) print out the customer name, address and a list of all projects with project code, project name, start date and end date. Produce a simple I/O Structure to merge with the input structure derived from the Enquiry Access Path.
b) *Staff Allocation Sheet.* For a given project print out the customer name and number; the project code and description and the staff working on the project; their name, grade and the number of days that they are working on it. An I/O Structure was produced for the Staff Allocation Sheet as the answer to Exercise 4.4.2 and is in Appendix D.

5.9   Assemble Logical Design (step 540)

Introduction

Each of the SSADM stages, from Stage 0, Feasibility, through to Stage 6, Physical Design, is completed by a formal process involving the users (and other experts) in making decisions and in accepting end-products. The Business Systems Options and Technical System Options stages are completed by the users making a decision regarding the future directions of the system (and project). All the other stages end with a step called 'Assemble...'. This 'Assemble...' step involves checking the accuracy, completeness, and consistency of the end-products of the stage. The products are checked both individually and as a whole. This checking is normally performed by a formal quality assurance review—strictly speaking the actual review is not part of this step which concentrates on the preparation for the review. Techniques for quality control are outside the remit of SSADM and are the responsibility of the project management method (e.g. PRINCE) used. Further discussion of an approach to quality control is given in Chapter 7, Management Aspects. As a result of quality control, some end-products may need amendment and further review.

All SSADM end-products are defined by Product Descriptions in the SSADM Reference Manual. This contains quality criteria for each product: at the lowest level of each Product Breakdown Structure, quality criteria are defined for individual parts of the product; at higher levels of the breakdown structure, quality criteria define consistency and completeness of logically related groups of products. In each of the sections dealing with the 'Assemble...' steps we discuss the objectives of the review and identify some of the most important points to which users and technical experts should pay particular attention. For a full description of quality criteria see Part 4 of the SSADM Reference Manual.

Stage 5 products to be reviewed

In this step all the products that comprise the Logical Design are brought together, checked, reviewed formally, and published. It is the last step in the Logical Systems Specification module and ensures that a complete and accurate specification is passed on to the Physical Design module of the project.

Figure 5.62 shows the Product Breakdown Structure for the Logical Design document. Several of the products shown here were developed during Requirements Specification and reviewed at the end of that module. In this step we need to ensure that these are consistent with the new products developed in this stage and that any amendments to the earlier products identified during this stage have been made.

The criteria that can be applied to quality checking to products that are carried forward from the Requirements Specification were discussed in Sec. 4.9—these same criteria apply here. Below we concentrate on the products developed during Logical Design and how these inter-relate with the earlier products.

The Function Definitions are central to the packaging of the Logical Process Model. Each Function Definition should be supported by the event/enquiry processing (Effect

Correspondence Diagram, Update Process Model, Enquiry Access Path, Enquiry Process Model) by its input/output processing (I/O Structures and dialogues) and by any other processing defined for it (e.g. common processing defined as Elementary Process Descriptions). These should be packaged and reviewed together to ensure that they are fully complete and consistent with one another. Essentially the Function Definition summarizes all of the specifications for the function, the detail of which will be found in the other associated documents listed above.

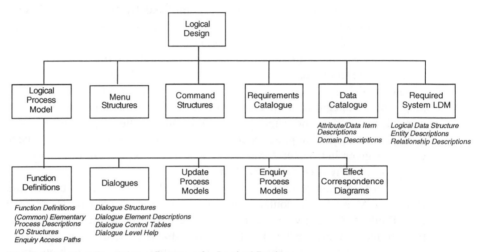

Fig. 5.62 Product Breakdown Structure for Logical Design

We also need to ensure that the detailed processing is consistent with other components of the dialogue design for the system—Menu Structures and Command Structures should define how functions are linked together in a way that they can be accessed by each particular user role. The data design of the new system is contained in the Required System Logical Data Model and Data Catalogue. These are carried forward from Stage 3 but some modifications may be necessary in the light of more detailed processing design in Stage 5. The Requirements Catalogue is also carried forward from earlier stages and should be re-examined to ensure that all functional requirements have been met and that these are consistent with the design documentation that describes their solution. By this stage everything in the Requirements Catalogue should be resolved (some technical aspects during Stage 4). Particularly we should ensure that any requirements associated with the human–computer interface have been met by the dialogue design work in Stage 5.

We now consider each of the new products that were produced in Stage 5 discussing the quality criteria that may be applied to each.

Dialogues
These should be consistent with the Function Definitions that they belong to. Each individual dialogue should consist of a Dialogue Structure (derived from the I/O Structure associated with the Function Definition in Stage 3), Dialogue Element

Descriptions (derived from the I/O Structure Description), a Dialogue Control Table, and Dialogue Level Help. These components of the dialogue should fit together and be consistent with all Logical Groupings of Dialogue Elements corresponding to the Dialogue Element Descriptions and to the Dialogue Control Table. The Dialogue Structure should follow the Jackson conventions with the dialogue name and the user role being given at the top. The attributes (data items) shown on the Dialogue Element Descriptions should correspond to those in the Data Catalogue and the groupings shown should correspond to those in the Dialogue Structures and in the Dialogue Control Tables. Dialogue Level Help should be described for each dialogue—if it is deemed unnecessary then some reason should be given for this.

Enquiry and Update Process Models
These should be named consistently with the names given in the Function Definitions. They should follow the Jackson conventions for these models with all operations and conditions being provided. Integrity errors and error outputs should be fully defined. Any structure clashes that occur should be identified and suggested resolutions described. Operations should not hang off iteration or selection nodes (some organizations may also not allow them to hang off sequence nodes).

Menu Structures and Command Structures
These define the navigation between dialogues. A Menu Structure is developed for each user role and should be validated with a user representative. Command Structures show how, within a user role, navigation can be managed from one dialogue to another. The user representative should validate that the likely paths between dialogues are documented. Dialogue names on Command Structures and Menu Structures should be consistent with the Dialogue Structures and the Function Definition. Menu Structures and Command Structures should be consistent with each other.

6 Physical Design

6.1 Introduction

The review of the detailed logical data and process design at the end of Logical Systems Specification marked the end of the logical stages of SSADM. The method now moves from this logical design to a physical design. The Physical Design module contains only Stage 6, Physical Design. The logical design could be implemented on any hardware or suitable software—in other words it is implementation independent. In Stage 6 this implementation-independent design is converted into a design specific for the particular hardware and software configuration selected. This implementation-dependent design is known as the *physical* design.

> **Warning** In Physical Design SSADM can get very technical. To be able to understand this chapter fully you will need a good understanding of at least one database management system, an understanding of the general principles involved in database systems, and some knowledge of software engineering. These topics are covered by many books and some recommendations are given in the Bibliography.

Objectives

In the earlier stages of an SSADM project considerable effort went into ensuring that the requirements of the user for functionality and information content were correctly determined, and into designing a system that would meet these agreed requirements. These requirements are carried through to Stage 6. There are three main objectives to this stage:

- to ensure that all the system components and plans are ready to enable system construction and implementation to be completed;
- to ensure that application and installation standards are set and followed throughout the project;
- to produce a tuned design that meets performance requirements.

Products of Physical Design

Figure 6.1 shows the Product Breakdown Structure for the Physical System Specification which contains the major products of the Physical Design module. Each of these products is briefly described below.

This product set for the Physical System Specification is a guideline only. SSADM is a flexible method that encourages developers to tailor it to their specific project circumstances. The first step of the Physical Design stage produces plans, Product Breakdown Structures, and Product Descriptions for the physical design, construction and testing phases of the project. The general approach that the project will take is outlined by the Physical Design Strategy (see Sec. 6.2).

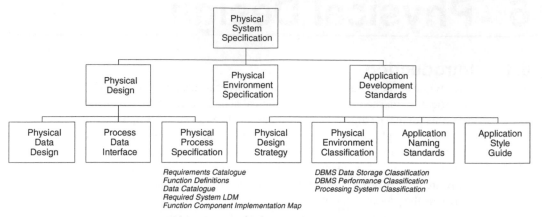

Fig. 6.1 Product Breakdown Structure for Physical System Specification

Application Development Standards
There are a great variety of tools that can be used to construct a working system such as: programming languages, database management systems, transaction processing software, tailored application packages, operating systems, screen painters, report writers, query languages, data dictionaries, expert system shells, automatic testing tools, and data communications software. The first step in Physical Design is to define the Application Development Standards—how the particular mix of tools determined in the Selected Technical System Option is going to be used in the project.

The individual products that form the Application Development Standards are discussed in the next section which deals with step 610, *prepare for Physical Design*.

Physical Environment Specification
This specifies the hardware and software products, their configuration, and the services that will be supplied by a service provider. The service provider would normally produce this specification based upon a contract which has been drawn up by the projects' management (or procurement team) with the organizations who have been selected to provide these services. Typically, it will include details of all hardware and software products that are due to be supplied; the hardware and software configurations, operating documentation, and reference manuals. Some fourth generation software suppliers (e.g. Oracle) provide product-specific guides describing how their software can be used with SSADM.

Essentially the Physical Environment Specification follows from good contractual procedures that the organization should enforce upon its suppliers. It is essentially an advance delivery note that ensures that the project team know exactly what they are due to get.[1]

Physical Design

The remaining products of the stage are concerned with the conversion of the logical specification into a design appropriate for the technical environment. This product set often requires considerable tailoring to the particular project environment. For instance, standards will need to be set for program specifications.

The Physical Data Design is derived from the Required System Logical Data Model—ensuring it conforms to the constraints of the data management software and meets the performance requirements.

The Process Data Interface specifies the interaction between the physical database design and the processing that operates on it. The 'logical' processing, in the form of Function Definitions, Update and Enquiry Process Models, is defined by the earlier stages of SSADM. As a result of constraints of the physical database system and of tuning of the overall system performance, the logical data design (around which the 'logical' processing was designed) may be compromised by physical design. An interface is developed to avoid respecifying all of the logical processing to be consistent with the tuned physical data design. This software is specified to interface between the 'logical' specification and the physical data structure—it is known as the Process Data Interface. This allows the designer to implement logical processes directly as physical programs independent of the physical database structure; thus easing maintenance and construction of the system.

The Physical Process Specification is derived from the Logical Systems Specification components (from Stage 5). Essentially, these components of the Physical Process Specification form a logical, idealized specification of the system which can be used in the future as the documentation base for testing, maintenance, enhancement, end-user support, error handling, and help desk activities.

The Data Catalogue would normally be implemented in a data dictionary package. The Function Definitions would now include physical design related information. The Requirements Catalogue would include any design compromises (e.g. on performance) made during Physical Design. The Required System Logical Data Model would be unchanged. The means of keeping all this documentation up-to-date (i.e. configuration management), and the level of detail required, will depend upon the tools available, the organization's internal standards, and the importance of the project.

The Function Component Implementation Map shows how the components of each function are physically implemented and packaged. It also attempts to remove duplication and promote re-use. It will be discussed in detail in Sec. 6.4.

---

[1] This may seem obvious but there have been many cases of projects being delivered with unexpected hardware and software.

Approach

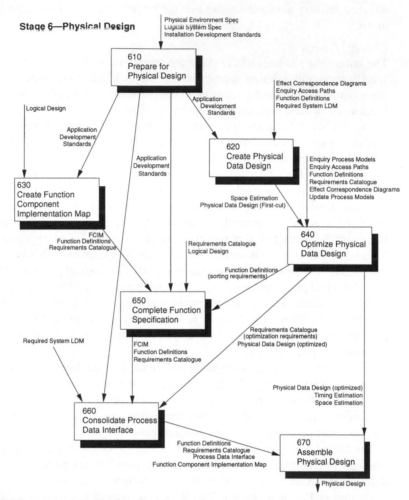

Fig. 6.2 Structure of the Physical Design module

Figure 6.2 shows the steps of the Physical Design module. Step 610, *prepare for physical design*, sets the standards and approach for the rest of the stage. Because the approach to physical design is so dependent upon the project, the installation, and the technology employed, SSADM cannot be too prescriptive about Stage 6. Step 610 defines the approach to be taken for the particular project.

The project team attempts to understand and classify the physical environment. Standards are defined for the use of programming languages, fourth generation environments, data management software, and any other development tools that will be used. Performance statistics for timing and space utilization are obtained for the hardware/software combination. Naming standards are defined for the elements of the system. Finally, plans for Physical Design are developed.

Step 620, *create physical data design*, turns the Required System Logical Data Model into a data design specific for the particular database or file management package. This is done in a prescriptive way without regard for system performance. SSADM suggests that this first-cut data design is developed in two phases. First, a general physical design applicable to all data management software is developed. Second, product-specific rules appropriate for the chosen hardware/software environment are applied to produce a detailed physical data design.

Step 630, *create function component implementation map*, develops the process specification from Stage 5. We identify how each function is physically implemented; deal with common processing: specify physical formats, physical dialogues, and syntax and control error handling. Any processing which was not designed previously is specified in this step. The only exception to this is the detailed specification of the function components which are to be implemented in procedural program code—these are specified in step 650.

In step 640, *optimize physical data design*, the performance of the first-cut Physical Data Design is measured against performance objectives set by the users. The physical design may not meet these objectives: it is optimized, or tuned, until it meets them. Tuning is an iterative process in which several cycles of design, measurement, and redesign may be repeated before a satisfactory conclusion is reached. If the objectives cannot be met with the planned hardware and software then modification of the objectives will be discussed with the users.

Step 650, *complete function specification*, considers the components of a function that cannot be specified in a non-procedural way; those that need a detailed specification for programming in a procedural language. The Function Component Implementation Map, developed in step 630, shows how each function component is to be physically implemented.

Step 660, *consolidate Process Data Interface*, specifies the interaction between the physical database design and the processing that operates on it. The 'logical' processing, in the form of Function Definitions, Update and Enquiry Process Models, was defined in the earlier stages of SSADM. As a result of constraints of the physical database software and of tuning of the overall system performance, the logical data design (around which the 'logical' processing was designed) may be compromised by physical design. To avoid respecifying all of the logical processing to be consistent with the tuned physical data design, software is developed to interface between the 'logical' specification and eventual code, and the physical data structure—this interface software is known as the Process Data Interface. This allows the designer to implement logical processes directly as physical programs independent of the physical database structure; thus easing maintenance and construction of the system.

Finally step 670, *assemble physical design*, brings together all of the physical design products ensuring that they are complete and consistent. These are then published and the project can continue onto the construction and testing stages, which are not covered by SSADM.

6.2   Prepare for physical design (step 610)

Introduction

The first step in Stage 6, Physical Design, is to tailor the stage to the particular project environment. Every project is different, requiring some modifications to the SSADM approach, but perhaps these project variations are greatest in physical design. Software and hardware technologies, organizational standards, and the application under development can all vary considerably from project to project. When these technological, organizational, and project factors combine, as they do in physical design, then the project variations are magnified.

Step 610 involves a variety of activities concerned with understanding the physical environment, defining standards on how it is to be used, and creating detailed plans and descriptions for the end-products of Stage 6. The main products of the step is the Application Development Standards, comprising the Physical Environment Classification, the Application Naming Standards, the Application Style Guide, and the Physical Design Strategy. The Product Breakdown Structure was shown as part of Fig. 6.1.

The Physical Design Strategy is perhaps the most important product of the step. It defines how physical design will be carried out for the particular project. Detailed plans (Activity Descriptions) and Product Descriptions are developed for the Physical Design Stage—these are normally based on the standard SSADM set. Standards are defined for program specifications, appropriate to the construction tools selected. Some projects may decide to determine the Physical Design Strategy at the end of Stage 4, Technical System Options, and then tailor Stage 5, Logical Design.

Physical Environment Classification

The Physical Environment Specification describes the hardware and software, and their configurations which were contractually agreed with suppliers. This information is used to understand and classify the physical environment in the Physical Environment Classification so that the Physical Design Strategy can be defined.

The Physical Environment Classification is composed of three components; the DBMS Data Storage Classification, the DBMS Performance Classification, and the Processing System Classification. SSADM forms are available to assist these classifications.[1] Once the DBMS performance and data structuring characteristics have been understood then space and timing estimation forms can be designed to calculate and tune performance in step 640, *optimize physical data design*.

If, as in many large projects, there are several different database management systems and processing systems used, then classifications should be developed for each product type. Sometimes the development environment will be different from the

---

[1] Some of the terminology used in the SSADM forms is rather idiosyncratic; we have attempted to explain it in rather more general terms. However, this is an area rife with jargon—from suppliers and from computer scientists.

operating environment (e.g. based on a different operating system), so a migration path between these should also be defined. Software suppliers may provide SSADM interface guides which define this information. These should be checked to ensure that they are valid for the current versions of the software and are consistent with the operating systems' environment in which they are to be employed.

Each of the classifications is described below.

DBMS Data Storage Classification
This defines the data storage and retrieval mechanisms for the selected database management software or file handler. It shows how the storage software physically implements entities and relationships, how it manages keys, and how it physically implements access mechanisms. Figure 6.3 shows an example of a completed DBMS Data Storage Classification form.[1]

DBMS/file handler The name of the database management system or file handler on which the software is to be built. In Fig. 6.3 we show typical details of a CODASYL product such as IDMS or IDMSX. Each particular product will implement the various categories in slightly different ways. For instance, IDMSX allows the use of secondary indexes, whereas some other CODASYL products do not.

Relationship representation There are three basic ways—tables, lists, and phantom—by which data management products physically store the relationships between entity occurrences. In *tables*, a separate record contains the physical or logical keys of the two occurrences participating in the relationship. In *lists*, or linked lists, the relationship between master and detail occurrences is represented by a list of keys including the keys of the master and each detail entity—pointers connect each entry in the list to the next entry. In relational databases, relationships are maintained through holding the primary key of the master occurrence (acting as a foreign key) with the key of the detail occurrence, usually alongside all of the detail entity's attributes. Because this data about the relationship is not specified explicitly, it is referred to as a *phantom* relationship.

Amalgamation of entity and relationship data In most database management systems it is possible to store the data about entities and that about relationships separately. However, in some products, the data can be amalgamated. In CODASYL databases, relationships become SETs, which are defined separately from the RECORDs storing entity occurrences. Pointers are held in the RECORDs pointing to the NEXT occurrence, PRIOR occurrence, and OWNER occurrence associated with the particular occurrence in the relationship. In relational products, relationship data can be stored separately, or can be stored as foreign key information within the detail occurrence.

---

[1]Note that this form is an indication only of the information that should be collected. It does not provide a comprehensive set of information about all database products. For instance, information is not held about the methods of implementation of many-to-many relationships or of all kinds of optional or exclusive relationships—these can be managed within some advanced database products. Similarly, DBMS facilities for enforcing database integrity rules to do with deletions and transference of relationships are not recorded in this form. All SSADM forms are guidelines only and can be adapted to particular project circumstances.

Key representation in relationship (logical or physical) A physical key indicates the disk address of the data. A logical key may only point to an index or require searching in other ways. Logical keys are often called symbolic pointers. Generally CODASYL databases operate through pointer chains which contain the physical address of the occurrence participating in the relationship. Relational databases usually work by using logical keys and manage relationships through joins of foreign key and primary key values. In the example shown in Fig. 6.3, pointer chains are used to manage all relationships, but if the entity is in Third Normal Form, then the logical key will be present.

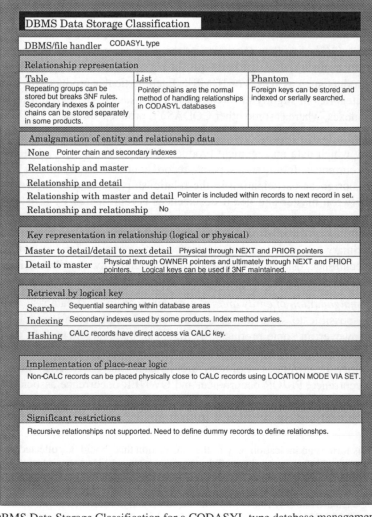

Fig. 6.3 DBMS Data Storage Classification for a CODASYL type database management system

Retrieval by logical key This documents the mechanism for finding the logical key. The three basic mechanisms are: searching serially, sequentially, or in binary modes (which techniques are possible depends upon the construction of the file); indexing, which may involve binary searching of the index; and using hashing algorithms to determine the physical address from the logical key. In CODASYL databases the primary means of access will be through the CALC hashed key, but many CODASYL products support secondary indexing, and if all else fails, then serial searches through parts of the whole database can be used.

Implementation of place-near logic Many database management products allow the designer to specify that related entity occurrences, of the same or of different types, can be stored physically near to a particular occurrence. This obviously has an impact on performance since one occurrence and its related occurrences can be retrieved much more rapidly. CODASYL databases specify that non-CALC records can be placed physically close to CALC records using the LOCATION MODE VIA SET data definition statement. Relational databases vary in their use of place-near logic, most support a form of clustering which is based upon clustering indexes together.

Significant restrictions Any restrictions on handling normal data structures that the database management software may impose. For instance, most CODASYL databases cannot implement relationships between occurrences of the same type (recursive relationships). These have to be handled by creating a separate record to deal with the information about the relationship. This restriction may be quite significant if the Required System Logical Data Model shows recursive relationships.

DBMS Performance Classification
In order to estimate the performance of the system in terms of its response times and turn-around times for batch processing, then we need hard information about the performance of the product on the chosen hardware/software platform. This information can be documented on the DBMS Performance Classification form. Further information may be available from the supplier in subject guides. However, it should always be borne in mind that this information is hard to come by with the most accurate figures being provided by comparison with similar technical architecture. Figure 6.4 shows an example of the form completed for a CODASYL type DBMS using relatively low-performance hardware.

DBMS/File Handler The name of the database management system or file handler being used. Often the performance may be affected by other software resident in the computer at the same time, such as the operating system. The hardware to which the figures relate should also be documented. If a distributed system is being designed with different processors then several of these forms may need to be completed.

Transaction logging overhead A journal is often maintained of transactions being processed. This is useful for audit and recovery purposes. Often the performance overhead is negligible as transaction logs are written to a separate disk drive—if it is significant then figures for the different types of transaction logging should be recorded.

DBMS Performance Classification

DBMS/file handler   CODASYL type

Transaction logging overhead

Transactions logged for all updates. Estimate .5 ms processor time.

Commit/backout overhead

Before and after imaging and checkpointing available. Estimate 3 disk accesses per update.

Space management overhead

Null values compressed, assume 4 bytes for all pointers, 32 bytes per page for page management, pages not recommended to be over 70% full.

Dialogue context save/restore overhead

Context saved in memory.

Standard timing factors

Disk operation:	Time:	Comment:
Read:	30 ms	
Write:	30 ms	

Overflow overhead:

DBMS operation	DBMS CPU time	TP monitor CPU time
All reads	2 ms	

Performance parameters for available sort packages

Fig. 6.4 DBMS Performance Classification Form

Commit/Backout Overhead Commit and backout (or rollback) were discussed in the context of logical success units in Sec. 5.7. Most sophisticated database management systems have a variety of strategies to maximize recovery. These include: before imaging, where the state of the database is recorded before update; after imaging, where the state is stored after update; and check-pointing, where the state of the database and the state of all progressing transactions are stored. Each of these strategies will have an overhead in terms of performance. Any extra disk accesses required for these should be recorded.

Space management overhead Figures are required for page management, pointer length, etc. in order to calculate space requirements. Strategies used by the DBMS for space management can be recorded here.

Dialogue context save/restore overhead This is necessary in case there is a fault during the dialogue to enable the system to recover. The dialogue context could be stored in main memory of the machine or, for added security, periodically on disk. These would enable recovery from line failures and processor breakdowns. Any impacts on performance of dialogues in terms of extra disk accesses required should be recorded.

Standard timing factors The disk figures have the greatest impact on the overall performance of the system. They include the average time taken to read from and write to the disk. The processor figures include the time taken by the database management software to perform a DBMS call[1] and the time taken by the transaction processing monitor, if one is used, to queue and remove from the queue input and output calls. These processor figures can be wildly inaccurate, and of course are very dependent upon the central processing unit and instruction set being used. We should also add in figures for the time taken for the processor to perform any additional application program code. Usually we can add an overhead of around half the time taken for performing the DBMS call (in this case 1 ms). Obviously, this figure depends upon the kind of processing being carried out. If complex calculations are required, it could be considerably increased.

Performance parameters for available sort packages Any timing details for sort packages used prior to update or for outputs before printing should be recorded. This is particularly appropriate in batch processing. Some discussion of sorting requirements was given in Sec. 4.4 which discussed sorting within functions.

Processing System Classification
The Processing System Classification form provides an outline of the features that should be understood about the processing physical environment (Fig. 6.5). This could be a programming language, third or fourth generation, which allows embedded links to database software and to dialogue or batch process handling software.

Classes of tool feature The names of the tools that are provided and the operating environment in which they will be used.

Procedural/non-procedural Some languages may permit a combination of procedural code and non-procedural code (e.g. SQL and COBOL being combined into the same program). This box should be ticked if they can be combined.

On-line/off-line Some tools will allow a mix of on-line and off-line processing within the same program or function, others require them to be separated. This box is ticked if both can be provided within the same function.

---

[1] A DBMS call refers to embedded database language statements in compiled programs. The DBMS will call into action subroutines which access the requested data from disk, manipulate in the required way and then write it back to disk. All of this processing is completely hidden from the application program.

Processing System Classification		
Classes of tool feature		
3GI with embedded CODASYL commands.		
Procedural/non-procedural ☐		On-line/off-line ☐
Success units		
Explicit COMMIT under program control.		
Error handling		
Defined through data dictionary.		
Process components		
Linked before run-time.		
Database processing		
Reports and enquiries through separate Report writer and end-user Query Language		
Update ☐	Enquiry ☐	
I/O processing		
No generation. No restrictions on screen handling.		
Dialogue processing		
Embedded Transaction processing Management System (TPMS) calls.		
Dialogue navigation		
Flexible, under program control using TPMS calls.		
Process data interface		
No generation possible, sub-schemas used in application programs.		
Distributed systems		
Locations must be explicitly defined.		

Fig. 6.5 Processing System Classification form

Success units Sometimes known as commit units, these are the mechanism that databases use to ensure that the integrity of their data is preserved. A piece of processing must either succeed or fail as a whole. This means that success units must be designed so that the data is always left in a consistent state. There are several physical ways in which a database can do this, particularly when involved in distributed processing. The approach taken by the particular software should be defined.

Error handling Some software has in-built error handling and error messages, e.g. for users pressing the wrong key. Some error handling may be defined through the data dictionary, with validation checks and messages defined for particular attributes. Some relational databases will handle referential integrity checks and display errors. The designer may wish to trap these errors and report on them in a different way, or to suppress the checks.

Process components This describes how processes can be combined, copied, and generated at run-time. Other issues that should be considered include: use of subroutines, data linkages between different modules, and use of common code.

Database processing It may be possible to generate enquiry and update processing, in which cases the boxes should be ticked. Other factors to consider are: whether the generated processing can be modified, the performance overheads of generated database processing, and what happens if the generated processing contradicts the Update and Enquiry Process Models.

I/O processing For batch programs it may be possible to generate the I/O processing. For on-line processing we can specify the ways in which attributes from different entities can be related together on one screen.

Dialogue processing The different ways in which dialogue components can be generated or combined. The following should be considered: generation and combinations of display, create, update, deletes of entity occurrences, and of error handling processing.

Dialogue navigation A description of the mechanisms available for dialogue navigation. The following should be considered: automatic generation of menus from function hierarchies, mechanisms for defining function keys, access to menu options, and passage of data between different dialogue components.

Process Data Interface A description of the extent to which a Process Data Interface can be generated using a non-procedural language and can later be modified or extended.

Distributed systems If the data is distributed can the designer ignore the physical distribution of data?

Physical Design Strategy

This defines the approach to the rest of the stage. It includes standards for the use of the processing and database environments, standards for the Function Component Implementation Map and for program specifications, and detailed plans for Stage 6. The Physical Design Strategy, particularly its planning aspects, should be agreed by senior project management and the project board.

Product-specific first-cut data design rules
Having classified the data management and processing software we need to specify how these are to be used in the development. In step 620, *create physical data design*, the Required System Logical Data Model is converted to a first-cut data design for the chosen data management software. This conversion is done in two stages; first, by applying general rules appropriate for all file handling software, and second, by applying product-specific rules to the general physical model. In step 610, *prepare for physical design*, the product-specific design rules used in the second of these stages are specified. Normally the product will have been used on a previous project and these

rules will be available from the supplier—they may be contained in a product-specific guide detailing how the particular software can be used with SSADM. Some CASE tools will automatically perform the transformation to a first-cut physical data design—this is discussed in Sec. 6.3 which deals with step 620.

Timing and space estimation forms
In step 640, *optimize physical data design*, we estimate the performance of critical transactions, measuring these against the Service Level Requirements. These calculations of performance use timing forms (which are usually set up in spreadsheet software). These forms are designed during step 610.

Also in step 640, calculations are made of the space requirements using space estimation forms. Information from the DBMS Data Storage Classification and from the DBMS Performance Classification are used to design the space estimation forms in step 610. Examples of space estimation and timing estimation forms are given in Sec. 6.5 which deals with step 640, *optimize physical data design*.

Function Component Implementation Map
The Function Component Implementation Map shows how the components of each function are physically implemented and packaged. It also attempts to remove duplication and promote re-use in the future system. There is no SSADM standard for this product, although some suggestions are made in Sec. 6.4. Its format depends on the development environment and standards for the project are developed in step 610.

Modern software development environments enable bespoke software for business applications to be developed from high-level languages. These 'fourth generation' languages are often non-procedural in that the programmer does not need to declare variables before use nor define the exact sequence in which commands are executed by the computer. These environments can greatly simplify and speed the task of constructing systems. The designer needs to decide which of the functional components can be developed using non-procedural code and which components need development in procedural languages such as COBOL or C. The criteria for making these decisions will depend on a large number of factors including the complexity of the functions, the capabilities of the tools available, and the circumstances of the project. These criteria form part of the Physical Design Strategy developed in step 610.

Program specification standards
The software will probably be developed using a mixture of procedural and non-procedural code. The detail of the specification will probably be greater for those components requiring procedural implementation. Non-procedural code may be developed by the designers responsible for the logical design—little further specification would then be required.

However, if the code is to be developed by specialist programmers unfamiliar with the application (and possibly unfamiliar with SSADM) then detailed specification will be necessary. The degree of translation from SSADM notations and terminology necessary, the amount of physical design related information, and the formats required will depend on a great variety of factors. Some guidelines are given in Sec. 6.6 which deals with step 650, *complete function specification*.

Physical Design Strategy and development environments
The way physical design is carried out will depend greatly on the kind of software used for the construction. Figure 6.6 shows different development environments and their impact on the cost of changes.

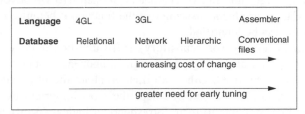

Fig. 6.6 Impacts of implementation environment on the Physical Design Strategy

If assembler and conventional files are used, the cost of making changes to improve the performance (or for any other reason) will normally be much higher than if high-level languages and a relational database are used. It also costs much more to make changes later in the development cycle (i.e. a change in the live system costs more than a change in the construction stage which costs more than a change in the design). Thus the more primitive the technology being used for construction, the more important it is to tune the system before construction begins. The traditional SSADM approach of 'paper' tuning before construction is particularly appropriate for a third-generation development in COBOL using a hierarchical database, network database, or conventional files.

If, however, the software used is so sophisticated that changes are easy to implement then the cost of early tuning may outweigh any benefits achieved. It then makes sense to develop a 'first-cut' design into working code and tune the system throughout the construction stage.

Another method is to follow the traditional SSADM approach but to construct a prototype database and develop code for critical transactions. This prototype can then be tuned and can form the basis for the complete construction of the system.

The approach used will be documented in the plans for the stage.

Planning the development
A full set of plans are developed for the Physical Design stage based upon the approach identified in step 610. Product Descriptions and Product Breakdown Structures are developed for the data design and for program specifications based upon the components of the Physical System Classification. These products are not specified by SSADM because they are specific to the project and to the chosen hardware/software environment. An Activity Network and Activity Descriptions are developed for the remaining activities in the stage. SSADM provides a generalized set which gives good guidelines on how the stage should be approached. However, these guidelines will need to be customized to the particular project—probably to a much greater degree than those for any of the earlier SSADM stages.

Application Naming Standards

A great variety of physical components will be developed during the project including: database records, temporary files, screens, reports, modules, programs, etc. Each of these must be named, observing the restrictions placed by the particular software, e.g. on name length and use of characters. In step 610 we develop naming standards for each of these products ensuring that the function it belongs to, its version number, and its owner, can be identified.

Data dictionary (or repository) software should be used, if possible, to hold information about the physical design components—standards should be agreed as to how this can be used. Other information about the physical fragment, apart from its name, should also be held. Perhaps the most important aspect of this is to link the physical components to their corresponding logical specification components. In this way, maintenance can be simplified and re-use promoted.

Application Style Guide

The other product included in the Application Development Standards is the Application Style Guide. The style guide contains standards for the design of the human–computer interface. It was developed as part of Stage 4, Technical System Options, and is carried through to step 610. Minor changes to the style guide might be necessary to ensure that it is consistent with the dialogue handling specified in the Processing System Classification.

User, operations, and training manuals

User, operations, and training manuals will need to be prepared for the final system. Some work on these may have been started earlier in the project, particularly associated with the Selected Technical System Option. However, only when the Physical Design is finalized can we be sure exactly how the new system will work and the detailed information required in these manuals be finalized. The preparation of these manuals should be started in this step, though the products will probably be developed by separate teams and be subject to separate product life cycles, which extend into the construction and take-on phases of the project. Normally Product Breakdown Structures, Activity Descriptions, and Activity Networks will be developed for these in this step.

SUMMARY

- Step 610, *prepare for physical design*, customizes the SSADM approach to the specific project.
- The Physical System Classification defines the way in which the data management software, the processing software, and their performance are characterized.
- Plans are developed for the remainder of the stage based upon the hardware/software products to be used in the project.
- Naming standards are specified for the application.
- The Physical Design Strategy defines the approach to the Physical Design stage and is agreed with senior management.

6.3   Create physical data design (step 620)

Introduction

The second step of Stage 6 involves turning the Required System Logical Data Model into an executable file or database design. This is achieved by the application of simple rules, particular to the database management software (DBMS) or file handler used. The initial executable design is known as the 'first-cut' because it is a first attempt at the physical data design. There may be several later versions of this design as it is tuned for optimum performance in step 640. This first-cut design is usually represented by a diagram supported by the amended Entity Descriptions.

Objectives

There are two basic criteria that the first-cut design should meet:

1. It can be directly transformed to the data definition constructs of the software to be used.
2. It should contain sufficient information about the physical placement of data to enable performance calculations to be made.

The first criterion is concerned with being able to create a working system. All data dictionary systems, all database management systems, most programming languages, and most operating systems have constructs that enable data structures to be defined. The software then manages the placement and retrieval of that data on disk (or other physical storage media). These data definition constructs may be part of the programming language (as in COBOL), or may be a separate language (as with SQL or the CODASYL standard for network databases). Thus the first-cut design diagram and supporting information can be transformed into the data definition syntax. This route is shown in Fig. 6.7.

Many CASE tools (supporting SSADM and other methods) can automatically produce data definition statements from the logical data design held on the tool. This route is shown by the dotted lines on Fig. 6.7 below. Note that data definition statements can only be produced when data item lengths and formats are known.

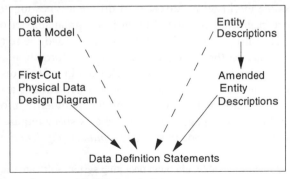

Fig. 6.7 Approaches to first-cut physical data design

In SSADM we normally develop a diagram as an intermediate stage before producing the statements because it is easier to apply the tuning to a diagrammatic representation. Monitoring the impact of various changes to the diagram is easier than monitoring the impact of changes to data definition statements. When the database design has been finalized the data definition statements are produced.

The second criterion is concerned with calculating the performance of the system. The time taken to perform certain critical transactions and batch programs needs to be calculated. Also the total space taken up by the system on backing storage needs to be calculated. To calculate both space and timings we need to know how the data is physically stored on disk.

Physical storage on disk

Database management systems and file handlers usually store and retrieve data in the form of fixed size *pages* or *blocks*[1] on disk. Figure 6.8 shows a simplified representation of how this works. A page is read from the disk into main memory (or into a main memory buffer or cache—on PCs the term RAM is invariably used). This can then be operated on by the application program (which will have requested the retrieval of the data). The end-user, or other software, may also be interacting with the program. If an update to the data occurs then the page is written back to disk.

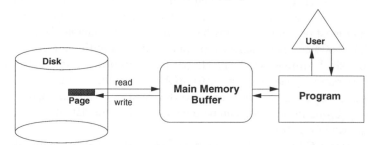

Fig. 6.8 Retrieval of pages from disk

Similar groups of data (some software might call these *records*) are then stored on the same page. Often several entity occurrences can be stored on a single page. Sometimes it is possible to cluster occurrences of different types together on the same page. The way these pages are organized often has a great impact on the performance of the system. Thus if the Customer entity occurrence and the related Order occurrences are stored together on the same page then all the information associated with a particular customer and his or her orders can be retrieved in a single disk access.

The first-cut data design needs to show which entities are clustered together so that entities can be allocated to pages. Using the volumetric information collected in Stage 3, the total number of pages, and thus the disk space required, can be calculated. All of these calculations are made in step 640, *optimize physical data design*.

---

[1] These terms are used interchangeably, although operating system software usually refers to it as a block, and database management system software refers to it as a page.

Generic approach to first-cut physical data design

The approach to developing a first-cut physical data design is determined by the Physical Design Strategy. SSADM suggests a two-stage transformation, whereby the Required System Logical Data Model is first transformed into a generic physical design. Then product-specific rules are applied to transform to a design for the particular data management product being used.

This approach enables analysts, unfamiliar with a particular product, to assist in the physical design.[1] The idea of generic design makes the assumption that all data management software has the following common features:

- Entity occurrences are stored as records (i.e. all of the data associated with a particular entity occurrence is stored together and is identifiable as a separate unit). Entity types are thus represented by record types.
- Records are stored together on disk as *blocks* or *pages.* Each block is the unit of disk storage and of disk access, so that when data is written to disk or retrieved from disk it is retrieved as a single block. Thus all the records on a particular block will be retrieved together.
- Records can be physically grouped together. This means that records of the same type or of different types can be clustered together either on the same block or nearby. This enables an entity occurrence and related occurrences to be retrieved or stored in a minimal number of disk accesses.
- All relationships are supported by the software. Relationships within the same physical group, where the records are clustered together, are known as *primary* relationships. Relationships between records in different physical groups are known as *secondary* relationships.

First-cut design rules

The development of the first-cut design is an eight-step process: the first seven steps develop the generic design, then the last step converts it to a product-specific design.

1. Identify the features of the Required System Logical Data Model that are required for physical data design.
2. Identify the required entry points and distinguish those that are non-key.
3. Identify the roots of physical hierarchies.
4. Identify the allowable physical groups for each non-root entry.
5. Apply the least dependent occurrence rule.
6. Determine the block size to be used.
7. Split the physical groups to fit the chosen block size.
8. Apply the product-specific data design rules using the decisions about the use of DBMS facilities taken in step 610, *prepare for physical design.*

---

[1]It seems to us there is little advantage in this two-stage process as product-specific physical design has to be achieved at some point, and transforming from the generic design to the product-specific design is really no more difficult than transforming to it from a Logical Data Model. Many CASE tools are capable of automatically performing this transformation.

We apply these rules to the Yorkies Required System Logical Data Model (repeated below in Fig. 6.9) to develop a generic first-cut design for Yorkies.

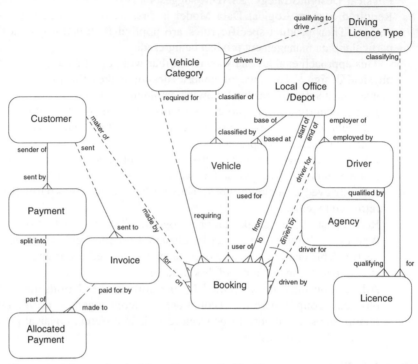

Fig. 6.9 Required System Logical Data Structure for Yorkies

1.   Identify features of the Logical Data Model required for Physical Design
The Logical Data Model contains more semantic information than can be represented in most database management systems.[1] Several features can be removed from the Required System Logical Data Structure to bring it closer to a physical data design.
* Relationship names are removed.
* Optionality is only shown at the detail (many) end. Optionality is shown by an 'o' on the relationship line close to the detail entity—this indicates that a master occurrence may not exist for a detail occurrence. Dashed lines are not used for optional relationships in this diagram.
* Exclusion arcs are removed from the diagram.
* Any remaining one-to-one relationships are converted to one-to-many relationships (this should have been done in the earlier steps).

---

[1] This is an assumption that SSADM makes, but it is not always true. Some modern object-oriented or semantic databases actually hold more semantic information than SSADM describes, so we should be cautious about applying this approach if an advanced product is being used.

- Volumetric information (discussed in Sec. 4.7) assists first-cut design and is shown. The number inside the box is the average total number of occurrences of the entity. The numbers shown on relationship lines are the average ratios of master and detail occurrences.

The Yorkies physical diagram is shown below in Fig. 6.10. Notice that each box is 'hard' (square-cornered)—this helps indicate their physical nature. Each of the optional relationships at the detail end has been shown by an 'o'. Relationship names have been removed and the number of occurrences of the relationship shown next to the line. The numbers inside the boxes indicate the total number of occurrences of each entity.

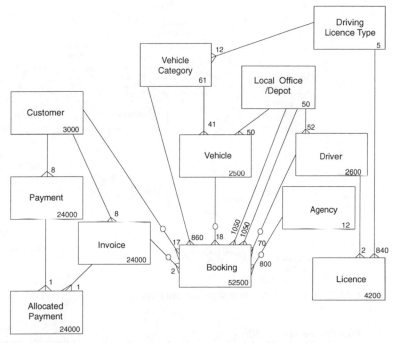

Fig. 6.10 Yorkies data structure showing features required for Physical Design

2.   Show entry points—key and non-key

Effect Correspondence Diagrams showed event triggers and Enquiry Access Paths showed enquiry triggers. These listed the attributes whose values were supplied by the function to the event or enquiry. The entity containing the attributes can be thought of as an *entry point* for access to systems data. SSADM recommends that a version of the Required System Logical Data Structure is annotated with these entry points during step 360, *develop processing specification*.

Key entry points are those where access is required through a supplied value of the primary key attributes. These are shown in Fig. 6.11 by the 'ballooned' arrows (other graphical conventions could also be used and the names of the key attributes may also be shown).

Non-key entry points are those where attribute values are supplied which do not correspond to keys. These are indicated by lozenge shapes containing the name of the attribute.[1] As there may be several entity occurrences for one value of the attribute, then a crow's foot is shown at the entity end.

In Yorkies to produce the Daily Departure List access is required to Booking by the non-key attributes Date Booking Starts and Date Booking Ends. Figure 6.11 shows that there will be many Booking occurrences for a given Date Booking Starts.

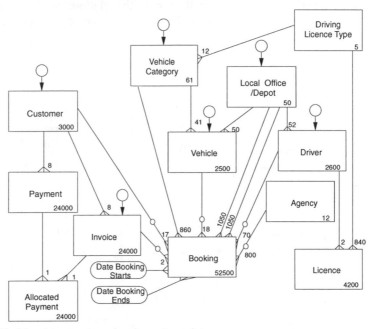

Fig. 6.11 Yorkies data structure showing entry points

3. Identify the root entities

Groups of entity occurrences may be physically clustered together (in other words, placed close to each other on the disk). The *root entity* is the one around which all the related occurrences are physically grouped. Root entities are shown by a stripe at the top of the box—as in Customer, Vehicle Category, and Driving Licence Type, etc., in Fig. 6.12.

For example, in the Yorkies model shown below in Fig. 6.12 the root occurrence of Customer could have the associated occurrences of Payment and Allocated Payment clustered around it. This would enable a customer, their payments and allocated payments to be retrieved with the minimum of disk accesses.

There are two rules for identifying root entities:

---

[1] Readers familiar with earlier versions of SSADM will recognize these as 'operational masters'.

1. All entities that are at the top of the data structure (i.e. those without master entities) become root entities.

By this rule Customer, Driving Licence Type, Local Office/Depot, and Agency all become root entities.

2. Each entity which is a key entry point becomes a root entity.

Thus, Invoice, Booking, Driver, Vehicle Category, Vehicle, and Booking all become root entities.

There is one exception to rule 2, which is associated with entities which are key entry points and have compound primary keys. If the compound key of the directly accessed entity includes the primary key of a master entity which is itself a root entity then the compound key entity is **not** made a root entity. The compound key entity need not be directly related to the root entity which contains the component of the compound key as its primary key.

There are no examples of the exception in the case study. Consider the entities (primary keys shown in brackets): A(a), AB(ab), ABC(abc), and ABCD(abcd). A and ABCD are both key entry points, but because of the exception to rule 2, only A is a root entity.

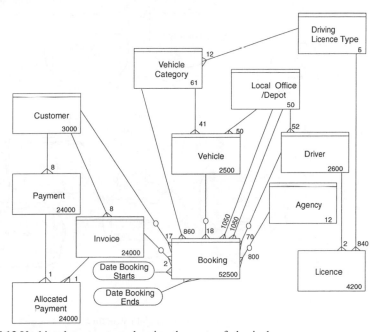

Fig. 6.12 Yorkies data structure showing the roots of physical groups

4.   Show the allowable physical groups for non-root entities
Each non-root entity (those not marked by a stripe) must belong to one or more physical groups. This step identifies which group or groups they can belong to.

A group is created for each root entity and all detail entities are included, unless they are already root entities, or they have an optional relationship with the master entity. Root entities cannot be grouped with other root entities, because it is physically impossible to cluster them together.

An optional relationship indicates that a detail occurrence can exist without an associated master occurrence. If this is possible, it means that there could be no master to cluster the detail with. Thus entities at the optional end of relationships cannot be in the same physical group as their optional master.

In Fig. 6.13 we show the allowable physical groups for the Yorkies data structure. Notice that Invoice cannot be grouped with Customer, because both are root entities. Even if Booking were not a root entity, it could not be grouped with its optional masters of Invoice, Customer, etc. Licence can be grouped in two different ways, either with Driver or with Driving Licence Type. A similar situation applies to Allocated Payment. The groups are shown by circling.

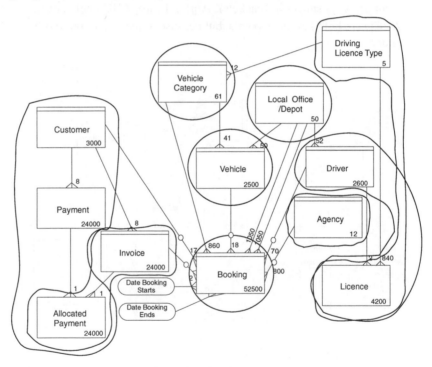

Fig. 6.13 Possible physical groups in the Yorkies data structure

5. Apply the least dependent occurrence rule

In Step 4 entities can be assigned to more than one physical group. The least dependent occurrence rule enables us to decide which physical group the entity can belong to. Each entity can only belong to one physical group—this makes sense as it is only possible to place an occurrence physically close to one root occurrence.

The least dependent occurrence rule states that *when an entity can be stored in more than one physical hierarchy, it is placed in the hierarchy in which it occurs the least number of times.* This is a rule of thumb which produces acceptable results in most cases—with the least number of occurrences, the designer has a better chance of being able to cluster entity occurrences together.[1]

In Fig. 6.13 Licence and Allocated Payment are each shown in two physical groups. In the Driver group, Licence occurs two times, whereas in the Driving Licence group it occurs 840 times—the least dependent occurrence rule places Licence close to Driver.

Allocated Payment could go either with Invoice or with Customer. There is an average of one Allocated Payment per Invoice. There is an average of one Allocated Payment per Payment, but there are eight Payments per Customer, meaning that there are eight Allocated Payments per Customer. Applying the least dependent occurrence rule then puts Allocated Payment with Invoice. Figure 6.14 shows the physical groupings after applying the least dependent occurrence rule.

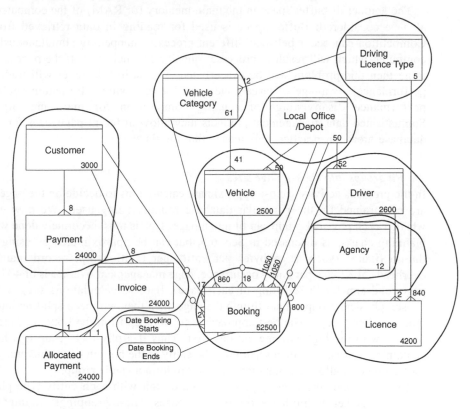

Fig. 6.14 Physical Data Structure after applying the least dependent occurrence rule

---

[1] Other approaches to clustering are usually determined by frequency of access which is more likely to lead to faster performance of the first-cut design.

6.   Determine the page size

The database management system software or the operating system may support a range of pre-determined block or page sizes. Typical page sizes range from 512 bytes to 32 kilobytes. The size of each physical group, identified in step 5, can be roughly estimated by multiplying the number of occurrences by the length. Thus the Customer Payment group is 1 x 150 (average length of the Customer occurrence) plus 8 (average number of payments per Customer) x 50 (average length of a Payment occurrence). This gives an average size for the data in the group of 550 characters. Allowing some room for pointers, indexes, and other mechanisms would mean that the minimum size that the group could fit into would be 1K. The designer should aim to use a page size that accommodates the largest groups that are frequently used. The frequency of usage of physical groups can be determined from the Function Definitions (these contain volumetric information) and their associated Enquiry Access Paths and Effect Correspondence Diagrams (these show which entities are being accessed).

The amount of buffer space in the main memory (or RAM) of the computer should also be considered. Buffer space is used for reading in data retrieved from disk. Competition can occur between different processes happening simultaneously in the computer, which will result in processes queuing for their turn. If the page size is too large then this problem will be exacerbated. The skilful designer will trade-off the performance advantage of large page sizes for retrieving information against their performance disadvantage of causing competition for main memory space. Sophisticated data management products may allow different page sizes for different database areas (in practice, this means that the database is spread over several disk drives with a particular page size for each drive).

7.   Fit groups into chosen page sizes

In the previous activity we use approximate calculations to decide on the page size, or are constrained by the particular database product being used. We now calculate whether each physical group can fit into a page. This is most accurately done with page planning charts, as discussed in Sec. 6.5, but can be approximated by using rule-of-thumb figures (such as: 6 bytes per entity per relationship, record management overheads of 8 bytes per entity occurrence, page management overheads of 40 bytes per page, and aim for 70% filling of each page). If these calculations suggest that the chosen physical group cannot fit into the page, then they will need splitting into two or more smaller groups. The best approach is to work up from the bottom of the model, dealing with the high-volume entities first. Thus if a physical group is a hierarchy containing four entities then separating the entity at the bottom of the hierarchy into its own group may allow the other three entities to form a viable group.

This completes the generic physical data design with each entity type physically grouped together with other entity types in pages. These groupings are important for performance calculations because they indicate which data can be retrieved and updated with minimal disk access.

8. Apply product-specific rules

These product-specific rules will have been defined by the supplier or by database experts during step 610, *prepare for physical design*. Below we describe general rules for the different classes of database products: hierarchical, CODASYL, and relational.

Product-specific first-cut rules

Although the rules are specific to a particular software product, they are very similar within classes of products. Thus all relational database management systems will have similar first-cut rules. Below we give some classes of database management software and some general principles which the product-specific first-cut rules follow.

Rather than use the full Yorkies model, the basic principles are demonstrated using the simpler hospital example used in Chapter 4. Figure 6.15 shows the Logical Data Model and Fig. 6.16 the generic design resulting from application of the above seven rules. With a page size of 1K each physical group can fit onto a single page. (The reader might try applying the rules to Fig. 6.15 as an exercise.)

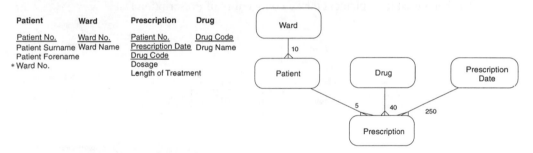

Fig. 6.15 Hospital Logical Data Model

Note that the whole area of data management is riddled with technical jargon. DBMS vendors and computer scientists often use different words to mean the same things and the same words to mean different things. We have tried to be consistent and generally use the SSADM terms when describing the classes of product rather than the technical term. When technical terms are used they are explained (we have shown the reserved words of the DBMS products in upper-case letters).

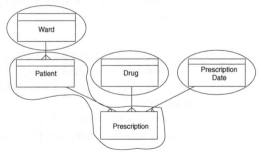

Fig. 6.16 Hospital generic first-cut physical data design

Hierarchical databases

The best-known example is IBM's IMS/VS which, although its use is declining, probably still holds a very large proportion of the world's data. The database that underlies the fourth-generation environment of FOCUS is also hierarchical (although the FOCUS language can also interact with many other DBMSs).

These are the most complicated to convert to the physical design. This is because hierarchical databases only allow a record to have one physical master. The same groupings are used as in the generic physical design. Patient is therefore picked as the physical owner of Prescription and Drug becomes the logical master. (Parent and child are the terms used by IMS to describe master and detail.)

The data structure is divided into a number of physical segments following the groupings of the generic design. The root entity becomes the top of the segment and is known as the root segment. The linking across segments is provided by the use of logical pointers and secondary indexes. However, the rules for the use of these are complex, with several obvious ways of linking entities being illegal. A secondary index has been used to implement the key only entity of Prescription Date.

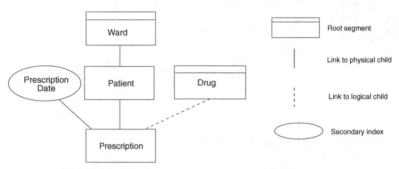

Fig. 6.17 First-cut IMS design

Figure 6.17 shows the first version of the IMS model of the hospital database; however, this is not yet an executable model as a logical child (Prescription) is not allowed to have a secondary index. To 'cure' this a 'Link' segment is created as physical child to Prescription whose logical parent is Drug. Further details of the precise rules for mapping logical data designs onto hierarchical databases will be found in the database books listed in the Bibliography.

Network databases

The most popular network database management systems are those that conform to the CODASYL standard set by the Database Task Group in 1971. The two most popular network database products in the UK are CA's IDMS and ICL's IDMSX, both of which follow the CODASYL standard.

The rules for converting the generic design into a CODASYL design are very simple although there are a number of options concerning placement of RECORDs.

The basic rules are as follows:

• All entities become RECORDs.

- All relationships become SETs.

The remaining rules are concerned with placement of RECORDs. These can be placed in one of two ways:

CALC The RECORD is placed on the disk by a hashing algorithm which is applied to the key of the RECORD to give a physical disk address at which the RECORD is stored. The RECORD is retrieved by using the same algorithm.

LOCATION MODE VIA The RECORD is placed on the disk near its master in the specified SET. This is how the physically groupings are specified in CODASYL databases.

All RECORDs that are root entities are placed by the CALC mechanism. CALC RECORDs are indicated in the diagram in the same way as root entities—by a stripe across the top. This is the notation SSADM uses; it is related to but not the same as notations used by the vendors of CODASYL databases.

In the hospital example Ward, Drug, and Prescription Date are all at the top of the structure and are access entry points. Patient is an access entry point. All these RECORDs are placed by the CALC mechanism.

All other RECORDs must be placed VIA a SET. Thus the Prescription RECORD must be placed VIA a SET. Here there are three possible SETs that Prescription could be placed VIA. It can only be placed VIA one of these: in this example Prescription occurrences can only be placed close to their master Patient, or to their master Drug, or to their master Prescription Date. The least dependent occurrence rule, applied in generic design, placed Prescription in the same group as Patient. Thus Prescription is placed physically close to Patient, LOCATION MODE VIA the SET linking them together. The SSADM notation is to show the SET the RECORD is placed VIA by a continuous arrow. Other SETs, which do not indicate placement, are shown by dotted arrows. Figure 6.18 shows the CODASYL representation of the hospital database.

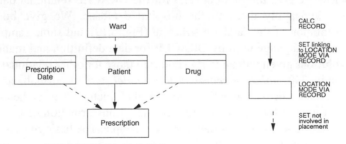

Fig. 6.18 First-cut CODASYL physical design

Modern versions of these CODASYL databases include a secondary indexing facility. This is particularly useful in that it means that non-key entry points (or key only entities) can be implemented directly rather than by creating a separate CALC RECORD. Thus in the hospital database we would create an index on Prescription of Prescription Date. The secondary index would be shown as an oval, as in the hierarchical data base example above.

Relational databases

In Chapter 4 we discussed relational data analysis and began Sec. 4.5 by explaining some aspects of the relational model. This model is that used by relational database management products such as ORACLE, INGRES, DB2, and many more. Relational databases are now widely accepted as the preferred approach with most projects using SSADM being implemented using a relational DBMS. All data is represented and manipulated as tables with relationships between tables of different types being managed by matching the values of data items in one table with those in another. A single language, usually SQL, is used for data definition and data manipulation.

Although there is an ISO standard for SQL, there is considerable theoretical debate over the limitations of the standard, with some experts claiming the standard to be a 'lowest common denominator'. However, although there are many implementations of SQL they follow the standard sufficiently for the first-cut rules to apply to most relational DBMSs.

Where relational DBMS products show greatest variation is in the underlying mechanisms used for storage and retrieval of data. Although these are hidden from the programmer or end-user who interacts with the system through SQL, they have a great impact on the performance of the system. Products vary greatly in the control they allow to the database administrator over such things as storage structures (INGRES allows tables to be organized as B*-trees, hash files, indexed sequential files, sequential files, or as heap files; ORACLE organizes all tables as B*-trees), indexing, page size, and clustering of records. With some products, particularly those from third-party vendors such as ORACLE and INGRES which run under a large range of operating systems, some of these storage issues will be dependent on the operating system rather than the database management system. The first-cut rules for determining the underlying storage will therefore be different for each product and operating system combination. These may, of course, be subject to change with later software releases.

Below we give the first-cut rules for the ORACLE relational database management system and apply these to the hospital database. We give both a diagrammatic representation of the database structure (Fig. 6.19) and some sample SQL (Fig. 6.20). This is the language used by ORACLE for data definition and manipulation. The rules and solutions given will be fairly similar to those for other relational products.

In step 340, *enhance required data model*, a well-normalized data structure was produced and checked with the Logical Data Structure. This is then in a form very close to that required by relational products. The transformation of the generic design to a relational first-cut design is therefore very simple. The basic rules are:

For all SSADM Required System Logical Data Model entities create tables (with the **CREATE** command) thus:

(1) For *simple (one attribute) primary keys* specify the column with the **NOT NULL** and **PRIMARY KEY** constraints.
(2) For *compound primary keys* specify all the primary key columns as **NOT NULL** and add a table **PRIMARY KEY** constraint containing the columns.

(3) For *simple foreign keys* specify the column with the **NOT NULL** (except for columns derived from an optional relationship) and **REFERENCES** (this gives the relevant primary key) constraints.

(4) For each *compound foreign key* specify the columns with the **NOT NULL** constraint (except for columns derived from an optional relationship) and add an appropriate table **FOREIGN KEY** constraint.

(5) Create a **UNIQUE INDEX** over each *simple primary key* column and a **UNIQUE INDEX** over all columns which are part of the *compound primary keys*.

To illustrate how straightforward it is to develop the data definition statements for relational databases we give the SQL PLUS statements for this database in Fig. 6.20. We have used the default options for INDEXes; these would probably be changed in the tuning step. We have allowed the non-key data items to default to allowing NULL values; it would be sensible to enforce values if this was required.

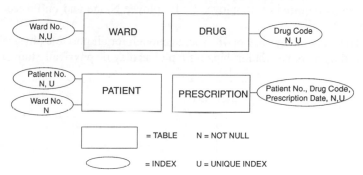

Fig. 6.19 Diagrammatic representation of a relational database

```
CREATE TABLE Ward (
Ward_No NUMBER (5) NOT NULL PRIMARY KEY,
Ward_Name CHAR (20))
CREATE TABLE Patient (
Pat_No NUMBER (5) NOT NULL PRIMARY KEY,
Pat_Surname CHAR (20),
Pat_Forename CHAR (20),
Ward_No NUMBER (5) NOT NULL REFERENCES Ward(Ward_No))
CREATE TABLE Drug (
Drug_Code CHAR (5) NOT NULL PRIMARY KEY,
Drug_Name CHAR (30))
CREATE TABLE Prescription (
Pat_No NUMBER (5) NOT NULL REFERENCES Patient (Pat_No),
Drug_Code CHAR (5) NOT NULL REFERENCES Drug (Drug_Code),
Prescription_Date DATE NOT NULL, Dosage CHAR (20),
Len_Trtmnt NUMBER (3),
PRIMARY KEY (Pat_No , Drug_Code , Prescription_Date))
CREATE UNIQUE INDEX Patient_PK ON Patient (Pat_No)
CREATE UNIQUE INDEX Ward_PK ON Ward (Ward_No)
CREATE UNIQUE INDEX Drug_PK ON Drug (Drug_Code)
CREATE UNIQUE INDEX Prescription_PK ON Prescription ( Pat_No , Drug_Code , Prescription_Date)
```

Fig. 6.20 SQL for data definition in the hospital example

SUMMARY
- A First-Cut Physical Data Design is produced by applying simple rules to the Required System Logical Data Model.
- These first-cut rules are specific to the DBMS or file handler used.
- No attempt is made to optimize performance with the first-cut design.
- The first-cut design is sufficiently detailed to allow performance predictions to be made and enable data definition statements to be produced.

Exercise

6.3.1   Scapegoat Systems–generic first-cut rules exercise

a) Complete the volumetric information on the diagram shown below in Fig. 6.21.

b) Develop a generic first-cut design.

Direct access is required by the primary key on Employee and on Project. Non-key access is required on Employee by Employee Name and on Project by Project Finish Date.

The chosen page size of 4K is large enough for all possible physical groups. Consider how the recursive relationship on Employee may be physically implemented.

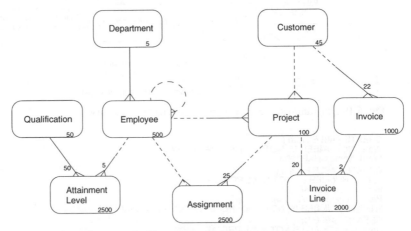

Fig. 6.21 Logical Data Structure for Scapegoat showing some volumes

6.4   Create function component implementation map (step 630)

Introduction

The object of this step is to complete the specification of each function; designing the components not included in the logical design, showing how each function component is physically implemented, and considering common processing and promoting re-use.

The Function Component Implementation Map shows how each component in a function is physically implemented and how each component is related to others.

The SSADM technique of *physical process specification* is concerned with the development of the Function Component Implementation Map, the production of detailed program specifications, and the development of the Process Data Interface. Unlike many of the other SSADM techniques, physical process specification is not prescriptive. Indeed, its first activity, performed in step 610, *prepare for physical design*, is to determine exactly how it should be performed in the particular project environment. The underlying principles of physical process specification are to:

* minimize development and maintenance staff costs;
* keep implementation structures and mechanisms simple;
* simplify the interface between the users and stored data;
* provide the users with adequate performance levels;
* complete the specification of functions;
* specify the processing to the level required by the constructor in whatever development environment is being used to develop working program code.

Functions

Functions are the way in which SSADM packages its processing. The universal function model, repeated below in Fig. 6.22, shows the various *components* that make up each function. In the earlier stages of SSADM most of these components have been specified at a logical level. Within each function, there may be components that occur within other functions. The design team should map these common functions and ensure that duplication of development, effort, and processing does not occur.

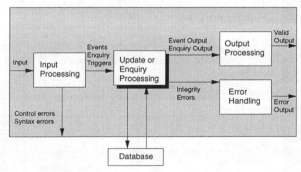

Fig. 6.22 The Universal Function Model

In this step we complete the specification for those components not previously designed. Usually this is the syntax error handling, the controls, and control errors.

Each component of each function is then considered as to how it should be physically implemented. In modern software environments there is a great range of possibilities for implementation, ranging from assembler code to very high-level languages. Having decided how each component is to be physically implemented, we then need to specify the component at a physical level appropriate to the construction tool being used.

The product that links together all of these physical specifications of function components is referred to as the Function Component Implementation Map. In step 610, *prepare for physical design*, decisions were made about the format of the Function Component Implementation Map.

Function Component Implementation Map

Like many of the physical design products, there is no pre-determined format for this. It is more than a map, perhaps an atlas, showing for the physical system how every processing component is physically implemented and inter-related to every other processing component. In practice, several ways of documenting features of the Function Component Implementation Map can be used.

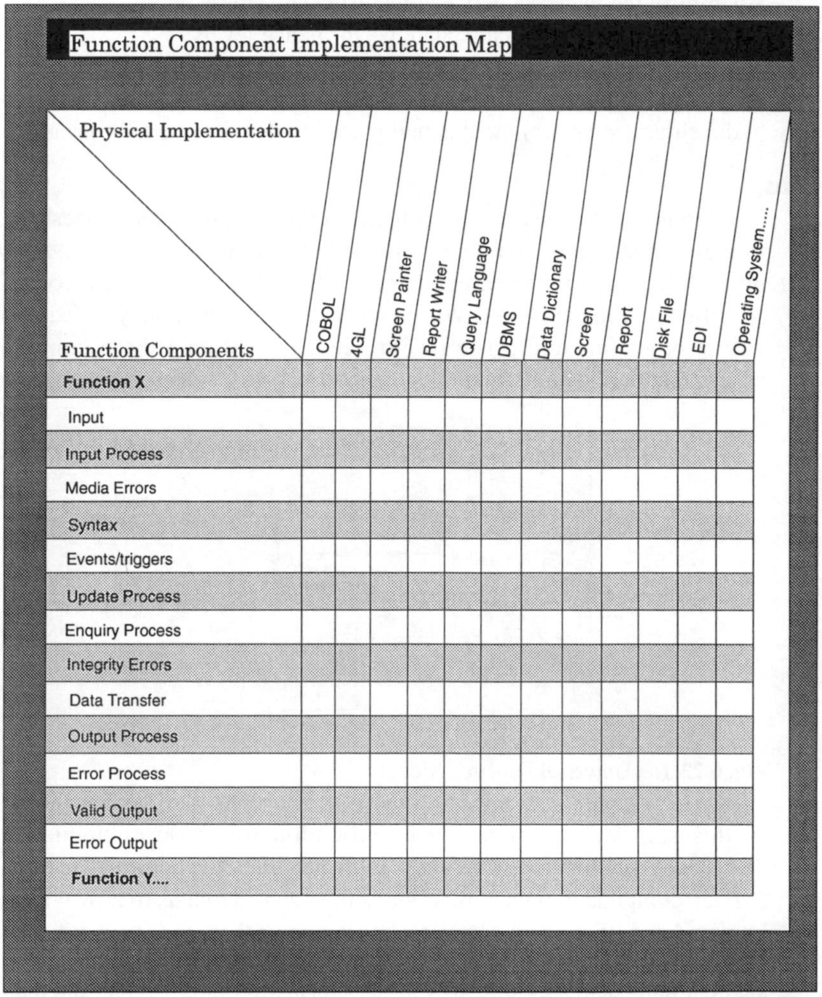
Function Component Implementation Map
Physical Implementation
Function Components
COBOL
4GL
Screen Painter
Report Writer
Query Language
DBMS
Data Dictionary
Screen
Report
Disk File
EDI
Operating System.....
Function X
Input
Input Process
Media Errors
Syntax
Events/triggers
Update Process
Enquiry Process
Integrity Errors
Data Transfer
Output Process
Error Process
Valid Output
Error Output
Function Y....

Fig. 6.23 Function Component Implementation Map showing how components are implemented

Figure 6.23 represents the Function Component Implementation Map as a matrix showing how each component of each function is physically implemented. Such a representation helps decide on the best implementation mechanism for each function.[1] Obviously, the physical implementation mechanisms will vary between physical environments and the types of function components will vary between different systems. One of the most important tasks of step 630 is to decide which components need detailed specification for procedural code, and which can be developed in non-procedural code (e.g. using fourth generation languages and application generators). Those components requiring procedural specifications are developed in step 650, *complete function specification*.

Common processing

Much has been written recently about software re-use.[2] Throughout an SSADM project we attempt to identify common processes—where the same process is used in different functional areas of the system. These common processes can either be low-level (such as algorithms to perform complex calculations or transformations of data from one format to another) or high-level (such as the ability to include a particular enquiry in several different update functions).

Duplication of processing, where the same procedure is designed and coded more than once, is undesirable. Apart from involving unnecessary work, it may cause consistency problems with each procedure operating in a slightly different way. Even if the code is duplicated by producing an exact copy, maintenance problems can occur when one copy is modified but others are not. As far as is possible, duplication of specification, design, and code should be avoided throughout the system. The SSADM approach, by using events as the basis for specification, helps to avoid duplication and promote re-use across the system.

Identification of common processing

Throughout the project, opportunities for re-use and common processes are identified. In the early stages, common processes may be identified when drawing Data Flow Diagrams (from current physical through to required) and documented as Common Elementary Process Descriptions. In later stages, the high-level common processes become functions, events, or enquiries, and are defined once and once only in the system—because SSADM uses an event-based approach to process definition the problems of duplication of function are less likely to occur than when pure functional decomposition techniques are used. Low-level common processes, such as routines for calculation, validation, formatting, and conversion, are documented as Elementary Process Descriptions and referenced in each of the Function Definitions in which they occur.

The whole system can be thought of as a network of inter-connected components, as in Fig. 6.24. Common processing is shown in this diagram at all levels. Function C is

---

[1] Many projects find it useful to identify the implementation mechanisms for functions before Stage 6. By making these decisions in Stage 4, Technical System Options, the project can redefine its approach to Stage 5, Logical Design.

[2] Particularly within the context of object-orientation which is claimed to promote re-usability.

used by both super functions, I/O and database processes are used by several functions, etc.

This diagram shows the different kinds of processing components: super functions, functions, database processes, I/O processes, and common processes. Database processes map to the Enquiry and Update Process Models defined in Stage 5. I/O processes map to dialogue designs, I/O Structures and the processing associated with those, described along with the Function Definitions. *Super functions* are a concept that was not met in the earlier stages of SSADM. For on-line processing they will represent the code that links together several dialogues as a menu structure or as a command processing structure. For off-line processing they will link together several functions (eventually programs and modules) which will form part of a batch run, and which will share common files.

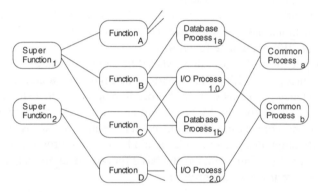

Fig. 6.24 Hierarchy of functional components represented as a network to show common processing

The network diagram (Fig. 6.24) can also be viewed as a hierarchy with super functions at the top being composed of functions, which are then composed of I/O processes and database processes, each of them using common processes defined at a low level. This network of processing depicted in Fig. 6.24 is another manifestation of the Function Component Implementation Map. It is unlikely that such a diagram would be drawn for the whole of the system's processing, it would be too big and complex. However, the interlinking of components should be documented and managed through support software such as a repository or data dictionary, ideally integrated with a CASE tool. An important part of the work in step 610, *prepare for physical design*, is to define the way the Function Component Implementation Map is managed.

Some care should be taken with defining processes as common. Making code and specifications re-usable does take extra time, care, and effort. It may be that the processing is not that similar and greater effort is involved in producing a generic design than would be required to produce several specific designs. These problems should not be considered lightly in large projects; separate teams should have responsibility for selecting and defining re-usable components. Object-oriented approaches (and SSADM uses many object-oriented ideas, although not their terminology) may offer some advantages in building re-usable components but many experts consider the major problems in production of re-usable components to be organizational and managerial rather than technical.

Enquiry-event pairs
A very common procedure is for the user to perform an enquiry and then, based on the information received, perform an update (event). For instance in Yorkies, the Booking Clerk will need to find out whether vehicles are available for a booking, and then follow the enquiry immediately by creating the booking and assigning the vehicle.

The enquiry-event pair provides a particular problem in defining common processing; because frequently the enquiry, the event, and the enquiry-event pair can each be performed in isolation. Thus there is potential for either duplicating or re-using specifications and program code.

There are three ways in which the enquiry-event pair could be designed and implemented:

1. Separate Enquiry and Update Process Models could be defined within one single function. This could enable either to be re-used elsewhere in the system.
2. Separate functions could define the enquiry and the update. The functions would need to be linked together in a super function which ensured that the data could not be updated by another process before the associated update took place. Each function would also need to operate in stand-alone mode.
3. Both enquiry and update processing could be combined into one single Update Process Model. This offers least flexibility in that the additional enquiry and update processing would need to be specified—leading to some duplication of specification and, potentially, of code.

The approach to physical implementation could follow directly from these different specifications. Probably the best way of preserving the integrity of the system's data, providing good performance and usability of the dialogue, is to implement as one total procedure. However, this is also the most awkward approach as far as re-use is concerned. (Although not impossible, the same coded procedure could be called by each program.)

There may be a tendency for the designer to specify the enquiry by duplicating the update, merely omitting the update operations. This could cause serious problems in maintenance, performance, and usability—it should therefore be avoided.

Further specification of physical components
Much of the logical specification can be carried over to the physical system unchanged. For example, database processing defined by Update and Enquiry Process Models can be implemented directly if Process Data Interface software is built. However, no conversion of these process models to implementation specific specifications is performed until step 660, *consolidate process data interface*. The major components of physical processing design that need to be developed in this step are:
- physical success units (also known as commit units);
- error handling;
- physical interface design.

Physical success units

Each event, and therefore Update Process Model, is regarded as a logical success unit. The whole set of processing associated with the event must be completed (succeed) to leave the system's data in a consistent state. In other words, if several entity and relationship occurrences are being changed by the event then the situation where some change and some do not change **must not** be allowed to happen. Thus, the processing must either succeed completely or fail completely (i.e. not happen). Some enquiries are also success units if it is essential that totally accurate and consistent data is supplied to the user (then the enquiry data cannot be updated during the enquiry).

Most database management software supports physical success units; locking the data that is being updated to ensure consistency until the unit has succeeded. It is not always possible to directly map the logical success units to the physical system. Performance reasons might mean that lengthy success units are undesirable—other users will have to wait for another's processing to succeed if they are sharing the same data. The data management software may impose constraints on the size of success units.

An example of this could be an order entry system where a large number of products, say over 100, can be entered on a single order. Normally there would be one event 'Order Acceptance' and one logical success unit. However, physically this will take a long time to enter, which has serious consequences for any other transactions wanting to access the stock records which are being depleted by the acceptance of the order. Recovery of the data may also be a problem if a software failure were to occur after entry of item No. 99 on the order: then all 99 could need re-entry. For these reasons, the physical designer might decide to split the logical success unit into smaller physical success units, say of 10 order items each.

Error handling

Syntax error handling

Syntax errors occur when the data input into the computer system is inconsistent with what it expects. In the Yorkies system we have defined an attribute, Vehicle Registration Mark (abbreviated to Veh Reg Mark). If the user inputs a value for Veh Reg Mark of '1C,3bd!' we would expect the computer system to reject it as a syntax error.

Validation checks for syntax (and other) errors are defined in the Attribute Descriptions in the Data Catalogue. During step 630 we specify precisely, using the language of the processing system, these validation checks. These could be in the data definitions used by the database management system or by the data dictionary or repository that supports the database management system. It is best not to define the validation and syntax errors too precisely early in the project, since a particular language for describing them will probably form part of the development environment. For example, the data dictionary definition for Vehicle Registration Mark might be:

Valid format: A999AAA
Error message: 'Invalid format for registration mark'.

Another way of defining syntax errors is within the input/output processing, particularly the screen definitions. Errors which are specific to a particular function must either be specified in this way or in the program that performs the function. Error messages are best stored in the database or data dictionary. They can then be used consistently by several programs. Storing them centrally also eases modification and maintenance.

Integrity errors and integrity error messages are associated with ensuring that the database is in a consistent state and that updates to system data are consistent with the business rules identified in Entity Life Histories. Business rule integrity is normally maintained through the use of state indicators and was specified in Stage 5, Logical Design.

Controls and control errors

This can be divided into control of data and control of processing. Control of data errors are related to the syntax and integrity errors discussed above, differing by being more concerned with consistency of groups of input data. These data control errors can be managed through specific audit functions, which ensure that correct and consistent data is entered and that it is in the right order for processing. One control technique is to use batch totals, where values of the individual items in a batch are totalled before input and then compared with the total after input. This ensures that all the data that is expected to be input is actually present. Error procedures will need to be designed for re-entry of data, or for termination of functions.

Control of processing should consider the navigation through the functional structure of the system. For on-line components of the system, this needs to consider: how a given user role can navigate through their menus or their commands, how security is managed, what errors can arise, and what error messages should be displayed. For batch processing: the possible sequences of functions should be considered, any possible errors (such as missing files) identified, and error procedures defined.

The Physical Design Strategy should consider how to develop these areas of integration between programs (e.g. using operating system commands for batch processing, or menu generators for on-line processing) and indicate how these controls should be physically implemented.

Physical interface design

Interface design before Stage 6

I/O Structures and I/O Structure Descriptions were first developed in step 330, *derive system functions*. Critical functions were subjected to specification prototyping in step 350—some physical screen designs may be preserved through to physical design, particularly if the same construction tools are used for the full development as for developing the prototype.

In Stage 4, Technical System Options, an Application Style Guide was developed which defined the standards for human–computer interaction, both for dialogues and for other outputs. This is primarily concerned with providing a standard interface to the computer system in terms of screen design, function key assignments, message formats, menu structures, etc. In step 510, *define user dialogues*, navigation paths through individual dialogues and connecting dialogues together, through menus or commands, were defined. Some projects, knowing the implementation environment, define physical I/O formats at this point.

During step 510, *define user dialogues*: I/O Structures became dialogue structures, Logical Groupings of Dialogue Elements (LGDEs, equivalent to logical screens) were identified, and navigation paths through dialogues were shown on Dialogue Control Tables. Also in step 510, Menu Structures, Command Structures and Dialogue Level Help were defined.

Physical I/O formats
These can be divided into two types: those formats associated with on-line processing, such as dialogues and screens; and those associated with off-line processing, reports, output files, and handling of input files.

In Physical Design, all physical I/O formats are designed, including error messages and error reports. Physical dialogue design is also completed in this step, and this is discussed below.

Input and outputs from off-line functions must be physically designed; these may be communicating with printing facilities, with other computerized systems, and with backing storage. External standards, such as those for electronic data interchange or for document interchange, should be observed where necessary.

Physical dialogue design
This is a complex area, the possibilities depending greatly on the technical environment. Interfaces can also have a tremendous effect on the user's performance and acceptance of the system. The latest fashion has been for Graphical User Interfaces[1] (GUIs) using software such as Windows, Apple Macintoshes, and UNIX front-ends (e.g. Open Look and OSF/Motif). The SSADM approach to dialogue design is geared to the older style of interfaces associated with form filling.

Physical dialogue design can be greatly influenced by the facilities available in the development environment. Fourth generation environments often include features such as screen painters, screen generators, validation and error handling routines linked to data dictionaries or to screen definitions. These features make it very easy for designers to build interfaces quickly, but these interfaces may not meet the requirements of users.

This is because the development environment may impose certain limitations on what can easily be provided in the interface. For instance, the generation facilities may limit the number of different entity types from which data can be retrieved to a particular screen, or they may impose restrictions on the way that physical success units (commit units) interact with the screens. Limitations may be imposed on the use of windows within a screen. Menu and command structures may be limited by only allowing hierarchical navigation of menus or by not allowing data to be passed directly from one dialogue to another.

---

[1] International SSADM User's Group (1994) *SSADM and GUI Design: A Project Manager's Guide* (HMSO, London)—for a good description of the techniques of HCI design see Browne, D. (1994) *STUDIO: STructured User-interface Design for Interaction Optimization*, Prentice Hall, Hemel Hempstead.

These kinds of features were examined when selecting the Technical System Option is Stage 4 and were revisited in defining the Physical Design Strategy in step 610, *prepare for physical design*. Other decisions about the way in which the construction software could influence the user interface design might have been made at Business System Options or during step 350, *develop specification prototypes*. However, it is now that we must take final decisions as to how dialogues are to be implemented in the full knowledge of the construction medium and of the Logical Systems Specification.

Screen design

In Physical Design we need to convert the logical specifications to a physical implementation, making best use of the facilities of the construction environment. Physical screens must accommodate the Logical Groupings of Dialogue Elements. Detailed layout should follow the guidelines specified in the Application Style Guide. Each physical screen may contain several groupings or alternatively a grouping may be split over several physical screens. As Physical Design progresses these groupings may need to be redesigned. Obviously the best approach is to implement the LGDEs directly, but this may not be possible in the physical environment.

Event handling in dialogues

A common feature of application generators is for them to deal with data at an entity occurrence level. Thus it will be easy to generate software that allows creation, modification, deletion, and display of all the data about a single occurrence, possibly all on one screen. Although such features are very useful, they can cause certain problems for the designer working from an SSADM specification. SSADM specifications are based around events which often require more complex processing and validation than simple entry of single-entity occurrences.

For example, in the Yorkies system, the Booking entity has relationships, maintained through foreign keys, with Invoice, Vehicles, Local Office (twice), Vehicle Category, Customer, Driver, and Agency. Using a relational database and application generator a screen could easily be built to create, modify, and delete a Booking occurrence. This could allow modification of all the foreign keys, in effect allowing the user to create and change relationships with other occurrences at will. However, the Entity Life History of Booking shows that the sequence in which these relationships with other occurrences are created is important to the way that the business works. For instance, we would not want to create an invoice before the booking had been completed. Using these kind of data entry and modification screens can allow us to perform several events in one go—creating one success unit for them. The designer must decide whether this is desirable.[1]

Another strategy, 'more in the spirit of the Entity Life Histories', is to deal with each event occurrence separately. In this way, only the attributes directly affected by the event would be updated. (Other attributes might be shown on screen to assist the user,

---

[1] If it is, then the Entity Life Histories were probably seriously flawed—if the user did not require the kind of complex validation prescribed by the Entity Life History, then such complexity should not appear. Poor user education and over-zealousness of the analyst/designer are probably the faults.

but it would not be possible to over-write their values.) Again the physical environment may offer specific facilities to handle it in this way, although this is much more sophisticated in terms of the requirements from the processing language than the case discussed above. It may be necessary for parts of the processing to be constructed in procedural code. In this case, each event would map to a single physical success unit.

A third way of dealing with this data is for several events to be input but for the processing system to deal with each event separately. The Update Process Models, specified for each of the events, would then be performed successively with error and progression messages being passed to the user.

All of these dialogue design strategies (and we have taken a relatively simple case here) have a great impact on how the system works. The user should be closely involved with making these decisions—if the dialogue is critical, then it should have been prototyped during the Requirements Specification module. Any critical dialogues that are recognized at this late stage in the project should be carefully considered by the user—possibly requiring the use of further prototyping.

Error handling in dialogues

Error handling was discussed earlier in this section. The three kinds of errors that can arise—syntactic, control, and integrity—should be integrated into the whole physical dialogue. Fourth-generation environments often include sophisticated facilities for attribute validation and error reporting (syntactic errors). The database management system may offer some facilities for handling integrity errors, but it is unlikely that these facilities will have sufficient sophistication to deal with the complex rules specified within the Entity Life Histories—ensuring this kind of integrity may require procedural code. Control error handling may also require procedural code as these facilities are rarely provided by fourth generation software. If error messages are defined as separate fields within the database (recommended if they cannot be handled by the construction environment) then additional entities and navigation will be required to handle the retrieval and display of error messages.

Dialogue navigation

This describes how the user may move the input cursor around screens and move from dialogue to dialogue. Certain features may be provided by the screen generation facilities of the development environment. Some examples of these are being able to move forward and back between fields and between groups of fields, being able to move to any specified field or groups of field on the screen, being able to jump out of the dialogue to a menu or to another dialogue, etc. The use to which these mechanisms will be put depends upon the specification: sometimes the designer may need to make them unavailable, at other times they may need to be extended. This can be difficult if the development environment is inflexible and may require the development of procedural code.

In step 510, Dialogue Control Tables were developed to define the different navigation paths through a dialogue—these need to be physically specified and implemented. Again the method of implementation depends totally on the development environment. Some possibilities include: use of control tables, including procedural statements in non-procedural code; and defining function keys. If it is necessary to use procedural code then specifications can be produced using control tables, decision tables, or using Jackson structures for the whole dialogue (these will probably require extensive use of quits and resumes to enable the user to deal with predictable but unusual sequences).

In step 510, *define user dialogues*, Menu Structures and Command Structures were developed. The processing that implements these structures might be regarded as a super function linking together the functions that provide the individual dialogues. Menu Structures are generally providing the user with a choice of functions. In some cases, it may be necessary to lead the user through a set of functions that naturally follow one another, passing data from one function to another. In either case the controlling structure can be regarded as a super function—this follows the hierarchical/network view of the Function Component Implementation Map shown in Fig. 6.24.

Help

Dialogue Level Help was defined in step 510, *define user dialogues*. This covered the contextual information available to the user to support with a particular dialogue. This now needs to be built into the dialogue processing software and further 'help' defined. Fourth generation environments may offer facilities for including help within the dialogue. This may be provided at a screen level and at an individual field level. The Application Style Guide should have covered issues such as how the help messages are defined and accessed. If the development environment does not satisfactorily support the incorporation of help messages into dialogues then procedural specification of access to these messages, including their incorporation into the database, will need to be specified. This is potentially a very significant task, but a very important one since for systems with many users, good help facilities can ensure acceptance of the system and reduce reliance on training and technical support.

Program specification

Throughout step 630, non-procedural components (or fragments) are specified by using the language of the development environment itself. This means that as they are specified using the construction language, they are in effect implemented, and can be demonstrated to and discussed with users. No further specification of these fragments is necessary as the idea of such tools is that the detailed processing is generated by the fourth generation environment and need not be specified in great detail by the designer or programmer.

Components which will need to be built using procedural code, using languages such as COBOL or C, do need further detailed specification. This is completed in step 650, *complete function specification*.

The only exception to this implementation using non-procedural code is for database access components—the logical specification of these is provided by the Enquiry and Update Process Models. The database access components may be revised by changing the physical data structure during step 640, *optimize physical data design*. In step 660, *consolidate process data interface*, the interaction of the processing with the database is defined to take account of any tuning of the physical data structure. At this time, the mapping of the logical database processes to physical fragments can be established. This can be done either using non-procedural code, such as SQL,[1] or procedural code.

SUMMARY

- The Function Component Implementation Map shows how the logical components of functions are physically implemented.
- The functional components are regarded as a network with common processes and functions being used wherever appropriate.
- All functions are reviewed to remove duplicate processing and to maximize sharing of common processing.
- Each function is specified to the detail required by the non-procedural development environment.
- Non-procedural function components can be physically implemented during this step.

The following are specified:

- physical success units;
- syntax error processing;
- control mechanisms and error handling;
- the physical format of all system interfaces (with other systems, reports, data storage, users, etc.);
- physical dialogues including navigation within dialogues and between dialogues using menus and command structures.

6.5   Optimize physical data design (step 640)

Introduction

The objective of this step is to produce a physical data design that meets the performance objectives agreed with users. These performance objectives were initially identified as non-functional requirements and documented as part of the Requirements Catalogue. During Stages 3 and 4 of the project they were further refined as the detailed specification was developed and the technical architecture selected. Requirements for storage were documented in the Requirements Catalogue. Requirements for the speed of computer processing for each function were documented as part of the Service Level Requirements in each Function Definition. The minimum failure rates and minimum times for restoring the system after failure were also identified and documented.

In step 640, *optimize physical data design*, the performance of the first-cut Physical Data Design is measured against performance objectives set by the users. The physical design may not meet these objectives: it is optimized, or tuned, until it meets them. Tuning is an iterative process in which several cycles of design, measurement, and redesign may be repeated before a satisfactory conclusion is reached. If the objectives

---

[1] Many projects may decide not to follow this route and may construct their SQL programs much earlier than is advocated by formal SSADM. Often, Enquiry Access Paths and Effect Correspondence Diagrams can form the non-procedural specification required for an SQL implementation.

cannot be met with the planned hardware and software then modification of the objectives will be discussed with the users.

There is an analogy here with the design of car engines. We may have a requirement to build a sports car that has a top speed of 150 m.p.h. and an acceleration of 0–60 m.p.h. in less than 8 seconds. There will be other considerations that compete with these objectives such as the cost of building the car and the desired engine capacity. To produce a car that meets all these objectives the designers will go through several stages. They will design the engine on paper (nowadays probably using computer-aided design), they will model its performance, and will adjust the design until the modelled performance meets their objectives. Only then will they build a prototype engine, and test and fine tune its performance.

A similar approach is followed in systems development. In SSADM we develop a model of the physical system and then measure the performance of that model against objectives set by the users. When we have a model that performs in a satisfactory way then we are ready to go ahead and build the system, and test and fine tune it. The same reasoning underlies the thinking of the system developer and the engineer: developing and tuning of a model is cheaper and less risky than building several prototypes, and testing and tuning each one. Operating on a model also has the advantage that a much greater range of possibilities can be tested.

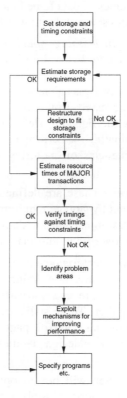

Fig. 6.25 Physical Design Control

The basic approach to achieving this is to measure the performance of the initial physical design for data and processing against the performance objectives. These designs can then be adjusted until the objectives are met. This process is known as physical design control (illustrated by the flowchart in Fig. 6.25). If it is impossible to modify the design sufficiently to meet the requirements then changes to these requirements will need to be discussed with users. This may mean a reduction in service levels or the purchase of additional hardware.

Physical design control is an expensive, time-consuming activity requiring considerable technical expertise. It should be **avoided** if possible. For many development projects, the additional cost of buying high-performance hardware and software with generous disk storage far outweighs the cost incurred by an extensive physical design control exercise.

Inputs and outputs

There are four basic inputs to the step.

First-Cut Physical Data Design Developed in step 620 as the first attempt at developing an executable data design. It is sized in terms of the storage space required. The time taken for critical transactions to be performed on it is estimated. This design will be modified if it does not, as is usually the case, meet the performance requirements. The volumes of data to be held, documented in the Logical Data Model, are also required for both space and timing estimation.

Enquiry and update processing specifications These comprise the Function Definitions, Enquiry Access Paths, Enquiry Process Models, Effect Correspondence Diagrams, and Update Process Models. They are needed because to estimate the time taken by the machine to process an enquiry or update then we first estimate the number of entity occurrences accessed, from which we can then estimate the number of disk accesses. Additionally the Function Definitions will contain details of the input and output processes—estimating the performance of these is particularly important for off-line processing. Frequencies of enquiries and updates are also required from the Function Definitions.

Performance objectives These are defined by Service Level Requirements in the Function Definitions and by storage requirements in the Requirements Catalogue. The users, assisted by the development team, defined objectives for data storage, timings for critical transactions, recovery, and information.

Hardware and software performance statistics These are needed to calculate the storage requirements and transaction timings. Installations should develop statistics for their own range of hardware and software, otherwise this information should be available from the supplier. These statistics were collected in step 610, *prepare for physical design*. Also during step 610, page planning charts for space estimation and timing estimation forms were designed—these are used in step 640, *optimize physical data design*.

The outputs from the step will be: an optimized Physical Data Design, a Space Estimation, a Timing Estimation, possibly a modified Requirements Catalogue showing changes to space requirements, and possibly agreed changes to the Service Level Requirements in the Function Definitions.

Measuring performance against requirements

The performance of the system is measured against the Service Level Requirements set in Stages 3 and 4 (these are described in Sec. 4.4). Initially this means estimating the performance of enquiries and updates against the first-cut Physical Data Design. If the performance requirements are not met then these designs will be modified and estimated again. This iterative process of performance estimation and design modification is continued until either the objectives are met or it becomes apparent that no improvement is possible.

Some requirements that may be still unmet from the Requirements Catalogue, such as those for information or portability of software, are not directly measurable and are not considered here. The performance requirements for storage space, function timing, and recovery are quantifiable. We describe below how the performance of the system can be estimated against each of these in turn.

Estimation of storage requirements

Most projects will make some estimates of the space required as part of the project justification. These will usually be very rough estimates based on the number of occurrences of the major entities. As more information is collected and a more detailed view of the new system is developed, then more accurate sizing can be done. In Stage 4 each of the technical options is sized and the sizing of the chosen option is often used as the basis for the storage space requirement.

In this step the first-cut Physical Data Design is sized in a more detailed and accurate way. The sizing is based upon the allocation of entity occurrences to specific areas of disk storage.

Below we describe the information that is required for this detailed sizing. This basically comes from three sources: the Logical Data Model, the first-cut Physical Data Design, and from the hardware and software environment to be used.

From the Required System Logical Data Model detailed information about the data volumes are extracted:

* data space for each entity;
* volumes of each entity;
* volumes of relationships;
* variance of volumes over time;
* which data needs to be on-line (from the Function Definitions).

From the first-cut Physical Data Design we need to know:

* how entities are clustered together;
* volumes of any new records introduced in first-cut design. [1]

Factors required from the hardware and software environment (normally collected in step 610, *prepare for physical design*) are:

---

[1] These are often required with hierarchical database management systems.

- possible page sizes, buffer allocation;
- DBMS overheads for page management;
- DBMS overheads for indices, pointers, hashing;
- handling of insertions, deletions, overflow, etc.;
- DBMS data type handling and data compaction possibilities.

The way that most database management systems, file handlers, and operating systems handle the retrieval and organization of data on disk is through a set of fixed size *pages* (operating systems usually refer to them as *blocks*). The page is the unit of disk I/O, with data written to main memory a page at a time to be manipulated and then written back to disk for update. The allocation of entities to pages therefore has a great impact on the speed of retrieval as well as on the space required.

Generally each system software product handles page management in a different way. Differences occur in a number of areas such as: possible page sizes, how each page is organized, and in the numbers of different entities that can be stored on a single page. In order to plan the allocation of entities to pages it is suggested that in step 610, *prepare for physical design*, page planning charts are developed specific to the software. One of these charts will then be completed for each cluster in step 640, *optimize physical data design*.

CODASYL page planning chart

Page size: 8k   Page type: Customer   No. CALC RECORDs: 3000   No. Pages: 3000   Expansion by 40 % = 4200 pages

RECORD	Data size	DBMS o'head	Pointers				Total pointer space	Total RECORD space	No. RECORDs per CALC	Space per CALC	Comment
			CALC	NEXT	PRIOR	OWN					
Customer	124	6	4	4			8	138	1	138	
Payment	43	6		8		4	12	61	27	1647	
Invoice	57	6		12		4	16	79	28	2212	
Allocated Payment	18	6		8		8	16	40	28	1120	

Total	5117
CALCs / page	1
Total data space	5117
Page space	5149

+ 32

Fig. 6.26 Completed CODASYL page planning chart for a portion of the Yorkies first-cut Physical Data Design

In Fig. 6.26 we have shown a completed CODASYL page planning chart for a portion of the Yorkies first-cut Physical Data Design.[1] A chart is compiled for each cluster group in the first-cut Physical Data Design. As each one shows the total number of pages occupied by the cluster, adding all these up gives the total number of pages occupied by the database. Then multiplying by the page size gives the database size in bytes. All these calculations are most conveniently performed using spreadsheets.

Because this chart is for CODASYL databases it shows space for pointers. Many relational databases (e.g. ORACLE, DB2) use indexes as their primary organization. For these there would be two types of page planning charts, one for the index pages and one for the data pages.

Estimation of function timings

Some rough estimates of function timing will have been done in Stage 4, Technical System Options. These may have been used to help define the performance requirements. In this step the timings for the critical functions are estimated in more detail.

There is no need to estimate the performance of every update or enquiry. This would be very time consuming and expensive for very little advantage—as was discussed earlier, many projects will avoid physical design control completely. If physical design control is considered necessary (and this decision would have been incorporated in the Physical Design Strategy developed in step 610, *prepare for physical design*) then a only small proportion of the system's processing need be controlled. The project team should identify the processing whose performance is critical to the success of the overall system. Modern software environments can offer great flexibility to the performance tuner and this can be exploited for the less critical processing.

Identification of critical functions

In most systems there are a few transactions or batch programs which are executed many times, occupying perhaps 80% of the computer's resources but only comprising perhaps 20% of the actual program code. The performance of these programs is therefore critical to the performance of the system as a whole. It is important to identify these critical functions and particularly the most frequent transactions within them. It is these transactions that will have their performance measured and possibly improved.

Other transactions may be critical, not because of their frequency but because a fast response is required—perhaps for rapid decision making or as a 'real-time' component of the system.

Thus the basic criteria for selecting the processing whose performance needs to be estimated in detail and then tuned are:

- high-volume on-line transactions;
- major off-line (batch) processing runs;
- on-line transactions requiring a fast response or real-time transactions.

---

[1] For the technically minded: we have assumed 4 bytes for all pointers, only implemented NEXT and OWNER pointers in the first-cut design, and each CALC record belongs to a system-owned SET.

To decide what processing falls into the above categories we use some of the volumetric information collected in the earlier stages of the project. Some sizing of the processing load will have been performed in the technical options stage and these calculations should be reviewed as part of the selection of critical transactions. Priorities in the Requirements Catalogue and the Service Level Requirements should also help identify the critical transactions of the system.

In step 330, *derive system functions*, the Function Definitions were begun; they included maximum and average frequencies for functions, events, and enquiries. These volumes may have been refined during the technical options and detailed process design stages. Volumetric information about the enquiry transactions is often hard to predict, particularly with management information or decision support systems, since users may use the system in a very different way from that anticipated. Some indications may come from the way the current system is used and from the users' estimates of enquiry frequency. The Function Definitions indicate whether transactions are to be performed in on-line or off-line mode, and if off-line which processing cycle they belong to.

Using the above approach we can determine which transactions are the most frequent and when they are going to be run. Thus the high-volume on-line transactions, the critical transactions, and the major daily batch runs can be found.

Information required for timing calculations
Below we describe the information that is required for these detailed timings. This basically comes from four sources: the detailed processing design (Enquiry Access Paths, Enquiry Process Models, Effect Correspondence Diagrams, and Enquiry Process Models), the first-cut Physical Data Design, the Function Definitions, and the hardware and software environment to be used.

For timing the critical on-line transactions we need to work through the Enquiry or Update Process Model (as appropriate). The operations on the process model show the 'reads' and 'writes' of each entity occurrence involved in the process. For each entity we need to estimate the number of 'reads' and 'writes' required—this information can be estimated from the volumetric information associated with the Logical Data Model. (In Sec. 4.7 we described how a version of the Logical Data Structure was annotated with volumetric information.) From the 'reads' and 'writes' the number of disk accesses are estimated. Processing time also needs to be estimated for any computation and screen handling performed. By applying figures appropriate to the hardware and software used we estimate the total CPU processing time and disk access time required for each transaction. An example of this technique is given later in this section.

A batch processing cycle will incorporate many transactions of the same kind and normally many transactions of different kinds. To estimate the time taken by the batch process we need to total the estimates for each individual transaction. The mix and volumes of transactions in a batch process can be determined from the Function Definitions. Several functions may have been combined into one super-function during step 630, *create Function Component Implementation Map*. A systems flow chart might also have been developed for the super function showing how the separate functions (which might become batch programs) interact.

The first-cut Physical Data Design and the page planning charts tell us which records are clustered together.

Factors required from the hardware and software environment are:

* CPU time per DBMS call;
* CPU time for application program per DBMS call;
* CPU time per message pair (for on-line);
* disk access time;
* record locking mechanisms;
* security overhead time (for preventing unauthorized access, etc.);
* recovery overhead time (for writing to transaction logs, etc.);
* data communication line speeds.

These kinds of figures can be quite hard to come by. If the installation is using the same hardware and software for another system and has a good performance monitor,[1] then installation standards can be set for the above. If hardware and software are to be purchased, the above statistics may be available from the supplier or there may be benchmark figures available from which these statistics can be derived. These figures were collected in step 610, *prepare for physical design*, and some were included in the DBMS Performance Classification (see Fig. 6.4).

Timing calculations
The prediction of overall system performance is a difficult area and is generally left to specialist staff known as *capacity planners*. A brief discussion of capacity planning and its interface to Stage 4, Technical System Options, was given in Sec. 5.3. There are several simulation programs and expert systems programs available which attempt to predict and improve system performance either generally or for specific hardware and software.

The basic approach to timing is to calculate the disk access time and CPU utilization time for each critical transaction. The actual average elapsed time taken by a transaction (or response time for an on-line transaction) will probably be several times larger than that calculated. The elapsed time will be affected by such factors as queuing time, record locking, the overall machine loading which may governed by other systems using the same machine, and by peaks and troughs of activity. Capacity planning information should enable estimates of the elapsed time from the disk access time and CPU utilization time for the transaction.

For critical on-line transactions the timings calculated can be compared with the Service Level Requirements set for those transactions. For batch functions the times taken to perform each individual enquiry or update are aggregated to give a total for the function. All the functions within the batch processing cycle can then be aggregated to give a figure for the whole cycle.

---

[1] Software (and possibly hardware) which monitors the performance of the machine, Typically they provide statistics such as CPU utilization, number of disk accesses per second, etc.

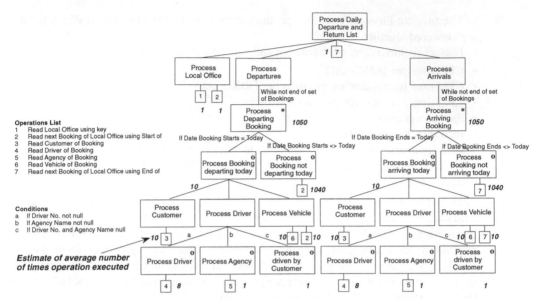

Fig. 6.27 Enquiry Process Model for Departure and Return List showing estimated average number of times each operation will be executed

To demonstrate a timing calculation we use the Daily Departure and Return List enquiry that was used as an example for the development of Enquiry Access Paths and Enquiry Process Models. Figure 6.27 shows the Enquiry Process Model developed for the Daily Departure and Return List—annotated by estimates of the number of times each operation is likely to be executed. These estimates are derived from the volumetric information associated with the Logical Data Model. Thus the figure of 1050 indicates the number of times that the iteration of reading the Booking occurrence is expected to happen—this figure follows from there being an average of 1050 bookings starting from or ending at a given local office. The figures given under the selections are estimates of the number of times the path will be followed. Thus an estimated average of 10 of the 1050 bookings will be on the date in question.

These figures provide an estimate of the numbers of read statements that the application program must perform. For each read (or write) statement we also need to estimate how many disk accesses are required. This will depend upon the actual organization of the data on the disk. A direct access could be achieved in one disk access (if hashing is used), or in two or more (if indexes are used—at least one to read the index and at least one to read the data). When going from the master occurrence to its associated detail occurrences (or vice versa) then each read may require several disk accesses (for both indexes and data) for every occurrence. However, in circumstances where the master occurrence and detail occurrences are on the same page of the disk then it is sometimes possible to read all master and detail occurrences with a single disk access. In all cases, reasonable estimates of the number of disk accesses required per read or write statement can only be made with good knowledge and understanding of the physical organization of data and mechanisms for storing and accessing it. The page planning charts completed for space sizing show which RECORDs are on the same page and can therefore be retrieved with a single disk access.

In Fig. 6.28 we illustrate a transaction timing form that can be used to estimate the performance of transactions on a CODASYL database. It shows 50 (one for each office) Daily Departure and Return Lists being produced daily off-line. The 'Process Verb' column shows the Data Manipulation Language (DML) process verbs that are used in the application program to access the data.[1] The 'Read Path' column shows the method used by the DBMS for navigation—hashing algorithms (CALC), pointer chains (NEXT, PRIOR, and OWNER), and sometimes indexes are used in CODASYL database products. Examination of the process verbs and read paths used can help check the calculations and help identify improvements.

The 'No. DBMS calls per trans' column shows the estimate of the of the number of read or write statements that the program will perform for each RECORD type each time the transaction (event or enquiry) is performed. The figures in this column are derived from those used to annotate the Enquiry Process Model. The 'Disk Transfers' columns on the timing form show estimates of the number of disk reads and writes for each RECORD type retrieved.[2] The total number of disk accesses is multiplied by the average disk access time (in this case 30 ms) to give the total time required for disk access by the transaction. If an index-based DBMS is used (many relational products use indexes) then columns should be added to the form to show the disk transfers associated with index reading and writing.

The 'CPU time' columns show the estimated time taken for the computer's Central Processing Unit (CPU) to perform each of the individual operations that make up the transaction. A figure is given for the CPU time taken to perform a DBMS call. (We have used the same figure for all process verbs but better estimates could be obtained by using a more precise figure for each process verb.) An estimate has been made that the time taken to execute the part of the application program associated with the DBMS call will be, on average, half the time taken by the CPU to process the DBMS call. (This is reasonable for typical information systems—if considerable calculation is required, the proportion could be increased.) The 'TP monitor' column refers to the processing required to support screen handling by a transaction processing (TP) monitor such as IBM's CICS. The time given here is per *message pair*—a message from the computer to the screen and back from the end-user via the screen to the computer. Other figures could be added in (but haven't been here) for factors such as communication line speeds and recovery overheads.

Throughout the tuning phase these timing forms may need to modified many times as the performance is recalculated after each change in design. One way of making this

---

[1]CODASYL uses FIND to place a cursor on the RECORD and then GET brings the RECORD into working storage, OBTAIN does a FIND followed by a GET. In this case we have needed to examine all the RECORDS found so OBTAIN has been used, represented by an 'O'.

[2]Note that for a write, at least two disk transfers will be required; one to read in the page and another to write it back.

process of recalculation less painful is to set up these timing forms on spreadsheet packages so that recalculation can be performed automatically.

The figures given below for database performance and disk access are reasonable at the time of writing. They could be recorded on the DBMS Performance Classification form developed in step 610, *prepare for physical design*. Some typical timing figures for CODASYL and hierarchical[1] databases are:

No. of instructions/DBMS call	~2000
No. of application program instructions/DBMS call	~1000
No. of instructions/message pair	~1000
Disk access time	~30 ms

For a 1 MIP machine (1 million instructions per second) this gives:

Time/DBMS call	2 ms
Time application program/DBMS call	1 ms
Time/message pair	1 ms

Codasyl transaction timing form

Transaction: Daily Departures and Returns List **No.** 50 **Frequency:** daily Off - line/ On-line

Process Verbs: F - FIND, G - GET, O - OBTAIN, M - MODIFY C - CONNECT, D - DISCONNECT, E - ERASE, S - STORE **Read Path:** C - CALC, N - NEXT pointer, P - PRIOR pointer, O - OWNER pointer

RECORD	DBMS		No. DBMS calls per trans	Disk Transfers			CPU time				Comments
	Process Verb	Read Path		Read	Write	Total	DBMS	TP Mon	App Prog	Total	
Local Office / Depot	O	C	1	1		1	2		1	3	
Booking	O	N	1051	1051		1051	2102		1051	3153	Need to read 1050 + 1 to ensure entire set read
Vehicle	O	O	10	10		10	20		10	30	
Customer	O	O	10	10		10	20		10	30	
Agency	O	O	1	1		1	2		1	3	
Driver	O	O	9	9		9	18		9	27	
Booking	O	N	1051	1051		1051	2102		1051	3153	Need to read 1050 + 1 to ensure entire set read
Vehicle	O	O	10	10		10	20		10	30	
Customer	O	O	10	10		10	20		10	30	
Agency	O	O	1	1		1	2		1	3	
Driver	O	O	9	9		9	18		9	27	

Total No. disk transfers: 2163 Total CPU time: 6487ms

Total I/O time: 34.890s **Total resource time: 41.377s**

Fig. 6.28 CODASYL timing form for the enquiry Daily Departure and Return List

[1] It is not possible to give these figures for SQL-based relational products because the language works in a non procedural-way—the number of instructions and disk accesses required to execute a SELECT statement will depend on the query.

Accurate timings for transactions run on relational DBMSs are often more difficult to estimate than for other DBMS products or conventional file handlers. This is because the physical access navigation and retrieval mechanisms are controlled by relational DBMS software. Thus without a very good knowledge of the internal workings of a particular product it is almost impossible to predict the performance. It is more accurate and much easier to build and populate a prototype database and then run the SQL for the critical transactions on it. The timings for the full system can then be estimated by extrapolation from the prototype timings.

Estimation of recovery times

It is difficult to predict how often system failures will occur. Suppliers may quote and contractually guarantee failure rates for hardware but it is harder to predict software and human errors. What is needed is planning for the various types of failure in the knowledge that they will occur.

The times taken for recovery should be estimated for the following types of failure: system crashes (e.g. power failure), disk failures (e.g. head crash), and program or transaction failures (e.g. overflow error). These estimates will be based upon the following factors:

- frequency of dumping;
- DBMS facilities for restoring, checkpointing, and transaction logging;
- extent to which these facilities are used;
- acceptable errors or missing data (determined by the users).

In case of prolonged loss of the system (e.g. through fire), the performance of back-up manual and/or stand-by computer sites should also be estimated and measured against the users' objectives.

Improving performance

Initially the performance of the first-cut physical data and process designs are estimated and compared with the requirements. If these requirements are not met then these designs will need to be examined and improvements made. After each modification the performance of the system, in all areas likely to be affected by the change, should be recalculated. When the performance meets the objectives then the project can proceed to full development.

It is important to realize that making improvements in one area of performance may lead to a degradation in another area. For instance, a reduction in the storage space made by removing some indexes will slow down those transactions which used the indexes.

Below we give some brief hints on how performance can be improved in storage space, timings, and recovery. System software will vary greatly in the extent to which these are possible. Generally a detailed knowledge of the system software and hardware is required to get optimum performance from the technical environment. The project may choose to buy expertise in the form of consultancy from, usually, the software supplier.

Reducing the storage space requirements
This means operating on the first-cut Physical Data Design and the Logical Data Model. Some possible reductions can come from:

- codifying data;
- compressing data, e.g. dates as 2 bytes, A/N as 5 bits, removing trailing spaces;
- archiving earlier;
- dropping rarely used data;
- relying on data in other systems;
- reducing the number of pointers and indexes;
- removing redundant or derived data held for timing reasons;
- removing duplicated foreign keys in non-relational databases.

Speeding up transactions
There are two major ways to improve the speed of transactions: first, by modifying the program design to make it more efficient, and second, by modifying the data design to make retrieval faster. It is always preferable to take the first approach if at all possible. Modifying the data structure will have effects on the performance in all areas, including other timings.

Some possible ways to speed up transactions are suggested below:

- ensure access paths in programs are efficient;
- modify clusters by adjusting allocation to pages to reduce disk accesses;
- introduce more access methods, e.g. extra pointers, indexes;
- drop indexes before batch updates and recreate afterwards;
- modify the depth and structure of B* indexes;
- unnormalize data in relational databases;
- use read-only snapshots to reduce locking overheads;
- perform functions in a different (faster) way from that specified by the user;
- introduce new entities (not on the data design) to reduce access paths;
- increase buffer space;
- reduce the frequency of dumping and checkpointing.

In the Daily Departure and Return List example discussed earlier there are several ways of improving performance. First, the Booking record could be indexed on the Date Booking Starts and Date Booking Ends attributes (these were identified as entry points during the development of the first-cut Physical Data Design). The process could then directly access only those bookings starting or leaving the selected office on the appropriate day. Another possibility, particularly appropriate with CODASYL databases, is to create sorted sets of the bookings of the office ordered by the Date Booking Starts (in the case of the 'from' set—the departing bookings) and ordered by the Date Booking Ends (in the case of the 'to' set—the arriving bookings). Using sorted sets means that the pointer to the next booking occurrence will find those departing on the same day together—thus ensuring that far fewer records (probably about 50) than the first estimated 1051 records in Fig. 6.28 will need to be read. A similar situation occurs with the arriving bookings.

Improving recovery

Recovery times can be improved by increasing the frequency of dumps, by increasing the frequency of checkpointing, and by maintaining transaction logs, before-image and after-image logs. Note that these will increase both the space requirement and the transaction timings.

Changing requirements

If it becomes apparent that the Service Level Requirements set in Stage 3 cannot be met, then a case for changing them is presented to the users who originally set the requirements. The development team should prepare a list of possible changes and present them to the users. The sort of changes that might be suggested are:

- reductions in the amount of historical data held;
- increased response times or batch run-times;
- increased hardware performance (i.e. spend more money);
- a reduction in the functions offered by the system.

Changes to the requirements should really be regarded as a last resort rather than a normal course of action.

SUMMARY

- Physical design control is an expensive activity which should be avoided if at all possible.
- Service Level Requirements are set for functions in Stage 3, for timing and recovery.
- The Requirements Catalogue details the storage space requirements for the computer system.
- The storage space required by the first-cut physical data design is estimated and compared with the requirements.
- The performance of critical processes is estimated and compared against the Service Level Requirements.
- Critical processes are ones that have a significant impact on the performance of the system, particularly high-volume, on-line transactions and major batch runs.
- Improve performance to meet requirements by modifying the process and data designs.
- After each change the performance is estimated.
- The final design will usually be a compromise between objectives.
- If requirements cannot be met then changes to them are agreed with users.
- When the performance is acceptable the project can proceed to full development.

6.6 Complete function specification (step 650)

In step 630, *create function component implementation map*, all components of the processing system, with the exception of database accesses (these are handled in step 660, *consolidate process data interface*), that could be specified and implemented non-procedurally were built. In step 650, *complete function specification*, any remaining components which require procedural specification, again excepting database access components, are specified. The format of the function specifications[1] to be developed in this step should have been determined in step 610, *prepare for physical design*, as part of the Physical Design Strategy. Much of the work involved in this step requires detailed technical knowledge of the development environment and of program design methodologies. The organizational standards for program design will also influence the approach. It is unlikely that this work could be performed by analysts/designers only experienced with SSADM.

Specific function models and batch processing

Considerable work will be required in this step for specifying large batch (off-line) processing programs. These tend to have gone out of fashion with end-user computing through cheap PCs becoming the normal approach, but such programs will always be the most efficient mechanism for processing very high volumes of similar data, e.g. creation of gas bills or benefit payments. Although such programs can sometimes be developed using non-procedural code the main languages used for batch programs are procedural, with the most popular being COBOL.

In general it is more complex to specify batch programs than on-line programs. This is because there will usually be greater interaction between the various transactions which the program controls. There is also greater interaction between programs, with output from one program input to another. It may also be necessary to define various transaction files and specify how they are used.

The universal function model provided by SSADM, which regards each function as having an input process and an output process, may need to be extended to specific function models for this type of program. These could be represented by system flow charts or Data Flow Diagram type specifications. The important thing is that the flows of data and files and the interconnecting processes are defined.

The design of each batch processing cycle is usually represented by a systems flowchart. This uses a wide range of symbols to show different kinds of storage media, different ways of processing data, and different kinds of input and output. It is a good and standard way of showing the typical activities in a batch cycle·such as sorts, merges, and use of transaction files. Systems flowcharts differ from Data Flow Diagrams in that they explicitly show sequences and decisions.

The individual program structures for dealing with the inputs and outputs could be specified using Jackson Structured Programming techniques.[2] Structure clashes (discussed in more detail in Sec. 5.8) are more likely to occur with batch processing

---

[1] The term *function specification* is used rather than *program specification*. Often the terms are interchangeable with most functions becoming programs. However, the mappings between superfunctions, functions, compiled modules and programs, and physical run-units depend upon both the physical environment used for construction and the organizational standards for development. The detail of how exactly each function component maps to a physical fragment is maintained by the Function Component Implementation Map.

[2] Of course, other styles of program specification could be used such as Yourdon and Constantine structure charts, Warnier–Orr diagrams, or action diagrams. The decision will depend on local standards and expertise. The best fit to SSADM Version 4 is provided by Jackson techniques.

because the requirements for input and output data are more likely to conflict with the structure imposed by the Logical Data Model.

Batch program specification

We need to consider all of the major processing cycles such as the daily, weekly, and end-of-month runs. The first step in batch program specification is to decide the basic sequence of programs within each cycle. System input and output processing and their associated transaction files can then be considered. In this way a run flowchart can be built up, in a step-wise way, for each processing cycle.

1. Define the basic run flows Each batch processing cycle, which could be thought of as a superfunction, will be composed of functions, each of which will be composed of events and enquiries. The basic run flow will need to define the order in which these are processed. There are two basic possibilities: either the data can be sorted so that all of the processing associated with a particular occurrence and its associated occurrences can be processed together; or the particular events and enquiries that make up each function can be processed in turn. There are 'in-between' approaches whereby the data can be sorted for particular functions, groups of functions, or groups of events. Any sorts should be added to the system flowchart as it is being built up. Deciding upon the approach for each run flow we need to take into account such factors as: performance, ensuring the integrity of the data, the ways in which the input data and output data are organized, and the characteristics of the processing environment.

Within each function we need to decide on the transaction sequence, i.e. in what order the events are going to be processed. A frequent technique used in batch processing is to sort the input transaction file by entity occurrence. Thus if we were updating a Customer master file we would sort the input transactions by Customer No. and perform all of the processing for each Customer before passing onto the next one. The traditional order is then to perform the deletions first followed by the insertions and modifications. In this way, if Customer Nos. are being re-used, there is no possibility of a new customer being created and deleted within the same processing cycle. The function specifications may need to be structured in a different way from the process models if a batch program is to be performed in this way.

Some specification of run flows may have been provided by the Function Definitions, the supporting Elementary Process Descriptions, and possibly by the Required System Data Flow Diagrams (if these have been maintained from step 310). Any sequencing of events for the same entity occurrences implied by the run flow should be consistent with the Entity Life Histories. It is particularly important to ensure that changes to entity occurrences occur in the order in which they happened in the real world. (A simple, though perhaps unrealistic, example could be a customer notifying a change of address twice in the same batch cycle—if they were processed in the wrong order then the wrong address would be stored.) One way of avoiding these problems is to time stamp every transaction as it is received. The software can then ensure that the transactions are processed in the order in which they are received (as they normally are for on-line processing).

2. Deal with input transaction files First these need to be identified. The source data for each batch program will be either the database or transaction file(s) or both. Some transaction files may be shown on the Required System Data Flow Diagrams. We need to specify these files in terms of their data content, organization, and storage medium. Information associated with the Function Definitions such as the I/O Structures and the Elementary Process Descriptions (and the Required System Data Flow Diagrams if these are kept up to date) will help create the file specification and the function specification.

3. Deal with program output Output transaction files from a program may be input to other programs in the same system; they may be used by other systems inside or outside the organization; or they may be reports and log outputs going to spooling or printing systems. These outputs need to be specified in terms of their format and content—I/O Structures will help with this task. The function specifications created in task 2 above will need to be amended and extended to take account of this output processing. The run flowchart will also be extended by showing the output processing and transaction files.

4. Transaction file creation and maintenance Some large systems might use on-line creation of transaction files before database update. There may be other transaction file maintenance to be considered such as input edits, transaction file reformats, and extensions. Function specifications will be based on the Function Definitions and their supporting documentation. These functions/programs are added to the run flow.

Combining procedural and non-procedural code

Often the development environment allows a mixture of procedural and non-procedural code to be combined. For instance, a COBOL component may contain embedded SQL commands, or a fourth generation language program may call subroutines which are written in a procedural language, such as C or Assembler. Careful consideration should be given to how different fragments are specified/implemented and then combined.

Physical run-units

A big impact is made upon programs by the approach taken in the implementation environment towards physical run-units. A physical run-unit can be thought of as a set of processing that once initiated must run through to a conclusion (equivalent to a physical success unit in on-line processing). It may combine several separately compiled modules, possibly written in different programming languages, which are combined together. Various strategies of using co-routines, subroutines, and program inversion are possible but the extent to which these may be applied depends greatly on the tools being used.

SUMMARY

- Function components, except database accesses, which are to be implemented using procedural program code are specified during this step.
- Batch programs are more complex to specify because each processing cycle and many transaction files have to be defined.

- Batch programs often require a specific function model which is often a systems flowchart.
- A run flow of functions within a batch processing cycle is developed.
- The run flow is expanded to include the processing of input and output transaction files.
- Some programs may combine non-procedural and procedural code.
- The way in which physical run-units are combined should be considered carefully.

6.7   Consolidate process data interface (step 660)

Introduction

Specification of the physical database access components is performed in this step. The Physical Data Design has been optimized in step 640 and the processes that write to it and read from it can now be designed.

The Process Data Interface specifies the interaction between the physical database design and the processing that operates on it. The 'logical' processing, in the form of Function Definitions, Update and Enquiry Process Models, is defined by the earlier stages of SSADM. As a result of constraints of the physical database system and of tuning of the overall system performance, the logical data design (around which the 'logical' processing was designed) may be compromised by physical design. The Physical Data Design may look nothing like the Logical Data Model from which it originated.

An interface is developed to avoid respecifying all of the logical processing to be consistent with the tuned physical data design. This software is specified to interface between the 'logical' specification and the physical data structure—it is known as the Process Data Interface. This allows the designer to implement logical processes directly as physical programs independent of the physical database structure; thus easing maintenance and construction of the system. In order for these 'logical' processes to operate on the physical data, then the interface software must operate to translate the logical structure required by the processing to the physical structure in which the data is actually held. This interface software could be written in procedural languages, such as COBOL, C, or Assembler, or non-procedural languages, particularly SQL.

This approach is similar to that taken by database management system vendors over the years. Databases have become progressively more 'logical' and are more able to implement directly Logical Data Models. Indeed with relational databases there may be little need for a Process Data Interface. However, even with these highly logical models, sometimes performance tuning can take the physical structure far away from the Logical Data Model.

Figure 6.29 shows how the Process Data Interface fits in with the universal function model, sitting between the processing and the physical database.

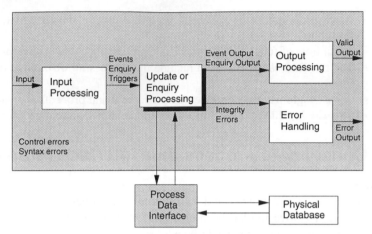

Fig. 6.29 The Process Data Interface and the universal function model

There are several benefits that may be achieved by the use of a Process Data Interface:

• it preserves the Logical Data Model view;
• it eases maintenance since only the logical view may need modification;
• it helps document any design decisions;
• if the design is optimized still further only the Process Data Interface will need changing, not the logical processing.

The above benefits are really associated with improved data independence. A logical view of the system's data is preserved so that performance tuning does not require changes to the programs themselves, but only to the Process Data Interface. On the other hand, producing a sophisticated Process Data Interface can be a time-consuming and expensive activity.

If it is unnecessary for the project to optimize the data design, then the Process Data Interface will simply be a physical implementation of the process models. An example of this kind of Process Data Interface is given later for the Daily Departure and Return List from the Yorkies system. Optimization can be avoided by ensuring that the hardware and software has sufficient capacity to perform the processing—this is often cheaper, particularly in small systems, than performing complex design optimization and developing a Process Data Interface. With large systems the story might be different. These kind of issues should be resolved during technical options and specified in the Physical Design Strategy.

The Process Data Interface is built by comparing the access requirements for function components specified in the Function Component Implementation Map against the optimized Physical Data Design. The physical keys of master and detail entities for each mismatch are identified and a physical access map (which could be similar to an Enquiry Access Path or Effect Correspondence Diagram) is developed. Comparing this with the Update or Enquiry Process Model will enable processing to be specified to handle the mismatch. This needs to be done for each set of processing changed by the development of the Physical Data Design. Combining together the new processing components to identify common processes would lead to the specification of the Process Data Interface. All the new processing components for the Process Data Interface are included in the Function Component Implementation Map, defining their interactions with the logical view of the processing. If serious performance problems occur, some of this may need to be coded in low-level languages, such as assembler.

Example—Daily Departure and Return List

This is a list of the vehicle departures and returns expected at a particular Yorkies depot on a particular day. It is printed at the end of a previous day's business at the office and collected by the depot staff before starting work in the morning. The list is separated into departures and returns; detailing the vehicles, drivers, or agencies, or otherwise used by the booking. This list was used as a example for normalization (Sec. 4.5), for Enquiry Access Paths (Sec. 4.7), for Enquiry Process Models (Sec. 5.6), and for transaction timing (Sec. 6.5). We repeat below the Enquiry Access Path and the Enquiry Process Model developed for the enquiry in steps 360 and 530.

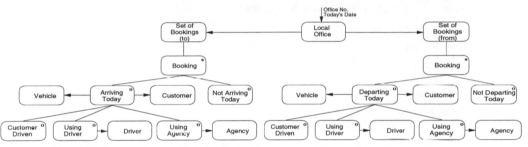

Fig. 6.30 Enquiry Access Path for Daily Departure and Return List (Version 1)

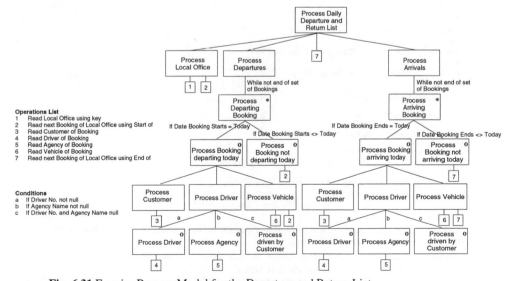

Fig. 6.31 Enquiry Process Model for the Departure and Return List

If the Yorkies system were to be implemented with a relational database (e.g. ORACLE) then the enquiry would be normally coded in SQL. The first-cut Physical Data Design is unchanged by optimization (either it was deliberately omitted or no changes were required) and reflects directly the Logical Data Model. In this case the Process Data Interface becomes simply the SQL code necessary to retrieve the data required by the enquiry.

Figure 6.32 below shows an ORACLE SQL query to retrieve information required for the Daily Departure and Return List. This query could be embedded in a programming language (e.g. C) or a report generator (e.g. SQL*Report). The retrieved values would then be put into variables and printed using the programming language or report generator facilities. The departures can be separated from returns in a number of ways: e.g. those with Start_Date=sysdate or Start_Mileage is null for departures and not null for returns.

```
SELECT
Office-No,
Office_Name,
Depot_Address,
sysdate,/* an ORACLE pseudo-column - today's date */
Booking-No,
Booking.Customer-No,
Customer_Name,
Veh_Cat_Req,
Start_Date,
Finish_Date,
Driver_Req,
Veh_Reg_Mark,
Agency_Name,
Booking.Driver-No,
Driver_Name,
Start_Mileage,
Date_Time_Collected,/* date type includes time */
Office-No_Start,
Office-No_Finish
FROM
Local_Office,
Booking,
Customer,
Driver
WHERE
Booking.Customer-No = Customer.Customer-No(+)
AND
Booking.Driver-No = Driver.Driver-No(+)
AND
((Start_Date = trunc(sysdate)
        AND
Office-No=Office-No_Start)
OR
(Finish_Date = trunc(sysdate)
        AND
Office-No=Office-No_Finish))
AND     Office-No = local_office_no /* value to be supplied */
```

Fig. 6.32 SQL for Daily Departure and Return List[1]

---

[1] Where the relationship is optional (i.e. the foreign key can be null), an outer join ((+)) is used to ensure that the rows with null foreign keys are also selected.

The pseudo-column sysdate has the time truncated to zero. This is because:
(a)   time is taken into account when comparing date types;
(b)   when date types are entered without the time, the time is set by ORACLE to zero (e.g. Start_Date and Finish_Date).

Several conclusions can be drawn from this example. We can see that the Enquiry Access Path and the Enquiry Process Model are hardly non-procedural, 'logical' models. (They work very well as a specification of the access paths required in hierarchical or CODASYL databases.) The physical implementation in SQL is in many ways more compact and 'logical'—but has the further advantage of actually working; enabling testing, demonstration to users, and performance evaluation of a prototype database. Increasingly database vendors are providing easy-to-use front-ends for generation of SQL[1]—some CASE products enable generation from Enquiry Access Paths. Many projects, knowing that a relational database will be used for implementation, will not develop process models in Stage 5, but will develop the access routines that make up their Process Data Interface using SQL in Stage 6 (or sometimes earlier).

SUMMARY

- Database access components are specified (and often built) during step 660, *consolidate process data interface*.
- The Process Data Interface acts as a filter enabling logical processes to operate on the physical database.
- The Process Data Interface enables process design to stay as logical as possible thus enhancing data independence.
- The Process Data Interface becomes working software which may be implemented in procedural or non-procedural languages.
- In many software environments (e.g. relational) the physical design may be so closely related to the Logical Data Model that the Process Data Interface is simply the software that interacts with the database.

6.8 Assemble physical design (step 670)

Like all of the other 'assemble' steps, this involves preparation for a quality review of the end-products of the stage. Quality criteria are difficult to specify for this step as the products are so dependent upon the Physical Design Strategy. The following set of products are recommended for review:

- Function Component Implementation Map;
- Function Definitions;
- Physical Data Design (optimized);
- Required System Logical Data Model;
- Requirements Catalogue;
- Space Estimation;
- Timing Estimation;
- Process Data Interface.

---

[1] A good example is Microsoft's Access. A user can define the navigation path on a diagram (very similar to a Logical Data Structure) and automatically generate the SQL required.

This review needs to be very carefully managed, as a considerable amount of technical information is involved. User input is very important, although it is unlikely that users would be able to understand the technical details of all the products. Consequences of any decisions made during the physical design, particularly those concerning performance and user interface requirements, should be presented to the users in as understandable a fashion as possible. Technical experts will need to ensure the technical accuracy and consistency of the majority of the products of this stage.

7 Management Aspects

The objective of this chapter is to consider some of the issues relevant to the manager of a project using SSADM. This embraces pure management issues, such as the staffing and planning of the project, to technical issues, such as how the method should be used with a CASE tool. The chapter is divided into three sections dealing with project management, customizing SSADM, and computer assisted systems engineering (CASE).

Section 7.1 discusses project management. We deal with the general issue of quality standards and consider how SSADM fits in. This section also discusses how the PRINCE (PRojects IN a Controlled Environment) method supports and integrates with SSADM. Issues such as project organization, planning, quality control, project control, and configuration management are addressed in the context of the PRINCE method. Other project management issues with which SSADM must interface are also discussed such as estimating, and risk assessment and management.

Section 7.2 discusses customizing SSADM. Every SSADM project is different, involving different organizations, problems, technology, and people. Because of this, it has always been necessary to customize SSADM. First, we discuss what SSADM is, attempting to define the core of the method around which it may be customized or tailored to particular project circumstances. Each SSADM module is then considered and opportunities for customization identified.

Throughout this book we have promoted the use of CASE (Computer Assisted Systems Engineering). In Sec. 7.3 we discuss the kind of features that can be expected with a CASE tool that supports an SSADM project and briefly discuss how such a tool might be used within a project.

7.1 Project management

In 1986 the UK government surveyed project managers about their use of SSADM. Perhaps unsurprisingly its most appreciated feature was that it aided project management. The detailed structure and definition of techniques have always been seen as a benefit to a project manager. The 'divide and conquer' approach taken by SSADM enables the manager to plan tasks, allocate resources, and monitor end-products throughout a project. Moreover, a standard approach is maintained, which once understood, improves communication in many ways. Analysts, designers, programmers, project managers, and users all speak the same language and understand the same types of diagrams.

SSADM and quality

One of the major buzz words in management circles in the 1990s has been 'quality'. Systems development has not escaped this attention with many IT organizations adopting cultural change initiatives such as Total Quality Management. Recently many software suppliers and consultancies have become certified to quality standards such as BS 5750 and ISO 9001. These quality standards are increasingly important in contractual negotiations, and often purchasers will only deal with certificated suppliers. Many software developers have used the quality procedures embedded in SSADM and PRINCE to achieve their quality certification.

In the United States an alternative software development quality model has become significant, known as the software process maturity model. Adopting this model measures an organization's capability to deliver software in five levels—most surveys indicate that 90% of organizations are at the bottom (level 1). Adopting methods like SSADM and PRINCE have been shown to raise an organization to at least level 2.

SSADM itself has been subjected to various quality standards which monitor the supply of its services. The Information Systems Examinations Board of the British Computer Society manage a scheme for certificating SSADM practitioners and accrediting training organizations. The CCTA has developed a scheme whereby an independent body measures the conformance of CASE tools to SSADM. A British standard has been developed for SSADM—this is primarily useful in the customer/supplier relationship where the customer can ensure that the standards of SSADM are being followed by the supplier.

PRINCE and SSADM

PRINCE (PRojects IN a Controlled Environment) is an open method for managing and controlling IT projects. Like SSADM it was developed by the UK government and is now an open standard with many organizations offering training and support.

PRINCE and SSADM Version 4 were designed together at approximately the same time. SSADM considers the technical aspects of developing a full specification of a system whereas PRINCE considers the management aspects. It is thus clear that SSADM was never intended to encompass project management activities. However, because of the need to embed links to a project management method there is probably more management control in SSADM than in any other systems development method. Its relatively prescriptive nature and its detailed Product Descriptions and Product Breakdown Structures considerably help management.

In any case, the management and the development are intimately linked with each other and it is often difficult to identify a component as 'management' or 'technical'. The management aspects of a project are usually far more critical in ensuring its success than the technical aspects. PRINCE consists of several components:

• organization;
• products;
• plans;
• controls;
• activities.

Each of these components is important in a project using SSADM whether PRINCE or any other approach is used for project management. In the sections below we describe each of these components from a PRINCE and SSADM perspective. PRINCE is a synthesis of many project management ideas—the concepts described here could be applied whether PRINCE was used, whether another formal project management method was used or whether more informal procedures were developed. However, because large projects involve many different roles and individuals, formal management structures and controls are critical to their success.

Project organization

Figure 7.1 shows a typical project organization for an SSADM project being managed under PRINCE. Each box describe a role in the project. Roles are first defined and later individuals assigned to them. The match of individuals to roles depends upon project size and/or organizational factors. In small projects one individual can take on several roles, and in much larger projects a particular role may be split between several individuals. Personnel may also be planned to change during the development as different skills are required.

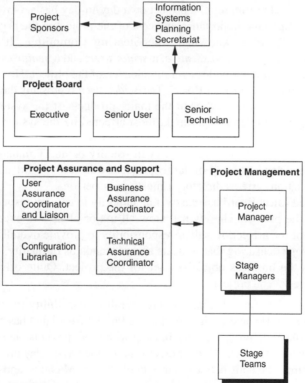

Fig. 7.1 Roles in a PRINCE project

It is possible that the individuals taking these roles may belong to different organizations. PRINCE standards can be applied in contracts to define the work required of different individuals or organizations. Below we briefly describe each of these roles.

Project Sponsors These are the individuals who have responsibility for paying for the development. They may be physically paying, or may be authorizing financial authority for the project. They will usually have ultimate responsibility for the parts of the organization which will be affected by the system. By their nature, these tend to be very senior people and must be kept informed of progress.

Information Systems Planning Secretariat There is an assumption that each project should be within an overall strategy governed by an information systems strategy plan which is in turn governed by the business plans. This Secretariat monitors the links between the individual project and the overall information systems plan or strategy. They also have responsibility for coordinating the links between projects in the strategic plan. Often further developments will be dependent upon this project.

Project Board The Project Board would be appointed by the Project Sponsors to have overall control of the project (it is possible that Project Sponsors may be part of this Board). Members of the Project Board will be managers themselves and are not usually be involved in running the project on a day-to-day basis. Obviously their seniority will depend upon the importance and cost of the project to the organization. Sometimes the Project Board is known as the Steering Committee. It comprises three senior management roles: an *executive*; a *senior user*; and a *senior technician*.

The *executive* provides overall guidance of the project. He or she will normally act as Chairman of the Project Board. The *senior user* represents the users of the system (both current and future) and/or of the major products of the system. Often this will be the manager of the user department most affected by the system under development. The *senior technician* represents the technical side of the development of the system and of its future operations. He or she will usually be an IT manager from the information systems department. For large projects this role would normally be taken by the information systems director or most senior person.

The Project Board has the overall authority to commit resources to and take resources from the project. They will review all major plans and exceptions, authorizing each stage of the project. It is their responsibility to provide overall direction and guidance to the project ensuring that it meets agreed standards of quality, time, and cost, and that it meets the business objectives set for the project. Quite often the Project Board will oversee several projects.

Project Manager This person has overall responsibility for the day-to-day running of the project. He or she will report to the Project Board and has responsibility for planning the project, defining controls, liaising with other projects, and defining configuration of management aspects. If the project is large, the day-to-day project management role will sometimes be split between an overall Project Manager and several Stage Managers. More typically project and stage management roles are combined, although the individual taking this role may change as different stages in the development will require different expertise. If the roles are distinguished then the Project Manager will take a more strategic view and the Stage Manager will take a more staff management view, managing the project teams. As SSADM is divided into modules, some of which are then subdivided into stages, it is more appropriate to designate these individuals as Module Managers rather than as Stage Managers.

Project Assurance Team
This group of roles is involved in quality assurance of all products and all plans. Thus they are involved in business, technical, and project management issues. This team splits into three roles:
- Business Assurance Coordinator;
- Technical Assurance Coordinator;
- User Assurance Coordinator.

A further role associated with the Project Assurance Team is the Configuration Librarian who has overall responsibility for configuration management of the project. They act as the custodian for all master copies of products produced by the project and are the focus for change control. Configuration management within SSADM is described later in this chapter.

Business Assurance Coordinator This is usually someone with financial and administrative knowledge including experience of cost/benefit analysis. They are primarily responsible for assessing the business aspects of the project which would include resourcing, and also act as the focal point for the administration of quality assurance and configuration management.

Technical Assurance Coordinator This is usually someone with considerable technical experience who is not directly associated with the project. In an SSADM context, this is often an experienced SSADM practitioner, possibly from another project, or sometimes an outside consultant. Their primary responsibility is to monitor and report on all technical assurance aspects of the project and ensure that the technical standards defined by the project are met.

User Assurance Coordinator This is someone with user knowledge of the business environment and of the individuals affected by the project. They are responsible for representing the users on the project on a day-to-day basis and coordinating their activities. Typically this involves: selecting which users should receive which products for review, determining the training needs for users in SSADM, deciding which users should be involved in prototype evaluations. They coordinate and agree any response from the users to any products developed. In an SSADM project this person would require some knowledge of SSADM and information systems in general, as well as good knowledge of the user area. They also need to be good communicators who command respect within the user community.

Products

PRINCE is a product-driven project management method. A project is judged on what it delivers so the emphasis is on products rather than on the activities that produce them. Thus for each stage in the project, we define a hierarchy of products to be produced, shown in a Product Breakdown Structure, and for each product we produce a Product Description. A PRINCE Product Description should have the following components: purpose; composition (i.e. what is included in the product); derivation (from which other products is this particular product derived?); and quality criteria. The Project Assurance Team ensure the quality of the products delivered by applying the quality criteria in review of SSADM end-products.

The SSADM Reference Manual contains a default set of Product Descriptions. So for every SSADM end-product, e.g. Required System Logical Data Model or Function Definition, there is a Product Description supplied in the Reference Manual. These are default descriptions, and every project will need to customize these to their own environment. Default Product Breakdown Structures are provided for each stage in SSADM—we have used these at the beginning of each chapter (e.g. see Fig. 6.1) to show which products are to be produced and how they are inter-related.

Planning

In PRINCE these Product Breakdown Structures are used to produce Product Flow Diagrams which show the derivation of each product from others and the inter-dependencies between products. This Product Flow Diagram is then used to produce an Activity Network showing which activities are needed to produce the products in the Product Flow Diagram. The activities required to produce the products can be written on the arrows connecting the products together.

Default Activity Networks are supplied in the SSADM Reference Manual and we have shown these, in a slightly different form, in the diagrams given at the beginning of each chapter showing each module, stage and step of SSADM.

Once an Activity Network has been built we can then attempt to estimate each of the activities. Based on the estimates we allocate resources of time, cost, and people to the activities. Most projects will use sophisticated planning tools (available relatively cheaply on PCs, e.g. Microsoft Project and Hoskyn's Project Manager Workbench) which help manage these activity networks through critical path analysis techniques. These project management tools use activity network diagrams and bar charts to display various aspects of time management, resource management, and cost management of the project. Sophisticated tools allows presentation of the underlying data in a variety of different ways and support project and resource planning techniques such as critical path analysis. A full description of these techniques is given by Meredith and Mentel.[1]

Under PRINCE several types of plan are required. A *Technical Plan* schedules the activities needed to produce the products and a *Resource Plan* shows the amount and cost of each resource needed. Technical plans can be represented graphically by Gant charts and network diagrams. These should be supported by a description of the responsibilities and methods for monitoring and reporting performance. The plans should also detail the frequency and nature of reporting on project performance to senior managers and the Project Board. The technical plans should also outline the quality control procedures and define at which points in the plan they are to be applied. Resource plans can be presented by various charts such as resource histograms and bar charts.

---

[1] Meredith, J. and Mentel, S. (1989) *Project Management: A Managerial Approach* 2nd edn (Wiley, New York).

It is impossible to set a detailed plan for the entire project from the outset. However, an overall project plan in outline should be developed, identifying the major milestones and delivery dates. Overall resources should also be allocated. For every project there will be a hierarchy of plans, with the overall project plan at the top and at lower levels detailed activity planning and resource planning. Detailed planning should be undertaken for the next module or phase of the project, outline planning for the later phases. As we move through the project then we will become more certain about what is to be done and what the risks are.

The *Quality Plan* defines the quality assurance standards to be followed by the project, the quality control methods to be applied, and which products will be subject to quality review or formal testing. Outline quality plans are produced for the whole project and detailed plans for the next phase .

Also produced should be a *Configuration Management Plan* which describes the way in which configuration management should be applied to the project. Configuration management and SSADM is discussed later in this section.

Levels of tolerance should also be set for the plans. If the resources or timescales move beyond the percentage tolerance then the project manger would raise a formal Exception Report to the Project Board.

Any assumptions underlying plans should also be documented. The project will be influenced by a variety of external factors and will, in turn, influence the business. The project may depend upon other projects and other projects may depend upon this particular project. Other prerequisites such as the delivery of hardware and software by external suppliers can affect the plans. Any business risks in the successful implementation of the plan should be described.

Exception Plans will need to be raised when the inevitable happens and problems arise with the original plans. Exception Plans should be produced by the project manager explaining why the exception has arisen, and what the effects are on the project if no action is taken. It will examine different options and recommend recovery action. This Exception Plan will need to go to the Project Board for approval.

Project control

Control is necessary to ensure that the project stays on schedule, within budget, and delivers a quality product. PRINCE defines various control points at which reports and/or meetings occur; identifying the different roles involved and specifying how they should be involved.

Project control operates at two levels: technical and management . Technical controls are generally associated with the quality of products, and how well they meet the users' requirements. These will normally be identified through quality reviews in the SSADM phase of the project (others will be identified during testing). The approach to technical control is discussed under the heading of quality assurance later in this chapter.

Management control is mainly concerned with schedules and resources—it is exercised at senior and junior levels. The senior level involves the Project Board, the Project Manager, the Stage Manager, and the Project Assurance Team. Junior management control involves the Stage Manager, their teams and team leaders in both meetings and written reports.

Control Mechanisms

At the senior level meetings and assessments are held at the major milestones of the project: Project Initiation, Project Closure, and End Stage (possibly Mid Stage). In each case, plans and authority for the next stage are reviewed and performance during the previous stage assessed.

Project Initiation involves a meeting and a review of the Project Initiation Document to ensure that the project starts on a firm business footing with clear objectives. All staff concerned should understand their responsibilities and have the necessary authority. At the end of each stage an End Stage Assessment occurs. This reviews the performance of the stage which has just been finished against budget and schedule, and the status and quality of the end-products of the stage.

Frequent *Highlight Reports* will be produced by the Project/Stage Manager and circulated to the Project Board and Project Assurance Team. These summarize the progress on the stage so far, highlighting any problems, real or potential, and forecasting progress. Frequency of Highlight Reports would be determined by the Project Board and will depend upon the size, importance and risk of project—they should be at least monthly.

At a more junior level, *Checkpoint Meetings* are held by the Stage Manager and involve the team members. They review progress against work plans, to discuss any technical problems, and to identify targets for the next checkpoint meeting. Checkpoint Meetings are normally held weekly. Members of the Project Assurance Team may also be involved if issues of interest to them are likely to be discussed. Minutes of Checkpoint Meetings can form the basis for Highlight Reports.

Exception Reporting

Several types of exception are defined within PRINCE, and these may result in Exception Plans being raised to the Project Board.

A *Project Issue Report* can be raised at any point during the project by anyone associated with the project and could cover anything related to the project. This could be errors in the system, failure to meet requirements, ideas for improvements, changes in organization or business practice. It could also be related to management issues. Project Issue Reports are considered by the Stage Manager and Project Assurance Team. The Project Manager has final responsibility on what should happen to a Project Issue Report.

An *Off-Specification Report* documents any technical situation where the system fails to meet its specification. These are authorized by the Project Manager based on recommendations from the Project Assurance Team after their analysis of Project Issue Reports. Some assessment is required of the work needed to correct the Off-Specification Report and its impacts. Ultimately a decision will be authorized by the Project Board as to how the problem should be corrected.

Configuration management

A software project involves development of a variety of complex inter-linked products, each of which is subject to change. The process of controlling those products, ensuring that the right version is used and managing changes to products is known as configuration management. It covers the management tracking of all technical products.

Configuration management is particularly significant when it comes to the delivery of a released system. This will comprise hardware, software, data, and documentation. Unless this complex configuration is managed and controlled, chaos can occur with different team members using different versions of documents, plans, software, etc. In the PRINCE structure (Fig. 7.1) we showed the role of a configuration librarian who has overall responsibility in the project for configuration management.

Configuration Items

Configuration Items are those products, critical to the workings of the system, which must be subject to formal configuration control procedures. The project team must identify which products will become Configuration Items. The default set of Configuration Items is defined by the Product Breakdown Structures which SSADM provides for the end-products of each SSADM module. Typically these comprise any products which are carried forward into the next stage of the project. Ultimately the Configuration Items will be those that comprise the final system.

A good example of such a product in SSADM is the Required System Logical Data Model—changes to this may necessitate major changes to other products such as Entity Life Histories, Update and Enquiry Process Models, etc. This would become a Configuration Item when it passes through quality control at the end of the Requirements Specification module (however, the Project Manager could decide to 'freeze' the data model as a Configuration Item at an earlier point). It is important not to overdo the identification of Configuration Items as configuration control provides a large overhead and is normally sensible only for highly significant products on which other products are dependent.

Baselines

A released set of Configuration Items forms a system *baseline* defining a fixed reference point in the development, usually at the end of a stage. Baselines can be established at any time in the project and will be an important part of the Configuration Management Plan. This must consider which SSADM stages would become a baseline, (normally the end of each module), and which SSADM products would become Configuration Items.

Once a product has been baselined then control of it passes to the configuration librarian and a version number is allocated. Requests to change baselined products must follow formal configuration control procedures through Requests For Change or Off-Specification Reports. In this way, changes to baselined products must be sanctioned by project management.

SSADM and Configuration Management

As far as SSADM is concerned it is important that a clear definition of Configuration Items and procedures to manage them are defined early in the project in the

Configuration Plan. Roles and responsibilities for Configuration Management should also be established early. CASE tools will have considerable impact, with sophisticated tools offering some Configuration Management facilities.

Estimating

One of the most difficult tasks in Project Management is estimating the time and resources required to perform each of the activities. Usually a combination of approaches are used, ranging through the highly scientific, the completely intuitive, to the pragmatic.

As a project is being developed to meet a business need then the business must know when its need can be satisfied and how much it will cost. The business can then make decisions about whether additional resources should be applied and whether the costs justify the end-result.

Some form of estimating is necessary in the very early stages of a project in order to decide whether it is worth while to continue. Of course, estimating early in the life cycle is inherently inaccurate: the scope of the project is not completely known, technology and skills available may change, requirements may change, and unforeseen problems may arise. As the project progresses then estimates should become progressively more accurate.

Initial estimates

Early in the project life, estimating must be done top-down. We rely upon the experience of the estimator and the organization. He or she must look at the whole project, including the size of the application, the technology to be employed, and the development team. With reference to past history and previous experience, they develop an estimate based on analogy, and/or more scientifically (apparently) by calculation.

The pragmatic Project Manager will look at the required delivery date, and work backwards using the resources that he or she has. Of course, this presumes that some resources and time have already been allocated to the project, which then presumes that some estimation of the effort required has been made. These estimates may have been made by waving a finger in the air and coming up with the magical number of person months. Hopefully the estimator has some experience of similar projects on which to base an estimate.

Refined estimates

The other approach to estimation, perhaps more applicable later in the development, is a bottom-up approach. In this, the project is broken down into low-level activities and the effort for each activity is estimated. This form of estimation is necessary for planning the next phase of the development or for the whole project when a full set of requirements are known.

Function Point Analysis

A more scientific approach to estimation is to use techniques such Function Point Analysis Mark 2[1] (usually abbreviated as FPA Mark II). In FPA a metric is developed,

---

[1] Symons, C. R. (1991)*Software Sizing and Estimating: Function Point Analysis Mark 2* (Wiley, Chichester).

known as a *function point*—systems can be compared in terms of their function point counts. A 1000 function point system should have twice as much functionality as a 500 function point system. Function Point Analysis has been used quite extensively in conjunction with SSADM and seems to provide a fairly effective approach to estimating the time taken to develop software from an SSADM Requirements Specification. Function points can be simply calculated from components of the SSADM specification.

The Mark 2 Function Point method calculates the size of a system by first estimating the number of unadjusted function points, and then multiplying these by an adjustment factor for technical complexity to give a total size of the system. The unadjusted function points map very closely to the SSADM events and enquiries. These are known in FPA as 'logical transactions'. Their size is based upon the number of input and output data items and the number of different entity types navigated in the transaction. We can simply go through our Enquiry Access Paths and Effect Correspondence Diagrams along with the I/O Structures to give an estimate of unadjusted function points.

The adjustment applies 19 Technical Complexity Adjustment factors, plus any others that are specific to the particular project or organization. These factors include data communications, training needs, transaction rates, and others—using various criteria the level of each adjustment is determined.

Once the system size has been estimated using function point analysis then we can estimate the effort required by dividing the size by the productivity. Productivity is measured in person hours per function point. Productivity can be first estimated and then calibrated by measuring previous projects with similar characteristics and environments. From the anticipated effort in person hours then elapsed time can be calculated by taking into account other factors, such as the number of person hours available, including such factors as holidays, dependency upon other projects or delivery of other products.

Other factors need also to be taken into account which may be unpredictable, such as relations with users, staff expertise, the time taken to adapt to new methods and tools, etc. You can only estimate effectively if you have a history of past projects. It is thus most important to collect metrics about your organization's performance on previous projects. Many organizations fail to collect any metrics—they cannot learn effectively from experience.

Some CASE tools include facilities for calculating function points from the specification built by the CASE tool. There are also specific estimating tools which are stand-alone. Some project management support tools also include facilities for estimation.

Early estimation in a project can be based around the initial Logical Data Structures and Data Flow Diagrams. These can give approximate function point counts which can then be refined as the project progresses. These approximations can be used as the basis for detailed estimating of the next phase of the project and for high-level estimating for the whole project. As the project progresses, the estimates should become more detailed and hopefully more accurate.

Quality assurance

It is very important to ensure that the products from each stage are technically correct and that they meet the objectives of the users. Each stage builds on the work done in the previous stage. Obviously, with poor foundations, there is a high risk that all subsequent work will be poor.

At the end of each SSADM stage a formal quality assurance review of its end-products is suggested. This involves: identifying and educating reviewers, sending them documentation and responding to any queries, a formal meeting and follow-up actions, and eventual sign-off of products to the next stage of the project. This should be done on a formal basis, to force the correction of errors identified by the reviewers before work is allowed to proceed to the subsequent stages.

A sign-off by a group consisting principally of users emphasizes the joint responsibility for the project of both the users and the project team. This ensures the continuing active interest of the users in the project and helps avoid the situation commonly met in systems development when poor communication between the project team and the users leads to an implemented system that does not meet the users' requirements.

Products from each stage should be reviewed by a team of responsible and representative users who can authorize changes in the working environment. The review team should include at least one 'technical reviewer' who has a good understanding of systems development and SSADM (this may be the Technical Assurance Coordinator).

There is a danger that users may feel 'rail-roaded' or 'blackmailed' into signing-off large specification documents which they haven't had time to read and barely understand. Project and user management has a clear responsibility to ensure that this does **not** happen. This means that users are trained to review SSADM products, that users are informally 'walked through' all significant products before the formal review, that users are given sufficient time to read and digest the documentation, and that users' views are listened to, understood, and acted upon by the project team.

Review Procedures

The following procedures are an example of how a quality assurance review might be undertaken in a project using SSADM.

Before the review The project team and the Project Assurance Team select the reviewers and fix a time and place. All participants receive a Quality Review Invitation one week in advance of the meeting, together with a neat copy of all the documents they will be required to review.

If any of the reviewers is unfamiliar with the conventions of the diagrams, then the analysts might arrange to explain the aspects of the diagrams that are relevant to a reviewer. This can be done on a one-to-one basis, but can be achieved more efficiently, when a number of people are involved, by organizing a presentation to state the purpose and basic conventions of the diagrams with a more general discussion about quality assurance review procedures.

The reviewers study the product and note errors. The SSADM Reference Manual provides default Product Descriptions and review checklists which can be used to guide reviewers in what to look for. These quality criteria may have been revised in the quality plan.

The review meeting The actual review should not be more than two hours long. The chairman is either a user who has been closely involved with the project or the project team manager. The meeting begins with the circulation of an agenda, possibly some introductions, and a clear statement of the objectives of the meeting. The meeting should not attempt to solve errors, but simply to highlight them for subsequent resolution away from the meeting. An analyst from the project team talks through the documentation being reviewed and invites comments from the reviewers. A list of errors is compiled by the chairman on the Follow-Up Action List and agreed by the meeting.

The reviewers may decide that the documentation contains no errors and meets its objectives, in which case they will sign the stage off at this meeting. More commonly, there will be a number of non-critical errors detected, in which case the documentation may be signed off provided that certain follow-up action is taken and subsequently agreed by the reviewers out of the meeting. If there are many severe errors, and the reviewers are not confident that the project team have met the objectives of the stage, then a date for another quality assurance review is set and the documentation failed.

After the review Any necessary corrections are made to the documentation within a week of the review and circulated to the members of the review team. If the errors are only minor, the reviewers may sign it off individually. If the errors are more serious, the documentation is reviewed again.

The resources required to hold a quality assurance review are significant and should not be underestimated when planning. At least three elapsed weeks should be allowed for each formal review, and one to two weeks for informal reviews. It is tempting to cut this time when project timescales are tight. But compared to the weeks or months that might be wasted later in the project sorting out compounded errors arising from poor quality assurance, it is time well spent.

Risk analysis

Risk analysis attempts to determine the risks to a project. Risk management minimizes the chance of risks occurring and contains them if they do occur.

In all projects some risk analysis should be undertaken. In the largest projects it should be a significant exercise. As with estimating, the level of risk can be assessed more accurately as the project progresses. We recommend that all projects conduct some risk analysis at the end of each SSADM stage.

Two major methods are employed in risk analysis: a qualitative approach using questionnaires, or a quantitative approach using statistical analysis. Questionnaire approaches can be specific to the organization and to the type of project—they are based on experience and some commercial PC packages are available. These help identify and rank the different risk factors applicable to the project. The qualitative approach can be used to decide what the main threats are and then quantitative techniques can be used to forecast how big the problem actually is. In practice, it is often sensible to use a combination of the two approaches.

The most significant risks are always difficult to spot until after they have happened but a good project manager should be aware of all risks and the factors that could cause them. Most importantly they must communicate these risks to their managers and to their project team to help avoid or contain them if they do occur.

Management need to be convinced that the cost of risk containment is justified. For example, we might assess as high risk the fact that the users will not accept the system we deliver. To contain this risk we could involve the users more with prototyping, hold more progress meetings with our users, spend longer on training, and put more effort into quality assurance with users. All this extra effort will cost—a management decision needs to be made as to whether the risks should be taken or contained, but it is better to decide in knowledge rather than in ignorance.

7.2   Customizing SSADM

In this book we have presented SSADM as if we work through every task of every stage of the method. In practice, development projects do not work like this. Every SSADM project that we have seen has customized the method to some degree.

The structural model presented in this book should be regarded as a default—the normal model is a customized one. Of course, to customize you must understand what the basic approach is. Our aim has been to teach the standard approach so that you understand how the techniques and activities defined by SSADM fit together. With this understanding you are in a strong position to adapt the method to your particular project circumstances.

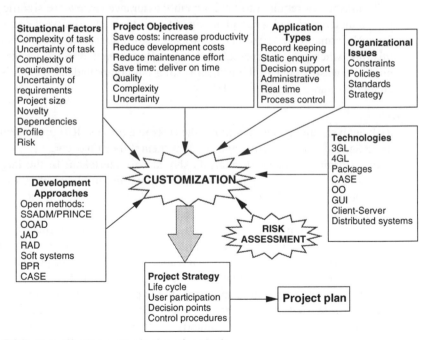

Fig. 7.2 Factors affecting customization of methods

In Fig. 7.2 we summarize some of the influences that can lead to customization of any development approach. Clearly there are a huge number of factors that can affect a project—to discuss fully the ideas involved in Fig. 7.2 would require an entire book.

This section discusses some of the ways in which the structural model and the techniques can be adapted. We also discuss some combinations of SSADM with other information systems ideas.

What is SSADM?

This may seem a rather strange question. To customize SSADM we need to have an idea about what is **core** so that we can preserve its basic ideas and still regard the approach that we have used as SSADM.

Most opponents of SSADM will attack the complex structure of SSADM in terms of its steps and stages. However, SSADM should not be seen as a pure structural model that has to be followed religiously. Two other models of SSADM have recently been developed which can help us to understand what is core and key to SSADM. Below in Fig 7.3 we show the Systems Development Template. This attempts to represent the concerns of information systems development that SSADM addresses.

In the centre is a conventional systems life cycle from Investigation to Specification and ultimately to Construction. The Investigation phase maps in the default structural model to the Feasibility and Requirements Analysis modules of SSADM. The Specification phase maps to: Requirements Specification, Logical Systems Specification, and Physical Design. The Construction phase is only partially covered by SSADM although many projects may use CASE to generate elements of the construction in the Specification phase.

The Decision Structure in the template encompasses any of the decision-making processes that are part of the SSADM structure. These include Feasibility Options, Business System Options, and Technical System Options.

The User Environment includes the definition of User Roles and their interaction with the system. Not fully covered by SSADM, although highly relevant to the success of the new information system are features such as the training of users and any manual organizational structure changes required for the new information system.

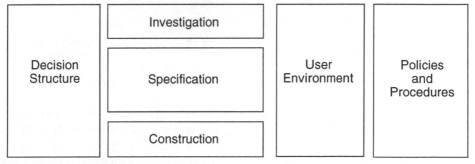

Fig. 7.3 The Systems Development Template

Policies and Procedures cover any installation or system-wide standards that apply to the development. These may include style guides, naming standards, technical standards, and quality standards. In this book we have described the Installation and Application Style Guides which are the only policies and procedures explicitly defined by SSADM.

The Systems Development Template is a useful way of looking at the aspects of development considered by SSADM. Other activities, not covered by SSADM, could be brought into the template to handle specific concerns for the project. For example, Soft Systems Analysis, Job Design, and Task Analysis could all find a place under User Environment for some projects; Government procurement standards could be appropriate under Policies and Procedures; and for some projects a Package Selection Technique could be useful in Decision Structure.

Three Schema Specification Architecture

The key SSADM techniques produce the specification models which can be represented by the *Three Schema Specification Architecture* (Fig. 7.4). This concentrates on the products which will turn into executable program code. It divides the specification into three components: the conceptual model; the external design; and the internal design.

The *external design* reflects the users' perspective of the system through menus, dialogues, screens, reports, and batch processing. Function Definitions and their associated I/O Structures will provide a detailed view of how the user interacts with the system. Associated with these will be the Dialogue Designs including Dialogue Structures, Command and Menu Structures. In Physical Design these become the Function Component Implementation Map,

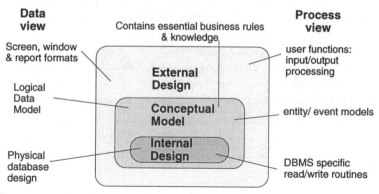

Fig. 7.4 Components of the Three Schema Specification Architecture

The *conceptual model* represents the underlying model of the system; it comprises the data model and the event and enquiry processing associated with it. The conceptual model reflects the business rules that constrain the system—whatever interface or functionality are developed. The SSADM products associated with this would be the Logical Data Model, Entity Life Histories, Effect Correspondence Diagrams, Enquiry Access Paths, and the Enquiry and Update Process Models.

The *internal design* considers how we map onto storage technology by defining the Physical Data Design and how the event and enquiry processing is handled by the physical database. It thus includes the Physical Data Design and the Process Data Interface. Performance considerations will be considered in the internal design. To a large extent the activities concerned with producing the internal design are part of the Physical Design module.

This Three Schema Architecture is a very powerful way of visualizing SSADM. Figure 7.5 shows how the SSADM specification products are interlinked and how they fit into the architecture. The Three Schema Architecture also gives us a good basis for customizing SSADM. We can use it to add in additional products or remove products as appropriate to particular project circumstances.

Dependence on certain time-consuming techniques can be reduced for rapid development. For instance, we could base our specification on the Effect Correspondence Diagrams and Enquiry Access Paths. We could base our external design directly on Function Definitions without going through the intermediate step of developing Data Flow Models.

We can use the Three Schema Architecture as a basis for incremental delivery. Having defined a conceptual model, we can select functions for external design and construction, and can select parts of the conceptual model for internal design and construction. In this way, we can deliver business benefits to our users early in the project but with a sound foundation for integrating further increments later.

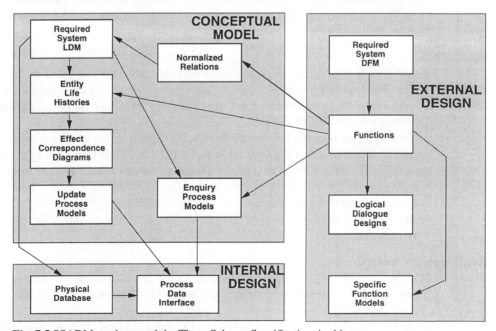

Fig. 7.5 SSADM products and the Three Schema Specification Architecture

The Three Schema Architecture maps closely to the Client-Server model. Server data and processing are defined by the conceptual model and mapped into the internal design. The Client would be defined by the external design which would include all of the dialogue design, screen definitions, and screen validation processing.

Much new systems development is based around graphical user interfaces (GUIs) and the International SSADM Users Group has developed a guide on how SSADM can be used in these environments.[1] This suggests additional techniques, such as user object modelling and interface prototyping within the external design component. It also extends the User Environment part of the template to include task modelling.

Customizing the SSADM Structural Model

The SSADM structural model consists of the stages, steps, and tasks of each of the SSADM modules. Throughout Chapters 3, 4, 5, and 6 of this book we have followed this structure using examples from the Yorkies case study. The first section in each of these chapters gave the structural model for the module and further sections were devoted to each of the steps.

There are many possibilities for customizing the different modules of SSADM. It can involve the addition of new techniques to deal with particular project circumstances, such as a requirement to define detailed manual procedures within the SSADM project, or to define complex human–computer interfaces. It can involve attempts to reduce the resources required for analysis and design whilst minimizing the risk of failure to deliver a satisfactory product. It could involve attempts to shorten the delivery time but by adding considerable resources. Below we consider each of the SSADM modules and discuss how they might be customized.

Feasibility

Feasibility is regarded as an optional phase within SSADM and many projects do not use it. The feasibility of these projects could be determined by an information systems strategy or perhaps the project is a 'must have'. In this book we have only dealt with Feasibility briefly in Appendix E.

Some project managers may feel that the SSADM approach to Feasibility is rather overkill. The production of Logical and Required Data Flow Diagrams is perhaps hard to justify. The minimum set of products produced should be a prioritized Requirements Catalogue, an Outline Data Model, and a Context Diagram. From these a set of combined Technical and Business Systems Options must be presented to the user, each containing a Cost/Benefit Analysis and an Impact Analysis, although they may be at a very high level.

Requirements Analysis

The key objective of this step is to understand the current system in sufficient detail to produce a prioritized set of requirements to build different designs of the system at

[1] International SSADM User's Group (1994) *SSADM and GUI Design: A Project Manager's Guide* (HMSO, London).

Business Systems Options. If a Feasibility Study has been performed this will reduce the work and constrain the options produced by this module.

The default structural model for the module involves the construction of Current Physical Data Flow Diagrams and conversion to a logical set. One way of customization is to move directly to the development of a Logical Data Flow Model, though this can require skilled analysts and can be more difficult to validate with users. More radically, Data Flow Models might be omitted entirely from the step with solely a Requirements Catalogue and Context Diagram produced.

Other ways of customizing the analysis are to incorporate techniques such as soft systems analysis[1] to help gain a clearer idea of the requirements and to investigate the human activity systems that surround the information system. Soft systems, by its use of rich pictures and holistic analysis, can look more at the human side of the information system—one that is often critical to its success. Other forms of business activity modelling such as those associated with business process re-engineering may also be introduced into the module.

Other extensions could include using Joint Applications Definition (JAD). This involves setting up intensive sessions with a small group of users and analysts to thrash out requirements. Typically two or three analysts (with CASE tools and administrative support) plus five or six senior and middle managers from the user organization ensconce themselves in a interruption-free environment for a set period of time. They aim to produce a detailed prioritized set of requirements for the new system, plus a Logical Data Structure and Data Flow Model.

Another possibility is to bring some of the SSADM techniques used later into the early stages of the analysis. For example, relational data analysis might be used to help produce the current environment data model, specification prototyping might be used to clarify some of the requirements, or to demonstrate some of the business options. If reduced reliance was placed on data flow diagramming then perhaps some early event identification could help specify the functionality of the system.

The techniques themselves can be adapted and extended. For example, Data Flow Diagrams could be extended by the use of some of the real-time notations if these were appropriate. Use of process hierarchy diagrams[2] instead of a full set of Data Flow Diagrams might reduce the workload without substantially increasing the risk to the project.

We feel it is most important that a Business Systems Option stage is considered as this involves the clients of the project in determining its direction and ensuring that the development meets the business need. Of course, the extent to which the Business System Options are developed will depend upon the size and profile of the project.

Requirements Specification

As this module is the most complex in SSADM, it offers the most scope for customization. The development of the Requirements Specification module involves

---

[1] Checkland, P. and Scholes, J.E. (1991) *Soft Systems Methodology in Action* (Wiley, Chichester).

[2] These show each process with its sub-processes. They can be shown by a hierarchy diagram or, more conveniently, by indented lists—easily produced on a word processor with an outline facility.

considerable iteration between functions and event/entity models. The system is portrayed in a variety of different ways: a conceptual view through the Logical Data Model and the event/entity models, and a user/external view through the Function Definitions. Each shift in perspective may identify further changes.

The Required System Data Flow Model is not an end-product of the stage and could be left out—Function Definitions being produced directly from the chosen Business System Options and the Logical Data Flow Model. Functions will be validated later by event-entity modelling. However, it is important to define any input and output processing which would normally have been documented on the Elementary Process Descriptions that went with the Data Flow Models. Many projects do find Data Flow Diagrams very useful and another form of customization might be to combine the steps that produce the Required System Data Flow Model and the functions together. There would then be a very close mapping between the functions and the processes.

SSADM specifically requires certain customization within this module. For instance, the amount of prototyping and relational data analysis to be performed is determined by project management—only critical functions are subjected to these analyses. If the team were confident that their Logical Data Model was fully normalized and that they had identified all attributes they might omit step 340, *enhance required data model*, altogether.

Some customization often occurs with event-entity modelling. This can include leaving this out altogether—but many experts would consider that **not** SSADM. The production of Entity Life Histories can be time consuming and difficult. The team must be certain that the complex interdependencies of events reflect the business rules that the software should satisfy. We have seen projects that have produced extremely complex Entity Life Histories only for them to be ignored by the constructors of the system.

The Entity/Event Matrix, although not formally required as an end-product of the stage, can be extremely useful. The matrix can be used to customize the event-entity modelling technique—selecting only those entities with the most complex lives for further analysis. For these entities only some events may need to be modelled in the life history (those we are interested in validating the previous states of)—this approach can simplify Entity Life Histories but it is not pure SSADM. Similarly we can identify from the matrix the events which interact with many different entities and only build the complex Effect Correspondence Diagrams.

If very rapid development is required, the Event/Entity Matrix plus some brief event description (perhaps including the Effect Correspondence Diagram) could be the specification mechanism for all update processing. Enquiries could be coded directly in SQL from Function Definitions.

Less dramatic customization of event-entity modelling also occurs. Some popular modifications are: adding state indicators early (normally done in Stage 5) to help check that the structures are correct, using a different syntax for the operations, adding operations to and showing the type of effect on Effect Correspondence Diagrams (whether Create, Modify, Delete, or Read).

If a Graphical User Interface is being developed then further techniques might be employed to produce a better design. The GUI guide (see page 458) suggests that user object modelling, task analysis, task modelling, and more extensive use of prototyping are incorporated into the Requirements Specification module.

Logical Systems Specification

The Technical Systems Options stage is of minor significance to some projects as their hardware and software architecture is already determined. However, a decision should be made at this point about the project's future. There will also usually be some technical decisions to be made.

The approach to dialogue design in SSADM works well for traditional character-based interfaces but for Graphical User Interfaces we recommend following the approach of the previously mentioned GUI guide.

Many projects using relational databases find the use of Update and Enquiry Process Models unnecessary. These projects will often construct directly from Effect Correspondence Diagrams and Enquiry Access Paths—adding operations to these from the Entity Life Histories.

Physical Design

This module explicitly requires customization in its first step 610, *prepare for physical design*. As all development environments are different it is even harder to give specific guidance to this phase of the project. Each of the steps in Stage 6 is designed to be customized using the Physical Design Strategy developed at the beginning of the stage. This customization was described in Chapter 6, Physical Design.

7.3   Computer Assisted Systems Engineering (CASE)

Imagine the following scenario. You are sitting with a user in front of your PC with a high-definition graphic screen and a Windows environment. While discussing with the user you identify several entities and draw them on the screen using the mouse. You draw relationships between the entities. You then decide that the positioning is not quite right, maybe you have a dead crow! You point at the entity box and move it towards the bottom of the screen, its relationships' lines follow. You then decide to define some attributes for the entity. You double-click with your mouse on the entity box and a new window opens, prompting you to enter attributes. You have already entered some attributes associated with input and output data flows. This list is available to you, so you select several attributes to include in your entity and define a primary key.

You then switch to the Data Flow Model because you have identified further attributes that belong to the entity which the CASE tool tells you are not included in the Data Catalogue. You need to define some new flows which contain these attributes in the Data Flow Diagram. You open the Data Flow Diagram, displaying it on the screen at level 1. You identify the appropriate process to handle this data flow, double click on the level 1 process, to display the level 2 diagram. Selecting a particular icon you create a new process box, name it, draw an input flow from an existing external entity. Double-clicking on the data flow arrow allows you to include some attributes that you have already defined to go with your new entity. You then run a consistency check on the diagram and it tells you that you have an input flow to a process but no output flow, identifying which process is incomplete.

Later on in the project you move on to event/entity modelling. To help you identify events the CASE tool produces a report of input data flows updating data stores. From this you identify events and with the aid of the cross-reference between the data stores and entities you identify which entities are updated by the events. In this way you start to build your Event/Entity Matrix. When you are satisfied with the level of detail in your matrix, you then move on to developing Entity Life Histories and by selecting an entity in the matrix, you display all the events that affect it.

You then build a Jackson structure around these events—the CASE tool ensures that you conform with the proper Jackson syntax. You add operations and can generate Effect Correspondence Diagrams from the complete set of Entity Life Histories. As you progress you can generate Update Process Models from the Effect Correspondence Diagrams carrying through the operations that you first defined on the Entity Life Histories.

At any time you may choose to print out high-quality documentation and submit it to the user. Other members of the project team will have access to your model in the CASE tool but sophisticated access control procedures prevent them from updating it without your permission. At a later point in the development, you may decide to generate your database design—the CASE tool can produce the SQL definitions which will create the database structure.

From the Enquiry Access Paths or Enquiry Process Models the CASE tool will generate the SQL necessary to perform the enquiries. Skeleton screens might be produced from I/O Structures held on the tool. You can then position them on the screen to suit the user's requirements and demonstrate a prototype to the user for validation.

All of these features are available today in some CASE tools supporting SSADM. At the time of publication there are more than ten products that claim to support SSADM. These range from highly sophisticated, expensive, integrated CASE tools that will generate working COBOL code on mainframes to stand-alone products on PCs that help to draw Data Flow Diagrams and are available as shareware. There is a general set of features that you can expect in a CASE tool that supports SSADM such as diagramming facilities, reporting facilities, cross-checking, and generation of code. Products vary in how well they provide such features. Below we discuss some of these features suggesting how they fit within an SSADM context.

Diagramming facilities

We should be able to show all SSADM diagram types with specific icons for each of the symbols. There should be a good interface on the screen for drawing and repositioning objects. When we reposition an object then all of the connecting lines, and their labels, should follow. We should be able to zoom in and pan out on diagrams so that we can progress from a detailed level to an overview level in the same picture.

Once we have drawn any diagram we should be able to record the objects in the underlying repository and recreate the diagram. Some tools have generation facilities that provide automatic redrafting of diagrams with a more aligned look about them. Another facility is that of drawing direct lines rather than orthogonal lines, angling text to align with the line. The diagramming tool should support the underlying semantics of the model. For example, Data Flow Diagram drawing tool should not allow direct flows between two data stores and an Entity Life History drawing tool should not permit children of different types (e.g. mixing selections and iterations).

Repository

A repository[1] is where all of the information about the development is stored. Ideally this would include everything from users' initial requirements through to working program code. In all the SSADM phases of the project, the repository is a database that includes all of the SSADM products interlinked in the way prescribed by the method. To do this the underlying database should follow the meta model of SSADM. This means that there will be entities in the meta model called 'entities', 'relationships', 'events', 'effects', 'processes', 'functions', 'data flows', etc.

The graphics should interact with the repository. Thus, when we draw an entity in a diagram, its corresponding database record should also be created. When we further describe that entity with an Entity Description the attributes held on the repository are displayed for entry into the entity. This will only be possible if there are good links between the repository and diagramming facilities.

Holding the information in a structured way in a repository allows a variety of important things to be done: the information can be represented in other ways, consistency and completeness checks can be applied, complex reports can be produced, data definition and program code can be generated.

Repository information can be exchanged with other CASE tools via standard interchange formats. This allows a variety of CASE tools to be used on the same project, each being best of breed for their particular stage. Thus a tool with a good graphical interface could be used in the analysis and design stages and that information ported into a mainframe repository or data dictionary package, and other components passed to a fourth generation environment for construction.

Representing the data

Because the information is held in the repository we can view that information in many different ways. For example, the information associated with the Data Flow Models is a hierarchy of processes. We might prefer to show that information, instead of as a set of Data Flow Diagrams decomposing at each level, as a process hierarchy whereby we see which processes our Level 1 processes break into, and so on down the hierarchy.

We may also wish to switch on and off certain features of the diagram for formal presentation to users. For example, we might prefer not to show relationship statements on the Logical Data Structure, or we might choose to pick only part of the data structure

---

[1]Repositories are also known as systems encyclopaedias or, rather less grandly, data dictionaries. However, these terms have slightly different connotations—since IBM's ill-fated A/D Cycle project, repository has become the preferred term.

for printing and presentation to users. A good CASE tool should allow different representations of the underlying data held in the repository to be generated.

The same is true of reporting facilities. There should be in-built reports, such as lists of attributes in each entity showing primary and foreign keys, but a degree of customization should be possible to present these reports in whatever way is most useful to the analyst or user.

Generation of other products

Having the information in a repository in a structured format allows various forms of generation to be performed by the CASE tool. Because some of the transformations required in SSADM are relatively mechanical then a degree of computer assistance can be provided to these from CASE software. For instance, some products are able, given a full set of Entity Life Histories with operations, to produce Effect Correspondence Diagrams and then convert them into Update Process Models. Generation of state indicator values from the Entity Life History is also possible.

Most CASE products have the ability to generate database schema definitions from the Logical Data Model. Thus the Entity Descriptions, Relationship Descriptions, and Attribute Descriptions held in the repository can be transformed to different variants of SQL for various relational database products. Some products can generate skeleton screens for prototyping from the I/O Structures or I/O Descriptions held in the tool using the formats given in the Attribute/Data Item Descriptions. The analyst can lay the various fields out on the screen and add messages as appropriate. Some CASE products generate working procedural program code from the various processing models used in SSADM. At the time of writing no product has particularly sophisticated facilities in this area.

Appendix A   SSADM Glossary

Acknowledgement

This Appendix contains the official SSADM glossary reprinted from the SSADM Version 4 Reference Manual with full permission.

Conventions

Headings for glossary entries have been shown in bold. Within each glossary entry cross-references to other glossary entries are shown in italics.

We have followed the conventions used by the SSADM Version 4 Reference Manual concerning the use of capitalization:

The following terms do use capitals:

- *product* names
- *Module, Stage* and *Step* names
- acronyms
- the words/terms Module, Stage, Step, Project Procedures, Procedural Standards and Structural Standards.

The following terms do not use capitals:

- techniques
- *'objects'*, such as *enquiry function.*

Terms and definitions

1NF see *normal form.*

2NF see *normal form.*

3NF see *normal form.*

acceptance (testing) criteria These criteria set out the details of how the final implemented *system* is required to perform specific tasks so that the users are satisfied that it caters for their needs. Initial details will be compiled based on SSADM documentation, but will require further development outside of SSADM .

access path This is the route to be taken through the *Logical Data Model* from an entry point to the *entity*, or *entities*, required for a particular piece of processing.

The *Logical Data Model* is constructed with a view to implementing update processing, so 'update processing *access paths*' are not documented separately (*Effect Correspondence Diagrams* show this detail). 'Enquiry processing *access paths*' need to be documented explicitly.

Action Plan see *Plan.*

Activity Descriptions Activities within SSADM Steps all *effect* transformations in one or more *products.* The description for an 'activity' details what the transformation is, the inputs, the references, and the participants.

Activity Network Places all of the activities into logical sequence, thus enabling timescales to be estimated and work to be scheduled.

***ad-hoc* enquiry** An enquiry which is not pre-defined but is created by the user as and when it is needed.
Ad-hoc enquiries are documented for each applicable *user role* as individual *Function Definitions.*

Analysis of Requirements This forms the *Module Product* from the *Requirements Analysis Module.* It consists of the *Current Services Description, Requirements Catalogue, User Catalogue* and the *Selected Business System Option.*

Application Development Standards Defines the standards which apply to the *physical design* and development activities, for this *project*/application.

Application Naming Standards Defines the naming conventions for all aspects of the application under development, with particular emphasis being placed on constraints imposed by the (physical) implementations environment.

Application Style Guide Should be regarded as a set of standards, covering the user interface, to be followed within a particular application development. This document is based on the *Installation Style Guide* and tailored to the specific needs of this *project.*

Assemble Investigation Results Step 160. The aim is to compile the *Current Services Description,* ensuring there is consistency across *products.*

Assemble Logical Design Step 540. The aim is to compile the *Logical Design,* ensuring there is consistency across *products.*

Assemble Physical Design Step 670. The aim is to compile the *Physical Design,* ensuring that there is consistency across *products.*

Assemble Requirements Specification Step 380. The aim is to compile the *Requirements Specification,* ensuring there is consistency across *products.*

Assemble the Feasibility Report Step 040. The aim is to present the *feasibility options* so that a recommended solution is proposed and the *process* documented in the *Feasibility Report.*

attribute A characteristic property of an *entity* type, that is, any detail that serves to describe, qualify, identify, classify, quantify or express the state of an *entity.* If possible the logical *attributes* for an *entity* will be translated directly into *data items* within the physical representation.

An *attribute* may be optional for an *entity*, meaning that it does not apply to all occurrences of the *entity*.

Attribute/Data Item Description Each description within this set documents all known details about an *attribute (data item)* in the logical *system*. Details are later translated into the physical *data item(s)* for the implementation of the *system*.

baseline A snapshot of the state of a *configuration item* and its *component configuration items* at an instant in time. *Baselines*, plus approved changes from those *baselines,* constitute the current identification of a *configuration item.*

batch A logical grouping of *events* (or *functions*) which always happen within the same time-frame. See *group of events.*

bottom-level process A *process* on a *Data Flow Diagram* which is not further decomposed into another *Data Flow Diagram.*

business role A unit of knowledge about the business *requirements* expressed in the *Logical Design*. A *business role* may be detailed within any aspect of the *Logical Design*, for example on the *Required System Logical Data Model, Data Catalogue*, and the *Update Process Model.*

BSO see *business system option*, or *Business System Options* or *Selected Business System Option*

business system option Is the means by which users agree the new application's desired functionality with developers. *BSOs* are used to define the functionality needs and the boundary for the *system*, with reference to the business needs.

Business System Options Stage 2. The aim is to take the *Requirements Catalogue, Current Services Description* and *User Catalogue* and use this information as the basis on which to decide the most appropriate way for development to meet the business needs.
This stage has two steps:
210—Define Business System Options
220—Select Business System Option.

Business System Options The set of *Business System Options* which is compiled so that a selection can be made.

capacity planning Used to predict the (hardware/software) configuration required to satisfy the constraints and *requirements* of the proposed *system*.
It is also used to assist in the development of service level agreements (outside of SSADM).

Capacity Planning Input Processing and data information is passed outside of SSADM activities to *capacity planning* techniques, explicitly during development of *Technical System Options.*

CBA see *Cost/Benefit Analysis.*

CI see *configuration item.*

CM see *configuration management.*

Command Structure Shows the directions that control can take when a user decides to complete or terminate a particular *dialogue*. This allows navigation to be implemented with or without *menus*.

common process An aspect of processing which is identified as common to several *processes* (or *functions*) within an SSADM *system* specification. Functionality such as a calculation of entitlement under a benefits scheme or discount arrangements may occur in more than one *process* or *function.*

Details for each *common process* need to be documented in an *Elementary Process Description* with the relevant cross-references. These may be carried forward as part of the *Function Definitions* within the *Requirements Specification. Common processes* are vital *components* of the *Physical Design,* documented in the *Function Component Implementation Map.*

Complete Function Specification Step 650. The aim is to specify the procedural *components* of the *Function Component Implementation Map,* and resolve outstanding structure clashes.

component An *object* represented in the *Function Component Implementation Map*, usually typed as one of the following: *super function, function, I/O process, database process, common process.*

composite data flow A *data flow* on a *Data Flow Diagram* which is decomposed into 'simpler' *data flows* on a lower-level *Data Flow Diagram.*

configuration item A *component* of a configuration that has a defined *function* and is designated for *configuration management. Configuration items* may vary widely in complexity, size, and type from a complete *system* including hardware, software and documentation, to an algorithm shared by several *programs.*

configuration management A set of techniques and procedures which provide the mechanisms for managing a configuration (a logically related set of modules which need to be managed as a composite set). It is used to ensure that *configuration items* are produced as required for a *project.*

Within SSADM this technique can be assumed to control *product* access to the *Structural Model information highway.*

Confirm System Objectives Step 370. The aim is to ensure that all the *functional requirements* on the *Requirements Catalogue* have the relevant *non-functional requirements* associated with them.

Consolidate Process Data Interface Step 660. The aim is to specify all aspects of the *Process Data Interface,* if one is required.

Context Diagram This may be drawn to illustrate the initial scope of the proposed *system* The diagram concentrates on the major inputs and outputs of the *system* and shows the external sources and recipients of *system* data.

control flow On the *Structural Model, control flows* indicate explicit management control being exerted over the activities being undertaken. This may be to stop, start or repeat activities.

Core SSADM   This is the central, fundamental, part of SSADM and refers to the following *Modules:*

Feasibility Study	(FS)
Requirements Analysis	(RA)
Requirements Specification	(RS)
Logical System Specification	(LS)
Physical Design	(PD).

Cost/Benefit Analysis   A formal *Cost/Benefit Analysis* is an objective way to judge the merit of one option against another. This forms the vital financial part of the specification of each option (business or technical).

Create Function Component Implementation Map   Step 630. The aim is to specify those *components* of *functions* which were not included in the *Logical Design*.

Create Physical Data Design   Step 620. The aim is to develop a *Physical Data Design* that implements the *Required System Logical Data Model* on the target *DBMS*. This is a *product* specific 'first-cut' design and not the optimized *version*.

current environment   A generic term for the *current services* (computer and manual) and the 'wish list' for the future *system*. Where no current *system* exists this will simply reflect the 'wish list' for the new *system*.

Current Environment Logical Data Model   Provides a detailed description of the information used or produced by the *current environment*. It is developed during the *Requirements Analysis Module* and forms part of the *Current Services Description*. See *Product Description* for *Logical Data Model*.

Current Physical Data Flow Model   Shows how the *current services* are organized and processing is undertaken. An overview of *current services* is provided by documenting only the level 1 *Data Flow Diagram*. See *Product Description* for *Data Flow Model*.

current services   A generic term which encompasses all existing processing within the business area being addressed by the *project*, irrespective of whether those *functions* are manual or computerized.

Current Services Description   Provides the details of the logicalized current *system* which, with the *Requirements Catalogue* and *User Catalogue*, is output from *Stage 1: Investigation of Current Environment*.

Data Catalogue   The central repository for all the descriptive information about items of data. This includes physical details which may be found during *data flow modelling* activities as well as *physical design* activities. *Logical data modelling* will provide information about *attributes* (the logical equivalent to *data items*). See *Attribute/Data Item Description* and *Grouped Domain Description*.

data flow   Shows where data is being passed between different elements on a *Data Flow Diagram*. The name associated with the *data flow* should be meaningful to those reviewing the *Data Flow Diagram*.

Data flows will pass into and out of the *system* and between *processes* (generally via *data stores* except on the *Current Physical Data Flow Model* where *process*-to-*process* flows may reflect inadequacies in the current *system*). When the *system* boundary is being defined there may even be *data flows* between external entities.

At the lowest level of the *Data Flow Diagram* these are 'simple' *data flows*, though they may be combined into *'composite data flows'* on higher-level diagrams.

Data Flow Diagram Shows how services are organized and processing is undertaken. It should be a simple diagram that is readily understood, so that it can act as an effective means of communication between analysts and users. See *Data Flow Model*.

Data Flow Model A set of *Data Flow Diagrams* and their associated documentation. The diagrams form a hierarchy with the *Data Flow Diagram* level 1 showing the scope of the *system* and the lower-level diagrams expanding the detail as appropriate. Additional documentation provides a description of the processes, input/output *data flows* and external entities.

data flow modelling Is used to help define the scope of the *system* and ensure that the analysts have a clear understanding of the user's problems and *requirements*.

The technique is used to build a model of the information flows and not to define the detail of the processing performed by the *system*.

data item An element or field of a *data store* (which should be held within an *entity* type on the *Logical Data Structure*). A *data item* is any detail that serves to describe, qualify, identify, classify, quantify or express the state of the *data store*. The logical *attributes* for an *entity* will, in general, translate directly into *data items* within the physical representation.

Data Item/Attribute Description Synonym for *Attribute/Data Item Description*.

data store A collection of any type of data in any form as represented on a *Data Flow Diagram*. This may be a computer file or a box of documents or any other means of storing data. *Data stores* may be standing, long-term files such as sales and purchase ledgers, or short-term accumulations such as daily *batches* of documents.

Database Management System The mechanism for managing data held within a computerized *system*. Conceptually data is held within one file regardless of how the content is physically organized.

database process A physical *process* to be applied to the implemented database. The valid *processes* will vary depending on the *DBMS* used for implementation. They will include read and write *operations* to varying levels of sophistication.

DBA abbreviation for Database Administrator.

DBMS see *Database Management System*.

DBMS Data Storage Classification For analysing and recording data storage and retrieval mechanisms of *DBMS* or file handler.

DBMS Performance Classification Records the factors which impact on the performance of a *DBMS* or file handler.

Define Business System Options Step 210. The aim is to compile several *Business System Options,* in outline, covering the possible solutions to all or part of the user *requirement*.

Define Enquiry Processes Step 530. The aim is to expand the description of processing *requirements* for all the enquiry *functions* identified within the *Requirements Specification.*

Define Required System Processing Step 310. The aim is to update the *Logical Data Flow Model* so that it fits within the scope of the *system* as set in the *Selected Business System Option.*

Define Technical System Options Step 410. The aim is to compile several *Technical System Options* which address the issues raised in the *Requirements Specification.*

Define the Problem Step 020. The aim is to identify the new *requirements* and existing problems that are to be satisfied by the proposed *system.*

Define Update Processes Step 520. The aim is to expand the description for all the *events* (database updates) identified within the *Requirements Specification.*

Define User Dialogues Step 510. The aim is to compile the documentation for *dialogues* between users and *system functions.*

Definition of Requirements Stage 3. The aim is to take the *Analysis of Requirements* and produce the *Requirements Specification* within the boundary identified in the *Selected Business System Option.*
This stage has eight steps:
310—Define Required System Processing
320—Develop Required Data Model
330—Derive System Functions
340—Enhance Required Data Model
350—Develop Specification Prototypes
360—Develop Processing Specification
370—Confirm System Objectives
380—Assemble Requirements Specification.

Derive Logical View of Current Services Step 150. The aim is to update the physical description of the existing *system* and logicalize it. Details of desired/required functionality will be documented in the *Requirements Catalogue.*

Derive System Functions Step 330. The aim is to compile a complete set of documentation about the *functions* identified for the *system.*

detail entity Where two *entities* are connected by a '1:m' *relationship*, a single instance of one *entity* is related to several instances of the other. The *entity* at the several end is deemed the *detail entity*. See *master entity.*

determinant Values for some of the *attributes* within an *entity* (instance) are directly dependent on the value of a group of specific *attributes* (possibly a group of one), which effectively identify this occurrence of the *entity*. The identification *attributes* are known as the *determinant* within *relational data analysis.*

Develop Processing Specification Step 360. The aim is to compile the *Processing Specification*. This involves cross-checking several major *products* already produced and may identify additional tasks which need to be undertaken within previous steps. The major techniques applied within this step are *entity life history analysis* and *effect correspondence diagramming*.

Develop Required Data Model Step 320. The aim is to modify and extend the *Current Environment Logical Data Model,* with the *Selected Business System Option* details and new *system requirements*, to produce the *Required System Logical Data Model*.

Develop Specification Prototypes Step 350. The aim is to use *specification prototyping* to ensure that the user has correctly specified the *requirements* for the *system*.

DFD see *Data Flow Diagram*.

DFM see *data flow modelling* and *Data Flow Model* .

dialogue The on-line activity required by a particular *user role* so that they can action (perform) a particular *function*.

Dialogue Control Table Used to identify and capture the navigation between the 'logical groupings of *dialogue elements'* under ' normal conditions'. This *table* also details the different order in which particular aspects of the *dialogue* may be undertaken.

dialogue design Is used to define the on-line activity of the *system*. *Dialogues* are identified as part of the *Requirements Specification* and then logically designed explicitly as part of the *Logical Design*. Physical *dialogue design* activities are undertaken during the *physical design* activities to complete the design prior to *system* implementation.

dialogue element A section of an input or output *data flow* which may consist of many *data items*. Each *dialogue element* is represented as a box on a *Dialogue Structure*.

Dialogue Element Description Used to describe a *dialogue element*. A set of these provides the detailed documentation for a *Dialogue Structure*.

Dialogue identification Is used to identify the complete set of the *requirements* for *dialogues* within the proposed *system*. *Dialogues* which are identified as critical in step 330: *Derive System Functions* will be subjected to *specification prototyping* (in *step 350: Develop Specification Prototypes*).

Dialogue Level Help Is used to detail the level of *help* that the user (*user role*) requires to progress through this *dialogue*.

Dialogue Structure A diagrammatic representation of a *dialogue*. Each box on the *Dialogue Structure* equates to a *dialogue element*. Input/output *operations* are allocated to *dialogue elements*.

Dialogues Is used to package together details of all identified *dialogues* within the *system*.

Document Flow Diagram Shows how documents pass around the *system*. This may be the initial diagram drawn within the *data flow modelling* technique to assist in defining/identifying the boundary of the *system*. This diagram will be produced if the current *system* is predominantly clerical and involves the passing of information using *forms* or other documents.

domain A 'pool of values' from which the actual values for an *attribute* can be drawn.

EAP see *Enquiry Access Path.*

ECD see *Effect Correspondence Diagram.*

EED see *External Entity Description.*

effect Is the change caused to a single *entity* because of a single *event.* An *effect* can be one of four kinds: create (birth), modify (update), logical delete (death) or update of *state indicators*.

The '*effect*' must be qualified where an occurrence of an *entity* is affected in one of severally mutually exclusive ways by an *event.* The qualifier is bracketed after the *event* name.

Note: brackets should differ in nature to those used to qualify an *event* by its role.

Effect Correspondence Diagram Shows all the affects an *event* has on data within the *system* and how those *effects* impact upon each other.

Effect Correspondence Diagrams provide the *access path* details for *update functions* which is used in logical design activities.

effect correspondence diagramming Used to analyse and document how *effects* are related to each other for each *event.*

elementary process The lowest-level *process* on a *Data Flow Diagram* which relates directly to the user (business) environment in which the *system* (computerized or manual) is to be operated. It will assist in the identification of *functions*.

Whole, or partial, *elementary processes* may be regarded as common across a number of *processes.* In which case they will be separately described.

Elementary Process Description Used to describe the business environment in which the *process* is trying to operate.

A *requirement* for *common processing* may also be described within an *Elementary Process Description* and cross-referenced to the *elementary processes* or *functions* which use it.

ELH see *Entity Life Histories* and *entity life history analysis*

Enhance Required Data Model Step 340. The aim is to validate the *Required System Logical Data Model* using *relational data analysis* techniques.

Enquiry Access Path The route through the *Logical Data Model* from an entry point to the *entity,* or *entities,* required for a particular *enquiry function.*

enquiry element (or enquiry) An element which requires information to be read from the database but involves no update processing. Some *update functions* contain enquiries as well as updates (*events*); these elements are also called enquiry elements.

enquiry function A *function* which requires information is read from the database but involves no associated update processing.

Enquiry Process Model Consists of a structure diagram for an enquiry processing *requirement* and the associated *Operations List*. The structure is based on the *Enquiry Access Path*.

enquiry trigger The *data items* that must be input to the *system* to initiate an enquiry.

Entity Is something, whether concrete or abstract, which is of importance to the area of business being investigated.

    Logical data modelling identifies types of *entity*, not individual occurrences; i.e. 'Tenant' and 'Applicant' not 'John Smith'.

Entity Description Documents all of the details concerned with an *entity* on the *Logical Data Structure,* including details of *state indicators* which are applied during *entity life history analysis.*

    There will be associated *Relationship Descriptions* for each related *entity* on the *Logical Data Structure.*

Entity/Event Matrix Synonym for *Event/Entity Matrix.*

entity-event modelling Is the combination of *entity life history analysis* and *effect correspondence diagramming.*

Entity Life Histories Structure diagrams for all *entity life histories* identified within the *system*. An *Entity Life History* is a structure combining all possible 'lives' of every possible occurrence of the *entity.*

entity life history Charts all of the *events* that may cause a particular *entity* to be changed in any way. It shows the valid structure of *events* (initially identified through use of *data flow modelling* and *function definition* techniques) affecting an *entity* on the *Logical Data Structure.*

entity life history analysis Brings together and validates the processing and data *requirements* of the *system*. This is done by investigating the *Required System Logical Data Model*. *Events* which affect the *entity* lives are documented showing the sequence of *effects* which take place.

Entity/Logical Data Store cross-reference Synonym for *Logical Data Store/Entity* cross-reference.

Entity/Process Matrix Synonym for *Process/Entity Matrix.*

entity roles If a single *event* affects more than one occurrence of a particular *entity* and the *effects* are different for each occurrence affected, the *entity* is deemed to be assuming different 'roles'.

    Each possible 'role' must be separately identified on the *ELH* diagram for the relevant *entity*, as separate processing will have to be specified for each role. The qualifier for the role is placed in brackets after the *event* name to provide a complete identification of the *entity role.*

    Note: brackets should differ in nature from those used to qualify an *event* by its *effect.*

EPD see *Elementary Process Description.*

EPM see *Enquiry Process Model.*

Establish Analysis Framework Step 110. The aim is to scope the investigation within the limits laid down by management. Also planning information is provided to management.

event An *event* is identified as whatever triggers a *process* (on a *Data Flow Diagram*) to update the values or status of the *system*. An *event* may cause more than one *entity* to be changed.
   In the logical *system*, an *event* initiates an update *process.*

Event/Entity Matrix A grid that is used to identify which entities are affected by a particular *event*. It provides two checks, that is: that each *event* affects at least one *entity* and that each *entity* is affected by at least one *event.*

exclusive relationship group If the participation of an *entity* occurrence in one *relationship* precludes its participation in one or more other *relationships* this identifies an '*exclusive relationship group*'.

expression A statement which can be evaluated. The statement may be forming a comparison between individual items. An *expression* may itself consist of several 'sub-expressions' linked by 'and' or 'or'.

external entity Is a source or recipient (or both) of data which exists outside the boundary of the defined *system* but which communicates with the *system*. An *external entity* may be another *system*, an organization, an individual or a group of people.
   These are documented within the *Data Flow Model.*

External Entity Description Used to explain, briefly, the relevance of an *external entity* in *relation* to the existing or proposed *system*. The detail will cover responsibilities or *functions* of the *external entity* and any constraints on the interface with the proposed *system*.

FCIM see *Function Component Implementation Map.*

FDs see *Function Definitions.*

Feasibility Stage 0. The objective is to investigate the *requirements* laid down within the *Project Initiation Document* and suggest the way ahead.
   This stage has four steps:
   010—Prepare for the Feasibility Study
   020—Define the problem
   030—Select Feasibility Options
   040—Assemble Feasibility Report.

feasibility Is used to investigate the possibilities for future work in a particular area of the business. The scope of the study will be laid down within the *Project Initiation Document*. Much of the analysis will be done using other techniques including *logical data modelling*, *data flow modelling*, *requirements definition* and *dialogue design.*

Feasibility Options The set of *Feasibility Options* which is compiled so that a selection can be made. Each option documents the *functions* to be incorporated and details implementation *requirements*. Each description is textual with some planning information.

Feasibility Report This is the *Module Product* from the *Feasibility Study Module*. It documents the possible approaches to the *system* development and assesses the impact of each so that the most appropriate way ahead can be fully investigated.

Feasibility Study Module The *Module* whose objective is to produce the *Feasibility Report* which will suggest the way ahead for the *project*. The activities form a short assessment of a proposed information *system* to determine whether the *system* would be feasible and appropriate to the business needs of the organization. *Feasibility* is assessed in terms of the managerial, business, financial, technological and cultural needs of the organization. This Module has one Stage—Stage 0: Feasibility.

first normal form see *normal form*.

form A *form* is the standard item of documentation used to hold details so that future work can be based on what has been covered in the past. In SSADM sample *forms* are illustrations of the information needs required to assist the analysis and design activities.

   Forms need not be paper-based; it is the content not the format which is of fundamental importance.

fragment A defined processing element which has a specific identity, purpose, set of inputs, outputs and correspondences. May be at any level. 1:1 with *component* or 1:1 with *operation*, e.g. Read Master. It may be in support of a *process*, or a data group, screen or error message.

function A set of *system* processing which the users wish to schedule together, to support their business activity.

Function Component Implementation Map A classification and specification of all implementation *fragments* for all *function components* defined in the *Function Definitions* to meet the processing *requirements*. See *component*.

Function Definition Is the description of the *function* and provides a cross-reference to other associated SSADM *products*.

function definition Identifies and documents *functions* which are the units of processing carried forward to *physical design*.

Function Definitions Is the packaging of all details about *functions* to be included in the *Requirements Specification*. These details are further expanded during *physical design* activities.

   Basic information about a *function* consists of a *Function Definition* with one or more *I/O Structures*. Further information may be found in *Enquiry Access Paths* (for *enquiry functions*) and (common) *Elementary Process Descriptions*.

function type There are three ways of categorizing *functions*:
- processing requirements: update or enquiry
- access details: on-line or off-line
- method of initiation: user or *system*.

Function/User Role Matrix Synonym for *User Role/Function Matrix*.

functional area The users will have a view of the processing *system* based upon the tasks which they undertake. Each of these views will represent one or more *'functional areas'* depending upon how widely the individual user uses the *system*. Each *functional area* will be directly related to a specific task which the user undertakes, e.g. 'monitoring of arrears' in the example documented throughout the manual set.

functional dependency *Attribute* A is said to be functionally dependent on *attribute* B if, and only if, it is true that for each distinct value of A there is necessarily exactly one distinct value of B (at any given time).

functional requirement A *requirement* for a particular facility or feature which describes 'what' the *system* should do. Examples include updates, enquiries and reports.

Generic Blank Form For use on an 'as required' basis for information recording. It has the bare minimum of identification necessary to meet the criteria for an SSADM *form*.

Generic Matrix Form For use on an 'as required' basis wherever two classes of *object* need to be cross-referenced diagrammatically using a grid.

grouped domain A 'pool of values' associated with validation rules and formats common to several *attributes*.

Grouped Domain Description Used to document validation rules and formats common to several *attributes*.

group of events A collection of *event* occurrences containing more than one *event* type. There may be more than one occurrence of each *event* type. The term is used to describe the batching or grouping of data for input to a *function*.

help *Help* facilities may be provided in the implemented *system* to guide the user through the options available to them at any point in time.

   Dialogue level 'help' may be associated with *Dialogue Structures* so that the need to consider (and implement) these features can be passed forward into the *physical design* activities.

I/O Descriptions Are used to document all *data flows* which cross the *Data Flow Model* system boundary.

I/O Ds see *I/O Descriptions*.

I/O S see *I/O Structures*.

I/O process A *process*, documented in the *physical design*, for producing detail to or accepting information from a specific piece of functional processing.

I/O Structure Documents the input to and outputs from a *function*, or part of a *function*.
   Also see *product descriptions* for *I/O Structure Diagram* and *I/O Structure Description*.

I/O Structures (for all functions) Is the packaging of all *I/O Structures* for all identified *functions*. This *product* exists because some SSADM activities do not require the complete set of documentation for all *functions*.

Impact Analysis Describes the *effects* of the option (business or technical) on the user environment and will cover issues concerned with organization, procedures, and implementation factors. This *product* is used to document the ramifications of pursuing a particular course of action.

information highway Is the mechanism by which the practitioner and management processes communicate with each other. All items on the *information highway* must have been reviewed to ensure the required *quality criteria* are satisfied.

When *configuration management* techniques are applied to a *project*, they are applied within the *information highway*.

Input/Output Description see *I/O Descriptions.*

Input/Output Structure see *I/O Structure.*

installation development standards Input to Step 610. Documents the criteria which should be used during the development of all *Information Systems* within the organization/installation. Note precise details of the contents of this *Product* are not given within this manual set.

Installation Style Guide Is a set of standards about the nature, approach and style of the human factors aspects of computerized *systems.* The standards should be followed by all *projects* undertaken within an organization.

integrity errors The data in a database must be consistent for the *system* to be able to function correctly. Where inconsistency arises the database is not maintaining 'referential integrity' of the database.

Investigate and Define Requirements Step 120. The aim is to compile the basic *requirements* for the proposed *system*.

Investigate Current Data Step 140. The aim is to produce a detailed description of the information used in and produced by the *current environment*, in the form of a *Logical Data Model.*

Investigate Current Processing Step 130. The aim is to compile a view *(Data Flow Model)* of the processing within the *current services*.

Investigation of Current Environment Stage 1. The aim is to look at the existing services and *requirements* and produce a logical view of the processing *requirements*.

This stage has six steps:
110—Establish Analysis Framework
120—Investigate and Define Requirements
130—Investigate Current Processing
140—Investigate Current Data
150—Derive Logical View of Current Services
160—Assemble Investigation Results.

key A *key* is an *attribute* or a combination of *attributes* which can be used to uniquely identify an *entity*. There are several classes of *key* which are fully described in the *logical data modelling*, *relational data analysis*, and *physical data design* chapters.

LDM see *Logical Data Model* and *logical data modelling.*

LDS see *Logical Data Structure.*

LGDE see *logical grouping of dialogue elements.*

list The *relationship* between master and detail entities is represented by a *list* of *keys*, including the *key* of the master and the *key* of each *detail entity* with pointers connecting each entry in the *list* to the next entry.

logical database process design Is used to translate the information gathered during the *Requirements Specification Module* into a logical specification which can then be translated into a *physical design* for the *system* in any implementation. This also provides a logical definition of the *system* which assists in maintenance of the implemented *system.*

 This technique covers the definition of the processing for data input to, and output from, the database.

Logical Data Flow Model Is produced during *logicalization* in Stage 1 (Step 150). It combines the existing services and the desired processing *requirements,* removing all physical considerations. See *Data Flow Model.*

Logical Data Model Provides an accurate model of the information *requirements* of all or part of an organization. This serves as a basis for file and database design, but is independent of any specific implementation technique or *product.*

 The *Logical Data Model* consists of a *Logical Data Structure, Entity Descriptions* and *Relationship Descriptions.* Associated descriptions of *attribute/data items* and *grouped domains* are maintained in the *Data Catalogue.*

logical data modelling Is used to produce a conceptual model of the information *requirements* of all or part of an organization.

Logical Data Store/Entity cross-reference Is a matrix showing the correspondence between logical *data stores* in the *Data Flow Model* and the entities on the *Logical Data Model.* This is used to ensure that a *main data store* corresponds to an *entity* or group of *entities.* Also each *entity* on the *Logical Data Model* must be held completely within one and only one *main data store. (Transient data stores* are not included on this matrix.)

Logical Data Structure A diagrammatic representation of the information needs of an organization in the form of *entities* and the important business relationships between them.

Logical Design The *Stage Product* from *Stage 5: Logical Design.* It packages the logical view of processing with the *Required System Logical Data Model* and the *Requirements Catalogue.*

Logical Design Stage 5. The aim is to take the *Requirements Specification* and further develop the processing *requirements* in such a way as to be implementation independent prior to *physical design* activities.

 This stage has four steps:
  510—Define User Dialogues
  520—Define Update Processes
  530—Define Enquiry Processes
  540—Assemble Logical Design.

logical grouping of dialogue elements *Dialogue elements* within a particular *Dialogue Structure* are grouped together where input/output *requirements* suggest that there are benefits to be gained by doing so, such as simpler processing.

logicalization Is a sub-technique of *data flow modelling*, used in step 150, which converts the *Current Physical Data Flow Model* into a logical model with no physical implications.

logical key Is meaningful to the users of the *system* and is usually allocated by them. Such a *key* is its unique identifier; it enables the *system* to distinguish the record from all others. It does not tell the *system* where the data is physically stored. See *physical key*.

Logical/Physical Data Store cross-reference A matrix that is used within the *data flow modelling* technique (*logicalization*) to construct the logical view of data organization from the current (physical) services.

Logical Process Model Is used to package all processing details within the *Logical Design*.

logical success unit see *success unit*.

Logical System Specification The *Module product* from the *Logical System Specification Module*. It consists of the *Selected Technical System Option,* the *Technical Environment Description* and the *Logical Design*.

Logical System Specification Module The objective is to produce the *Logical System Specification*. The *Selected Technical System Option* and the *Technical Environment Description* define the scope of the physical implementation; this detail must be consistent with the *Logical Design*. The *Application Style Guide* is also developed during this *Module*.

This module has two stages:

Stage 4—Technical System Options

Stage 5—Logical Design.

main data store Represents the data that is held centrally in a *system* so that it can be used by a number of different *processes*. These are elements on *Data Flow Diagrams*. Entities on the *Logical Data Model* must reside in one and only one *main data store*. Each *main data store* must have one or more entities associated with it.

master entity Where two *entities* are connected by a 1:m *relationship*, a single instance of one *entity* is related to several instances of the other. The *entity* at the 'single' end is deemed the *master entity*.

After step 340, all *relationships* on the *LDM* must be represented as 1:m *relationships*. This provides a clear hierarchic structure to provide the necessary input to the following techniques: *entity life history analysis, logical database process design* and *physical design*. See *detail entity*.

menu A hierarchical structure used to provide a user (role) with access to available, and applicable *functions*.

Menu Structure Provides a diagrammatic representation of the *menus* to be used within the *system*.

message pair An exchange between the user and the *system* comprising an input message and an output message.

Module The SSADM framework requires a *project* to be sub-divided into a number of *Modules* each of which consists of one or more *Stages*.

Each *Module* forms a distinct unit for management purposes. A *Module* has a defined set of *products* and activities, a finite lifespan and an organizational structure. The production of the defined end *products*, to agreed *quality* standards, signals the completion of the *Module*.

non-functional requirement A *requirement* which describes how, how well or to what level of *quality* a facility of the *system* should be provided. Examples include *service level requirements*; access restrictions; security; monitoring; audit and control; and constraints.

non-procedural specification Generally used with a *program* generator, it is the specification of a *process* (or entire *function*) which may contain no more than the specification of the inputs and outputs, and the correspondences between them.

normal form Is the result of applying *relational data analysis* techniques. There are several stages of *normalization*; relations are translated into:

first normal form (1NF)
second normal form (2NF)
third normal form (3NF)
fourth normal form
fifth normal form.

SSADM recognizes the existence of *fourth and fifth normal form* but does not tend to put them to practical use.
Refer to Sec. 4.5 for further information.

normalization Is effectively *relational data analysis*, and uses rules to analyse the way items of data depend upon one another for their meaning.

In a 'normalized *Logical Data Model'* all entities, considered as *relations*, must be in *third* (or higher) *normal form*.

normalized relation Is the result of *normalization*. It is a group of data (items) which are a convenient package for access and manipulation purposes. The information held within a *normalized relation* will be concerned with particular concept.

object Similar to an *entity* but having a defined range of behaviours. Typically, a *function component* (e.g. *I/O process*) or an element type supported in *physical environment* (screen).

off-line function A *function* where all the data is input and the whole of the *database processing* for the *function* is completed without further interaction with the user.

on-line function A *function* where the *system* and the user communicate through input and output messages, i.e. *message pairs*. The *system* responds in time to influence the next input message. *On-line functions* may include off-line elements such as printing an off-line report.

operation These are discrete pieces of processing which combine to constitute *effects*. Initially identified during *entity life history analysis* and expanded during update process modelling.

Operations are also used within *dialogue design*.

Operations List Is a list of all the *operations* which are detailed on a processing structure which may be for an enquiry or an update. See *Enquiry Process Model* and *Update Process Model*.

Optimize Physical Data Design Step 640. The aim is to validate the *Physical Data Design* against information in the *Function Definitions* and the *Requirements Catalogue*. Where there are likely to be performance problems the data design is optimized.

Outline Current Environment Description A brief description of the *current services* and any existing problems. Produced during the *Feasibility Study*. The analysis reflects that carried out in Stage 1, but is not completed to the same level of detail.

Outline Development Plan Provides management with information on the development strategy for the remainder of the *project* for the specific *Technical System Option*, so that provisional timescales and resource *requirements*, and therefore development costs, can be estimated. See *Plan*.

Outline Required Environment Description A brief description of the *requirements* to be included within the proposed *system*. Produced during the *Feasibility Study*. *The* analysis reflects that carried out in Stage 1, but is not completed to the same level of detail.

Overview Logical Data Structure Describes the eight to twelve major entities and their *relationships* within the area of the investigation. See Logical *Data Model*.

PBS see *Product Breakdown Structure*.

parallel structure Appearing on *Entity Life Histories*, this is used to show where certain *events* will definitely happen within the lifetime of an *entity*, but not in a prescribed order.

PDD see *Physical Data Design* or *physical data design*.

PDI see *Process Data Interface*.

PES see *Physical Environment Specification*.

Physical Data Design The definition for the physical database which is to be implemented. The design is developed in two steps; the first produces a 'first-cut' design based on applying rules about the *DBMS* to the *Requires System Logica Data Model*; the second is a design optimized for performance reasons.

physical data design Takes the *Required System Logical Data Model* and translates it into a *product* specific database design within the chosen technical environment with consideration having been given to performance and space constraints.

Physical Design Is the *Module product* from the *Physical Design* module which defines the data and processing elements of the implementable *system*.

Physical Design Stage 6. The objective is to specify the physical data and physical processes using the language and features of the chosen implementation environment and incorporating installation standards.

This stage has seven steps:
610—Prepare for Physical Design
620—Create Physical Data Design

630—Create Function Component Implementation Map
640—Optimize Physical Data Design
650—Complete Function Specifications
660—Consolidate Process Data Interface
670—Assemble Physical Design.

physical design Takes the *Logical Design* and develops it into a specification for the implementation which is wholly dependent on the technical environment as documented in the *Physical Environment Specification.* This technique has two aspects: *physical data design*, and *physical process specification.*

Physical Design Module The objective is to produce the *Physical Design* for the *system* based on the *Logical System Specification* and the *Physical Environment Specification*, i.e. it will be implementation dependent.
      This module has one stage:
      Stage 6—Physical Design.

Physical Design Strategy Documents all aspects relating to designing the physical implementation of the application. This includes all planning documentation.

physical environment The implementation environment where appropriate will include the development environment and the migration path between them.

Physical Environment Classification Classifies the environment in which the application is to be implemented. Also describes the development environment and migration path necessary. See *DBMS Data Storage Classification, DBMS Performance Classification* and *Processing System Classification.*

Physical Environment Specification Specifies the hardware and software *products* and services to be supplied, commissioned and made available for implementation. Generally this will be provided by the vendor.

physical key Often called a 'pointer', this tells the *system* the address on the magnetic disk where this record is to be found.

Physical Process Specification Packages all of the specifications for processing which are required in the proposed *system*.

physical process specification Takes the *Logical Design* and tailors it to the *physical environment* to produce the specification for all necessary processing (*programs*).

Physical System Specification Comprises the *Physical Design, Application Development Standard* (both from SSADM) and the *Physical Environment Specification* (which is likely to be the response to a procurement exercise).

PID see *Project Initiation Document.*

Plan Contains details of all the required resources for any one particular *project, Module , Stage* or possibly *Step*. A *Plan* is produced and presented to the *project* board for approval prior to the formal commencement of the work. After approval this *Plan* is used to report actual financial expenditure and resource usage against the original estimated plan. *Plans* are the basis for controlling costs and resource usage.

Prepare for the Feasibility Study Step 010. The aim is to ensure that the *requirements* for the study are understood, achievable, and agreed with the *project* board. The major activities are in planning for the rest of the *Feasibility Study*.

Prepare for Physical Design Step 610. The aim is to classify the relevant aspects of the *physical environment* and then plan for the rest of the *physical design* activities.

Problem Definition Statement A statement of the user *requirement* for the *system* which may include charts and diagrams to supplement the detail. Produced during the *Feasibility Study* it is essentially a summary of the SSADM details and has not been explicitly documented in this manual set.

procedural specification Probably a Jackson programming structure, based on the input and output data, with *operations* and conditions allocated to it.

process Transforms or manipulates information (data) in a *system*.

Process Data Interface Documents how the *Logical Data Model* can be mapped onto the *Physical Data Design*, showing how it interfaces with the *Physical Processing Specification*. It allows the designer to implement the logical update and enquiry *processes* as physical *programs*, independently of the physical database structure.

Process/Entity Matrix Is a cross-check that all *entities* are used as the basic information for at least one *process* and to identify logical groupings of bottom-level *processes* during *logicalization* of the *Data Flow Model*.

Processing Specification The *Step Product* from step 360: *Develop Processing Specification*. This *product* is not shown explicitly on the SSADM structural model. It exists to identify the *quality criteria* associated with the close links between *entity-event modelling* results and the *products* being input to this *Step*. Development of this *product* may identify errors in other *products* and force previous *Steps* to be revisited.

Processing System Classification Classifies the details of the processing environment which is to be used for implementation. Where appropriate, it also defines the development environment.

product May be an item of software, hardware, or documentation and may itself be a collection of other *products*. Each *product* is pre-defined and its production is planned within the *project*.

Within the *Product Breakdown Structure* there is a distinction between *Management Products* (which are produced as part of the management of the *project*), *Technical Products* (which are those *products* which make up the *system*) and *Quality Products* (which are produced for or by the *quality process*).

Product Breakdown Structure Identifies the *products* which are required and which must be produced by a *project*. This document describes the *system* in a hierarchic way, decomposing it through a number of levels down to the *components* of each *product*.

Product Description Describes the purpose, form and *components* of a *product*, and lists the *quality criteria* which apply to it.

product flow Shows how *products* are passed around between *processes* to provide details needed to create new *products* or transform the existing ones.

Product Flow Diagram Is used to describe the technical strategy of a *project* in terms of a diagram showing the *products* of the *project* and how they are derived from each other. It is essentially a working document produced by planners for their own benefit.

program A package of *fragments* assembled to meet the *requirements* of one or more *functions*.

Progress Report Used to report back to management details of the current status of the *project*, highlighting relevant issues.

project A *project* is regarded as having the following characteristics:
- a defined and unique set of technical *products* to meet the business needs
- a corresponding set of activities to construct those *products*
- a certain amount of resources
- a finite lifespan
- an organizational structure with defined responsibilities.

Project Initiation Document Is approved by the project board at 'project initiation'. It defines the terms of reference and objectives for the *project*. It is used to identify business *requirements*, as well as organizational and general information needs, security aspects and an initial *Project Plan*.

project management Is used to monitor and control the resources allocated to a *project*, ensuring that any constraints for the *project* are imposed.

Project Plan see *Plan*.

project procedures The activities which surround and support an SSADM *project* to ensure that sufficient control (managerial and *quality*) are imposed on the *project*. Interfaces to other techniques or methods, such as *risk analysis*, and capacity planning, are handled within the *project management* activities.

prototype Provides the user with an animated view of how the *system* being developed will work. It enhances user understanding, allowing better identification of discrepancies and deficiencies in the user *requirement*.

Prototype Demonstration Objective Document One of these is completed prior to any *prototype* demonstration for each *Prototype Pathway*. Assumptions and queries for each *menu*, screen and/or report are listed under their respective *component* number. This document lists the points of discussion to be addressed between the user and the analyst during the *prototype* demonstration.

Prototype Pathway Once screen and report *components* have been identified within the *prototyping* activities, they can be combined with the existing *menus* to form *Prototype Pathways*. The pathways are a script for the *prototyping* session and hence use a limited and simple serial diagrammatic representation to convey the structure.

Prototype Result Log Used to record the results of the *prototype* demonstration This document is used in a similar capacity to minutes of a meeting. Each request made by the user is documented on the log, with a change grade, and the log is updated later to show what changes are required.

prototyping A variety of techniques which may be used to produce *prototypes.* See *specification prototyping.*

Prototyping Report Is prepared by the technical manager of the *prototyping* exercise to report back to the *project* board. It sets out whether the objectives for the exercise were achieved, or alternatively, the reasons why they were not. It includes estimates of the value of the work done and where necessary suggests whether more work would (or would not) be beneficial.

Prototyping Scope Is used by the *project* board to define the boundaries and objectives for the *prototyping* activities.

QA see *quality assurance.*

quality Is defined in ISO 8402 (BS 4778) as: 'the totality of features and characteristics of a *product* or service which bear on its abilities to satisfy a given need'—that is, fitness for purpose.

quality assurance *quality assurance* dictates how *quality* is achieved and assured. The mechanisms are:
- specification of cost-effective *quality control processes*
- consistent use of these procedures
- external surveillance and audit of the *quality control* practice.

  quality assurance is a guarantee to users that the developers and management aim for *quality*.

quality control The process of ensuring that:
- required qualities are built into the *product*
- defects are detected and removed
- the process of production is itself corrected to remove defects
- errors and non-conformance are brought to the attention of management.

  Mechanisms include inspection, review, checking and testing.

quality criteria Characteristics of a *product* which determine whether it meets *requirements*, and thus define what '*quality*' means in the context of that *product*. These are defined in the *Product Description* and agreed with the *project* board before development of the *product* commences.

quality review Is a means whereby a *product* (or group of related *products*) is checked against an agreed set of *quality criteria*. Those criteria are defined for every *product* (on the *Product Description*) and may be supplemented with other documents.

  For some *products* it may be sufficient to 'review' them as they are being developed, for others more rigorous formal review is necessary.

quit and resume Appearing on an *Entity Life History* to show how the prescribed sequence of *events* for an *entity* may be altered in particular circumstances. It shows processing being stopped and restarted at another point on the structure.

random event An *event* which may occur at any point either during the life of an *entity* or during a particular stage of an *entity* life.

RDA see *relational data analysis.*

RDA Working Paper Is used to document the progress through *relational data analysis*, taking *relations* which are unnormalized through to *third normal form.*

relation A *relation* is a group of *data items* (or *attributes*). When the *Logical Data Model* is validated using *relational data analysis*, a relation equates to an *entity.*

relational data analysis Is a method of deriving data structures which have the least redundant data and the most flexibility. The flexibility is achieved by breaking down the data groups into smaller groups without losing any of the original information. It is the objective of this technique to transform all *relations* into at least *third normal form.*

relationship Is an association between two entities, or one *entity* and itself (recursion/ involution), to which all instances (occurrences) of the *relationship* must conform.

relationship degree Where two entities are directly related, the degree indicates the number of instances of each such *entity* that may participate in one instance of the *relationship.*

Relationship Description Documents the details of a *relationship* between two entities on the *Logical Data Structure.*

release A full set of some *product* (e.g. documentation or software) made available to the recipient, is termed a *release.* A *release* is issued for a specific purpose to those authorized to receive it (developers, users) as required to assist in some aspect of the *project* life cycle. A subsequent *release* usually implies a significant change in functionality or style since the preceding *release.*

Report Format Shows the layout of a printed report as desired by the user.

Required System Data Flow Model Shows how the proposed services are to be organized and what processing is to be undertaken. See *Data Flow Model.*

Required System Logical Data Model Provides the detail of the proposed *system* information *requirements.* It is developed during the *Requirements Specification* and *Logical System Specification Modules.* See *Logical Data Model.*

requirement Describes a required feature of the proposed *system.* *Requirements* may be functional (describing what the *system* should do) or non-functional (describing how a facility should be provided, or how well, or to what level of *quality*). See *functional* and *non-functional requirements.*

Requirements Analysis Module The objective is to produce the *Analysis of Requirements.* Within this the *Selected Business System Option* will define the scope of further investigation.
    This module has two stages:

Stage 1—Investigation of Current Environment
Stage 2—Business System Options.

Requirements Catalogue Is the central repository for information covering all identified *requirements*, both functional and non-functional. Each entry is textual and describes a required facility or feature of the proposed *system*.

requirements definition The focus of this technique is on the future, required *system*. It is used to identify and describe *requirements* for the proposed *system* which meet the needs of users, and of the business as a whole.

As the *project* progresses *requirements* are 'resolved' using more formal techniques, such as *function definition*.

Requirements Specification Is the *Module product* from the *Requirements Specification Module*, packaging all of the details which are required in order to decide upon the technical direction of the *project*.

Requirements Specification Module The objective is to produce the *Requirements Specification*. This module has one stage:
Stage 3—Definition of Requirements.

Resource Flow Diagram Documents how resources move within an organization. This may be the initial diagram drawn within the *data flow modelling* technique to define the boundary of the *system*. This diagram will be produced if the current *system* is predominantly concerned with movement of physical objects, e.g. goods.

risk analysis This involves identifying and assessing the level of risk, which is calculated from:
• the assessed value of assets (hardware and software)
• threats to these assets
• vulnerability of the assets to these threats.
Risk management involves identifying and adapting security counter-measures with the aim of reducing risk to a known and acceptable level There is a need to justify the counter-measures by the identified level risk.

Screen Format This shows the layout that the user requires on the visual display unit screen.

second normal form see *normal form*.

Select Business System Option Step 220. The aim is to select and fully develop a single *Business System Option*. This option may be made up of parts from several of the proposed options.

Select Feasibility Options Step 030. The aim is to identify and outline several options which satisfy the *requirements* and recommend action for the future.

Select Technical System Options Step 420. The aim is to present the *Technical System Options* to the *project* board to enable the selection of a technical solution to the *system requirement*. This selection is then fully documented.

Selected Business System Option This is a description of a chosen *system* development direction. The description documents the *system* boundary, inputs, outputs and the transformation taking place within the boundary. Essentially the description is textual with supporting (annotated) elements from the *Current Services Description*.

Selected Technical System Option Documents the selection process with the planning details. The technical details are placed in the *Technical Environment Description*.

service level requirement A *non-functional requirement* which states the required *quality* of service the user expects from a functional aspect of the *system*. The *service level requirement* may be associated with *Function Definitions*.

SI see *state indicator*.

SLR see *service level requirement*.

Space Estimation Is used to assess the storage *requirements* of the data design using a particular implementation environment.

  The relevant information will vary widely depending upon the technical environment and must be designed and compiled for each application.

specific function model Is a model of the *components* of a particular SSADM *function*.

specification prototyping Is used to identify and trap errors in the specification of the user *requirement* and enhance them prior to detailed logical design activities being undertaken.

SSADM Structure Diagram Used to represent structures diagrammatically in terms of sequences selections, and iterations. May be extended to include parallel constructs and *operations lists*.

Stage The SSADM framework requires a *project* to be sub-divided into a number of *Modules* each of which consists of one or more *Stages*.

  A *Stage* is a unit of activity with a single goal and rationale.

State indicators Are used as a re-expression of the structure of an *Entity Life History*, in a format which will be used during the *Logical Design Stage* to enforce the defined sequence of *events*. A *state indicator* should be thought of as an additional *attribute* within each *entity*.

Step The SSADM framework requires a *project* to be sub-divided into a number of *Modules* each of which consists of one or more *Stages*, each of which consists of one or more *Steps*.

  A *Step* has a defined set of *products* and activities.

Structural Model Diagram For SSADM provides a record of *system processes* and messages and material flows in the form of a flowchart drawn to highlight the sequencing, nesting and control of the *processes* and the converging and diverging of message and material flows.

Study Plan see *Plan*.

Style Guide see *Application Style Guide* and *Installation Style Guide*.

success unit Is a set of processing which must succeed or fail as a whole within the *system*. When a failure occurs the *system* is restored to the state it was in immediately before the '*success unit*' began.

super function A *function* which is composed of several 'lower-level' *functions*.

system This is, the complete technical output of the *project* including all technical *products* (that is, all hardware, software, documentation, etc.). The *system* will live beyond the life of the *project* and, in the case of an enhancement *project*, will have existed before the *project*.

System Description Shows how the *Requirements Specification* is met by the *Technical Environment Description* for a particular *Technical System Option*. In many cases the major decisions in this area will have already been taken in choosing a *Business System Option*.

table The *relationship* between master and detail entities is represented by physical contiguity of the *key* of the *master entity* and the *keys* of each of its detail *entities* in a *table*.

Take-On Requirements Description Is compiled during *technical system option* activities, and details the conversion *requirements* which must be implemented before a fully working *system* can be available.

Technical Environment Description Provides the specification of the technical environment which is produced once the *Technical System Option* has been selected. This detail is then passed on to *physical design* activities.

technical system option Is the means by which users agree the new application's implementation strategy incorporating the desired functionality, as defined in the *Requirements Specification*. Several *Technical System Options* are developed and one is selected (or combined elements from several). It gives the technical direction for future development.

Technical System Options The set of *Technical System Options* which has been developed so that the *system* development direction can be chosen.

Each option documents the *functions* to be incorporated and details implementation *requirements*. Each description is textual with some planning information. Functional elements are taken directly from the *Requirements Specification*.

Technical System Options Stage 4. The aim is to take the *Requirements Specification* and decide on the most appropriate way for development to meet the technical needs.

410—Define Technical System Options
420—Select Technical System Options.

TED see *Technical Environment Description*.

Testing Outline Is compiled during *technical system option* activities, and documents the basic *requirements* for testing the implementable *system* so that it will meet user *requirements*.

Testing Timing Factors Definition Is used to identify the *DBMS* read and write *operations* that will be used to implement the types of logical reads and writes used in the logical update and enquiry *processes*.

Disk and processor performance information is required for all relevant *operations*.

Third normal form see *normal form*.

Timing Estimation Is used to assess the timing *requirements* using the data design within a particular implementation environment. The relevant information will vary wildly depending upon the technical environment and must be compiled for each application.

Training Requirements Description Is compiled during *technical system option* activities, and documents the amount of training required for the staff who will be using/working on the new *system*, so that they will be fully effective at the appropriate time (that is, when the *system* is available for use).

transient data store Transient data is held for a short time before being used by a *process* and then deleted. Data held in *transient data stores* may not be structured the same way as the data in a *main data store*.

These are elements of a *Data Flow Diagram*, but are not reflected in the *Logical Data Model*. They are likely to be used to overcome a constraint within the physical *system* implementation.

TSO see *technical system option* and *Selected Technical System Option* and *Technical System Options*.

UFM see *universal function model*.

universal function model Is a standard model used to identify the general *components* of an SSADM *function*.

update function Contains some update processing of the database. This may also include some *enquiry functions*.

Update Process Model Is a structure diagram for the update (*event*) processing and the associated *operations list*. This is based on the *Entity Life Histories*, which provide a data-oriented view of the *system*, and the associated *Effect Correspondence Diagrams*, which provide an *event*-oriented or *process*- oriented view of the *system*.

UPM see *Update Process Model*.

User Catalogue Provides a description of the on-line users of the proposed *system*. It includes details of job titles and the tasks undertaken by each of the identified users.

User Manual Requirements Description Is compiled during *technical system option* activities, and documents the basic information which can be supplied from the SSADM *products* and other available sources. It relates to the *system* and its smooth running from the user's point of view.

user role A *user role* is defined as a collection of job holders who share a large proportion of common tasks.

User Role/Function Matrix *Dialogues* are identified as being the cross-reference between *user roles* and *on-line functions* (either enquiry or update). The matrix maps correspondences between *functions* and *user roles,* thus identifying these *dialogues*.

Reading down from the *user roles* axis also provides the (initial) *Menu Structure* for the *system*.

User Roles Is used to document the details for each *user role* identified as having direct interest in the required *system*.

version A *configuration item* may have a number of *versions* relating to the continuing development of that configuration item.

Appendix B   Bibliography

Systems analysis and design

Avison, D.E. and Fitzgerald, G. (1988) *Information Systems Development: Methodologies, Techniques and Tools* (Blackwell Scientific).

CCTA (1990) *SSADM Version 4 Reference Manual* (NCC-Blackwell).

Yeates, D., Shields, M., and Helmey, D. (1994) *Systems Analysis and Design* (Pitman).

Database systems

Date, C. J. (1995) *An Introduction to Database Systems* 6th edn (Addison-Wesley).

Project management

Bradley, K. (1993) *PRINCE: A Practical Handbook* (Butterworth-Heinemann).

Gilb, T. (1988) *Principles of Software Engineering Management* (Addison-Wesley).

Humphrey W. (1989) *Managing the Software Process* (Addison-Wesley).

Meredith, J. and Mentel, S. (1989) *Project Management: A Managerial Approach* 2nd edn (Wiley).

Symons, C. R. (1991) *Software Sizing and Estimating: Function Point Analysis Mark 2* (Wiley).

Yeates, D. (1991) *Project Management for Information Systems* (Pitman).

Soft systems

Checkland, P. and Scholes, J.E. (1991) *Soft Systems Methodology in Action* (Wiley).

Galliers, R. (Ed.) (1987) *Information Analysis: Selected Readings* (Addison-Wesley).

Software engineering and CASE

Dixon, R. (1992) *Winning with CASE* (McGraw-Hill).

Sommerville, I. (1994) *Software Engineering* 4th edn (Addison-Wesley).

Yourdon, E. (1992) *Decline & Fall of the American Programmer* (Prentice Hall).

Interface design

Browne, D. (1994) *STUDIO: STructured User-interface Design for Interaction Optimization* (Prentice Hall).

Object orientation

Goodland, M. (1994) SSADM: An object-oriented method? in *Object development methods* (Ed. A. Carmichael), (SIGS Books Inc.).

Graham, I. (1994) *Object-Oriented Methods* 2nd edn (Addison-Wesley).

Rumbaugh, J., Blaha, M., Premelani, W., Eddy, F., and Lorensen, W. (1991) *Object-Oriented Modeling and Design* (Prentice Hall).

Appendix C   Yorkies case study

Terms of reference

1. To design a computer system to support the vehicle rental, driver administration, customer records, and invoicing areas of Yorkies.
2. To investigate ways of improving the efficiency of the operations of the company in those areas specified in 1.
3. To investigate extending the system to include the administration of one-way hires and the acceptance of non-registered customers

Background information

Yorkies are a medium-sized organization dealing with the hire of vehicles ranging in size from vans to articulated lorries. They have a Head Office (HQ) and 50 Local Offices with a depot attached to each Local Office. They deal with a large number of regular local customers over the whole of the UK mainland. The organization chart for Yorkies is shown in Fig. C.1.

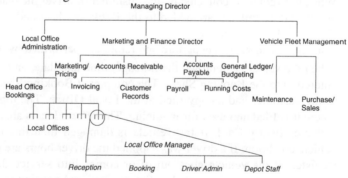

Fig. C.1 Organization chart for Yorkies

Description of the current system

1. Customers may make telephone or written bookings of vehicles to reception staff in the Local Offices. These are passed to the booking staff where they are first checked against the local Customer List to ensure the customer is accredited and that the booking does not exceed the maximum value bookable for that customer. If the booking is unacceptable the customer is referred to HQ.
2. If the booking is satisfactory the Vehicle Booking Diary is checked to ensure that a suitable vehicle is available for the days required; if no vehicle is available the unfillable booking is passed to HQ who use the Empty Vehicle Log to find an office that can satisfy the booking.

3. If a vehicle is available a Booking Sheet is partially filled out and the booking number and the vehicle category entered into the Vehicle Booking Diary. The Booking Sheet is in four parts; the bottom, partially filled copy, is sent to the customer as confirmation of his or her order. Any instructions to the driver are filed in order of the date required and stored separately until required. If a driver is required the driver administration staff are notified.

4. The Empty Vehicle Log is amended by HQ every second working day from sheets filled out by the Local Offices detailing the number of vehicles of each category currently available for hire for each of the next 20 working days.

5. Any previously unfilled bookings filled by HQ using the Empty Vehicle Log are passed to the Local Office able to satisfy the booking. They fill out a Booking Sheet and deal with the booking in the normal way. If HQ fill the booking using the Empty Vehicle Log they inform the customer directly.

6. If a driver is required the Local Office finds a suitable driver from the Driver/Agency Register held at each Local Office and contact him by telephone to determine whether he is available for the days required. When a driver is 'booked' the booking details are entered into the Driver Register and the driver name onto the Booking Sheet. The driver instructions on the Booking Sheet are sent to the driver as confirmation. If no driver can be found the Local Office contacts an agency who supply drivers.

7. When the vehicle is collected by the customer or driver the date and time collected, and departure mileage are added to the Booking Sheet and to the Vehicle History Card. The booking number is also added to the Vehicle History Card. The activities concerned with vehicle departure and return are performed by the depot staff.

8. When the vehicle is returned the mileage, time and date, and vehicle condition are entered onto the Booking Sheet. The completed Booking Sheet (copy 2) is passed to the customer and a copy filed at the Local Office. The top copy is sent to HQ where it is filed and used for invoicing. The return details are also entered onto the Vehicle History Card. If the vehicle is damaged then this is recorded with the vehicle condition. If a driver was supplied the driver hours are entered in the Driver Register. If the vehicle goes out of or comes into service this is notified to the booking staff and written on the History Card and notified to fleet maintenance at HQ.

9. The accounts section is based at HQ and uses a microcomputer accounts package to produce invoices and to hold customer records. This uses two files: the Customer File and the Invoice File.

10. The Customer List is printed out monthly and sent to each Local Office. Every week a list of amendments are printed and sent to each Local Office. Maintenance of the Customer File (e.g. adding new customers, changing their details, etc.) is carried out by HQ accounts staff.

11. Copy A of the completed Booking Sheet is sent by the depot staff to HQ accounts and is used to produce the invoice. Customers are invoiced on individual bookings

but also receive monthly statements and reminders if they have not paid in the last 30 days. Completed Booking Sheets are filed for archival.

12. When payment is received the remittance is recorded and reconciled against the invoice in the Invoice File.

13. The amount owing at the end of each month is recorded on the Customer File—this information is also on the monthly statement sent to the customer.

Information currently held

Customer List (Local Offices) The invoicing of customers is carried out centrally at HQ using a microcomputer which produces monthly a list of accredited customers that is sent to each of the Local Offices who use it when accepting and confirming bookings. It contains customer number, customer name and address, and a maximum value bookable. About 500 customers are dealt with on a regular basis. Weekly amendments to this list are sent out by HQ.

Driver Register (Local Offices) This is used when Yorkies are requested to supply a driver with the vehicle. It contains the driver's name, address, telephone number, and the type of licence held (HGV I, II, or III). Bookings for the driver are entered with the booking number and dates required. When the vehicle is returned the hours worked are added.

Booking Sheets (Local Offices and HQ) The Booking Sheet, when completed, contains the following information: office issuing, booking number, booking date, customer number, customer name and address, category of vehicle required, vehicle make and model, vehicle registration number, date and time required, date and time collected, mileage when collected, date and time to be returned, date and time when actually returned, mileage when returned, vehicle condition, driver name, driver instructions.

Vehicle History Cards (Local Offices) Each office keeps a set of cards for each vehicle it is responsible for. They are filed by make and model within category (e.g. van, articulated lorry, etc.). The following information is held: make and model, vehicle category, registration number, date purchased; and information relating to each hiring: the booking number, date and mileage when sent out, date and mileage when returned, the driver name (if Yorkies supplied the driver), and any comments about the condition. Information about the various vehicle categories is kept with the History Cards.

Vehicle Booking Diary (Local Office) This is used when acceptance or rejecting bookings. Each day that a vehicle (and driver, if required) is booked is recorded.

Empty Vehicles Log Diary of unbooked vehicles kept at HQ and used to fill bookings that could not be filled by the Local Office that they were originally submitted to. This is kept 20 working days forward and for each day holds for each office the number of vehicles of each category that are currently unfilled.

Customer File PC file held at HQ which holds customer number, name and address, telephone number, maximum amount bookable, and amount owing at end of previous month.

Invoice File   PC file held at HQ which holds invoice number, customer number, customer name and address, booking number, cost of booking, date payment received, amount paid, date of booking, and date of invoice.

Current problems

- Customer List held at Local Offices is frequently out of date. This causes customers to be wrongly accepted or rejected.
- Current microcomputer invoicing system is very heavily overloaded and could not handle any expansion in the business. It is a single-user system that uses an invoicing package and it is not possible to upgrade it to a multi-user system.
- It is not straightforward to accept 'off-the-street' customers.
- Customers cannot be informed immediately whether vehicles are available for them. If a booking has been referred to Head Office it may take several telephone calls to check on its progress.
- The summary Booking Sheets created by Head Office take a long time to prepare and are often inaccurate. This causes booking requests to be sent by HQ to the Local Offices for vehicles already booked or out of service.
- Expensive agency drivers are often used in some offices when other offices may not make full use of the drivers on their register.
- There is no standard way of dealing with cancelled bookings; each Local Office has developed its own procedure.
- It is difficult, with the current accounting procedures, to calculate the relative profitabilities of the Local Offices.
- Statistical reports are often late and require considerable clerical effort for their production.

New requirements

1. Ability to deal with one-way hires and to track vehicles.
2. Have a central pool of drivers organized regionally who are allocated to vehicles.
3. Investigate the possibility of setting up regional offices to administer groups of Local Offices.
4. Extend the business to allow one-off customers to hire vehicles for removals, etc.

Volumetrics

- Currently about 3000 customers are dealt with per year, although there are 5250 on the Customer List. This is growing at the rate of 5% per year.
- There are currently 50 Local Offices operating. This has increased recently due to a company merger, but is expected to remain constant in the foreseeable future.
- An average of 50 vehicles per Local Office—2500 in all.
- There are currently 61 vehicle category codes in use. This is not expected to change.
- An average of five permanent drivers are attached to each office. Each Local Office register lists about 50 drivers.
- About 1800 bookings are accepted every year by each Local Office.

Appendix D   Suggested answers

3.4.1   CAt Breeding Agency (CABA)

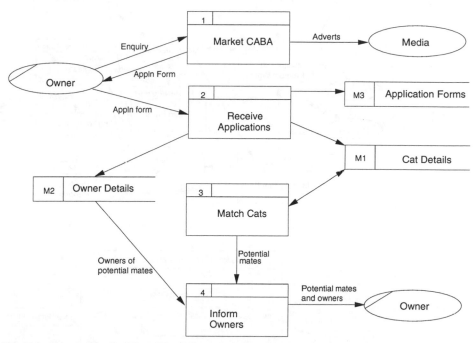

Fig. D.1 Current Physical Data Flow Diagram for the CAt Breeding Agency

Note there are many possible solutions to this exercise. You may have left the marketing out—a different system boundary. We prefer to keep the scope wide at the beginning of a project to ensure we don't miss anything.

You might have expanded Processes 2 and 3; either to another level or into several processes at the same level. It's best not to go beyond the description—in a real project we would **ask**.

3.4.2   Reckitt Repairs

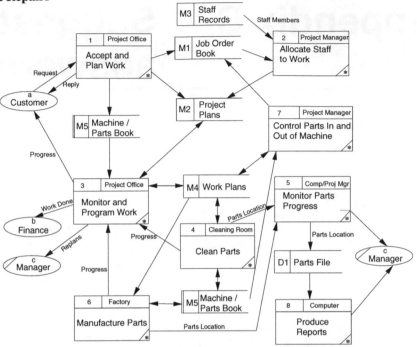

Fig. D.2 Level 1 Current Physical Data Flow Diagram for Reckitt Repairs

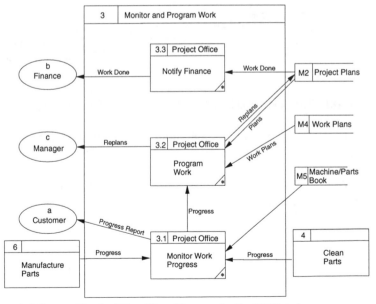

Fig. D.3 Level 2 Current Physical Data Flow Diagram for Reckitt Repairs

3.5.1   Scapegoat Systems

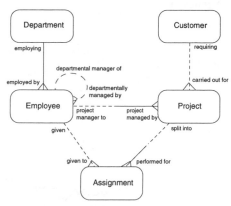

Fig. D.4 Logical Data Structure for Scapegoat Systems

The recursive relationship is shown on Employee because each employee is allocated one manager within the department. An additional 'one-to-many' relationship is required between Employee and Project to show that one employee can manage many projects but that each project can have only one project manager.

The relationship between Customer and Project is optional because some projects are internal and are therefore are not done for a customer—it also assumes that no joint projects between several customers are required. Assumptions are made on the optionality of the relationships: Employee–Assignment and Project–Assignment (that projects are split into assignments before employees are assigned).

3.5.2   Reckitt Repairs

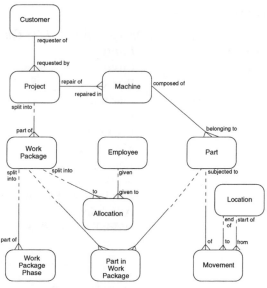

Fig. D.5 Reckitt Repairs Logical Data Structure

3.5.3   CAt Breeding Agency (CABA)

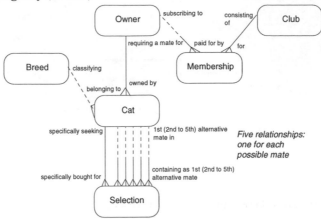

Fig. D.6 Logical Data Structure for CABA

This is a tricky exercise. The difficulty is in deciding how to represent the selection itself. Our solution uses a separate entity which in effect represents the information about the selection contained on the cat card. This Selection entity has one master occurrence for the cat on the application and five master occurrences for the five possible mates. Another way to represent this would be to represent the relationship between Selection and Cat as a 'many-to-many' and create a link group. This would be less accurate as precisely five cats are recommended, but it would be more flexible in that if CABA wanted to offer six or more mates it would be easier to make the change.

3.6.1   Reckitt Repairs

1. Determine the main Logical Data Stores from LDS Entities and Cross-reference:

Logical Data store		Entity
D1	Projects	Customer
		Project
D2	Machine Details	Machine
		Part
D3	Movements	Location
		Movement
D4	Employees	Employee
D5	Work Details	Work Package
		Part in Work Package
		Allocation
		Work Package Phase

Cross-reference Logical Data Stores and Physical Data Stores

Logical Data Store		*Physical Data Store*	
D1	Projects	M1	Job Order Book
D2	Machine Details	M5	Machine / Parts Book
D3	Movements	D1	Parts File
D4	Employees	M3	Staff Records
D5	Work Details	M2	Project Plans
		M4	Work Plans

2. Rationalize bottom-level processes

a) Processes which only retrieve data

Process 8 produces reports for Management and can be removed from the Logical DFD provided an appropriate retrieval requirement is recorded in the Requirements Catalogue. Similarly, process 3.3 can be removed from the Logical DFD. Data flows to Management and Customer can be also removed and replaced by appropriate retrieval requirements.

b) Processes containing subjective decision making

Processes 1, 2 and 3.2 contain an element of work that requires some subjective decision making. Such processes should be split and the external element of work represented by an external entity and data flows communicating with the process.

c) Duplicated processing

In processes 3.1, 4, 5, 6 and 7 there is duplication of processing in that the movements are monitored twice—by the current computer system and by the manual system in the Factory and Cleaning Room. One Record Parts Movement process will be sufficient to replace all the data updating performed by these processes. The retrievals required by these processes can be logged in the Requirements Catalogue (e.g. Work Details to Factory).

New bottom-level logical processes:
Record/Update Projects
Record/Update Work Programme
Record/Update Allocation of Staff
Record Parts Movements

The following retrievals should be logged in the Requirements Catalogue:
Reply to Customers acknowledging receipt of work request.
Progress reports to Customers
Replans to Management
Current and planned parts locations to Management
Work done details to Finance
Employee and Project details to Project Manager
Work Details to Project Manager, Project Office, Factory and Cleaning Room.
Machine and Parts details, and Parts Movements to Project Office, Factory and Cleaning Room.

3. Logical Data Flow Diagram

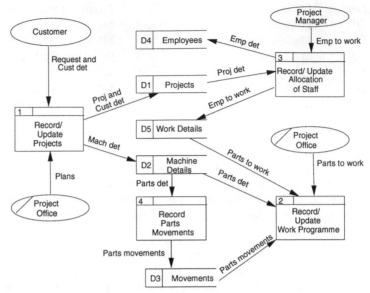

Fig. D.7 Reckitt Repairs Level 1 Logical Data Flow Diagram

4.3.1   Scapegoat Systems

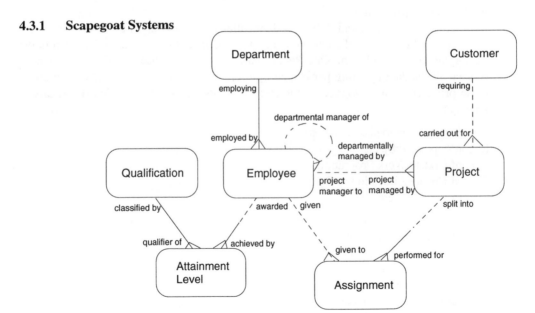

Fig. D.8 Scapegoat Systems Required System Logical Data Structure

4.4.1 Scapegoat Systems—I/O Descriptions

I/O Descriptions

From	To	Data Flow Name	Data Content	Comments
3.2 Allocate Staff	d Project Manager	Staff Allocation Sheet	Project Code Project Description Customer No. Customer Name	Sent to Project Manager to confirm staff allocated to Project.
				If internal project marked as such here.
			Staff No. Staff Name Grade No. of days	The next group of data items are repeated for each employee allocated to the project.
5.1 Produce Invoice	a Customer	Invoice	Invoice No. Invoice Date Customer No. Customer Name Customer Address	Active customers are sent an invoice once a month for the work performed in the previous month.
			Proj Desc Start Date Finish Date Mon Proj Cost Mon Proj Man Days	The next set of items are repeated for each project being currently performed for the customer.
			Inv Total Cost	This item appears on its own as a total cost for the invoice.

Fig. D.9 I/O Descriptions for the staff allocation sheet and invoice from Scapegoat Systems

Note: the details of Scapegoat Systems have been omitted from these descriptions. This assumes that we are developing a single system for the Scapegoat Systems. If Scapegoat was one of a group of companies all having the same invoicing system then it would be sensible to include this information as data items in the Data Catalogue.

4.4.2 Scapegoat Systems—I/O Structures and I/O Structure Descriptions

I/O Structure Description

Data flows represented   Allocate Staff (3.2)→Project Manager (d)   Staff Allocation Sheet

I/O structure element	Data item	Comments
Project Details	Proj Code Proj Description	
Customer Details	Cust No. Cust Name	Optional
Internal Project		Message "internal project" if no customer
Employee Allocation	Staff No. Staff Name Grade No. of Days	May be several staff allocated to project

Fig. D.10 I/O Structure Description for the Staff Allocation Sheet

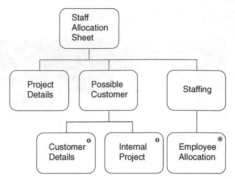

Fig. D.11 I/O Structure for the Staff Allocation Sheet

I/O Structure Description		
Data flows represented	Produce Invoice (5.1)→Customer (a) Invoice	
I/O structure element	**Data item**	**Comments**
Invoice Details	Invoice No. Invoice Date	
Customer Details	Customer No. Customer Name Customer Address	
Invoice Line	Proj Desc Start Date Finish Date Mon Proj Cost Mon Proj Man Days	
Invoice Total Cost	Inv Total Cost	

Fig. D.12 I/O Structure Description for the Invoice

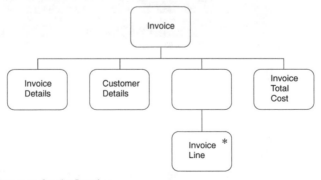

Fig. D.13 I/O Structure for the Invoice

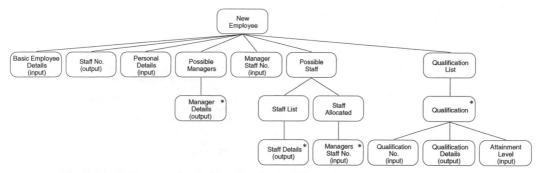

Fig. D.14 I/O Structure for the New Employee dialogue

Note: in this example, unlike the one in the Sec. 4.4, we have not shown the decisions made by the user—to display potential managers or staff.

SSADM is unclear as to whether data that is not to be permanently stored should be shown on dialogue structures. We have shown it on the Yorkies enquiry example because the input data defines the response given. On this example the input is simply a confirmation keystroke so it seems hardly worth adding the extra input boxes.

4.4.3   Yorkies—I/O Structures and I/O Structure Descriptions

I/O Structure Description		
Data flows represented Local Office Vehicle Report (not on DFD)		
I/O structure element	Data item	Comments
Office Details	Local Office ID Local Office Name Local Office Address Depot Address	
Vehicle Category Details	Vehicle Cat Code Veh Cat Description No. of Vehicles	
Vehicle Details	Vehicle Reg Mark Make of Veh Model No Date of Reg Date of Purchase End Month Mileage Insurance Class Insurance Renewal Date MOT Date Condition	

Fig. D.15 I/O Structure Description for Yorkies Local Office Vehicle Report

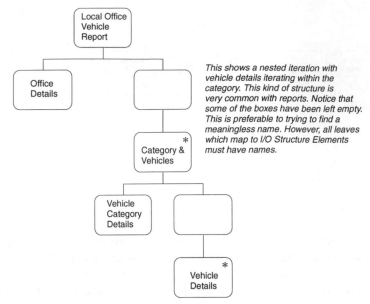

This shows a nested iteration with vehicle details iterating within the category. This kind of structure is very common with reports. Notice that some of the boxes have been left empty. This is preferable to trying to find a meaningless name. However, all leaves which map to I/O Structure Elements must have names.

Fig. D.16 I/O Structure for Yorkies Local Office Vehicle Report

4.5.1   Scapegoat Systems—relational data analysis

a) Staff Allocation Sheet

UNF	1NF	2NF	3NF
Proj Code	Proj Code	Proj Code	Proj Code
Proj Desc	Proj Desc	Proj Desc	Proj Desc
Cust No.	Cust No.	Cust No.	*Cust No.
Cust Name	Cust Name	Cust Name	
Staff No.			Cust No.
Staff Name	Proj Code	Proj Code	Cust Name
Grade	Staff No.	Staff No.	
No. of Days	Staff Name	No. of Days	Proj Code
	Grade		Staff No.
	No. of Days	Staff No.	No. of Days
		Staff Name	
		Grade	Staff No.
			Staff Name
			Grade

Fig. D.17 Relational data analysis of the Staff Allocation Sheet.

b) Invoice

UNF	1NF	2NF	3NF
Invoice No.	Invoice No.	Invoice No.	Invoice No.
Invoice Date	Invoice Date	Invoice Date	Invoice Date
Cust No.	Cust No.	Inv Total Cost	Inv Total Cost
Cust Name	Cust Name	Cust No.	*Cust No.
Cust Address	Cust Address	Cust Name	
Proj Desc	Inv Total Cost	Cust Address	Cust No.
Start Date			Cust Name
Finish Date	Invoice No.	Invoice No.	Cust Address
Mon Proj Man Days	Proj Desc	Proj Desc	
Mon Proj Cost	Start Date	Mon Proj Cost	Invoice No.
Inv Total Cost	Finish Date	Mon Proj Man Days	Proj Desc
	Mon Proj Man Days		Mon Proj Cost
	Mon Proj Cost	Proj Desc	Mon Proj Man Days
		Start Date	
		Finish Date	Proj Desc
			Start Date
			Finish Date

Fig. D.18 Relational data analysis of the Invoice.

c) Rationalized relations

Invoice
Invoice No.
Invoice Date
*Customer No.
Total Cost

Invoice Line
Invoice No.
Project Code
No. of Man Days
Project Cost

Allocation
Project Code
Staff No.
No. of Days

Customer
Customer No.
Customer Name
Customer Address

Project
Project Code
Project Description
*Customer No.
Start Date
Finish Date

Employee
Staff No.
Staff Name
Grade

Fig. D.19 Rationalized relations from Scapegoat

Note: in rationalization the candidate key of Proj Desc identified in analysis of the invoice has been replaced by Proj Code. This determines Proj Desc and is a better primary key.

d) Relational Data Structure Diagram

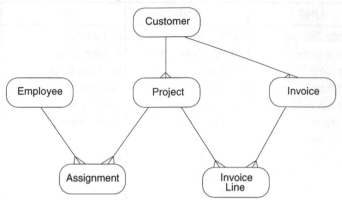

Fig. D.20 Scapegoat Relational Data Structure Diagram

e) Required System (enhanced) Logical Data Structure

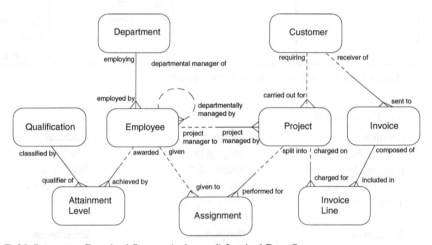

Fig. D.21 Scapegoat Required System (enhanced) Logical Data Structure

It is interesting that we have got so close to the Logical Data Structure by analysing just two inputs. The extra data identified by relational data analysis (Invoice and Invoice Line) was not identified in the Logical Data Structure because this information was not provide in the system description.

If we had analysed further I/O Structures we would have confirmed other entities and relationships on the Logical Data Structure.

4.7.1   Entity Life Histories

a) & b)   *Project Entity Life History with operations*

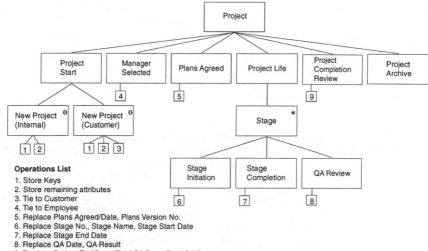

Operations List
1. Store Keys
2. Store remaining attributes
3. Tie to Customer
4. Tie to Employee
5. Replace Plans Agreed/Date, Plans Version No.
6. Replace Stage No., Stage Name, Stage Start Date
7. Replace Stage End Date
8. Replace QA Date, QA Result
9. Replace Project End Date, Final QA Date, Final QA Result

Fig. D.22 Project Entity Life History with operations

Note that we have not shown the 'gain' operations on this model. These would have required additional effects: Assignment of Staff (with the operation Gain Assignment) and New Invoice (with the operation Gain Invoice Line).

c) Handling of stages in the project

The way stages are handled seems inadequate in the above solution. The description refers to multiple stages and we see a Stage iteration in the Entity Life History. This is correct with the modification of the attributes in Project which are overwritten with each new stage.

A better solution, after discussion with the user, would probably be to create a separate Stage entity as a detail of the Project. It is quite common that developing the Entity Life Histories may lead to changes in the Logical Data Model.

d) Employee Entity Life History

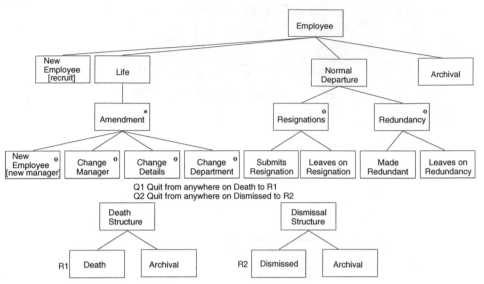

Fig. D.23 Employee Entity Life History

There are several possible ways of dealing with redundancy, resignation, death and dismissal. Because yours is different doesn't mean that it is necessarily wrong—but it may be!

The New Employee[New Manager] event reflects the change in the value of foreign key attribute Employee No.(manager)—this is an example of a simultaneous effect as the role [recruit] is also affected, the 'recruit' gaining the employees who they will now manage. The event Change Manager would have a similar effect on the Employee entity.

4.7.2 Effect Correspondence Diagrams

a)

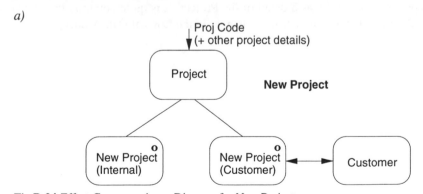

Fig D.24 Effect Correspondence Diagram for New Project

b)

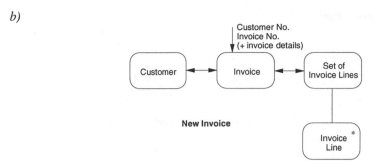

Fig D.25 Effect Correspondence Diagram for New Invoice

Note that the function supplying the data to the process would need to compute the invoice line amounts and the totals.

c)

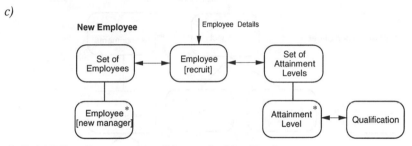

Fig D.26 Effect Correspondence Diagram for New Employee

The linking to the employee who is to be the manager of the new employee (say, Bloggs) is not shown as the manager (say, Smith) is only affected by 'Gaining' Bloggs. No value in Smith's occurrence is changed by the event occurrence.

However, the linking of the employees (say, Brown and Jones) who are to be managed by Bloggs is shown—the value of the Employee No. (manager) will be changed in both the Brown and Jones occurrences. This is a good example of the simultaneous effect where one event occurrence affects several different entity occurrences of the same type.

4.7.3   Enquiry Access Paths

a)

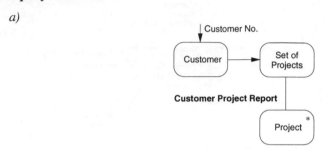

Fig D.27 Enquiry Access Path for Customer Project Report

b)

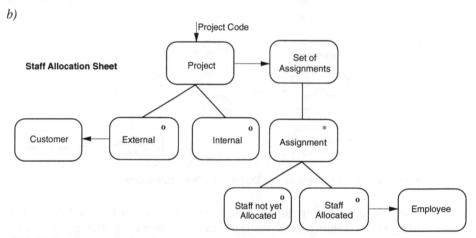

Fig D.28 Enquiry Access Path for Staff Allocation Sheet

Note the optional relationships on the Logical Data Structure. The Project–Customer is optional because a project may be internal—this results in the optional accesses from Project in the Enquiry Access Path. The Assignment–Employee relationship is optional because staff are allocated after the assignment is set up—this results in the optional accesses from Assignment.

c)

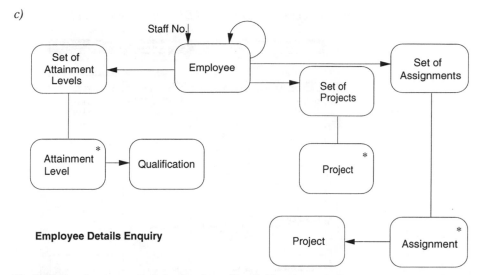

Employee Details Enquiry

Fig D.29 Enquiry Access Path for Employee Details Enquiry

1. Need to find employee's manager so use recursive link—shown on diagram by arrow pointing back to Employee entity. (Another, possibly better, way would be to show a one-to-one correspondence of Employee with an access on the entity role Employee [manager].)
2. Project accessed by two different routes, via the Assignment and directly via the 'project manager to' relationship—note these will be a different set of occurrences.

Scapegoat Dialogue Design

5.6.1   Logical Groupings of Dialogue Elements

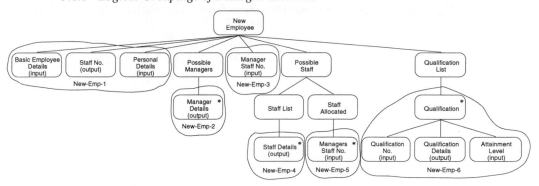

Fig. D.30 Dialogue Structure for New Employee showing LGDEs

5.6.2 Dialogue Element Descriptions and Dialogue Control Table

Dialogue Element Descriptions		Scapegoat	
Dialogue name New Employee (PM)			
User role Personnel Manager		**Function** New Employee	
Dialogue element	Data item	Logical grouping of dialogue elements ID	Mandatory/ optional LGDE
Basic Employee Details	Employee Surname Grade Department No.	New-Emp-1	M
Staff No.	Staff No.		
Personal Details	Employee Forename Address Date of Birth		
Manager Details	Staff No. Employee Surname Empoyee Forename Grade Job Title	New-Emp-2	O
Manager Staff No.	Staff No.	New-Emp-3	M
Staff Details	Staff No. Employee Surname Employee Forename Grade Job Title	New-Emp-4	O
Manager Staff No.	Staff No.	New-Emp-5	O
Qualification No.	Qualification No.	New-Emp-6	M
Qualification Details	Name of Qualification Subject		
Attainment Level	Date passed Level attained		

Fig. D.31 Completed Dialogue Element Description showing mandatory and optional LGDEs

Dialogue Control Table			Scapegoat				
Dialogue name New Employee (PM)							
Logical grouping of dialogue elements ID	Occurrences			Default pathway	Alternative pathways		
	min	max	ave		alt 1	alt 2	alt 3
New-Emp-1	1	1	1	X	X	X	X
New-Emp-2	0	20	10	X		X	
New-Emp-3	1	1	1	X	X	X	X
New-Emp-4	0	40	20			X	
New-Emp-5	0	10	5			X	X
New-Emp-6	0	20	5	X	X	X	X
Percentage path usage				70	5	10	10

Fig. D.32 Dialogue Control Table for New Employee

5.6.3   Menu Structure

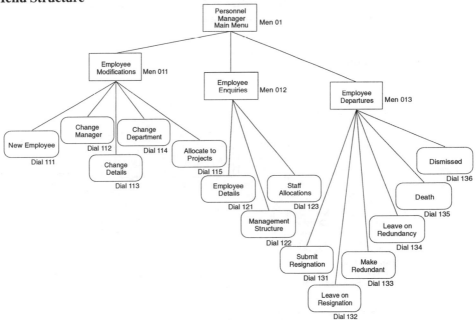

Fig. D.33 Menu Structure for the user role Personnel Manager

Obviously there are many different ways of designing this Menu Structure. This answer follows the description very closely. Further discussion with the users and possibly prototyping should ensure a satisfactory structure.

5.6.4   Command Structure

Command Structure		Scapegoat

Dialogue name	New Employee
User role	Personnel Manager

Option	Dialogue or menu	Dialogue/menu name
Add another Employee	Dialogue	New Employee (PM) (Dial 111)
Allocate Employee to Projects	Dialogue	Allocate to Projects (PM) (Dial 115)
Quit to Employee Modifications	Menu	Employee Modifications (Men 011)
Quit to Main Menu	Menu	Personnel Manager Main Menu (Men 01)

Fig D.34 Command Structure for New Employee

5.7.1   State indicators

a)

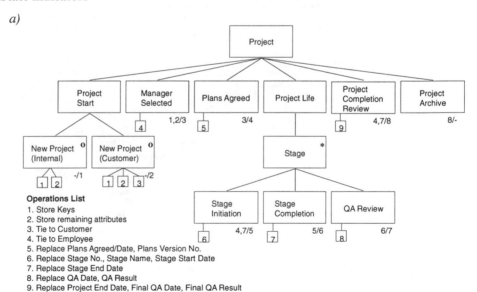

Operations List
1. Store Keys
2. Store remaining attributes
3. Tie to Customer
4. Tie to Employee
5. Replace Plans Agreed/Date, Plans Version No.
6. Replace Stage No., Stage Name, Stage Start Date
7. Replace Stage End Date
8. Replace QA Date, QA Result
9. Replace Project End Date, Final QA Date, Final QA Result

Fig. D.35 Project Entity Life History showing state indicators

5.7.2   Update Process Models

a)

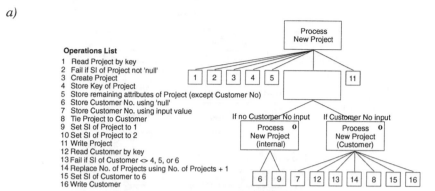

Operations List
1   Read Project by key
2   Fail if SI of Project not 'null'
3   Create Project
4   Store Key of Project
5   Store remaining attributes of Project (except Customer No)
6   Store Customer No. using 'null'
7   Store Customer No. using input value
8   Tie Project to Customer
9   Set SI of Project to 1
10 Set SI of Project to 2
11 Write Project
12 Read Customer by key
13 Fail if SI of Customer <> 4, 5, or 6
14 Replace No. of Projects using No. of Projects + 1
15 Set SI of Customer to 6
16 Write Customer

Fig. D.36 Update Process Model for the New Project event

b)

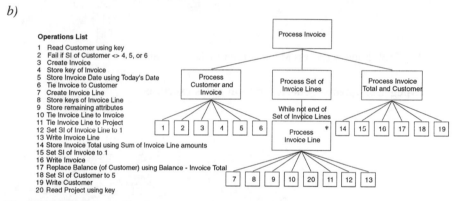

Operations List
1   Read Customer using key
2   Fail if SI of Customer <> 4, 5, or 6
3   Create Invoice
4   Store key of Invoice
5   Store Invoice Date using Today's Date
6   Tie Invoice to Customer
7   Create Invoice Line
8   Store keys of Invoice Line
9   Store remaining attributes
10 Tie Invoice Line to Invoice
11 Tie Invoice Line to Project
12 Set SI of Invoice Line to 1
13 Write Invoice Line
14 Store Invoice Total using Sum of Invoice Line amounts
15 Set SI of Invoice to 1
16 Write Invoice
17 Replace Balance (of Customer) using Balance - Invoice Total
18 Set SI of Customer to 5
19 Write Customer
20 Read Project using key

Fig. D37 Update Process Model for the New Invoice event

5.8.1   Scapegoat Enquiry Process Models

a)

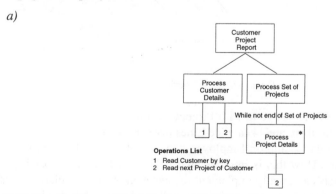

Operations List
1   Read Customer by key
2   Read next Project of Customer

D.38 Enquiry Process Model for Customer Project Report

b)

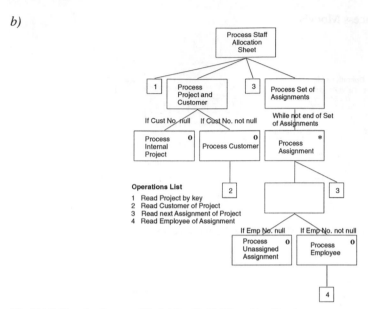

Fig. D.39 Enquiry Process Model for Staff Allocation Sheet

6.3.1   Scapegoat Systems—generic first-cut rules exercise

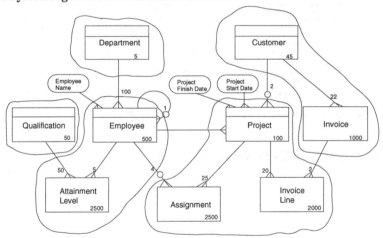

Fig. D.40 Scapegoat First-Cut Data Design—Generic

Note that Invoice Line has gone with Project because there are only 20 Invoice Lines per Project whereas there are 44 Invoice Lines per Customer.

The recursive relationship on Employee does not allow employees to be physically clustered together. How this is implemented will depend upon the particular DBMS. Relational products can usually implement recursive one-to-many relationships directly, with other types of product a new entity type will need to be introduced.

Appendix E Feasibility Study

Introduction

'A Feasibility Study is a short assessment of a proposed information study to decide whether the system can effectively meet the specified business requirements of the organization and whether a business case exists for developing such a system.'

The SSADM Reference Manual so describes a Feasibility Study. Feasibility Studies are recommended for all projects except for those of very low risk. In practice, feasibility is often carried out by means of a strategy study which identifies several potential systems (projects), and performs a very short Feasibility Study on each of them (perhaps less than one person week). The SSADM approach to feasibility is rather more comprehensive and feasibility for a large project could require as much as one person year of effort (although to be effective we would argue that it should not last more than three elapsed months). Because of the preceding short strategy study, Feasibility Studies in SSADM projects following exactly the SSADM recommended structural model are rare. Most projects entering an SSADM full study (beginning with the Requirements Analysis module) will have determined the feasibility in some way.

We do not go into great detail on SSADM's approach to feasibility. None of the SSADM techniques used in feasibility are unique to that phase of the project—as they have been described in their relevant sections, we do not describe them or their detailed use in this Appendix. Outline models or documents are produced, sufficiently detailed to assess the feasibility of the project.

It is perhaps important to realize that in the Feasibility Study non-SSADM techniques and skills are perhaps used more than in any of the other SSADM modules. Interaction with users is a most important part of feasibility. The analyst will actively be involved in interviewing, holding workshops, thinking creatively about the future system, and in presenting to users.

An SSADM Feasibility Study is in some ways rather like a shortened, less detailed approach to the Requirements Analysis module with some Technical Systems Options work combined with the Business Systems Options in the final phase. The end of the module is a decision-making point at which the senior users and the project board must decide the future of the project. A range of options, both business and technical, will be presented to them and they will make a decision to select one of these, a combination of these, or to terminate the project.

Structure of module

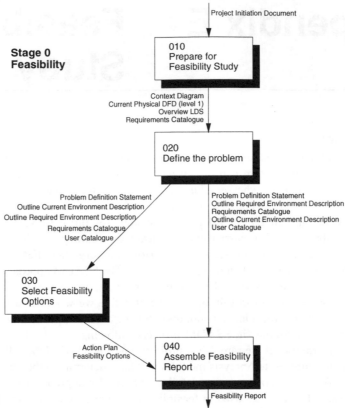

Fig. E.1 Structure of Feasibility Study module

Figure E.1 shows the structure of the Feasibility Study module which contains only one stage: Stage 0, Feasibility. Below we briefly describe each of the four steps in a Feasibility Study discussing how the SSADM techniques are applied to each one.

Step 010, *prepare for the study* This reviews any documentation already produced for the project such as the Project Initiation Document which should include the terms of reference. An initial Requirements Catalogue is produced. The outline boundaries of the project are developed using Data Flow Models to produce Context Diagrams, a Level 1 Current Physical Data Flow Diagram, and an Overview Logical Data Structure. Plans are developed for the Feasibility Study which include roles for both analysts and users, activities, and products to be produced. These will include many non-SSADM activities such as interviews and workshops.

Step 020, *define the problem* The current and required environments are described textually and using SSADM models. A more detailed current physical data flow diagram and a more detailed Logical Data Structure are both produced. The users of the future system are identified and defined in the User Catalogue. New functions, data, and non-functional requirements are identified and recorded in the Requirements Catalogue. A Problem Definition Statement is produced and agreed with the project board and senior user management. This summarizes the requirements and ranks their priority in relation to the business objectives.

Step 030, *select feasibility options* This step combines the Business Systems Options and Technical Systems Options techniques to produce a minimum of two feasibility options for recommendation to the project board—who will choose an option (or combination). The suggested approach is to first identify the minimal requirements, then to produce some outline Business Systems Options, then to produce outline Technical Systems Options each satisfying one Business System Option. Combined options are produced and reduced to a manageable number (ideally three). Descriptions are prepared for each option containing an outline Cost/Benefit Analysis, an Impact Analysis, and an outline Development Plan. These are presented to the project board and senior users who will make a decision and finalize an action plan for the development.

Step 040, *assemble the Feasibility Report* Like all of the other 'assemble...' steps in SSADM this checks the completeness and consistency of the Feasibility Study module products. These consist of the Action Plan, Feasibility Options, Outline Current Environment Description, Outline Required Environment Description, Problem Definition Statement, Requirements Catalogue, and User Catalogue. These are brought together to produce the Feasibility Report.

An SSADM Feasibility Report is quite a detailed document that records all decisions made and forms the basis for a full study for the project. It should be produced in accordance with the organization's standards (if any) for internal reports. It contains the following sections:

- Introduction
- Management/Executive Summary
- Existing business and IS support to the business
- Future IS support required by the business
- Options considered but rejected
- Financial assessment
- Project plan
- Conclusions and recommendations
- Appendices, supporting documentation which includes SSADM documents such as those specified above.

Appendix F   Further information and materials

International SSADM User Group

SSADM has a very active users group with over 500 member organizations. They publish a quarterly newsletter and an annual Technical Journal. Two conferences are held every year and several active sub-groups hold regular meetings.

Details can be obtained from:

International SSADM User Group
11 Burlings Lane
Knockholt
Kent
TN14 7PB
United Kingdom

SSADM Certificate

As SSADM became an 'open' standard its use increased and demand for experienced practitioners grew. To ensure the quality of practitioners a Certificate in SSADM was introduced by the Information Systems Examination Board (ISEB) of the British Computer Society. To obtain the Version 4 SSADM Certificate candidates need to:

* have at least one year's systems development experience
* complete an ISEB accredited course
* pass written and oral examinations

Details of accredited courses are available from:

Information Systems Examination Board
7 Mansfield Mews
London
W1M 9FJ

The materials in this book have been used to produce an ISEB accredited Distance Learning course. This involves: self-assessment work; interaction with tutors via post, telephone, fax, and/or e-mail; and two residential weekends. Details are available from:

Metadata
1A Loubet Street
London
SW17 9HD
Tel 0181–767 7337

Course materials—distance learning package and OHP slides

An entire distance learning package is also available at low cost for use by universities and colleges. This comprises: instructions and objectives for each topic; self-assessment questions and answers; assessments and model answers; and a fully worked case study based on an estate agency. These are provided in electronic form (Word 6) allowing easy adaptation.

A set of OHP slides (approx. 500) for the entire course is available in electronic format (Powerpoint 4) allowing adaptation to different teaching programmes.

These materials have been used by various organizations to help gain accreditation from the ISEB to deliver SSADM Certificate courses in a conventional mode (80 hours face-to-face teaching) and in a distance learning mode. Further details are available from:

Metadata
1A Loubet Street
London
SW17 9HD
Tel 0181–767 7337

Index